Rethinking the Age of Emancipation

Rethinking the Age of Emancipation

Comparative and Transnational Perspectives on Gender, Family, and Religion in Italy and Germany, 1800–1918

Edited by

Martin Baumeister, Philipp Lenhard, and Ruth Nattermann

berghahn
NEW YORK • OXFORD
www.berghahnbooks.com

First published in 2020 by
Berghahn Books
www.berghahnbooks.com

© 2020, 2025 Martin Baumeister, Philipp Lenhard, and Ruth Nattermann
First paperback edition published in 2025

All rights reserved. Except for the quotation of short passages
for the purposes of criticism and review, no part of this book
may be reproduced in any form or by any means, electronic or
mechanical, including photocopying, recording, or any information
storage and retrieval system now known or to be invented,
without written permission of the publisher.

Library of Congress Cataloging-in-Publication Data

A C.I.P. cataloging record is available from the Library of Congress

Library of Congress Cataloging in Publication Control Number:
2019051619

British Library Cataloguing in Publication Data

A catalogue record for this book is available from the British Library

EU GPSR Authorized Representative

LOGOS EUROPE, 9 rue Nicolas Poussin, 17000, LA ROCHELLE, France
Email: Contact@logoseurope.eu

ISBN 978-1-78920-632-6 hardback
ISBN 978-1-83695-075-2 paperback
ISBN 978-1-83695-210-7 epub
ISBN 978-1-78920-633-3 web pdf

https://doi.org/10.3167/9781789206326

Contents

List of Illustrations   viii

Acknowledgments   ix

Introduction   1
   Martin Baumeister, Philipp Lenhard, and Ruth Nattermann

Section 1. Concepts and Perspectives

1. Nineteenth-Century Italy and Germany beyond National History   35
Amerigo Caruso

2. Rethinking Nation and Family   58
Ilaria Porciani

Section 2. Family and Nation

3. The Morenos between Family and Nation: Notes on the History of a Bourgeois Mediterranean Jewish Family (1850–1912)   85
Marcella Simoni

4. Portrait of a "Political Lady": Family Ties and National Activism around 1848 in the Italian and German States   105
Giulia Frontoni

5. Emancipation, Religious Affiliation, and Family Status around 1900   119
Angelika Schaser

Section 3. Religion and Education

6. The Legacy of Adam and Eve: Morality and Gender in Jewish "Catechisms" in Nineteenth-Century Germany   139
Philipp Lenhard

7. The Transformation of Jewish Education in Nineteenth-Century Italy: The Meaning of "Catechisms"   163
Silvia Guetta

8. Religion and Nation: Catholic and Protestant Female Education and Cultural Models in Germany (1871–1914)   179
Sylvia Schraut

9. Women for the Homeland: Comparing Catholic and Protestant Female Education in Italy (1848–1908)   198
Liviana Gazzetta

Section 4. Politics of Women's Emancipation

10. Denomination Matters: Strategies of Self-Designation of the German Women's Movement   219
Anne-Laure Briatte

11. German and Italian Advocates for Women's Emancipation at the International Congress on Women's Achievements and Women's Endeavors in Berlin (1896)   241
Magdalena Gehring

Section 5. Patriotism and Gender

12. Historian between Two Fatherlands: Robert Davidsohn and World War I   263
Martin Baumeister

13. Between Motherhood and Patriotic Duty: Marital Correspondence as a Key Source for the Understanding of French-Jewish Women's Perspectives on World War I   287
Marie-Christin Lux

Section 6. War and Violence

14. "An Expression of Horror and Sadness"? (Non)Communication of War Violence against Civilians in Ego Documents (Austria-Hungary)   309
Christa Hämmerle

15. Hunger, Rape, Escape: The Many Aspects of Violence against Women and Children in the Territories of the Italian Front   332
Nadia Maria Filippini

Section 7. War Experience and Memory

16. The Construction of the Enemy in Two Jewish Writers: Carolina Coen Luzzatto and Enrica Barzilai Gentilli 353
    Tullia Catalan

17. Heroic Fathers, Patriotic Mothers, Fallen Sons: National Belonging and Political Positioning in Italian-Jewish Families' Versions of World War I 376
    Ruth Nattermann

18. The Commemoration of Jewish Soldiers in Austria 395
    Gerald Lamprecht

Index 415

Illustrations

Figure 10.1. Front page of *Zeitschrift für Frauen-Stimmrecht* (Women's Suffrage Magazine), 15 January 1907 — 225

Figure 10.2. Emblem of Deutscher Verband für Frauenstimmrecht (German Association for Women's Suffrage), advertisement for the suffrage stamp, 1905 — 226

Figure 10.3. Jean-Jacques Le Barbier, *La Déclaration des Droits de l'Homme et du Citoyen* (The Declaration of Human and Citizens' Rights), 1791 — 227

Figure 10.4. International Women's Peace Conference in The Hague, April–May 1915 — 227

Figure 10.5. *From left to right:* Anita Augspurg, Marie Stritt, Lily von Gizycki, Minna Cauer, and Sophia Goudstikker, around 1894 — 228

Table 8.1. Contents of the courses of instruction for history lessons in the German *Volksschule* in Prussia and Bavaria — 185

Table 8.2. German historical biographies for girls — 189

Table 8.3. *Die Jugend großer Frauen* (The Youth of Great Women), Konstantin Holl, 1912 — 190

Acknowledgments

This book is the outcome of a joint venture between the international DFG-network "Gender—Nation—Emancipation: Women and Families in the 'Long' Nineteenth Century in Italy and Germany," the German Historical Institute in Rome, and the Wissenschaftliche Arbeitsgemeinschaft des Leo Baeck Instituts. Our central goal was to rethink the Age of Emancipation by incorporating perspectives of both gender and Jewish history, asking about processes of participation and exclusion in the crucial period between 1800 and 1918. Thus, we intended to create an original work on nation building, nationalism, and war based on an "integrated history" that deconstructs the essentialism of national history. We also decided to widen the Italian-German comparison toward a transnational context, especially regarding the closely entangled spheres of the Habsburg Empire, France, and Northern Africa.

We wish to express our profound gratitude to each of the individual contributors for their ongoing commitment to this joint effort. The present volume is the result of their precious work and fruitful collaboration, which has created an innovative historiographical approach toward the Age of Emancipation.

We want to thank very much the Deutsche Forschungsgemeinschaft, the German Historical Institute in Rome and the Wissenschaftliche Arbeitsgemeinschaft des Leo Baeck Instituts for their continuous, generous support. Warm thanks go to Michael Brenner, Lutz Klinkhammer, Guido Lammers, and Stefanie Schüler-Springorum, who have been immensely helpful in shaping the intellectual and organizational parameters of the project. From the very outset of this international academic enterprise, Margit Szöllösi-Janze has fully supported its guiding ideas. She and Paula-Irene Villa have provided their expert knowledge and valuable advice in many stages of the working process.

We are indebted to the staff of the German Historical Institute in Rome and the History Department at the Ludwig Maximilians University of

Munich for assisting us in organizing several conferences and workshops that took place between April 2015 and June 2017 in Rome and Munich. The intellectual input by Patrizia Dogliani, Axel Körner, Philipp Nielsen, Ilaria Porciani, Angelika Schaser, Andrea Sinn, and Perry Willson have greatly inspired our discussions and helped us to refine our questions.

The Fondazione Centro di Documentazione Ebraica Contemporanea (CDEC) in Milan showed an early interest in our project. We would like to express our sincere gratitude to Laura Brazzo and Gadi Luzzatto Voghera for their gentle collaboration and helpful counsel.

Our language editors Ela Harrison and Stuart Oglethorpe have been indispensable for correcting, improving, and fine-tuning the contributions of this volume. We wish to thank them very much for their tireless, excellent work, as well as for their patience and kindness with this transnational, multilingual, and culturally heterogeneous group of authors. Without Ela Harrison's invaluable support, the book would have remained far from its present shape.

Finally, we want to express our appreciation to the staff of Berghahn Books. From the very beginning, Marion Berghahn has shown trust in our project and was instrumental in discussing relevant aspects of the publication at an early stage. We would like to extend our thanks to Chris Chappell for many pieces of thoughtful advice and his kind support in helping us to bring the book to fruition, and to Mykelin Higham for her competent assistance and uncomplicated way of dealing with seemingly intricate issues. We are further grateful to the anonymous reviewers for their valuable suggestions.

Martin Baumeister, Philipp Lenhard, and Ruth Nattermann

Introduction

Martin Baumeister, Philipp Lenhard, and Ruth Nattermann

In 1792, the German essayist Karl Philipp Moritz, one of the leading writers of the proto-Romantic *Sturm und Drang* movement, published his travelogue of several journeys to different parts of Italy and Germany. Moritz described the moment of astonishment that came over him when he finally reached the Saint Gotthard Pass. He had hoped to arrive in Italy by the next day upon descending from Saint Gotthard, but although he stood there at a height of over two thousand meters, he could not spot anything similar to what he had expected to see. Instead of a "paradisiac land," he saw only "bare rocks, a simple inn, far and wide no sight or trace of vegetation, and I was freezing in my German overcoat in the middle of the summer . . ."[1] Deeply disappointed, Moritz asked a Capuchin friar, whom he met on the mountain, where the "entrance to Italy" was. The monk replied laconically with a Latin phrase: "Hic est Italia, hic est Italia." Moritz was bewildered by the apparent tautology of this answer, but suddenly a distinction came into his mind, namely the difference between "the Italy of the geographers" and "the Italy of the poets."[2] In other words, Moritz distinguished between the political construct of Italy, with its artificial borders, and the literary or philosophical image of Italy. As one of the forefathers of German Romanticism, Moritz caught a glimpse of the modern concept of "the nation." At the exact time when France constituted itself as a modern nation-state, Germans and Italians were still uncertain about what the terms "Germany" and "Italy" actually meant and which regions and populations of central and southern Europe should be part of those "countries."

Scholars of modern European history time and again have described both Italy and Germany as "late-coming nation-states."[3] Not least with regard to the mutual influence and interconnectedness of the German and Italian nationalist movements in the nineteenth century, traditional historiography has emphasized the apparent parallels in the processes of nation-building, as well as the historical roles of "great men" such as Ernst Moritz Arndt and Giuseppe Mazzini, Otto von Bismarck and Camillo Benso di Cavour. This tradition was interrupted by World War I, only to be revived and politicized as the infamous Rome-Berlin Axis in the wake of the World War II and until the German occupation of Italy in 1943. During the 1950s, after a period of profound disruption and deep resentments on both sides, the concept of a parallel history came back to life in both Germany and Italy as an expression of shared European experiences. Bearing in mind that the first postwar European institutions, above all the European Economic Community founded in 1957, emerged in the same period, we can see that the detection of similarities and shared heritages was based mainly on political rather than on scholarly deliberations. Hence, it is not surprising that the founding document of the Treaty of Rome of 1957 starts with the assurance "to establish the foundations of an ever closer union among the European peoples" and to foster "the economic and social progress of their countries by common action in eliminating the barriers which divide Europe."[4] As a result, the strong emphasis on the historical and political commonalities, not only between Italy and Germany but among all of the European nations, concealed the social, cultural, and economic differences between them. However, in the 1950s and 1960s, most historians, as well as the European public, had not forgotten what had heinously divided Europe only twenty years earlier. In contrast to a unifying project, which Mazzini already had envisioned as the "United States of Europe," historiography and popular opinion tended to perceive European history as a juxtaposition of distinct national histories.[5] In West Germany, Fritz Fischer and Hans-Ulrich Wehler became well known for their thesis of a "special path" (*Sonderweg*) of German history, according to which Nazism was the product of the "partial modernization" of Prussian militarism. In Italy, the Roman historian Renzo De Felice and his disciples began to historicize Fascism in a similar way, trying to insert it into an alleged normality of Italian history and underlining its continuities with liberal Italy in order to deconstruct the master narrative of the Italian resistance.

Comparative and Integrated History

Particularly after the turn of the millennium, historians such as Sabine Behrenbeck, Gabriele Clemens, Christof Dipper, Patrizia Dogliani, Oliver Janz, Marco Meriggi, Alexander Nützenadel, Ilaria Porciani, Wolfgang Schieder, Pierangelo Schiera, and Edoardo Tortarolo initiated comparative studies on nineteenth- and twentieth-century Italy and Germany, highlighting the social, economic, cultural, or political fabric of these two national communities from a comparative perspective.[6] These pioneering works corrected the traditional image created by both the "parallel history" and the "special path" thesis, offering a new, more nuanced view of the fundamental differences in the processes of Italian and German nation-building. However, German and Italian comparative history still lacks a perspective that questions the story of two separate but allegedly homogenous entities.

Therefore, the volume at hand adopts the approach of an "integrated history" in order to deconstruct the essentialism of national history. The concept of an "integrated history" has been developed first and foremost in two separate historiographical fields: East Asian History on the one hand and the history of the Holocaust on the other. While historians of East Asia have to cope with a great variety of cultural, social, and religious reference systems,[7] scholars of the Holocaust, most prominently Saul Friedländer, have tried to "integrate" the Jewish perspective into a narrative that has been dominated for decades by the perspective of the perpetrators.[8] Building upon the results of these two relatively new historiographical traditions, this volume not only incorporates religious and cultural diversity but takes the multilayered texture of Italian and German society as the basis of research. Two aspects are at the center: while the *gender perspective* rectifies a still male-dominated historiography of nationalism, the *Jewish perspective* focuses on the multireligious structure of both societies and highlights the mechanisms of inclusion and exclusion of minorities.

Hardly any attempt has been made up until now to employ methods of gendered or Jewish history for a comparative study of Italian and German history. In fact, both German and Italian scholars discovered the analytical category of gender very late. It was not before the 1980s that German historians became interested in the complex relationship between gender and nation, between women's emancipation movements, nationalism, and war, thus gaining access to a large group of historical protagonists that had been ignored in relevant literature so far.[9] In Italian historiography, this process took even longer. Only toward the end of the 1990s could a new tendency be seen to emerge, stimulated above all by the studies by Ilaria Porciani, who rejected the categorical division between public and private spheres and who, by way of contrast, emphasized the central role of women, families, and parental networks for the construction and representation of imagined national communities.[10] Paul Ginsborg has stressed the discursive connection between gender, family, and nation, quoting Giuseppe Mazzini, according to whom families represented "the temple of the modern nation" while a woman stood at the center of the family, an angel-like figure who facilitated everyday duty and pain with a mysterious influence of grace and love.[11]

What is true for the lack of a gendered perspective on Italian and German history applies to a Jewish perspective as well.[12] Although the exchange and interaction between Jewish intellectuals, rabbis, communities, and institutions in "Italy" and "Germany" dates back to the Middle Ages, transnational research so far has focused on the intersections between French-Jewish and German-Jewish history.[13] Other recent studies have emphasized the role of German rabbis in the modernization processes of Eastern European Jewish life or have examined the migration movement of German Jews to North America after 1848.[14] However, despite the widely spread myth of an Italian-Jewish *Sonderweg*, this history was always connected to that of the central European Jews.[15] Jews originating in the German lands have been part of Italian-Jewish communities for ages. As Anna Esposito has shown, even the venerable Jewish community of Rome included German Jews since the sixteenth century.[16] In the early modern period, as Lois Dubin has demonstrated, the port city of Trieste—belonging to the Habsburg Empire but encircled by the mainland of the Venetian Republic and Venetian Istria—also became a focal point of an emerging proto-Haskalah among urban, educated Jewish merchants.[17] In the nineteenth century, Jewish intellectuals like Samuel David Luzzatto, who was born in Trieste and later worked as a lecturer at the famous Collegio Rabbinico Italiano in Padua, and Naphtali Herz Homberg, born in a Bohemian town near Prague and active as a schoolteacher, reformer, and writer in Trieste in the 1780s, were mediators between the two cultures. Luzzatto maintained friendly correspondence with the chief rabbi of Prague, Salomo Judah Rapoport, and with Leopold Zunz, one of the founders of the Wissenschaft des Judentums (Science of Judaism). Homberg's books were translated into Italian and had a great impact on the reform of the Jewish school system in both Germany and Italy.

Starting from our approach of an integrated and comparative history, we purposefully take these processes of interaction and exchange between contemporary Italian and German, Italian-Jewish, and German-Jewish spheres, protagonists, and concepts under consideration. The main chronological and thematic focus of the present volume is on the period between 1800 and the crucial years of World War I, which allows for a critical and long-term reassessment of notions, discourses, and narratives concerning nation-building, nationalism, and war. The binational comparison has deliberately been inserted into and widened toward a transnational context. This includes above all the Habsburg Empire and France, whose histories are inextricably entangled with the German and Italian spheres, but it also reaches as far as North Africa when it comes to the characteristic transnational parental and commercial networks of Italian-Jewish families.

The contributions by Amerigo Caruso and Ilaria Porciani reflect from two related angles on central *concepts and perspectives* of this historiographical approach. Caruso makes a plea for new methodological approaches toward writing national histories, which is supported also by Porciani in the conclusion of her chapter. Caruso's chapter discusses the impact of comparative and transnational history on traditional interpretations. He focuses on the classical paradigm of Italian and German national "parallel history," considering in particular more recently emerging tendencies toward gendered and Jewish perspectives. Based on significant case studies in the German and Italian contexts, Caruso presents key strategies for countering teleological approaches to the nation-state, based on a persistent methodological nationalism. His contention is that national history, particularly regarding nineteenth-century Italy and Germany, has frequently overlooked the plurality of collective identities, of multiple political and cultural affiliations in the processes of nation-building, instead of reflecting on the construction of national identities, the problem of multiple social, political, and cultural loyalties, as well as the tensions and conflicts between national emancipation and the emancipation of minorities, all of which represent central aspects discussed by the authors in this volume. He highlights the major role of transnational and nonstate elements in the process of nation-building, stressing the complexity of patriotic discourse developed by transnational elites who referred to transnationally circulating emotions, experiences, and narratives of nationalism. In order to create new approaches toward national historiography, Caruso calls for the consideration of marginal traditions, informal groups, and the plurality of social and cultural micro- and intermediate spheres that are often removed from the master narrative of nationalism and the nation-state. His chapter makes the case for combining comparative and transnational perspectives and suggests searching for new concepts of periodization in order to overcome methodological nationalism and to reassess ingrained interpretative paradigms of national histories.

Porciani emphasizes the idea that during the "long" nineteenth century, family and nation were strictly entwined in the same patriotic discourse, cutting through divisions between male and female, public and private. Nations are imagined as a family; the family is considered the seat of national honor, while the nation is seen as the benchmark of family honor. Her chapter offers an extensive historical panorama on the respective interrelations in contemporary public debates and representations. Based on a wide range of sources from juridical texts to visual evidence, the contribution adopts a transnational perspective with particular attention toward Germany, Italy, France, and the United States, stressing the importance of a broader comparison when looking at the complex interplay between family, national discourse, and national identities.

The nation is not only militarized and masculinized but also "familiarized." Porciani highlights the role of the family as a key institution of national identity, of the health of the nation, and of national morality in public discourse, as well as in the process of nation-building. The family figures as a center of gravity in patriotic painting as well as in national pedagogics. Porciani observes the politicization of home and family affecting the emerging bourgeoisie as well as traditional dynasties forced to come to terms with the postrevolutionary political order. Further, she stresses the role of the family as a symbol of national reassurance in times of crisis like war. Within her comparative assessment, there appear many common features in a certain transnational dynamic of the "familiarization" of the nation, constructed as a "patriarchically and hierarchically organized folk family" (Ruth Roach Pierson), while at the same time she points to important differences regarding, among others, the relevance of religion or denomination to the complex relationship between nation and family, with far-reaching consequences for the family as a symbolic and social order, as in the case of the laicism of Republican France and the anti-Catholic Italian Risorgimento nationalism compared to the concept of nation within the German Kaiserreich, deeply imbued by Protestantism. For the Jewish minority, the ties between family and nation were particularly important, where national unification and Jewish emancipation were considered to develop in unison, as in the case of Italy.

Rethinking the Age of Emancipation

The guiding question, which is implicitly present in all the contributions to this volume, concerns social and cultural as well as political participation and exclusion in the processes of nation-building, nationalism, and war. It is this ongoing tension between those who are supposed to belong to the imagined communities and those who do not belong that strikingly characterizes the "Age of Emancipation," whose legal reforms and egalitarian concepts eventually did not succeed in bringing equality to everyone.[18] We understand the notion of emancipation in its characteristic complexity and consider its manifold implications reaching from legal and political equality in the strict sense toward acculturation and bourgeoisification. The latter, rather long-term and irregular historical processes represent the common focus of our rethinking the "Age of Emancipation" between 1800 and 1918.

Speaking of Jewish emancipation in the legal sense, both Italian and German Jews were emancipated in the second half of the nineteenth century (with the exception of the short period under Napoleonic occupation)—their emancipation in terms of social and cultural integration, however, remained incomplete even after the end of World War I. Civic equality had been granted to Italian Jews as early as 1848 in the Kingdom of Sardinia-Piedmont and was extended between 1859 and 1870 to the subsequently conquered territories of the Kingdom of Italy, which was proclaimed in 1861. Nevertheless, in spite of the long-lasting narrative of an unproblematic, almost idyllic integration of Jews into Italian society,[19] recent studies have shown that liberal Italy was by no means free from antisemitism and that the alleged "success story" of Italian Jewry proves to be erroneous, especially when applying a gender perspective that considers the incomplete emancipation of Italian-Jewish women.[20]

Similarly to the Italian context, German Jews too were emancipated gradually. After they had been granted civic equality in several smaller South German states at the beginning of the 1860s, the legal emancipation process was concluded with the creation of the Dual Monarchy and the foundation of the North German Confederation in 1867 in Austria and Prussia as well. Two years later, Judaism was declared equal to all other confessions in the law regarding the *Gleichberechtigung der Konfessionen in bürgerlicher und staatsbürgerlicher Beziehung*. With the foundation of the Empire in 1871, it became valid in the whole of Germany.[21] In Italy, it was not before 1889 that the penal code included the equality of all confessions, among them also the Jewish faith, as officially recognized and legally protected religious communities.[22] Thus, the legal emancipation process for Jews was concluded both in the German and in the Italian context toward the end of the nineteenth century, while the social and cultural integration processes continued on uneven paths until far into the twentieth century. The case of Jewish women stands out, since they did not achieve equal citizenship as did their male counterparts. Their integration processes as Jews *and* as women followed patterns and strategies that differed considerably from the emancipation paths of Jewish men.

In both cases, the struggle and negotiations for emancipation occurred within the framework of nation-building and were closely connected to the creation of national consciousness. What is more, they formed an essential element of the history of families, influencing attitudes of national and cultural belonging, of gender as well as religious identities. Marcella Simoni presents an intriguing example of the relationships between emancipation, family, and nation in her contribution on the Livornese Jewish family Moreno, who migrated to Tunis in 1830. Based on the papers of the Moreno family recently donated to the Livorno State Archives, Simoni looks at the interplay between nationality and religion—i.e. Italian and Jewish identities—within the evolving colonial context of fin de siècle Tunis. The story of the Moreno family represents the transnational experience of Italian Jews in the nineteenth century, which has inevitably been linked to migration.

While Simoni sets the Moreno family into a broader context of Italian-Jewish and colonial history and focuses mostly on men as agents of emancipation processes, the contribution by Giulia Frontoni analyzes the political role of upper-class women during the revolution of 1848–49 in the Italian and German states. She distills two competing concepts, the "mother of the nation" and the "political lady," both of which assumed a decisive role in the self-empowerment of women as political players. By integrating the religious and social background of political activists and writers who participated in national movements, Frontoni provides evidence of the widespread belief in the middle of the nineteenth century that women should help to forge the nation in a manner befitting their social status.

Angelika Schaser adds an important element to the discursive and conceptual interrelationships between emancipation, family, and nation by looking into contemporary feminist ideas of motherhood, which were supposed to reconcile family status and intellectual work. They stood in opposition to the conventional perception of motherhood as a national task and to the necessary subordination of intellectual work under family duties. Her chapter is based on an analysis of a contemporary key document in German, the book *Motherhood and Intellectual Work: A Psychological and Sociological Study*, written by two educated German-Jewish women, Adele Gerhard and Helene Simon, and published in 1901. Their survey included well-known female protagonists from all over Europe and the United States as study participants. Schaser demonstrates that in spite of the emancipatory claims of the authors, their findings eventually emphasized traditional views of gender and family orders. In fact, it was seen as risky to combine motherhood and a demanding occupation. Motherhood and raising children were interpreted as the most important national duty for women across all social classes. Hence, the welfare of the respective nation was ranked higher than the needs of (Jewish) minorities, particular families, and individuals.

Picking up especially on Frontoni's and Schaser's portrayal of gender roles in very diverse social and religious contexts, several chapters in this volume are concerned with issues of *religion and education*, particularly the question of how different religious backgrounds of women evoked specific gender models within the broader framework of the nation-building processes in Italy and Germany. Liviana Gazzetta underlines the fact that the Risorgimento and the later national movement in Italy had to cope and compete with the idea of a "Catholic nation." This development allowed Protestant and Jewish women to become active and equal members of the movement. Resting upon an analysis of sources like instructional materials for young women, Gazzetta shows that in the Protestant and Jewish communities, female involvement in the Risorgimento process at the same time promoted proximity to and often involvement in the feminist movement, unlike what tended to happen in the Catholic world. In general, she concludes, Jewish and Protestant female gender roles provided women with more agency in the public sphere than the traditional or liberal Catholic models.

Sylvia Schraut, by contrast, points to the strong Protestant imprint of the German Kaiserreich. The dominant gender model there was strongly influenced by Protestant values and norms, which is why Schraut argues that the so-called "German" gender model was in fact a Protestant one. Based on a thorough examination of instruction books and reading materials from the late nineteenth century, Schraut suggests that two aspects in particular were incompatible with leading Catholic concepts: first of all, the Protestant gender model only accepted married women as full women, whereas Catholic culture knew three female gender models: the wife, the nun, and the widow. Second, the Protestant gender model drafted a female life as a life that took place first and foremost within the family, while the Catholic model ranked living in a convent much higher than mere family life. In addition, as members of a convent, women were able to practice a profession, for example as a nurse or a teacher. Gazzetta's and Schraut's chapters complement one another, although their results contrast somewhat: in Catholic Italy, Protestant and Jewish women were more inclined to live a self-determined life, whereas in Protestant Germany, especially Prussia, Catholicism offered alternative models of womanhood that transcended the narrow role of a mother.

The transformation of the traditional ideal of womanhood in Judaism into a modern, bourgeois one is the focus of the contributions by Philipp Lenhard and Silvia Guetta. Starting in the early modern period, Lenhard shows that traditional Judaism did not separate primarily between the private and the public sphere but between different functions in religious and professional life. Initially, Jewish women were active in business together with their husbands or fathers and took care of religious observance within the household, while studying the Torah was restricted to men. It was only in the course of the emancipation process that Jewish gender ideals "assimilated" to dominant bourgeois norms and values. On the basis of a large corpus of modern Jewish "catechisms," Lenhard suggests that Jewish emancipation in Germany thus implied the relegation of women to the household.

Silvia Guetta takes a deeper look at the new genre of the "Jewish catechism" as well, but from an Italian-Jewish angle. The focus of her chapter is the transformation of Jewish education in Italy in the nineteenth century. As in Germany, Jewish emancipation resulted in a new self-definition as a mere "community of faith," which was clearly distinct from an ethnic or national identity. Funneling this modern concept of a "Jewish religion" to the next generation was a central aspect of Jewish education. Guetta performs an in-depth analysis of several Jewish journals, among which *L'Educatore Israelita* and its successor *Il Vessillo Israelitico* are the most important. These and other publications shared the same agenda, namely teaching Jewish history and literature on a popular level in order to foster and reshape Italian-Jewish identity.

Further crucial aspects investigated by Guetta are the reform of the Jewish school system and the advocacy of a new family ideal. If the traditional Jewish community dissolved in the era of emancipation, education became indispensable. Jewish children had to learn about their religion and their origins not only in school but also at home. As a result, the Jewish mother came to be expected to pass on the torch of Judaism to her children. Modern Jewish education in both Italy and Germany thus included a reformulation of gender roles. The process of emancipation did not necessarily occasion more freedom for women.

As a matter of fact, the demands for women's rights remained unfulfilled even after emancipation had been granted to Jews. For women, whether Jewish or not, emancipation implied civic equality and political participation. At the same time, however, the concept of women's emancipation was associated with detachment from a traditionally given social integration, which depended on their husbands and/or families. In Italy as well as in Germany, contemporary law defined women's status in society. The Italian Civil Code, enacted in 1865, included the *autorizzazione maritale* (marital authorization) set by the Piedmontese Code of 1837, which itself drew heavily on the Napoleonic Code dating back to 1804. It legally emphasized the inferiority of women to men within the family and the young nation-state, and was not abolished until the passing of the *legge Sacchi* in July 1919.[23] In the German context, the *Geschlechtsvormundschaft*, i.e. the legal dependence of women on their fathers, husbands, or male relatives, existed until the end of the nineteenth century, while the *eheliche Vormundschaft*, whose implications were comparable to the Italian *autorizzazione maritale*, prevailed until far into the twentieth century.[24] Against this background, emancipation meant liberation from patriarchal social orders, family constraints, and hierarchies. Men and women had defined places in the cultural construct of the bourgeois societies of the "long" nineteenth century, divided according to their status as man or woman and positioned within a strict hierarchical ranking. Thus, the demand for "women's emancipation," a term that had been in use throughout Europe and the United States since the beginning of the nineteenth century, was above all directed against the division of male and female spheres. As Sylvia Paletschek and Bianka Pietrow-Ennker have argued, the contemporary notion of women's emancipation meant the fight for self-determination and improvements in the legal, social, cultural, and political positions of women. It comprised both feminist and potentially feminist discourse, which is why the authors in this volume deliberately call the protagonists of the early movements "feminists." What is more, the first women's emancipation movements also included men who committed themselves to the cause of women's emancipation.²⁵ In fact, the desired realization of the emancipation of women depended on a profound inner change within society and its capacity for development.²⁶ Integration here meant the achievement of personal responsibility and independence as well as access to hitherto exclusively "male" spaces: suspension of legal dependence, access to secondary schools, universities, and qualified professions, as well as the right to political participation.²⁷

It was these topics that stood at the center of contemporary politics of women's emancipation. The first women's emancipation movements in Europe, whose protagonists conceived, developed, and discussed the respective issues within the framework of associations, journals, writings, and conferences, considerably shaped and characterized the period between 1848 and World War I.²⁸ The number of middle-class Jewish women who participated in these movements was above average. Their usually high level of education as well as their unfulfilled demand for civic equality, which was gradually being granted to Jewish men, made numerous Jewish women participate, frequently as central actors, in first-wave feminism in the German-speaking areas, Italy, France, and many other European countries.²⁹

While the forerunners of the early women's emancipation movements date back to the period of the Enlightenment and the French Revolution, the European revolutions of 1848 marked the beginning of the first women's emancipation movements in the Italian and the German contexts too. As in many other European countries, however, a continuous organization of German and Italian feminists developed only from the end of the nineteenth century. The foundation of the Allgemeiner Deutscher Frauenverein (ADF) in 1865 by Louise Otto-Peters and Auguste Schmidt in Leipzig preceded the creation of the first Italian women's organization, the Lega promotrice degli interessi femminili, in 1881 by Paolina Schiff and Anna Maria Mozzoni in Milan. The ADF concentrated on women's education and the improvement of working conditions for women, while the Lega promotrice, sixteen years younger and politically left wing, also explicitly aimed at the political emancipation of women. The fight for women's suffrage represented one of its main purposes.³⁰

A key to understanding the ambiguous developments and often-conflicting concepts associated with women's demands for the rights to self-determination and equal citizenship in the period leading up to World War I can be found within different uses of the term "emancipation" among contemporary protagonists of the respective movements. Focusing on the politics of women's emancipation, Anne-Laure Briatte's chapter in this volume analyzes the denominating strategies of German middle-class feminists in contemporary discourse. Briatte shows how the term "emancipation" fell into disrepute in nineteenth-century Germany, bringing women close to the alleged "outsiders" of the national community—Jews, workers, and unionists, all of whom were seen as a danger by the supporters of law and order. Consequently, the term was banned from the vocabulary of middle-class protagonists. However, after Bismarck's dismissal and the relative liberalization of the political context around 1890, German feminists began to combine different strategies to suggest emancipation without expressing it openly. They made use of historical parallels, iconographic references, and alternative ways of life, implying emancipatory claims for civil rights, economic and social independence, and the liberation of the body. By doing so, Briatte concludes, middle-class German feminists developed sophisticated public relations and emancipated themselves from social and cultural rules and norms that excluded them from the public sphere. Hence, they created participatory spaces for themselves outside the political arena, which remained inaccessible to them at least until 1918.

Magdalena Gehring complements Briatte's view in her comparative study on the contemporary politics of women's emancipation among German and Italian feminists during the late nineteenth century. Her chapter deals with central debates during the international congress on Women's Achievements and Women's Endeavors in Berlin in 1896. Gehring demonstrates that although German and Italian feminists had a similar understanding of women's emancipation, Italian and German protagonists expressed the development of their movements very differently. Their discussions reflected the disparities in each country's position and the different structure of their movements: the distinct regional diversity in unified Italy allowed there to be more radical feminists in the women's movement than in its German counterpart, along with closer cooperation between social classes. At the same time, like the Italian protagonists, German feminists placed themselves deliberately on the international stage in order to raise consciousness and develop the approach of the advocates of women's emancipation. Gehring's analysis also emphasizes the transnational orientation of the politics of women's emancipation in Europe at the turn of the century, for which international congresses represented an important forum. In the prewar period, however, nationalist ambitions also increased within women's organizations throughout Europe. World War I put a temporary stop to the transnational alignment of the German and Italian women's emancipation movements, whose protagonists eventually found themselves on enemy sides and within conflicting alliances.

Gender and Jewish Perspectives on World War I

Notions of gender, nation, and emancipation are central to an in-depth understanding of World War I. Nevertheless, mainstream historiography still all too often neglects both gender issues and Jewish experiences and memories of the conflict. One recent contribution that successfully employs the analytical category of gender is the volume of essays *Gender and the First World War*, edited by Christa Hämmerle, Oswald Überegger, and Birgitta Bader Zaar.[31] Regarding Jewish war experience and memory, especially in the German, the Austrian, and the Eastern European contexts, scholars such as Marsha L. Rozenblit, Petra Ernst-Kühr, Eleonore Lappin-Eppel, Gerald Lamprecht, Ulrich Wyrwa, Gideon Reuveni, and Edward Madigan have initiated significant research and publications that emphasize the place of World War I as a turning point of the Jewish experience in the twentieth century.[32] In Italy, historians have just begun to reassess the Italian-Jewish perspective of World War I, touching upon questions such as the approaches of Jewish protagonists toward interventionism, Jewish soldiers' testimonies, and relief work of Jewish communities.[33] Only recently, there has also been an increasing interest in the political attitudes and discourses of Italian-Jewish women during the war.[34] The chapters in this volume dealing with conflicts of national loyalty and belonging, gender relationships, narratives of violence, family dynamics, and the role of religion in discourses of remembrance with regard to World War I form a crucial part of our reassessment of the Age of Emancipation in terms of gender and Jewish history. The twofold perspective allows us to focus on neglected, silenced, or forgotten actors, narratives, and sources, thereby creating a counterhistory to simplified master narratives of the global conflict.

In Italy and Germany, as in the Habsburg Empire, France, and most European countries, the war was extensively supported by middle- and upper-class women. They were convinced that their war effort and relief work could eventually prove their right and fitness for citizenship. This tendency frequently resulted in an increasingly aggressive nationalism among women's organizations and their protagonists. Numerous feminists distanced themselves from pacifist positions and the conspicuously transnationalist orientation that had characterized the politics of women's emancipation movements since the nineteenth century. From the beginning of the twentieth century onward, a major part of German, Austrian, and Italian women's organizations began to legitimize their activities by way of the national principle instead of via the traditions of human rights, thus maintaining the characteristic exclusive and aggressive elements inherent in nationalism. The realization of a constructive and long-term internationalism within the early women's emancipation movements, which had represented one of the main goals of first-wave feminists, was doomed to failure in the face of the predominance of contemporary nationalisms. As soon as their "own" nation seemed to be threatened in its existence, the great majority of feminist actors gave priority to national aspirations in preference to pacifist and feminist principles, which had aimed at an international understanding.[35] Middle-class German-Jewish and Italian-Jewish women usually participated in these developments in the same way as non-Jewish protagonists. Jewish feminists in particular hoped that the conflict would not only continue and further the process of Jewish integration but also eventually lead to the emancipation of women as well.

For Jewish men and women in general, World War I represented an outstanding opportunity to prove their national solidarity toward their home countries. As Sigmund Freud maintained in 1915, however, it brought an end to the ideal of "Kulturweltbürgertum," the idea of a transnational cosmopolitan community of the educated elite, shared particularly by members of the Jewish bourgeoisie. As a diasporic people, Jews had often been viewed as quintessentially cosmopolitan, moving in transnational networks of family, economic relations, and worlds of learning.[36] With the rise of the nation-states during the century before 1914, which ran parallel to the political emancipation of Jews as well as to a new wave of antisemitism, the tensions between loyalties to one's native country and a transnational, cosmopolitan outlook had increased, since anticosmopolitanism represented an important element of antisemitic discourse and propaganda. The war brought a severe crisis for the mobile lives and hybrid identities of Jews, as can be illustrated by the case of the German-Jewish historian Robert Davidsohn (1853–1937). The chapter by Martin Baumeister questions the interpretation of the protagonist—who had lived in Florence since 1889, considering Italy his "fatherland by adoption," and was forced to return to Germany at the outbreak of the war—as a forerunner of a transnational, particularly European utopia in the era of nationalism. Based on Davidsohn's largely unpublished ego documents, Baumeister's chapter looks into the scholar's activities and experiences between 1914 and 1918. The war in particular is revealed as a challenge both to his ideals of national belonging—his patriotic loyalties and the love for his chosen second fatherland—and to his ideas of a bourgeois male identity. Baumeister's close reading of the sources shows that Davidsohn's Italian affinity, binational career, left-liberal convictions, and cosmopolitan sociability did not prevent him from taking an uncritical stance toward the official German interpretation of World War I as a defensive struggle against an overwhelmingly hostile alliance that included Italy. In fact, the scholar's attachment to his German fatherland took precedence over a cosmopolitan outlook during the global conflict and resulted in a profound war patriotism. This attitude was closely connected to the historian's effort to reaffirm a masculine bourgeois identity, since due to his age he was unable to enter active military service and thereby prove his solidarity toward Germany as a citizen-soldier on the battlefield. Baumeister concludes that Davidsohn's increasingly nationalist viewpoint during

World War I in fact reveals the fragility and contradictions of his transnational biography and professional project.

The wartime attitudes of acculturated French-Jewish female intellectuals such as the educationalist Alice Hertz and the artist Laure Isaac show parallels to Davidsohn's strong patriotic attachment to his native country, which eventually prevailed over a cosmopolitan outlook. Despite being part of transnational parental and professional networks, including German-Jewish connections, these women expressed a deeply rooted patriotism and unconditional support for the French Republic during the war, as Marie-Christin Lux explains. In contrast to the German-Jewish *Grenzgänger* Davidsohn, however, the patriotic sentiments of her protagonists, coined by republicanism, did not develop into nationalist viewpoints. Lux's in-depth analysis of unpublished wartime letters by Alice Hertz and Laure Isaac to their husbands, the sociologist Robert Hertz and the historian Jules Isaac, both of whom fought on the Western Front, emphasizes the benefits of using marital correspondences as sources for reassessing middle-class Jewish women's perspectives on World War I. By following personal narratives within these private letters, the study reveals how the protagonists tried to (re)define themselves and their roles within the war effort between being wives and mothers, French citizens, and Jewish women. Whereas the scholar Robert Hertz supported the concept of Jewish self-sacrifice as a citizen-soldier, oriented toward a masculine bourgeois identity similarly to Robert Davidsohn, the feminists Alice Hertz and Laure Isaac worked and volunteered in order to actively support their countries' war efforts and to prove their patriotism. As wives and mothers, however, they did not identify with the idea of self-sacrifice as did their male counterparts. The two case studies give a significant insight into the close and often ambiguous interrelationship between *patriotism* and *gender*, offering a frequently neglected view of the war that deconstructs the binary concept of front and home front.

The gender perspective also allows us to focus on forgotten or repressed narratives of war violence against women and children. In World War I, civilians experienced various forms of violence, including rape, famishment, internment, air raids, etc., to an extent hitherto unknown. Christa Hämmerle and Nadia Maria Filippini demonstrate how war violence was communicated or silenced in wartime correspondence, autobiographical texts, and official documents by female and male protagonists. Whereas Hämmerle's chapter deals with texts from the Austrian-Hungarian sphere, Filippini's chapter starts from Italian documents and testimonies. By offering important insights into war violence against civilians within areas of conflicting alliances, the two complementary chapters emphasize the reverse perspectives of perpetrators and victims in the respective national contexts. Hämmerle's contribution concentrates on areas of mobile warfare, as in the case of the Isonzo battles, and investigates diverse manifestations of war-related violence against civilians on the basis of mostly unpublished and largely neglected ego documents from family archives and institutionalized collections. Her detailed analysis of letters and diaristic war accounts by men and women, among them soldiers and war nurses, also asks about signs of patriotism and nationalism in these sources, i.e., whether they reflected the official national discourse about the alleged "clean" and defensive war of the Habsburg Monarchy. Hämmerle concludes that the examination of various forms of ego documents proves the difficulties in finding a coherent language for the experiences of war violence during World War I. In the Austrian context, discursive struggles in war diaries and diaristic texts remained private in the postwar era too and had no impact on public memory. The hegemonic culture of war remembrance became increasingly revisionist by glorifying the defeated Habsburg army. At the same time, civilian victims were largely forgotten after 1918, as they predominantly belonged to non-German ethnicities or were refugees, often Jews, from "mixed" areas of the Habsburg Monarchy that no longer belonged to the new Austrian state.

Nadia Maria Filippini extends this view and the interpretation of hitherto-neglected contemporary sources on war violence by focusing on the perspective of victims in the Italian context. Her study does not concentrate on ego documents but on testimonies and protocols from the Italian commission of inquiry regarding crimes committed by the enemy against civilians and prisoners of war, established in 1918. The thematic and geographical emphasis lies on the area of Veneto and Friuli, which became a war zone even before Italy's entry into the war and from May 1915 onward experienced profound and long-lasting social disruption. Filippini's analysis detects war atrocities against the local civilian population in the context of invasion and occupation by Austro-German forces, pointing to forgotten and repressed accounts by women and children whose lives were shattered by the experience of war. Like Hämmerle, Filippini also considers related social issues within the immediate postwar period, which regarded the reintegration process of civilian refugees and returning soldiers to Italy. Gendered readings of war experience, she affirms, reflect not only trauma, violence, and victimhood but also the self-determination, courage, and resistance of female protagonists who protected their children and families in the extreme circumstances of war.

What applies to a gendered history of World War I, which uncovers subtle narratives and highly diversified realities, is true for a Jewish perspective as well. There was no such thing as one common Jewish experience and memory of World War I. For Jewish minorities in the belligerent countries, the war became a sort of a testing ground for their sense of belonging, their loyalties to nation and state, and their will to maintain a particular religious and cultural identity. In their respective societies, Jews shared the experiences of mobilization, warfare, violence, and bereavement, as well as the collective efforts to come to terms with the traumas of war and to commemorate mass death according to their social position and their political and ideological convictions. Primary sources, hitherto often unknown or neglected in relevant research, reveal the rich facets of their self-images as well as political and cultural viewpoints that emerged in the course of the global conflict. Up to now, the place and function of Jewish commemoration of war within public memory discourse and practices, as well as the creation of national collective identity in war and postwar societies, have not yet been sufficiently studied.

In her contribution, Tullia Catalan shows how Jewish women could engage in aggressive nationalism and how their nationalist stance could further radicalize in the context of the war. She presents a case study of two female Italian-Jewish writers in the borderlands of Austria-Hungary close to Italy, addressing an audience of women and children, whose irredentist nationalism went hand in hand with a strong commitment to the cause of women's emancipation. Under the impact of ethnic and religious conflict in the Habsburg border region and the rise of political antisemitism on the eve of the war and particularly during the war, their nationalist credo became increasingly aggressive, assuming racist overtones and preparing the path to fascism.

Ruth Nattermann focuses on the same milieu as Catalan, bourgeois national Jews; however, she focuses on those living in their homeland, not in what Italian nationalists considered their "unredeemed lands." In her chapter, she stresses the crucial role of personal choice and the closely knit unit of the family for individual political and ideological developments. She too considers World War I as a turning point for Italian nationalism and—referring to three Jewish family stories, in particular three prominent women, Margherita Sarfatti, Gina Lombroso, and Amelia Rosselli, as mothers and wives—illustrates how the experience of war violence and the loss of a beloved person, one's own son, on the battlefield could lead into fascism, glorifying and politicizing the soldiers' death as a sacrifice for a fatherland to be reborn, or, on the contrary, into antimilitarism, antifascist resistance, and exile.

Whereas Catalan and Nattermann deal with secular Jews who passionately embraced the cause of (Italian) nationalism while preserving at the same time a particular collective identity based on ethical values, ideas of a common origin, and shared family memories, Gerald Lamprecht discusses the constraints and barriers the Austro-German Jewish community had to confront when claiming public recognition and representation of their fallen soldiers and victims of war during wartime, i.e. during the last years of the Habsburg Monarchy and the crisis-ridden Austrian Republic from 1918 until 1938. Lamprecht's chapter highlights the Jewish community's insoluble dilemma between the willingness in principle to participate in public commemorations and the endeavor to preserve a Jewish particularism. Both in the late Empire and in the new national state it was difficult, if not impossible, for Jews to reconcile their sense of belonging as Jews with their declared patriotism and loyalty to the monarchy or, later, to the republican state, where remembrance was dominated by Christian traditions and practices. During the war as well as the interwar period, Jewish discourses about military service and war memory were always linked to the defense against the menace of antisemitism, the pursuit of social acceptance, and the state's formal guarantee and protection of civil rights. Austria, in this way, preceded Fascist Italy, where, from 1938 onward, the Racial Laws gave the ultimate evidence for the impossibility of integrating Jews into the national heroic narrative, created and propagated by male and female, Jewish and gentile advocates of Risorgimento nationalism, and deceptively sealed by the unconditional participation in the national war effort.

Martin Baumeister has been the director of the German Historical Institute in Rome since 2012. From 2003 until 2017, he held the Chair in Contemporary European History at the Ludwig-Maximilians-Universität of Munich. His current research interests are the history of contemporary Southern Europe and the Mediterranean, urban history, the history of religion, and the history of historiography. Among his recent publications is an annotated edition of *Robert Davidsohn, Menschen, die ich kannte: Erinnerungen eines Achtzigjährigen* (Berlin: Duncker & Humblot, 2019), edited together with Wiebke Fastenrath Vinattieri in collaboration with Wolfram Knäbich.

Philipp Lenhard is assistant professor (*Wissenschaftlicher Assistent*) of Jewish history and culture at the University of Munich. In 2015–16, he was a visiting scholar at the University of California, Berkeley. In 2016–17, he was a visiting professor of medieval and modern Jewish history at the Martin Buber Institute for Judaic Studies in Cologne. Lenhard published the monographs *Nation or Religion? The Emergence of Modern Jewish Ethnicity in France and Germany, 1782–1848* (Goettingen/Bristol: Vandenhoeck & Ruprecht, 2014) and *Friedrich Pollock: The Grey Eminence of the Frankfurt School* (Berlin: Jüdischer Verlag, 2019) in German.

Ruth Nattermann is assistant professor (Privatdozentin) at the Department of European History at the University of Munich. She held postdoctoral positions at the LMU Munich and the German Historical Institute in Rome, and has been principal investigator of the DFG-network

"Gender—Nation—Emancipation." Among her latest contributions are *Jüdinnen in der frühen italienischen Frauenbewegung 1861–1945. Biographien, Diskurse und transnationale Vernetzungen* (Rome: Bibliothek des Deutschen Historischen Instituts in Rom, 2020); "The Female Side of War: The Experience and Memory of the Great War in Italian-Jewish Women's Ego-Documents," in *The Jewish Experience of the First World War*, ed. Edward Madigan and Gideon Reuveni (Basingstoke/New York: Palgrave Macmillan, 2018), 233–54.

Notes

1. Karl Philipp Moritz, "Reise über den St. Gotthardsberg, und durch das Livinerthal: Eine der wildesten gegenden Italiens," in *Italien und Deutschland in Rücksicht auf Sitten, Gebräuche, Litteratur und Kunst: Eine Zeitschrift*, ed. Karl Philipp Moritz (Berlin, 1792), 62.
2. Ibid., 63.
3. From 1866 onward at the latest, historiography continued to reproduce the image of the two "late-coming nation-states." On this argument, see especially the critical assessment by Christian Goeschel, "A Parallel History? Rethinking the Relationship between Italy and Germany, ca. 1860–1945," *Journal of Modern History* 88 (2016): 610–32. See also Christof Dipper, "Italien und Deutschland seit 1800: Zwei Gesellschaften auf dem Weg in die Moderne," in *Europäische Sozialgeschichte: Festschrift für Wolfgang Schieder*, ed. Christof Dipper, Lutz Klinkhammer, and Alexander Nützenadel (Berlin: Duncker & Humblot Verlag, 2000), 493f.; Christof Dipper, "Revolution und Risorgimento: Italien 1848/49 aus deutscher Perspektive," in *Die Revolutionen von 1848 in der europäischen Geschichte: Ergebnisse und Nachwirkungen*, ed. Dieter Langewiesche (Munich: Oldenbourg Verlag, 2000), 73–89; Christof Dipper, *Ferne Nachbarn: Vergleichende Studien zu Deutschland und Italien in der Moderne* (Vienna: Böhlau, 2017); MacGregor Knox, "The First World War and Military Culture: Continuity and Change in Germany and Italy," in *Imperial Germany Revisited. Continuing Debates and New Perspectives*, ed. Cornelius Torp and Sven Oliver Müller (New York, Oxford: Berghahn Books, 2011), 213; Axel Körner, *Politics of Culture in Liberal Italy: From Unification to Fascism* (London: Routledge, 2008), 3f.; Dieter Langewiesche, *Reich, Nation, Föderation: Deutschland und Europa* (Munich: C. H. Beck, 2008), 146f.; Adrian Lyttelton, "The 'Crisis of Bourgeois Society' and the Origins of Fascism," in *Fascist Italy and Nazi Germany: Comparisons and Contrasts*, ed. Richard Bessel (Cambridge: Cambridge University Press, 1996), 14; Daniel Ziblatt, *Structuring the State: The Formation of Italy and Germany and the Puzzle of Federalism*. (Princeton, NJ: Princeton University Press, 2006), 7.
4. Treaty establishing the European Economic Community (Rome, 25 March 1957), http://www.cvce.eu/obj/treaty_establishing_the_european_economic_communi ty_rome_25_march_1957-en-cca6ba28-0bf3-4ce6-8a76-6b0b3252696e.html.
5. Giuseppe Mazzini, "From a Revolutionary Alliance to the United States of Europe," in *A Cosmopolitanism of Nations*, ed. Steffano Reccia and Nadia Urbinati (Princeton, NJ: Princeton University Press, 2009), 131–35. For this topic, see

the interesting perspective of Alexander Tchoubarian, *The European Idea in History in the Nineteenth and Twentieth Centuries: A View from Moscow* (New York, London: Routledge, 1994), 46–61.

6. See, among others, *Inszenierungen des Nationalstaates: Politische Feiern in Deutschland und Italien seit 1860/71*, ed. Sabine Behrenbeck and Alexander Nützenadel (Cologne: SH Verlag, 2000); Gabriele B. Clemens, *Sanctus Amor Patriae: Eine vergleichende Studie zu deutschen und italienischen Geschichtsvereinen im 19. Jahrhundert* (Tübingen: Max Niemeyer Verlag, 2004); Christof Dipper, *Ferne Nachbarn; Zentralismus und Föderalismus im 19. und 20. Jahrhundert, Deutschland und Italien im Vergleich*, ed. Oliver Janz, Pierangelo Schiera, and Hannes Siegrist (Berlin: Duncker & Humblot, 2000); *Dalla città alla nazione: Borghesie ottocentesche in Italia e in Germania*, ed. Marco Meriggi and Pierangelo Schiera (Bologna: Il Mulino, 1993); Edoardo Tortarolo, *La ragione interpretata: La mediazione culturale tra Italia e Germania nell'età dell'Illuminismo* (Rome: Carocci Editore, 2003).

7. Jonathan L. Lipman et al. (eds.), *Modern East Asia: An Integrated History* (New York: Pearson, 2012); Barbara Molony et al. (eds.), *Gender in Modern East Asia: China, Korea, Japan; An Integrated History* (Boulder, CO: Westview Press, 2016); Sisir Kumar Das, "Integrated History of Indian Literature: A Draft Working Paper," in *A History of Indian Literature: 1800–1910; Western Impact, Indian Response*, Sisir Kumar Das (New Delhi: Sahitya Akademi, 1991), 341–66; Charles Holcombe, *A History of East Asia: From the Origins of Civilization to the Twenty-First Century*. (Cambridge: Cambridge University Press, 2011.)

8. See by way of example Saul Friedländer, "An Integrated History of the Holocaust: Possibilities and Challenges," in *Years of Persecution, Years of Extermination: Saul Friedländer and the Future of Holocaust Studies*, ed. Christian Wiese and Paul Betts (New York: Bloomsbury, 2010), 21–29, and Zoë V. Waxman, "Towards an Integrated History of the Holocaust: Masculinity, Femininity, and Genocide," in ibid., 311–21; Tomasz Frydel, "The Devil in Microhistory: The 'Hunt for Jews' as a Social Process 1942–1945," in *Microhistories of the Holocaust*, ed. Claire Zalc and Tal Bruttmann (New York, Oxford: Berghahn Books, 2017), 171–89.

9. See especially Ute Frevert, ed., *Bürgerinnen und Bürger: Geschlechterverhältnisse im 19. Jahrhundert* (Göttingen: Vandenhoeck & Ruprecht, 1988); Svenja Goltermann, *Körper der Nation: Habitusformierung und die Politik des Turnens 1860–1890* (Göttingen: Vandenhoeck & Ruprecht, 1998); Sylvia Paletschek, *Frauen und Dissens: Frauen im Deutschkatholizismus und in den freien Gemeinden 1841–1852* (Göttingen: Vandenhoeck & Ruprecht, 1990); *Nation, Politik und Geschlecht: Frauenbewegungen und Nationalismus in der Moderne*, ed. Ute Planert (New York: Campus Verlag, 2000).

10. See Ilaria Porciani, ed., *Famiglia e Nazione nel lungo Ottocento Italiano: Modelli, strategie, reti di relazioni* (Rome: Viella, 2006); Paul Ginsborg and Ilaria Porciani, "Famiglia, società civile e Stato tra Otto e Novecento," special issue, *Passato e Presente* 57 (September–December 2002).

11. Paul Ginsborg, "Romanticismo e Risorgimento: l'io, l'amore e la nazione," in *Storia d'Italia: Annali 22. Il Risorgimento*, ed. Alberto Mario Banti and Paul Ginsborg (Turin: Einaudi, 2007), 25.

12. Rare examples are Ulrich Wyrwa, *Juden in der Toskana und in Preußen im Vergleich: Aufklärung und Emanzipation in Florenz, Livorno, Berlin und Königsberg i. Pr.* (Tübingen: Mohr Siebeck, 2003); Ulrich Wyrwa, *Gesellschaftliche Konfliktfelder und die Entstehung des Antisemitismus: Das Deutsche Kaiserreich und das Li-

berale Italien im Vergleich (Berlin: Metropol Verlag, 2015); Mario Toscano, ed., *Integrazione e identità: L'esperienza ebraica in Germania e Italia dall'illuminismo al fascismo* (Milan: Franco Angeli, 1998); Lois C. Dubin, "The Rise and Fall of the Italian Jewish Model in Germany: From Haskalah to Reform, 1780–1820," in *Jewish History and Jewish Memory: Essays in Honor of Yosef Hayim Yerushalmi*, ed. Elisheva Carlebach et al. (London: Brandeis University Press, 1998), 271–95; Cristiana Facchini, "Living in Exile: *Wissenschaft des Judentums* and the Study of Religion in Italy (1890s–1930s)," in *Italian Jewish Networks from the Seventeenth to the Twentieth Century: Bridging Europe and the Mediterranean*, ed. Francesca Bregoli et al. (New York: Palgrave Macmillan, 2018), 101–26; Asher D. Biemann, "'Thus Rome shows us our True Place': Reflections on the German Jewish Love for Italy," in *German-Jewish Thought between Religion and Politics: Festschrift in Honor of Paul Mendes-Flohr on the Occasion of His Seventieth Birthday*, ed. Christian Wiese and Martina Urban (Boston: De Gruyter, 2012), 241–62.

13. Michel Espagne, *Les juifs allemands de Paris à l'époque de Heine: La translation ashkénaze* (Paris: PUF, 1996); Michael Brenner et al., eds., *Jewish Emancipation Reconsidered: The French and German Models* (Tübingen: Mohr Siebeck, 2003); Philipp Lenhard, *Volk oder Religion? Die Entstehung moderner jüdischer Ethnizität in Frankreich und Deutschland, 1782–1848* (Göttingen: Vandenhoeck & Ruprecht, 2014); Ari Joskowicz, *The Modernity of Others: Jewish Anti-Catholicism in Germany and France* (Stanford, CA: Stanford University Press, 2014).

14. Tobias Grill, *Der Westen im Osten: Deutsches Judentum und jüdische Bildungsreform in Osteuropa (1783–1939)* (Göttingen: Vandenhoeck & Ruprecht, 2013); Tobias Brinkmann, *Von der Gemeinde zur "Community": Jüdische Einwanderer in Chicago 1840–1900* (Osnabrück: Universitätsverlag Rasch, 2002).

15. The emergence of an Italian-Jewish "Sonderweg" is analyzed by Carlotta Ferrara degli Uberti, *Making Italian Jews: Family, Gender, Religion and the Nation, 1861–1918* (London: Palgrave MacMillan, 2017). The myth of the Italian-Jewish "Sonderweg" has been challenged by Asher Salah, "Steinschneider and Italy," in *Studies on Moritz Steinschneider (1816–1907)*, ed. Gad Freudenthal and Reimund Leicht (Leyden, Boston: Brill, 2011), 411–56. For an overview, see Stanislao G. Pugliese, ed., *The Most Ancient of Minorities: The Jews of Italy* (Westport, CT: Greenwood Press, 2002); Elizabeth Schächter, *The Jews of Italy, 1848–1915: Between Tradition and Transformation* (Portland, OR: Vallentine Mitchell, 2011); Shira Klein, *Italy's Jews from Emancipation to Fascism* (Cambridge: Cambridge University Press, 2018).

16. Anna Esposito, "Gli ebrei aschenaziti a Roma nel primo Rinascimento," *Quellen und Forschungen aus italienischen Archiven und Bibliotheken* 91 (2011), 249–76.

17. Lois C. Dubin, *The Port Jews of Habsburg Trieste: Absolutist Politics and Enlightenment Culture* (Stanford, CA: Stanford University Press, 1999).

18. On the characteristic tension between participation and exclusion, or rather aggression, with regard to nationalism, see Dieter Langewiesche, "Nationalismus im 19. und 20. Jahrhundert: zwischen Partizipation und Aggression," in *Nation, Nationalismus, Nationalstaat in Deutschland und Europa* (Munich: C. H. Beck, 2000), 35–54.

19. This version was supported especially by Renzo De Felice, *Storia degli ebrei sotto il fascismo* (Turin: Einaudi, 1961). The important studies by Enzo Collotti and Michele Sarfatti have corrected this distorted view and demonstrated that the Racial Laws in 1938 did not represent a sudden change within Italian society

toward antisemitism but rather the climax of a long-term development; see Enzo Collotti, *Il Fascismo e gli ebrei: Le leggi razziali in Italia* (Rome: Laterza, 2004); Michele Sarfatti, *The Jews in Mussolini's Italy: From Equality to Persecution* (Madison: University of Wisconsin Press, 2006). On this argument, see also the works by David Bidussa and Filippo Focardi on the "myth" of the "good Italian": David Bidussa, *Il mito del bravo italiano* (Milan: Il Saggiatore, 1994); Filippo Focardi, *Il cattivo tedesco e il bravo italiano: La rimozione delle colpe della seconda guerra mondiale* (Rome: Laterza, 2013).

20. Among the studies that distance themselves explicitly from the "success story" of Italian Jewry, see Wyrwa, *Gesellschaftliche Konfliktfelder*; Elizabeth Schächter, *The Jews of Italy, 1848–1915: Between Tradition and Transformation* (Portland, OR: Vallentine Mitchell, 2011); Martin Baumeister, "'Ebrei fortunati?': Juden in Italien zwischen Risorgimento und Faschismus," in *Italien, Blicke: Neue Perspektiven der italienischen Geschichte des 19. und 20. Jahrhunderts*, ed. Petra Terhoeven (Göttingen: Vandenhoeck & Ruprecht, 2010), 43–60. On the incomplete emancipation process of Italian-Jewish women, see Ruth Nattermann, *Jüdinnen in der frühen italienischen Frauenbewegung 1861–1945. Biographien, Diskurse und transnationale Vernetzungen* (Rome: Bibliothek des Deutschen Historischen Instituts in Rom, 2020).

21. See Michael Brenner, "Zwischen Revolution und rechtlicher Gleichstellung," in *Deutsch-jüdische Geschichte in der Neuzeit*, vol. 2, ed. Michael Brenner, Stefi Jersch-Wenzel, and Michael A. Meyer (Munich: C. H. Beck, 1996), 287–302; Arno Herzig, *Jüdische Geschichte in Deutschland: Von den Anfängen bis zur Gegenwart* (Munich: C. H. Beck, 1997), 185.

22. See Collotti, *Il Fascismo e gli ebrei*, 13f.

23. See Karen Offen, *European Feminisms 1700–1950: A Political History* (Stanford, CA: Stanford University Press, 2000), 121; Perry Willson, *Women in Twentieth-Century Italy* (New York: Palgrave Macmillan, 2010), 57.

24. On the status of contemporary German women within marriages and families, see Angelika Schaser, *Frauenbewegung in Deutschland 1848–1933* (Darmstadt: Wissenschaftliche Buchgesellschaft, 2006), 11; Ernst Holthöfer, "Die Geschlechtsvormundschaft: Ein Überblick von der Antike bis ins 19. Jahrhundert," in *Frauen in der Geschichte des Rechts: Von der Frühen Neuzeit bis zur Gegenwart*, ed. Ute Gerhard (Munich: C. H. Beck, 1997), 390–451; Martina Kessel, "Individuum/Familie/Gesellschaft in der Neuzeit," in *Europäische Mentalitätsgeschichte: Hauptthemen in Einzeldarstellungen*, ed. Peter Dinzelbacher (Stuttgart: Alfred Kröner Verlag, 1993), 38–53.

25. See Sylvia Paletschek and Bianka Pietrow-Ennker, "Introduction," in *Women's Emancipation Movements in the 19th Century*, ed. Sylvia Paletschek and Bianka Pietrow-Ennker (Stanford, CA: Stanford University Press, 2004), 6. On the contemporary use of the term "women's emancipation," see Offen, *European Feminisms*, 112f., as well as Anne-Laure Briatte's chapter in this volume. On Offen's proposal to use the term "feminism" to define women's emancipation movements of the nineteenth century, see *European Feminisms*, 19–21; Karen Offen, "Challenging Male Hegemony: Feminist Criticism and the Context for Women's Movements in the Age of European Revolutions and Counterrevolutions," in *Women's Emancipation Movements*, 29.

26. On this argument, see Barbara Vogel, "Inklusion und Exklusion von Frauen: Überlegungen zum liberalen Emanzipationsprojekt im Kaiserreich," in *Liberalis-*

mus und Emanzipation: In- und Exklusionsprozesse im Kaiserreich und in der Weimarer Republik, ed. Angelika Schaser and Stefanie Schüler-Springorum (Stuttgart: Franz Steiner Verlag, 2010), especially 200, 204.

27. The respective dates and processes of these achievements differed considerably in the German and the Italian contexts. Whereas in Italy women were allowed to enter secondary schools and universities from 1884 onward, it was not before 1900 that German universities, and at first only the ones in Freiburg and Heidelberg, accepted female students. With the introduction of the *legge Sacchi* in 1919, Italian women were allowed to practice all professions (with certain exceptions), while such access was still restricted for women in Germany. However, Italian legal reforms in the aftermath of World War I excluded the vote for women, while in Germany women's suffrage was introduced in November 1918; see especially James C. Albisetti, *Schooling German Girls and Women: Secondary and Higher Education in the Nineteenth Century* (Princeton, NJ: Princeton University Press, 1988); *Geschichte der Mädchen- und Frauenbildung*, vol. 2: *Vom Vormärz bis zur Gegenwart*, ed. Elke Kleinau and Claudia Opitz (New York: Campus Verlag, 1996); Simonetta Polenghi and Carla Ghizzoni, eds., *L'altra metà della scuola: Educazione e lavoro delle donne tra Otto e Novecento* (Turin: Einaudi, 2008); Simonetta Soldani, ed., *L'educazione delle donne: Scuole e modelli di vita femminile nell'Italia dell'Ottocento* (Milan: Franco Angeli, 1989).

28. In spite of their political, social, and cultural relevance, many of the protagonists and organizations of the early movements have been rather forgotten by European historiography and collective memory. Only from the beginning of the twenty-first century, especially German-speaking historiography has begun to examine thoroughly the biographies and writings of several central protagonists of the first women's emancipation movements; see especially Angelika Schaser, *Helene Lange und Gertrud Bäumer: Eine politische Lebensgemeinschaft* (Vienna: Böhlau, 2000); Susanne Kinnebrock, *Anita Augspurg (1857–1943): Feministin und Journalistin zwischen Journalismus und Politik; Eine kommunikationshistorische Biographie* (Herbolzheim: Centaurus Verlag, 2005); Britta Konz, *Bertha Pappenheim (1859–1936): Ein Leben für jüdische Tradition und weibliche Emanzipation* (New York: Campus Verlag, 2005). Recently, there has been a new trend toward the rediscovery of European first-wave feminism and its protagonists; see e.g. Johanna Gehmacher, Elisa Heinrich, and Corinna Oesch, eds., *Käthe Schirmacher: Agitation und autobiographische Praxis zwischen radikaler Frauenbewegung und völkischer Politik* (Vienna: Böhlau Verlag, 2018); Angelika Schaser and Sylvia Schraut, eds., *Frauenbewegungen in Europa (19.-20. Jahrhundert): Narrative, Traditionsstiftung und Vergessen* (New York: Campus Verlag, 2019).

29. The Italian and German cases represent important examples. The most important Italian women's association, the Unione Femminile Nazionale (UFN), founded in 1899 in Milan, had about 10 percent Jewish membership until the passing of the Fascist Racial Laws in November 1938; see Liana Novelli-Glaab, "'Zwischen Tradition und Moderne': Jüdinnen in Italien um 1900," in *"Denn in Italien haben sich die Dinge anders abgespielt": Judentum und Antisemitismus im modernen Italien*, ed. Liana Novelli-Glaab and Gudrun Jäger (Berlin: Trafo Verlag, 2007), 110. Approximately one-third of the participants in the early German women's movement were Jewish. In contrast to the numerous left-wing Italian-Jewish feminists, they mainly belonged to the moderate middle-class groups. Out of ninety-four women's associations that existed in Berlin in 1893, thirty were led by Jewish

women; see Stefanie Schüler-Springorum, *Geschlecht und Differenz* (Paderborn: Schöningh, 2014), 97.

30. Compared to the German, French, and British movements, the first emancipation movement in Italy, its protagonists, concepts, and associations, as well as its distinct transnational orientation, has receded rather into the background in the relevant historiography. Among the standard works, see Franca Pieroni Bortolotti, *Alle origini del movimento femminile in Italia 1848–1892* (Turin: Einaudi, 1963); Franca Pieroni Bortolotti, *La Donna, La Pace, L'Europa: L'Associazione internazionale delle donne dalle origini alla prima guerra mondiale* (Milan: Franco Angeli, 1985); Annarita Buttafuoco, *Cronache femminili: Temi e momenti della stampa emancipazionista in Italia dall'Unità al fascismo* (Arezzo: Dipartimento di studi storico-sociali, 1988); Annarita Buttafuoco, *Le Mariuccine: Storia di un'istituzione laica; L'asilo Mariuccia* (Milan: Franco Angeli, 1985). Among the more recent studies, see Elisabeth Dickmann, *Die italienische Frauenbewegung im 19. Jahrhundert* (Frankfurt am Main: Domus Editoria Europaea, 2002); Gabriele Boukrif, *"Der Schritt über den Rubikon": Eine vergleichende Untersuchung zur deutschen und italienischen Frauenstimmrechtsbewegung* (Münster: LIT Verlag, 2006); Willson, *Women in Twentieth-Century Italy*.

31. Christa Hämmerle, Oswald Überegger, and Birgitta Bader Zaar, eds., *Gender and the First World War* (New York: Palgrave Macmillan, 2014). See also Susan R. Grayzel and Tammy M. Proctor, eds., *Gender and the Great War* (Oxford: Oxford University Press, 2017). In spite of its frequent neglect by mainstream historiography, the international research over the past several decades on women's and gender history in World War I has produced numerous valuable publications, among them Gail Braybon and Penny Summerfield, eds., *Out of the Cage: Women's Experiences in Two World Wars* (New York: Routledge & Kegan Paul, 1987); Françoise Thébaud, *La femme au temps de la guerre de 14* (Paris: Éditions Stock, 1986); Ute Daniel, *The War from Within: German Working Class Women in the First World War* (Oxford: Berg, 1997); Susan R. Grayzel, *Women and the First World War* (London: Pearson Education, 2002); Karen Hagemann and Stefanie Schüler-Springorum, eds., *Home/Front: The Military, War and Gender in Twentieth-Century Germany* (New York: Berg, 2002). In the last few years, several important works have appeared on the closely enmeshed Italian, German, and Austrian-Hungarian spheres; see Christa Hämmerle, *Heimat/Front: Geschlechtergeschichte/n des Ersten Weltkriegs in Österreich-Ungarn* (Vienna: Böhlau Verlag, 2014); Stefania Bartoloni, ed., *La Grande Guerra delle italiane: Mobilitazioni, diritti, trasformazioni* (Rome: Viella, 2016); Stefania Bartoloni, *Donne di fronte alla guerra: Pace, diritti e democrazia (1878–1918)* (Rome: Laterza, 2017); Nadia Maria Filippini, ed., *Donne dentro la guerra: il primo conflitto mondiale in area veneta* (Rome: Viella, 2017).

32. See especially Marsha Rozenblit, *Reconstructing a National Identity: The Jews of Habsburg Austria during World War I* (Oxford: Oxford University Press, 2001); Petra Ernst and Eleonore Lappin-Eppel, eds., *Jüdische Publizistik und Literatur im Zeichen des Ersten Weltkriegs* (Innsbruck: Studienverlag, 2016); Petra Ernst, Jeffrey Grossman, and Ulrich Wyrwa, eds., "The Great War: Reflections, Experiences and Memories of German and Habsburg Jews (1914–1918)," special issue, *Quest: Issues in Contemporary Jewish History; Journal of Fondazione CDEC* 9 (October 2016), http://www.quest-cdecjournal.it/index.php?issue=9; Gerald Lamprecht, Eleonore Lappin-Eppel, and Ulrich Wyrwa, eds., *Jewish Soldiers in*

the *Collective Memory of Central Europe: The Remembrance of World War I from a Jewish Perspective* (Vienna: Böhlau Verlag, 2018); Edward Madigan and Gideon Reuveni, eds., *The Jewish Experience of the First World War* (New York: Palgrave Macmillan, 2018).
33. See Caterina Quareni and Vincenzo Maugeri, eds., *Gli ebrei italiani nella grande guerra (1915–1918): Atti del Convegno del Museo Ebraico, Bologna, 11 novembre 2015* (Florence: Giuntina, 2017).
34. See Tullia Catalan, "Linguaggi e stereotipi dell'antislavismo irredentista dalla fine dell'Ottocento alla Grande Guerra," in *Fratelli al massacre: Linguaggi e narrazioni della Prima Guerra Mondiale*, ed. Tullia Catalan (Rome: Viella, 2015), 39–69; Ruth Nattermann, "Zwischen Pazifismus, Irredentismus und nationaler Euphorie: Italienische Jüdinnen und der Erste Weltkrieg," in *Jüdische Publizistik und Literatur im Zeichen des Ersten Weltkriegs*, ed. Petra Ernst and Eleonore Lappin-Eppel (Innsbruck: Studienverlag, 2016), 247–63; Ruth Nattermann, "The Female Side of War: The Experience and Memory of the Great War in Italian-Jewish Women's Ego Documents," in *The Jewish Experience of the First World War*, 233–54; Monica Miniati, "Donne in guerra: Il contributo femminile ebraico nella Prima Guerra Mondiale," in *Gli ebrei italiani nella grande guerra (1915–1918)*, 127–47.
35. See Ute Planert, "Vater Staat und Mutter Germania: Zur Politisierung des weiblichen Geschlechts im 19. und 20. Jahrhundert," in *Nation, Politik und Geschlecht*, 50; Ruth Nattermann, "Frauen in der europäischen Friedensbewegung. Die Association Internationale des Femmes (1868–1914)," *Themenportal Europäische Geschichte* (2015), http://www.europa.clio-online.de/2015/Article=744.
36. See Michael L. Miller and Scott Ury, "Cosmopolitanism: The End of Jewishness," *European Review of History* 17, no. 3 (2010): 344f. For the recent discussion regarding the relationship between cosmopolitanism and Judaism, see, among others, Cathy S. Gelbin and Sander L. Gilman, *Cosmopolitanisms and the Jews* (Ann Arbor: University of Michigan Press, 2017); Cathy S. Gelbin and Sander L. Gilman, eds., *Jews on the Move: Modern Cosmopolitanist Thought and Its Others* (New York: Routledge, 2018); Michael L. Miller and Scott Ury, eds., *Cosmopolitanism, Nationalism and the Jews of Central Europe* (New York: Routledge, 2014).

Bibliography

Albisetti, James C. *Schooling German Girls and Women: Secondary and Higher Education in the Nineteenth Century*. Princeton, NJ: Princeton University Press, 1988.
Bartoloni, Stefania, ed. *La Grande Guerra delle italiane: Mobilitazioni, diritti, trasformazioni*. Rome: Viella, 2016.
———. *Donne di fronte alla guerra: Pace, diritti e democrazia (1878–1918)*. Rome: Laterza, 2017.
Baumeister, Martin. "'Ebrei fortunati?': Juden in Italien zwischen Risorgimento und Faschismus." In *Italien, Blicke: Neue Perspektiven der italienischen Geschichte des 19. und 20. Jahrhunderts*, edited by Petra Terhoeven, 43–60. Göttingen: Vandenhoeck & Ruprecht, 2010.
Behrenbeck, Sabine, and Alexander Nützenadel, eds. *Inszenierungen des Nationalstaates: Politische Feiern in Deutschland und Italien seit 1860/71*. Cologne: SH Verlag, 2000.

Bidussa, David. *Il mito del bravo italiano*. Milan: Il Saggiatore, 1994.
Biemann, Asher D. "'Thus Rome Shows Us Our True Place': Reflections on the German Jewish Love for Italy." In *German-Jewish Thought between Religion and Politics: Festschrift in Honor of Paul Mendes-Flohr on the Occasion of His Seventieth Birthday*, edited by Christian Wiese and Martina Urban, 241–62. Boston: De Gruyter, 2012.
Boukrif, Gabriele. *"Der Schritt über den Rubikon": Eine vergleichende Untersuchung zur deutschen und italienischen Frauenstimmrechtsbewegung*. Münster: LIT Verlag, 2006.
Braybon, Gail, and Penny Summerfield, eds. *Out of the Cage: Women's Experiences in Two World Wars*. New York: Routledge & Kegan Paul, 1987.
Brenner, Michael. "Zwischen Revolution und rechtlicher Gleichstellung." In *Deutsch-jüdische Geschichte in der Neuzeit*, vol. 2, edited by Michael Brenner, Stefi Jersch-Wenzel, and Michael A. Meyer, 287–302. Munich: C. H. Beck, 1996.
Brenner, Michael, Vicki Caron, and Uri R. Kaufmann, eds. *Jewish Emancipation Reconsidered: The French and German Models*. Tübingen: Mohr Siebeck, 2003.
Brinkmann, Tobias. *Von der Gemeinde zur "Community": Jüdische Einwanderer in Chicago 1840–1900*. Osnabrück: Universitätsverlag Rasch, 2002.
Buttafuoco, Annarita. *Le Mariuccine: Storia di un'istituzione laica; L'asilo Mariuccia*. Milan: Franco Angeli, 1985.
———. *Cronache femminili: Temi e momenti della stampa emancipazionista in Italia dall'Unità al fascismo*. Arezzo: Dipartimento di studi storico-sociali, 1988.
Catalan, Tullia. "Linguaggi e stereotipi dell'antislavismo irredentista dalla fine dell'Ottocento alla Grande Guerra." In *Fratelli al massacro: Linguaggi e narrazioni della Prima Guerra Mondiale*, edited by Tullia Catalan, 39–69. Rome: Viella, 2015.
Clemens, Gabriele B. *Sanctus Amor Patriae: Eine vergleichende Studie zu deutschen und italienischen Geschichtsvereinen im 19. Jahrhundert*. Tübingen: Max Niemeyer Verlag, 2004.
Collotti, Enzo. *Il Fascismo e gli ebrei: Le leggi razziali in Italia*. Rome: Laterza, 2004.
Daniel, Ute. *The War from Within: German Working Class Women in the First World War*. Oxford: Berg, 1997.
De Felice, Renzo. *Storia degli ebrei sotto il fascismo*. Turin: Einaudi, 1961.
Dickmann, Elisabeth. *Die italienische Frauenbewegung im 19. Jahrhundert*. Frankfurt am Main: Domus Editoria Europaea, 2002.
Dipper, Christof. "Italien und Deutschland seit 1800: Zwei Gesellschaften auf dem Weg in die Moderne." In *Europäische Sozialgeschichte: Festschrift für Wolfgang Schieder*, edited by Christof Dipper, Lutz Klinkhammer, and Alexander Nützenadel, 485–503. Berlin: Duncker & Humblot Verlag, 2000.
———. "Revolution und Risorgimento: Italien 1848/49 aus deutscher Perspektive." In *Die Revolutionen von 1848 in der europäischen Geschichte: Ergebnisse und Nachwirkungen*, edited by Dieter Langewiesche, 73–89. Munich: Oldenbourg Verlag, 2000.
———. *Ferne Nachbarn: Vergleichende Studien zu Deutschland und Italien in der Moderne*. Vienna: Böhlau Verlag, 2017.
Dubin, Lois C. "The Rise and Fall of the Italian Jewish Model in Germany: From Haskalah to Reform, 1780–1820." In *Jewish History and Jewish Memory: Essays in Honor of Yosef Hayim Yerushalmi*, edited by Elisheva Carlebach, John M. Efron, and David N. Myers, 271–95. London: Brandeis University Press, 1998.
———. *The Port Jews of Habsburg Trieste: Absolutist Politics and Enlightenment Culture*. Stanford, CA: Stanford University Press, 1999.

Ernst, Petra, and Eleonore Lappin-Eppel, eds. *Jüdische Publizistik und Literatur im Zeichen des Ersten Weltkriegs*. Innsbruck: Studienverlag, 2016.
Ernst, Petra, Jeffrey Grossman, and Ulrich Wyrwa, eds. "The Great War: Reflections, Experiences and Memories of German and Habsburg Jews (1914–1918)." Special issue, *Quest: Issues in Contemporary Jewish History; Journal of Fondazione CDEC* 9 (October 2016).
Espagne, Michel. *Les juifs allemands de Paris à l'époque de Heine: La translation ashkénaze*. Paris: PUF, 1996.
Esposito, Anna. "Gli ebrei aschenaziti a Roma nel primo Rinascimento." *Quellen und Forschungen aus italienischen Archiven und Bibliotheken* 91 (2011): 249–76.
Facchini, Cristiana. "Living in Exile: *Wissenschaft des Judentums* and the Study of Religion in Italy (1890s–1930s)." In *Italian Jewish Networks from the Seventeenth to the Twentieth Century: Bridging Europe and the Mediterranean*, edited by Francesca Bregoli et al., 101–26. New York: Palgrave Macmillan, 2018.
Ferrara degli Uberti, Carlotta. *Making Italian Jews: Family, Gender, Religion and the Nation, 1861–1918*. London: Palgrave MacMillan, 2017.
Filippini, Nadia Maria, ed. *Donne dentro la guerra: Il primo conflitto mondiale in area veneta*. Rome: Viella, 2017.
Focardi, Filippo. *Il cattivo tedesco e il bravo italiano: La rimozione delle colpe della seconda guerra mondiale*. Rome: Laterza, 2013.
Frevert, Ute, ed. *Bürgerinnen und Bürger: Geschlechterverhältnisse im 19. Jahrhundert*. Göttingen: Vandenhoeck & Ruprecht, 1988.
Friedländer, Saul. "An Integrated History of the Holocaust: Possibilities and Challenges." In *Years of Persecution, Years of Extermination: Saul Friedländer and the Future of Holocaust Studies*, edited by Christian Wiese and Paul Betts, 21–29. New York: Bloomsbury, 2010.
Frydel, Tomasz. "The Devil in Microhistory: The 'Hunt for Jews' as a Social Process 1942–1945." In *Microhistories of the Holocaust*, edited by Claire Zalc and Tal Bruttmann, 171–89. New York: Berghahn Books, 2017.
Gehmacher, Johanna, Elisa Heinrich, and Corinna Oesch, eds. *Käthe Schirmacher: Agitation und autobiographische Praxis zwischen radikaler Frauenbewegung und völkischer Politik*. Vienna: Böhlau Verlag, 2018.
Gelbin, Cathy S., and Sander L. Gilman, *Cosmopolitanisms and the Jews*. Ann Arbor: University of Michigan Press, 2017.
———, eds. *Jews on the Move: Modern Cosmopolitanist Thought and Its Others*. New York: Routledge, 2018.
Ginsborg, Paul. "Romanticismo e Risorgimento: l'io, l'amore e la nazione." In *Storia d'Italia: Annali 22. Il Risorgimento*, edited by Alberto Mario Banti and Paul Ginsborg, 5–67. Turin: Einaudi, 2007.
Ginsborg, Paul, and Ilaria Porciani, eds. *Famiglia, società civile e Stato tra Otto e Novecento*. Special issue, *Passato e Presente* 57 (September–December 2002).
Goeschel, Christian. "A Parallel History? Rethinking the Relationship between Italy and Germany, ca. 1860–1945." *Journal of Modern History* 88 (2016): 610–32.
Goltermann, Svenja. *Körper der Nation: Habitusformierung und die Politik des Turnens 1860–1890*. Göttingen: Vandenhoeck & Ruprecht, 1998.
Grayzel, Susan R. *Women and the First World War*. London: Pearson Education, 2002.
Grayzel, Susan R., and Tammy M. Proctor, eds. *Gender and the Great War*. Oxford: Oxford University Press, 2017.

Grill, Tobias. *Der Westen im Osten: Deutsches Judentum und jüdische Bildungsreform in Osteuropa (1783–1939)*. Göttingen: Vandenhoeck & Ruprecht, 2013.
Hagemann, Karen, and Stefanie Schüler-Springorum, eds. *Home/Front: The Military, War and Gender in Twentieth-Century Germany*. New York: Berg, 2002.
Hämmerle, Christa. *Heimat/Front: Geschlechtergeschichte/n des Ersten Weltkriegs in Österreich-Ungarn*. Vienna: Böhlau Verlag, 2014.
Hämmerle, Christa, Oswald Überegger, and Birgitta Bader Zaar, eds. *Gender and the First World War*. New York: Palgrave Macmillan, 2014.
Herzig, Arno. *Jüdische Geschichte in Deutschland: Von den Anfängen bis zur Gegenwart*. Munich: C. H. Beck, 1997.
Holcombe, Charles. *A History of East Asia: From the Origins of Civilization to the Twenty-First Century*. Cambridge: Cambridge University Press, 2011.
Holthöfer, Ernst. "Die Geschlechtsvormundschaft: Ein Überblick von der Antike bis ins 19. Jahrhundert." In *Frauen in der Geschichte des Rechts: Von der Frühen Neuzeit bis zur Gegenwart*, edited by Ute Gerhard, 390–451. Munich: C. H. Beck, 1997.
Janz, Oliver, Pierangelo Schiera, and Hannes Siegrist, eds. *Zentralismus und Föderalismus im 19. und 20. Jahrhundert, Deutschland und Italien im Vergleich*. Berlin: Duncker & Humblot, 2000.
Joskowicz, Ari. *The Modernity of Others: Jewish Anti-Catholicism in Germany and France*. Stanford, CA: Stanford University Press, 2014.
Kessel, Martina. "Individuum/Familie/Gesellschaft in der Neuzeit." In *Europäische Mentalitätsgeschichte: Hauptthemen in Einzeldarstellungen*, edited by Peter Dinzelbacher, 38–53. Stuttgart: Alfred Kröner Verlag, 1993.
Kinnebrock, Susanne. *Anita Augspurg (1857–1943): Feministin und Journalistin zwischen Journalismus und Politik; Eine kommunikationshistorische Biographie*. Herbolzheim: Centaurus Verlag, 2005.
Klein, Shira. *Italy's Jews from Emancipation to Fascism*. Cambridge: Cambridge University Press, 2018.
Kleinau, Elke, and Claudia Opitz, eds. *Geschichte der Mädchen- und Frauenbildung*. Vol. 2: *Vom Vormärz bis zur Gegenwart*. New York: Campus Verlag, 1996.
Knox, MacGregor. "The First World War and Military Culture: Continuity and Change in Germany and Italy." In *Imperial Germany Revisited: Continuing Debates and New Perspectives*, edited by Cornelius Torp and Sven Oliver Müller, 213–25. New York: Berghahn Books, 2011.
Konz, Britta. *Bertha Pappenheim (1859–1936): Ein Leben für jüdische Tradition und weibliche Emanzipation*. New York: Campus Verlag, 2005.
Körner, Axel. *Politics of Culture in Liberal Italy: From Unification to Fascism*. London: Routledge, 2008.
Kumar Das, Sisir. "Integrated History of Indian Literature: A Draft Working Paper." In *A History of Indian Literature: 1800–1910; Western Impact, Indian Responses*, Sisir Kumar Das, 341–66. New Delhi: Sahitya Akademi, 1991.
Lamprecht, Gerald, Eleonore Lappin-Eppel, and Ulrich Wyrwa, eds. *Jewish Soldiers in the Collective Memory of Central Europe: The Remembrance of World War I from a Jewish Perspective*. Vienna: Böhlau Verlag, 2018.
Langewiesche, Dieter. "Nationalismus im 19. und 20. Jahrhundert: Zwischen Partizipation und Aggression." In *Nation, Nationalismus, Nationalstaat in Deutschland und Europa*, 35–54. Munich: C. H. Beck, 2000.
———. *Reich, Nation, Föderation: Deutschland und Europa*. Munich: C. H. Beck, 2008.

Lenhard, Philipp. *Volk oder Religion? Die Entstehung moderner jüdischer Ethnizität in Frankreich und Deutschland, 1782–1848*. Göttingen: Vandenhoeck & Ruprecht, 2014.

Lipman, Jonathan L., et al., eds. *Modern East Asia: An Integrated History*. New York: Pearson, 2012.

Lyttelton, Adrian. "The 'Crisis of Bourgeois Society' and the Origins of Fascism." In *Fascist Italy and Nazi Germany: Comparisons and Contrasts*, edited by Richard Bessel, 12–22. Cambridge: Cambridge University Press, 1996.

Madigan, Edward, and Gideon Reuveni, eds. *The Jewish Experience of the First World War*. New York: Palgrave Macmillan, 2018.

Mazzini, Giuseppe. "From a Revolutionary Alliance to the United States of Europe." In *A Cosmopolitanism of Nations*, edited by Steffano Reccia and Nadia Urbinati, 131–35. Princeton, NJ: Princeton University Press, 2009.

Meriggi, Marco, and Pierangelo Schiera. *Dalla città alla nazione: Borghesie ottocentesche in Italia e in Germania*. Bologna: Il Mulino, 1993.

Miller, Michael L., and Scott Ury. "Cosmopolitanism: The End of Jewishness." In *European Review of History* 17, no. 3 (2010): 337–59.

———, eds. *Cosmopolitanism, Nationalism and the Jews of Central Europe*. New York: Routledge, 2014.

Miniati, Monica. "Donne in guerra: Il contributo femminile ebraico nella Prima Guerra Mondiale." In *Gli ebrei italiani nella grande guerra (1915–1918)*, edited by Caterina Quareni and Vincenzo Maugerix, 127–47. Florence: Giuntina, 2017.

Molony, Barbara, Janet Theiss, and Hyaewoi Choi, eds. *Gender in Modern East Asia: China, Korea, Japan; An Integrated History*. Boulder, CO: Westview Press, 2016.

Moritz, Karl Philipp. "Reise über den St. Gotthardsberg, und durch das Livinerthal: Eine der wildesten gegenden Italiens." In *Italien und Deutschland in Rücksicht auf Sitten, Gebräuche, Litteratur und Kunst: Eine Zeitschrift*, edited by Karl Philipp Moritz, 62–94. Berlin, 1792.

Nattermann, Ruth. "Frauen in der europäischen Friedensbewegung Die Association Internationale des Femmes (1868–1914)." *Themenportal Europäische Geschichte* (2015), http://www.europa.clio-online.de/2015/Article=744.

———. "Zwischen Pazifismus, Irredentismus und nationaler Euphorie: Italienische Jüdinnen und der Erste Weltkrieg." In *Jüdische Publizistik und Literatur im Zeichen des Ersten Weltkriegs*, edited by Petra Ernst and Eleonore Lappin-Eppel, 247–63. Innsbruck: Studienverlag, 2016.

———. *Jüdinnen in der frühen italienischen Frauenbewegung 1861–1945. Biographien, Diskurse und transnationale Vernetzungen*. Rome: Bibliothek des Deutschen Historischen Instituts in Rom, 2020.

———. "The Female Side of War: The Experience and Memory of the Great War in Italian-Jewish Women's Ego Documents." In *The Jewish Experience of the First World War*, edited by Edward Madigan and Gideon Reuveni, 233–54. New York: Palgrave Macmillan, 2018.

Novelli-Glaab, Liana. "Zwischen Tradition und Moderne: Jüdinnen in Italien um 1900." In *"Denn in Italien haben sich die Dinge anders abgespielt": Judentum und Antisemitismus im modernen Italien*, edited by Liana Novelli-Glaab and Gudrun Jäger, 107–28. Berlin: Trafo Verlag, 2007.

Offen, Karen. *European Feminisms 1700–1950: A Political History*. Stanford, CA: Stanford University Press, 2000.

———. "Challenging Male Hegemony: Feminist Criticism and the Context for Women's Movements in the Age of European Revolutions and Counterrevolutions." In *Women's Emancipation Movements in the 19th Century*, edited by Sylvia Paletschek and Bianka Pietrow-Ennker, 11–30. Stanford, CA: Stanford University Press, 2004.

Paletschek, Sylvia. *Frauen und Dissens: Frauen im Deutschkatholizismus und in den freien Gemeinden 1841–1852*. Göttingen: Vandenhoeck & Ruprecht, 1990.

Paletschek, Sylvia, and Bianka Pietrow-Ennker. "Introduction." In *Women's Emancipation Movements in the 19th Century*, edited by Sylvia Paletschek and Bianka Pietrow-Ennker, 3–10. Stanford, CA: Stanford University Press, 2004.

Pieroni Bortolotti, Franca. *Alle origini del movimento femminile in Italia 1848–1892*. Turin: Einaudi, 1963.

———. *La Donna, La Pace, L'Europa: L'Associazione internazionale delle donne dalle origini alla prima guerra mondiale*. Milan: Franco Angeli, 1985.

Planert, Ute. "Vater Staat und Mutter Germania: Zur Politisierung des weiblichen Geschlechts im 19. und 20. Jahrhundert" In *Nation, Politik und Geschlecht*, edited by Ute Planert, 15–50. New York: Campus Verlag, 2000.

———, ed. *Nation, Politik und Geschlecht: Frauenbewegungen und Nationalismus in der Moderne*. New York: Campus Verlag, 2000.

Polenghi, Simonetta, and Carla Ghizzoni, eds. *L'altra metà della scuola: Educazione e lavoro delle donne tra Otto e Novecento*. Turin: Einaudi, 2008.

Porciani, Ilaria, ed. *Famiglia e Nazione nel lungo Ottocento Italiano: Modelli, strategie, reti di relazioni*. Rome: Viella, 2006.

Pugliese, Stanislao G., ed. *The Most Ancient of Minorities: The Jews of Italy*. Westport, CT: Greenwood Press, 2002.

Quareni, Caterina, and Vincenzo Maugeri, eds. *Gli ebrei italiani nella grande guerra (1915–1918): Atti del Convegno del Museo Ebraico, Bologna, 11 novembre 2015*. Florence: Giuntina, 2017.

Rozenblit, Marsha. *Reconstructing a National Identity: The Jews of Habsburg Austria during World War I*. Oxford: Oxford University Press, 2001.

Salah, Asher. "Steinschneider and Italy." In *Studies on Moritz Steinschneider (1816–1907)*, edited by Gad Freudenthal and Reimund Leicht, 411–56. Boston: Brill, 2011.

Sarfatti, Michele. *The Jews in Mussolini's Italy: From Equality to Persecution*. Madison: University of Wisconsin Press, 2006.

Schächter, Elizabeth. *The Jews of Italy, 1848–1915: Between Tradition and Transformation*. Portland, OR: Vallentine Mitchell, 2011.

Schaser, Angelika. *Helene Lange und Gertrud Bäumer: Eine politische Lebensgemeinschaft*. Vienna: Böhlau Verlag, 2000.

———. *Frauenbewegung in Deutschland 1848–1933*. Darmstadt: Wissenschaftliche Buchgesellschaft, 2006.

Schaser, Angelika, and Stefanie Schüler-Springorum, eds. *Liberalismus und Emanzipation: In- und Exklusionsprozesse im Kaiserreich und in der Weimarer Republik*. Stuttgart: Franz Steiner Verlag, 2010.

Schaser, Angelika, and Sylvia Schraut, eds. *Frauenbewegungen in Europa (19.-20. Jahrhundert): Narrative, Traditionsstiftung und Vergessen*. New York: Campus Verlag, 2019.

Schüler-Springorum, Stefanie. *Geschlecht und Differenz*. Paderborn: Schöningh, 2014.

Soldani, Simonetta. *L'educazione delle donne: Scuole e modelli di vita femminile nell'Italia dell'Ottocento*. Milan: Franco Angeli, 1989.

Tchoubarian, Alexander. *The European Idea in History in the Nineteenth and Twentieth Centuries: A View from Moscow*. New York: Routledge, 1994.

Thébaud, Françoise. *La femme au temps de la guerre de 14*. Paris: Éditions Stock, 1986.

Tortarolo, Edoardo. *La ragione interpretata: La mediazione culturale tra Italia e Germania nell'età dell'Illuminismo*. Rome: Carocci Editore, 2003.

Toscano, Mario. *Integrazione e identità: L'esperienza ebraica in Germania e Italia dall'illuminismo al fascismo*. Milan: Franco Angeli, 1998.

Vogel, Barbara. "Inklusion und Exklusion von Frauen: Überlegungen zum liberalen Emanzipationsprojekt im Kaiserreich." In *Liberalismus und Emanzipation: In- und Exklusionsprozesse im Kaiserreich und in der Weimarer Republik*, edited by Angelika Schaser and Stefanie Schüler-Springorum, 199–218. Stuttgart: Franz Steiner Verlag, 2010.

Waxman, Zoë V. "Towards an Integrated History of the Holocaust: Masculinity, Femininity, and Genocide." In *Years of Persecution, Years of Extermination: Saul Friedländer and the Future of Holocaust Studies*, edited by Christian Wiese and Paul Betts, 311–21. New York: Bloomsbury, 2010.

Willson, Perry. *Women in Twentieth-Century Italy*. New York: Palgrave Macmillan, 2010.

Wyrwa, Ulrich. *Juden in der Toskana und in Preußen im Vergleich: Aufklärung und Emanzipation in Florenz, Livorno, Berlin und Königsberg i. Pr.* Tübingen: Mohr Siebeck, 2003.

———. *Gesellschaftliche Konfliktfelder und die Entstehung des Antisemitismus: Das Deutsche Kaiserreich und das Liberale Italien im Vergleich*. Berlin: Metropol Verlag, 2015.

Ziblatt, Daniel. *Structuring the State: The Formation of Italy and Germany and the Puzzle of Federalism*. Princeton, NJ: Princeton University Press, 2006.

Section 1
CONCEPTS AND PERSPECTIVES

Chapter 1

Nineteenth-Century Italy and Germany beyond National History

Amerigo Caruso

"The natural intellectual superiority of Italy and Germany can easily be demonstrated, and we urgently need to nurture the feeling of affinity between these two great nations of Central Europe."[1] In 1873, just a few years after the formation of Italy and Germany as nation-states, the historian Heinrich von Treitschke wrote to the Italian diplomat Anselmo Guerrieri Gonzaga with these chauvinistic ideas. Treitschke projected his radical nationalist credo from the German into the Italian context, and from the late nineteenth century onward, several generations of commentators, entrenched in the narrative tradition of national history, held in common the conviction that the two nations shared a parallel history.[2] A wealth of supposed parallels contributes to this enduring narrative: the retrospective notion of "belated" nation-building; the trauma of national humiliation at the peace negotiations after World War I; the affinities between the Fascist and Nazi regimes; the transition to democracy and the "economic miracle" in the aftermath of World War II; from the early 1970s on, the consequences of the end of the long postwar boom; and, finally, the terrorist campaigns by the radical left-wing Baader-Meinhof Group and the Red Brigades.[3] The persistent tradition of parallel Italian and German histories is permeated by teleological thinking, which has inevitably influenced the approach of comparative history that emerged during the 1970s and became a mainstream methodology in the 1990s. Because comparative studies on the two countries have been influenced by the tradition of parallel history, a comparative analysis of Italian and German history can not only explicitly reproduce political and ideological nationalism, as in the case of Treitschke, but also perpetuate a less evident methodological nationalism.

During the last four decades, comparative research projects have put forward new interpretative and methodological approaches that are without doubt a far remove from Treitschke's radical nationalism. However, the end of national history may have been too hastily declared after the comparative and transnational turn. The two main purposes of this chapter are to highlight the persistence of methodological nationalism and to present some "best practices" employed by the new historiography that has moved on from purely national histories. I start by discussing the impact of comparative and transnational history on the traditional interpretative paradigms of Italian and German nation-building and, in particular, on more recent approaches such as gendered and Jewish perspectives. I then analyze the way that national histories have been constructed in time and space. In my third section, I explore the issue of whether methodological nationalism can be avoided by using combined approaches, such as that of comparison, transfer, and entanglement history. How can this three-step method be employed in practice? My concluding remarks examine the vitality of national history, which still tends to overlook the manifold foundations and plurality of collective identities, not just national, in nineteenth-century Italy and Germany. The construction of national identities, the problem of multiple social, political, and cultural loyalties, and the tensions between national emancipation and the emancipation of minorities are some of the key aspects discussed in this volume.[4]

New Interpretative Paradigms and the Persistence of Methodological Nationalism

In the field of the history of nationalism, one significant reason for the persistence of interpretative traditions that focus on the national is the assumption, either deliberate or unconscious, that this is the most important dimension of history.[5] This methodological nationalism has particularly weighty implications in the cases of Italy and Germany, because it overlaps with the tradition of parallel history. The persistence of methodological nationalism is strongly connected to the narrative impact of nationalism during the nineteenth century. Especially in the second half of the century, nationalist poets, artists, historians, and politicians employed teleological thinking to imagine and present the nation-state with great success as a consensual, natural, and modern historical outcome. In the final decades prior to World War I, there were also aggressive claims of cultural superiority and racial exclusivity made by more-radical nationalists. Despite the emergence of these racist and chauvinistic views, the rise of nationalism in nineteenth-century Europe was in fact a transcultural, transnational, highly contested, and open-ended phenomenon. The multiple foundations and contradictions of nationalism and nation-building had often been ignored, and they still pose a major challenge for historical studies.

A further methodological problem is posed by the plurality of historical identities in Europe and their close relationship to "essentially contested concepts" such as nation, religion, gender, race, ethnicity, and class.[6] In John Breuilly's view, historians should study the nation and nationalism as mutually independent concepts in order to overcome the analytical challenge of examining nationalism and nation-building. He emphasizes that nationalism should not be considered as the expression of a unique national history but as a "distinct phenomenon with general characteristics which is productive for the national."[7] Achieving the aim of detaching nation from nationalism is particularly difficult in the case of Italy and Germany, because of the apparently simultaneous emergence of nationalism and nation-building on both sides of the Alps during the nineteenth century. As a result of the enduring influence of national and parallel histories, nationalism and the creation of the nation-state appeared to historians to be connected exceptionally closely in these "belated" nations. For this reason, binational comparisons are still the dominant approach to studying Italian and German history, while surprisingly few studies follow the more recent approaches of transnational and transfer history.[8] To some extent, the comparative method belongs within the tradition of parallel history, while transnational and transfer studies have more explicitly rejected the national framework.

Despite historians such as Federico Chabod proclaiming the cultural differences between German and Italian nationalism after World War II, the traditional paradigm of parallel history launched by Treitschke and Croce still influences historiographical and public discourses. Use of the lenses of parallel history and, at least in some cases, of comparative history has often led to an underestimation of the differences between Italian and German national ideology and nation-building. These include the role played by nineteenth-century history in the national culture of remembrance and the role of volunteers in the nation-building process, both of which are given greater prominence by Italian historians than by their German colleagues.[9] In addition, female education and assumptions about gender roles were significantly different in nineteenth-century Germany and Italy, primarily because German culture was predominantly Protestant.[10] Parallel history tends to unduly emphasize the similarities between the Italian and German national paths, but without dislodging the stereotypes regarding the different "national characters" that emerged in the nineteenth century and grew stronger during the twentieth.

The persisting narratives of parallel history can be challenged by using a combination of the methods of comparative, transnational, and entangled history, and by adopting an approach that is equally open to the local, regional, national, and global scales of history. However, before further discussion of these methodological and theoretical steps, this chapter explores the main trends in research regarding nationalism and nation-building in Italy and Germany. During the last four decades, there has been impressive development in this field of research due on the one hand to the emergence of comparative and transnational history, and on the other to the attention that historians have given to marginal traditions as well as to cultural and gender history. Alberto Banti's monograph *L'onore della nazione* remains one of the most comprehensive and controversial studies on the connections between masculinity, nationalism, and violence in European nationalism during the long nineteenth century.[11] Banti argues that racially exclusive and heterosexual masculinity was deeply connected to the construction and representation of nationhood. Taking the perspective of cultural history, he demonstrates that ideas about gender and sexual identity circulated transnationally as common ways of thinking within emerging national and patriotic discourses. Banti's interest in narrative structures was recently complemented by feminist scholars who have examined "the specific forms of women's participation in the patriotic movement" and charted "the multiple connections between the ostensibly private realm of the family and the emerging political sphere of the nation."[12]

Recent publications on nationalism and nation-building have rejected the dichotomy between public and private spheres and reassessed interpretative traditions regarding the construction of imagined communities. Ilaria Porciani's studies show that nationalism implied a broad process of imposing order on domestic life as well as on the nation's public affairs.[13] In the wake of the pioneering work by George Mosse on nationalism and sexuality, Karen Hagemann's book on the gendered history of war and nation-building in postrevolutionary Prussia and Ute Planert's studies on women's emancipation, antifeminism, and nationalism in Imperial Germany were major influences on the development of a gendered perspective on national history.[14] This and subsequent work by Hagemann clearly demonstrate that the modern world's understanding of gender roles was deeply interwoven with narratives of national identity and nation-state formation in nineteenth-century Europe. The gendering of national history was a transnationally circulating element common to many national metanarratives. Its clearest expression was in the "routine feminisation of enemies, and the positive self-ascription of allegedly male, manly values."[15]

In order to rethink the mainstream themes of national history such as war, diplomacy, monarchy, and high politics, recent studies on historians and nationalism stress the importance of examining marginal traditions.[16] A focus on the themes mentioned still prevails and is "in itself an unconscious legacy of nineteenth-century nationalist historical traditions."[17] In the case of Italy and Germany, informal networks and nonmainstream ideas were of fundamental importance to the initial galvanization of national movements. Nationalism only became politically dominant in the late nineteenth century; in the meantime, on the one hand, nationalist ideas were disseminated from above, while on the other the transnational and nonstate component played a major role in the process of nation-building.[18] The importance of women, families, and wider family networks for both the spread of nationalist emotions and the cultural representation of the Italian nation-state is convincingly demonstrated in recent research by Ruth Nattermann, Giulia Frontoni, and Karoline Rörig.[19] Furthermore, an interdisciplinary group of scholars led by Lucy Riall has broadly surveyed nineteenth-century Italian sexuality, shedding more light on personal and political relationships, gender roles, and transnational encounters.[20]

Other scholars, including Abigail Green and Sarah Panter, have made outstanding contributions to the discussion of gendered and Jewish perspectives on nation-building and modernity.[21] These approaches now seem to have become well-established ways of interpreting the history of nationalism. However, the pioneering studies by Banti and Hagemann explaining the paradigms of masculinity and honor in Italian and German nationalism are still less than twenty years old. Transnational and gendered perspectives are very recent developments in the research into nationalism and its political significance, which is at least 150 years old. Since its "geopolitical explosion" in the late nineteenth century, and despite the revelation of its full destructive potential in the two World Wars, nationalism continues to play a key role in European history and politics.[22] Even the German historian Theodor Schieder, who was strongly criticized because of his Nazi past, observed that the traditional nationalism of European nations did not completely change after World War II.[23] Historians should never underestimate the persistence of interpretative traditions, and the recent right-wing populist revival in Europe has been a reminder of the vitality and adaptability of nationalist discourses. Since the late 1970s, innovative methods and new research interests have contributed to reassessment of the traditional interpretative paradigms of nationalism and nation-building. However, they have not fully dismantled deep-seated nationalist teleologies; for this reason, the legacy of methodological nationalism can still influence historiographical discourse.

Why has the change in interpretative traditions regarding nationalism been slower and less comprehensive than might have been imagined? One reason is that nationalism and nation-states are politically very sensitive concepts, and scholarly work in this field is to some extent always vulnerable to influence from the field of politics. From the theoretical developments in historiography during the nineteenth century onward, "historical practice was tightly linked to institutional frameworks that in turn were deeply influenced by political developments."[24] Furthermore, the professionalization and academic institutionalization of the discipline of history were strongly related to the growing nationalization of historical writing, as well as to the exclusion of women from the profession of history.[25] After 1848, pragmatism and the claim of objectivity dominated the language of politics; correspondingly, "historians were more effective politically when they could lay claim to professionalism and scientificity."[26] From the end of the nineteenth century, professional historians became more authoritative and proclaimed their impartiality; however, historiography was no less politicized.

The entanglements between nationalism, historiography, and politics still leave their traces today. The state-supported revival of nationalism when the anniversary of Italian unification was celebrated in 2011, for example, served to perpetuate the myth of Verdi as the bard of the Risorgimento, notwithstanding the convincing rejection of this view of the early Verdi as an "image constructed to a large extent *a posteriori*."[27] Although patriotic commemoration of "national awakening" during the long nineteenth century has played a different and substantially smaller role in Germany than in Italy, there too national histories experienced a revival after the Wiedervereinigung in 1990. Biographies of Bismarck are still among the most popular history books, and Ulrich Herbert's recently published comprehensive work on the history of twentieth-century Germany begins by stating that "Europe is our present, but our history remains rooted in the national."[28] Furthermore, and paradoxically, the new series of books on contemporary European history issued by the large German publisher Beck presents a very traditional history of the "old continent" as the history of nation-states.[29]

Countercurrents to the decline of methodological nationalism have come not only from the fields of politics and journalism but also from historiography itself: from the need to adapt to the requirements of publishers and the market, and from lack of communication between historians. Some pioneers of the new cultural history have dismissed the integration of the traditional narrative of the Risorgimento into the transnational perspective. By contrast, the discipline of cultural studies and the "linguistic turn" have been harshly criticized by traditional scholarship.[30] Despite the fact that historians have been trying, at least since the Cold War ended, to detach themselves from the traditional commitment to national histories, there are important reasons to continue analyzing the problem of methodological nationalism. In a recent essay, David Armitage pointed out that "like most other social scientists, [historians] assumed that self-identifying nations, organized politically into states, were the primary objects of historical study."[31] The preferential attention given by European historians to the state, which is a crucial precondition for methodological nationalism, was closely related to the standardization and institutionalization of the discipline of history during the nineteenth century, at the same time as the emergence of nationalism.

Three main options, mutually complementary, are available in order to deal effectively with the persistent tradition of methodological nationalism. First, because the focus on state, high politics, diplomacy, and monarchy has been one of the main components of national history's metanarrative,[32] political history should look further than state institutions and their formal decision-making processes.[33] Its field of inquiry should also be extended to the semantic and affective aspects of politics, and to a variety of social arenas and semiformal political networks. Furthermore, this new political history and its enhanced methodology should be integrated with intellectual and cultural history, and also with the history of communication and conceptual history. The new approaches to political history have understood the study of political discourses in a "constructivist" way, emphasizing "the cultural and medial constructedness of the political."[34] However, there should also be more critical questioning of the cultural turn, especially in the case of Risorgimento historiography. The intention to develop the approach further "does not necessarily mean to abandon cultural history, but rather to cross-fertilize cultural history with social and political history and vice-versa."[35]

The second option, aimed at reassessment of the interpretative traditions of nation-building, is to place both the political history of nation-states and the intellectual history of nationalism within a transnational and global framework. Later in this chapter, I return to this theme by discussing comparison, transfer, entanglement, and global history as possible antidotes to methodological nationalism.

The third way of addressing this is to focus on marginal traditions and histories from below, which have been obscured by the metanarrative of the nation-state. Systematic exploration of the role played in nation-building processes by women, religious minorities, and localist movements, and also by exile, migration, and internal enemies, offers historians great advantages for critical revision of the great narratives of nations. These "outsider" topics are some of the most vibrant and controversial themes in contemporary academic discourse and will be further discussed in the sections that follow.

The Many Faces of "National" History

Invented national traditions resulted from the clash and reciprocal influence of many different types of allegiance and belonging in spatially, temporally, politically, socially, and culturally diverse contexts. In his respected work on the Italian Risorgimento, the French historian Gilles Pécout argues that if we think of Italian nation-building as a linear and nonconflictual process, then we will not understand the Risorgimento at all.[36] One major analytical problem for the study of nationalism is that its hybrid narrative structure resolutely proclaimed itself as the exclusive, natural, and widely desired product of a specific national identity. Despite the "strong presence of ethnic, and thus determinist, components in the Italian imagining of the national community," patriotic discourse was developed by cosmopolitan elites, who referred to transnationally circulating emotions, experiences, and narratives of patriotism.[37] A second analytical problem is that perceptions of nationalism had customarily been linked to the narratives of progress, liberalism, and modernity, whereas the new nation-states in Italy and Germany were the result of a conservative-led convergence of very varied expectations and experiences of nationhood. After the shock of the European revolutions of 1848, a new alliance of moderate liberals and conservatives formed that hoped to legitimate its constitutional reformism and stave off further insurrection by claiming continuity with the earlier tradition of enlightened monarchical state-building.

Nationalism was conceptually embedded in manifold traditions across different eras, not only in the "late" nations of Italy and Germany but also elsewhere in Europe. On the one hand, narratives of nationhood intertwined with the new experiences and expectations of modernity. On the other, "modern" nationalist discourses included elements typical of traditional patriotism based on religion, paternalism, family, an ethos of public service, and monarchism. Many elements that contributed to nationalism were closely connected to the ideals of liberalism and political participation, but at the same time also to the elite-based symbolic language of honor and loyalty. The emerging political culture of the nation-state attempted to legitimate itself with moderate constitutionalism and nationhood, adapting traditional patriotic discourses based on paternalism, religion, ethnicity, and class.[38]

The historiography's commitment to political and methodological nationalism has created profound distortions in collective memory and identity. Many students of German history hold the belief that the inappropriately named "Liberation Wars" of 1813 were the origin of modern nationalism. Ute Planert's studies on Napoleonic Germany have instead shown that "national currents . . . intensified during the anti-Napoleonic wars without, however, prevailing completely."[39] Italian and German soldiers who served in the Grande Armée were not "unpatriotic," and those who fought against Napoleon had patriotic but also liberal, religious, and monarchist sentiments, and in some cases were simply demonstrating their hostility toward military service. Between 1813 and 1848, the debate over the legacy of the Revolutionary and Napoleonic period and the struggle for constitutional reform were much more important than the activities of early nationalist organizations such as the Italian *Carbonari* and German *Burschenschaftler*, whose significance has been hugely overestimated in the past by nationalist historians. Recent studies on the Napoleonic Empire have shown that on the left bank of the Rhine, as well as in the Kingdom of Westphalia, the German-speaking urban elites cooperated very closely with the new regime.[40] After the Congress of Vienna, the elites in the Rhineland were fighting to maintain the Napoleonic Code and to defend their political autonomy against Prussification. In the southern German states of Baden, Bavaria, and Württemberg, patriotism was primarily related to the regional state, the monarchy, and the constitution that had been imposed from above. Regional patriotism, the maintenance of law and order, and pragmatic reformism also prevailed in the imperial departments of Napoleonic Italy. Comparative studies on Piedmont and the Rhineland have shown that administrative efficiency, police authority, and a modern justice system were more important than the construction of regional and national patriotism for securing political authority in Napoleonic Europe.[41] In the age of state-building, the process of ensuring public order and the safety of a country's citizens was no less relevant than the construction of identity.[42]

Like the Liberation Wars of 1813, the history of the German Confederation created at the Congress of Vienna in 1815 illustrates how memory was shaped by later interpretations. The birth of this new entity was retrospectively condemned by much of German historiography after 1871 as the negation or antithesis of German national sentiments and aspirations, but since 2000, historians have started to unpick its poor reputation. Jürgen Müller emphasizes that this association of thirty-nine German states was much more the product of federalist traditions in German state-building than a rejection of the struggle for unification.[43] Another important corrective to methodological nationalism came from the studies by Marco Meriggi and Francesca Brunet that challenged the hitherto negative portrayal of Austria's domination of northern Italy.[44]

Despite the different Italian and German experiences of constitutional models and political culture, the impact of the Age of Revolution has traditionally been seen as the prelude to nation-building on both sides of the Alps.[45] Ugo Foscolo's epistolary novel *Last Letters of Jacopo Ortis*, published in 1816, expressed frustration with Italian localism and the internal conflicts within the peninsula. Mazzini "attributed the discovery of Italy as his fatherland to his reading of Foscolo's *Le ultime lettere di Jacopo Ortis* . . . [and] acknowledged in Foscolo the merit of linking literature to politics."[46] However, the great majority of Italians did not share Mazzini's opinions. Michael Broers points out that Liguria (Mazzini's homeland) was "seeking first the renewal of its independence, and then—in a real gasp of desperation—reunion with France" in order to avoid annexation by Piedmont after 1814.[47] In 1848, the popular patriotic songs that were circulating in Turin and Berlin, such as "Inno al re," "La coccarda," "Preußenlied," and "Schwarz und Weiß," had as their primary references the regions and dynasties of Piedmont and Prussia.[48]

These observations on Italy and Germany, first during the Napoleonic era and then after the Congress of Vienna, allow us to draw two partial conclusions. First, patriotism, nationalism, and the struggle for liberal reform were not interchangeable during the first half of the nineteenth century. While most German and Italian patriots were fighting for liberal and constitutional reform, the more contentious quest for national unification within a new nation-state was not always of primary importance in the political discourse of mid-nineteenth-century Germany and Italy.[49] From the late nineteenth century onward, influential historians such as Benedetto Croce, who saw Fascism as a parenthesis in Italian history, customarily linked nation-building and liberal reform as mutually dependent elements of progress toward modernity. The issue of the conflation of nationalism and liberal reformism can be dealt with by avoiding premature application of the terminology of the nation-state to the beginning of the long nineteenth century rather than to its end. Was the relationship between nation-building and emancipation movements established retrospectively by the master narrative of nationalism in order to legitimize the nation-state? Or can we instead establish a profound relationship between emancipatory discourses, political participation, and the process of nation-building? The contributions to this volume provide innovative responses to these enduring questions because they analyze nationalism and nation-building from the perspective of nonstate actors, transnational groups, and religious minorities, exemplified by the Morenos, an Italian Jewish family who left Livorno for Tunis in 1830.[50]

One of the principal objectives of transnational history is to "displace the focus on the nation state by studying non-governmental institutions, informal groups and individual actors."[51] The transnational approach can thus help to reexamine national history without obscuring the plurality of historical dimensions, including the local, regional, European, Atlantic, imperial, and global. Several recent publications have contributed to the growing field of transnational intellectual history, revisiting the genealogy of nineteenth-century nationalism and liberalism.[52] These studies stress that multiple cultural and political affiliations, as well as dual national belonging and imperial ideologies, continued to exist in the so-called "age of nationalism."[53] In other words, the construction of national identities emerged from multiple loyalties and the mutual hybridization of different political cultures. Transnational intellectual history can help to reveal the transcultural nature of European nationalism and its development without following any predetermined path.

Three Ways to Counter Methodological Nationalism: Comparison, Transfer, and Entanglement

The emergence of comparative and transnational history as widely used methodologies has led to a continuing debate among historians.[54] Comparative history, transfer studies, and entangled history are distinct but partially overlapping approaches, all of which require the important features of flexibility and reflexivity. According to Michael Werner and Bénédicte Zimmermann, reflexive induction, which is linked to the paradigm of *histoire croisée*, leads to historicization of both the objects and categories of analysis.[55] This can play an important role in challenging methodological nationalism. Some key assumptions of the entangled history approach, such as the high permeability of national boundaries and the importance of mutual transfer processes, are already well established in historiographical discourse. However, *histoire croisée* offers the possibility of critical reflection on the potentially deterministic construction of the units of comparison or transfer. After four decades of comparative and transnational studies, we can not only identify the achievements and limitations of these approaches but also clearly understand their role in an era of global history and postcolonial studies.

In a recent essay, Jörn Leonhard argues that for analyzing European history and its global interconnections, the best methodological framework available is a non-nation-specific transnational history in combination with cultural transfer and a comparative approach. He argues that the "common tendency to think through the prism of results comes with high analytical costs, leading scholars to ignore the historical alternatives embedded in the 'past future.'"[56] Traditional comparative history has generally assumed that the nation-state was a fixed category of analysis and perpetuated a parallel teleology of nation-building: a simple comparison between imagined national communities. For this reason, comparative studies need to co-opt analytical assistance from transfer and entanglement history.[57] If used together, these three methodological approaches will support a critical rethinking of the spatial and temporal categories of national history. Furthermore, not only is transnational history open toward European, Atlantic, and global dimensions, but it can also grasp the local and regional dimensions beyond the nation-state. The transnational approach can help to reduce the persistent influence of methodological nationalism by taking into account informal groups and marginal traditions. An approach combining comparative and transnational perspectives has been productively employed in some of the case studies presented in this volume, including those on the activism of "political ladies" in 1848, the history of the international women's movement, and the transformation of Jewish and female education in nineteenth-century Europe.[58]

In addition to the three approaches of comparison, transfer, and entanglement, there are other types of "best practice" for limiting the influence of methodological nationalism. One of these is related to the lack of correspondence between the temporalities of the many different paths into modernity, and the challenge this has presented to traditional periodization. The conceptualization of historical time always predetermines historical narration. Lucian Hölscher's studies on historiography's conceptualization of time highlight "the need for more 'neutral' concepts of time in today's globalised historiography in order to bring contradicting and conflicting ideas, developments and perspectives together without fostering any pre-determined meaning for interpretation of history."[59] Hölscher's observations about the order of time are of particular importance for the reassessment of longstanding interpretative traditions relating to nationalism and the nation-state. Another form of "best practice" that helps to challenge the teleological thinking of historians in relation to nation-building and modernity is to shift the focus away from "national" turning points by exploring structural change and long-term trends. As Lutz Raphael has recently suggested, the best possible answer to the persistent problem of retrospective teleology seems to be a more open and fluid approach to periodization in relation to the location of modernity between the mid-eighteenth century and the end of the twentieth.[60] Methodological nationalism is often linked to specific turning points in history, such as the events of 1789 and 1848, or it can relate instead to the narrative construction of continuity and progress. The use of neutral concepts and open periodization as the basis for research is closely associated with other types of "best practice" to counter methodological nationalism; these include integrating political, social, and cultural history; working with multiple categories of analysis (gender, religion, generation, and ethnicity); combining comparison, transfer, and entanglement; reassessing the traditional boundaries between modernity and pre-modernity, and between local, national, European, and global history.[61]

The deep-seated link between the narratives of modernity and nationalism has influenced the increasingly wearisome debate between traditionalists and modernists on the roots of nationalism. Scholars employing the cultural approach are mostly modernists, who "regard the nation as a quintessentially modern political phenomenon."[62] Traditionalists, by contrast, had been discredited as practitioners from the old school of national history, which had argued that nationhood existed before modernity and had invented the tradition of the new nation-states. More recently, scholars have criticized the hegemony of modernism, on the one hand, and, on the other, have shown a growing interest in the traditionalist approach.

In the wake of influential publications by Caspar Hirschi and Azar Gat, a large number of new studies on nationalism have explored a range of interpretative approaches that lie somewhere between the modernist and traditionalist perspectives.[63] Without the retrospective distinction between modernity and pre-modernity, it will be possible to initiate a more complex interpretation of the origins of nationalism. Ute Planert makes a convincing argument for adopting the concept of a "national Sattelzeit" in order to overcome the dichotomy of modernity and pre-modernity and to allow neutral investigation of the origins and spread of nationalism. In both Italy and Germany, the construction of national identities was just part of a broader picture that involved the development of key political concepts in the context of an increasing gap between expectations and experience.

The Mosaic of Loyalties: Historiography beyond National History

To criticize methodological nationalism is not necessarily to say that writing national histories is always wrong and misleading. Ulrich Herbert's magnum opus on German history, mentioned earlier, is clearly a national history, but the author largely succeeds in avoiding methodological nationalism. He assures us that he is well aware of the many and entangled connections both between German and European history and between European and global history.[64] He condemns the uncritical orientation of historians toward national history as outdated; I would argue that this is particularly inappropriate with regard to study of the nineteenth century, when nation-states and nationalism were less firmly established. It is noteworthy that until a few years ago, a focus on national history needed no justification, whereas scholars working on national history now have to critically question their subject of study and be prepared to reconsider national boundaries and temporalities.

Are the interpretative models for Italian and German nation-building still national? The demise of national history still seems a long way off. However, historians now have effective tools for challenging methodological nationalism. Drawing on numerous case studies in German and Italian history, this chapter has presented key strategies for countering teleological approaches to the nation-state. The first piece of "best practice" is the integration of traditional comparative studies with the transnational and entangled approaches. The three methodological tools of comparison, transfer, and entanglement not only allow for exploration of political history and the process of state-building, which are the fields of traditional comparative history, but also enable the analysis of nonstate actors, informal networks, and minority communities. The use of these three methods leads to rethinking and potentially revising the chosen spatial and temporal framework by historicizing the objects and the categories of analysis. As well as discussing the potential contribution of comparative, transnational, and entangled history, which form the necessary starting point for historiography's struggle against methodological nationalism, this chapter has briefly introduced five additional strategies for reassessing interpretative traditions regarding nationalism and nation-building. The first is the methodological and theoretical development of the new political history. The second piece of "best practice" draws on the growing interest of historians in topics removed from the master narrative of nationalism and the nation-state, such as gender, religion, Jewish history, migration, exile, and internal "others." Two further approaches that counter methodological nationalism are the quests for neutral concepts of time and for open chronological boundaries. The fifth and final approach involves the revival of imperial, global, transatlantic, and Mediterranean history, which generates a fresh understanding of cultural affiliations and collective identities. The notions of empire and nation were deeply interwoven not only in France's Third Republic, the British Empire, and Austria-Hungary but also in Italy and Germany, where the "process of nation-building coincided with a push for empire-building."[65]

The contributions to this volume shed more light on the variety of gender models and the plurality of social, political, and cultural loyalties in nineteenth-century Italy and Germany. Despite the lack of a widely accepted concept of loyalty, this notion has great potential for revealing how individuals, groups, and societies dealt with multiple and changing elements of identity formation, such as family, religion, identification with the monarchy, class, ethnicity, and nationality. Jana Osterkamp and Martin Schulze Wessel have recently offered a broad discussion of the analytical potential of this concept; they advance a range of reasons for its adoption and further development to aid historical research on nationalism, some of which are closely connected to the elements of "best practice" employed by other contributors to this volume. First, the notion of loyalty is an element of patriotism and subnational affiliations, but it can also apply to nongovernmental and even oppositional identities such as membership of the church, the trade unions, and other political or social networks. Second, loyalty is a useful tool for investigating the many forms of allegiance within nation-states, but also in multinational empires, and in informal groups; the use of the concept does not assume that the only "modern" form of attachment is to the nation-state. Third, a focus on loyalty helps to shed light on the multiple temporalities and nonsimultaneity of allegiances in European history, including not only nationalism but also concurrent, complementary, and alternative identifications. Fourth, loyalty refers both to top-down or vertical relationships and to horizontal bonds, and it can also relate to both individual and collective emotions.[66]

Osterkamp and Schulze Wessel are enthusiastic about the analytical potential of loyalty, which highlights the plurality and interrelationships of social and political identities. Some empirical studies that productively employ the concept of loyalty have already been published.[67] Although the theoretical debate on loyalty is not yet very well developed, the concept can help us to rethink the teleological, Eurocentric, and state-centered framework of nationalism. However, we do need to consider some critical points regarding the flexibility and huge extension of the notion of loyalty. Is its analytical conceptualization too diffuse to provide accuracy and clarity? There is a danger that "loyalty," like "identity," will evolve into a "plastic notion," which is Lutz Niethammer's sarcastic expression for the excessive use and meaningless imprecision of the latter concept.[68]

The topics and approaches chosen by the contributors to this volume explore some of the best practices for writing modern Italian and German history that supersede national history. Some of the overarching themes that pervade these contributions are the problem of multiple loyalties, the emancipation of minorities, the relevance of social class, and the relationship between violence and identity. A common aspect of these themes is that they only indirectly or partially belong within the interpretative traditions of national histories. This volume analyzes a set of case studies and transnational aspects that for many decades had been intentionally passed over by nationalist historians or passively overlooked by methodological nationalism. The contributions to this volume attempt to go beyond parallel history and clearly show that a thorough understanding of nation-building and of the emergence of nationalism cannot be reached without consideration of marginal traditions, informal groups, and the plurality of social and cultural microspheres. This chapter has therefore made the case for adopting elements of "best practice," such as the approaches that combine comparative and transnational perspectives and the search for less loaded concepts of time in order to reassess deep-seated interpretative paradigms of national histories.

Amerigo Caruso is lecturer in modern European history at Saarland University. His current research project investigates how different political regimes reacted in times of turmoil and widespread insecurity during the nineteenth and early twentieth centuries. He is the author of *Nationalstaat als Telos? Der konservative Diskurs in Preußen und Sardinien-Piemont 1840–1870* (Berlin: De Gruyter, 2017), an exploration of conservative discourses and nation-building in mid-nineteenth-century Italy and Germany.

Notes

1. Ernst Deuerlein, "Die Konfrontation von Nationalstaat und national bestimmte Kultur," in *Reichsgründung 1870/71: Tatsachen, Kontroversen, Interpretationen*, ed. Theodor Schieder and Ernst Deuerlein (Cologne: Seewald, 1961), 239.
2. On the enduring tradition of parallel Italian and German history, see Christof Dipper, *Ferne Nachbarn: Vergleichende Studien zu Deutschland und Italien in der Moderne* (Cologne: Böhlau Verlag, 2017), 323–56; Christian Goeschel, "A Parallel History? Rethinking the Relationship between Italy and Germany, ca. 1860–1945," *Journal of Modern History* 88 (2016): 610–32. On the problem of national framing in historiography, see Philipp Ther, "Beyond the Nation: The Relational Basis of a Comparative History of Germany and Europe," *Central European History* 36 (2003): 45–73.
3. On the post-boom crisis in the 1970s, see Lutz Raphael, "The 1970s—A Period of Structural Rupture in Germany and Italy?," in *Cities Contested: Urban Politics, Heritage, and Social Movements in Italy and West Germany in the 1970s*, ed. Martin Baumeister, Bruno Bonomo, and Dieter Schott (Frankfurt am Main: Campus Verlag, 2017), 31–50. On the terrorist groups, see Christian Jansen, "Brigate Rosse und Rote Armee Fraktion: ProtagonistInnen, Propaganda und Praxis des Terrorismus der frühen siebziger Jahre," in *Personen, Soziale Bewegungen, Parteien: Beiträge zur Neuesten Geschichte; Festschrift für Hartmut Soell*, ed. Oliver von Mengersen (Heidelberg: Manutius, 2005), 483–500.
4. At the time when nationalism was at its peak, between the late nineteenth and mid-twentieth centuries, nation-states provided the political and legal justification for policies of forced cultural assimilation and the population transfer of national minorities. See Matthew Frank, *Making Minorities History: Population Transfer in Twentieth-Century Europe* (Oxford: Oxford University Press, 2017).
5. See Stefan Berger, *The Past as History: National Identity and Historical Consciousness in Modern Europe* (Basingstoke: Palgrave, 2015), 2. On methodological nationalism, see also George Vasilev, "Methodological Nationalism and the Politics of History-Writing: How Imaginary Scholarship Perpetuates the Nation," *Nation and Nationalism* 25 (2019): 499–522.
6. Berger, *Past as History*, 13.
7. John Breuilly, *Nationalism, Power and Modernity in Nineteenth-Century Germany* (London: German Historical Institute, 2006), 9.
8. Goeschel, "Parallel History," 630.
9. Stefan Berger, *The Search for Normality: National Identity and Historical Consciousness in Germany since 1800* (New York: Berghahn Books, 2003), 12.
10. See Sylvia Schraut's contribution to this volume.
11. Alberto Mario Banti, *L'onore della nazione: Identità sessuali e violenza nel nazionalismo europeo dal XVIII secolo alla Grande Guerra* (Turin: Einaudi, 2005).
12. Silvana Patriarca and Lucy Riall, "Introduction: Revisiting the Risorgimento," in *The Risorgimento Revisited: Nationalism and Culture in Nineteenth-Century Italy*, ed. Silvana Patriarca and Lucy Riall (Basingstoke: Palgrave, 2012), 4. See also Ilaria Porciani's chapter in this book.
13. Ilaria Porciani, "Disciplinamento nazionale e modelli domestici nel lungo Ottocento: Germania e Italia a confronto," in *Storia d' Italia: Annali; Il Risorgimento*, ed. Alberto M. Banti and Paul Ginsborg (Turin: Einaudi, 2007), 97–125. See

also Ilaria Porciani, "Famiglia e nazione nel lungo Ottocento," *Passato e Presente* 57 (2002): 11–39.

14. Karen Hagemann, *Männlicher Muth und teutsche Ehre: Nation, Militär und Geschlecht zur Zeit der antinapoleonischen Kriege Preußens* (Paderborn: Ferdinand Schöningh, 2002). See also Ute Planert, *Antifeminismus im Kaiserreich: Diskurs, soziale Formation und politische Mentalität* (Göttingen: Vandenhoeck & Ruprecht, 1998); Ute Planert, "Nationalismus und weibliche Politik: Zur Einführung," in *Nation, Politik und Geschlecht: Frauenbewegungen und Nationalismus in der Moderne*, ed. Ute Planert (Frankfurt am Main: CampusVerlag, 2000), 9–14.
15. Berger, *Past as History*, 363.
16. For discussion of the need for more research on marginal traditions, see Monika Baár, *Historians and Nationalism: East-Central Europe in the Nineteenth Century* (Oxford: Oxford University Press, 2010).
17. Shane Nagle, *Histories of Nationalism in Ireland and Germany: A Comparative Study from 1800 to 1932* (London: Bloomsbury, 2017), 3.
18. On nationalism and the rise of the modern state, see John Breuilly, *Nationalism and the State* (Chicago: University of Chicago Press, 1985).
19. As well as the contributions by Nattermann and Frontoni to this volume, see Ruth Nattermann, "Jüdinnen in der frühen italienischen Frauenbewegung," in *150 Jahre Risorgimento—geeintes Italien?*, ed. Gabriele B. Clemens and Jens Späth (Trier: Kliomedia, 2014), 127–46; Karoline Rörig, *Cristina Trivulzio di Belgiojoso (1808–1871): Geschichtsschreibung und Politik im Risorgimento* (Bonn: Röhrig, 2013); Giulia Frontoni, "Heute gehe ich zum Parlament: Frauen im Publikum des piemontesischen Parlaments," in *150 Jahre Risorgimento—geeintes Italien?*, ed. Gabriele B. Clemens and Jens Späth (Trier: Kliomedia, 2014), 107–26.
20. See Valeria P. Babini, Chiara Beccalossi, and Lucy Riall, "Introduction," in *Italian Sexualities Uncovered, 1789–1914*, ed. Valeria P. Babini, Chiara Beccalossi, and Lucy Riall (Basingstoke: Palgrave, 2015), 1–12.
21. See Abigail Green, "Spirituality, Tradition and Gender: Judith Montefiore, the Very Model of Modern Jewish Womanhood," *History of European Ideas* 40 (2014): 747–60; Sarah Panter, *Jüdische Erfahrungen und Loyalitätskonflikte im Ersten Weltkrieg* (Göttingen: Vandenhoeck & Ruprecht, 2014).
22. Oliver Zimmer, *Nationalism in Europe, 1890–1940* (Basingstoke: Palgrave, 2003), 1.
23. Theodor Schieder, *Nationalismus und Nationalstaat. Studien zum nationalen Problem in Europa* (Göttingen: Vandenhoeck & Ruprecht, 1992), 145.
24. Berger, *Past as History*, 358.
25. Ibid., 359.
26. Ibid., 361. See also Christopher Clark, "After 1848: The European Revolution in Government," in *Transactions of the Royal Historical Society* 22 (2012): 171–97.
27. Axel Körner, *Politics of Culture in Liberal Italy: From Unification to Fascism* (New York: Routledge, 2009), 224.
28. Ulrich Herbert, *Geschichte Deutschland im 20. Jahrhundert* (Munich: C. H. Beck, 2014).
29. See Stefan Troebst, "European History," in *European Regions and Boundaries: A Conceptual History*, ed. Diana Mishkova and Balázs Trencsényi (New York: Berghahn Books, 2017), 235–57.
30. See Alison Chapman, *Networking the Nation: British and American Women's Poetry and Italy, 1840–1870* (Oxford: Oxford University Press, 2015), 34. See also Oli-

ver Janz and Lucy Riall, "Introduction: The Italian Risorgimento, Transnational Perspectives," *Modern Italy* 19 (special issue) (2014): 1–4. On the new Risorgimento historiography, see Maurizio Isabella, "Rethinking Italy's Nation-Building 150 Years Afterwards: The New Risorgimento Historiography," *Past and Present* 217 (2012): 247–68.

31. David Armitage, "The International Turn in Intellectual History," in *Rethinking Modern European Intellectual History*, ed. Darrin M. McMahon and Samuel Moyn (Oxford: Oxford University Press, 2014), 232.
32. Berger, *Past as History*, 362.
33. See Willibald Steinmetz and Heinz-Gerhard Haupt, "The Political as Communicative Space in History: The Bielefeld Approach," in *Writing Political History Today*, ed. Willibald Steinmetz, Ingrid Gilcher-Holtey, and Heinz-Gerhard Haupt (Frankfurt am Main: Campus Verlag, 2013), 11–33.
34. Ibid., 32.
35. Patriarca and Riall, "Introduction," 13.
36. Gilles Pécout, *Naissance de l'Italie contemporaine, 1770–1922* (Paris: Colin, 2002).
37. Patriarca and Riall, "Introduction," 3.
38. See Oliver Zimmer, *A Contested Nation: History, Memory and Nationalism in Switzerland* (Cambridge: Cambridge University Press, 2003). See also Amerigo Caruso, "Resilient in Adversity: The Monarchical State in Prussia and Sardinia-Piedmont, 1847–51," in *Transnational Histories of the Royal Nation*, ed. Milinda Banerjee, Charlotte Backerra, and Cathleen Sarti (Basingstoke: Palgrave, 2017), 45–66.
39. Ute Planert, "International Conflicts, War, and the Making of Modern Germany, 1740–1815," *The Oxford Handbook of Modern German History*, ed. Helmut Walser Smith (Oxford: Oxford University Press, 2011), 110.
40. Gabriele B. Clemens, "Entre opposition et intégration: les départements du Rhin dans la première phase de la restauration (1814–1832)," *Revue d'Allemagne et des pays de langue allemande* 47 (2015): 151–62. See also Claudie Paye, "Cassel, prisme de l'identité westphalienne ou petit Paris au bord de la Fulda? Pratiques identitaires et frictions culturelles au royaume de Westphalie, 1807–1813," in *Erbfeinde im Empire? Franzosen und Deutsche im Zeitalter Napoleons*, ed. Gabriele B. Clemens, Jacques-Olivier Boudon, and Pierre Horn (Ostfildern: Thorbecke, 2016), 33–50.
41. Lutz Klinkhammer, "Kontrolle und Identität. Die Grenzen der Freiheit im Rheinland und in Piemont unter französischer Herrschaft," in *Napoleonische Expansionspolitik: Okkupation oder Integration?*, ed. Guido Braun et al. (Berlin: De Gruyter, 2013), 120–37.
42. See Eckart Conze, "Securitization: Gegenwartsdiagnose oder historische Analyseansatz," *Geschichte und Gesellschaft* 38 (2012): 453–67.
43. Jürgen Müller, *Der Deutsche Bund 1815–1866* (Munich: Oldenbourg, 2006). See also Daniel Ziblatt's comparative study on nation-building and federalism in Italy and Germany: Daniel Ziblatt, *Structuring the State: The Formation of Italy and Germany and the Puzzle of Federalism* (Princeton, NJ: Princeton University Press, 2006).
44. Marco Meriggi, *Amministrazioni e classi sociali nel Lombardo-Veneto, 1814–1848* (Bologna: Il Mulino, 1983); Francesca Brunet, "Die Begnadigungen der Hochverräter im vormärzlichen Lombardo-Venetien: Politische und kommunika-

tions-theoretische Perspektiven," *Römische Historische Mitteilungen* 53 (2011): 303–14.
45. See Geoffrey Ellis, *The Napoleonic Empire* (Basingstoke: Palgrave, 2003).
46. Stefano Jossa, "Politics vs. Literature: The Myth of Dante and the Italian National Identity," in *Dante in the Long Nineteenth Century: Nationality, Identity, and Appropriation*, ed. Aida Audeh and Nick Havely (Oxford: Oxford University Press, 2012), 34.
47. Michael Broers, "Transformation and Discontinuity from the Old Order to the Modern State in Piedmontese and Ligurian Départements of Napoleonic Italy," in *Napoleonische Expansionspolitik: Okkupation oder Integration?*, ed. Guido Braun et al. (Berlin: De Gruyter, 2013), 50.
48. See Caruso, "Resilient in Adversity," 56.
49. See Janz and Riall, "Introduction," 1–4.
50. See Marcella Simoni's contribution to this volume.
51. Janz and Riall, "Introduction," 1.
52. Lucy Riall's monograph on the popular cult of Giuseppe Garibaldi and Eveline Bouwers's book on the nation-state's public pantheons, for example, have provided new insights into the cultural and transnational aspects of nation-building. See Lucy Riall, *Garibaldi: Invention of a Hero* (New Haven, CT: Yale University Press, 2007); Eveline G. Bouwers, *Public Pantheons in Revolutionary Europe: Comparing Cultures of Remembrance, c.1790–1840* (Basingstoke: Palgrave, 2012).
53. See Maurizio Isabella and Kostantina Zanou, eds., *Mediterranean Diasporas: Politics and Ideas in the Long 19th Century* (London: Bloomsbury, 2015).
54. Hartmut Kaelble, "Die Debatte über Vergleich und Transfer und was jetzt?," *Connections: A Journal for Historians and Area Specialists* (8 February 2005), http://www.connections.clio-online.net/article/id/artikel-574.
55. Michael Werner and Bénédicte Zimmermann, "Beyond Comparison: Histoire Croisée and the Challenge of Reflexivity," *History and Theory* 45 (2006): 30–50.
56. Jörn Leonhard, "Comparison, Transfer and Entanglement, or: How to Write Modern European History Today?," *Journal of Modern European History* 14 (2016): 153.
57. Ibid., 162. See also Michael Werner and Bénédicte Zimmermann, "Vergleich, Transfer, Verflechtung: Der Ansatz der Histoire croisée und die Herausforderung des Transnationalen," *Geschichte und Gesellschaft* 28 (2002): 607–36.
58. See the contributions to this volume by Giulia Frontoni, Magdalena Gehring, Philipp Lenhard, Silvia Guetta, Liviana Gazzetta, and Sylvia Schraut.
59. "Tagungsbericht: Analysing Historical Narratives," retrieved 10 October 2017 from http://www.de/conferencereport/id/tagungsberichte-6782. See also Lucian Hölscher, *Semantik der Leere: Grenzfragen der Geschichtswissenschaft* (Göttingen: Wallstein, 2009).
60. "Gesellschaftswandel und Modernisierung, 1800–2000: Autoren-Workshop des Archivs für Sozialgeschichte," retrieved 10 October 2017 from http://www.hsozkult.de/event/id/termine-32285.
61. The editorial statement for Palgrave's War, Culture and Society 1750–1850 series provides a very good summary of some of the best practices that counter methodological nationalism. See Rafe Blaufarb, Alan Forrest, and Karen Hagemann, "Aim of the Series," in Joshua Meeks, *France, Britain, and the Struggle for the Revolutionary Western Mediterranean* (Basingstoke: Palgrave, 2017).

62. Lotte Jensen, "The Roots of Nationalism," in *The Roots of Nationalism: National Identity Formation in Early Modern Europe, 1600–1815*, ed. Lotte Jensen (Amsterdam: Amsterdam University Press, 2016), 10.
63. See Caspar Hirschi, *The Origins of Nationalism: An Alternative History from Ancient Rome to Early Modern Germany* (Cambridge: Cambridge University Press, 2012); Azar Gat, *Nations: The Long History and Deep Roots of Political Ethnicity and Nationalism* (Cambridge: Cambridge University Press, 2013).
64. Herbert, *Geschichte Deutschland im 20. Jahrhundert*, 19.
65. Goeschel, "Parallel History," 612.
66. Jana Osterkamp and Martin Schulze Wessel, "Texturen von Loyalität: Überlegungen zu einem analytischen Begriff," *Geschichte und Gesellschaft* 42 (2016): 553–73.
67. See Panter, *Erfahrungen*.
68. See Lutz Niethammer, *Kollektive Identität: Heimliche Quellen einer unheimlichen Konjunktur* (Hamburg: Rowohlt, 2000).

Bibliography

Armitage, David. "The International Turn in Intellectual History." In *Rethinking Modern European Intellectual History*, edited by Darrin M. McMahon and Samuel Moyn, 232–52. Oxford: Oxford University Press, 2014.

Baár, Monika. *Historians and Nationalism: East-Central Europe in the Nineteenth Century*. Oxford: Oxford University Press, 2010.

Babini, Valeria P., Chiara Beccalossi, and Lucy Riall. "Introduction." In *Italian Sexualities Uncovered, 1789–1914*, edited by Valeria P. Babini, Chiara Beccalossi, and Lucy Riall, 1–12. Basingstoke: Palgrave, 2015.

Banti, Alberto Mario. *L'onore della nazione: Identità sessuali e violenza nel nazionalismo europeo dal XVIII secolo alla Grande Guerra*. Turin: Einaudi, 2005.

Berger, Stefan. *The Search for Normality: National Identity and Historical Consciousness in Germany since 1800*. New York: Berghahn Books, 2003.

———. *The Past as History: National Identity and Historical Consciousness in Modern Europe*. Basingstoke: Palgrave, 2015.

Blaufarb, Rafe, Alan Forrest, and Karen Hagemann. "Aim of the Series." In Joshua Meeks, *France, Britain, and the Struggle for the Revolutionary Western Mediterranean*. Basingstoke: Palgrave, 2017.

Bouwers, Eveline G. *Public Pantheons in Revolutionary Europe: Comparing Cultures of Remembrance, c.1790–1840*. Basingstoke: Palgrave, 2012.

Breuilly, John. *Nationalism and the State*. Chicago: University of Chicago Press, 1985.

———. *Nationalism, Power and Modernity in Nineteenth-Century Germany*. London: German Historical Institute, 2006.

Broers, Michael. "Transformation and Discontinuity from the Old Order to the Modern State in Piedmontese and Ligurian Départements of Napoleonic Italy." In *Napoleonische Expansionspolitik: Okkupation oder Integration?*, edited by Guido Braun, Gabriele B. Clemens, Lutz Klinkhammer, and Alexander Koller, 41–52. Berlin: De Gruyter, 2013.

Brunet, Francesca. "Die Begnadigungen der Hochverräter im vormärzlichen Lombardo-Venetien: Politische und kommunikations-theoretische Perspektiven." *Römische Historische Mitteilungen* 53 (2011): 303–14.

Caruso, Amerigo. "Resilient in Adversity: The Monarchical State in Prussia and Sardinia-Piedmont, 1847–51." In *Transnational Histories of the Royal Nation*, edited by Milinda Banerjee, Charlotte Backerra, and Cathleen Sarti, 45–66. Basingstoke: Palgrave, 2017.

Chapman, Alison. *Networking the Nation: British and American Women's Poetry and Italy, 1840–1870*. Oxford: Oxford University Press, 2015.

Clark, Christopher. "After 1848: The European Revolution in Government." *Transactions of the Royal Historical Society* 22 (2012): 171–97.

Clemens, Gabriele B. "Entre opposition et intégration: les départements du Rhin dans la première phase de la restauration (1814–1832)." *Revue d'Allemagne et des pays de langue allemande* 47 (2015): 151–62.

Conze, Eckart. "Securitization: Gegenwartsdiagnose oder historische Analyseansatz." *Geschichte und Gesellschaft* 38 (2012): 453–67.

Deuerlein, Ernst. "Die Konfrontation von Nationalstaat und national bestimmte Kultur." In *Reichsgründung 1870/71: Tatsachen, Kontroversen, Interpretationen*, edited by Theodor Schieder and Ernst Deuerlein, 226–58. Cologne: Seewald, 1961.

Dipper, Christof. *Ferne Nachbarn: Vergleichende Studien zu Deutschland und Italien in der Moderne*. Cologne: Böhlau Verlag, 2017.

Ellis, Geoffrey. *The Napoleonic Empire*. Basingstoke: Palgrave, 2003.

Frank, Matthew. *Making Minorities History: Population Transfer in Twentieth-Century Europe*. Oxford: Oxford University Press, 2017.

Frontoni, Giulia. "Heute gehe ich zum Parlament: Frauen im Publikum des piemontesischen Parlaments." In *150 Jahre Risorgimento—geeintes Italien?*, edited by Gabriele B. Clemens and Jens Späth, 107–26. Trier: Kliomedia, 2014.

Gat, Azar. *Nations: The Long History and Deep Roots of Political Ethnicity and Nationalism*. Cambridge: Cambridge University Press, 2013.

Goeschel, Christian. "A Parallel History? Rethinking the Relationship between Italy and Germany, ca. 1860–1945." *Journal of Modern History* 88 (2016): 610–32.

Green, Abigail. "Spirituality, Tradition and Gender: Judith Montefiore, the Very Model of Modern Jewish Womanhood." *History of European Ideas* 40 (2014): 747–60.

Hagemann, Karen. *Mannlicher Muth und teutsche Ehre: Nation, Militär und Geschlecht zur Zeit der antinapoleonischen Kriege Preußens*. Paderborn: Ferdinand Schöningh, 2002.

Herbert, Ulrich. *Geschichte Deutschland im 20. Jahrhundert*. Munich: C. H. Beck, 2014.

Hirschi, Caspar. *The Origins of Nationalism: An Alternative History from Ancient Rome to Early Modern Germany*. Cambridge: Cambridge University Press, 2012.

Hölscher, Lucian. *Semantik der Leere: Grenzfragen der Geschichtswissenschaft*. Göttingen: Wallstein, 2009.

Isabella, Maurizio. "Rethinking Italy's Nation-Building 150 Years Afterwards: The New Risorgimento Historiography." *Past and Present* 217 (2012): 247–68.

Isabella, Maurizio, and Kostantina Zanou, eds. *Mediterranean Diasporas: Politics and Ideas in the Long 19th Century*. London: Bloomsbury, 2015.

Jansen, Christian. "Brigate Rosse und Rote Armee Fraktion: ProtagonistInnen, Propaganda und Praxis des Terrorismus der frühen siebziger Jahre." In *Personen, Soziale Bewegungen, Parteien: Beiträge zur Neuesten Geschichte; Festschrift für Hartmut Soell*, edited by Oliver von Mengersen, 483–500. Heidelberg: Manutius, 2005.

Janz, Oliver, and Lucy Riall. "Introduction: The Italian Risorgimento, Transnational Perspectives." *Modern Italy* 19 (special issue) (2014): 1–4.

Jensen, Lotte. "The Roots of Nationalism." In *The Roots of Nationalism: National Identity Formation in Early Modern Europe, 1600–1815*, edited by Lotte Jensen, 9–27. Amsterdam: Amsterdam University Press, 2016.

Jossa, Stefano. "Politics vs. Literature: The Myth of Dante and the Italian National Identity." In *Dante in the Long Nineteenth Century: Nationality, Identity, and Appropriation*, edited by Aida Audeh and Nick Havely, 30–50. Oxford: Oxford University Press, 2012.

Kaelble, Hartmut. "Die Debatte über Vergleich und Transfer und was jetzt?" *Connections: A Journal for Historians and Area Specialists* (8 February 2005), http://www.connections.clio-online.net/article/id/artikel-574.

Klinkhammer, Lutz. "Kontrolle und Identität: Die Grenzen der Freiheit im Rheinland und in Piemont unter französischer Herrschaft." In *Napoleonische Expansionspolitik: Okkupation oder Integration?* edited by Guido Braun, Gabriele B. Clemens, Lutz Klinkhammer, and Alexander Koller, 120–37. Berlin: De Gruyter, 2013.

Körner, Axel. *Politics of Culture in Liberal Italy: From Unification to Fascism*. New York: Routledge, 2009.

Leonhard, Jörn. "Comparison, Transfer and Entanglement, or: How to Write Modern European History Today?" *Journal of Modern European History* 14 (2016): 149–63.

Meriggi, Marco. *Amministrazioni e classi sociali nel Lombardo-Veneto, 1814–1848*. Bologna: Il Mulino, 1983.

Müller, Jürgen. *Der Deutsche Bund 1815–1866*. Munich: Oldenbourg, 2006.

Nagle, Shane. *Histories of Nationalism in Ireland and Germany: A Comparative Study from 1800 to 1932*. London: Bloomsbury, 2017.

Nattermann, Ruth. "Jüdinnen in der frühen italienischen Frauenbewegung." In *150 Jahre Risorgimento—geeintes Italien?*, edited by Gabriele B. Clemens and Jens Späth, 127–46. Trier: Kliomedia, 2014.

Niethammer, Lutz. *Kollektive Identität: Heimliche Quellen einer unheimlichen Konjunktur*. Hamburg: Rowohlt, 2000.

Osterkamp, Jana, and Martin Schulze Wessel. "Texturen von Loyalität: Überlegungen zu einem analytischen Begriff." *Geschichte und Gesellschaft* 42 (2016): 553–73.

Panter, Sarah. *Jüdische Erfahrungen und Loyalitätskonflikte im Ersten Weltkrieg*. Göttingen: Vandenhoeck & Ruprecht, 2014.

Patriarca, Silvana, and Lucy Riall. "Introduction: Revisiting the Risorgimento." In *The Risorgimento Revisited: Nationalism and Culture in Nineteenth-Century Italy*, edited by Silvana Patriarca and Lucy Riall, 1–17. Basingstoke: Palgrave, 2012.

Paye, Claudie. "Cassel, prisme de l'identité westphalienne ou petit Paris au bord de la Fulda? Pratiques identitaires et frictions culturelles au royaume de Westphalie, 1807–1813." In *Erbfeinde im Empire? Franzosen und Deutsche im Zeitalter Napoleons*, edited by Gabriele B. Clemens, Jacques-Olivier Boudon, and Pierre Horn, 33–50. Ostfildern: Thorbecke, 2016.

Pécout, Gilles. *Naissance de l'Italie contemporaine, 1770–1922*. Paris: Colin, 2002.

Planert, Ute. "International Conflicts, War, and the Making of Modern Germany, 1740–1815." In *The Oxford Handbook of Modern German History*, edited by Helmut Walser Smith, 91–118. Oxford: Oxford University Press, 2011.

———. "Nationalismus und weibliche Politik: Zur Einführung." In *Nation, Politik und Geschlecht: Frauenbewegungen und Nationalismus in der Moderne*, edited by Ute Planert, 9–14. Frankfurt am Main: Campus Verlag, 2000.

———. *Antifeminismus im Kaiserreich: Diskurs, soziale Formation und politische Mentalität*. Göttingen: Vandenhoeck & Ruprecht, 1998.
Porciani, Ilaria. "Disciplinamento nazionale e modelli domestici nel lungo Ottocento: Germania e Italia a confronto." In *Storia d' Italia: Annali; Il Risorgimento*, edited by Alberto M. Banti and Paul Ginsborg, 97–125. Turin: Einaudi, 2007.
———. "Famiglia e nazione nel lungo Ottocento." *Passato e Presente* 57 (2002): 11–39.
Raphael, Lutz. "The 1970s—A Period of Structural Rupture in Germany and Italy?" In *Cities Contested: Urban Politics, Heritage, and Social Movements in Italy and West Germany in the 1970s*, edited by Martin Baumeister, Bruno Bonomo, and Dieter Schott, 31–50. Frankfurt am Main: Campus Verlag, 2017.
Riall, Lucy. *Garibaldi: Invention of a Hero*. New Haven, CT: Yale University Press, 2007.
Rörig, Karoline. *Cristina Trivulzio di Belgiojoso (1808–1871): Geschichtsschreibung und Politik im Risorgimento*. Bonn: Röhrig, 2013.
Schieder, Theodor. *Nationalismus und Nationalstaat: Studien zum nationalen Problem in Europa*. Göttingen: Vandenhoeck & Ruprecht, 1992.
Steinmetz, Willibald, and Heinz-Gerhard Haupt. "The Political as a Communicative Space in History: The Bielefeld Approach." In *Writing Political History Today*, edited by Willibald Steinmetz, Ingrid Gilcher-Holtey, and Heinz-Gerhard Haupt, 11–33. Frankfurt am Main: Campus Verlag, 2013.
Ther, Philipp. "Beyond the Nation: The Relational Basis of a Comparative History of Germany and Europe." *Central European History* 36 (2003): 45–73.
Troebst, Stefan. "European History." In *European Regions and Boundaries: A Conceptual History*, edited by Diana Mishkova and Balázs Trencsényi, 235–57. New York: Berghahn Books, 2017.
Vasilev, George. "Methodological Nationalism and the Politics of History-Writing: How Imaginary Scholarship Perpetuates the Nation." *Nation and Nationalism* 25 (2019): 499–522.
Werner, Michael, and Bénédicte Zimmermann. "Beyond Comparison: Histoire Croisée and the Challenge of Reflexivity." *History and Theory* 45 (2006): 30–50.
———. "Vergleich, Transfer, Verflechtung. Der Ansatz der Histoire croisée und die Herausforderung des Transnationalen." *Geschichte und Gesellschaft* 28 (2002): 607–36.
Ziblatt, Daniel. *Structuring the State: The Formation of Italy and Germany and the Puzzle of Federalism*. Princeton, NJ: Princeton University Press, 2006.
Zimmer, Oliver. *A Contested Nation: History, Memory and Nationalism in Switzerland*. Cambridge: Cambridge University Press, 2003.
———. *Nationalism in Europe, 1890–1940*. Basingstoke: Palgrave, 2003.

CHAPTER 2

Rethinking Nation and Family
Ilaria Porciani

Family and Nation: The Same Patriotic Discourse

In the long nineteenth century, family and nation were strictly entwined in the same patriotic discourse. They sustained each other, cutting through the traditional divisions of public and private, male and female. Scholarship from recent decades has questioned the rigid distinction into separate spheres and shown how porous the boundary between them was. The public sphere entered the home. Often, national feelings were generated in the semiprivate space of associations and clubs, as well as in the private space of salons or living rooms, where so many discussions on nation-building took place and where patriotic songs were first performed. Families became a crucial space for nation-building.

Moreover, in the nineteenth century, national narratives focused on the defense of the purity of the people, who were often ethnically defined. Hence the fear of mixed marriages, which might threaten the purity of the national lineage. Here again, family was crucial. The defense of the fatherland equaled the defense of the family, as Giuseppe Garibaldi put it bluntly when he appealed to the *tropos* of the national family contaminated by the enemy.[1]

Family and nation became closely connected in the real world, and even more so in the many metaphors and symbols in currency. Jurists codified this discourse. Heinrich Ahrens's *Cours de droit naturel* was explicit: "Man always belongs to a nation as he belongs to a family; he senses its mysterious influence in his entire way of thinking, feeling, acting, and speaking. Everyone supports his own nation as he supports his own family."[2] Johann Caspar Bluntschli pointed out, "The history of the nation merges with that of the family."[3] The opposition between "domestic" (home nation and household) and "foreign" was crucial. The perimeter of the great national family became the border of the nation-state, inclusive, highly exclusive, and often ethnic.

Domesticity took on a key role in the ideology of nationalism. In the United States, the feminine skill and virtue governing the family state became a mainstay of conquering the West. Not only was the family fitted to the nation, the nation was also a reference point for the running of the home. The hierarchical and vertical family pattern, so important for defining the monarchic nation, was not the only framework; equally important was the horizontal one that defined the "democratic and republican universe"[4] in the country as well as in exile. In monarchical countries, the king was the good father of the homeland, the prime example of the legal figure for the new codification as the *good family father*. Yet in republican countries, what occured was not so different; republican America set up a public cult around the founding fathers. Washington was the father of the nation, while women gathered into the significantly labeled association Liberty's Daughters. In the French Third Republic, albeit more feebly, the model of the president's family was held up and displayed in the illustrated press much like a family portrait; one could not be a good citizen without being a good father, or at least a good husband.

This web of concepts and discourses, which I started investigating years ago,[5] seems to me to still be coherent and valid. Benedict Anderson recalled, quoting Jules Michelet, how the nation-state and its educational institutions helped the French to learn the "family history" of the nation[6]: "The emerging nation may have been militarized and masculinized, but it was also 'familialized,' constructed as a 'patriarchically and hierarchically organized folk family.'"[7] It is in the years between the American and the French Revolutions that the model of strong links between family and nation took form. This model would then enjoy a very long success, as it is possible to see in the World Wars and in the decolonization rhetoric.

In Europe, the image of the family played a decisive role in shifting the notion of honor and building up a kind of aristocracy of nationhood. The family was the seat of national honor as the nation was the benchmark of family honor. This was true for the aristocrats. As Isacco Artom reported in *La Nazione* on 24 July 1862, Cavour used to say, "Those of illustrious birth must buy back the privilege of that birth by benefits and services rendered to the fatherland." This was even more the case for those aspiring to join the new elites by dint of services rendered to the nation. As the biologist and philosopher Jean Rostand would comment, "Families just like nations have their own moral physiognomy. Individuals have no right . . . to disfigure it."[8] One sought distinction partly for one's family or defended the family honor as much as one's own.

This strategy was important for the rising Jewish families wherever proclamation of the nation-state coincided with enfranchisement and the chance to contract marriages recognized by the state, practice the liberal professions, and gain admission to the university and army. In such cases too, it became important to tie one's family story to the process of national unification. Heroism—an important concept throughout the long nineteenth century—became a symbolic legacy to hand on.

Both the editors' introduction and the other chapters in this book underline the specificity of the case of the Jews. In Italy, after the turning point of 1848, the concept of fatherland significantly shifted in fiction and in literary works from "stepmother" to "mother," and the Jews were welcomed as "brothers" by the Piedmontese people.[9] One of the proposed paths was obviously assimilation. Women should never marry a foreigner, an enemy—a trope well developed in novels and poetry of the age of Restoration.[10] For the well-known author of some of the most influential historical novels of the Risorgimento, the anticlerical democrat Francesco Domenico Guerrazzi, Italian women had the task of creating mixed families by marrying Jewish men, of mixing and sharing the hopes and the hates through marriage. For Italian Jews as well as for the Italian patriotic Catholics (and Protestants), family was a shrine. Austere domestic *pietas*, the intimate discipline of belonging, and *Disziplinierung* created a strategic pedagogical space capable of strongly imprinting the patriotic feelings of the extended family of the nation, which deserved the same love and respect as the biological one. For the rabbi Marco Mortara, "devoted to the nation's interests, the Jew repudiates the name of nation to his stock."[11] The participation of Jewish women in the process of constructing often pivotal institutions of child education in nineteenth-century Italy[12] should probably also be reconsidered under this perspective of vicarious motherhood in relation to the nation, as did Laura Orvieto, the author of influential children's books for bourgeois mothers.[13]

Like the nation, the family came into conflict with the phenomenon (and the fear) of the anonymous, dangerous masses. Lucien Febvre stressed the importance of the homeland in injecting the warmth and strength of family feeling into the public arena, transferring family attachment "to all persons of the same country" and recalling how even Auguste Comte, who thought in terms of mankind, saw the fatherland as useful in combating a sense of rootlessness.[14] Here again, as in the many cases of gendered nations studied in the past twenty years or so, the novel was decisive for its reference to private life: Walter Scott wrote a national novel as the "private lives of our ancestors" and defined the family milieu as the proper "home" on which national character is built.[15]

"Us" stands directly opposed to "me," constructing what Norbert Elias considers to be a strong "Wir-Gefühl" forming a bridge leading from a society of corporate bodies, in which the individual as such does not exist, toward a society where the bodies have disappeared, leaving a void. Textbooks or illustrated weeklies set the stage: grandfather should relate the deeds of heroic battles, father should point to the sovereign's portrait, mother should school the little ones in patriotic history. The family enabled society to be represented in a more reassuring way than would be the case, on the one hand, with individuals and, on the other, with masses. But its role extended further. Thinking of the dual meaning of the word "represent," one is tempted to make passing reference to those occasions when there was a proposal for voting "by families."

In the United States: The Republican Wife and Mother

Beginning with the United States enables us to place the family role issue within an emerging republican nation, to focus on some real instances of Republican Motherhood, and, lastly, to raise the complex question of cultural transfer. To Alexis de Tocqueville, family was more united in America's democratic society, and there were fewer differentiations based on age and sex within it. Some of the characteristics of the democratic family (strong domestic intimacy and affection, fewer ties with the past, a shared vision) also became attributes of the new nation in revolutionary France, the Italian sister republics, and in Germany during the wars of liberation against Napoleon. Increased family intimacy within an antifeudal tendency to value bourgeois ethics and the close-knit conjugal family grew together with national feelings.

In the United States, the myth of Republican Motherhood[16] is the center of the family on which the American identity forms. The seeds of women's political engagement were present right from the days of the Revolution when distinctions were blurred and "home and the community were one and the same thing."[17] Despite their "apolitical" status, women had taken part in the revolution, kept the farms and businesses going while the men were away, successfully boycotted English products, and nursed soldiers and supported widows. Massachusetts expressly encouraged the wives of men who sided with the English to declare their loyalty to the republic and break their marital bonds.[18] It was as though the new republican nation was allowing them to cast off a bond that contradicted their loyalty to the nation.

Genre painters from the mid-nineteenth century portrayed the "domestic bliss" of the young couple immersed in nature, who somehow epitomize the youthful American nation.[19] Republican mothers also had a central role in pictures like *Old '76 and Young '48* by Richard Caton Woodville, dating from 1848, not to mention the *Madonna of the Prairie* by Wilhelm Heinrich Detlev Koerner[20] or *Daniel Boone Escorting Settlers* by George Caleb Bingham. War presents a need to describe the nation as a home and prompts comforting images and metaphors like that of the family, as in *Reading of an Official Dispatch (Mexican War News)* by John L.

Magee. It is interesting to compare these American works where the woman seems to occupy center stage with *The Volunteers* (1860), where the English painter Frederick Daniel Hardy shows a group of children playing at soldiers with a drum and their father's busby while he, in uniform, sits and watches with the youngest boy on his knee. Here, significantly, the womenfolk are onlookers on the sidelines; one is almost out of the picture, the other is in a cone of shadow as if to denote her subordinate role. At any rate, they are engrossed in their domestic tasks. For America, the family is the great symbol of reassurance during the crisis of the Revolution or the great panic of 1837 or the war with Mexico. It is the ever-present metaphor, finding its way into official language, as when the annexation of Texas is described as a harmonious and spontaneous "marriage,"[21] the family here becoming an allegory of the youthful republic.

The theme of family and nation intertwines with the American home. In 1846, Sarah Josepha Hale launched a campaign to celebrate Thanksgiving as the national holiday commemorating unification, expansion, and inclusion—and one might also say exclusion of the other. The campaign intensified significantly during the Mexican War. *Godey's Lady's Book*—the American woman's bible of domestic science that would see out the century—urged its readers to support this important influential ritual with its roots in domestic life.

In the United States as elsewhere, war mobilized the families themselves, though after the war, politicians and opinion-makers would encourage women to stay at home and forget all they had learned during the fighting.[22] However, out of the indemnities that the nation awarded its soldiers or their wives and mothers, there developed the germinal phase of American welfare, which began with federal pensions for the widows and relations of union veterans or victims of the Civil War.[23] This established a practice that would become a central policy elsewhere: for example in the German Reich or, in token form rather than as a legal right, in the Kingdom of Italy, where endowments were granted and provisions made for veterans' dependents; these were indirect ways of acknowledging and indemnifying families that had laid down their lives for their country.

Family and Citizenship: France

In France, legislation was so sensitive to the institution of the family that there was tax relief for fathers from the third child on (law passed 9 January 1805) and state help in maintaining the seventh child. Though the drafters of the Napoleonic Code did not see fit to dignify the subject with a chapter of its own, they made deep and decisive innovations, above all concerning marriage and filiation, to what would become *family law*.[24]

The Constitution of Year III laid down that one could not be a good citizen without being a good husband and father. After the end of the Republican regime, the fatherland was replaced by the nation.

With the Revolution and extending therefrom to the sister republics, the national colors found their way into male and female clothing as part of the new symbolism. Again, the fashion newspapers—illustrating the gravely pensive faces of women thinking of the fatherland[25]—proposed patriotic phrases for wives and fiancées to embroider. The republic and nation penetrated to the rooms where women began to sew flags. This image was popular in every war during the nineteenth and early twentieth centuries.

Images referring to the participation of women in political events appeared often in Italy during the long "Forty-Eight" biennium and again in the years of unification between 1859 and 1861—one thinks of paintings by Girolamo Induno, Odoardo Borrani, and many others. They figured in the German Forty-Eight and again in the Empire, when revolution was a distant memory and the nation was firmly rooted. Here too, the visual arts marked the bond between the family hearth and a country at war.

For mainstream historical painting in the Revolution and Napoleonic periods, the family seems to me one of the centers of gravity, along with patriotism. Jacques-Louis David's *Oath of the Horatii*,[26] *The Lictors Bring Back to Brutus the Bodies of His Son*, or the *Intervention of the Sabine Women* show how the state mentality affected the family and recorded the woman's new role[27] in national pedagogics. It would be intriguing to track the course of celebratory painting, beginning from an important portrayal of power and the body politic like the coronation of Napoleon, in which the Emperor wanted his mother to be shown though she was actually absent.[28] The aim, presumably, was to bring the sovereign's family, the mother at whose knee he learned, into a picture that was principally a political manifesto. At the same time, Louis-Léopold Boilly was launching a new season in genre painting that would have echoes in other countries, including the United States. His *Lecture du Bulletin de la Grande Armée* captures an 1806 scene. The family, gathered around the usual table, follows the bulletin of battle on a map (the bulletin was an institution in Napoleonic France). The reference to nationhood is obvious as an ideal extension of the scene depicted.

Girls began to be groomed to be good mothers, not just of a family but of a nation. The institute of Écouen, founded by Napoleon and managed by Henriette Campan, implemented the national education policy for girls as future mothers of citizens. Rousseau's ideas began to be pressed into service, exploiting his glorification of motherhood, and the nation is at the center of the argument. We are clearly poles apart from the Jesuits' education.

France in 1848 spoke the language of the Republic, not the nation. Article 4 of the Constitution reads, "The Republic has the family for its basis." The two words began to be used together from 1871 on, both in the public utterances of the still composite republican front and on the conservative, monarchical side with its frankly reactionary and somewhat racist mentality. Scholars like Karen Offen have picked up certain similarities, thickly underlining their implications for women.[29] In the French Revolution, the broad family paradigm formed the ideological terrain upholding both the revolutionary and the counterrevolutionary positions.[30] At the root of such treatment is the great aberration of the Paris Commune, the *pétroleuse*, woman in revolt going beyond the limits of her sex—something the new republican wanted to forget. There is also the demographic fall, which was by no means limited to the French but was keenly felt in the wake of defeat. Specific concern for a shrinking population to the detriment of the nation combined with the need for a consolatory archetype: the metaphor of the family after the fratricidal war. In the Third Republic, the allegorical figure of Marianne transformed into a prosperous philoprogenitive woman, often suckling a child. Jules Simon insisted on the idea of the good family as the pillar of the state, especially for the republicans. The definition of such themes is shaped in part by Hippolyte Taine, who advocated strong authority rooted in local communities and families.[31] However, what counts for more is the work of Frédéric Le Play, who accused Rousseau and the omnipotence of the Revolutionary State of destroying the authority of the paterfamilias, which alone can form the "social link" by which the young learn respect and obedience. The pivot of his plan was to revive the "famille souche," an appurtenance by no means exclusive to France but nevertheless "the oldest and deepest of our national institutions."[32] National identity and the health of the nation thus both fell back on the structure of the family.

Le Play's sociology found many adherents, and not only in the reactionary camp. Many progressives and republicans like Émile Zola and Marcel Prévost would directly or indirectly come to acclaim the family, denounce feminism as a dangerous foreign importation, and praise the wives of the republic who generated so many children for the nation.[33] In harking back to Rousseau and the problem of reviving national morality, the republicans themselves thought that the cornerstone of the state was the family and not the individual; they were keen for women to be educated and removed from control by the Church. In this light one can read both the reintroduction of divorce (1804)—proclaiming state authority over civil marriage—and the issue of "family wages," where those in favor were not just Catholics but also many republicans and socialists who were equally convinced that men should be the sole breadwinners.

It would be interesting to know how the card of the traditional family was played during electoral campaigns. A hint comes from the way that president of the Republic, Raymond Poincaré, was portrayed upon election. The newspaper *Le Petit Journal* presented him as the center point of the "milieu familial," which holds the "safest and sweetest joys of life."[34] This is more than the automatic attitude of a newspaper that had supported l'Alliance Républicaine Démocratique since 1901. Shortly after the law was passed changing Article 340 of the Code Civil to allow for natural paternity suits in a republic shaken by its falling birth rates in the social classes and by the low fertility of its women, at a moment when war was beginning to be in the wind, the family was still part of the reassuring republican image.[35]

Quite dissimilar was the appeal to the family made by the conservatives. The conservative front was largely made up of hostility to the republic under the lead of Léon Gambetta, the *métèque*, the accidental Frenchman. A republic born in the café, as the antirepublican and propagandist writers claimed, was a dangerous haunt of mischief and social disorder. Alcoholism and republicanism were made to seem like two sides of the same coin, a reminder of the Commune, which was "a monstrous excess of acute alcoholism."[36] The popular imagination could thus quite naturally contrast these dens of vice with the walls of the home, the republic versus the nation *tout court*. Paul Bourget worked on these phantasms in his outrage at "de-Catholicized" France, where religious practice as a source of family virtue had quite dried up. Like the Action Française movement, he wanted to stop the rot that began with Revolution when it opened the door to dissociated individuals and foreigners. According to Bourget, against "revolution and democracy, those two minions of death,"[37] one had to say with Le Play: "Loving France means, sooner or later, recognizing the values of the French family." Everything had to be subordinated to that now-endangered cell of regeneration.[38] Maurice Barrès, too, saw France in terms of spiritual families destined to merge in time of war. At the battlefront, *la nation juive* itself formed part of a united France.[39]

Germany: War and Religion

In Germany, and Prussia above all, the experience of *Befreiungskriege* was etched into the national DNA. Mass call-up and general mobilization not only forged a masculine brand of patriotism centering on the figure of the soldier,[40] they also made new room for the family as the breeding ground for the national conscience and the patriotic upbringing of children, a sacred shrine from which one is torn away to fight the foreign foe. As would be stressed a few years later by the entry "Nation" in *Rheinisches*

Conversations-Lexicon (published in Cologne in 1826), women—whose honor was to be safeguarded like that of the nation—had the job of rearing the family in *Sittlichkeit* (morality), civility, and civil rigor within a domestic moral code. For that, they needed to be good patriotic mothers and raise their children in national customs, cultivating German culture in language as in dress. It was during the wars of liberation that a German national costume began to be devised as an explicitly anti-French statement, just as esteem for the German language and choosing traditional names for one's offspring was anti-French.[41] The "politicization" of the home and family and a feminine ideal charged with national significance coalesced into a classic repertoire suitable for the bourgeois woman's involvement in national work. The family analogy made it seem less of a directly political unit, and this helped women to take part in the cause. The female associations actively alive during the Anti-Napoleonic War spread appreciation for the specific nature of female work (knitting socks for soldiers, nursing them, cooking, etc.) as being complementary to men's. This began to set up a model enshrining fixed coordinates that would last down to World War I in a national framework, one that was alert to the internal "enemy" (social democracy) as well as to the colonies. The Reichsverband gegen die Sozialdemokratie (Association against Social Democracy), the Deutscher Flottenverein (German Navy League), and Deutscher Kolonialverein (German Colonial Association) called on women to stand up for national values in Germany as in the colonies.

The time of the liberation wars also saw the beginnings of a cult formed around Queen Louise of Prussia, wife of King Frederick William III.[42] Painters and writers popularized her sweet, charitable image. Novalis held her up as a model for mothers and daughters, and there were great expectations that the royal couple would engender authentic patriotism from the blend of their public and domestic life.[43] The royal couple's coordinates for self-representation changed on a bourgeois model and filtered through new channels like the family weeklies (in Germany the *Gartenlaube* founded in 1853[44]), which targeted the average bourgeois family. In the pages of the magazine, the royal couple (or family) continued to be held up as a model for the middle classes. Recurrently, with peaks in crucial years like 1866 or 1870–71, the *Gartenlaube* featured the return of the wounded soldier or widows of the wars of liberation, alternating these with peaceable but also nationalist shots of the German family in the heart of the countryside. It published images of German couples with the legendary Rhine in the background or the Kyffhäuser, or depictions of the original, traditional German family glimpsed through rituals, especially the kind connected with marriage.[45] It also printed letters written by Bismarck to his wife at key moments (1848, 1870–71), which combined information on political events with remarks of an intimate, even delicate kind, while the etchings accompanying the text showed, for example, an affectionate Bismarck recounting history to his grandchildren. One last picture deserves attention, the *Return of the Conscript* by Moritz Oppenheim,[46] a popular artist in the last quarter of the century. In it we learn the Jewish identity of the family from certain objects, while the young volunteer's uniform reminds us of war. German Jews fought in the patriotic war without feeling that it clashed with their group and religious identity.

When World War I broke out, the *Gartenlaube* carried propaganda to the effect that Germany was not responsible for the war. It harped on service and office—*Amt*—described as "our people's oldest word," and family. It urged all Germans to "band together in links and chains of steel, to harbor wives, children, enfeebled parents, and sisters who need help from our soldiers since this is a German state and a question of being German. . . . We went through 1813 and God was our strength. In 1870 we got by with God's help."[47]

The quotation from psalm 46 "Ein feste Burg ist unser Gott" is a Lutheran favorite and as such is often found engraved inside churches of the Gründerzeit.[48] Religion was as decisive for the national identity as war, well ahead of the *Kulturkampf*. Protestantism played an important role in sealing national identity with the model of the family. Treitschke in his Berlin lectures on *Politik* dwelled insistently on the deeply Protestant nature of the Prussian state and also on the masculine (*einseitig männlich*) character of the Reformation.[49] References to religion were common, especially the figure of Martin Luther, a key symbol of German identity. When the talk of intimacy and privacy was at its height, with domestic Biedermeier at the apogee, the family of Luther began to be depicted. The setting in Gustav Adolph Spangenberg's portrait *Luther im Kreise seiner Familie* (Luther in the circle of his family) was private, yet, although shut within the walls of the house, it represented a political and national portrait too. Once again, there are specific gender issues that should not be glossed over: Luther's thoughts on marriage entailing the wife's strict submission to her husband were clearly present, albeit edulcorated in a formula of which Spangenberg's portrait is a typical example (this again dates from a significant year: 1866). In it, Luther is strumming a stringed instrument; his children are singing along with him (choral singing was a classical German way of teaching, even in the home); from his wife's belt hang purse and keys, symbols of the woman's domestic role as custodian of the home economy; in her arms she cradles the youngest child who is seraphically asleep. The colors prevailing in the picture—red, black, and gold—are an overt reference to the flag. We could also cite the portrait *Luthers Winterfreuden im Kreise seiner Familie* (Luther's winter joys in the circle of his family) by Gustav König, or the great fresco *Dr. Martin Luther auf einem Familienfest* (Dr. Martin Luther at a Family Festivity) by

Anton von Werner.[50] By the end of the eighteenth century, it had been established that Luther, the husband, father, and citizen, was the reformer of his country's domestic life, the family, and education, as well as an upholder of marriage for love and a family man attentive to his children. In a phase of nationalization of Protestantism, the pastor's house became an object of national identification,[51] and his family became a model for the German middle class. This archetypal image is to some extent borne out in reality: 57 percent of those included in the *Allgemeine deutsche Biographie* are children of pastors; a widely circulating newspaper bore the very name *Das Pfarrhaus*, and the home metaphor is neatly confirmed by "the pastor's house."

This section would not be complete without reference to two other factors. First, the debate over the Bürgerliches Gesetzbuch (German civil code) that came into force in 1900 would repay study; it concerned the outcry when the lawyer and politician Gottlieb Planck—editor of the family law section—was accused of being too "un-German." Although the proposal expressed by the legal scholar and historian Otto von Gierke to adopt a rigidly national code did not pass, the German tradition of the *mundium* and *Schlüsselgewalt* continued to be deeply felt.[52]

The second point regards the protection of maternity. It would be interesting to hunt up the references to nationhood in relation to the women's movement and their demands, which in Germany focused on safeguarding maternity, as from the 1904 Bund für Mutterschutz on.[53]

In Italy

In Italy, the Bologna Constitution of 1796 echoed the French Year III Constitution: "There is no being a good citizen without being a good son, good brother, good father, good friend, good husband"; the same went for the other sister republics, the representatives of which were often expected to be married men or widowers.[54] Ugo Foscolo expressed the same idea in his outline of a constitution for the Ionian isles. Only family men would be able to govern, since "by their progeny they are obliged to think for the future, to fear dishonor and exile." "No-one can govern the State who has not proved he can govern his own family."[55] The periodicals of the time insisted on the profound renewal of the family institution[56]: a new family characterized by a strong ideal bond cementing the union of the couple.

Le Ultime lettere di Jacopo Ortis (The last letters of Jacopo Ortis) illustrates these sentiments in the striking form of an epistolary novel, which would make a huge impact on the imagination, feelings, and values of a whole generation. Boys and girls learned its opening pages by heart throughout the nineteenth century. The text begins with a strong sense of liberty and nationality—something that a patriot's child born in exile would tragically lack:

> Were the dear friend even to be the mother of my children, my children would have no fatherland; and the dear companion of my life would sigh to realize as much. Alas! On top of the other passions that cause young girls grief at the dawn of their fleeting day there is added this unhappy love of the fatherland.[57]

As one of the most influential Italian poets of the 19th century Giosuè Carducci recalled, "A thrill of assent exploded every time lines like Monti's resounded, 'Italians are we to a man, one sole people / one sole family. Italians all and brothers.'"[58] In 1847, Goffredo Mameli, the author of the future Italian national anthem "Il canto degli italiani," would probably have had these lines in mind.

In the constitution of the united Italian provinces, voted in on 14 May 1831 but destined to last less than a month, there shines the idea of lands and provinces that at long last know the experience of "union in one sole state, in one sole family." The metaphor expresses the reality of a composite Italy that patriots longed to recognize as a nation while realizing all its enormous diversity. This metaphor was also a suitable way of representing the federalist designs of 1848. Alberto Mario had reason to quote Carlo Cattaneo on the "almost family variety of the States and regions," which in no way detracted from the national inheritance. "Every political family must have its own separate patrimony, its magistrates, its arms; yet it must . . . sit in free and sovereign representation at the fraternal congress of the whole nation, and deliberate in common on the laws paving . . . the indestructible unity and cohesion of the whole."[59] Long after the collapse of federalist designs, that metaphor would be employed in the national exhibition in 1911, where the family of the nation would be represented by families typifying the various Italian regions.

The year 1848 was decisive also for the construction of the family-nation pair. Private letters, memoirs, and later biographies pointed at the many real patriotic love stories that had their origins on the barricades. But 1848 and its failure, while the democratic Risorgimento gave way to the monarchic leadership, marks a turning point also for women's participation in politics. True, Gian Luca Fruci has pointed out both the desire and the practice of women's voting, at least in the plebiscites.[60] However, I believe Simonetta Soldani is right in affirming that after 1848 there was a retreat from women's active participation in the political struggle. Women found other, more indirect roles for themselves. The new "patriotic" national family was one of those roles, maybe the first one, along with the new extension of maternity through the role of primary school teacher that many women were assigned in the new educational system. I have already pointed out another way for Italian women to participate in the Risorgimento: the writing of family memoirs and history.[61]

Also in the postunification years, the notion of the fatherland took on Manzionian accents. "Italy—in the dual role of mother and daughter—evokes the King of unification in the guise of a corresponding twofold figure: father of the country and its most illustrious son."[62] The family of the nation has a father: the monarch. The idea of monarchy also transpired in the debate surrounding the citizens of the Pisanelli Code of 1856. Giuseppe Pisanelli's own address is especially rich in meaning: "The orator presenting the legislating body with the reasons for the tribuneship's vote on the law concerning *patria potestas* would say that every family is a 'small republic' where father and mother are the natural heads. I prefer to depict the family as the archetype of the small monarchy, the father of which is the sovereign."[63] The arguments of the jurists bring to light key features of the national debate; thus, the lawyer and politician Guido Fusinato claimed that "indissoluble marriage is a historic national concept of ours," and the journalist Rocco De Zerbi spurred his colleagues to the lofty mission of restoring "the religion of the family, as it existed in ancient Rome."[64] The same context brought references to the decline of the Roman Empire, which was enfeebled by the practice of divorce, as part of the weakening of the age-old institution of the family that underpinned it. If we return from the land of the jurists to the language of rhetoric and the emotions, we should recall not only much-studied novels but the arias of opera. *William Tell* throws the persuasive power of music into creating a climax: "un esclave n'a point de femme / un esclave n'a point d'enfants" (A slave can have no wife / a slave can have no children).

In such a climate, Giuseppe Mazzini thought the family should set an example and encourage patriotism, while "mothers who call themselves Christian" should ponder "that book of Maccabees which seems ordained for the Italians."[65]

Many postunification memoirs recall that it is the democrats who participate most in this heroic atmosphere that forges the link between family and nation. The Italian patriot Luigi Settembrini spoke of his father handing down the family memoir of the Parthenopean Republic and also the 1820 uprising as moments decisive in forming the nation. The politician Giovanni Giolitti insisted on his liberal uncles' example in his upbringing. Biographies of Mazzini joined in stressing the mother-son relationship as opening his mind to the idea of nationhood and highlighting the role of Maria Drago. Marietta Campo, Zellide Fattiboni, and other women historians have told their family stories in the light of the nation.[66]

While the Lutheran Church was decisive in forming the national awareness in the Reich, the Catholic Church in Italy played exactly the opposite part. For its part, the liberal movement promoted the family, with special emphasis on women's education, as from 1847 to 1848. Later, after unification and, more particularly, from the mid-1870s on, the galleries of famous women—the feminine Plutarchs—would foster the theme of the nation in compositions by authors like Pietro Fanfani, while Francesco Berlan focused on the lives of women patriots, those done to death by the Bourbon or Papal regimes.[67] The national spirit came in with models like Adelaide Cairoli and later Anita Garibaldi, though the latter's life was duly censored and presented as entirely exceptional.

The nation was beginning to be used as a benchmark to discipline the family, which appears as undisciplined and infertile to more than one observer. In this I see a significant parallel with Republican France. The ethics of self-sacrifice are weighed in relation to the nation. Though it is the family where sacrifice is practiced, formation of values allegedly needed defending and strengthening. National values tended to be instilled more by the schools, which viewed the family as a target for education in the new values via the child. Yet the family did preserve its own educational corner, which was diligently fed by anthologies and popular weeklies of a didactic kind.

"Family and nation" were "indissoluble companion principles."[68] This idea would continue to circulate even after the hiatus brought by the Commune, though with a shift in meaning. The key example would be the obituary of Mazzini in the *Rivista Europea*, which put its finger on "how love of the family and nation are stepping-stones to a higher love of mankind; as opposed to the recent doctrine that seeks through property to destroy love of family or fatherland."[69] The family—like the nation—became an object of contention, a stake in the game. The designs of an authoritative source like the *Digesto* were quite transparent: "In seeking to replace the private family by a great universal family, the socialists are going against nature, morality, the existence of the State."[70] Some years later—one among many examples we might cite—a daily newspaper would propose a series of pen portraits of women "devoted to the family and fatherland" against the onset of "social disorder" and a "dire disease spreading through France and beginning to invade the popular classes." The lower classes, "divorced from all attachment, no longer accept any moral code, or religion of duty, no social hierarchy, no country, no freedom."[71] Once again, the family was the key to it all. It stood as a terrain on which to act. Through their natural calling to moderation, women were targeted as the force that could ward off the peril of socialist subversion.

Conclusion: Rethinking Objects

I would like to make a plea for a broader comparison. In spite of the centrality of the cases recalled above, the examples of Belgium, Greece, and

Hungary—but also of Britain, in its imperial dimension—would be crucial to better understand the national specificity of the family and nation complex in Europe, following the suggestions of the exhibition *Mythen der Nationen*. Even more telling would be non-European cases, such as Cuba, India, or Japan.[72]

In short, I invite adoption of a wide angle in three directions: space, time, and source materials. In the first years of interest in the topic of nationalism, research focused essentially on words and written sources. Now it is time to increasingly focus on objects and "things" rather than on images. Many years ago, historians started to pay attention to material culture in collaboration with archaeologists, sociologists, folklorists, anthropologists, and, more recently, experts in museum studies. Recent works[73] have pointed out the importance of objects, artifacts, and things, even when they seem to be banal and connected to everyday use, as well as the intimate relation between objects and people. A global turn has also suggested a closer consideration of countries such as Japan in the Meiji Restoration. It was then that a "modern" object of everyday use appeared for the first time: the dining table, up to then unknown in Japanese households. The new habit of having common family dinners, synecdochized by the table, was a way of strengthening family bonds within the framework of the new state.

Rabindranath Tagore's (and the well-known Satiajit Raj movie) *The Home and the World* sets the perfect stage for this. In an early twentieth-century Indian home, a young Indian man who went to university in Britain tries to open up the boundary between men's and women's spaces in order to develop a more intimate and confident relationship with his wife, and to make her feel part of his intellectual and political world. Yet, how national is the home? Or, is the home (and therefore the family) national enough? A friend of the husband, a political activist for the national movement, raises the issue of the "nationality" of imported goods (and indirectly of the domestic objects, which connote the inner side of the home, its hearth).

Patriotic objects, originally private, then become public, and museum collections have recently attracted the attention of scholars such as Enrico Francia and Alessio Petrizzo, who focused more specifically on albums.[74] Silvia Cavicchioli has explored the shifting of meaning of objects from private homes to a collective memory of the Risorgimento in Piedmont, and has investigated the ways in which these relics of a domestic cult become national relics. Especially women (wives, sisters, mothers, or daughters) created this musealization and constructed a patriotic heritage out of their private belongings: letters, clothes, pictures—small memory tokens, apparently. They also contributed to make it alive, curating the Risorgimento museums or parts of them.[75] The pairing of family and nation appears here in a very strong way. In those family collections, as in the civic Risorgimento museums, family history is rewritten through a series of symbolic objects, which soon become objects of veneration; in short, family archeology thus becomes patriotic, national archaeology.

It is not possible here to delve deeply into the intimate links between the practice of archaeology and the representation of the nation as a family. However, it will probably be useful to suggest at least two possible grounds for testing this topic.

The first case would be national archaeology in regions claimed as national before World War I, where archaeology did not intend to discover "precious" artifacts but rather the signs of an extensive, pervasive presence of national ancestors in territories claimed as part of the nation. Istria would be the perfect case in point.[76] The second case would be a later one. Especially at the end of Nazi rule, archaeologic as well as ethnographic exhibitions had the task of proclaiming the Nordic race and the German character of the people of the area. Models of ancient families, blond and with bright blue eyes, were displayed in order to give the mark of truth to this propaganda statement at universities or in exhibitions.[77]

Family and nation are the warp and woof of a single discourse. The emotional complex that they form appears in an even stronger way in the relatively recent museums of the repatriated. There our topic is complicated and magnified by the haunting image of the lost home and, to some extent, the lost fatherland.[78] The study of very special *period rooms*, such as the ones set up by the Italians who left Istria and Dalmatia after World War II, is extremely telling. In 1946, the Italians from Pola who boarded the last ship to Trieste took with them literally every item in the household. Some of them even took the coffins containing the remains of their relatives, which they had dug out of the cemetery for that purpose.[79] The message was clear: the national family should not and could not leave anybody—dead or alive—behind, and the family should be symbolically reconstituted within the national borders. The museums that testify to this forced migration still have much to tell on the ways that family and nation were part of the same construct.[80]

After 1945 and after 1962, that is, exactly in the same years as the long migration across the Italian northeastern border, expellees (*Vertriebene*), and Eastern Germans (*Ostdeutsche*) arrived in both East and West Germany. The Federal Republic of Germany developed a policy of incorporation. Hence, the *Länder* decided to keep and protect their tangible as well as intangible heritage in an appropriate manner.[81] The many *Heimatsammlungen* both in East and West Germany[82] were followed by others, which continued to develop in the 1980s and 1990s.

How is the family represented in all these museums? Is its tight bond to the nation represented, and how? Objects are firstly tokens of symbolic exchange. Implicitly, families who carried the objects with them are the ones that carried the duty of constructing this complex dimension, which involves the memory of catastrophic events, longing, desire, and praise for the fatherland, and, last but not least, the concept of a community of destiny: a *Schicksalsgemeinschaft*. To be sure, family, community, ethnicity, habits, and nation are intertwined, merging with the imagination and the desire for a lost dimension of belonging to a specific place.

Looking at these museums, one discovers that there are new paths to explore in order to better understand how the discourse on the family and that on the nation merged and sustained each other well into the twentieth and maybe the twenty-first century.

Ilaria Porciani teaches modern and contemporary history at the University of Bologna. She has published widely on the history of education, culture, the university, historiography, museums, and nation-building, often incorporating a gender approach. Her present research interests focus on history museums and food history. Among her latest contributions is *Cibo come patrimonio* (https://storicamente.org/porciani-cibo-come-patrimonio-storia); she has also edited the volume *Food Heritage and Nationalism in Europe* (London and New York: Routledge, 2019).

Notes

1. Lucy Ryall, *Garibaldi: L'invenzione di un eroe* (Rome: Laterza, 2011), 281.
2. Heinrich Ahrens, *Cours de droit naturel: Théorie du droit public* (Leipzig: F. A. Brockhaus, 1875), 308.
3. Quoted in Guido Bortolotto, "Nazione," in *Il digesto italiano: enciclopedia metodica e alfabetica di legislazione, dottrina e giurisprudenza* (Turin: Unione Tip.-Editrice Torinese, 1905–10), 16:40.
4. Catherine Brice, ed., *Frères de sang, frères d'armes, frères ennemis : la fraternité en Italie (1820–1924)* (Rome: Ecole française de Rome, 2017).
5. See Ilaria Porciani, "Famiglia e nazione nel lungo Ottocento," in "Famiglia, società civile e stato," edited by Paul Ginsborg and Ilaria Porciani, special issue, *Passato e Presente* 57 (2002): 11–39. The present contribution draws on this work.
6. Benedict Anderson, *Imagined Communities* (London: Verso, 1991), 198 and *passim*.
7. Ruth Roach Pierson, "Nations: Gendered, Racialized, Crossed with Empire," in *Gendered Nations: Nationalisms and Gender Order in the Long Nineteenth Century*, ed. Ida Blom, Karen Hagemann, and Catherine Hall (New York: Oxford International Publishers, 2000), 46.
8. Jean Rostand, *Les familiotes et autres essais de mystique bourgeoise* (Paris: Bibliothèque-Charpentier, 1925), 23, 43.
9. Carlotta Ferrara degli Uberti, *Fare gli ebrei italiani* (Bologna: Il Mulino, 2011), 20.
10. See Barbara Armani and Guri Schwarz, "Premessa," in *Ebrei borghesi: Identità*

familiari, solidarietà e affari nell'età dell'emancipazione, Quaderni Storici 14 (2003): 621–52; David M. Myers, ed., *Acculturation and Its Discontents: The Italian Jewish Experience between Exclusion and Inclusion* (Toronto: University of Toronto Press, 2008); Elizabeth Schächter, *The Jews of Italy (1848–1915): Between Tradition and Transformation* (London: Vallentine Mitchell, 2010).
11. Ferrara degli Uberti, *Fare gli ebrei*, 101–2.
12. Ilaria Porciani, ed., *Le donne a scuola* (Florence: Il Sedicesimo, 1987).
13. Ruth Nattermann, "The Italian-Jewish Writer Laura Orvieto (1876–1955) between Intellectual Independence and Social Exclusion," *Quest: Issues in contemporary Jewish History; Journal of Fondazione CDEC* 8 (November 2015): www.quest.cdecjournal.it.
14. See Lucien Febvre, *"Honneur et Patrie": Une enquête sur le sentiment d'honneur et d'attachement à la patrie (1945–46)* (Paris: Librairie Académique Perrin, 1996), 129.
15. See James Chandler, *England in 1819: The Politics of Literary Culture and the Case of Romantic Historicism* (Chicago: Chicago University Press, 1998), 15.
16. See Margaret A. Nash, "Rethinking Republican Motherhood: Benjamin Rush and the Young Ladies' Academy of Philadelphia." *Journal of the Early Republic* 17 (1997): 171–91.
17. Paula Baker, "The Domestication of Politics: Women and American Political Society, 1780–1920," *American Historical Review* 89 (1984): 622.
18. See Linda Kerber, *Women of the Republic* (Chapel Hill: University of North Carolina Press, 1980), 124f.
19. See Peyton Boswell, *Modern American Painting* (New York: Dodd, Mead & Company 1940); Herman W. Williams, *Mirror of the American Past: A Survey of American Genre Painting* (New York: New York Graphic Society, 1973), 81.
20. See Annette Stott, "Prairie Madonnas and Pioneer Women: Images of Emigrant Women in the Art of the Old West," *Prospect* 21 (1996): 299–325.
21. See Glenda Riley, *Inventing the American Woman: A Perspective on Woman's History; 1607–1877* (Arlington Heights, IL: Harlan Davidson, 1986).
22. Riley, *Inventing the American Woman*, 128.
23. See Theda Skocpol, *Protecting Soldiers and Mothers* (Cambridge, MA: Harvard University Press, 1992); Amy E. Holmes, "Such Is the Price We Pay: American Widows and the Civil War Pension System," in *Towards a Social History of the American Civil War: Exploratory Essays*, ed. Maris Vinovskis (New York: Cambridge University Press, 1990), 171–95.
24. See Marcel Garaud, *La Révolution française et la famille* (Paris: Presses Universitaires de France, 1978).
25. See Annemarie Kleinert and Gretel Wagner, "Mode und Politik," in *Waffen und Kostümkunde* 31 (1989): 24–38.
26. See Thomas E. Crow, *Emulation: David, Drouais, and Girodet in the Art of Revolutionary France* (New Haven: Yale University Press, in association with the Getty Research Institute Los Angeles, 1995), 49–51.
27. See, for example, Christopher Prendergast, *Napoleon and History Painting: Antoine-Jean Gros's "La bataille d'Eylau"* (Oxford: Clarendon Press, 1997), 44–45.
28. Ibid., 45.
29. See the works of Karen Offen, in particular, Karen Offen, "Depopulation, Nationalism and Feminism in Fin-de-Siècle France," *American Historical Review* 89 (1984): 648–76.

30. Roddey Reid, *Families in Jeopardy: Regulating the Social Body in France 1750–1910* (Stanford, CA: Stanford University Press, 1993), 38.
31. See Michele Battini, *L'ordine delle gerarchie: I contributi reazionari e progressisti alla crisi della democrazia in Francia 1789–1914* (Turin: Bollati Boringhieri, 1995), 191.
32. Frédéric Le Play, *L'organisation de la famille selon le vrai modèle signalé par l'histoire de toutes les races et de tous les temps* (Paris: Bibliothécaire de l'oeuvre Saint-Michel, 1871), xi, xvi, xx, 112.
33. Offen, *Depopulation, Nationalism and Feminism*, 662–63.
34. See Supplément illustré, *Le Petit Journal* 24, no. 1139 (1913).
35. See Madeleine Rebérioux, *La République radicale, 1898–1914* (Paris: Éditions du Seuil, 1975), 54.
36. Jérôme Grevy, *La République des opportunistes 1870–1885* (Paris: Perrin, 1998), 173.
37. Paul Bourget, "Les Mémoires d'un patriote," in *Pages de critique et de doctrine*, vol. 2: *Thèses traditionalistes* (Paris: Plon-Nourrit et cie, 1922), 39.
38. Ibid., 33, 88–89.
39. See Maurice Barrès, *Les diverses familles spirituelles de la France* (Paris: Editions Émile-Paul Frères, 1917), 79ff.
40. Karen Hagemann, "A Valorous Volk Family: The Nation, the Military, and the Gender Order in Prussia in the Time of the Anti-Napoleonic Wars, 1806–1815," in Blom, Hagemann, and Hall, *Gendered Nations*, 179–205.
41. Ute Planert, *Nation, Politik und Geschlecht: Frauenbewegung und Nationalismus in der Moderne* (New York: Campus Verlag, 2000), 289, 29–30.
42. See Wulf Wülfing, "Die heilige Luise von Preußen: Zur Mythisierung einer Figur der Geschichte in der deutschen Literatur des 19. Jahrhunderts," in *Bewegung und Stillstand in Metaphern und Mythen: Fallstudien zum Verhältnis von elementarem Wissen und Literatur im 19. Jahrhundert*, edited by Jürgen Link and Wulf Wülfing (Stuttgart: Klett Cotta Verlag, 1984), 209–14.
43. See Horst Möller, *Fürstenstaat oder Bürgernation, Deutschland 1763–1815* (Berlin: Siedler, 1988).
44. See Dieter Barth, *Zeitschrift für alle: Das Familienblatt im 19. Jahrhundert. Ein sozialhistorischer Beitrag zur Massenpresse in Deutschland* (Münster: Institut für Publizistik der Universität Münster, 1974). Heidemarie Gruppe, *"Volk" zwischen Politik und Idylle in der "Gartenlaube" 1853–1914* (Frankfurt am Main: Peter Lang, 1976), esp. 43.
45. See *"Gartenlaube"* 14–24 (1882): 371; *Allerlei Hochzeitsgebrauchen* 36 (1885): 589.
46. See Russell A. Berman, "Citizenship, Conversion and Representation: Moritz Oppenheim's Return of the Volunteer," in *Cultural Studies of Modern Germany: History, Representation and Nationhood* (Madison: Wisconsin University Press, 1993), 46–72.
47. A. Sperl (writing from Würzburg in August 1914), "Du liebes deutsches Volk," in *"Gartenlaube"* (1914), II Sonderbeilage, 4.
48. See Michael Fischer, *Religion, Nation, Krieg. Der Lutherchoral "Ein feste Burg ist unser Gott" zwischen Befreiungskriegen und Erstem Weltkrieg* (Münster: Waxmann Verlag, 2014).
49. Heinrich von Treitschke, *Politik. Vorlesungen, gehalten an der Universität zu Berlin*, ed. Max Cornicelius (Leipzig: Hirzel, 1911).

50. See Werner Hager, "Leben mit Geschichte," in *Anton von Werner: Geschichte in Bildern*, ed. Dominik Bartmann (München: Hirmer Verlag, 1993), 17.
51. See Oliver Janz, "Das evangelische Pfarrhaus," in *Deutsche Erinnerungsorte*, ed. Etienne François and Hagen Schulze, 3:229 (Munich: C. H. Beck, 2001).
52. See Marianne Weber, *Ehefrau und Mutter in der Rechtsentwicklung* (Tübingen: J. C. B. Mohr, 1907), 411–12.
53. See Kay Goodmann, "Motherhood and Work: The Concept of Misuse of Women's Energy, 1895–1905," in *German Women in the Eighteenth and Nineteenth Centuries: A Social and Literary History*, ed. Ruth Ellen Joeres and Mary Jo Maynes (Bloomington: Indiana University Press, 1986), 110–11.
54. Alberto Acquarone et al., eds., *Le costituzioni italiane* (Milan: Edizioni di Comunità, 1958), 169, 177, 228.
55. Quoted in Paolo Ungari, *Storia del diritto di famiglia, dalle costituzioni giacobine al Codice civile del 1942* (Bologna: Il Mulino, 1974), 95.
56. *La Decade cisalpina: Giornale filosofico-politico-letterario*, 10 Frimale year VII (30 November 1798) (Milan: 1997), 85–86.
57. Ugo Foscolo, letter of 17 March [1798], in *Le Ultime lettere di Jacopo Ortis* (1802), retrieved 30 November 2019 from https://www.liberliber.it/mediateca/libri/f/foscolo/ultime_lettere_di_jacopo_ortis/pdf/foscolo_ultime_lettere_di_jacopo_ortis.pdf.
58. Quoted in Giuditta Comani Mariani, *Compendio di storia*, vol. 2, part 2: *Storia contemporanea* (Florence: Sansoni, 1910), 124.
59. Alberto Mario, "Carlo Cattaneo," in *Il Risorgimento italiano*, ed. Leone Carpi (Milan: Vallardi, 1884), 238–39.
60. Gian Luca Fruci, "Cittadine senza cittadinanza: La mobilitazione femminile nei plebisciti del Risorgimento (1848–1870)," in "Una donna, un voto," ed. Vinzia Fiorino, special issue, *Genesis* 5, no. 2 (2006): 21–56.
61. See Ilaria Porciani, "Les historiennes et le Risorgimento," in *Mélanges de l'École française de Rome, Italie et Méditerranée* 112 (2000): 317–57.
62. Bruno Tobia, *L'altare della patria* (Bologna: Il Mulino, 1998), 22.
63. Ungari, *Storia del diritto di famiglia*, 168.
64. See Silvano Montaldo, "Il divorzio: Famiglia e nation building," *Il Risorgimento* 52 (2000): 26.
65. Giuseppe Mazzini, "Ricordi dei fratelli bandiera" [1844], in *Scritti editi e inediti* (Imola: Cooperativa Tipografica-Editrice, 1921), 31:40–41.
66. See Porciani, "Les historiennes," 330–57.
67. See Porciani, *Le Donne a scuola*, 45–46.
68. Pasquale Stanislao Mancini (1851), cited in Bortolotto, "Nazionalità," 16:11.
69. Ludmilla Assing, "Giuseppe Mazzini," *Rivista europea* 3 (1872): 209–16.
70. Giuseppe Manfredini, "Famiglia," in *Il digesto italiano: enciclopedia metodica e alfabetica di legislazione, dottrina e giurisprudenza* (Turin: Unione Tip.-Editrice Torinese 1895), 434.
71. *Il Piccolo: Giornale politico della sera* 22 (1889): 1.
72. Christopher Hill, *National History and the World of Nations: Capital, State, and the Rhetoric of History in Japan, France, and the United States* (Durham, NC: Duke University Press, 2008). The book convincingly points out transnational stereotypes and models from among the cases considered.
73. Arjun Appadurai, ed., *The Social Life of Things: Commodities in Cultural Perspective* (New York: Cambridge Studies in Social and Cultural Anthropology, 1986);

Aleida Assmann, *Erinnerungsräume: Formen und Wandlungen des kulturellen Gedächtnisses* (Munich: C.H.Beck, 1999); Mary C. Beaudry and Dan Hicks, eds., *Oxford Handbook of Material Culture Studies* (Oxford: Oxford University Press, 2010); Remo Bodei, *La vita delle cose* (Rome: Laterza, 2014); Timothy Brook, *Vermeer's Hat: The Seventeenth Century and the Dawn of the Global World* (London: Profile, 2007); Victor Buchli, ed., *The Material Culture Reader* (New York: Bloomsbury Academic, 2002); Victoria de Grazia and Ellen Furlough, eds., *The Sex of Things: Gender and Consumption in Historical Perspective* (Los Angeles: California University Press, 1996); James Epstein, *In Practice: Studies in the Language and Culture of Popular Politics in Modern Britain* (Stanford, CA: Stanford University Press, 2003); Anne Gerritsen and Giorgio Riello, eds., *Writing Material Culture History* (London: Bloomsbury, 2014); Paul Graves Brown et al., eds., *Oxford Handbook of the Archeology of the Contemporary World* (Oxford: Oxford University Press, 2013); Ludmilla Jordanova, *The Look of the Past: Visual and Material Evidence in Historical Practice* (New York: Cambridge University Press, 2012); John Styles and Amanda Vickery, eds., *Gender, Taste and Material Culture in Britain and North America 1700–1830* (New Haven, CT: Yale University Press, 2006); Victoria & Albert Museum, *Europe 1600–1815*, http://www.vam.ac.uk.

74. See Enrico Francia, "'Oggetti patriottici': Una ricerca sulla cultura materiale del Risorgimento," *Passato e Presente* 35, no. 100 (2016): 35–42.
75. See Massimo Baioni, *La "religione della patria": Musei e istituti del culto risorgimentale (1884–1918)* (Quinto di Treviso: Pagus, 1994), 194.
76. Ilaria Porciani, "Rappresentanza e patrimonio culturale: Dalla Dieta del Nessuno al museo di Parenzo," in *Per continuare il dialogo: Gli amici ad Angelo Varni*, ed. Alberto Malfitano, Alberto Preti, and Fiorenza Tarozzi (Bologna: BUP, 2014), 1:111–22.
77. Anne-Marie Adam et al., eds., *L'archéologie en Alsace et en Moselle au temps de l'annexion (1940–1944)* (Strasbourg: Musées de Strasbourg, 2001).
78. See Patrizia Audenino, *La casa perduta: La memoria dei profughi nell'Europa del Novecento* (Rome: Carocci, 2015).
79. Fondazione Giorgio Perlasca, "Pola, una città che muore," YouTube, 31 May 2012, retrieved 1 September 2017 from https://www.youtube.com/watch?v=ppQILLUSwHw.
80. Ilaria Porciani, "Exilescapes in a Hangar—Exilescapes in a Camp: Period Rooms from the Lost Nation," in *The Period Rooms: Allestimenti storici tra arte, collezionismo e museologia*, ed. Sandra Costa, Dominique Poulot, and Mercedes Volait (Bologna: BUP, 2016), 199–206.
81. Cornelia Eisler, *Verwaltete Erinnerung, symbolische Politik: Die Heimatsammlungen der deutschen Flüchtlinge, Vertriebenen und Aussiedler* (Munich: De Gruyter Oldenbourg, 2015), 42.
82. See Tim Völkering, *Flucht und Vertreibung im Museum: Zwei aktuelle Ausstellungen und ihre geschichtskulturellen Hintergründe im Vergleich* (Berlin: LitVerlag, 2008).

Bibliography

Acquarone, Alberto, et al., eds. *Le costituzioni italiane*. Milan: Edizioni di Comunità, 1958.
Adam, Anne-Marie, et al., eds. *L'archéologie en Alsace et en Moselle au temps de l'annexion (1940–1944)*. Strasbourg: Musées de Strasbourg, 2001.
Ahrens, Heinrich. *Cours de droit naturel: Théorie du droit public*. Leipzig: F. A. Brockhaus, 1875.
Anderson, Benedict. *Imagined Communities*. London: Verso, 1991.
Appadurai, Arjun, ed. *The Social Life of Things: Commodities in Cultural Perspective*. New York: Cambridge Studies in Social and Cultural Anthropology, 1986.
Armani, Barbara, and Guri Schwarz. "Premessa." In *Ebrei borghesi: Identità familiari, solidarietà e affari nell'età dell'emancipazione, Quaderni Storici* 14 (2003): 621–52.
Assing, Ludmilla. "Giuseppe Mazzini." *Rivista europea* 3 (1872): 209–16.
Assmann, Aleida. *Erinnerungsräume: Formen und Wandlungen des kulturellen Gedächtnisses*. Munich: C.H.Beck, 1999.
Audenino, Patrizia. *La casa perduta: La memoria dei profughi nell'Euopa del Novecento*. Rome: Carocci, 2015.
Baioni, Massimo. *La "religione della patria": Musei e istituti del culto risorgimentale (1884–1918)*. Quinto di Treviso: Pagus, 1994.
Baker, Paula. "The Domestication of Politics: Women and American Political Society, 1780–1920." *American Historical Review* 89 (1984): 620–47.
Barrès, Maurice. *Les diverses familles spirituelles de la France*. Paris: Editions Émile-Paul Frères, 1917.
Barth, Dieter. *Zeitschrift für alle: Das Familienblatt im 19. Jahrhundert; Ein sozialhistorischer Beitrag zur Massenpresse in Deutschland*. Münster: Institut für Publizistik der Universität Münster, 1974.
Battini, Michele. *L'ordine delle gerarchie: I contributi reazionari e progressisti alla crisi della democrazia in Francia 1789–1914*. Turin: Bollati Boringhieri, 1995.
Beaudry, Mary C., and Dan Hicks, eds. *Oxford Handbook of Material Culture Studies*. Oxford: Oxford University Press, 2010.
Berman, Russell A. "Citizenship, Conversion and Representation: Moritz Oppenheim's Return of the Volunteer." In *Cultural Studies of Modern Germany: History, Representation and Nationhood*. Madison: Wisconsin University Press, 1993.
Bodei, Remo. *La vita delle cose*. Rome: Laterza, 2014.
Bortolotto, Guido. "Nazionalità." In *Il digesto italiano: enciclopedia metodica e alfabetica di legislazione, dottrina e giurisprudenza*. Turin: Unione Tip.-Editrice Torinese, 1898.
———. "Nazione." In *Il digesto italiano: enciclopedia metodica e alfabetica di legislazione, dottrina e giurisprudenza*. Turin: Unione Tip.-Editrice Torinese, 1905–10.
Boswell, Peyton. *Modern American Painting*. New York: Dodd, Mead & Company, 1940.
Bourget, Paul. "Les Mémoires d'un patriote." In *Pages de critique et de doctrine*. Vol. 2: *Thèses traditionalistes*. Paris: Plon-Nourrit et cie, 1922.
Brice, Catherine, ed. *Frères de sang, frères d'armes, frères ennemis : la fraternité en Italie (1824–1924)*. Rome: Ecole française de Rome, 2017.
Brook, Timothy. *Vermeer's Hat: The Seventeenth Century and the Dawn of the Global World*. London: Profile, 2007.

Buchli, Victor, ed. *The Material Culture Reader*. New York: Bloomsbury Academic, 2002.
Chandler, James. *England in 1819: The Politics of Literary Culture and the Case of Romantic Historicism*. Chicago: Chicago University Press, 1998.
Comani Mariani, Giuditta. *Compendio di storia*. Vol. 2, part 2: *Storia contemporanea*. Florence: Sansoni, 1910.
Crow, Thomas E. *Emulation: David, Drouais, and Girodet in the Art of Revolutionary France*. New Haven: Yale University Press, in association with the Getty Research Institute Los Angeles, 1995.
de Grazia, Victoria, and Ellen Furlough, eds. *The Sex of Things: Gender and Consumption in Historical Perspective*. Los Angeles: California University Press, 1996.
Eisler, Cornelia. *Verwaltete Erinnerung, symbolische Politik: Die Heimatsammlungen der deutschen Flüchtlinge, Vertriebenen und Aussiedler*. Munich: De Gruyter Oldenbourg, 2015.
Epstein, James. *In Practice: Studies in the Language and Culture of Popular Politics in Modern Britain*. Stanford, CA: Stanford University Press, 2003.
Febvre, Lucien. *"Honneur et Patrie": Une enquête sur le sentiment d'honneur et d'attachement à la patrie (1945–46)*. Paris: Librairie Académique Perrin, 1996.
Ferrara degli Uberti, Carlotta. *Fare gli ebrei italiani*. Bologna: Il Mulino, 2011.
Fischer, Michael. *Religion, Nation, Krieg. Der Lutherchoral "Ein feste Burg ist unser Gott" zwischen Befreiungskriegen und Erstem Weltkrieg*. Münster: Waxmann Verlag, 2014.
Foscolo, Ugo. *Le Ultime lettere di Jacopo Ortis* [Last letters of Jacopo Ortis]. 1802. Retrieved 30 November 2019 from https://www.liberliber.it/mediateca/libri/f/foscolo/ultime_lettere_di_jacopo_ortis/pdf/foscolo_ultime_lettere_di_jacopo_ortis.pdf.
Francia, Enrico. "'Oggetti patriottici': Una ricerca sulla cultura materiale del Risorgimento." *Passato e Presente* 35, no. 100 (2016): 35–42.
Fruci, Gian Luca. "Cittadine senza cittadinanza: La mobilitazione femminile nei plebisciti del Risorgimento (1848–1870)." In "Una donna, un voto," edited by Vinzia Fiorino. Special issue, *Genesis* 5, no. 2 (2006): 21–56.
Garaud, Marcel. *La Révolution française et la famille*. Paris: Presses Universitaires de France, 1978.
Gerritsen, Anne, and Giorgio Riello, eds. *Writing Material Culture History*. London: Bloomsbury, 2014.
Goodmann, Kay. "Motherhood and Work: The Concept of Misuse of Women's Energy, 1895–1905." In *German Women in the Eighteenth and Nineteenth Centuries: A Social and Literary History*, edited by Ruth Ellen Joeres and Mary Jo Maynes, 203–23. Bloomington: Indiana University Press, 1986.
Graves Brown, Paul, et al., eds. *Oxford Handbook of the Archeology of the Contemporary World*. Oxford: Oxford University Press, 2013.
Grevy, Jérôme. *La République des opportunistes 1870–1885*. Paris: Perrin, 1998.
Hagemann, Karen. "A Valorous Volk Family: The Nation, the Military, and the Gender Order in Prussia in the Time of the Anti-Napoleonic Wars, 1806–1815." In *Gendered Nations: Nationalisms and Gender Order in the Long Nineteenth Century*, edited by Ida Blom, Karen Hagemann, and Catherine Hall, 179–205. New York: Oxford International Publishers, 2000.
Hager, Werner. "Leben mit Geschichte." In *Anton von Werner. Geschichte in Bildern*, edited by Dominik Bartmann, 11–18. München: Hirmer Verlag, 1993.

Gruppe, Heidemarie. *"Volk" zwischen Politik und Idylle in der "Gartenlaube" 1853–1914.* Frankfurt am Main: Peter Lang, 1976.
Hill, Christopher. *National History and the World of Nations. Capital, State, and the Rhetoric of History in Japan, France, and the United States.* Durham, NC: Duke University Press, 2008.
Holmes, Amy E. "Such Is the Price We Pay: American Widows and the Civil War Pension System." In *Towards a Social History of the American Civil War: Exploratory Essays,* edited by Maris Vinovskis, 171–95. New York: Cambridge University Press, 1990.
Janz, Oliver. "Das evangelische Pfarrhaus." In *Deutsche Erinnerungsorte,* edited by Etienne François and Hagen Schulze, 3:221–38. Munich: C. H. Beck, 2001.
Jordanova, Ludmilla. *The Look of the Past: Visual and Material Evidence in Historical Practice.* New York: Cambridge University Press, 2012.
Kerber, Linda. *Women of the Republic.* Chapel Hill: University of North Carolina Press, 1980.
Kleinert, Annemarie, and Gretel Wagner. "Mode und Politik." *Waffen und Kostümkunde* 31 (1989): 24–38.
Le Play, Frédéric. *L'organisation de la famille selon le vrai modèle signalé par l'histoire de toutes les races et de tous les temps.* Paris: Bibliothécaire de l'oeuvre Saint-Michel, 1871.
Manfredini, Giuseppe. "Famiglia." In *Il digesto italiano: enciclopedia metodica e alfabetica di legislazione, dottrina e giurisprudenza.* Turin: Unione Tip.-Editrice Torinese, 1895.
Mario, Alberto. "Carlo Cattaneo." In *Il Risorgimento italiano,* edited by Leone Carpi, 238–39. Milan: Vallardi, 1884.
Mazzini, Giuseppe. "Ricordi dei fratelli bandiera" [1844]. In *Scritti editi e inediti,* 31:40–41. Imola: Cooperativa Tipografica-Editrice, 1921.
Möller, Horst. *Fürstenstaat oder Bürgernation, Deutschland 1763–1815.* Berlin: Siedler, 1988.
Montaldo, Silvano. "Il divorzio: Famiglia e nation building." *Il Risorgimento* 52 (2000): 5–57.
Myers, David M., ed. *Acculturation and Its Discontents: The Italian Jewish Experience between Exclusion and Inclusion.* Toronto: University of Toronto Press, 2008.
Nash, Margaret A. "Rethinking Republican Motherhood: Benjamin Rush and the Young Ladies' Academy of Philadelphia." *Journal of the Early Republic* 17 (1997): 171–91.
Nattermann, Ruth. "The Italian-Jewish Writer Laura Orvieto (1876–1955) between Intellectual Independence and Social Exclusion." *Quest: Issues in contemporary Jewish History, Journal of Fondazizone CDEC* 8 (November 2015): www.quest.cdecjournal.it.
Offen, Karen. "Depopulation, Nationalism and Feminism in Fin-de-Siècle France." *American Historical Review* 89 (1984): 648–76.
Planert, Ute. *Nation, Politik und Geschlecht: Frauenbewegung und Nationalismus in der Moderne.* New York: Campus Verlag, 2000.
Porciani, Ilaria, ed. *Le donne a scuola.* Florence: Il Sedicesimo, 1987.
———. "Les historiennes et le Risorgimento." *Mélanges de l'École française de Rome, Italie et Méditerranée* 112 (2000): 317–57.
———. "Famiglia e nazione nel lungo Ottocento." In "Famiglia, società civile e stato," edited by Paul Ginsborg and Ilaria Porciani. Special issue, *Passato e Presente* 57 (2002): 11–39.

———. "Rappresentanza e patrimonio culturale. Dalla Dieta del Nessuno al museo di Parenzo." In *Per continuare il dialogo: Gli amici ad Angelo Varni*, edited by Alberto Malfitano, Alberto Preti, and Fiorenza Tarozzi, 1:111–22. Bologna: BUP, 2014.

———. "Exilescapes in a Hangar—Exilescapes in a Camp: Period Rooms from the Lost Nation." In *The Period Rooms: Allestimenti storici tra arte, collezionismo e museologia*, edited by Sandra Costa, Dominique Poulot, and Mercedes Volait, 199–206. Bologna: BUP, 2016.

Prendergast, Christopher. *Napoleon and History Painting: Antoine-Jean Gros's "La bataille d'Eylau."* Oxford: Clarendon Press, 1997.

Rebérioux, Madeleine. *La République radicale, 1898–1914*. Paris: Éditions du Seuil, 1975.

Reid, Roddey. *Families in Jeopardy: Regulating the Social Body in France 1750–1910*. Stanford: Stanford University Press, 1993.

Riley, Glenda. *Inventing the American Woman: A Perspective on Woman's History, 1607–1877*. Arlington Heights, IL: Harlan Davidson, 1986.

Roach Pierson, Ruth. "Nations: Gendered, Racialized, Crossed with Empire." In *Gendered Nations: Nationalisms and Gender Order in the Long Nineteenth Century*, edited by Ida Blom, Karen Hagemann, and Catherine Hall, 41–61. New York: Oxford International Publishers, 2000.

Rostand, Jean. *Les familiotes et autres essais de mystique bourgeoise*. Paris: Bibliothèque-Charpentier, 1925.

Ryall, Lucy. *Garibaldi: L'invenzione di un eroe*. Rome: Laterza, 2011.

Schächter, Elizabeth. *The Jews of Italy (1848–1915): Between Tradition and Transformation*. London: Vallentine Mitchell, 2010.

Skocpol, Theda. *Protecting Soldiers and Mothers*. Cambridge, MA: Harvard University Press, 1992.

Stott, Annette. "Prairie Madonnas and Pioneer Women: Images of Emigrant Women in the Art of the Old West." *Prospect* 21 (1996): 299–325.

Styles, John, and Amanda Vickery, eds. *Gender, Taste and Material Culture in Britain and North America 1700–1830*. New Haven, CT: Yale University Press, 2006.

Supplément illustré. *Le Petit Journal* 24, no. 1139 (1913).

Tobia, Bruno. *L'altare della patria*. Bologna: Il Mulino, 1998.

Ungari, Paolo. *Storia del diritto di famiglia, dalle costituzioni giacobine al Codice civile del 1942*. Bologna: Il Mulino, 1974.

Völkering, Tim. *Flucht und Vertreibung im Museum: Zwei aktuelle Ausstellungen und ihre geschichtskulturellen Hintergründe im Vergleich*. Berlin: LitVerlag, 2008.

von Treitschke, Heinrich. *Politik. Vorlesungen, gehalten an der Universität zu Berlin*, edited by Max Cornicelius. Leipzig: Hirzel, 1911.

Weber, Marianne. *Ehefrau und Mutter in der Rechtsentwicklung*. Tübingen: J. C. B. Mohr, 1907.

Williams, Herman W. *Mirror of the American Past: A Survey of American Genre Painting*. New York: New York Graphic Society, 1973.

Wülfing, Wulf. "Die heilige Luise von Preußen: Zur Mythisierung einer Figur der Geschichte in der deutschen Literatur des 19. Jahrunderts." In *Bewegung und Stillstand in Metaphern und Mythen: Fallstudien zu, Verhältnis von elementarem Wissen und Literatur im 19. Jahrhundert*, edited by Jürgen Link and Wulf Wülfing, 209–14. Stuttgart: Klett Cotta Verlag, 1984.

Section 2
FAMILY AND NATION

CHAPTER 3

The Morenos between Family and Nation
Notes on the History of a Bourgeois Mediterranean Jewish Family (1850–1912)

Marcella Simoni

Introduction: The Interplay of Some Questions of Identity and Belonging

In this chapter, I would like to take as a point of departure the history of the Moreno family from Livorno (Leghorn), who settled in Tunis in 1830, to discuss some broader questions regarding the religious and national affiliation of an Italian *and* Jewish family between the end of the nineteenth century and the first decades of the twentieth. The patriarch of the family—Moisè Moreno—left Livorno for Tunis in 1830 to open a pharmacy; as we shall see, by the end of the century, the Morenos had grown in number, thrived economically, expanded within society through commercial and marriage networks, and risen to political prominence, becoming one of the main Italian-Jewish families in all of Tunisia.

This linear path disguises a more complex picture, which raises manifold questions about the positioning of a Jewish family in a changing social and political context vis-à-vis their own identity as Jews, as Italians, as *grana* (Jews from Livorno), as part of Tunisia's commercial elite, and, after 1881—when Tunisia became a French protectorate—as foreigners in a colonial context that they (together with many others) had strongly believed would become Italian instead. And although it may seem that Tunisia's complex domestic and international situation would make this family a good case study for the dynamics of situational ethnicity, as we shall see, its history could also be seen as a case of situational nationalism.[1] Situational ethnicity is defined here as a case where an ethnic identity is displayed or concealed depending on its usefulness in a given situation, allowing for people to participate in their ethnic heritage while still maintaining membership of the broader, mainstream culture.

Within this framework, I will discuss how issues of religious and national identity were at play in the internal and external dynamics of this family (and by extension, in that of the group of Jews who were part of the same social and national milieu) at a time when Italy's colonial aspirations were rebuffed with the Treaties of Bardo (1881) and La Marsa (1883) (which made Tunisia a French protectorate), or when they were later bolstered with the Italian colonial conquest of Libya in 1911. Though the tension between religious and national affiliation runs through the following pages, other equally important tensions emerge from the many relations that this family entertained: for example, that between this group of Italian Jews and the local Jews, which falls into the well-known set of relations between the *grana* (the Jews originally from Livorno/Leghorn [*gurni*, pl. *grana*]) and the *twansa* (the Jews from Tunis [*tunis*, pl. *twansa*]); or that between this group of Italian Jews and the non-Jewish Italians who migrated to Tunisia in vast numbers at the end of the nineteenth century, whether permanently or as seasonal workers, especially from nearby Sicily. Finally, in the changed institutional colonial context post-1881, a new tension emerged between the Italian economic elite and the French authorities. These tensions played out in different ways in various historical moments of the Morenos' century-long residence in Tunisia, and I will therefore deal with some of them in greater detail than others.

The Background: Some Numerical and Geographical Data

As mentioned above, the history of the Morenos began in Livorno in 1830 and can be considered part and parcel of the broader picture of Jewish and Italian migration in the Mediterranean in the nineteenth century. This was a voluntary migration motivated by economic considerations; it was not limited to male individuals; it often included women and children; it originated in the commercial/diplomatic treaties between Tuscany and the Ottoman Empire that pre-dated the regime of the Capitulations; and it placed Tuscan subjects in Tunisia under the jurisdiction of the Grand Duke's law.[2] This situation resulted in a constant, steady growth in the Jewish presence in Mediterranean ports during the second half of the nineteenth century, contributing to the development and further enrichment of what has been termed a "Mediterranean Jewish Diaspora."[3] After Italian unification was complete, Italy and the Bey signed the Regime of Capitulations in 1868 (for a twenty-eight-year term), which bestowed on Italians the same privileges accorded to foreigners in other areas of the Ottoman Empire: Italians in Tunisia maintained their nationality and were subject to consular jurisdiction in matters of private and commercial law; in practice, this translated to their commercial enterprises having the status of extraterritoriality.

The studies by Daniela Pennacchio[4] on Jewish migrations from Livorno to twelve Mediterranean ports confirm the centrality of Livorno as the single port from which more than five thousand Jews migrated elsewhere in the Mediterranean between 1825 and 1865: Alexandria, Algiers, Constantinople, Jerusalem, Marseilles, following the alphabet all the way to Tunis.[5] Alexandria, in Egypt,[6] was the port that received the highest number of Jewish migrants (1,370 individuals), immediately followed by Tunis (1,313) and then by Marseilles (1,044). Interestingly enough, Jerusalem scored second last in this period, with only eight Jews traveling from Livorno to Palestine, a number that challenges the normative homeland-diaspora model of Jewish relations. Here, "home" was quite simply Italy, with Livorno as its capital, while the diaspora was defined in reference to that original home. In this context, Tunis—imagined as a would-be Italian colony—became the point of departure for many economic and political activities that further strengthened the relationship between Italy and Tunisia through a continuous exchange.

If we look at the original group of Jews who transited from Livorno and migrated to Tunis, we see that 62 percent of the Jewish migrant population was engaged in trade. Trade was followed as an employment category by two others that reveal the changing needs of the European trading families in Tunis throughout the nineteenth century and their upward social mobility. As Pennacchio shows, the second category of employment for Jews in Tunis was that of *domestici* (servants, cooks), catering to the needs of the rising European middle classes of Tunis—which included many Jews. The third-largest professional grouping among Jews who emigrated from Livorno to Tunis is classified in the registers as *scritturali*, i.e. a large body of scribes, clerks, notaries, and accountants, which provided for the legal, accounting, and secretarial jobs of this emerging mercantile middle class. They were much needed indeed if, between 1861 and 1881, Italy, France, and the United Kingdom handled 92 percent of the commercial volume of the whole country.[7] As is well known, another field in which the Jewish presence dominated in Tunis was the medical sciences. Here, Italian Jews were in the good company of many French Jews.[8]

This Mediterranean Jewish diaspora was not only composed of a rising merchant elite but also of Jews engaged in more modest professions; the story of Salomone Hasdà represents a good example. In 1852, Hasdà— one of four brothers—a poor tailor from Livorno working in Tunis who had already twice been assisted economically by the Jewish community of Livorno, was requesting further help to relocate to another "scalo of Berberia [port of the Berber lands] to find better luck in his tailor's craft." One of his brothers was working as a petty trader in Algiers until 1829;

another was working for the government in Alexandria until 1837, while the third brother was still living in Livorno.⁹

Obviously, Italian migration to Tunis was not only a Jewish phenomenon, nor did it necessarily originate from Livorno. In the first half of the nineteenth century, the Italian community was the largest among the European communities in Tunisia and, in the mid-nineteenth century, one-third of the Europeans in Tunis were Italians—about 8,000 people. According to data published by William Shorrock, "in 1881, of 20,000 Europeans (out of a total population of some 1 1/2 million), 11,000 were Italian; only some 700 were French."¹⁰ Almost 90,000 Italians were counted in the census of 1926.¹¹

Many details attest to this centrality: some quarters of Tunis became known as Piccola (Little) Sicilia, Piccola Calabria, Piccola Venezia, Piccola Sardegna; Italian was the commercial language, and diplomatic papers were written in Italian (including for the Austrian and French consulates); passports were in Italian and so were medical certificates. Italian was spoken at the court of the Bey, and many Italians worked at the court in various capacities.¹² From the 1840s on, during the Risorgimento, many Italian political exiles found refuge in Tunisia. Some of them were Jews, like the well-known patriot and physician Giacomo Castelnuovo.¹³ Others were not Jews, nor did they belong to the upper and middle classes, as the studies of Daniela Melfa and others have shown.¹⁴ With the help of Leone Carpi, a Jewish political economist and a well-known supporter of the Risorgimento—who was in turn quoting a report from the Italian consul in Tunis in 1874—we can sum up the situation as follows: "The Italian community in Tunis is composed of three main groups: the Tabarkini (those who migrated from Genoa to Tabarka to pick coral), the Israelites from Livorno (who came to trade among Arabs and Christians), and more recently, the Sicilians."¹⁵

The Moreno family enters this picture and this world of circulation and exchange in 1830, when the pharmacist Moisè Moreno from Livorno was invited by one of the physicians working at the court of the Bey;¹⁶ he moved to Tunis with his wife Grazia Sonsino and his two children, Sara and Aaron Daniele, and he opened the first pharmacy in town.¹⁷

The Morenos in Tunis, the *Grana* and the *Twansa*

The Moreno family's stay in Tunisia spans over a century, from their establishment in Tunis in 1830 through the momentous decades until their departure between 1948 and 1956 after the anti-Jewish riots of 1947, and after Tunisia achieved independence from France. In the nineteenth century, Italy's loss of Tunisia to France probably represented the most significant event that left an indelible mark on the family in terms of identity. As we shall see in the next paragraph, it strengthened an already quite marked sense of Italian national identity (if not nationalism) that they carried right on into the following century, whose first decades inevitably further strengthened the national feelings of the various members of this family in various ways. The Italian colonial conquest of Libya in 1911 and World War I represent the first two crucial moments of this transformation. Shortly after, Fascism seduced many members of the Italian Tunisian colony (Jews and non-Jews alike); for many of these, that fascination was over by the mid-1930s. In 1935, with the Franco-Italian Agreement, Italy renounced any claim to Tunisia in exchange for an area on the border between Libya (Italian) and Chad (French), a move that many Italians viewed as the ultimate betrayal of their country.[18] Shortly after, another betrayal would affect the Morenos not as Italians but as Jews, when the Racial Laws of 1938 led to the confiscation of some of their property in Italy. The war would bring not only other confiscations of property for military use (in Tunisia)[19] but also the deportation and extermination of one family member at Auschwitz.

The trajectory of the Morenos throughout the 120 years of their residence in Tunisia and throughout the Mediterranean is too long and complicated to be fully analyzed in the space of this chapter; I will therefore sketch a picture of this family at the peak of its influence, i.e. between the end of the nineteenth century and the first decade of the new one. In my conclusions, I will point to some other directions for more detailed and deeper research on the Moreno family.

The son and grandsons of Moisè Moreno—Aaron Daniele, Raffaello, and Leone—did not follow in their father's and grandfather's footsteps; they joined the trading bank of Isacco Coriat, and in 1876 they established a joint trading society (A. D. Moreno Figli & C.ie). That company was passed down to the Moreno descendants under various names and lasted one century altogether.[20] Along the way, new members of the family became associated, and the company expanded and diversified the type of commercial activities in which they engaged, the real estate they owned, and the geography of their presence in Tunisia. These ranged from the timber trade (Raffaello, son of Aaron Daniele)—which was the Morenos' initial field of operations—to moneylending (including to the Bey) (Daniel Cardoso, brother in law of Raffaello), from agricultural development and the construction of a mill in Zeghouan (Leone, brother of Raffaello) to management of the concession for extracting the precious yellow marble of Chemtou. Toward the end of the century, Raffaello was the head of the family, and his two sons—Ugo and Giacomo—had become lawyers. The Morenos were connected to a tight professional and family network that linked several middle- and upper-class commercial Jewish families—the Coriats, Lumbrosos, Molcos, Morpurgos, Boccaras, Cardosos, etc. Most of them were *grana*; some of them, like Dr. Funaro, led the Italian freemasons in Tunis; a few were upper-class educated *twansa*, like the Cattans. The Moreno women tended to marry other *grana* or educated *twansa* and were usually involved in philanthropy, mainly for Italian institutions (Italian Red Cross, etc.) and some Jewish associations (education, etc.).

Many studies have analyzed the multilayered relationship between *grana* and *twansa* both per se and through the prism of the colonial presence, through the relations one or the other group entertained with the local non-Jewish population or with the Jews of other countries in the (French) Maghreb.[21] Two studies are worth mentioning in more detail in this context: the work of Keith Walters—who summarizes the differences and connections between the two groups in a concise and clear table within the framework of a broader study on the spread of French in Tunisia through the education of Jewish girls between the end of the nineteenth century and the beginning of the twentieth,[22] and the analysis of Yaron Tsur. Describing the relations between the two communities in the provincial Tunisian town of Mahdia, Tsur captures the essence of the distinction between the two groups, as well as their connections. In his words:

> The Grana were distinguished not only by their Italian-Jewish ethnicity but also by their social status. . . . They were concentrated in the higher strata of society. . . . The Grana elite, which from the 17th century onwards specialized in trade, leasing and finance, succeeded in keeping contact with Livorno, and sometimes even in securing for themselves the legal status of European merchants (and hence subject to consular justice). . . . Furthermore, the Grana became the elite of the Italian colony in Tunisia and several of its members filled political positions in the service of the Italian kingdom. It appears that more than any other factor, what determined the connection with one group or the other was economic status. The crucial distinction had to do with access to Western economy. Being a "native" meant participation in economic activities of the local market only, while the quasi-European had access to both local and world market. The Grana were active in business by mainly with Europe.[23]

In 1905, the French archaeologist Eusèbe Vessel gave a contemporary description of this very situation, in which he emphasized both the sense of community and the presence of the *grana* elite in the public sphere:

> If it is true that the Israelites in Tunisia form a State within a State, then one should add that i livornesi [those from Livorno] have established a State within the Jewish State [Jewish community].[24]

Such presence and influence in the public sphere came to the fore in 1881, when Italy lost Tunisia to France, thus precipitating both the *grana* elite and the other upper-class Italians into a defensive corner. Despite themselves, their identity, and all their work for Tunisia as a *colonia italiana*—the same name by which they defined themselves—overnight they became the economic ruling class of another nation.

La Colonia Italiana and the New Colonial Context

In 1831, a political refugee from Livorno, Pompeo Sulema, and his sister Ester, opened the first Italian school in Tunis. At the end of the nineteenth century, there were twenty-one Italian state schools in Tunisia; thirteen were in Tunis, three in La Goulette, three in Sousse, and two in Sfax. Five of them were nursery schools, eleven were primary schools, and five were secondary schools.[25] At the end of the nineteenth century, a whole other colonial network of Italian factories, economic ventures, trading companies (such as the Morenos'), banks (Credito Italiano), hospitals (Ospedale Italiano), railways (Rubattino), theater companies, etc., was ready to turn Tunisia into an Italian colony; moreover, as mentioned above, the Italian population vastly outnumbered the French.[26] However, after 1881, the French colonial administration provided the new institutional framework in which the *granas* (and everyone else) had to operate.

Following the establishment of the French Protectorate, the Italian press of Tunis launched an intense campaign to defend Italian economic interests. The publication that led the campaign was *L'Unione*, an expression of the liberal middle classes and in particular of the *grana* elite. *L'Unione* was the publication of the Italian Chamber of Commerce of Tunis, and Raffaello Moreno was its president.[27] Many issues, articles, and clippings from this (first weekly and then daily) newspaper have been preserved among the Moreno family papers. Three types of articles in particular are circled and underlined: those that speak about protection of the commercial interests of the Italians in Tunisia against French protectionist policies; those that remark on the role of one or the other Moreno in representing their interests with the Italian authorities at Rome; and some official speeches concerning the situation of the Italian community (*la colonia italiana*) in Tunisia after 1881. Raffaello Moreno was described in *L'Unione* in 1900 as someone "guided in his every action by peace of mind and a firm conscience, with high aims":

> The Colony does not ignore the diligence, the lack of self-interest with which he defends its prosperity and rights. He is always the first to act in ways aimed at maintaining our name intact and respecting it. Many of the existing Italian institutions . . . owe him their existence . . . and without boasting of it, he perseveres in his mission, i.e. to be a most faithful and intelligent servant of our Consular authorities.[28]

Raffaello Moreno preserved not only the articles from Tunis that spoke (usually very highly) of himself but also those from Italy that described the situation of the Italians in Tunis. Indeed, *L'Unione* is not the only paper preserved in the Moreno archive. As a testimony to continuous contact and exchange with Italy, one also finds *La Gazzetta Livornese*, *Il Fanfulla* (published in Florence and then in Rome), and *Il Mezzogiorno* (from Southern Italy), publications that were delivered to his address in Tunis. In 1895, for example, *Il Mezzogiorno* presented Cavaliere Moreno as the "representative of the Italian Colony of Tunis." And it was during one of his visits to the Italian foreign ministry in Rome that the ministry had applauded the patriotism of the Italian colony of Tunis, surely with a view to Raffaello's own activities.[29] A few years later, in 1901, he clipped an article from the *Gazzetta Livornese* concerning the sale of the Tunis-Goletta railway, which had originally belonged to the Italian Rubattino Society; the article expressed the great sadness with which the Italian population of forty thousand received the news:

> The Italians of Tunis were once more made aware of the apathy and negligence of the Italian government in defending our interests abroad, so much so that, through their continuous neglect, they will make our life unbearable indeed in all those countries where Italian emigration is more abundant. After selling the Post, after the shameful political surveillance imposed on our subjects (including those holding important posts in the regency and who are quite rightly esteemed by everyone), in manifestly clear violation of the latest treaties, after the subsequent loss of all our rights here, this final palm of Italian land has now also been handed over to France. . . . We are told that in a country where our influence has become nothing, it is useless to maintain a railroad that costs the state 150 thousand lire per year and they believe that they can shut our mouths with this lie and with this silly argument![30]

The Morenos were always at the forefront of patriotic celebrations like the *Festa dello Statuto* to commemorate the Statuto Albertino (1848) or the anniversary of 20 September (1871)—the capture of Rome that marked the political unification of the kingdom. The speeches of Raffaello Moreno, for example, for the usually very well-attended *Festa dello Statuto*, were reported as an example of balance and vision. As the studies of Ilaria Porciani have demonstrated in a different context, the latter (more than the former) was the Italian celebration par excellence.[31] Considering both Livorno and Tunis, the *Festa dello Statuto* was celebrated in the squares, at the consulate, in sports and music circles, and, interestingly enough, also in the synagogues.[32] This is clearly very significant in terms of identity; on the days of Italian national celebration, the *grana* micro-identity allowed for the Italian macro-identity to fully emerge both at "home" and "in the new home." The capture of Rome was described by *L'Unione* in enthusiastic terms:

> Today marks a memorable date for the Italians, solemnized in Italian with great affection and harmony. For the entry of the Italian troops into Rome marked the end of a theocratic rule that had weighed on past generations like a nightmare, clipping . . . the positive impulse of human thought.[33]

Describing 20 September as it was celebrated in Tunis in more detail, *L'Unione* gave a complete picture not only of how the celebrations were organized but also of who attended them, summarizing how the Italian society of Tunis was structured as well as the very compatible and mixed roles of Jews and non-Jews within its ranks. Given the completeness of this portrait, it is interesting to read it directly from *L'Unione* (almost) in full:

> Again this year the highest sentiment of patriotism inspired the Italians of Tunis on the occasion of the recurrence of the wonderful event of the centuries, i.e. Rome's return to civil power as the capital of a free and united Italy. The Colonia Italiana also responded today with its usual alacrity to the appeal by the Representative of the Patriotic Government, and this morning the House of Italy was celebrating, its descendants in Tunis crowded together from the rich to the poor in an affectionate communality. As is customary, the first to be received are the teachers in our schools, on behalf of whom the notable Cav. Liscia, the high school principal, speaks in the most elevated tones. Today's solemnity, which is an unshakeable consecration of completed actions and a guarantee of immutable rights, finds faith and sincerity in the national institutions, and the Italian Homeland can certainly count on them. With no less fervor, the Consul General adds his voice to these sentiments, defining the elementary schools as the guardians of successful [national] unity and of free thinking. Immediately after comes the Italian freemasonry, led by the distinguished Dr. Funaro. For his part, he clarifies the aims of the association and declares that the freemasons . . . will faithfully cooperate with the authorities, ready to make sacrifices for the triumph of honorable and upright causes. . . . Later on, the notable Cav. Mr. Vignale speaks for the Workers' Society, and then his beloved president, the notable Cav. R. Moreno, President of the Chamber of Commerce, also speaks. . . . For the hospital, its director, Dr. Morpurgo speaks, succeeded by Dr. Cardoso for the Military Society of Discharged Soldiers, of which he is president. . . . The Dante Alighieri society is represented by the Notable Cav. Ravvisano. . . . Our most esteemed Consul General Comm. Botteghini . . . made our hearts vibrate with the notes of a very lively love of Italy, to which our hearts always tend, and regard for which this distinguished officer embodies so nobly, keeping it revered and beloved and respected by us, her children and by foreign colonies and their natives alongside us, among whom our labor of civilization and work is peaceful and profitable.[34]

As other articles from *L'Unione*—and much personal correspondence—show, the connection between Italy and the Colonia Italiana was one that fits the home-diaspora paradigm well. Without entering into a debate on the possible definitions and variations of this paradigm, the classic brief description by Gabriel Sheffer is perhaps the one that best suits this case.

Sheffer defines an "ethno-national diaspora" as a "social-political formation" that resulted from "either voluntary or forced migration, whose members regard themselves as of the same ethno-national origin and who permanently reside as minorities in one or several host countries." In his definition, diasporas "maintain a common identity, identify as such, showing solidarity with their group and their entire nation, and they organize and are active in the cultural, social, economic, and political spheres. Among their various activities, members of such diasporas establish trans-state networks that reflect complex relationships among the diasporas, their host countries, their homelands, and international actors."[35]

Once again *L'Unione* fits such a perspective:

> We always consider an occasion auspicious that allows us to gather around the Representative of Italy, to hear his authoritative voice speak of our beloved homeland and of memories of the past, of new hopes, to feel ourselves bonded and strengthened in our aspirations, in our confidence in the best and most glorious destinies for our Italy. And to realize this dream of glory, which is at the same time a desire for human progress, because the progress and civilization of the world are reasons for Italy's greatness. And Italians abroad are proud they can make their modern and by no means negligible contributions. In the peaceful struggle any nation might fight today to increase its influence beyond its borders, the first factors that lead to success are the colonies. . . . With industriousness, with seriousness in undertaking the task they have been assigned, they contribute to maintaining the high prestige and name of the distant homeland.[36]

If we look at these quotes through the lens of the home-diaspora relations, it is very evident to which homeland the *grana* in Tunis felt they belonged, even though some philanthropic concessions to Zionism eventually appeared in the twentieth century. As the documentation in the Central Zionist Archives in Jerusalem shows, Leone Moreno in 1923 accommodated the request of the Jewish National Fund (JNF) for help acquiring land for the new colony (*moshav*) of Nahalal "to add to the inalienable land patrimony of Eretz Israel" with a contribution of 10,000 French francs.[37] Interestingly enough, this donation was contemporaneous with a much larger contribution to the Italian colonial enterprise in Libya. The extent of the support to the national colonial project can also be gathered from the correspondence exchanged by various members of this family, if not from the text of their letters, for example, from the choice of postcards that they sent one another. One of them depicts the image of Italy as a proud woman standing tall on a pedestal, extending her benevolent hand to another woman of darker complexion representing Libya; the former is crowned with a tower and laurel; the other wears a turban and crescent; two men (King Vittorio Emanuele III and Sultan Mohammed V, wearing a fez, the symbol of the new Turkish modernity) look down on the two women, almost shaking hands, while the caption of the postcard reads: "Peace between Italy and Turkey for civilization and for the progress of Libya."[38] If we read these words through the prism of colonialism, we find most of the buzzwords that evoke a colonialist worldview: the "glorious destinies," "the human progress," "the civilization of the world," "the peaceful struggle to increase influence beyond borders," "the prestige of the distant land."

As in other colonial contexts, schools and hospitals represented a means for the elite to educate and cure themselves and their children with Western standards. At the same time, it is well known to what extent health and education represented major tools for importing and imposing cultural normative notions of what was healthy/unhealthy and educated/uneducated, along with a normative Western modernity.[39] In the context of the post-1881 anti-French polemic, Italian schools and hospitals were absorbed in the same rhetoric. The speech by Senator Di San Giuliano delivered at the Chamber of Deputies on 29 June 1896, which Raffaello saved in his personal papers, reflects this kind of thought. Here, emphasis was placed more on the schools than on the hospitals, in keeping with an Italian sentiment:

> France aims . . . to hit our associations and schools. And this is what we must prevent. For our associations and schools are the institutions that keep the Italian spirit alive in Tunisia. The patriotic spirit of the majority of our colony would be weakened without them, and those who have retained Italian citizenship would be less numerous today.[40]

The single largest donor and supporter of the Italian school of Tunis was Raffaello Moreno. All the Moreno boys studied there and later became involved not only in the selection of teachers but also in drafting the school syllabi. Raffaello's brother Leone, as well as their sons Ugo and Giacomo, were members of the Dante Alighieri society. Leone, who appears to have been more nationalist than his brother, only employed seasonal Italian workers[41] in the mill that the family established in Zaghouan. If we look at other Italian societies, we find more than a few Jews directing them; as we saw in the 20 September *L'Unione* article quoted above, the president of the Italian hospital was Dr. Morpurgo, and the president of the "Società Militari in congedo" (Society of Discharged Soldiers) was Dr. Cardoso.[42] These very same national themes also recur in the private correspondence between members of the family. It is not by chance that many of them were decorated with various Italian and Tunisian titles: Giuseppe Di Vittorio (a Sicilian entrepreneur), Luigi Rey (born in Tunis to an immigrant from a village north of Turin, Piedmont, Italy, who ran a construction company), and the Jewish medical doctor Giacomo Castelnuovo were awarded both the title of *Cavaliere dell'Ordine della Corona d'Italia* by the Italian king and the title of *Nichan Iftikhar* by the Bey of Tunis, as were Raffaello and Leone Moreno.[43]

Conclusion

The angle through which I have sketched a partial profile of the Morenos in Tunis is the public and political sphere in which they moved at the end of the nineteenth century, a time of great political and economic change for Tunisia and its inhabitants, the locals as well as the foreigners who resided there for various (mainly economic) reasons. This public aspect is the one that emerges more immediately from the family papers deposited in the State Archive of Livorno. An intimate and more private portrait of the family seems more difficult to sketch, for the late nineteenth century at least. Considering this period, it is quite evident that the dynamics of situational ethnicity and situational nationalism played an important role in orienting their individual and family identity, a factor that was further enhanced by their not being at "home" but in "diaspora." It could easily be argued that it was exactly this (dis)placement that made them more nationalist, monarchic, and attached to Italy, that made them oftentimes stress their attachment to the royal family and to an image of Livorno that corresponded to its idealized and frozen memory.

Further research could offer a different—and certainly more complete—picture of the history of this family, for example by taking a different temporal framework, another geographical focus, or other methodological perspectives. I will only mention here a few examples of the possibilities that other frameworks could lead to. After 1936, the family was no longer based in Tunisia alone, triangulating instead, as the family correspondence shows us, for travel, real estate, trade, and family relations between Italy, France, and Tunisia. Moving away from the binary home-diaspora framework to a larger Mediterranean framework would allow for broader focus on the private and public family dynamics and thus reveal a much larger network of relations that this family was able to develop, well beyond Livorno and Tunis.

Changing the time frame of this study could also lead to new conclusions, revealing how ethnicity played out differently in other situations. Just looking at the period of World War II—when several members of the Moreno family found a safe haven in South America, in Brazil, Uruguay, and Argentina—could show how their identity as Italians and Jews came to be confronted with other kinds of diasporas, such as the Italian diaspora that had migrated to South America since the nineteenth century and the more recent Jewish diaspora that was fleeing Nazi-Fascist Europe.[44]

Adopting a different methodological perspective would also help build a more complex and nuanced picture: for example, if we consider the role of women, both in the family, in the relationship between *grana* and *twansa*, and in the broader society in Tunis at the end of the nineteenth century, or later on in other moments. Connected to this last point is the perspective on interethnic or national philanthropy. As the studies of Luisa Levi D'Ancona, Mirella Scardozzi, and others have shown, philanthropic donations in the nineteenth century from upper-class Jewish families on the one hand became a form of Jewish affiliation; on the other, they helped in the development of what we would call welfare associations today—organizations and foundations that were open to all and not limited to a needy Jewish public.[45] Equally interesting would be an investigation into the ways in which the *granas* as an upper-class economic elite helped shape some of the architecture and spaces of the Tunisian cities in which they operated, considering not only the real estate properties but also their commercial activities and the sites where they exercised their philanthropy.[46] This section would also include an investigation of the long and complicated history that led to the construction of the synagogue of Tunis, from the acquisition of the land to the realization of a building that recalled the same Moorish style that was being used for synagogue construction in Europe and in the French Maghreb during the same period.[47] Finally, a comparative perspective could also be useful for a better understanding of the relations between *grana* and *twansa*, especially if we consider that similar class imbalances between local and newly arrived Jews in colonial contexts were quite common, for example in French Algeria, British India, or, later, in Italian Libya.

The context in which the Moreno story developed is generally well known, and much research into French, Arabic, and Italian private and public sources has painted a picture in which all the characters of this history are well represented—*grana* and *twansa* Jewish families, the local population, French authorities, Italian immigrants, traders, bankers, and religious authorities—as well as their whereabouts and the points where they crossed paths. The Moreno story represents another important piece in this multifaceted picture. One aspect that could not find a place in this chapter but is well known and, I think, worth underlining yet again is the low-level religious tension between groups, despite the national enthusiasms that the unfulfilled colonial context (with the expected Italian colonizers being replaced by the French) nurtured. I refer in particular to the coexistence of different religious groups—Catholics, Muslims, and Jews—which was reflected in the pages of *L'Unione* in various ways. One such example is a small section on its very last page providing the date according to the Hijiri and Hebrew calendars, the saints of the day, and notable events that happened on the same day in a different year. Despite this being only an insignificant box on the last page of a newspaper, it is revealing of a tradition and practice of tolerance that remains one of Tunisia's traits of historical continuity.

Marcella Simoni lectures at Ca' Foscari University of Venice and at NYU in Florence. She obtained her PhD from the University of London (UCL, 2004) and has held various postdocs in Los Angeles, Oxford, Paris, and Jerusalem. She has published on health and welfare in Mandatory Palestine (Cafoscarina, 2010), on the relations between Italy and Israel (ECG, 2010), and on civil society and grassroots mobilization in the Israeli-Palestinian conflict. Her research focuses on the dynamics of violence and nonviolence in the Israeli-Palestinian conflict on the one hand and on the history of Jews in South, East, and Southeast Asia on the other.

Notes

1. For a standard reference on situational ethnicity, see Jonathan Y. Okamura, "Situational Ethnicity," *Ethnic and Racial Studies* 4 (1981): 452–65; for a partially comparable study, see Till Van Rahden, "Intermarriages, the "New Woman" and the Situational Ethnicity of Breslau Jews from the 1870s to the 1920s," *Leo Baeck Institute Yearbook* 46 (2001): 125–50.
2. Tunisia had become part of the Ottoman Empire in 1574; the Commercial Treaty with Tuscany was signed in 1710, and Tuscany opened a consulate in Tunis in 1815.
3. Liana E. Funaro, "A Mediterranean Diaspora: Jews from Leghorn in the Second Half of the Nineteenth Century," in *L'Europe Méditerranéenne/Mediterranean Europe*, ed. Marta Petricioli (Brussels: Peter Lang, 2008), 95–110.
4. Daniela Pennacchio, "Ebrei fra Livorno e altri porti del Mediterraneo secondo i registri delle emigrazioni dell'Archivio Storico della Comunità Israelitica," in *Studi Mediterranei ed extraeuropei*, ed. Vittorio A. Salvadorini (Pisa: Epistudio, 2002): 221–45.
5. This number should be considered a minimum estimate, as the alphabetical lists from A to H for the decade 1843–53 are missing in the Archives of the Jewish Community of Livorno; in ibid., 222.
6. On Jews in Egypt, see Dario Miccoli, *Histories of the Jews of Egypt: An Imagined Bourgeoisie, 1880s–1950s* (London: Routledge, 2015).
7. See Michele Luzzati, ed., *Ebrei di Livorno tra i due censimenti (1841–1938): Memoria familiare e identità* (Livorno: Belforte, 1990).
8. Lucien Moatti, *La mosaïque médicale de Tunisie 1800–1950* (Paris: Éditions Glyphe, 2008).
9. Quoted in Maurizio Vernassa, *All'ombra del Bardo: Presenze toscane nella Tunisia di Ahmed Beÿ (1837–1855)* (Pisa: Edizioni Plus, 2005), 175.
10. William I. Shorrock, "The Tunisian Factor in Franco-Italian Relations 1881–1940," *Proceedings of the Meeting of the French Colonial Historical Society* 8 (1985): 167–77, 170.
11. Paul Sebag, *Tunis: Histoire d'une ville* (Paris: Harmattan, 1998).
12. See also Alessandro Triulzi, "Italian Speaking Communities in Early Nineteenth Century Tunis," *Revue de L'Occident e de la Méditerranée* 9 (1971): 153–84.
13. Treccani, "Castelnuovo Giacomo," retrieved 4 October 2017 from http://www.treccani.it/enciclopedia/giacomo-castelnuovo (Dizionario-Biografico)/. Castelnuovo, born in Livorno in 1819, had fled from Italy in 1841, initially to Egypt,

where he founded two Italian newspapers—*Lo Spettatore Egiziano* and *Il Progresso d'Egitto*—and then to Tunis. Here, he became the Bey's personal physician. He later returned to Italy to fight in Italy's wars for unification. He became the king's personal physician and then senator of the newly established Kingdom of Italy in 1871, and again in 1874. He died in La Goulette in 1886.

14. Daniela Melfa, *Migrando a sud: Coloni italiani in Tunisia (1881–1939)* (Rome: Aracne, 2008). See, for example, the pages on Tuscan wet nurses working in French and Italian families in Tunis and in other North African countries by Lucilla Briganti, "L'emigrazione 'stagionale' dalla Toscana alla Tunisia fra Ottocento e Novecento," in *Tunisia e Toscana*, ed. Vittorio A. Salvadorini (Pisa: Edistudio, 2002), 151–70, esp. 169–70.

15. Leone Carpi, *Delle colonie e delle migrazioni di Italiani all'estero sotto l'aspetto dell'industria, del commercio, agricoltura, e con trattazione d'importanti questioni sociali* (Milan: Editrice Lombarda, 1874). See also Alessio Loreti, "La diffusion de la culture Italienne en Tunisie: Imprimerie et édition entre 1829 et 1956," *Rivista trimestrale di studi e documentazione dell'Istituto italiano per l'Africa e l'Oriente* 62 (2007): 443–55.

16. Massimo Sanacore, *L'Archivio della Famiglia Moreno (1819–2006), Introduzione*, retrieved 4 October 2017 from http://www.archiviodistatolivorno.beniculturali.it/index.php?it/175/archivio-moreno, p. 3. See also Massimo Sanacore, "Storia della famiglia Moisè Moreno," and Giuliana Moreno, "Descrizione dell'archivio (1819–2006)," both in *Nuovi Studi Livornesi* 18 (2011): 347–53 and 338–41.

17. Liana E. Funaro, "Percorsi attraverso l'Archivio Moreno," *Nuovi Studi Livornesi* 18 (2011): 333–38.

18. Charles Monchicourt, *Les Italiens de Tunisie et l'accord Laval-Mussolini de 1935* (Paris: Recueil Sirey, 1938); Shorrock, "Tunisian Factor," 171.

19. Archivio di Stato di Livorno (henceforth ASLi), Moreno Family Collection (henceforth Moreno), b. 5, *Danni di Guerra e Requisizione Magazzini Legname 28 Rue de Besançon*, 31 May 1943; see also b. 13 for the documents related to the confiscation of the Moreno real estate, goods, bank accounts, and stocks as citizens of an enemy country in 1943, and for the use of the Moreno property by the British and French armies in 1944 and 1945.

20. ASLi, Moreno, b. 5. On 31 July 1899, Leone Moreno withdrew from the company, and Raffaello changed its name to "Maison Raffaello Moreno et C.ie"; a few years later, in 1913, Raffaello added his son and his brother-in-law (Daniele Cardoso), and the company's new name became "Moreno fils et C.ie."

21. Lucette Valensi and Abraham L. Udovitch, *Juifs en terre d'islam: Les communautés de Djerba* (Paris: Archives contemporaines, 1991); Jacques Taïeb, *Être juif au Maghreb à la veille de la colonisation* (Paris: Albin Michel, 1994); Jacques Taïeb "Les juifs livournais de 1600 à 1881," in *Histoire communautaire: Histoire plurielle, la communauté juive de Tunisie: Actes du colloque de Tunis organisé les 25-26-27 Février 1998 à la Faculté de la Manouba*, ed. Abdelkrim Allagui and Habib Kazdaghli (Tunis: Centre de publication universitaire, 1999), 153–64; Paul Sebag, *Histoire des Juifs de Tunisie: Des origines à nos jours* (Paris: L'Harmattan, 2000); Jacques Taïeb, *Sociétés juives du Maghreb moderne (1500–1900)* (Paris: Maisonneuve et Larose, 2000); Elia Boccara, "La comunità ebraica portoghese di Tunisi (1719–1944)," *La Rassegna Mensile di Israel* 66 (2000): 25–98; Denis Cohen-Tannoudji, *Entre Orient et Occident: Juifs et musulmans en Tunisie* (Paris: Éditions de l'Éclat, 2007); Albert-Armand Maarek, *Les Juifs de Tunisie entre 1857*

et 1958: histoire d'une émancipation (Paris: Glyphe, 2010); for a broader comparative perspective in geographical and chronological terms, see *Jewish Culture and Society in North Africa*, ed. Emily Benichou Gottreich and Daniel J. Schroeter (Bloomington: Indiana University Press, 2011).

22. Keith Walters, "Education for Jewish Girls in Late Nineteenth and Early Twentieth Century Tunis and the Spread of French in Tunisia," in Gottreich and Schroeter, *Jewish Culture and Society*, 257–281, esp. 260–61
23. Yaron Tsur, "Haskala in a Sectional Colonial Society: Mahdia (Tunisia) 1884," in *Sephardi and Middle Eastern Jewries: History and Culture in the Modern Era*, ed. Harvey E. Goldberg, (Bloomington: Indiana University Press, 1996), 151–53.
24. Pennacchio, "Ebrei fra Livorno," 232.
25. Giulia Barrera, "Third-Grade Pupils of the Italian State-Funded Giovanni Meli Primary School in Tunis," in "Sharing History: Arab World-Europe, 1815–1918," Museum with No Frontiers, 2017, retrieved 5 October 2017 from http://www.sharinghistory.org/database_item.php?id=object;AWE;it;117;enSource.
26. Shorrock, "Tunisian Factor," 170.
27. Comitato della Camera Italiana di Commercio ed Arti, *Gli Italiani in Tunisia* (Tunis: Imprimerie typo lithographique de l'Association Ouvrière, Frédéric Weber, 1906).
28. ASLi, Moreno, f. 19, f. 2, *L'Unione—Giornale Politico Quotidiano—Ufficiale per gli atti della Camera di Commercio Italiana, ed autorizzato*, 10 June 1900.
29. ASLi, Moreno, f. 19, f. 1, "Note Tunisine," *Fanfulla*, 30 March 1899.
30. ASLi, Moreno, f. 19, f. 1, "Cose Tunisine," *Gazzetta Livornese*, 24–25 July 1898.
31. Ilaria Porciani, *La festa della nazione: Rappresentazione dello Stato e spazi sociali nell'Italia unita* (Bologna: Il Mulino, 1997).
32. Funaro, "Percorsi," 95, 98–99.
33. ASLi, Moreno, f. 19, f. 2, "XX Settembre," *L'Unione*, 20 September 1901.
34. ASLi, Moreno, f. 19, f. 2, Bottesini, "Il XX Settembre a Tunisi," *L'Unione*, 20 September 1901.
35. Gabriel Sheffer, *Diaspora Politics at Home and Abroad* (Cambridge: Cambridge University Press, 2003). For a more critical outlook on this term and its usage, see Rogers Brubaker, "The 'Diaspora' Diaspora," *Ethnic and Racial Studies* 28 (2005): 1–19.
36. ASLi, Moreno, f. 19, f. 2, C.F., "Il valore e la mobilità," *L'Unione*, 4 June 1900.
37. Central Zionist Archives, Jerusalem, *Moreno* AK 807. In the same correspondence, Leone Moreno explains the difficulty about fundraising for the JNF in the French Maghreb (19 and 20 December 1923).
38. ASLi, Moreno, f. 19, f. 5.
39. Among the many available texts on this question, see the classic Bryan S. Turner, *Medical Power and Social Knowledge* (London: Sage Publications, 1987) and the more recent Poonam Bala, ed., *Medicine and Colonialism: Historical Perspectives in India and South Africa* (London: Pickering and Chatto, 2014).
40. ASLi, Moreno, f. 19, f. 15, *Discorso del Deputato di San Giuliano pronunciato alla Camera dei Deputati nella seduta del 29 giugno 1896* (Rome: Tipografia della Camera dei Deputati, 1896), 18.
41. On Italian seasonal workers from Tuscany to Tunisia, see Briganti, "L'emigrazione 'stagionale.'"
42. ASLi, Moreno, f. 19, f. 2, Bottesini, *Il XX Settembre a Tunisi*, "L'Unione," 20 September 1901.

43. Massimo Sanacore, "A Tunisian Decoration (on the Right) and an Italian Decoration (on the Left) Awarded to a Member of the Moreno Family," in Museum with no Frontiers, "Sharing History: Arab World-Europe, 1815–1918," retrieved 9 October 2017 from http://www.sharinghistory.org/database_item.php?id=object;AWE;it;111;en.
44. The bibliography on this subject is extremely vast; for a few examples, see Fábio Bertonha, *Sob a sombra de Mussolini: Os italianos de São Paulo e a luta contra o fascismo, 1919–1945* (São Paulo: Annablume, 1999); Eleonora Maria Smolensky and Vera Vigevani Jarach, *Tante voci, una storia: Italiani ebrei in Argentina, 1938–1948* (Bologna: Il Mulino, 1998); Clara Aldrighi, *Antifascismo italiano en Montevideo: El dialogo entre Luigi Fabbri y Carlo Rosselli* (Montevideo: Departamento de Publicaciones de la Faculdad de Humanidades y Ciencias de la Educación, 1996); Clara Aldrighi, "Los Judìos Italianos in Uruguay," *Brecha*, 12 December, 2008, 20–21.
45. Mirella Scardozzi, "Una storia di famiglia: I Franchetti delle coste del Mediterraneo nell'Italia liberale," and Luisa Levi D'Ancora, "'Notabili e Dame' nella filantropia ebraica ottocentesca: Casi di studio in Francia, Italia e Inghilterra," in "Ebrei Borghesi: Identità famigliare e affari nell'età dell'emancipazione," ed. Barbara Armani and Guri Schwarz, special issue, *Quaderni Storici* 3 (2003): 697–740 and 741–76.
46. For a fascinating study of the role of the "Colonia Italiana" in shaping the architectural space of French Tunisia and of some of the personal residences of many *grana*, see, as a starting point, Ettore Sessa, "Italian Architects, Decorators and Contractors in French Tunisia: Continuity and Discontinuity in the Building Production of an Integrated Community," in *The Presence of Italian Architects in Mediterranean Countries: Proceedings of the First International Conference*, Bibliotheca Alexandrina, Chatby, Alexandria (Florence: Edizioni Maschietto, 2008), 103–15, retrieved 9 October 2017 from https://iris.unipa.it/retrieve/handle/10447/54938/42423/ANVUR percent20Atti_Alessandria percent20SESSA.pdf. See also Ahmed Sadaaoui, "Les synagogues de Tunisie: Recherches architecturales," in Allagui and Kazdaghli *Histoire communautaire: Histoire plurielle*, 181–201.
47. Massimo Sanacore, "Bond of 100 Francs Issued by the Caisse Générale de Secours et de Bienfaisance Israélite de Tunis, in Order to Raise Funds for the Construction of a New Synagogue in Tunis, and Bought by Leone Moreno," Museum with No Frontiers, "Sharing History: Arab World-Europe, 1815–1918," retrieved 9 October 2017 from http://www.sharinghistory.org/database_item.php?id=object;AWE;it;133;en;N. See also Un Tunisino, "Da Souk El Arba presso Tunisi," *Il Vessillo Israelitico* 45 (1897): 193–94, and Ivan Davidson Kalmar, "Moorish Style: Orientalism, the Jews, and Synagogue Architecture," *Jewish Social Studies* 7 (2001): 68–100.

Bibliography

Aldrighi, Clara. *Antifascismo italiano en Montevideo: El dialogo entre Luigi Fabbri y Carlo Rosselli*. Montevideo: Departamento de Publicaciones de la Faculdad de Humanidades y Ciencias de la Educación, 1996.

———. "Los Judìos Italianos in Uruguay." *Brecha*, 12 December 2008, 20–21.

Archivio di Stato di Livorno. "Massimo Sanacore, L'Archivio della Famiglia Moreno (1819–2006), Introduzione." Retrieved 4 October 2017 from http://www.archiviodistatolivorno.beniculturali.it/index.php?it/175/archivio-moreno.

Armani, Barbara, and Guri Schwarz, eds. "Ebrei Borghesi: Identità famigliare e affari nell'età dell'emancipazione." Special issue, *Quaderni Storici* 3 (2003).

Bala, Poonam, ed. *Medicine and Colonialism: Historical Perspectives in India and South Africa*. London: Pickering and Chatto, 2014.

Barrera, Giulia. "Third-Grade Pupils of the Italian State-Funded Giovanni Meli Primary School in Tunis." Museum with No Frontiers. "Sharing History: Arab World-Europe, 1815–1918." Retrieved 5 October 2017 http://www.sharinghistory.org/database_item.php?id=object;AWE;it;117;enSource.

Benichou Gottreich, Emily, and Daniel J. Schroeter, eds. *Jewish Culture and Society in North Africa*. Bloomington: Indiana University Press, 2011.

Bertonha, Fábio. *Sob a sombra de Mussolini: Os italianos de São Paulo e a luta contra o fascismo, 1919–1945* São Paulo: Annablume, 1999.

Boccara, Elia. "La comunità ebraica portoghese di Tunisi (1719–1944)." *La Rassegna Mensile di Israel* 66 (2000): 25–98.

Briganti, Lucilla. "L'emigrazione 'stagionale' dalla Toscana alla Tunisia fra Ottocento e Novecento." In *Tunisia e Toscana*, edited by Vittorio A. Salvadorini, 151–70. Pisa: Edistudio, 2002.

Brubaker, Rogers. "The 'Diaspora' Diaspora." *Ethnic and Racial Studies* 28 (2005): 1–19.

Carpi, Leone. *Delle colonie e delle migrazioni di Italiani all'estero sotto l'aspetto dell'industria, del commercio, agricoltura, e con trattazione d'importanti questioni sociali*. Milan: Editrice Lombarda, 1874.

Cohen-Tannoudji, Denis. *Entre Orient et Occident: Juifs et musulmans en Tunisie*. Paris: Éditions de l'Éclat, 2007.

Comitato della Camera Italiana di Commercio ed Arti. *Gli Italiani in Tunisia*. Tunis: Imprimerie typo lithographique de l'Association Ouvrière, Frédéric Weber, 1906.

Funaro, Liana E. "A Mediterranean Diaspora: Jews from Leghorn in the Second Half of the Nineteenth Century." In *L'Europe Méditerranéenne/Mediterranean Europe*, edited by Marta Petricioli, 95–110. Brussels: Peter Lang, 2008.

———. "Percorsi attraverso l'Archivio Moreno." *Nuovi Studi Livornesi* 18 (2011): 333–38.

Kalmar, Ivan Davidson. "Moorish Style: Orientalism, the Jews, and Synagogue Architecture" *Jewish Social Studies* 7 (2001): 68–100.

Levi D'Ancona, Luisa. "'Notabili e Dame' nella filantropia ebraica ottocentesca: casi di studio in Francia, Italia e Inghilterra. In "Ebrei Borghesi: Identità famigliare e affari nell'età dell'emancipazione," edited by Barbara Armani and Guri Schwarz. Special issue, *Quaderni Storici* 3 (2003): 741–76.

Loreti, Alessio. "La diffusion de la culture Italienne en Tunisie: Imprimerie et édition entre 1829 et 1956." *Rivista trimestrale di studi e documentazione dell'Istituto italiano per l'Africa e l'Oriente* 62 (2007): 443–55.

Luzzati, Michele, ed. *Ebrei di Livorno tra i due censimenti (1841–1938): Memoria familiare e identità*. Livorno: Belforte, 1990.
Maarek, Albert-Armand. *Les Juifs de Tunisie entre 1857 et 1958: Histoire d'une emancipation*. Paris: Glyphe, 2010.
Melfa, Daniela. *Migrando a sud: Coloni italiani in Tunisia (1881–1939)*. Rome: Aracne, 2008.
Miccoli, Dario. *Histories of the Jews of Egypt: An Imagined Bourgeoisie, 1880s–1950s*. London: Routledge, 2015.
Moatti, Lucien. *La mosaïque médicale de Tunisie 1800–1950*. Paris: Éditions Glyphe, 2008.
Monchicourt, Charles. *Les Italiens de Tunisie et l'accord Laval-Mussolini de 1935*. Paris: Recueil Sirey, 1938.
Moreno, Giuliana. "Descrizione dell'archivio (1819–2006)." *Nuovi Studi Livornesi* 18 (2011): 338–41.
Museum with No Frontiers. "Sharing History: Arab World-Europe, 1815–1918." Retrieved 5 October 2017 from http://www.sharinghistory.org/database_item.php?id=object;AWE;it;117;en&pageT=N&cp.
Okamura, Jonathan Y. "Situational Ethnicity." *Ethnic and Racial Studies* 4 (1981): 452–65.
Pendola, Marinette. *Gli italiani di Tunisia: Storia di una comunità (XIX–XX secolo)*. Foligno: Editoriale Umbra, 2007.
Pennacchio, Daniela. "Ebrei fra Livorno e altri porti del Mediterraneo secondo i registri delle emigrazioni dell'Archivio Storico della Comunità Israelitica." In *Studi Mediterranei ed extraeuropei*, edited by Vittorio A. Salvadorini, 221–46. Pisa: Epistudio, 2002.
Porciani, Ilaria. *La festa della nazione: Rappresentazione dello Stato e spazi sociali nell'Italia unita*. Bologna: Il Mulino, 1997.
Reiyman, Alyssa. "Claiming Livorno: Citizenship, Commerce, and Culture in the Italian Jewish Diaspora." In *Italian Jewish Networks from the Seventeenth to the Twentieth Century: Bridging Europe and the Mediterranean* edited by Francesca Bregoli et al., 81–100. London, New York: Palgrave MacMillan.
Sadaaoui, Ahmed. "Les synagogues de Tunisie: recherches architecturales." In *Histoire communautaire: Histoire plurielle, la communauté juive de Tunisie*, edited by Abdelkrim Allagui and Habib Kazdaghli, 181–201. Tunis: Centre de publication universitaire, 1999.
Sanacore, Massimo. "Storia della famiglia Moisè Moreno." *Nuovi Studi Livornesi* 18 (2011): 347–53.
———. "A Tunisian Decoration (on the Right) and an Italian Decoration (on the Left) Awarded to a Member of the Moreno Family." Museum with No Frontiers. "Sharing History: Arab World-Europe, 1815–1918." Retrieved 9 October 2017 from http://www.sharinghistory.org/database_item.php?id=object;AWE;it;111;en.
———. "Bond of 100 Francs Issued by the Caisse Générale de Secours et de Bienfaisance Israélite de Tunis, in Order to Raise Funds for the Construction of a New Synagogue in Tunis, and Bought by Leone Moreno." Museum with No Frontiers. "Sharing History: Arab World-Europe, 1815–1918." Retrieved 9 October 2017 from http://www.sharinghistory.org/database_item.php?id=object;AWE;it;133;en;N.
Scardozzi, Mirella. "Una storia di famiglia: I Franchetti delle coste del Mediterraneo nell'Italia liberale." In "Ebrei Borghesi: Identità famigliare e affari nell'età

dell'emancipazione," edited by Barbara Armani and Guri Schwarz. Special issue, *Quaderni Storici* 3 (2003): 697–740.

Sessa, Ettore. "Italian Architects, Decorators and Contractors in French Tunisia: Continuity and Discontinuity in the Building Production of an Integrated Community." In *The Presence of Italian Architects in Mediterranean Countries: Proceedings of the First International Conference*. Bibliotheca Alexandrina, Chatby, Alexandria, 103–15. Florence: Edizioni Maschietto, 2008. Retrieved 9 October, 2017 from https://iris.unipa.it/retrieve/handle/10447/54938/42423/ANVUR percent 20Atti_Alessandria percent20SESSA.pdf.

Sheffer, Gabriel. *Diaspora Politics at Home and Abroad*. Cambridge: Cambridge University Press, 2003.

Shorrock, William I. "The Tunisian Factor in Franco-Italian Relations 1881–1940." *Proceedings of the Meeting of the French Colonial Historical Society* 8 (1985): 167–77.

Smolensky, Eleonora Maria, and Vera Vigevani Jarach. *Tante voci, una storia: Italiani ebrei in Argentina, 1938–1948*. Bologna: Il Mulino, 1998.

Taïeb, Jacques. *Être juif au Maghreb à la veille de la colonisation*. Paris: Albin Michel, 1994.

———. "Les juifs livournais de 1600 à 1881." In *Histoire communautaire: Histoire plurielle, la communauté juive de Tunisie*: *Actes du colloque de Tunis organisé les 25-26-27 Février 1998 à la Faculté de la Manouba*, edited by Abdelkrim Allagui and Habib Kazdaghli, 153–64. Tunis: Centre de publication universitaire, 1999.

———. *Sociétés juives du Maghreb moderne (1500–1900)*. Paris: Maisonneuve et Larose, 2000.

Treccani. "Castelnuovo Giacomo." Retrieved 4 October 2017 from http://www.treccani.it/enciclopedia/giacomo-castelnuovo_(Dizionario-Biografico)/.

Triulzi, Alessandro. "Italian Speaking Communities in Early Nineteenth Century Tunis." *Revue de L'Occident e de la Méditerranée* 9 (1971): 153–84.

Tsur, Yaron. "Haskala in a Sectional Colonial Society: Mahdia (Tunisia) 1884." In *Sephardi and Middle Eastern Jewries: History and Culture in the Modern Era*, edited by Harvey E. Goldberg, 146–67. Bloomington: Indiana University Press, 1996.

Turner, Bryan S. *Medical Power and Social Knowledge*. London: Sage Publications, 1987.

Un Tunisino. "Da Souk El Arba presso Tunisi." *Il Vessillo Israelitico* 45 (1897): 193–94.

Valensi, Lucette, and Abraham L. Udovitch. *Juifs en terre d'islam: Les communautés de Djerba*. Paris: Archives contemporaines, 1991.

Van Rahden, Till. "Intermarriages, the "New Woman" and the Situational Ethnicity of Breslau Jews from the 1870s to the 1920s." *Leo Baeck Institute Yearbook* 46 (2001): 125–50.

Walters, Keith. "Education for Jewish Girls in Late Nineteenth and Early Twentieth Century Tunis and the Spread of French in Tunisia." In *Jewish Culture and Society in North Africa*, edited by Emily Benichou Gottreich and Daniel J. Schroeter, 257–81. Bloomington: Indiana University Press, 2011.

CHAPTER 4

Portrait of a "Political Lady"
Family Ties and National Activism around 1848 in the Italian and German States

Giulia Frontoni

In the nineteenth century, national movements articulated political visions linked to specific gender constructions. Women's and men's roles became politicized. Especially during the political and social upheavals that buffeted Europe in 1848–49, newly formulated ideals of womanhood emerged that were closely related to discourses of nationalism. This chapter focuses on the Italian and German national movements and highlights some of the differences and similarities in the construction of womanhood employed within the two national discourses. I discuss two specific images of womanhood in politics, namely that of the "mother of the nation" and that of the so-called "political lady." I argue that such ideals shaped women's political identities and how they participated in politics, whereas women's social backgrounds impacted their political behavior and social expectations. This chapter marks a first attempt at understanding the ideal of the "political lady" and analyzes how this ideal was part of the political diversification of the national movement which took place in the 1840s and 1850s.

In considering women's role in politics, it is essential to take their social and familial backgrounds into account, because people took part in the political and social changes in the mid-nineteenth century in different ways depending on their social and economic situations. Considering women's role during the political and social upheavals in this way requires thinking anew about contemporary discussions on women's role in society, in politics, and above all in the national movements, bearing in mind concepts like class and religion. A conceptualization that encompasses familial and social background can illustrate women's role in the promotion of national culture as well as in the differentiation of political debates. My aim is to show how upper-class women in the German and Italian states around 1848–49 were more than just observers of men's political activities. Rather, women were also expected to participate in the promotion of national values and to shape political discussions. As I will illustrate, women's political participation was grounded in ideals such as the mother of the nation and the political lady and was deeply interwoven with social backgrounds, national movements, and political debates.

Historians have done much to disclose how national discourses were gendered, both within and beyond Europe. Postcolonial scholars in particular have made important contributions to the understanding of gender in national discourses. As Nira Yuval-Davis and others have argued, within discourses of nationalism, women were associated with specific ideals of womanhood that were related to well-defined social functions: women were understood to be responsible for the biological and cultural reproduction of the national community, for imparting national ideals to children, and for supporting the men who were fighting for national freedom.[1] Yet, the social aspect of this ideal, which was significant for many national movements, has often been neglected in studies about women's participation in national movements, including studies about the German and Italian national movements that have focused on gender.[2] Historians have often written about women's participation as correspondents and salonnières or about women's associations in the national movements without paying much attention to the public that women wrote for. This is problematic, however, because social and biographical contexts mattered in significant ways for ideals of womanhood in politics. Activists often participated in national movements, for instance, in ways befitting their social status. While working and peasant women protested on the streets, bourgeois women used their writing skills to promote women's participation in national movements.[3] For this reason, it is important to ask what sort of public they wrote for. Not only female but also male writers wrote for upper-class readers with well-defined political and social expectations. Through ideals such as the mother of the nation and the political lady, national discourses framed women's participation and linked that participation to women's respective social backgrounds.

The Italian and German Cases: The Ideal of the Mother of the Nation

The ideal of the mother of the nation figured centrally in European national discourses throughout the nineteenth century. It became widespread in the aftermath of the French Revolution. Within the French national movement, pictures of mothers sacrificing themselves for the sake of their children during social upheavals or supporting fighting soldiers represented the cohesion of the French community against its enemies, as well as broader participation in contemporary political changes. These images promoted a new vision of gender roles: at the beginning of the nineteenth century, women were seen as mothers who should be able to preserve the stability of the national community and its progress. Nevertheless, to be a "mother" meant more than having children. Being a "mother" also implied that women should have a pedagogical commitment to the national community. This commitment entailed both childbearing for the nation and the promotion of national values.[4]

In this way, the ideal of the mother of the nation encouraged women's participation in the national movements during the nineteenth century. Together with other family-related metaphors, the ideal of the mother of the nation took root throughout Europe in the aftermath of the French Revolution.[5] In this period, many contemporaries, and women in particular, found it very appealing to use family-related images to promote social and political change and popular mobilization in Europe.[6] Nevertheless, the many layers of such familial images in contemporary political discussions in the German and Italian cases have received too little attention. Although the ideal of the mother of the nation circulated throughout the German and Italian states, it had regional traits—especially in the German states. In this following section, I describe the relevance of the ideal of the mother of the nation in the Italian and German national discourses and how women reacted to such an ideal in both national contexts, taking the local context into consideration.

As the formulation of a national discourse became appealing for broader groups in the Italian and German states, national cohesion was increasingly expressed through family-related metaphors that vividly and emotionally defined gender roles. Writers and intellectuals used the well-known ideal of the mother of the nation to frame women's social and political participation. Like other familial metaphors, the mother of the nation ideal had several discursive layers. A strong component was the religious one.

In the German national movement, the ideal of the mother of the nation implied a social commitment to Protestant or Catholic associations. During the nineteenth century, women's participation in religious associations was widespread in the German states. Stressing emotional aspects of religiosity, the Evangelical and the Catholic Churches strove for a religious revival among women, who were seen as active members of the religious community.[7] Through church associations, women appeared increasingly in public. As Sylvia Palatschek has shown, these women understood their activism as a way to improve the world they lived in and as a legitimated endeavor by their status as mothers and wives.[8] Such a strong pedagogical component also prevailed within the German national movement, because the ideal of the mother of the nation set a learning process in motion for women. Through involvement in church associations, women learned to be actively involved in public assemblies or to collect money. At the same time, upper-class women in the German states used their writing skills for the promotion of national values and social change. As Ann Taylor Allen has shown, German female writers like Malwida von Meysenburg defined womanhood in a new way to promote motherhood as a means to "self-fulfillment" and as a "basis for transformation of self and the world."[9]

In the Italian national movement, the Catholic element predominated, as historian Marina D'Amelia has shown.[10] Female writers such as Caterina Franceschi Ferrucci emphasized Catholic femininity. Women, Ferrucci argued, could support national struggles through their femininity. This meant they should do so through prayers, childbearing, and educating children in national and Catholic values. Ferrucci believed Catholicism made Italy a nation with a mission and a higher value system than other nations in Europe. For Ferrucci, as for many other liberal contemporaries from Tuscany, the struggles of the national and liberal movement were seen as legitimate because they were rooted in Catholicism, and because the Italian liberals aimed to establish a Catholic Italian nation. Above all, Ferrucci underscored in her books and articles the important role of women in education. In her view, being part of the Italian national community entailed a pedagogical commitment. This meant that even women of the upper class should devote energy to educating themselves, their children, and disadvantaged children. We thus find a pedagogical element in the Italian concept of the mother of the nation, a concept that Caterina Franceschi Ferrucci embedded in Catholicism.

Within the Italian and German national movements, women were expected to follow role models presented in articles and books. Such role models were often rooted in the past, in order to obtain public approval. For example, Ferrucci argued that women—trusting in God—should be willing to sacrifice themselves just as mothers did in ancient times. As she put it in 1855,

> We are born in peaceful times, live in the lap of luxury, follow the cult of pleasure, and regard the strength of Spartan and Roman mothers as unnatural. But they knew that, before being wives and mothers, they were citizens. And because all our affections are at one with the feeling that bound us to the nation, this latter must be loved more than our relatives and even our children.[11]

Mothers from ancient times, famous for their rigid education of children, should thus serve as role models for women in the Italian national movement.

This ideal of a strong Roman mother was quite typical for the Italian national movement. Indeed, it often served as a reference point, especially in the wars of 1848–49. This was evidenced in the many gazettes that were published by national activists around 1848 following the abolition of censorship. Even a newspaper for women (*La Donna Italiana*) was published in Rome, which featured articles about political activities for women within the national movement. Many periodicals directly addressed mothers. This is evident, for instance, in a 6 May 1848 article in *La Donna Italiana*, wherein mothers were encouraged to educate their children at the military school so that they could prepare themselves to fight against the enemies of the Italian national project.[12] Mothers were expected to follow the example of strong Roman women from the past. Through examples of mothers from ancient times, the Italian national discourse rooted the ideal of the mother of the nation in an imagined past. In this way, a tradition of women's willingness to sacrifice was built, while women's trust in God testified to the strength of their character. The ideal was often presented by women who became activists of the Italian national movement through their writing. They proposed such examples to generate greater support for national struggles among women and sought to guarantee the continuity of such support by educating children in national values.

German activists also looked to the past for local examples to promote broader participation in national struggles. For example, Prussian militants in the German national movement held up women from the Napoleonic war years as models. Women within the German national movement were empowered to write about the political activities and experiences of their female relatives—above all, their mothers—during the Napoleonic wars to learn from the past experiences. Women's support activities for the soldiers and their protests were often recalled to promote similar participation during the riots of 1848. In the northern German states, women pleaded for greater women's participation in support activities for soldiers during the war in Schleswig and Holstein. Women's activities during the Napoleonic wars figured prominently in such pleas. As two contemporaries in Hamburg wrote, "Ask those who remember what German women did during the patriotic wars. And let us admit that our mothers did more then than we have done up to now."[13] In this plea, the female authors promoted women's participation by recalling past experiences. They not only imagined a continuity between patriotic activities in the Napoleonic era and women's activism during 1848–49 but also called for a greater exchange between women and elderly people, so that women could learn strategies from the past and acquire political knowledge. This emphasis on intergenerational exchange promoted family cohesion during wartime, because women's political experiences during the Napoleonic wars were presented to the younger generation as patriotic examples worthy of emulation. By recalling the experiences of German upper- and middle-class women, the collective memory of women became part of the German national movement.

The Hamburg women who had written the plea came from the German upper class. This is significant, because historians have often talked about women's participation in the revolution of 1848–49 without paying much attention to their social background. Through their writing, these women saw themselves and other bourgeois women as members of the German national collectivity, with well-defined patriotic duties. Like other contemporaries, women in Hamburg addressed their pleas to upper-class women. Women, even the young ones, were expected to sacrifice themselves proportionally to their social background. Because of their bourgeois background, the plea writers suggested that women should sacrifice their demand for stylish clothes and instead donate to the soldiers or the poor families in the bombed territories in Holstein.

The ideal of the mother of the nation opened up new ways for women to participate in contemporary social changes, because it articulated politically the everyday experiences of women. Through examples from the past, mothers of the nation were represented as being committed to the struggles of their community. Childbearing, military education of children, and passing on national values through writing or in daily communication were seen in the German and Italian national discourses as a patriotic duty that women should perform to support the national project. Because of their familial duty and their own sex, women were expected to be responsible for national cohesion, and activists for the German and Italian national discourse expressed this through family metaphors such as the ideal of the mother of the nation.

The Ideal of the Political Lady: Political Diversification in the German and Italian National Movement

Next to the ideal of the mother of the nation, a new ideal of womanhood in politics emerged in the first half of the nineteenth century. In the beginning, the term "political lady" was used to criticize women's participation in political debates satirically. In fact, women's presence in political places like parliaments or clubs was viewed very critically.[14] In a historical and satirical book from 1840, the French conservative Horace De Viel-Castel referred to "political ladies" in a satirical way, and clearly defined this term in a chapter titled "La femme politique."[15] For De Viel-Castel, "la femme politique" was a well-born woman who read the newspapers, historical books, and the writings of her friends. She was also seen as a woman of age who held gatherings with political activists and politicians and was capable of networking and of influencing people. The description of the skills and the roots of the political lady are in fact evident in the salon culture of the eighteenth and early nineteenth centuries. For De Viel-Castel, political ladies took sides for one party or another; some women from the upper class invited, for example, republican writers for dinner to discuss political matters and give them advice about their writing, while other upper-class women debated with conservative politicians in their living rooms. In De Viel-Castel's view, moreover, women influenced political debate and contributed to the diversification of the political discussion through gatherings and remarks on the writings of friends.

Yet, De Viel-Castel used this ideal to argue against women's participation in national struggles. He wrote, for example, "I will not impose on all women the epitaph of the Roman matron *Domum mansit—lana fecit*; but I would rather read on the funeral stone of each, 'She died of too much dancing'!"[16] De Viel-Castel was thus critical of the growing participation of upper-class women in political discussions and suggested they should focus more on leisure than on political activities. His critique reveals a contemporary view of women in politics: the involvement of upper-class women in contemporary political disputes was seen as a way to intensify the diversification of political opinions rather than to narrow the gap between different political parties.

De Viel-Castel's writing spread abroad. His work was translated into English and was reviewed in newspapers in England and the United States.[17] Reviewers compared the French situation with their own local contexts. They looked for local examples of upper-class women involved in politics, held them up as political ladies, and argued against this notion, because they believed such women exaggerated when expressing their own political views. As the *London and Westminster Review* wrote, "Our political lady was walking backwards and forwards in a state of great agitation: 'my friend'—said she to a visitor with tears streaming from her eyes—'I am distracted: between my sick child and the affairs of the nation, I am almost mad.'"[18] The article connected two tasks contemporary upper-class women performed—the mothering of a child and the mothering of the nation—and suggested that women were overwhelmed by politics. It seems men used the ideal of the political lady to criticize satirically women's participation in political discussions. And of course, De Viel-Castel and his contemporaries brought this ideal into play to argue against women's participation in political activities and national struggles. In so doing, they nevertheless described a growing phenomenon that was also taking place in the 1840s in the German and Italian states.

Around 1848, German-speaking publications evidenced how upper-class women were becoming increasingly interested in politics. In her 1849 novel *Rom und Berlin*, the famous German author Therese von Bacheracht described the life of a middle-class wife in Berlin who loved political discussions, had her own political views, read many newspapers, and was well informed about society and social and political changes.[19] Bacheracht's character exemplifies some of the attitudes and political practices of upper-class women in the first half of the nineteenth century. This can be well illustrated with an example from the everyday life and activities of a woman in Berlin during the revolution of 1848, namely Ludmilla Assing.

Assing was born in Hamburg at the beginning of the nineteenth century and came from a prominent literary family. Her mother was Rosa Varnhagen, who held gatherings with writers and the literati in Hamburg, including Amalia Schoppe, Emilie Campe, and poets of Young Germany like Heinrich Heine. Her uncle was August Varnhagen von Ense, a diplomat and the husband of the famous salonnière Rahel Levin. She was, moreover, a cousin of Fanny Lewald, with whom she had a complicated relationship. It was within this liberal, intellectually stimulating family that Ludmilla Assing and her sister Ottilie were socialized.[20] The intellectual stimulation is linked to the family's Jewish background.[21] Some family members, including Assing's father and Rahel Levin, had converted from Judaism to Christianity. From a young age, both Ludmilla and her sister became accustomed to participating in political discussions. After the death of her parents, Ludmilla Assing moved to Berlin to live with her uncle, with whom she and her sister had a close relationship. Indeed, they worked closely together and held gatherings not only with liberal-minded Germans but also with liberals of the Italian national movement. Ludmilla's uncle had a significant influence on her political socialization. During her time in Berlin, Assing became accustomed to attending the theater and to discussing plays she saw and books she read, as we know from the letters she wrote to her friend Amalia Schoppe in Hamburg. Through her letter writing, moreover, Assing maintained a connection between Berlin and Hamburg and at the same time demonstrated that she was part of this liberal group.

During the revolution of 1848, Assing still lived in Berlin. She was close with the writers of the Young Germany movement and with liberal editors that were friends with her uncle, such as Gustav Kühne and August Lewald. She began to write articles for liberal newspapers. In her writing, she described the revolution in Berlin and her view of the nation: "Prussia has become German. . . . What is relevant is no longer the all-decisive, solitary 'I,' but rather the 'we' of the people."[22] For her, the March 1848 uprising in Berlin had brought to the fore the feelings of nationalism harbored by people in Prussia. In her writing, she also emphasized the participation of men and women in public ceremonies, such as the burial of those killed during the riots in Berlin. In so doing, she wanted to show how strongly people in Berlin felt about the German nation and how involved they were in the German national struggle.

Assing looked favorably on the participation of so many people in the German national struggle. She herself was rather curious about contemporary political events. She formed and defined her own political opinions around 1848. She did so, for example, by attending the discussions of the constitutional club in Berlin with liberal friends. By attending such discussions, she distanced herself from the liberal moderates and opted for more democratic views. She took part in the revolution through her political practices (e.g. her literary skills and ability to participate in political discussions) and proved herself to be a part of a liberal democratic group in which she played an important role after 1848.

By contrast, it seems that satirical references—or any other references—to "political ladies" were absent from Italian-speaking newspapers in 1848–49. One of the reasons for this apparent silence could lie in the different way that the Italian national movement was socially stratified. In the Italian case, many of the leading women in the movement were liberal aristocrats rather than bourgeois.[23] A further reason may be drawn from a brief reflection on the political discussion within the Italian and the German national movements. The Italian national discourse emphasized the cohesion of the national community during the revolution and later wars of 1848–49 and thus tried to erase political differences, while the German press often highlighted political diversification in the German national movement, even in the publications for and by women.[24] Nevertheless, German-speaking women underscored the significance of political cohesiveness when they wrote for a broader public. In the view of Ludmilla Assing, for example, the national democratic movement was based on the joint contributions of men and women. For her, both sexes had specific activist roles to play. Writing was one of the ways both sexes worked for democratic goals. She used her writing during and after the revolution to disseminate examples of women's participation. For Assing, women should always encourage men and the younger generations to take part in the German democratic movement, even if this led to disappointment.[25] Indeed, from Assing's perspective, political encouragement was the main duty for women in the German national movement.

Conclusion

Women like Ludmilla Assing or the other female writers discussed above had the financial means, the know-how, and the proper connections to initiate activities for the promotion of emergent national values. They made considerable use of their connections and skills in order to take sides for one party or another. By doing so, they staked out a strong political position and showed themselves to be precisely the sort of "political ladies" that authors had depicted satirically in print. At the same time, though, women understood their activism as a way to fulfill their pedagogical commitment to the nation. What is more, the very ideal of the mother of the nation empowered women to take part in the national movement.

In the first half of the nineteenth century, writers in the German and Italian states had advocated social and political commitment for women in specific contexts. The ideals of the political lady and the mother of the nation reflected this belief. Activists believed women should help forge the nation in a manner befitting their social status. In their writings, they took into account the social status of women, as my discussion of the political lady shows. Moreover, although the ideal of the political lady was used to criticize satirically women's influence on contemporary political debates, this influence was itself evidence of the mid-nineteenth-century diversification that took place within national movements. By contrast, the ideal of the mother of the nation symbolized a collectivity and social cohesion in face of the enemy. This ideal set in motion a learning process for women in the German states, who could speak openly about the past political activism of their mothers and other female relatives, while in the Italian states, the ideal of the mother of the nation reflected the political expectation of the upper classes, who were still struggling to legitimate the roots of their national ambitions.

Giulia Frontoni studied history, German, and English literature in Rome. She obtained her PhD at the University of Göttingen with a thesis on women's networking around 1848 in the German and Italian states. She has published on gender history, the history of emotions, and women's political participation around 1848. Frontoni collaborates with the Bismarck Foundation in Friedrichsruh and the Willy-Brandt-Haus in Lübeck.

Notes

I would like to thank Dean Bond for his editorial work, and Ruth Nattermann, Marion Kaplan, and the members of the DFG-Network for their contributions.
1. Nira Yuval-Davis, *Gender and Nation* (London: Sage Publications, 1997), 26–38.
2. The studies of Nadia Filippini and Ramona Myrrhe focus on the social background of women in the Italian and German national movements. See Nadia Maria Filippini, ed., *Donne sulla scena pubblica: Società e politica in Veneto tra Sette e Ottocento* (Milan: Franco Angeli, 2006); Ramona Myrrhe, *Patriotische Jungfrauen, treue Preußinnen, keifende Weiber Frauen und Öffentlichkeit in der ersten Hälfte des 19. Jahrhunderts in Sachsen-Anhalt* (Freiburg: Fördergemeinschaft wissenschaftlicher Publikationen, 2006).

3. See Carola Lipp, ed., *Schimpfende Weiber und patriotische Jungfrauen: Frauen im Vormärz und in der Revolution 1848/49* (Bühl-Moos: Elster Verlag, 1986).
4. In recent discussions about nationalisms in nineteenth-century Europe, the historian John Breuilly has suggested that nationalisms should be evaluated "by the criteria of the promotion of national identity or culture," because this would allow one to understand how such nationalisms spread. See John Breuilly, "Nationalism and National Unification in Nineteenth-Century Europe," in *The Oxford Handbook of the History of Nationalism*, ed. John Breuilly (Oxford: Oxford University Press, 2013), 149–74.
5. On the use of metaphors in national discourses, see Ida Blom, Karen Hagemann, and Catherine Hall, eds., *Gendered Nations: Nationalisms and Gender Order in the Long Nineteenth Century* (Oxford: Berg Publishers, 2000); Alberto Mario Banti, *L'onore della Nazione: Identità sessuali e violenza nel nazionalismo europeo dal XVIII alla Grande Guerra* (Turin: Einaudi, 2005); John Breuilly, "Risorgimento Nationalism in the Light of General Debates about Nationalism," in *Nation and Nationalism* 15 (2009): 439–45.
6. About the meaning of such images in European national movements, see Alberto Mario Banti, *L'onore della Nazione*. On strategies for people's mobilization, see Maarten Van Ginderachter and Marnix Beyen, eds., *Nationhood from Below: Europe in the Long Nineteenth Century* (Basingstoke: Palgrave MacMillan, 2012); Ilaria Porciani, "Disciplinamento nazionale e modelli domestici nel lungo Ottocento: Germania e Italia a confront," in *Storia d'Italia: Annali 22. Il Risorgimento*, ed. Alberto Mario Banti and Paul Ginsborg (Turin: Einaudi, 2007), 1:97–126.
7. On women's activism in German church associations, see Sylvia Paletschek, *Frauen und Dissens: Frauen im Deutschkatholizismus und in den freien Gemeinden, 1841–1852* (Göttingen: Vandenhoeck & Ruprecht, 1990).
8. Paletschek, *Frauen und Dissens*, 155–59.
9. Ann Taylor Allen, *Feminism and Motherhood in Germany, 1800–1914* (New Brunswick, NJ: Rutgers University Press, 1991), 41.
10. Marina D'Amelia, *La Mamma* (Bologna: Società Editrice il Mulino, 2005); Maria Cristina Morandini, *Scuola e nazione: Maestri e istruzione popolare nella costruzione dello Stato italiano, 1848–1861* (Milan: Vita e Pensiero, 2003), 159–61; Simonetta Soldani, "Il Risorgimento delle donne," in *Storia d'Italia: Annali 22. Il Risorgimento*, ed. Alberto Mario Banti and Paul Ginsborg (Turin: Einaudi, 2007), 183–224; Simonetta Soldani, "Italiane! Appartenenza nazionale e cittadinanza negli scritti di donne dell'Ottocento," *Genesis: Rivista della società italiana delle storiche* 1, no. 1 (2002): 85–124. As D'Amelia has noted, there was a focus on femininity and on female religiosity to promote Catholic consciousness as a political alternative to the secular nationalist thinking of the French Revolution, whereas the liberals in the Italian national movement saw Catholicism as a distinguishing mark that unified the different Italian states. In the first half of the nineteenth century, this discussion was largely animated by the writings of the abbot Vicenzo Gioberti. However, as historians Soldani and Morandini have shown, women also did much to shape this national ideal.
11. Caterina Franceschi Ferrucci, *Della educazione morale della donna italiana* (Turin: Unione Tipografico-Editrice, 1855), 40.
12. "Il battaglione della speranza. Preghiera alle madri," *La Donna Italiana*, 6 May 1848.

13. Hermine Speckter, *Aufruf ca. 1849*, Staatsarchiv Hansestadt Hamburg, Nachlass Speckter, 622–1/478 B3.
14. Some studies have pointed out how newspapers and many male writers viewed women's presence and participation in the national movement critically and satirized it. See Carola Lipp, "Die Frau in der Karikatur und im Witz der 48er Revolution," *Fabula* 32 (1991), 132–64; Stanley Zucker, *Kathinka Zitz-Halein and Female Civic Activism in Mid-Nineteenth-Century Germany* (Carbondale: Southern Illinois University Press, 1991), 70–78, 90–93.
15. Horace De Viel-Castel, "Les Femmes Politiques," in *Les Français peints par eux même*, ed. Henri-Léon Curmer (Paris: Henri-Léon Curmer, 1841), 41–48.
16. "Political Lady," in *The Corsair* 47, 1840, 751–52.
17. See Jules Gabriel Janin and Louis-Marie de Lahaye Cormenin, *Pictures of the French: A Series of Literary and Graphic Delineations* (London: W. S. Orr, 1840). For reviews, see "Les Francais Moeurs contemporaines," *The London and Westminster Review* 33, 1840, 162–81; "Political Lady," 751–52.
18. "Les Francais Moeurs contemporaines," 171.
19. Therese von Bacheracht, *Novellen: Rom-Berlin* (Leipzig: Brockhaus Verlag, 1849), 100.
20. On Ludmilla Assing, see Nikolaus Gatter, "'Letztes Stück des Telegraphen: Wir alle haben ihn begraben helfen . . .' Ludmilla Assings journalistische Anfänge im Revolutionsjahr," in *Internationales Jahrbuch der Bettina-von-Arnim-Gesellschaft* 11–12 (1999–2000), 101–20; Nikolaus Gatter, ed., *Makkaroni und Geistesspeise: Almanach der Varnhagen Gesellschaft e. V.* (Berlin: Berlin-Verlag Spitz, 2002).
21. On conversion from Judaism to Christianity as well as women's education in Jewish circles, see Deborah Hertz, *How Jews Became Germans: The History of Conversion and Assimilation in Berlin* (New Haven, CT: Yale University Press, 2007); Monica Rüthers, "Frauenleben verändern sich," in *Luftmenschen und rebellische Töchter: Zum Wandel ostjüdischer Lebenswelten im 19. Jahrhundert*, ed. Heiko Haumann (Cologne: Böhlau-Verlag, 2003), 223–308.
22. ."Die Märztage in Berlins, aus dem Tagebuche einer deutschen Frau," *Europa* 14, 1 April 1848, 233.
23. On the liberal orientation of the aristocracy in the Italian states, see Thomas Kroll, *Die Revolte des Patriziats: Der toskanische Adelsliberalismus im Risorgimento* (Tübingen: Niemeyer, 1999); Marco Meriggi, *Milano Borghese: Circoli ed élites nell'Ottocento* (Venice: Marsilio, 1992).
24. An example is the well-known *Frauenzeitung* (women's newspaper) published by Louise Otto-Peters. See Ute Gerhardt, Elisabeth Hannover-Drück, and Ramona Schmitter, eds., *"Dem Reich der Freiheit werb' ich Bürgerinnen": Die "Frauen-Zeitung" von Louise Otto* (Frankfurt am Main: Syndikat, 1979). About the heterogeneity of the political elites in the German states, see, for example, Thomas Kühne, "Professionalization or 'Amateurization,' Homogenization or Segmentation? The Parliamentary Elite in Germany, 1815–1918," in *Les familles politiques en Europe occidentale au XIXe siècle*, ed. Serge Bernstein (Rome: École Française de Rome, 1997), 391–408.
25. Assing began her career as a biographer by writing a book about Elisa von Ahlenfeld, who was the wife of Alfred Lützow, the commander of the Prussian volunteer corps during the Napoleonic wars. In her book about Elisa von Ahlenfeld, Assing showed how women's activism during the Napoleonic wars promoted a similar commitment to the nation among contemporary women. Ludmilla As-

sing, *Gräfin Elisa von Ahlefeldt, die Gattin Adolphs von Lützow, die Freundin Immermann's. Eine Biographie* (Berlin: Duncker, 1857).

Bibliography

Allen, Ann Taylor. *Feminism and Motherhood in Germany, 1800–1914*. New Brunswick, NJ: Rutgers University Press, 1991.
Assing, Ludmilla. *Gräfin Elisa von Ahlefeldt, die Gattin Adolphs von Lützow, die Freundin Immermann's: Eine Biographie*. Berlin: Duncker, 1857.
Banti, Alberto Maria. *L'onore della Nazione: Identità sessuali e violenza nel nazionalismo europeo dal XVIIII alla Grande Guerra*. Turin: Einaudi, 2005.
Blom, Ida, Karen Hagemann, and Catherine Hall, eds. *Gendered Nations: Nationalisms and Gender Order in the Long Nineteenth Century*. Oxford: Berg Publishers, 2000.
Breuilly, John. "Risorgimento Nationalism in the Light of General Debates about Nationalism." *Nation and Nationalism* 15 (2009): 439–45.
———. "Nationalism and National Unification in Nineteenth-Century Europe." In *The Oxford Handbook of the History of Nationalism*, edited by John Breuilly, 149–74. Oxford: Oxford University Press, 2013.
D'Amelia, Marina. *La Mamma*. Bologna: Società Editrice il Mulino, 2005.
De Viel-Castel, Horace. "Les Femmes Politiques." In *Les Français peints par eux même*, edited by Henri-Léon Curmer, 41–48. Paris: Henri-Léon Curmer, 1841.
"Die Märztage in Berlins, aus dem Tagebuche einer deutschen Frau." *Europa* 14, Leipzig, 1 April 1848, 233.
Franceschi Ferrucci, Caterina. *Della educazione morale della donna italiana*. Turin: Unione Tipografico-Editrice, 1855.
Filippini, Nadia Maria, ed. *Donne sulla scena pubblica: Società e politica in Veneto tra Sette e Ottocento*. Milan: Franco Angeli, 2006.
Gatter, Nikolaus. "'Letztes Stück des Telegraphen: Wir alle haben ihn begraben helfen . . .' Ludmilla Assings journalistische Anfänge im Revolutionsjahr." *Internationales Jahrbuch der Bettina-von-Arnim-Gesellschaft* 11–12 (1999–2000): 101–20.
———, ed. *Makkaroni und Geistesspeise: Almanach der Varnhagen Gesellschaft e. V.* Berlin: Berlin-Verlag Spitz, 2002.
Gerhardt, Ute, Elisabeth Hannover-Drück, and Romina Schmitter, eds. *"Dem Reich der Freiheit werb' ich Bürgerinnen": Die "Frauen-Zeitung" von Louise Otto*. Frankfurt am Main: Syndikat, 1979.
Hertz, Deborah. *How Jews Became Germans: The History of Conversion and Assimilation in Berlin*. New Haven, CT: Yale University Press, 2007.
"Il battaglione della speranza: Preghiera alle madri." *La Donna Italiana*, 6 May 1848.
Janin, Jules Gabriel, and Louis-Marie de Lahaye Cormenin. *Pictures of the French: A Series of Literary and Graphic Delineations*. London: W. S. Orr, 1840.
Kroll, Thomas. *Die Revolte des Patriziats: Der toskanische Adelsliberalismus im Risorgimento*. Tübingen: Niemeyer, 1999.
Kühne, Thomas. "Professionalization or 'Amateurization,' Homogenization or Segmentation? The Parliamentary Elite in Germany, 1815–1918." In *Les familles politiques en Europe occidentale au XIXe siècle*, edited by Serge Bernstein, 391–408. Rome: École Française de Rome, 1997.
"Les Francais Moeurs contemporaines." *The London and Westminster Review* 33, London, 1840, 162–81.

Lipp, Carola, ed. *Schimpfende Weiber und patriotische Jungfrauen: Frauen im Vormärz und in der Revolution 1848/49*. Bühl-Moos: Elster Verlag, 1986.

———. "Die Frau in der Karikatur und im Witz der 48er Revolution." *Fabula* 32 (1991): 132–64.

Meriggi, Marco. *Milano Borghese: Circoli ed élites nell'Ottocento*. Venice: Marsilio, 1992.

Morandini, Maria Cristina. *Scuola e nazione: Maestri e istruzione popolare nella costruzione dello Stato italiano, 1848–1861*. Milan: Vita e Pensiero, 2003.

Myrrhe, Ramona. *Patriotische Jungfrauen, treue Preußinnen, keifende Weiber Frauen und Öffentlichkeit in der ersten Hälfte des 19. Jahrhunderts in Sachsen-Anhalt*. Freiburg: Fördergemeinschaft wissenschaftlicher Publikationen, 2006.

Paletschek, Sylvia. *Frauen und Dissens: Frauen im Deutschkatholizismus und in den freien Gemeinden, 1841–1852*. Göttingen: Vandenhoeck & Ruprecht, 1990.

"Political Lady." *The Corsair* 47, New York, 1840, 751–52.

Porciani, Ilaria. "Disciplinamento nazionale e modelli domestici nel lungo Ottocento: Germania e Italia a confront." In *Storia d'Italia: Annali 22. Il Risorgimento*, edited by Alberto Mario Banti and Paul Ginsborg, 1:97–26. Turin: Einaudi, 2007.

Rüthers, Monica. "Frauenleben verändern sich." In *Luftmenschen und rebellische Töchter: Zum Wandel ostjüdischer Lebenswelten im 19. Jahrhundert*, edited by Heiko Haumann, 223–308. Cologne: Böhlau-Verlag, 2003.

Soldani, Simonetta. "Italiane! Appartenenza nazionale e cittadinanza negli scritti di donne dell'Ottocento." *Genesis: Rivista della società italiana delle storiche* 1, no. 1 (2002): 85–124.

———. "Il Risorgimento delle donne." In *Storia d'Italia: Annali 22. Il Risorgimento*, edited by Alberto Mario Banti and Paul Ginsborg, 22:183–224. Turin: Einaudi, 2007.

Speckter, Hermine. *Aufruf ca. 1849*. Staatsarchiv Hansestadt Hamburg, Nachlass Speckter. 622–1/478 B3.

Van Ginderachter, Maarten, and Marnix Beyen, eds. *Nationhood from Below: Europe in the Long Nineteenth Century*. Basingstoke: Palgrave MacMillan, 2012.

Von Bacheracht, Therese. *Novellen: Rom-Berlin*. Leipzig: Brockhaus Verlag, 1849.

Yuval-Davis, Nira. *Gender and Nation*. London: Sage Publications, 1997.

Zucker, Stanley. *Kathinka Zitz-Halein and Female Civic Activism in Mid-Nineteenth-Century Germany*. Carbondale: Southern Illinois University Press, 1991.

CHAPTER 5

Emancipation, Religious Affiliation, and Family Status around 1900

Angelika Schaser

In these days of postcolonial studies, the long-term impact of colonialization both in the colonized societies and in the societies of the former colonial powers is becoming clear. The same is true of discrimination against women, which did not simply come to an end when legal equity was established. This observation is rooted in history, and its content is the focus of this chapter. Although the opportunities for, and wishes of, women have changed a lot over the last century, we find even today that both self-perception and external perception of female intellectual work and parenthood vary between women and men. Around 1900, the two fields of housewife and mother were the goals of female education in the family and at school. This was also widely accepted by the members of the German women's movement. However, their goal was that gifted women should have access to higher education, academic studies, and professional work. Academic education and intellectual work for women were the key demands of the women's movement in the nineteenth century, first tentatively and then with growing intensity.

In this chapter, I have analyzed one key document by close reading. The leading questions are: (1) Around 1900, what opportunities for intellectual work did women see for themselves? (2) What criteria did they define for female expertise? (3) How were the results of female intellectual work presented? Why did the two female authors present only very few conclusions, leaving it to the readers to draw their own conclusions from the information presented? (4) Both authors were Jewish. Why did they not link the discourse on women's emancipation with the question of religious minorities? Finally, the reception and impact of the study are summarized.

Women and Intellectual Labor around 1900

Innumerable texts on women and intellectual work were published around 1900. The writings of scientists who denied that women had the capacity to study or to produce any intellectual achievements are well known and often quoted.[1] One of the best-known and most-quoted books is Adele Gerhard and Helene Simon's *Motherhood and Intellectual Work: A Psychological and Sociological Study; Based on an International Survey and on the Historic Development* (Berlin, 1901).[2]

Two German-Jewish women, born in 1868 (Gerhard) and 1862 (Simon), wrote about motherhood and intellectual labor in 1901. Gerhard was married and had two children (born in 1891 and in 1896); Simon was unmarried and had no children. They had known each other since their youth in Düsseldorf[3] and met again in Berlin in the context of the Verein für Socialpolitik (Association for Social Politics) and in the circles of Gustav Schmoller, whose seminars and lectures on national economic issues attracted numerous female guest students.[4] Schmoller was one of the few professors who not only encouraged women to study but also supported them in their endeavors. For example, he included in the yearbooks he edited studies conducted by women who—like Gerhard and Simon—mainly worked on an autodidactic basis with no formal education.[5]

Gerhard and Simon were among the pioneers, working scientifically and presenting their work in public even before women were admitted to universities. Gerhard had published her first novelette in 1894 and a study on consumer society and social democracy in the subsequent year. Simon, who is also said to have written novelettes in her youth,[6] started extensively publishing scientific texts after a visit to England (1896) and three semesters of study as a guest student at the Berlin University. In those days, both of them—thirty-three and thirty-nine years old, respectively—were probably at crossroads in their lives. Gerhard was attempting to combine motherhood with intellectual work. Simon, aged nearly forty, probably had the impression that she would have to live out her life unmarried and without children.

Their jointly published study can also be read autobiographically: both of them did intellectual work, one of them (Gerhard) as a mother and the other (Simon) as an unmarried woman. In their study, more than four hundred famous women (called experts) from the Western world (Europe and the United States) were asked about the compatibility of intellectual work and motherhood, with questions relating directly to their own lives.

Women as Experts

Gerhard and Simon were familiar with the ideas of social reform and the goals of the social democrats; they regarded solving the "social question" and the women's rights issue as relevant societal challenges. Both are known to have been in touch with leading representatives of the women's movement, but—as far as is known—neither of them personally engaged in its activities. Gerhard knew the problems arising out of the conflict between emancipation and socially mandated maternal obligations.[7] Simon was confronted with prevalent disdain toward unmarried women in society. Both of them belonged to the Jewish minority. Both of them were trying to find a place within society where they might combine their private lives with intellectual work. The study's autobiographically motivated intention was to demonstrate the compatibility of womanhood with intellectual work.

At the same time, it becomes clear that the two women regarded their work as a scientific production and saw their own role in the study as that of scientists. Just like Gustav Schmoller, they connected national-economic considerations with history. The focus was not on personal fate but on national economic and societal problems: women, and human beings in general, were seen as resources for society that should be put to effective use.

In order to underline the scientific nature of the study, Gerhard and Simon did not clamor for women's emancipation but strove for a balanced, objective presentation. There is extensive coverage of the opposition to women's emancipation. The work is introduced with consideration of the exceptional achievements of famous women since antiquity, but every chapter also describes the difficulties and conflicts brought about by combining motherhood with intellectual work. Gerhard and Simon held that large amounts of data would be necessary for their study. The women participating in their survey are presented by name in the appendix and are characterized as "experts."[8] Apparently, Gerhard and Simon made extra efforts to include well-known women from all over Europe and the United States as study participants. This was meant to add authority and respectability to their study. Thus, they equate female expertise with fame.

As for the study's acceptability in scientific circles, Gerhard and Simon were able to rely on support from several well-known professors at Berlin University and from abroad. In the preface, these professors are only listed by surname: "[Gustav] Schmoller, [Adolph] Wagner, [Max] Sering und [Werner] Sombart," all of them professors at the Department of Philosophy, University of Berlin. In addition, the physiologist Heinrich Herkner,[9] then professor in Zurich, was at the Technical University of Berlin from 1907 on. "Zuntz" probably refers to the animal physiologist Nathan

Zuntz, who at the time worked at the Königliche Landwirtschaftliche Hochschule Berlin. He came from a Jewish family and had converted to Protestantism in 1889. "Kemmerer" presumably refers to the American economist Edwin Walter Kemmerer, who interacted with German national economists.[10]

They were assisted in contacting famous women by Helene Lange, Clara Zetkin, Beatrice Webb (whom Simon had met in London), and Henriette von der Mey.[11] Gerhard and Simon expressed their special thanks to some members of the women's movement and to foreign scientists for providing international contacts.[12] In France, Käthe Schirmacher helped to recruit experts. Similarly, there were several contact persons (some of them German) in Scandinavia, Denmark, Italy, Belgium, the Netherlands, Switzerland, Hungary, Russia, Portugal, Austria, and Poland who helped search for female experts. Only for England and the United States were Gerhard and Simon able to utilize institutional support. In England, they were supported by the Women's Institute in London; in the United States, by the Students Reference Bureau, which maintained close connections to the Woman's Clubs[13] in various U.S. cities.[14]

Seven experts came from Italy: actress Adelaide Ristori (Marchesa Capranica del Grillo), writer Alinda Brunamonti, writer Virginia Mulazzi, Irma Melany Scodnik, scientist Rina Monti, lawyer Teresa Labriola, and Rosy Amadori. In the case of the Italian experts, only famous women were included in the study, and only two of them were quoted by name. The Italian writer Alinda Brunamonti confirmed that even during pregnancy she had been able to combine family duties with poetry.[15] Rina Monti, then lecturer at the University of Padua, underlined that "a woman is able to do intellectual work without any damage to health."[16] The case of the Italian experts demonstrates that the alphabetic listing of names in the book enhances the study's weight, even if only a small number of statements recorded in the book can be attributed to specific experts.

The Scientific Presentation of the Topic

Gerhard and Simon give a historical introduction on the topics of "the physical nature of the woman," "motherhood as an occupation," and "the intellectual work of the woman," building on the latest studies. In the second part of the book, they present the data. For this purpose, they classify the intellectual work of the woman into six occupational categories:

1. Acting
2. Music

3. Fine arts
4. Poetry
5. Science and humanities
6. Agitation, essay, and journalism

In doing so, they give the impression that it was possible for the expert women to be assigned to specific occupational categories, although as a rule they were self-taught and rarely held recognized training qualifications. The details of the questionnaire are not known, but the tables presented in the book allow for reconstruction of some of the questions.[17] The study participants were asked questions including: Are you married or unmarried? Do you have children? If yes, how many? Did you breastfeed your children? Did you have stillborn children? Were you sick due to overwork?[18] The questions indicate the context in which motherhood and intellectual work were discussed in those days, and they point to the relevance attributed to fertility, health, and breastfeeding.

On several occasions, the authors indicate serious deficiencies in the information received. For this reason, Gerhard and Simon resorted to published (auto)biographical texts from women artists, writers, and scientists on a comprehensive scale. Women who filled in the questionnaire did not always agree to be quoted by name. Therefore, verbal quotations are often attributed to anonymous "writers of international renown," etc. The case was different with Helene Lange, whom Gerhard and Simon classified as a scientist and who did not want her statements to be anonymized.[19] Not only in this case, the women's assignment to the occupational categories appears to be somewhat arbitrary; well-known women were frequently active in a variety of fields. The analysis makes a distinction between "reproductive" and "productive" occupations. It starts with the "reproductive" occupations such as acting and singing. Composing is seen as standing in the middle between the "reproductive" and the "productive" occupations. The "productive" occupations were poetry, science, and the umbrella category of agitation, essay, and journalism.

Acting, Music

In those days, female actors and singers were held in high esteem; their work was recognized and sometimes well paid. Within the artistic community, they were seen as irreplaceable. Public interest in these persons was further stimulated by stories of illegitimate children, extramarital affairs, or giving children away. High-level artistic performance, often associated with travel obligations, appeared scarcely reconcilable with a mother's duties.

Fine Arts

It was seen as easier for female fine artists to combine motherhood with intellectual work. Most of the married female artists had completed their studies before marriage, and as mothers they did not undertake long travel tours.[20] Fine artists, in most cases, were not in high societal esteem; only a very few became famous.

Poetry

The case was different for female poets (this term was used by Gerhard and Simon mostly for women writing novels and novelettes). Their activity was seen by Gerhard and Simon as a productive art and was more highly esteemed than the reproductive art of actors and singers.[21] In historical retrospect on the women in this group,[22] the authors speak only of female poets who "rose above mediocrity."[23] The authors had a deep respect for scientific opinions denying that women had the ability to perform independent intellectual work. This attitude is reflected, for example, in their focus on famous female writers. One example is Harriet Beecher-Stowe (1812–96), who is mentioned but is not classified as a poet. Why do Gerhard and Simon not recognize the author of the globally known bestseller *Uncle Tom's Cabin* as a poet? Imprudently, Beecher-Stowe had attacked Lord Byron. This "sin against one of the greatest geniuses of all times" had provided her with numerous enemies.[24] Apparently, this also led Gerhard and Simon to attest that she was "not truly rooted in poetry." She was only included in the historical sketch because, given the breadth of her influence, it is interesting to consider what she reports regarding the impact of her own maternal sufferings on *Uncle Tom's Cabin*.[25] This crudely demonstrates how only the contributions based on biological or intellectual motherhood were recognized as inventive and original.

It looked as if a serious and nearly insoluble problem would arise from "the union of poetic production with the maternal occupation."[26] Reportedly, a "female poet of international renown, belonging to the most well-known women of current times,"[27] claimed to concede the right of extramarital children to working mothers, as long as they were in a position to financially support their children. For Gerhard and Simon, this was definitely going too far. By no means was this Gerhard and Simon's vision of the "new woman."[28]

Science, Humanities

In the historical introduction to women in the sciences and humanities, they underline the female thirst for knowledge, and the "small number of individuals standing out from the background of a school or a scientific circle."[29] In the center of the chapter on "women in the sciences and humanities" are female teachers and academics as well as physicians and lawyers. In this category, many women did not see female occupational activity as reasonable as long as there were small children to be taken care of.[30] The female physicians' responses indicate that they saw the union of medical practice with motherhood as possible in principle, but also as difficult. Dr. Hope Bridges Adams Lehmann[31] makes it clear that only in a socialist society would it be possible for a woman to combine professional practice with maternal duties.[32]

Agitation, Essay, and Journalism

Due to the difficulties for mothers in the above categories, Gerhard and Simon saw the category "agitation, essay, and journalism" as appropriate for mothers: in their opinion, these fields did not require a more or less specific professional preparation, possibly regulated by the state. Nor do these fields—in contrast with truly creative work—require the complete involvement of one's personality.[33] Gerhard and Simon's reasoning for establishing these occupational groups is as follows: both the essayistic and the journalistic activity of women is mostly motivated by religious, philanthropic, sociopolitical, women's rights, and anti–women's rights agitation.[34] In this context, agitation was meant to include all activities that, in speaking or writing, "*directly* pursue a specific tendency."[35]

In this chapter, the first person mentioned was Olympe de Gouges. Gerhard and Simon succeeded in recruiting famous feminists such as Elizabeth Cady Stanton and Susan B. Anthony to participate in their study.[36] Auguste Schmidt,[37] Hanna Bieber-Böhm, Marie Stritt, Henriette Fürth,[38] and Clara Zetkin[39] agreed to be quoted explicitly. Gerhard and Simon underline that in these fields, no professional studies were needed; motherhood helped "gain knowledge of a more general nature," and all these activities were compatible "even with decades of interruption, without loss of quality."[40]

Irrespective of marital status, if women intended to work intellectually, according to Gerhard and Simon, the criterion for assessing their work was "the irreplaceable cultural value"—this should be the deciding factor in the "right to exist" for mothers working intellectually.[41] The presentation of results shows that among the experts, 37 percent were unmarried, and among the married women, 33 percent had no children. Gerhard and Simon kept insisting that motherhood implies the most demanding intellectual work. The material that mothers work with is the noblest material ever trusted to a creative hand.[42]

So, "motherhood" in this context would not necessarily mean biological motherhood but could refer to "spiritual motherhood" as well.

The idea was that women should get the vote in order to be honored as mothers and to be able to provide their experience and knowledge to society in a more effective way.[43] Women were supposed to be active based on motherhood; the fundamental experience of motherhood was seen as benefiting the whole of society.

The questions asked by Gerhard and Simon refer not to spiritual motherhood but to biological motherhood. The questions underline how important they deemed fertility and the ability to breastfeed babies for the societal recognition of working women.[44] Here, they indirectly discredit women who are not mothers. Their activity, even if defined as "spiritual motherhood," could not contribute directly to demographic development and to public health by breastfeeding. Other passages written in a highly defensive manner point out that "the female physical nature" does not prevent them from doing effective academic and artistic work.[45] This illustrates how laden with risk the arena of intellectual work was seen as being for women.

Even women's movement activists only had confidence in a successful combination of motherhood and intellectual work among "flexible, particularly strong women."[46] (Biological) maternal duties were deemed more important than intellectual work. Neither was a consecutive arrangement of a woman's life seen as a solution. Gerhard and Simon regarded postponing intellectual work to later phases of life as highly inappropriate.[47] They assumed that "damage" and "degeneration" would follow from this both for the individual women and for society at large.

Unmarried women, who were supposed to have no children, held a legitimate position in science and the humanities, in Gerhard and Simon's view.[48] For mothers, the situation was perceived as more difficult. Compatibility with motherhood appeared particularly problematic in the applied sciences and with work situations, which required extended absences from home. On the other hand, work intermissions of years or decades seemed to imply significant impairments of their occupational careers.[49] As a compromise, Gerhard and Simon identified the option of postponing essential creative activities to more mature years of life in selected work fields, where intermissions were common and "small versions" prevailed: the field of agitation, essay, and journalism.[50]

Two conclusions are offered. (1) A woman without children is an imperfect being: "Psychologically and physically, a woman can act out her life only as a mother."[51] By glorifying biological motherhood, Gerhard and Simon downgrade all women without children. This is not ameliorated by their concept of spiritual motherhood. (2) A mother intending to work as an artist, poet, scientist, writer, musician, or journalist has to achieve excellence. Only in this way, according to Gerhard and Simon, could the combination of motherhood with intellectual work be justified. So they adopted the dictum put forward by those who opposed women's higher education: female intellectual work would only be justified in society if it delivered extraordinary achievements.

Women's Emancipation and Jewish Minority

The study focuses on the women's emancipation discourse, on educational issues, and on the basic conditions of intellectual work and creativity for women. Religion and religious differences are hardly mentioned. In the paragraph about preachers, the well-known sentence from the Bible (1 Corinthians 14:34) is cited ("women should keep silent in the churches"), and relating to midwives, a phrase from the Jewish Mishnah (Kiddushin 1:7) is mentioned ("and every positive commandment which is time-dependent, men are obligated and women are exempt").[52] Although it was postulated that women played a very strong role in the spread of religions, especially the Christian religion,[53] no distinctions are made with respect to religion. Nor is there any discussion on the potential role of religion in educational opportunities for women. The few passages where the study discusses religion were only meant to demonstrate that women, historically, "were admitted early to join in (Christian) church singing,"[54] and they played such an important role for spreading religions that this statement necessitated no limitation with respect to specific religions, nor in terms of space or time. The situation of Jewish women or Jewish minorities was not addressed at all.

On the one hand, this was in tune with an attitude prevailing in the Protestant well-educated middle class, the German women's movement, and the Social Democratic Party (SPD) implying that religion was a private affair and had no role in public discussions or in the humanities. This omission, however, also illustrates the dilemma of Jewish emancipation, which gave equal rights to Jewish individuals but not to the Jewish community. This situation induced polarizations between liberal and orthodox tendencies within the Jewish population and caused the renunciation of a group of liberal and secular Jews from the Jewish communities to the point of conversions to Christianity.

Women are assigned a key role in these struggles concerning Jewish identity and assimilation.[55] Studies have also shown that Jewish women were overrepresented among female students and graduates.[56] However, Jewish women played an important role not only in the family and in the academic world but also in the German women's movement. Women's movements in Europe,[57] similar to Catholicism[58] and Liberalism,[59] proved somewhat resistant to antisemitism.

Therefore, when Shulamit Volkov defined antisemitism as a cultural code in 1978, she classified the women's movement as part of the emancipatory culture, opposed to antisemitism: "Antisemitism and antifeminism were almost invariably combined in Imperial Germany. Both were integral elements of the anti-emancipatory culture of a majority of Germans in the pre-war years."[60] More recent research has shown that, within the women's movement, the basic refusal of antisemitism was at times accompanied by a latent rejection and ambivalent attitude toward Jews. All this mostly caused Jewish women not to focus on their Jewish identity when acting beyond the local level. (The Jewish Women's Association [Jüdischer Frauenbund] was established only in 1904). Such considerations probably also prompted Gerhard and Simon not to discuss Jewishness in this book.

Reception and Impact

The study met with intensive responses; it was translated into Finnish in 1907, and a second edition was published in 1908.[61] Being of interdisciplinary interest, the study was discussed in daily newspapers and professional journals. In 1906, Max Weber wrote about Helene Simon: She "is *very* intelligent. Her book 'Motherhood and intellectual work' . . . counts among the greatest achievements."[62]

Scientists and politicians interpreted the work as verifying their respective views of the female role in society.[63] In the women's movement and among Social Democrats too, the study met with a lot of interest. August Bebel was impressed by the study and called it "inventive."[64] He concluded from the results that conflicts between family duties and occupation were not limited to women. In his view, only a new organization of the productive forces in society could open up an opportunity for transformation of marriage, education, and domestic economy that would allow women and men appropriate development potentials. Since the authors presented the information but restrained themselves from extensive comment, they provided ample evidence for all sides, including the opponents of female work and higher education.

Gerhard and Simon, leading emancipated lives at the time, covered their own external roles as women and Jews with the scientific habitus of objectivity. Their own situations and religious affiliations do not show through in the text. However, the adaptation of the two women to the dominant scientific habitus did not achieve the desired success. Gerhard and Simon were autodidacts and guest students without university degrees. The "specific logic" of the scientific field indissolubly interlinked the practices of their scholarly work with the authors' "specific capital," which was considered insufficient.[65]

The foreword is characterized by female modesty and self-doubt,[66] reflecting a typical feature of female scientific work. At that time, the authors were outsiders not only in German society and the scientific arena but also in the women's movement and in the SPD. Although they were in close contact with several members of the women's movement, their widely noticed study was marginalized only a few years later. They were criticized for having drawn no conclusions from their study, in contrast with Marianne Weber, whose approach to the problem was seen as more serious.[67] However, there was continued impact from the standards set by Gerhard and Simon concerning female intellectual work, how they handled the writings of opponents of female higher education and work, the issue of female modesty in science, and the fact that they did not address their own family status and religious affiliation. Even twenty-five years later, after receiving an honorary doctoral degree from Cologne University for her philosophical works, Else Wentscher chose to use the same title for her autobiography.[68] This text too reflects an overdose of modesty and obedient gratitude toward her husband and her teachers. Still in the 1920s, only good luck and nerves of steel were seen as facilitating the combination of motherhood and scientific work for women.[69]

After this publication, Gerhard and Simon went separate ways. For Gerhard, this study was her final scientific publication. She felt released and free to devote herself completely to her poetic work.[70] One year later, she left the Jewish community and converted to Protestantism in 1911. Simon, being a private scholar, began her career as "female theorist of social and welfare work," for which she would receive an honorary doctorate from the University of Heidelberg in 1922.[71] Due to their Jewish origins, both of them were forced to leave Germany in 1938; Gerhard immigrated to the United States, Simon to the United Kingdom.

Conclusion

The gender order of the nineteenth century in the Western world made it difficult for women to combine their womanhood with intellectual work and ambitious occupations. It was seen as highly risky to combine motherhood and a demanding profession. Adelheid Weber coined the phrase that such a combination would mean "lighting a candle at both ends." To Gerhard and Simon, this metaphor appeared the appropriate leitmotif for the answers returned to their questionnaire.[72]

On the one hand, the pioneers among the academic women tried to settle the claim to be better than the average (male) academic. In their eyes, only the creation of irreplaceable cultural values (*unersetzliche Kulturwerte*) justified the academic education and occupation of women. On the other hand, from the beginning, women were used to being modest and to combining their work with their duties as wives and mothers.

Motherhood was normally seen as a national task, while intellectual labor and occupation were seen as a business that must be subordinated to family duties. A mother must "make her family her first, nearest, and dearest duty."[73] Motherhood and raising children were seen as the most important national duty for women across all social classes. The welfare of the nation figured prominently on the agenda and was ranked higher than the needs of (Jewish) minorities and individual families and persons. Primarily intellectual work or occupation should support the nation and the family, not private satisfaction or happiness. This conditioning has had a long-term effect on the professional lives of women right up to the present. One can see the long-term effect in the gender pay gap in Europe even today. In summary, two outsiders, by integrating antifeminist prejudices and an attitude of exaggerated modesty, contributed to the view that female intellectual work was exceptional and not to be encouraged—a view with a long-term impact.

Angelika Schaser is professor of modern history at the Universität Hamburg. Her publications include studies on women's movements, minorities, collective memories, nation and gender in the German history of the nineteenth and twentieth centuries, religious conversions, the history of historiography, and auto/biographical research. Her recent publications include *Erinnern, vergessen, umdeuten? Europäische Frauenbewegungen im 19. und 20. Jahrhundert* (Frankfurt am Main/New York: Campus, 2019), edited together with Sylvia Schraut and Petra Steymans-Kurz, and "Geschlechtergeschichte der Universitäten und Geisteswissenschaften," *Jahrbuch für Universitätsgeschichte* 20 ([2017], 2019), edited together with Falko Schnicke.

Notes

1. See Katharina Rowold, *The Educated Woman: Minds, Bodies, and Women's Higher Education in Britain, Germany, and Spain, 1865–1914* (New York: Routledge, 2010).
2. Adele Gerhard and Helene Simon, *Mutterschaft und geistige Arbeit: Eine psychologische und soziologische Studie, Auf Grundlage einer internationalen Erhebung mit Berücksichtigung ihrer geschichtlichen Entwicklung* (Berlin: Reimer, 1901).
3. Walter Friedländer, *Helene Simon: Ein Leben für soziale Gerechtigkeit* (Bonn: Arbeiterwohlfahrt Hauptausschuss, 1962), 21; Rowold, *Educated Woman*, 123.
4. Daniela A. Frickel, *Adele Gerhard (1868–1956): Spuren einer Schriftstellerin* (Cologne: Böhlau Verlag, 2007), 183, 122f.
5. Sabine Bertram, "Frauen promovieren: Doktorandinnen der Nationalökonomie an der Berliner Universität, 1906–1936," *Jahrbuch für Universitätsgeschichte* 11 (2008): 131. From 1882 on, Schmoller was a university professor in Berlin.

6. Friedländer, *Helene Simon*, 12.
7. Frickel, *Adele Gerhard*, 190.
8. Gerhard and Simon, *Mutterschaft und geistige Arbeit*, 329–33. Several experts, however, insisted on their names not being listed there (Gerhard and Simon, *Mutterschaft und geistige Arbeit*, iv).
9. Already in 1899, Herkner supported female enrollment in national economy studies. See Heinrich Herkner, "Das Frauenstudium der Nationalökonomie," *Archiv für soziale Gesetzgebung und Statistik: Zeitschrift zur Erforschung der gesellschaftlichen Zustände aller Länder* 13 (1899): 227–54.
10. Gerhard and Simon, *Mutterschaft und geistige Arbeit*, iv–v.
11. Ibid., v. Henriette von der Mey = Henriëtte Rosina Dorothea van der Meij (1850–1945); in 1884, she was the first female journalist employed in the Netherlands, working with the liberal journal *Middelburgschen Courant*.
12. Gerhard and Simon, *Mutterschaft und geistige Arbeit*, v.
13. Henriette Greenbaum Frank and Amalie Hofer Jerome, *Annals of the Chicago Woman's Club for the First Forty Years of its Organization, 1876–1916* (Chicago: Chicago Woman's Club, 1916), 155.
14. Gerhard and Simon, *Mutterschaft und geistige Arbeit*, v.
15. Ibid., 172.
16. Ibid., 236.
17. Ibid., tables 170, 231, 252, 259, 285, 309.
18. "Erkrankung der Mutter durch Überarbeitung," ibid., 252.
19. Ibid., 237.
20. Ibid., 110.
21. Ibid., 116.
22. Ibid., 116–71. Presumably, it was Gerhard who wrote the history of the female poets, comprising fifty pages. Only twenty pages were dedicated to contemporary female poets.
23. Ibid., 127.
24. Ibid., 145.
25. Ibid.
26. Ibid., 185; ibid., 189.
27. Ibid., 192, 1f. This could have been Ricarda Huch, who gave birth to her only child in 1890 and was divorced soon after.
28. Ibid., 193.
29. Ibid., 200.
30. Ibid., 265.
31. Hope Bridges Adams Lehmann (1855–1916) was one of the first woman physicians in Imperial Germany. Adams Lehmann was born and grew up in England, studied medicine in Leipzig, and finished her studies as the first woman in Germany with a state examination in medicine. In 1901, she was married for the second time. She had two children from her first marriage. See Marita Krauss, "Die Lebensentwürfe und Reformvorschläge der Ärztin Hope Bridges Adams Lehmann (1855–1916)," in *Barrieren und Karrieren: Die Anfänge des Frauenstudiums in Deutschland: Dokumentationsband der Konferenz "100 Jahre Frauen in der Wissenschaft" im Februar 1997 an der Universität Bremen*, ed. Elisabeth Dickmann and Eva Schöck-Quinteros (Berlin: Trafo Verlag Weist, 2000), 143–57, and Marita Krauss, *Hope: Dr. Hope Bridges Adams Lehmann, Ärztin und Visionärin: Die Biografie* (Munich: Volk Verlag, 2009).

32. Gerhard and Simon, *Mutterschaft und geistige Arbeit*, 256.
33. Ibid., 267.
34. Ibid., 268.
35. Ibid. Emphasis in the original text.
36. Ibid., 284, 289f.
37. Ibid., 291.
38. Ibid., 292f.
39. Ibid., 303f.
40. Ibid., 305.
41. Ibid., 322.
42. Ibid., 324.
43. Ibid.
44. Ibid., 311.
45. Ibid., 312.
46. Helene Lange, *Die Frauenbewegung in ihren modernen Problemen* (Leipzig: Quelle & Meyer, 1907), 82.
47. Gerhard and Simon, *Mutterschaft und geistige Arbeit*, 321.
48. Ibid., 265.
49. Ibid., 266.
50. Ibid., 267–68.
51. Ibid., 191: "Psychisch und physisch lebt sich die Frau erst aus, wenn sie Mutter wird."
52. Ibid., 266.
53. Ibid., 268.
54. Ibid., 70.
55. Marion Kaplan, *The Making of the Jewish Middle Class: Women, Family, and Identity in Imperial Germany* (New York: Oxford University Press, 1991); Kirsten Heinsohn and Stefanie Schüler-Springorum, "Einleitung," in *Deutsch-Jüdische Geschichte als Geschlechtergeschichte: Studien zum 19. und 20. Jahrhundert*, ed. Kirsten Heinsohn and Stefanie Schüler-Springorum (Göttingen: Wallstein, 2006), 11–17; Angelika Schaser, "Antisemitismus und deutsche Frauenbewegung," *Querelles-Net* 2 (2000): https://www.querelles-net.de/index.php/qn/article/view/18/18; Angelika Schaser, "Einige Bemerkungen zum Thema Antisemitismus und Antifeminismus," *Ariadne* 43 (2003): 66–71.
56. Claudia Huerkamp, *Bildungsbürgerinnen: Frauen im Studium und in akademischen Berufen 1900–1945* (Göttingen: Vandenhoeck & Ruprecht, 1996), 24; Shulamit Volkov, *Germans, Jews, and Antisemites: Trials in Emancipation* (Cambridge: Cambridge University Press, 2006).
57. Ute Planert, "Liberalismus und Antifeminismus in Europa," in *Liberalismus und Emanzipation: In- und Exklusionsprozesse im Kaiserreich und in der Weimarer Republik*, ed. Angelika Schaser and Stefanie Schüler-Springorum (Stuttgart: Steiner, 2010), 73–91.
58. Olaf Blaschke, *Katholizismus und Antisemitismus im Kaiserreich* (Göttingen: Vandenhoeck & Ruprecht, 1997); Olaf Blaschke, *Offenders or Victims? German Jews and the Causes of Modern Catholic Antisemitism* (Lincoln: University of Nebraska Press, 2009).
59. Uffa Jensen, "Integrationalismus, Konversion und jüdische Differenz: Das Problem des Antisemitismus in der liberalen Öffentlichkeit des 19. Jahrhunderts," in *Liberalismus und Emanzipation*, ed. Schaser and Schüler-Springorum, 55–71; Bar-

bara Vogel, "Inklusion und Exklusion von Frauen: Überlegungen zum liberalen Emanzipationsprojekt im Kaiserreich," in *Liberalismus und Emanzipation*, ed. Schaser and Schüler-Springorum, 199–218; Volkov, *Germans, Jews, and Antisemites*.
60. Shulamit Volkov, "Antisemitism as a Cultural Code: Reflections on the History and Historiography of Antisemitism in Imperial Germany," *Leo Baeck Institute Yearbook* 23 (1978): 25–46.
61. Frickel, *Adele Gerhard*, 107.
62. Max Weber to Paul Siebeck, 19 May 1906, in *Max Weber Gesamtausgabe*, vol. 5, ed. Mario Rainer Lepsius (Tübingen: J. C. B. Mohr Siebeck 1990), 92–93. Emphasis in the original text.
63. Frickel, *Adele Gerhard*, 107–18; Sabine Klöhn, *Helene Simon: 1862–1947, Deutsche und britische Sozialreform und Sozialgesetzgebung im Spiegel ihrer Schriften und ihr Wirken als Sozialpolitikerin im Kaiserreich und in der Weimarer Republik* (Frankfurt am Main: Lang, 1982), 251–55; Rowold, *Educated Woman*, 124–25.
64. August Bebel, "Mutterschaft und geistige Arbeit," *Die Neue Zeit: Wochenschrift der deutschen Sozialdemokratie*, vol. 2 of 19 [1901] (repr. Glashütten im Taunus: Auvermann, 1973), 45–47.
65. See Pierre Bourdieu, *Die feinen Unterschiede: Kritik der gesellschaftlichen Urteilskraft* (Frankfurt am Main: Suhrkamp 1987), 143–47, 194.
66. Gerhard and Simon, *Mutterschaft und geistige Arbeit*, iii–v.
67. Anna Plothow, *Die Begründerinnen der deutschen Frauenbewegung* (Leipzig: Rothbarth, 1907), 199–200.
68. Else Wentscher, *Mutterschaft und geistige Arbeit* (Langensalza: Beyer & Söhne, 1926).
69. Wentscher, *Mutterschaft*, 28.
70. Adele Gerhard to Max Martersteig, 5 August 1908. Quoted in Frickel, *Adele Gerhard*, 117–18.
71. See Marina Sassenberg, "Helene Simon," *Jewish Women: A Comprehensive Historical Encyclopedia*, last modified 1 March 2009, https://jwa.org/encyclopedia/article/simon-helene.
72. Gerhard and Simon, *Mutterschaft und geistige Arbeit*, 182.
73. See Antoinette Brown Blackwell, "The First American Ordained Minister, Lecturer and Writer," in ibid., 265.

Bibliography

Bebel, August. "Mutterschaft und geistige Arbeit." In *Die Neue Zeit: Wochenschrift der deutschen Sozialdemokratie*. Vol. 2 of 19: 45–47. 1901. Reprint, Glashütten im Taunus: Detlev Auvermann, 1973.
Bertram, Sabine. "Frauen promovieren: Doktorandinnen der Nationalökonomie an der Berliner Universität, 1906–1936." *Jahrbuch für Universitätsgeschichte* 11 (2008): 111–33.
Blaschke, Olaf. *Katholizismus und Antisemitismus im Kaiserreich*. Göttingen: Vandenhoeck & Ruprecht, 1997.
———. *Offenders or Victims? German Jews and the Causes of Modern Catholic Antisemitism*. Lincoln: University of Nebraska Press, 2009.
Bourdieu, Pierre. *Die feinen Unterschiede: Kritik der gesellschaftlichen Urteilskraft*. Frankfurt am Main: Suhrkamp, 1987.

Frank, Henriette Greenbaum, and Amalie Hofer Jerome. *Annals of the Chicago Woman's Club for the First Forty Years of Its Organization, 1876–1916*. Chicago: Chicago Woman's Club, 1916.

Frickel, Daniela A. *Adele Gerhard (1868–1956): Spuren einer Schriftstellerin*. Cologne: Böhlau Verlag, 2007.

Friedländer, Walter. *Helene Simon: Ein Leben für soziale Gerechtigkeit*. Bonn: Arbeiterwohlfahrt Hauptausschuss, 1962.

Gerhard, Adele, and Helene Simon. *Mutterschaft und geistige Arbeit: Eine psychologische und soziologische Studie, Auf Grundlage einer internationalen Erhebung mit Berücksichtigung ihrer geschichtlichen Entwicklung*. Berlin: Reimer, 1901.

Heinsohn, Kirsten, and Stefanie Schüler-Springorum. "Einleitung." In *Deutsch-Jüdische Geschichte als Geschlechtergeschichte. Studien zum 19. und 20. Jahrhundert*, edited by Kirsten Heinsohn and Stefanie Schüler-Springorum, 11–17. Göttingen: Wallstein Verlag, 2006.

Herkner, Heinrich. "Das Frauenstudium der Nationalökonomie." *Archiv für soziale Gesetzgebung und Statistik: Zeitschrift zur Erforschung der gesellschaftlichen Zustände aller Länder* 13 (1899): 227–54.

Huerkamp, Claudia. *Bildungsbürgerinnen: Frauen im Studium und in akademischen Berufen 1900–1945*. Göttingen: Vandenhoeck & Ruprecht, 1996.

Jensen, Uffa. "Integrationalismus, Konversion und jüdische Differenz: Das Problem des Antisemitismus in der liberalen Öffentlichkeit des 19. Jahrhunderts." In *Liberalismus und Emanzipation: In- und Exklusionsprozesse im Kaiserreich und in der Weimarer Republik*, edited by Angelika Schaser and Stefanie Schüler-Springorum, 55–71. Stuttgart: Steiner, 2010.

Kaplan, Marion. *The Making of the Jewish Middle Class: Women, Family, and Identity in Imperial Germany*. New York: Oxford University Press, 1991.

Klöhn, Sabine. *Helene Simon: 1862–1947: Deutsche und britische Sozialreform und Sozialgesetzgebung im Spiegel ihrer Schriften und ihr Wirken als Sozialpolitikerin im Kaiserreich und in der Weimarer Republik*. Frankfurt am Main: Lang, 1982.

Krauss, Marita. "Die Lebensentwürfe und Reformvorschläge der Ärztin Hope Bridges Adams Lehmann (1855–1916)." In *Barrieren und Karrieren: Die Anfänge des Frauenstudiums in Deutschland, Dokumentationsband der Konferenz; "100 Jahre Frauen in der Wissenschaft" im Februar 1997 an der Universität Bremen*, edited by Elisabeth Dickmann and Eva Schöck-Quinteros, 143–57. Berlin: Trafo Verlag Weist, 2000.

———. *Hope: Dr. Hope Bridges Adams Lehmann, Ärztin und Visionärin, Die Biografie*. Munich: Volk Verlag, 2009.

Lange, Helene. *Die Frauenbewegung in ihren modernen Problemen*. Leipzig: Quelle & Meyer, 1907.

Planert, Ute. "Liberalismus und Antifeminismus in Europa." In *Liberalismus und Emanzipation: In- und Exklusionsprozesse im Kaiserreich und in der Weimarer Republik*, edited by Angelika Schaser and Stefanie Schüler-Springorum, 73–91. Stuttgart: Steiner, 2010.

Plothow, Anna. *Die Begründerinnen der deutschen Frauenbewegung*. Leipzig: Rothbarth, 1907.

Rowold, Katharina. *The Educated Woman: Minds, Bodies, and Women's Higher Education in Britain, Germany, and Spain, 1865–1914*. New York: Routledge, 2010.

Sassenberg, Marina. "Helene Simon." In *Jewish Women: A Comprehensive Historical Encyclopedia*, 1 March 2009. Jewish Women's Archive. https://jwa.org/encyclopedia/article/simon-helene.

Schaser, Angelika. "Antisemitismus und deutsche Frauenbewegung." In *Querelles-Net. Rezensionszeitschrift für Frauen- und Geschlechterforschung*, Nr. 2, 2000. https://www.querelles-net.de/index.php/qn/article/view/18/18.

———. "Einige Bemerkungen zum Thema Antisemitismus und Antifeminismus." *Ariadne* 43 (2003): 66–71.

Vogel, Barbara. "Inklusion und Exklusion von Frauen: Überlegungen zum liberalen Emanzipationsprojekt im Kaiserreich." In *Liberalismus und Emanzipation: In- und Exklusionsprozesse im Kaiserreich und in der Weimarer Republik*, edited by Angelika Schaser and Stefanie Schüler-Springorum, 199–218. Stuttgart: Steiner, 2010.

Volkov, Shulamit. *Germans, Jews, and Antisemites: Trials in Emancipation*. Cambridge: Cambridge University Press, 2006.

———. "Antisemitism as a Cultural Code: Reflections on the History and Historiography of Antisemitism in Imperial Germany." *Leo Baeck Institute Yearbook* 23 (1978): 25–46.

Weber, Max. *Max Weber Gesamtausgabe*. Vol. 5. Edited by Mario Rainer Lepsius. Tübingen: J. C. B. Mohr Siebeck, 1990.

Wentscher, Else. *Mutterschaft und geistige Arbeit*. Langensalza: Beyer & Söhne, 1926.

SECTION 3
RELIGION AND EDUCATION

Chapter 6

The Legacy of Adam and Eve
Morality and Gender in Jewish "Catechisms" in Nineteenth-Century Germany

Philipp Lenhard

As a result of the confessionalization of German Judaism in the course of the nineteenth century, Jewish "denominations" had to compete with each other over essential moral values and theological norms that were meant to guide Jews in a world of ongoing secularization and assimilation. Children and adolescents, especially, were seen as a resource for a brighter, enlightened, and emancipated, yet still *Jewish*, future, freed from the density of the ghetto and the "superstition" of Eastern European Ḥasidism.[1] Hence, the struggle over religious education became a key element of Jewish-internal politics. This process is reflected in the flood of Jewish "catechisms" that poured out of Western Europe in the early nineteenth century. Jewish catechisms were essentially religious primers for young wedding couples as well as for schoolboys and schoolgirls, especially for those who were preparing for their bar/bat mitzvah—back then called "confirmation" in many reform and modern orthodox congregations.[2] While there has been a long tradition not only of Jewish legal texts but also of *musar* (ethical) literature, the concept of "catechisms"—catalogues of central religious doctrines—was clearly adopted from Christianity.[3] In the Jewish context, however, catechisms were manifestations of bourgeois culture and aimed at reconciling its cultural virtues with inherited religious traditions. At the same time, the purpose of these textbooks was to teach the "essentials of Judaism" in a time of growing secularism.

Religious reformers and modern orthodox rabbis alike regarded the Jewish family as the basis for the continued existence of Judaism. Therefore they were anxious to strengthen the gender order. From the reformers' perspective, this goal demanded the inclusion of women into synagogue service and community institutions, while orthodox proponents argued that although the appropriate place of Jewish women was the household, there was urgent need for enhanced religious education for women in order for them to preserve the Jewish tradition.[4] Both factions agreed that only if women were capable of finding their way *as Jews* in a modernized world would it be possible to maintain the Jewish family under dramatically changing social and political circumstances. The nascent production of catechisms and primers was a means to this end—with unforeseen ramifications.

The crucial question to be answered in this chapter is to what extent a new literary genre (catechism) transformed traditional teachings (religious law) about gender into a new and decisively modern content (bourgeois morality).[5] Resting upon a thorough analysis of fifty-one "catechisms" written by Jewish men, most of them rabbis or teachers and all of them published between 1779 and 1859, this study demonstrates that gender issues played a central role in Jewish religious education in late eighteenth- and early nineteenth-century Germany.[6] Thus, the genre of Jewish catechisms illustrates the much-discussed "transformation of German Jewry" in the fields of morality and gender normativity.[7]

Jewish Law and the Basic Doctrines of Judaism

Jewish catechisms themselves were more or less an invention of the nineteenth century.[8] Still in 1783, Moses Mendelssohn in his famous book *Jerusalem, or on Religious Power and Judaism* differentiated between a religion of immutable truths, which was Christianity, and a religion of law, which, according to Mendelssohn, was Judaism. What is more, the great *maskil* and philosopher openly rejected the idea of religious doctrines:

> Judaism boasts of no exclusive revelation of immutable truths indispensable of salvation; of no revealed religion in the sense in which that term is usually taken. Revealed religion is one thing, revealed legislation is another. The voice which was heard on Sinai, on that memorable day, did not say, "I am the Lord, thy God, the eternal, self-existing Being, omnipotent and omniscient, who rewards men, in a future life, according to their works."[9]

Mendelssohn argued that God did not introduce Himself to the Jewish people by revealing His divine attributes. Instead, God's voice said, "'I am the Lord thy God, who led thee out of the land of Egypt; who delivered thee from bondage,' etc." This introduction, explained Mendelssohn, is based on a "historical fact, on which the legislation of that particular people was to be founded, since laws were to be revealed there; commandments, judgments, but no immutable theological truths."[10] That is, Mendelssohn defied the definition of Judaism as a religion in the Christian sense of a community of faith.[11] Consequently, throughout the text, he called the Bible a "divine code of law."

Scholars of the history of religion today widely agree that the name of their discipline is based on a terminological universalization of multiple and very diverse ritual orders, ideas of transcendence, hierarchies of religious experts, notions of holiness, and other pillars of the spiritual structures of premodern societies.[12] Thus, if we speak of "religions" in the plural, we knock these diverse orders into the shape of a nineteenth-century Western, Christian model.[13] Mendelssohn's book is so important in this regard because it draws a clear line between Christianity and Judaism. However, the rejection of "immutable truths" by Mendelssohn is only half the story. Jewish history also comprises a long rabbinical tradition of condensing the essence of Judaism, including the identification of the basic doctrines of Judaism. This tradition reaches back to the ancient Rabbanites and Rabbi Akiva's well-known dictum that the love of one's neighbor was the totality of the Torah, and continues with various catalogues of essential doctrines in the Middle Ages, like the first section of Maimonides's *Mishneh Torah* (repetition of the Torah) from the twelfth century and Joseph Albo's *Sefer ha-Ikkarim* (book of principles) from the fifteenth century, until early modern times.

In his remarkable dissertation of 1922, "Jewish Law: Towards a Sociology of Diaspora-Judaism," Erich Fromm highlighted what is so confusing about those Jewish catalogues of basic doctrines: "The first representative of Judaism who postulated a system of dogmata," elucidates Fromm,

> was the Jewish philosopher of religion, Maimonides. He formulated *thirteen* articles of faith, which served as indicators of one's belonging to Judaism. Maimonides's articles of faith found partial acknowledgment, but in part they were supplemented or shortened; sometimes they were even fiercely contradicted. Nachmanides for instance, formulates only *three* basic principles of Judaism . . .; Rabbi David ben Samuel d'Estella (1320) speaks of *seven* doctrines of faith, Rabbi David Yomtov Bilia adds another *thirteen* articles to Maimonides's *thirteen* articles [for a total of *twenty-six*]. Rabbi Josef recognizes only *one* basic demand of faith. Finally Rabbi Saul of Berlin, who died in 1794 and was a critic of Maimonides, stated that dogmata could be formulated only with regard to the necessities of each time.

"Dogmata," concludes Fromm, "did not acquire any further meaning than being an individual expression of opinion by singular leaders of the Jewish people. The total diversity of [systems of] dogmata proves this."[14] In short, the enormous diversity of Jewish catalogues of doctrines shows that Jewish tradition was unable to find a final answer to the question of what the basic principles of faith actually were. This of course stems from the fact that traditional Judaism, as Mendelssohn rightly points out, is not concerned primarily with *beliefs* but rather with halakhic *observance*.

It is well known that the early modern period experienced a revolution in cataloguing Jewish law. The sixteenth-century four-volume halakhic code *Shulḥan Arukh* (set table) by Yosef Karo with its supplement *ha-Mappah* (the tablecloth) by Moses Isserles compiled the 613 commandments in a dense form and, thanks to the invention of the printing press, made them easily accessible to everyone at a relatively low price.[15] Now every Jew without formal rabbinic education who was proficient enough in Hebrew and who owned a copy of the *Shulḥan Arukh* would be capable of figuring out what was forbidden and what was allowed according to religious law. Historically, the *Shulḥan Arukh* certainly became increasingly important first and foremost for religious experts, especially in the countryside, who did not own a Talmud themselves but nevertheless still had to adjudicate in their communities due to the corporatist structure of early modern Germany.[16] Not every community had its own rabbi. Most of the smaller communities in rural Germany employed a religious teacher with only a basic knowledge of Jewish law, and very often these teachers at the same time assumed the job of ritual slaughterer (*shoḥet*), circumciser (*mohel*), or cantor (*ḥazan*) as well. In all of these occupations halakhic expertise was necessary, at least to some extent. After the expulsion of the Jews from most German cities and the destruction of the majority of age-old Jewish communities, the *Shulḥan Arukh* became the most important instrument for maintaining medieval rabbinic jurisdiction.[17] It was the backbone of an already precarious ethnoreligious unity whose representatives yearned for clear guidance, particularly in regions where Jewish existence was far from the ideal of a fully-fledged Jewish community with its multifaceted infrastructure of religious institutions.

But given these vast social ravages, administering the halakhah would obviously not be enough. Jewish tradition was being challenged by the dissolution of Jewish community life yielded by expulsion and the dramatic increase in Jewish beggars and vagrants as a result of social and political exclusion. The majority of German Jewry in the seventeenth and eighteenth centuries lived at least temporarily on the roads and in the interspaces between legal Jewish communities.[18] Hence, not just Jewish law but similarly Jewish ideas and ethics had to be taught to the masses of Jews who traveled around in early modern Ashkenaz, homeless, far away from their families, from rabbinic schools, or from religious teachers who could have conveyed the norms and values of Jewish ethics and beliefs. This is not to say that the Jewish poor were not religious or pious; quite the opposite: they attended synagogue services on the holidays and spent their Shabbat nights as guests in Jewish households, which hosted them willy-nilly; they knew how to pray and were aware of basic religious rituals and symbols.[19] But a deeper knowledge of the religious aspects of Judaism was in danger of getting lost long before the era of actual

Jewish secularism began in the nineteenth century, as the case of Salomon Maimon suggests. In his fascinating autobiography, the great philosopher and Talmud scholar Maimon depicts an episode from his life in which he joined a Jewish beggar for several months after being refused admission to Berlin by the orthodox rabbinate:

> At night, I came to a tavern where I met a poor pedestrian, who was a begging Jew [*Betteljude*] *ex professo*. . . . I was a learned rabbi; he was an idiot. . . . I had an understanding of morality, decency, and civility, while he didn't know anything of it at all. I was ultimately of a healthy, yet weak body constitution, while he was a strong, stout guy, who could make the best sort of soldier. Despite all these differences, I decided to join him, since I was compelled to stray in a foreign country anyway in order to scrape up a living. On the tramp, I attempted to teach my fellow traveler terms of religion and true morality, and he in turn taught me the art of begging.[20]

Maimon wasn't very successful in his mission. The beggar was so concerned about his everyday problems of how to survive that he had neither the time nor the capacity to receive a good religious education—although he might have cherished this education personally. We can learn from this episode that the social misery of Central European Jewry brought massive consequences for the status of morality and religious education. What was needed, thus, was a guidebook of Jewish teachings in Hebrew or—as the unlearning of Hebrew continued over the centuries—in Judeo-German, which was easily accessible and readable for the *am ha-arets*, for the common people. This situation marked not only the rediscovery of the *musar* genre but also the beginning of Jewish catechisms.[21]

Lekaḥ Tov, or the First Jewish Catechism

In 1595, only a couple of decades after the publication of the *Shulḥan Arukh*, Abraham ben Ḥenanyah Yagel, a rabbi and physician from Italy, published his *Sefer Lekaḥ Tov* (Book of a Good Lesson) in Venice.[22] The book, initially produced for the children of a wealthy Jewish banker who had employed Yagel as a private teacher, was reprinted in Amsterdam in 1658 and appeared in forty-two editions in seven languages, including Judeo-German (Western Yiddish) and Yiddish, until the end of the eighteenth century. In the same spirit of facilitating Jewish tradition and making it accessible to everyone that had spawned the publication of the *Shulḥan Arukh*, Yagel wrote the first Jewish catechism or religious primer.[23] It was also a response to a situation in which the pressing social conditions of the absolutist policy toward the Jews made it difficult for the majority of the Jewish population in Germany to study the Torah in depth. Naphtali ben Samuel Pappenheim, the printer of the second edition of the *Lekaḥ*

Tov (Amsterdam, 1658), correspondingly complained "that the Torah is being forgotten because people are preoccupied by their pursuit of a living and do not study the Torah proficiently."²⁴ According to the wealthy Jewish merchant Isaac Wetzlar, writing in 1749, "*Lekaḥ Tov* has been printed in good Yiddish many times, so that everybody can understand it." "It had an effect on some people," Wetzlar summarized, "but the majority have no desire to see it. . . . Thousands of Jews do not know what they believe."²⁵

Like its Christian counterpart, the catechism of the Dutch Jesuit priest Peter Canisius, the *Sefer Lekaḥ Tov* was a compilation of questions and answers: simple questions of the ordinary man were presented and answered accordingly. Surprisingly, at first glance, it was a virtual "rabbi" who asked the questions and his "student" (*talmid*) who answered them, as if the text was the written transcript of an inquiry or an oral exam. The first question the rabbi poses is, "Tell me, my son, for what purpose has God created you in His honorable image?"²⁶ And the student replies, "I was created in order to serve my Creator, to love Him, and to fear Him because of His Honor [*kavod*]."²⁷

The book also contains several teachings regarding the nature of the two sexes. According to Yagel, God gave the commandment of loving thy neighbor in order to make "peace between a man and his wife."²⁸ Thus, the ideal relationship between men and women was matrimony. Only this legal institution allowed or even commanded sexual intercourse under specific circumstances and thus prevented men and women from falling for one of the gravest sins: "unchastity is the desire of the human heart for carnality and adultery."²⁹ While it is only natural that rabbinic tradition has emphasized the *legal* liability of fathers and husbands, Yagel focused on their *moral* responsibility. He painted a picture of women as human beings who—in contrast to men—are guided more by their natural desires than by spiritual or moral values. It is the responsibility of, first, their fathers, and then their husbands to make them refrain from sin.³⁰

The notion of marriage and sexual relations as established by Rabbinic Judaism differed significantly from Yagel's: according to the Talmud (and the *Shulḥan Arukh*), *both sexes* were in danger of going astray from the right path. Thus, the recommended age of marriage was the beginning of sexual maturity for both boys and girls (usually at the age of fourteen through sixteen). The main purpose of matrimony was neither love nor decency, but procreation. In this regard, Rabbinic Judaism was far from preaching sexual abstinence or asceticism. Within the limits of the commandments for religious purity, sexual intercourse was encouraged by the halakhah. Since intimacy between a husband and his wife is a mitzvah (included in Exodus 21:10), it is hardly surprising that in the early modern period, Friday night after the Shabbat meal was the preferred time for sexual intercourse.³¹

However, Yagel's focus on morality rather than law is just a glimpse of what would become a general trend two hundred years later. References to questions of gender relations are very scarce in his catechism because Jewish society in his day was still fundamentally shaped by a widely unquestioned gender order.[32] The distribution of gender roles was transmitted from parents to their children and promoted by religious literature of all sorts.[33]

Women were clearly dependent on their husbands' rulings and—within the framework of religious law—subject to their discretion.[34] Their inferior status was marked especially by denying them the right to study the Talmud, since rabbinic wisdom was still the highest value of early modern Jewish society. Yagel's book may have been written also for women, but in the first place it was a guideline for Jewish men.

With the dawning of the modern era at the turn of the nineteenth century, traditional Judaism faced yet another existential crisis. While the late-medieval expulsions from the cities had indeed challenged the Jewish communities profoundly, Jewish communal autonomy, as demonstrated, had been preserved in the estate-based societies of early modern Europe.[35] The French Revolution, in contrast, represented the radical dissolution of corporate autonomy and the coercive inclusion of all citizens into the nation-state on the basis of equality and individual freedom. For Jews, this development was highly ambivalent. While it meant political emancipation on the one hand, it completed the loss of the traditional community structure on the other.[36] Scholars of modern Jewish history have argued that the abolition of communal autonomy implied the end of rabbinic authority in its traditional sense.[37] The profession of rabbi shifted from an expert in Jewish law to a Jewish chaplain and preacher; ordinary Jewish men and women, in turn, became voluntary members of what were now called "Israelite congregations."

As a result of this development, rabbis and other male Jewish intellectuals in Central and Western Europe increasingly stopped producing halakhic books and resorted to a variety of moralistic, philosophical, historiographical, and devotional literature. Halakhah could no longer be enforced in secularizing societies in which the nation-state had a monopoly on the legitimate use of force. The rabbis' most effective instrument to impose sanctions on transgressors, the ban (*ḥerem*), was no longer available to them. Religious education and moral instruction began to take the place of halakhic regulation. At the same time, the traditional Jewish school system (*ḥeder*) was replaced by modern educational institutions, in which emphasis was put on secular knowledge like modern European languages, grammar, algebra, history, and geography rather than Bible and Midrash, or even Talmudic scholarship.[38] Jakob Petuchowski underlines that "the increasing number of secular subjects now studied by the Jewish child left him less time for the specifically Jewish disciplines."[39] Paradoxically, the efforts for a renewal of Jewish education led to Jewish tradition passing into oblivion. What was meant to strengthen Jewish identity in a modern world ultimately paved the way for Jewish secularism.[40]

The New Catechism: Bourgeois Morality and the Jewish Woman

It was in this very context that the idea of Jewish catechisms was revitalized and modernized. According to historian George Y. Kohler, about fifty catechisms had been published by 1832, and as many as 161 by 1889.[41] This flood of books and pamphlets was produced, firstly, for boys (*b'ney mitzvah*) and girls (*banot mitzvah*) in preparation for their "confirmation," and secondly for brides and grooms. One of the most fascinating and influential examples of these guidebooks is Naphtali Herz Homberg's *Bne-Zion: A Religious-Moral Primer for the Youth of the Israelite Nation*, published in 1812 and translated into Italian in two different versions in 1815 and 1828.[42] Homberg, an ardent supporter of the Jewish enlightenment movement (*haskalah*), was born in 1749 in a small town near Prague. He had attended several *yeshivot* (Talmudic academies) in Prague, Glogów, and Bratislava before moving to Berlin and Hamburg, where he studied philosophy, European languages, and mathematics. In 1782, the same year in which Emperor Joseph II promulgated the Edict of Tolerance, he moved to Vienna and assumed several state functions in favor of the reform of the Jews in the Habsburg Empire.[43] His primer *Bne-Zion* was meant to prepare young couples for their lives as newlyweds. But the content of the book was not merely suggestion. Rather, the couple had to learn its contents by heart and was obliged to undergo a test, with Homberg himself as the examiner who could deny couples the right to marry if they failed. Homberg had to face fierce corruption allegations and became one of the most hated men in the Jewish world of his time.[44]

Most of the basic principles of Judaism that Homberg's book contained were not particularly different from those of Christianity. Moreover, the book was at least as concerned with the duties of a decent citizen of the Habsburg Empire as it was with religious values. This included detailed explanations of what was to be expected from husbands and wives. Hinting at the biblical story of Adam and Eve, Homberg declared:

> Matrimony is the exact conjunction and friendship that unites two people, man and woman, for the preservation of the human race. Matrimony itself is brought about and blessed by God. Husband and wife promise each other solemnly that

they will live together for the easing of toil, for the happy pleasure of life, and for the education of children. They love each other more than anyone else, they help each other in business and in times of hardship, they support each other's luck and wish to make each other happy.[45]

Homberg's notion of a love marriage was doubtless modern in nature, an outcome of the sentimental turn in the era of Enlightenment, and a reflection of the ideal of the bourgeois nuclear family.[46] By the end of the eighteenth century, terms like "love" and "friendship" increasingly appeared in Jewish marriage contracts (*ketubbot*). An example from Metz from the year 1781 suggests that new formulae were incorporated into the prescribed Ashkenazi standard text: "Said couple should treat each other with love and devotion from now on, as it is the common custom. They neither divest nor hide something from the other, but they are equally entitled to manage their assets."[47] Although the idea of mutuality emerges in these marriage contracts, the new type of Jewish family was based on a modern distribution of gender roles:

> The man has to take care of a decent livelihood for the woman and the family by carrying on a profession in an orderly manner. He also has to provide for security and support. The woman, in contrast, shall look diligently to the order, tidiness, and wealth of the household. She is to show obedience and respect toward the man and shall be docile at any time.[48]

While it was the husband's duty to earn a living (rather than study), it was up to his wife to fulfill her role as mother and educator of her children, especially her daughters:

> Mothers have to teach their daughters kitchen affairs, handicrafts such as needlework, knitting, and so forth, and how to actually run a household. In addition to this, she shall guide her to female discipline, humility, and humbleness, and chasten her love of luxury and fashion. Righteous parents have to familiarize their children with industriousness, order, tidiness, domesticity, and sincerity, and must care for their greater luck and progress in the world, and make them learn something useful, a decent business, with which they can earn their living, in order to prevent them from being a burden on society.[49]

The "decent business" that women had to learn, according to Homberg, was only cautionary—it was to "prevent them from being a burden on society" in case their husband died. The actual place for women was the household. To be sure, Homberg's understanding of the gender order wasn't particularly Jewish. He instead reproduced very common bourgeois virtues and norms like obedience, humility, love, and loyalty, which he contrasted with the "cold formality" of a traditional Jewish marriage of convenience.

A similar approach was presented by the Jewish schoolteacher Moses Büdinger. In his book *Moreh le-Torah* (Teacher of the Torah), published in 1837, he argued that

> since the oldest times, matrimony, on which the welfare of the human kind rests, is a bond hallowed by the divine law of God. The greatest good on earth, domestic bliss, is based on the good consent and the mutual love and fidelity of matrimony, and a good and wise education of children emerges from it; and what could foster the welfare of humanity more than the good consent of parents and their teaching children the fear of God and virtue?[50]

Good consent, mutual love, domestic bliss—to almost all of the authors of Jewish catechisms, matrimony was more than a legal form of partnership; it was the heart of the family, and the family was the nucleus of a civil society.

But there were less harmonious opinions as well. Several catechisms display androcentric ideas or even sexist notions of masculinity. Wolf Schlessinger, for instance, the district rabbi of the famous Jewish community of Sulzbach-Rosenberg in the Upper Palatinate, elucidated in his very loose German translation of the *Sefer ha-Ikkarim*, published in 1844, that women "were created to support" their husband so that "he attains the perfection that lies dormant in his abilities since his creation."[51] And thus, it is not surprising that Schlessinger thought that "the love between a leader and his subordinates" was similar to the one between husband and wife. Although Schlessinger featured the bourgeois idea of the spouses mutually bestowing honor on one another, more traditional views, especially the image of the Jewish businesswoman, appear in his book as well. The man, he states, "has to take care of his wife's needs, he has to honor her, and to meet her requirements as best he can; she, on the other hand, has to serve him, honor him, has to take care of the business, and is not allowed to love anyone except him."[52]

Honoring a woman obviously did not necessarily mean seeing her as equal. In his *Systematic Catechism of the Israelite Religion*, Samuel Hirsch, one of the most prominent reform rabbis of the nineteenth century, voiced his opinion that "it is not the mission of women to serve through their actions as an example for the world, but rather to be an example in their homes. The Israelite mission toward the world can only be assumed by men."[53] Hirsch's distinction between female (home) and male (outside world) spaces revised the traditional distinction between the sacred (the religious sphere of studies, prayers, and services) and the profane (the sphere of business). His orthodox opponents phrased the modern idea that the natural space of women was inside the house in different words. The mother's place was at home with her children, wrote an anonymous author in the orthodox journal *Der treue Zions-Wächter* (The True Guard of Zion), because she was the "first and natural nurturer, guardian, caretaker, and educator of the helpless child."[54] But her divine mission to serve as an example in her home was foiled by the *Zeitgeist*; instead of having the time and leisure to care for her child as she was supposed to do, the Jewish mother of the modern era "has so many other duties and obligations."[55] As a result, the influence of the Jewish mother on her children had even become harmful: "How many spoilings, effeminacies, weaknesses of character, how many selfish aspirations of the sapling are due to what was taught to him by the mothers, grandmothers, aunts, nurses, and nannies!"[56] And there was no doubt that it was the father's duty to set things straight.

Even the preacher Eduard Kley from Hamburg, one of the most radical reformers in the nineteenth century, explained that God's providence becomes manifest only in the genius of male leaders: "Noah, Joseph, Moses, David, Daniel, on the whole, especially in the leadership of the people of Israel."[57] Even where he emphasized mutual duties between the husband and wife at first glance, Kley indicated that women were the man's appendix: "Husband and wife shall mutually beautify and perfect each other's lives through love and loyalty, harmony and concord, virtuousness and piety, because the man belongs to the woman, and *the woman is the man's most costly property and most beautiful adornment* [Ehrenschmuck]."[58]

These examples of an androcentric concept of Judaism revolve around the problem of social hierarchy, grounded in real or imaginary differences between the sexes. Thus, it is not surprising how much emphasis was put on the maintenance of gender differences in nineteenth-century catechisms. Again and again, authors quoted the prohibition from Deuteronomy 22:5: "The woman shall not wear that which pertaineth unto a man, neither shall a man put on a woman's garment: for all that do so are abominable unto the LORD thy God."[59] Consequently, Markus Beer Friedenthal argued in his 1836 essay "The Dignity of Women" that "nothing renders women less amiable, that is: unhappier, than to transgress the sublime antagonism of gender. . . ."[60]

It is important to note that this concept of femininity shouldn't be simply equated with the traditional Jewish notion of the woman's role in the premodern family. First of all, the primary obligation of the Jewish man is no longer to learn the Talmud. Instead, he is primarily a businessman and a good father. His wife, on the other hand, is dragged out of the public sphere, which is in contrast to the Middle Ages and the early modern period when women were active in the economy as well or even managed to care for the family's earthly needs alone.[61] With regard to the status of women in the medieval Jewish communities of Ashkenaz, the historian Avraham Grossmann notes:

Of all the factors leading to the improvement of the status of Jewish women in Christian Europe during the Middle Ages, this is in my opinion the most significant one, whose importance it is difficult to exaggerate. The woman's right to leave her home as she wished and to meet with traders and leaders of state was of great significance.[62]

The consequences of this major shift in the social and economic status of women lasted well into the early modern period. The famous seventeenth-century female entrepreneur Glikl bas Judah Leib, for example, tells in her autobiography about her participation in her husband's jewelry and gold business, and it is revealing that she knows every detail of the couple's economic situation.[63] Her function in the business was to redeem the pawns of contract partners. After her husband's death, she took over the business herself and established business contacts with merchants throughout Europe. At the end of her life, she had developed into a highly accepted woman in the Jewish community of Metz. In other words, the ideal of a mere housewife and mother is *bürgerlich*, not Jewish in the traditional sense.[64]

Thus, catechisms and guidebooks had the purpose of teaching boys and girls, young ladies especially, the norms and values of contemporary bourgeois culture. Their parents were not capable of conveying these values because they already belonged to a decaying Jewish past, as Samuel Hirsch complains in the introduction to his catechism:

> Unfortunately, such an outline [as this catechism] has to be considered necessary even for most of Israel's fathers and mothers of families, although the same principles and teachings [that appear in this catechism] were developed over several years on every Sabbath and on every holiday from the pulpit. A second local need . . . is that we have many Israelite families who live isolated in the countryside and, due to the lack of orderly religious tuition, are faced with the problem of what to teach their children from the religion of their fathers.[65]

Taking into account that Jewish catechisms essentially taught bourgeois virtues and merged them with relevant quotations from the Bible, it becomes understandable that these virtues were repeated mantra-like again and again. In his *Guidebook for Instructions in the Mosaic Religion*, published in Glogów in 1829, Michael Aron Arnheim, who was a cantor and rabbi in the Prussian village of Przemęt near Poznań, explained that morality and virtue required strict abstinence and self-discipline. What can save us from the "sin of unchastity" he asked? And his answer was:

> (1) To avoid everything that harms the shamefacedness, even if we think that there are no witnesses. (2) To flee from obscene sayings, writings, and images as if we were fleeing from pestilence; because they fill our souls with impure ideas and lure us to sin. (3) To be always active and try to stay sober. Idleness leads to licentious-

ness, our sages teach.⁶⁶ (4) That we deliberately abstain from a permitted pleasure in order to exercise ourselves in austerity and self-control.⁶⁷

What Arnheim recommended was a system of total self-discipline and self-sanction; a way of life that ironically reminds us of the Jewish *ḥasid*, the countermodel to the enlightened Jewish citizen of a Western state.⁶⁸

Empowerment of Women through Education

But the nineteenth century was also a time when women were "discovered" as responsible and autonomous subjects—as individuals. Despite being reduced to helpers of their husbands in most of the catechisms, women were acknowledged as having their own right to get educated, not *only* but *also* in a religious sense. This development reflects in some of the catechisms as well. To be sure, religious literature specially produced for Jewish women was not as new as it seems. Already in the thirteenth century, important works like Yonah Gerondi's *Dat ha-Nashim* (Religion of Women) were published, and the early modern period saw Benjamin Aron ben Slonik's halakhic compendium *Mitzvot ha-Nashim* (Commandments of Women), written in Yiddish and typeset in "Vaybertaytsh" with the subtitle *Eyn sheyn frouen bikhleyn* (A Lovely Book for Women), come to light.⁶⁹ The most popular book among early modern Jewish women was certainly Jacob ben Isaac Ashkenazi's Yiddish "Women's Bible" *Tse'enah u-Re'enah* (Go Forth and Look), published for the first time in 1616.⁷⁰ This easily readable midrashic paraphrase of the weekly portions (*parashot*) of the Pentateuch and the Haftarah appeared in over two hundred editions and spread all over the Ashkenazi world.

But while the "Women's Bible" was essentially narrative in its literary style, activists of the Haskalah movement took the first steps to combine these narrative elements with specifically didactic contents. David Friedländer's *Reading Book for Jewish Children*, published in 1779, contained not only "moralistic tales from the Talmud" but also Maimonides's thirteen articles of faith.⁷¹ Although the book was designed for male pupils of the Jewish Free School in Berlin only, its style was influenced by *Tse'enah u-Re'enah*, and its content was interesting for girls and young women as well. Besides the learning material, which included short stories and poems, the book also included educational and moralistic instructions for prospective brides and grooms, for instance Talmudic sayings and parables: "Marital love finds its place on a knife's edge; for marital hatred, even a bed sixty feet wide is too narrow."⁷² And in one of the poems, bourgeois boasting and superficiality is criticized: "Your girl glitters from her makeup; mine glitters from the [water of the] creek."⁷³ Only little is known about the reception of the book, which was published in a second edition in Prague in 1781, but one can assume that it was prevalent in many bourgeois Jewish households and thus also accessible to Jewish girls.[74]

Despite the focus on Jewish boys, with regard to the question of women's education, Friedländer's *Reading Book* and similar publications of the Haskalah movement were prefigurations and precursors of the craze for catechism literature. One example is the primer *Dat Moshe ve-Jehudit* (Mosaic and Jewish Religion) by the orthodox preacher and writer Salomon Plessner, who stated that a "cathetic religious education" was necessary "for the female youth, which has no access to the Holy Scriptures." Plessner quoted a tractate of the Mishnah, which declares that "no knowledge of law shall be taught to the female gender,"[75] and relativized this prohibition by arguing that it referred only to the "higher education of law or the halakhic part of the Bible, since the dame was exempted from the observance of many commandments."[76] According to Plessner, this prohibition did not mean to exclude women from learning "general doctrines of faith and duty." He quoted the twelfth-century *Sefer ha-Ḥassidim* (Book of the Pious) as a proof for his opinion: "The man has the obligation to inform his daughters about the prescriptions of law. . . . Because if she, for example, does not know the commandments for Sabbath, how can she observe it?"[77] Plessner referred to women's responsibility for preparing the Sabbath at home. Therefore, he explained, they had to know precisely what was forbidden and what was allowed. They had to be religious experts themselves, and thus Plessner's plea had the religious education of women as its consequence.

The staunchest defender of the empowerment of women through religious education was Hermann Engländer's book *Benot Zion* (Daughters of Zion), which was written in German in Hebrew letters and published in Vienna in 1828. Its introduction was written by the Jewish scholar Eduard Altschul, who opened straightforwardly by arguing

> that we actually owe the first education of our spirit, the primary rudiments of our heart's culture, solely to women. Greece's wise men were right to entrust their tender adolescents to the tender education of their wives, and even the belligerent legislator Lycurgus felt moved to do that. Because only they understand . . . how to honor the good at daytime with a wise hand and a tender sense, and how to inflame and enthrall our hearts for virtue and religiosity, for humaneness and human kindness, for everything which is beautiful and noble.[78]

Altschul continued by attacking women's enemies: "This beautiful part of humankind indeed found enough enemies who tried to contest its rights hallowed by nature, and even the wise Plato tended to deny the female soul. And the Talmud teachers declare that lectures about interpretations of law for women are futile."[79] Altschul didn't dare to confront Plato and the Talmudists openly, but rather chose an indirect rebuttal: "From my point of view," he argued,

> both did focus only on cold and strictly logical reflections. Indeed, this kind of preoccupation will always remain strange to the sentimental women. They don't appeal to their individuality, stand in disharmony with the sensibility of their gentle fabric of nerves, and will never be in accordance with them—hence, if this world sage's [Plato's] loveless judgment of the mental faculties of women should be acknowledged, then we have to understand that he only means the mathematical soul or the sense for higher calculations by that which he denies the female gender; and indeed, the dames of all times and all places have no love and desire for strictly logical studies of that kind.[80]

Altschul played the melody of sentimental women and logical, calculating men, but it is very important to realize that this melody here functioned as a discursive strategy in support of women's education. That is why Altschul added the example of "the sixteenth-century . . . princess [Elisabeth] of Wittenberg, who studied higher algebra, the Hebrew language, and even the Kabbala with her laudable diligence."[81] Elisabeth of Wittenberg is his example of an enlightened, modern woman. And her curriculum—algebra, Hebrew, Kabbalah—resembles his own plans for decent education for Jewish women. "So much on the generally acknowledged worth of women for our first moral education," concluded Altschul. "Having now determined the important impact of women on our earliest education of the heart, we have even more of a holy obligation to foster the intellectual culture of our girls and women."[82]

The transformation of German Jewry from an early modern ethnoreligious entity to a bourgeois community of faith implied the emergence of new ideals of gender and morality. Catechisms and religious primers functioned as a catalyst that helped to modify Jewish tradition in order to make it compatible with the challenges of a bourgeois, increasingly secularized society. The distribution of gender roles as propagated in the catechisms resembled that of its Christian counterpart, although the critical consideration of rabbinic sources remained vital. The most fundamental shift in the image of the Jewish woman was her ejection from the public sphere and her confinement to the household. Hence, the acculturation of German Jewry moved women into a position of weakness and subordination.

Philipp Lenhard is assistant professor (*Wissenschaftlicher Assistent*) of Jewish history and culture at the University of Munich. In 2015–16, he was a visiting scholar at the University of California, Berkeley. In 2016–17, he was a visiting professor of medieval and modern Jewish history at the Martin Buber Institute for Judaic Studies in Cologne. Lenhard published the monographs *Nation or Religion? The Emergence of Modern Jewish Ethnicity in France and Germany, 1782–1848* (Goettingen/Bristol: Vandenhoeck & Ruprecht, 2014) and *Friedrich Pollock: The Grey Eminence of the Frankfurt School* (Berlin: Suhrkamp/Insel, 2019) in German.

Notes

1. For the image of the *Ostjude*, see Steven E. Aschheim, *Brothers and Strangers: The East European Jew in German and German Jewish Consciousness, 1800–1923* (Madison: University of Wisconsin Press, 1982), 3–31.
2. See Benjamin Maria Baader, *Gender, Judaism, and Bourgeois Culture in Germany, 1800–1870* (Bloomington: Indiana University Press, 2006), 82–84; Michael A. Meyer, *Response to Modernity: A History of the Reform Movement* (Oxford: Oxford University Press, 1988), 40–43.
3. Among the most important books of *musar* literature is Baḥya ibn Pakudah's *Ḥovot ha-Levavot* (Duties of the Heart, 1040) and Yehudah ha-Levi's *Sefer ha-Kuzari* (Book of the Kuzari, 1140). In the early modern period, Moshe Ḥaim Luzzato's *Mesillat Yesharim* (Paths of the Upright, 1738) was widely read in the Jewish world. See Joseph Dan, *Sifrut ha-Musar ve-ha-Derush* [Ethical and Homiletical Literature] (Jerusalem: Keter, 1975).
4. See Abraham Geiger, "Die Stellung des weiblichen Geschlechtes in dem Judenthume unserer Zeit," in *Wissenschaftliche Zeitschrift für jüdische Theologie* 1 (1837): 1–14, especially 6f.; Samson Raphael Hirsch, "Das jüdische Weib" [1863], in *Gesammelte Schriften*, ed. Naphtali Hirsch (Frankfurt: J. Kauffmann, 1908), 4:160–208, especially 163f.
5. Orthodox rabbis knew very well about the dangers of the new medium of catechisms, although they used it themselves. According to Jay Berkovitz, a catechism manuscript by the German reformer Joseph Johlson was denied publication in 1812 by the French Consistory's orthodox rabbinate because its "emphasis on the pluralistic nature of religion was dangerous for the young child." See *The Shaping of Jewish Identity in Nineteenth-Century France* (Detroit: Wayne State University Press, 1989), 188.
6. After finishing the first draft of this chapter in the summer of 2016, I took account of Kerstin von der Krone's project *Educating the "Man," the "Jew," and the "Citizen": Transformations in Social Norms and Values in Nineteenth-Century Jewish Educational Media* at the German Historical Institute in Washington, DC; see Kerstin von der Krone, "The Duty to Know: Nineteenth-Century Jewish Catechisms and Manuals and the Making of Jewish Religious Knowledge," in *History of Knowledge* (3 June 2018): https://historyofknowledge.net/2018/06/03/the-duty-to-know/; Kerstin von der Krone, "Old and New Orders of Knowledge in Modern Jewish History," in *Bulletin of the German Historical Institute* 59 (2016): 59–82.
7. See David Sorkin, *The Transformation of German Jewry, 1780–1840* (Detroit: Wayne State University Press, 1999).
8. Hans-Jürgen Fraas provides general information about catechisms. See "Katechismus," in *Theologische Realenzyklopädie*, ed. Gerhard Müller and Horst Balz

(Berlin: De Gruyter, 1988), 17:710–44. For Jewish catechisms, see Alexander Altmann "Articles of Faith," in *Encyclopaedia Judaica*, 2nd ed. (Detroit: Macmillan Reference USA, 2007), 2:529–32.

9. Moses Mendelssohn, *Jerusalem: A Treatise on Ecclesiastical Authority and Judaism* [1783], trans. M. Samuels (London: Longman, Orme, Brown and Longmans, 1838), 102.
10. Ibid., 103f.
11. See Leora Batnitzky, *How Judaism Became a Religion: An Introduction to Modern Jewish Thought* (Princeton, NJ: Princeton University Press, 2011), 20.
12. See the critique by Timothy Fitzgerald in *The Ideology of Religious Studies* (Oxford: Oxford University Press, 2000), 3–32.
13. See Jakob J. Petuchowski, "Manuals and Catechisms of the Jewish Religion in the Early Period of Emancipation," in *Studies in Nineteenth-Century Jewish Intellectual History*, ed. Alexander Altmann (Cambridge, MA: Harvard University Press, 1964), 53.
14. Erich Fromm, *Das jüdische Gesetz: Zur Soziologie des Diaspora-Judentums* [1922], in *Schriften aus dem Nachlass*, ed. Rainer Funk (Weinheim: Beltz, 1989), 2:27f. Translation and emphasis mine.
15. See David B. Ruderman, *Early Modern Jewry: A New Cultural History* (Princeton, NJ: Princeton University Press, 2011), 99–110.
16. Already prior to the publication of the *Shulḥan Arukh*, several abbreviated codes of law circulated, most importantly Moses Maimonides's *Mishneh Torah* (1170–80) and Jacob ben Asher's *Arba'ah Turim* (early fourteenth century).
17. See Jonathan I. Israel, *European Jewry in the Age of Mercantilism, 1550–1750* (Oxford: Oxford University Press, 1989), 5–34.
18. According to Mordechai Breuer, 10 percent of the Jewish population in German lands in the eighteenth century consisted of vagrants; in Franconia and Swabia, it was more than a quarter of the population. In addition to this large group of vagrants, the even larger group of mobile retailers, peddlers, students, and job-seeking maidservants crowded the roads of early modern Germany. See Breuer, "Frühe Neuzeit und Beginn der Moderne," in *Deutsch-jüdische Geschichte in der Neuzeit*, vol. 1, *1600–1780*, ed. Michael A. Meyer (Munich: C. H. Beck, 2000), 235. See also Robert Liberles, "On the Threshold of Modernity, 1618–1780," in *Jewish Daily Life in Germany, 1618–1945*, ed. Marion A. Kaplan (Oxford: Oxford University Press, 2005), 61–69.
19. See Yacov Guggenheim, "Von den Schalantjuden zu den Betteljuden: Jüdische Armut in Mitteleuropa in der Frühen Neuzeit," in *Juden und Armut in Mittel- und Osteuropa*, ed. Stefi Jersch-Wenzel (Cologne: Böhlau Verlag, 2000), 55–69.
20. Salomon Maimon, *Geschichte des eigenen Lebens* (1792; Berlin: Schocken, 1935), 130f.
21. For the development of *musar* literature in the eighteenth and nineteenth centuries, see Sorkin, *Transformation*, 45–56.
22. See David B. Ruderman, *Kabbalah, Magic, and Science: The Cultural Universe of a Sixteenth-Century Jewish Physician* (Cambridge, MA: Harvard University Press, 1988).
23. Gadi Luzzatto Voghera, "I catechismi ebraici fra Sette e Ottocento," in *Le religioni e il mondo moderno*, vol. 2, *Ebraismo*, ed. David Bidussa (Turin: Giulio Einaudi editore, 2008), 444; footnote 15 also refers to a Yiddish edition of the book *Mitsvot Nashim* (Commandments for Women), printed in Venice in 1552.

24. Quoted in Morris M. Faierstein, "Abraham Jagel's 'Leqah Tov' and its History," in *Jewish Quarterly Review* 89, nos. 3–4 (1999): 323.
25. Ibid., 321f.
26. Abraham ben Ḥenanyah Yagel, *Sefer lekaḥ tov* (Leipzig: Joh. Friedrich Richtern, 1694), 1. Translations from the Hebrew text are mine.
27. Ibid.
28. Ibid., 43.
29. Ibid., 53.
30. The Mishnah tractate Sotah (1:2), which is concerned with adultery, is anxious to limit the husband's power of control: "If he [the husband] says to her before two [witnesses]: 'Do not speak with a certain man,' and she speaks with him, she is still permitted to her household and permitted to eat *t'rumah* [if she is married to a priest]. If she meets with him secretly in a house and stays with him long enough to become impure [*tum'ah*], she is forbidden to her house and forbidden to eat *t'rumah*."
31. See Jean Baumgarten, "Amour et famille en Europe central (fin du Moyen Age–XVIIIe siècle)," in *La société juive à travers l'histoire*, vol. 2, *Les liens de l'Alliance*, ed. Shmuel Trigano (Paris: Fayard, 1992), 426–33.
32. See Jacob Katz, *Tradition and Crisis: Jewish Society and the End of the Middle Ages* (Syracuse, NY: Syracuse University Press, 2000), 123f. However, there was, of course, a difference between ideals and reality, as Andreas Gotzmann shows in his illuminating chapter, "Respectability Tested: Male Ideals, Sexuality, and Honor in Early Modern Ashkenazi Jewry," in *Jewish Masculinities: German Jews, Gender, and History*, ed. Benjamin Maria Baader, Sharon Gillerman, and Paul Lerner (Bloomington: Indiana University Press, 2012), 23–49.
33. Robert Jütte, *Leib und Leben im Judentum* (Berlin: Suhrkamp, 2016), 175f. The author mentions a popular prayer book for women from mid-seventeenth-century Amsterdam in Judeo-German, which explained gender difference through the physical constitution of male and female bodies.
34. See Merry E. Wiesner, *Women and Gender in Early Modern Europe* (Cambridge: Cambridge University Press, 2000), 102–42.
35. See Katz, *Tradition and Crisis*.
36. See Philipp Lenhard, *Volk oder Religion? Die Entstehung moderner jüdischer Ethnizität in Frankreich und Deutschland 1782–1848* (Göttingen: Vandenhoeck & Ruprecht, 2014), 93–114.
37. See Andreas Gotzmann, *Jüdisches Recht im kulturellen Prozess: Die Wahrnehmung der Halacha im Deutschland des 19. Jahrhunderts* (Tübingen: Mohr Siebeck, 1997).
38. See Mordechai Eliav, *Jüdische Erziehung in Deutschland im Zeitalter der Aufklärung und der Emanzipation* (Munich: Waxmann, 2001); Shmuel Feiner, "Erziehungsprogramme und gesellschaftliche Ideale im Wandel: Die Freischule in Berlin, 1778–1825," in *Jüdische Erziehung und aufklärerische Schulreform: Analysen zum späten 18. und frühen 19. Jahrhundert*, ed. Britta L. Behm, Uta Lohmann, and Ingrid Lohmann (Münster: Waxmann, 2002), 69–105; Dirk Sadowski, *Haskala und Lebenswelt: Herz Homberg und die jüdischen deutschen Schulen in Galizien 1782–1806* (Göttingen: Vandenhoeck & Ruprecht, 2010), 167–204.
39. Petuchowski, *Manuals and Catechisms*, 48.
40. See Shmuel Feiner, *The Origins of Jewish Secularization in Eighteenth-Century Europe*, trans. Chaya Naor (Philadelphia: University of Pennsylvania Press, 2011), 219.

41. George Y. Kohler, ed., *Der jüdische Messianismus im Zeitalter der Emanzipation: Reinterpretationen zwischen davidischem Königtum und endzeitlichem Sozialismus* (Berlin: De Gruyter, 2014), 97n1.
42. Herz Homberg, *Bene Zion: Libro d'istruzione religioso-morale per la gioventù Israelitica del regno Lombardo-Veneto* (Venice: Giuseppe Molinari, 1828); Herz Homberg, *"Bne-Zion": Figli di Sion; Libro d'istruzione morale e religiosa per la gioventù della nazione israelita* (Trieste: Gasparo Weis, 1815).
43. From 1783 to 1784, Herz Homberg served as a teacher at the Jewish school in Trieste. For his biography, see Rachel Manekin, "Naphtali Herz Homberg: Ha-d'mut ve-ha-dimui" [The Personality and the Image], in *Zion* 71, no. 2 (2006): 153–202.
44. See Philipp Lenhard and Martina Niedhammer, "'Ohne Bewilligung': Vorgeschichte, Funktion und Auswirkungen der Judenmatrikel in Bayern (1813–1861) und der Familiantengesetze in den böhmischen Ländern (1726/27–1859)," in *Tschechien und Bayern: Gegenüberstellungen und Vergleiche vom Mittelalter bis zur Gegenwart*, ed. Milan Hlavačka, Robert Luft, and Ulrike Lunow (Munich: Collegium Carolinum, 2016), 145f.
45. Herz Homberg, *Bne-Zion: Ein religiös-moralisches Lehrbuch für die Jugend israelitischer Nation* (Vienna: K. k. Schulbücher-Verschleiß bey St. Anna, 1812), 156.
46. See Edward T. Potter, *Marriage, Gender, and Desire in Early Enlightenment Comedy* (Rochester, NY: Boydell & Brewer, 2012), 15–35.
47. Ketubbah between Feiks ben Yekel Levi and Keila bat Eisik Orchel, Cheschvan 13, 5542 (1 November 1781). AD Moselle 17 J 9, No. 68. Published in Pierre-André Meyer *Die jüdische Gemeinde von Metz im 18. Jahrhundert: Geschichte und Demographie* (Trier: Kliomedia, 2012), 445.
48. Homberg, *Bne-Zion*, 157.
49. Ibid., 160.
50. Moses Büdinger, *Moreh la-torah. Oder: Leitfaden bei dem Unterrichte in der israelitischen Religion, für Knaben und Mädchen, in Schulen und beim Privatunterrichte* (Kassel: Johann Christian Krieger, 1837), 68.
51. Joseph Albo, *Sefer Ikkarim. Grund- und Glaubenslehren der Mosaischen Religion* [Soncino 1485], ed. Wolf Schlessinger and Ludwig Schlesinger (Frankfurt am Main: s.n., 1844), 222.
52. Ibid., 400.
53. Samuel Hirsch, *Systematischer Katechismus der israelitischen Religion* (Luxemburg: V. Bück, 1856), 42.
54. "Cultur des religiösen Gefühls durch die Mutter," in *Der treue Zions-Wächter* 33 (17 August 1847): 265.
55. Ibid., 266.
56. "Cultur des religiösen Gefühls durch die Mutter," in *Der treue Zions-Wächter* 34 (24 August 1847): 274.
57. Eduard Kley, *Edut Adonai: Catechismus der mosaischen Religionslehre* (Leipzig: Voigt, 1840), 53.
58. Ibid., 133. Emphasis mine.
59. See, for example, Michael Aron Arnheim, *Leitfaden beim Unterricht in der mosaischen Religion zunächst für die Elementarschule in Glogau* (Głogów: C. Heymann, 1829), 29.
60. Markus Beer Friedenthal, "Die Würde der Frauen," in *Vermischte Aufsätze religiösen Inhalts* (Breslau: Schulz, 1841), 153. The chapter is based on a translation of a book by Wolfgang Menzel.

61. Although the Mishnah tractate Ketubbot (5:5) states, "These are the [kinds of] work which the woman [is obliged to] do for her husband. She grinds, and bakes, and washes [clothes]. She cooks, and nurses her child. She makes his bed, and works with wool," women were actually quite active in many businesses outside the household in the medieval and especially in the early modern periods. It is interesting to note that the Gemara contrasts the Mishnaic ideal of a working woman with Rabbi Ḥiyya's teaching that a "wife is only for beauty, and a wife is only for children, but not for household tasks." BT Ketubbot 59b.
62. Avraham Grossmann, *Pious and Rebellious: Jewish Women in Medieval Europe* (Hanover, NH: University Press of New England, 2004), 274f.
63. Glückel of Hameln, *The Memoirs of Glückel of Hameln*, trans. Marvin Lowenthal (New York: Schocken, 1977).
64. See Stefanie Schüler-Springorum, *Geschlecht und Differenz* (Paderborn: Ferdinand Schöningh, 2014), 13–15.
65. Hirsch, *Systematischer Katechismus*, i.
66. This is a reference to Mishnah Ketubbot 5:5.
67. Michael Aron Arnheim, *Leitfaden beim Unterricht in der mosaischen Religion zunächst für die Elementarschule in Glogau* (Glogów: C. Heymann, 1829), 29. See also Leopold Lammfromm, *Katechismus über die nothwendigsten Glauben- und Sittenlehren der biblisch-mosaischen Religion für die Mittelclassen der israelitischen Schulen* (Blaubeuren: Lubrecht, 1848), 48, and its emphasis on "diligence, modesty, and respectable manners."
68. Concerning the figure of the *ḥasid* in ancient and medieval Judaism, see the brief summary by Susanne Talabardon, *Chassidismus* (Tübingen: UTB, 2016), 17–28. For sexuality in the Ḥasidic movement, see David Biale, "The Lust for Asceticism in the Hasidic Movement," in *Jewish Explorations of Sexuality*, ed. Jonathan Magonet (New York: Berghahn Books, 1995), 51–64.
69. The latter book appeared in at least thirteen editions, including an Italian translation (Venice, 1616). See Marvin J. Heller, ed., *The Seventeenth Century Hebrew Book: An Abridged Thesaurus* (Leiden: Brill, 2011), 89.
70. Ya'akov ben Yitzḥak (Ashkenazi), *Tse'enah u-Re'enah Benot Tsiyon* (Sulzbach: s.n., 1798). See Simon Neuberg, "Ze'ena u-Re'ena," in *Enzyklopädie jüdischer Geschichte und Kultur*, ed. Dan Diner (Stuttgart: J. B. Metzler, 2015), 6:500–503.
71. David Friedländer, *Lesebuch für jüdische Kinder* (Berlin: Voss 1779), 9–13; 22–25.
72. Ibid., 34.
73. Ibid., 27.
74. See Britta L. Behm, "Moses Mendelssohns Beziehungen zur Berliner jüdischen Freischule zwischen 1778 und 1786: Eine exemplarische Analyse zu Mendelssohns Stellung in der Haskala," in Behm et al., *Jüdische Erziehung und aufklärerische Schulreform*, 128f.
75. Mishnah Sotah 3:4. In the original text, it doesn't say "female gender" (*weibliches Geschlecht*) but rather *bito* (his daughter).
76. Salomon Plessner, *Dat Moshe we-Jehudit oder jüdisch-mosaischer Religionsunterricht für die israelitische Jugend* (Berlin: L. Fernbach, 1838), xi–xii. It is quite telling that the word *dat*, which in modern Hebrew is used as the word for "religion," originally meant "legal prescription" in biblical Hebrew.
77. Judah ben Samuel he-Ḥassid, *Sefer ha-Ḥassidim* (Basel: Ambrosio Provinio, 1581), fol. 39b.

78. Eduard Altschul, "Foreword," in *Benot Zion: Ein moralisches Unterhaltungsbuch für Israels Söhne und Töchter*, ed. Hermann Engländer (Vienna: Anton Edler von Schmid, 1828), 1.
79. Ibid.
80. Ibid.
81. Ibid.
82. Ibid.

Bibliography

Albo, Joseph. *Sefer Ikkarim: Grund- und Glaubenslehren der Mosaischen Religion* [Soncino 1485]. Edited by Wolf Schlessinger and Ludwig Schlesinger. Frankfurt: s.n., 1844.
Altmann, Alexander. "Articles of Faith." In *Encyclopaedia Judaica*. 2nd ed. Vol. 2. Detroit: Macmillan Reference USA, 2007.
Altschul, Eduard. "Foreword." In *Benot Zion: Ein moralisches Unterhaltungsbuch für Israels Söhne und Töchter*, edited by Hermann Engländer. Vienna: Anton Edler von Schmid, 1828.
Arnheim, Michael Aron. *Leitfaden beim Unterricht in der mosaischen Religion zunächst für die Elementarschule in Glogau*. Głogów: C. Heymann, 1829.
Aschheim, Steven E. *Brothers and Strangers: The East European Jew in German and German Jewish Consciousness, 1800–1923*. Madison: University of Wisconsin Press, 1982.
Baader, Benjamin Maria. *Gender, Judaism, and Bourgeois Culture in Germany, 1800–1870*. Bloomington: Indiana University Press, 2006.
Batnitzky, Leora. *How Judaism Became a Religion: An Introduction to Modern Jewish Thought*. Princeton: Princeton University Press, 2011.
Baumgarten, Jean. "Amour et famille en Europe central (fin du Moyen Age–XVIIIe siècle)." In *La société juive à travers l'histoire*. Vol. 2: *Les liens de l'Alliance*, edited by Shmuel Trigano, 413–33. Paris: Fayard, 1992.
Behm, Britta L. "Moses Mendelssohns Beziehungen zur Berliner jüdischen Freischule zwischen 1778 und 1786: Eine exemplarische Analyse zu Mendelssohns Stellung in der Haskala." In *Jüdische Erziehung und aufklärerische Schulreform: Analysen zum späten 18. und frühen 19. Jahrhundert*, edited by Britta L. Behm, Uta Lohmann, and Ingrid Lohmann, 107–135. Munich: Waxmann, 2002.
Berkovitz, Jay R. *The Shaping of Jewish Identity in Nineteenth-Century France*. Detroit: Wayne State University Press, 1989.
Biale, David. "The Lust for Asceticism in the Hasidic Movement." In *Jewish Explorations of Sexuality*, edited by Jonathan Magonet, 51–64. New York: Berghahn Books 1995.
Breuer, Mordechai. "Frühe Neuzeit und Beginn der Moderne." In *Deutsch-jüdische Geschichte in der Neuzeit*. Vol. 1: *1600–1780*, edited by Michael A. Meyer, 85–247. Munich: C. H. Beck, 2000.
Büdinger, Moses. *Moreh la-torah. Oder: Leitfaden bei dem Unterrichte in der israelitischen Religion, für Knaben und Mädchen, in Schulen und beim Privatunterrichte*. Kassel: Johann Christian Krieger, 1837.

Dan, Joseph. *Sifrut ha-Musar ve-ha-Derush* [Ethical and Homiletical Literature]. Jerusalem: Keter, 1975.

Eliav, Mordechai. *Jüdische Erziehung in Deutschland im Zeitalter der Aufklärung und der Emanzipation*. Munich: Waxmann, 2001.

Faierstein, Morris M. "Abraham Jagel's 'Leqah Tov' and Its History." In *Jewish Quarterly Review* 89, nos. 3–4 (1999): 319–50.

Feiner, Shmuel. "Erziehungsprogramme und gesellschaftliche Ideale im Wandel: Die Freischule in Berlin, 1778–1825." In *Jüdische Erziehung und aufklärerische Schulreform: Analysen zum späten 18. und frühen 19. Jahrhundert*, edited by Britta L. Behm, Uta Lohmann, and Ingrid Lohmann, 69–105. Munich: Waxmann, 2002.

———. *The Origins of Jewish Secularization in Eighteenth-Century Europe*. Translated by Chaya Naor. Philadelphia: University of Pennsylvania Press, 2011.

Fitzgerald, Timothy. *The Ideology of Religious Studies*. Oxford: Oxford University Press, 2000.

Fraas, Hans-Jürgen. "Katechismus." In *Theologische Realenzyklopädie*, edited by Gerhard Müller and Horst Balz, 17:710–44. Berlin: De Gruyter, 1988.

Friedenthal, Markus Beer. "Die Würde der Frauen." In *Vermischte Aufsätze religiösen Inhalts*, 3:151–56. Breslau: Schulz, 1841.

Friedländer, David. *Lesebuch für jüdische Kinder*. Berlin: Voss, 1779.

Fromm, Erich. *Das jüdische Gesetz: Zur Soziologie des Diaspora-Judentums*. 1922. In *Schriften aus dem Nachlas*, edited by Rainer Funk, vol. 2. Weinheim: Beltz, 1989.

Geiger, Abraham. "Die Stellung des weiblichen Geschlechtes in dem Judenthume unserer Zeit." In *Wissenschaftliche Zeitschrift für jüdische Theologie* 1 (1837): 1–14.

Glückel of Hameln. *The Memoirs of Glückel of Hameln*. Translated by Marvin Lowenthal. New York: Schocken, 1977.

Gotzmann, Andreas. *Jüdisches Recht im kulturellen Prozess: Die Wahrnehmung der Halacha im Deutschland des 19. Jahrhunderts*. Tübingen: Mohr Siebeck, 1997.

———. "Respectability Tested: Male Ideals, Sexuality, and Honor in Early Modern Ashkenazi Jewry." In *Jewish Masculinities: German Jews, Gender, and History*, edited by Benjamin Maria Baader, Sharon Gillerman, and Paul Lerner, 23–49. Bloomington: Indiana University Press, 2012.

Grossmann, Avraham. *Pious and Rebellious: Jewish Women in Medieval Europe*. Translated by Jonathan Chipman. Hanover, NH: University Press of New England, 2004.

Guggenheim, Yacov. "Von den Schalantjuden zu den Betteljuden: Jüdische Armut in Mitteleuropa in der Frühen Neuzeit." In *Juden und Armut in Mittel- und Osteuropa*, edited by Stefi Jersch-Wenzel, 55–69. Cologne: Böhlau, 2000.

Heller, Marvin J., ed. *The Seventeenth Century Hebrew Book: An Abridged Thesaurus*. Leiden: Brill, 2011.

Hirsch, Samson Raphael. "Das jüdische Weib." 1863. In *Gesammelte Schriften*. Vol. 4, edited by Naphtali Hirsch, 160–208. Frankfurt: J. Kauffmann, 1908.

Hirsch, Samuel. *Systematischer Katechismus der israelitischen Religion*. Luxemburg: V. Bück, 1856.

Homberg, Herz. *Bene Zion: Libro d'istruzione religioso-morale per la gioventù Israelitica del regno Lombardo-Veneto*. Venice: Giuseppe Molinari, 1828.

———. *Bne-Zion: Ein religiös-moralisches Lehrbuch für die Jugend israelitischer Nation*. Vienna: K. k. Schulbücher-Verschleiß bey St. Anna, 1812.

———. *"Bne-Zion": Figli di Sion; Libro d'istruzione morale e religiosa per la gioventù della nazione israelita*. Trieste: Gasparo Weis, 1815.

Israel, Jonathan Irvine. *European Jewry in the Age of Mercantilism, 1550–1750*. Oxford: Oxford University Press, 1989.
Judah ben Samuel he-Ḥassid. *Sefer ha-Ḥassidim*. Basel: Ambrosio Provinio, 1581.
Jütte, Robert. *Leib und Leben im Judentum*. Berlin: Suhrkamp, 2016.
Katz, Jacob. *Tradition and Crisis: Jewish Society and the End of the Middle Ages*. Syracuse, NY: Syracuse University Press, 2000.
Kley, Eduard. *Edut Adonai: Catechismus der mosaischen Religionslehre*. Leipzig: Voigt, 1840.
Kohler, George Y., ed. *Der jüdische Messianismus im Zeitalter der Emanzipation: Reinterpretationen zwischen davidischem Königtum und endzeitlichem Sozialismus*. Berlin: De Gruyter, 2014.
Lammfromm, Leopold. *Katechismus über die nothwendigsten Glauben- und Sittenlehren der biblisch-mosaischen Religion für die Mittelclassen der israelitischen Schulen*. Blaubeuren: Lubrecht, 1848.
Lenhard, Philipp. *Volk oder Religion? Die Entstehung moderner jüdischer Ethnizität in Frankreich und Deutschland 1782–1848*. Göttingen: Vandenhoeck & Ruprecht, 2014.
Lenhard, Philipp, and Martina Niedhammer. "'Ohne Bewilligung': Vorgeschichte, Funktion und Auswirkungen der Judenmatrikel in Bayern (1813–1861) und der Familiantengesetze in den böhmischen Ländern (1726/27–1859)." In *Tschechien und Bayern: Gegenüberstellungen und Vergleiche vom Mittelalter bis zur Gegenwart*, edited by Milan Hlavačka, Robert Luft, and Ulrike Lunow, 131–49. Munich: Collegium Carolinum, 2016.
Liberles, Robert. "On the Threshold of Modernity, 1618–1780." In *Jewish Daily Life in Germany, 1618–1945*, edited by Marion A. Kaplan, 9–92. Oxford: Oxford University Press, 2005.
Luzzatto Voghera, Gadi. "I catechismi ebraici fra Sette e Ottocento." In *Le religioni e il mondo modern*. Vol. 2: *Ebraismo*, edited by David Bidussa, 437–55. Turin: Giulio Einaudi editore, 2008.
Maimon, Salomon. *Geschichte des eigenen Lebens*. 1792. Berlin: Schocken, 1935.
Manekin, Rachel. "Naphtali Herz Homberg: Ha-d'mut ve-ha-dimui" [The Personality and the Image]. In *Zion* 71, no. 2 (2006): 153–202.
Mendelssohn, Moses. *Jerusalem: A Treatise on Ecclesiastical Authority and Judaism*. 1783. Translated by M. Samuels. London: Longman, Orme, Brown and Longmans, 1838.
Meyer, Michael A. *Response to Modernity: A History of the Reform Movement*. Oxford: Oxford University Press, 1988.
Meyer, Pierre-André. *Die jüdische Gemeinde von Metz im 18. Jahrhundert: Geschichte und Demographie*. Translated by Rainer Prass. Trier: Kliomedia, 2012.
Neuberg, Simon. "Ze'ena u-Re'ena." In *Enzyklopädie jüdischer Geschichte und Kultur*, edited by Dan Diner, 6:500–503. Stuttgart: J. B. Metzler, 2015.
Petuchowski, Jakob J. "Manuals and Catechisms of the Jewish Religion in the Early Period of Emancipation." In *Studies in Nineteenth-Century Jewish Intellectual History*, edited by Alexander Altmann, 47–64. Cambridge, MA: Harvard University Press, 1964.
Plessner, Salomon. *Dat Moshe we-Jehudit oder jüdisch-mosaischer Religionsunterricht für die israelitische Jugend*. Berlin: L. Fernbach, 1838.
Potter, Edward T. *Marriage, Gender, and Desire in Early Enlightenment Comedy*. Rochester, NY: Boydell & Brewer, 2012.

R.-R. "Cultur des religiösen Gefühls durch die Mutter." In *Der treue Zions-Wächter* 33 (17 August 1847): 265–67.
———. "Cultur des religiösen Gefühls durch die Mutter." In *Der treue Zions-Wächter* 34 (24 August 1847): 274f.
Ruderman, David B. *Kabbalah, Magic, and Science: The Cultural Universe of a Sixteenth-Century Jewish Physician*. Cambridge, MA: Harvard University Press, 1988.
———. *Early Modern Jewry: A New Cultural History*. Princeton, NJ: Princeton University Press, 2011.
Sadowski, Dirk. *Haskala und Lebenswelt: Herz Homberg und die jüdischen deutschen Schulen in Galizien 1782–1806*. Göttingen: Vandenhoeck & Ruprecht, 2010.
Schüler-Springorum, Stefanie. *Geschlecht und Differenz*. Paderborn: Ferdinand Schöningh, 2014.
Sorkin, David. *The Transformation of German Jewry, 1780–1840*. Detroit: Wayne State University Press, 1999.
Talabardon, Susanne. *Chassidismus*. Tübingen: UTB, 2016.
von der Krone, Kerstin. "Old and New Orders of Knowledge in Modern Jewish History." In *Bulletin of the German Historical Institute* 59 (2016): 59–82.
———. "The Duty to Know: Nineteenth-Century Jewish Catechisms and Manuals and the Making of Jewish Religious Knowledge." in *History of Knowledge* (June 3, 2018), https://historyofknowledge.net/2018/06/03/the-duty-to-know/.
Wiesner, Merry E. *Women and Gender in Early Modern Europe*. Cambridge: Cambridge University Press, 2000.
Ya'akov ben Yitzḥak (Ashkenazi). *Tse'enah u-Re'enah Benot Tsiyon*. Sulzbach: s.n., 1798.
Yagel, Abraham ben Ḥenanyah. *Sefer lekaḥ tov*. Leipzig: Joh. Friedrich Richtern, 1694.

Chapter 7

The Transformation of Jewish Education in Nineteenth-Century Italy
The Meaning of "Catechisms"

Silvia Guetta

The nineteenth century was a time of great political, social, cultural, and religious changes for the Italian peninsula. This chapter explores and traces the myriad ways in which these general societal changes had an impact on Jewish education. First, this was the time of the unification of the Italian states into the nation of Italy, a process known as the Risorgimento. In addition, the region underwent economic and industrial development in certain areas during this century. The power of the Catholic Church declined, and the bourgeois class grew stronger. In the last quarter of the century, the first phase of Italian emigration to the United States began. This was also the time during which the process of emancipation for Italy's non-Catholic minorities (namely Protestants and Jews), which had tentatively begun in the eighteenth century, came to fruition. In this context, "emancipation" refers to a complex social, cultural, and political movement, which involved the granting of civil rights to previously disempowered groups. Emancipation affected multiple arenas of activity, including education and training. Emancipation changed the social bonds between majority and minority groups, many of which had existed for centuries. Every individual, community, and social group in Italy was affected. They all strove, from the perspective of their traditions, experiences, conditions, and convictions, to adapt to and embrace these rapid and significant changes.

Representatives of Jewish and Protestant communities of the pre-unification Italian states played leading roles in, and significantly contributed to, the process of emancipation and the recognition of civil rights for religious minorities,[1] although this is not always recognized in the historiography of pedagogy.² For Italian Jews, the granting of citizenship rights finally enabled them to live in a condition of social equality. As the governments of pre-unification states that supported the recognition of Jews' civil rights became more tolerant, new and stronger types of bonds, control, and dependency were created. Within a few decades, the geographical distribution of the Italian-Jewish population shifted, as Jews were able to move out of the ghettos to which they had been confined (with the exception of the Jewish community in Livorno) since the sixteenth century.

Furthermore, emancipation resulted in changes to the Jewish community's traditional patterns of thought, behaviors, and values. In the ghettos, the Italian-Jewish communities had developed an internal legislative system, which ensured a fair standard of living and focused strongly on educational and cultural continuity for the younger generations. The end of the era of ghettos, according to the historiography, was divided into two phases. The first took place in the late eighteenth century, reflecting the values espoused by the French Revolution and reinforced by the presence of Napoleon in Italy. The second, a profoundly and completely Italian phase, was generated by King Charles Albert of Sardinia's granting civil rights to the Jews of Piedmont-Sardinia. This gave the Italian-Jewish community the opportunity to participate in the cause of the Risorgimento and to enter fully into the sphere of political and social debate.

This emancipation process, which began in some European states at the end of the eighteenth century, affected complex issues regarding the relations between minority and majority cultures and within the minority communities themselves. The granting of equal civil rights was founded on the assumption that individuals belonged to a minority religion only as individuals, not as a community or nation, a perspective made explicit in the words of the French politician Stanislas Marie Adélaïde, Comte de Clermont-Tonnerre: "We must refuse everything to the Jews as a nation and accord everything to Jews as individuals. . . . They should not be allowed to form in the state either a political body or an order. They must be citizens individually."³ Clermont-Tonnerre's statement highlights some of the relevant aspects of the relations created between the postrevolutionary French state and the Jews. Namely, these relations required organizational change within the Jewish communities, acceptance of changed relations of power and social control, and acceptance of the "regeneration" process that implicitly meant confirming prejudices and stereotypes about Jews created by the Church over the course of many centuries.

The Jews of Europe in general and of Italy in particular desired the relatively more positive social and political status created by emancipation, as well as recognition for their social, economic, and cultural contributions. However, integration into the mainstream culture and elimination of distinctive subgroups within the dominant society caused a deterioration of Jewish identity and self-image and a "narrowing" of the complex cultural traditions that had been followed by previous generations. As required by the Catholic majority, Judaism was considered only a religious practice rather than a primary social and cultural reference point.

Thus, emancipation did not only mean easing oppression and marginalization. As Monica Miniati notes, "Judaism had the difficult task of rethinking and redefining its own role and spaces in the individuals' lives, as well as recreating a new balance between tradition and modernization during the emancipation process that would inevitably affect the main structures of reference and support of basic community life institutions as synagogue, school and family, changing its functions and contents."[4] Hidden behind the states' self-professed enlightenment and tolerance and the granting of rights was the implicit request that Jews give up their distinctive culture. They were expected to "abandon part of those 'anti-social' activities linked to religious precepts, quit some of the occupations classified as unproductive and immoral such as lending money and small business (both coming from the ghetto economy), and eventually urged to undertake permanent religious conversion and align themselves with Christian society."[5]

The Jewish communities of Italy reflected the general fervor for emancipation and the Risorgimento by redesigning the characteristics of the Italian-Jewish reality. This reality, due to its diverse history, gave rise to a multitraditional, articulated reference framework that could be seen more as a variety of positions and interpretations than as a monolithic and monochromatic representation.[6] The most internal processes of acculturation and identification were profoundly affected. The link between emancipation and integration rapidly caused widespread Jewish deculturation, accompanied by acculturation into the dominant Italian society. This significantly affected the content and style of Jews' cultural education in newly united Italy.

Jewish Perceptions of Emancipation

How the Jews of nineteenth-century Italy perceived the changes and challenges of this new era can be read firsthand in the numerous journals and periodicals the community published throughout the second half of the nineteenth century. In these publications, Italian-Jewish writers debated the merits and dangers of the possibilities and options opening up to them in the new era. They testify to the wide range of opinions that existed on emancipation in general and on related educational issues in particular. Important insights into the process of transformation and how it affected

Italian Jews in terms of education and Jewish instruction can be culled from these publications.

The publications that provided the greatest contributions to the cultural renewal of Judaism in the nineteenth century were *L'Educatore Israelita*, published between 1853 and 1876 in Vercelli, and its successor, *Il Vessillo Israelitico*, published in Casale Monferrato between 1876 and 1922.[7] These publications shared the same agenda, namely focusing on "the defense of the faith and of education, teaching Jewish history and literature, by means of articles of a prevalently popular level, providing news on Jewish life in Italy and abroad."[8] Around the beginning of the 1860s, the *Corriere Israelitico* was founded in Trieste, which aimed at publicizing Jewish and non-Jewish history and literature as broadly and completely as possible. The journal promoted the basic tenets and values of Jewish tradition. In 1915, the publication merged with the Florentine *La Settimana Israelitica*, a Zionist journal aimed at cultural renewal, which eventually became the newspaper *Israel*. During the same time period (1904–15), *La Rivista Israelitica* examined "the science and life of Judaism."

When reading the journals, one can perceive the ways in which Italian Judaism was attempting to find a new identity. The articles convey the reaction to an end to centuries of oppression; the appreciation of the new enjoyment of elementary rights by any individual, which was, however, most novel of all for Jews; the attraction exercised by Italian culture and history, which by then were much more easily available to the individual than before; and last but not least, the ambition for personal success—never before experienced—all of which speedily dismembered what had hitherto been the compact body of Italian Judaism. The result was the emergence of a large number of Jews who were isolated from their traditional communities and now felt lukewarm about their ancient ideal values.[9]

In 1860, the codirector of *L'Educatore Israelita*, Giuseppe Levi, attempted to define the condition of Jews in the past and in the present:

> In a world, from which hitherto Jews had been debarred, the ancient Jewish world is slowly falling apart and disappearing. . . . Thought is no longer content to graze in its accustomed pastures; our heart no longer beats to the ancient rhythms. Present and future assume different colors, as Jews have fallen greedily on this new field that has been opened to them. They want to drink from those waters and be warmed by this new sun. They want to experience this life and be inspired by those affections and passions, which constantly animate it . . . this is the supreme duty, the supreme need of present Jews. They must explain to themselves the true essence of their faith, unchanged by the insecure requirements of an age or of a country, but severed and distinct from the nationality that ancient circumstances used to legitimize. It was thus that exile and pain became teachers of faith for our forefathers. Now, however, that these terrible instructors have been removed, Jews must replace them with another intelligent, noble, and efficacious one. Without

this being done promptly, our young people, who do not want, nor are able to imbibe instruction from another strong source, would grow up, not as representatives of faith, but of the Jewish name. Faith would be left as a shadow, rather than a substance, a name replaced by a thing.[10]

Social Transformation and Educational Questions

Beginning in the early 1800s, pedagogic and educational activities were linked to the sociopolitical transformation of the pre-unification states, especially those in the northern and central parts of the region, as compared with the central zone, which was governed by the Vatican State. The fall of the Ancien Régime, the strengthening of the middle class, and increased industrialization initiated a process of "regeneration" for the Italian population, albeit belatedly compared to other parts of Europe. In terms of education, new school policies were developed with the goal of accelerating acculturation and training processes useful in constructing a unified state. Following the Risorgimento, pedagogues and enlightened educators outlined initiatives and reform projects. One broad goal was to address the issue of illiteracy, which was considered by liberal policymakers to be a major obstacle to development. The Casati Law of 1859 required two years of primary school education. The Coppino Law of 1877 increased compulsory education to four years and standardized curricula and regulations for public and private schools. Further, a rich dialogue on education, curriculum contents, and educational ideology was launched.[11]

The building of an Italian school system also affected the Jewish community. Education represented a key element for the study of the Jewish tradition in all its complexity. Thus, while civil society was debating the controversial matter of public education, the Jewish community redrafted its educational system and developed suitable programs and materials in light of this newly compulsory education.[12] Jewish schools revised and drafted curricula on subjects made mandatory by the new education laws, also doing so in light of the Church's positions on education. Notably, we see the creation of "Jewish catechisms." These pedagogic tools were simple, easy to read and comprehend, and particularly appropriate for educating young Jews on their new position as emancipated Italian citizens of Jewish faith.

As history clearly shows, individuals and groups need to change fundamentally the way they see themselves and others for emancipation to be fully achieved. This is strongly linked to public education. Changing the law is not sufficient to suppress prejudices or overturn the social exclusion and subjugation developed during centuries of separation and violence. For emancipation to succeed, it must be a priority to invest in reeducating all the groups involved—the majority culture and minority groups. Clear and transparent reconciliation activity is necessary. Therefore, it is impossible to separate reflection on the history of social processes of emancipation from analysis of its effects on education and schooling.[13] "Man is educated partly by himself, partly by domestic society . . ., partly by civil society, and finally partly by theocratic (religious) society," wrote Antonio Rosmini Serbati, an Italian Catholic priest and philosopher, in the first decades of the nineteenth century, predicting the mutual influence and close connections between education, society, culture, and history.[14]

In nineteenth-century Italy, the Jewish world was trying to discover how to provide younger generations with a Jewish education suitable for an Italian citizen. As Giuseppe Levi put it in 1860 in *L'Educatore Israelita*,

> There are two great schools for mankind: the family and society. It would perhaps be folly to measure their strengths and functions separately, encompassing exactly the confines of each. . . . Thus, without attempting any system, and describing their parts from their most important and efficacious aspects, I shall say that the mind is formed in the scholastic and practical societies, whereas the heart is shaped in the family.[15]

The idealization of the family led to the hope that it should continue to exist, in accordance with the teachings of the Jewish tradition, as a source of morality and faith. Parents were entrusted with the creation of a home as a "holy" place in which Jewish instruction could be steadily delivered to their children, even in times of change and in a society that had only recently opened its gates to them. As the periodicals and journals of the time stressed, a mere reminder of duties and obligations would be insufficient. Rather, "a practical treatise, describing the details of the domestic and religious life of a Jewish family should be created, to be used as a mirror and secure set of rules."[16] According to this view, a proper Jewish education had to abstain from any pre-defined formula and from any form of catechizing instruction. Some of those in favor of strengthening Jewish education were opposed to this approach, instead preferring presentation of prescribed religious disciplinary dogmas without promoting any inducement to personal study and interpretation. However, as will be shown, some rabbis from the beginning of the nineteenth century on started to publish textbooks promoting more modern concepts.[17]

The debate on how to preserve Jewish educational models was also promoted by the gradual departure from traditional centers of Jewish life. As families moved from ghettos to more comfortable residential areas, they also left behind the places in which the Jewish community provided instruction. From the second half of the nineteenth century on, the number of Jewish children in state schools increased considerably, and they came from families that were wealthy enough to move out of the ghettos.

In this way, Jewish community schools were left chiefly with the poorest children, whose families did not move. This led to a progressive decline in these schools and in the quality of teaching provided in them.[18]

At the same time, the journals drew alarmed attention to the education delivered in state schools and how it contravened or breached Jewish morals. They condemned improper behavior affecting Jewish pupils and rebuked parents for having failed to take responsibility for the supervision and protection of their children. The heaviest criticisms were directed at the instruction during the class hours dedicated to teaching the Catholic religion. According to the Casati Law of 1859 and Coppino Law of 1877, study of the Catholic religion was not compulsory for children of other faiths. The Casati Law envisaged compulsory religious instruction in state schools but allowed pupils professing another religion to obtain dispensation from these classes. The Coppino Law removed religious instruction from the list of compulsory subjects, replacing it with article 2, "the study of the initial notions regarding the duties of man and citizen."

Nonetheless, critical outbursts, indignation, and alarm are apparent in the Jewish journals of the period. In the words of one contributor to *L'Educatore Israelita*,

> There are such grave and widespread disgraceful occurrences in state educational institutions, and complaints are so justified and extensive, that one must have lost the last tittle of common sense, to leave things as they are. While these complaints are justified, is it not also true that the fault lies partly with the fathers of the families? As regards religious instruction, if one so desires, the firm wishes of the parents could prevent so many disgraceful episodes from occurring.[19]

The Necessity of Jewish Catechisms

Italian-Jewish families wanted to provide their children with the kind of instruction that would prepare them to cope successfully with the latest opportunities and developments made possible by social integration. At the same time, they wanted to preserve their Jewish identity and customs. Jewish schools faced the need for a profound change in order to coexist with the state schools, which were now an option for Jewish pupils. Unfortunately, lack of economic and educational investment in the school system prevented them from accomplishing this transformation, and throughout the nineteenth century, schools in the Jewish communities underwent a period of gradual decline in terms both of numbers of students and of quality of education. Nevertheless, much can be learned from examining the Jewish community's attempts to navigate their new reality.

Influenced by recent educational policies and legislation, Jewish schools began to modify their curricula and introduce secular subjects considered essential in preparing a Jewish student to be a good Italian citizen. The introduction of secular disciplines and the consequent reduction of time devoted to the teaching of Jewish subjects led to a deterioration and simplification of the contents of both. New teaching instruments were developed in order to impart the fundamentals of Judaism while conforming to the pedagogic model adopted by the prevailing educational system and the dominant paradigm of Catholic religious education. These may be called "Jewish catechisms." The first "Jewish catechism," arguably, was published in the sixteenth century in Venice by Abraham Jagel de Gallichi, based on the thirteen articles of faith delineated by Maimonides.[20]

In the Catholic world, catechisms are a method of religious education consisting of a set of questions with fixed answers. Their aim is religious indoctrination and memorization of the Catholic creed. Knowledge of the catechism is required for one to be recognized as a member of the Catholic community. In contrast, knowledge of Jewish tradition is not a matter of simply absorbing a few axioms or principles learned by heart as a child. Rather, knowledge is built up gradually throughout one's life. To gain full acceptance in the community, one must demonstrate competence in reading, singing, and interpretation of numerous texts.

Jewish catechisms were formulated to facilitate basic knowledge of the Jewish religion. The birth and spread of Jewish catechisms represented an attempt to apply a new, socially accepted teaching instrument to Jewish disciplines while serving as a counterpart to the Catholic catechism. In fact, the proposed catechisms could not easily be adapted to the teaching of the corpus of Jewish disciplines usually taught in the schools, which consisted of the Bible, Hebrew language, Jewish history, duties of Jewish life, Jewish holidays, and liturgical blessings. These subjects were distinct yet integrated. For example, knowledge of the Hebrew language is necessary to read biblical texts, and knowledge of biblical texts is essential to understanding the history of the Jewish people.

In the Jewish periodicals, the community discussed, with considerable imagination and curiosity, the best and most efficient methods for ensuring a solid and lasting acquisition of all these subjects, especially Hebrew. Rabbis published educational theories that reflected the trends of the time. For example, in 1862, the chief rabbi of Ferrara, Isacco Ascoli, published a three-hundred-page manual that included a historical summary of the Hebrew language, a grammar, a dictionary, a thesaurus, and collections of Jewish sayings and Italian-Jewish family dialogues.[21] The intention was the revitalization of Hebrew as an everyday language, although it does not explain how to teach the language, especially to young children. Guglielmo Lattes, one of the most attentive scholars of Jewish nineteenth-century educational requirements, emphasized the need to find "the best way of making study amusing from the earliest years of schooling, by not forcing the child to carry out arid exercises, which neither educate his intelligence nor his heart, but lead him to regard dealing with the study of the holy language as a torture."[22]

The teaching of "duties of Jewish life" was most strongly influenced by the catechism model used during Catholic religion class hours in public schools. The classes were designed to instill in children a sense of belonging to the Jewish people, and to convince them that all actions in Jewish daily life are subject to the dictates of the Torah, and that adherence to these dictates is necessary to guarantee justice and social harmony.

Some objected to applying the term "catechism" to Jewish learning. For example, Elia Samuele Artom stated:

> Catechism is, in effect, the exposition or enumeration, especially if in the shape of questions and answers, called therefore in "catechism form," of articles of faith and dogma. If, therefore, the Jewish catechism is chiefly an elementary exposition of the rites and cult practices, it is not only different from the catechism of other religions, but it is no catechism. If matters stand thus, one cannot understand why this very important aspect of our education should be defined by such an inappropriate term.[23]

Gadi Luzzatto Voghera analyzes how the production and publication of Jewish catechisms served as a response to the requirement for "regeneration" of the Italian-Jewish community.[24] The new declarations of tolerance imposed upon citizens a need to confirm their sincere and profound loyalty to the state. This loyalty was "reiterated every week in prayers and became the object of instruction in catechisms, according to models that did not markedly differ from the Talmud dictate of the so-called *dinà de malkhutà dinà* (Aramaic for 'the law of the kingdom is law'), but actually represented an important and novel element of the principles dictated in the catechism, related to the new social relationships that were spreading through bourgeois society."[25]

Marco Mordekai Mortara, the rabbi of Mantua between 1842 and 1894, a central and emblematic figure of this period, published numerous textbooks for teaching Jewish religion.[26] These texts introduced his readers to the essential elements of Jewish liturgy and provided an easily readable understanding of the text, more by virtue of the simplicity of his explanations than thanks to the structure of his texts. Rabbi Mortara's Jewish cultural background was influenced by the Habsburg Empire as well as by Jewish emancipation in Italy. He exhibited his opinions regarding the "transition of Judaism from its original rational-religious tenets to purely religious tenets."[27] His views on transition and integration with different cultural and political realities attributed to the Jews the ability to recognize themselves as "citizens of the world." This differs from the stereotype of the "wandering Jew" generated by the Church to emphasize the lack of peace the Jews endured in their wanderings that began with their exile in 70 CE.[28]

The extensive production of textbooks to be used in teaching the Jewish religion in nursery and elementary schools[29] is surprising given the small size of the Italian-Jewish school population of the time. In the first quarter of the twentieth century, Artom collected statistics on the education of Italian-Jewish children.[30] In the last quarter of the nineteenth century, participation in Jewish day schools and Sunday or afternoon classes did not amount to more than 10 percent. This dropped to 4 percent by the first decade of the twentieth century.[31] These statistics lead to several questions: For whom were these texts written? What was their real educational purpose? What methodological approaches made this new teaching aid practical?

Women and Girls in Italian-Jewish Education

The years leading up to and during emancipation elicited a particularly significant change regarding the role of women in the modernization process. The nineteenth century saw a series of complex and manifold changes regarding women's role in society and their own perception of it. This complexity may also be seen when comparing Jewish women's experiences with those of Catholic women.

Women's role in the modernization process was particularly notable in the transformation that took place in the Jewish educational system. As Miniati points out,

> During the second half of the 1870s, when the entire world of Italian Judaism was, at that point, definitively free from the period of ghettos, the interest toward the feminine "issue," which started to take shape in the late 1840s, came back with a renewed vigor, hereby constituting a moment that was anything but secondary in the wide-ranging debate that was increasingly developing within the Jewish universe. This debate concerned several issues on maintaining cohesion, and the religious and cultural specificity in a period of increasing integration with the surrounding society.[32]

Women found themselves living in a new relationship with the Jewish community and with Italian society. They became citizens of the state. As such, they no longer needed to be supported by their community. The Italian state discouraged bonding and belonging to anything other than the state. To experience freedom and the new public and civil commitment, women looked for new positions in society and tried to define new roles for themselves. Far from being secluded subjects, required to stay in the shadows, Jewish women participated in society in various ways, according to their social class and their roles as wives and mothers. Although they felt the weight of the majority culture, Jewish women found strategies to reaffirm their own distinctive presence in some areas. For example, in the 1840s, a female teacher by the name of Miss Rossi was part of the elementary school staff in Ferrara. Many women participated in community and educational associations, often as volunteers.

Anna Foa stresses that women took part in Jewish ritual activities and Italian-Jewish education, which had previously been limited to men:

> Among Jewish women's activities in Italy, there is documentary evidence of ritual slaughter of meat animals (*shechitah*). . . . We have permits for women stating that their diligence will be rewarded with male children and marriage. In one verdict, the women's ritual slaughter permit is connected to the license to testify in court. . . . In Italy, despite fundamental reticence and the frequent prohibitions of the halakhic laws, Jewish women continued and actually expanded the tradition that in practice allowed them to testify in court and that was sometimes ratified by legal innovations. As we have seen, they could also make a will quite independently, and could conclude firsthand agreements and notarial deeds.[33]

Young Jewish girls found themselves in the midst of a very complex emancipatory process. Even though the newly granted civil rights were only accorded to men, they affected family decisions on issues such as children's education. Women had to find their position in society outside the ghetto walls. They came into contact with a society in which they needed to build relationships and connections. This society, which had internalized Rousseau's ideal of woman as wife and mother, caught the attention of those in the Jewish world who feared that younger generations would distance themselves from the Jewish tradition. They thus entrusted women, precisely because of their roles as wives and mothers, with the task of defending Jewish values, morals, and ethics by educating their children from birth. Jewish newspapers of the time often published works that supported this role for Jewish women, strengthening and radicalizing an idealized portrayal of women essentially impossible to find in reality.

In the pages of *Vessillo Israelitico* from the late 1870s, a journalist who signed her works as R.L. supported the role of mothers in defending and transmitting tradition. As noted by Miniati, the purpose of R.L.'s call was to highlight one of the most passionate conflicts related to Jewish integration, specifically

> the difficulty of reconciling tradition, the "dogmatic sentiment" with liberal individualism, inseparable from critical sentiment. The verification of changes in customs among women, and also within families, rather than pushing R.L. toward a more detailed factual analysis or toward a mediation with the new habits, reinforced a blind stubbornness in her to desire to propose a specific feminine role at all costs and to impose on women both severe and schematic organization of their time and tasks, essentially aimed at a religious education.[34]

Beyond this debate on women's roles, Jewish periodicals often commended Jewish community schoolteachers and the results achieved by the Jewish students in school and in the public arena.[35] *L'Educatore Israelita* from 1868 in particular listed the positive results of a Florentine girls' boarding school. The writer comments on the necessity of giving future women the means to overcome difficulties in life. However, according to the periodical, this was possible only because of religious education. Therefore, young Jewish women should attend a school in which a Jewish education could be ensured. Elementary schools for boys existed in many Italian-Jewish communities, but girls' schools were rare. This situation was strongly criticized in *Il Vessillo Israelitico* in 1880. The writers linked public education to the progressive but inexorable decay and abandonment of Judaism. They stated that if girls were educated in public schools, far from a Jewish environment and its symbols, traditions, and teachings, the community would lose the opportunity to have good Jewish mothers for the next generation.

A point may also be made regarding the role of teachers. In Italian-Jewish communities with a few hundred students, male and female schools were organized separately. Although teachers could work in both facilities, none of them entrusted women with the teaching of *sacred* subjects. These disciplines, generally, were taught by a young rabbi trained for this task (in small cities), or by other male teachers.

However, even if the teachers in the boys' and girls' schools were the same, the programs and content taught in them were certainly different. The organization of the Jewish community required that male students prepare for participation in synagogue life, with hymns and readings. The purpose of girls' education, by contrast, was to raise good mothers and wives to guarantee the continuity of Judaism. Therefore, while noting that the Jewish press in the nineteenth century strongly supported girls' education, many authors expressed quite strong criticisms of the image of the modern woman.

In an article written to clarify the claims made by the Turin Jewish girls' school's headmistress, Adele Levi, it was reiterated that the kingdom of the woman should be in the house and that modern education, by getting women away from what they were really supposed to learn, was to be discouraged, "as the young girl's preciousness depends not on how educated she is, as they are taught in our girls' schools nowadays, but rather on how good she will be as housewife, as loving daughter, as modest wife and as excellent mother."[36]

Given this resistance and intransigence, upheld by the stereotyped portrayal of women in Catholic society, it took decades until women's role as teacher became socially and culturally recognized. Women were not allowed to teach Jewish subjects until the beginning of the twentieth century. At this time, in the Jewish Talmud Torah school of Florence, girls' and boys' schools were integrated into one complex, and teachers of both sexes were involved in the organization of teaching, the content of the programs, and the preparation of learning materials. Changes in girls' upbringing and education can be traced through documents and sources about the organization of schools.

Analysis of nonformal and informal education could make a significant contribution to understanding the complexity of different frameworks, as these provide a better understanding of how issues related to upbringing and education played an important part in the outcome of Jewish girls' and women's "squared emancipation" in nineteenth-century Italy.

Silvia Guetta, PhD, is associate professor in the Department of Science of Education and Psychology at the University of Florence, Italy. She teaches peace education as well as intercultural and interreligious education. Her research focuses on the history of Jewish education in Italy and on Holocaust education. She is a member of the Transdisciplinary UNESCO Chair "Human Development and Culture of Peace," of INEE (International Network Education Emergencies), and of IHRA (International Holocaust Remembrance Alliance). She was a fellow at the International Institute for Holocaust Research at Yad Vashem in Jerusalem. Her most recent publication is *Educating in Religious Pluralism through the Multiple Paths of Dialogue* (Lecce: Pensa Multimedia, 2018).

Notes

1. Claire E. Honess and Verina R. Jones, eds., *Le donne delle minoranze: Le ebree e le protestanti d'Italia* (Turin: Claudiana, 1999).
2. Silvia Guetta, "I contributi delle minoranze negli scenari della pedagogia italiana," in *Educazione, laicità e democrazia*, ed. Carmen Betti, Gianfranco Bandini, and Stefano Oliviero (Milan: Franco Angeli, 2014), 266–73.
3. Quoted after the translation by David Sorkin, *Jewish Emancipation: A History Across Five Centuries* (Princeton, NJ: Princeton University Press, 2019), 94. See also Maria Grazia Meriggi, "Le comunità ebraiche nella rivoluzione francese: Una rilettura delle tesi dell'Abate Grégoire," *La Rassegna Mensile di Israel* 66, no. 1 (January–April 2000): 7–46.
4. Monica Miniati, *Le "emancipate": Le donne ebree in Italia nel XIX e XX secolo* (Rome: Viella, 2008), 34.
5. Gadi Luzzatto Voghera, "I catechismi ebraici fra Sette e Ottocento," in *Le religioni e il mondo moderno*, ed. Giovanni Filoramo (Turin: Einaudi, 2008), 437–55.
6. Ibid.
7. Carlotta Ferrara degli Uberti, *Fare gli ebrei italiani: Autorappresentazioni di una minoranza (1861–1918)* (Bologna: Il Mulino, 2011).

8. Bruno Di Porto, "Marco Mordekai Mortara: Doresh Tov," in *Materia Giudaica*, ed. Mauro Perani (Florence: Giuntina, 2011), 15–16:249.
9. Attilio Milano, *Storia degli Ebrei in Italia* (Turin: Einaudi), 1963.
10. Giuseppe Levi, "L'ebreo del presente," *L'Educatore Israelita* (1860): 136.
11. Franco Cambi, *Storia della Pedagogia* (Rome: Laterza, 1995).
12. Voghera, "I catechismi ebraici."
13. Antonio Santoni Rugiu, *Storia sociale dell'Educazione* (Milan: Principato, 1979).
14. Antonio Rosmini Serbati, *Opere* (Naples: Batelli, 1844), 12:10.
15. Giuseppe Levi, "L'ebreo del presente," *L'Educatore Israelita* (1860): 162.
16. Giuseppe Levi, "Sull'educazione israelitica come creatrice e tutrice della famiglia," *L'Educatore Israelita* (1866): 136.
17. Voghera, "I catechismi ebraici."
18. Silvia Guetta, "La scuola ebraica dalla Emancipazione alle leggi razziali," in *E li insegnerai ai tuoi figli: Educazione ebraica in Italia dalle leggi razziali ad oggi*, ed. Anna Maria Piussi (Florence: Editrice Giuntina, 1997), 169–81.
19. *L'Educatore Israelita* (1872), 345
20. David B. Ruderman, *Kabbalah, Magic, and Science: The Cultural Universe of a Sixteenth Century Jewish Physician* (Cambridge, MA: Harvard University Press, 1988), 18.
21. *L'Educatore Israelita* (1862).
22. Guglielmo Lattes, *Educazione e civiltà israelitica* (Livorno: S. Belforte, 1892), 212.
23. Samuele Elia Artom, "L'insegnamento dell'ebraico e gli articoli di fede," in *La Settimana Israelitica*, no. 17 (29 April 1915): 2.
24. Voghera, "I catechismi ebraici."
25. Ibid.
26. Marco Mordekai Mortara, *La religione israelitica compediosamente esposta giusta i suoi dogmi e precetti* (Mantua: A. Beretta, 1853); Marco Mordekai Mortara, *Compendio della religione israelitica metodicamente esposto ad uso dell'istruzione domestica e della scuola* (Mantua: A. Beretta, 1855); Marco Mordekai Mortara, *Zarua: Corso di Istruzione religiosa infantile ed elementare* (Mantua: Giovanni Agazzi, 1857); Asher Salah, *L'epistolario di Marco Mortara (1815–1894)* (Florence: Giuntina, 2012); Mauro Perani, Ermanno Finzi, *Nuovi studi in onore di Marco Mortara nel secondo centenario della nascita* (Florence: Giuntina, 2016).
27. Di Porto, "Marco Mordekai Mortara," 139–67.
28. Ibid., 165.
29. Voghera, "I catechismi ebraici."
30. Samuele Elia Artom, "Le nostre scuole," in *Il Vessillo Israelitico*, no. 8 (30 April 1913).
31. Guetta, "La scuola ebraica."
32. Monica Miniati, *Les Emancipées: Les femmes juives italiennes aux XIXe et XXe siècles, 1848–1924* (Paris: Honoré Champion, 2003), 71.
33. Anna Foa, "Le donne nella storia degli ebrei in Italia," in *Le donne delle minoranze: Le ebree e le protestanti d'Italia*, ed. Claire E. Honess and Verina R. Jones (Turin: Claudiana, 1999), 22.
34. Miniati, *Les Emancipées*, 93–94.
35. Giulia di Bello, Silvia Guetta, and Andrea Manucci, eds., *Modelli e progretti educative nell'Italia liberale* (Florence: Centro Editoriale Toscano, 1998).
36. *L'Educatore Israelita* (1868), 252.

Bibliography

Archivi di Stato, Saggi 26. *Italia Judaica: gli ebrei nell'Italia unita 1870–1945*. Rome: Ministero per i beni culturali e ambientali, 1993.
Artom, Samuele Elia. "Le nostre scuole." *Il Vessillo Israelitico*, no. 8 (30 April 1913).
———. "L'insegnamento dell'ebraico e gli articoli di fede." *La Settimana Israelitica*, no. 17 (29 April 1915).
Barbieri, Nicola S. *La storia dell'educazione in prospettiva comparata*. Padua: CLEUP, 2013.
Betti, Carmen, Gionfranco Bandini, and Stefano Oliviero, eds. *Educazione, laicità e democrazia*. Milan: Franco Angeli, 2014.
Cambi, Franco. *Storia della Pedagogia*. Rome: Laterza, 1995.
Della Pergola, Sergio. *Anatomia dell'ebraismo*. Rome: Carucci, 1976.
Di Bello, Giulia, Silvia Guetta, and Andrea Mannucci, eds. *Modelli e progetti educativi nell'Italia liberale*. Florence: Centro Editoriale Toscano, 1998.
Di Porto, Bruno. "Il Corriere Israelitico: Uno sguardo di insieme." In *Materia Giudaica*, edited by Mauro Perani, vol. 9, issue 1–2: 249–63. Florence: Giuntina, 2004.
———. "Marco Mordekai Mortara: Doresh Tov." In *Materia Giudaica*, edited by Mauro Perani, 15–16:139–67. Florence: Giuntina, 2011.
Ferrara degli Uberti, Carlotta. *Fare gli ebrei italiani: Autorappresentazioni di una minoranza (1861–1918)*. Bologna: Il Mulino, 2011.
Foa, Anna. "Le donne nella storia degli ebrei in Italia." In *Le donne delle minoranze: Le ebree e le protestanti d'Italia*, edited by Claire E. Honess and Verina R. Jones, 11–30. Turin: Claudiana, 1999.
Guetta, Silvia. "La scuola ebraica dalla Emancipazione alle leggi razziali." In *E li insegnerai ai tuoi figli: Educazione ebraica in Italia dalle leggi razziali ad oggi*, edited by Anna Maria Piussi, 169–81. Florence: Casa Editrice Giuntina, 1997.
———. "I contributi delle minoranze negli scenari della pedagogia italiana." In *Educazione, laicità e democrazia*, edited by Carmen Betti, Gianfranco Bandini, and Stefano Oliviero, 266–73. Milan: Franco Angeli, 2014.
Honess, Claire E., and Verina R. Jones, eds. *Le donne delle minoranze: Le ebree e le protestanti d'Italia*. Turin: Claudiana, 1999.
Lattes, Guglielmo. *Educazione e civiltà israelitica*. Livorno: S. Belaforte, 1892.
Levi, Giuseppe. "L'ebreo del presente." *L'Educatore Israelita* (1860): 133–47.
———. "Sull'educazione israelitica come creatrice e tutrice della famiglia." *L'Educatore Israelita* (1866): 65–73.
Liscia Bemporad, Dora, ed. *L'emancipazione ebraica in Toscana e la partecipazione degli ebrei all'Unità d'Italia*. Florence: Edifir, 2012.
Meriggi, Maria Grazia. "Le comunità ebraiche nella rivoluzione francese: una rilettura delle tesi dell'Abate Grégoire." *La Rassegna Mensile di Israel* 66, no. 1 (January–April 2000): 7–46.
Milano, Attilio. *Storia degli Ebrei in Italia*. Turin: Einaudi, 1963.
Miniati, Monica. *Le "emancipate": Le donne ebree in Italia nel XIX e XX secolo*. Rome: Viella, 2008.
———. *Les Emancipées: Les femmes juives italiennes aux XIXe et XXe siècles, 1848–1924*. Paris: Honoré Champion, 2003.
Molinari, Maurizio. *Ebrei in Italia: Un problema di identità*. Florence: Casa Editrice Giuntina, 1991.

Mortara, Marco Mordekai. *La religione israelitica compediosamente esposta giusta i suoi dogmi e precetti*. Mantua: A. Beretta, 1853.

———. *Compendio della religione israelitica metodicamente esposto ad uso dell'istruzione domestica e della scuola*. Mantua: A. Beretta, 1855.

———. *Zarua: Corso di Istruzione religiosa infantile ed elementare*. Mantua: Giovanni Agazzi, 1857.

Ottonello, Pier Paolo. *Rosmini: l'ordine del sapere e della socetà*. Rome: Città Nuova, 1997.

Perani, Mauro, and Ermanno Finzi, eds. *Nuovi studi in onore di Marco Mortara nel secondo centenario della nascita*. Florence: Giuntina, 2016.

Ravenna, Leon. "La donna in Israello." *L'Educatore Israelita* (1858): 129–36.

Ruderman, David B. *Kabbalah, Magic, and Science: The Cultural Universe of a Sixteenth Century Jewish Physician*. Cambridge, MA: Harvard University Press, 1988.

Rugiu Santoni, Antonio. *Storia sociale dell'Educazione*. Milan: Principato, 1979.

Salah, Asher, *L'epistolario di Marco Mortara (1815–1894)*. Florence: Giuntina, 2012.

Serbati, Antonio Rosmini. *Opere*. Vol. 12. Naples: Batelli, 1844.

Servi, Flaminio. *Gli Israeliti di Europa*. Turin: Tipografia e Litografia Foà, 1872.

Sorkin, David. *Jewish Emancipation: A History Across Five Centuries*. Princeton, NJ: Princeton University Press, 2019.

Ulivieri, Simonetta. *Educare al Femminile*. Pisa: ETS, 1995.

Vivanti, Corrado, ed. *Storia d'Italia, Annali 11, Gli Ebrei in Italia*. Vol. 1. Turin: Giulio Einaudi Editore, 1996.

Voghera, Gadi Luzzatto. "I catechismi ebraici fra Sette e Ottocento." In *Le religioni e il mondo moderno*, edited by Giovanni Filoramo, 437–55. Turin: Einaudi, 2008.

CHAPTER 8

Religion and Nation

Catholic and Protestant Female Education and Cultural Models in Germany (1871–1914)

Sylvia Schraut

For a long time, German historical research analyzed the nineteenth century as a secular period. At the beginning of the century, the political power of the Catholic Church, its participation in the electoral body of the German emperor, and much of its property vanished with the breakdown of the German Empire. In general, historical researchers analyzed the following decades as marked by conflicts between liberal politicians or the nationalistic movement and the dynastic monarchs in the various German countries of the loose German Confederation. They analyzed the revolutions of 1848–49, in which the liberal and nationalistic movements failed to found a German constitutional national state, and they followed this development until the founding of the German Empire in 1870–71. The conflicts between the Catholic Church and the state during the so-called *Kulturkampf* (cultural struggle) were interpreted as conflicts over modern concepts of the separation between church and state.

Historians neglected the conflicts between the Protestant north and the Catholic south in the newly founded Protestant empire, which took over from the empire of the early modern era that was dominated by Catholics.[1] This apparently secular development, which accompanied the founding of a German national state in the nineteenth century, provided the background for historical research on the German educational systems and the women's movement.[2] Even gendered research on female and male agency usually neglects religious aspects. But more recent research shows that the nineteenth century was far from being a secular time. It reveals deep cultural and political differences between the predominantly Catholic or denominationally mixed south of Germany and predominantly Protestant Prussia. Prussia dominated the German Empire of 1870–71 because the exclusion of Austria resulted in two-thirds of the Empire's territory now being part of Prussia and its inhabitants predominantly Protestant. This is the reason why historical research often identifies Prussia with Germany. To sum up: due to the religious, cultural, and political determinants of the German Empire of 1870–71, we should always keep in mind that, in contrast to Italy, the Catholics and the Catholic Church in Germany were in the position of an oppositional milieu and an oppositional political power, at least during the last decades of the nineteenth century. These circumstances influenced the relationship of Catholicism to the nation as a whole.

The secularist historical perspective on the German Empire described above or, as we might say, its blind spots with regard to the role of religion have had some consequences for research on the topics this chapter is concerned with. In general, the educational system of Prussia is regarded as the educational system of the German Empire and not as a Protestant educational system; the dominant gender model is seen as a German gender model and not as a primarily Protestant German gender model; and the women's movement is seen as a secularist movement and not as a movement in which religion played an important role.[3]

In the following, I will therefore compare:

1. the so-called German gender model of the late nineteenth century—which, in fact, is a Protestant one—with the Catholic gender model;
2. the course of instruction for female pupils generally described as a German syllabus—which is in fact a German-Protestant one—with the German Catholic syllabus;
3. and Catholic and Protestant historical biographies as reading material for the female youth.

I will also raise the question of the consequences for the agency of Protestant and Catholic feminists in the national state.

The German Gender Model

The roots of the bourgeois gender model in Germany are more or less the same as in the other European countries that were influenced by the Enlightenment during the early modern era. The leading political and cultural group of the nineteenth century—the bourgeoisie and the bourgeois pedagogues—learned from Rousseau that rationality, activity, and the ability to differentiate are characteristics of male persons, while female persons are characterized by emotionality, passivity, and simplicity. It was taken for granted that women were by nature subordinated to male guardianship. In particular, the diametrically opposed gender characteristics of male and female persons were, according to Rousseau, the basis of the erotic attraction between men and women.[4] To compare the Christian European gender model of the early modern period with the model developing since the French Revolution, we can use a symbolic image: before the Enlightenment, man and wife stood side by side in front of God, and they were defined primarily by social status and of course by the gender hierarchy. In the first place, they had to be good Christians. With the Enlightenment, a diametrical gender model developed in which man and wife faced each other. We may widen this polar image into a triangle whose vertices represent man, wife, and their relationship with the nation.

Looking more closely at the development of Rousseau's ideas in Germany, we can see that Rousseau's concept of erotic relationships was altered into a relationship that emphasized the role of the mother.[5] In my view, this was, however, not a specific German development. Since the French Revolution, not only German liberals claimed that women were unable to act politically. Their sphere of activity was to be the family home, where they had to support their husbands.[6] But the leading German or European gender model did not mean that there was no place for women in the nation. A patriotic woman was primarily defined as a nationally minded woman who assisted her husband well and educated their children in a patriotic manner. Among other things, patriotic women were allowed to participate in the festivities of the nation as a decorative attachment to their husbands, and the women's movement in the second half of the century achieved the recognition of social work as national work. It is obvious that their subordinate role did not hinder women from feeling patriotic.[7]

But if we analyze this German gender model under religious aspects, it can be characterized as primarily Protestant. Two aspects in particular were incompatible with the leading Catholic concepts.

1. The German and, as I would say, the secular modern or Protestant gender model only accepted married women as full women. Unlike Protestantism, Catholic culture knew three female gender models: the wife; the unmarried woman who preferred a life close to God, such as a nun; and the widow who renounced a new marriage and committed herself to social work in the community. At least until the end of the nineteenth century, an unmarried woman ranked higher than a wife in the Catholic social hierarchy. Pope Leo XIII explicitly emphasized this perspective in an Apostolic Letter of 1899.[8] These differences between the Protestant and the Catholic image of unmarried women were, for example, at least one reason for the conversion of Elisabeth Gnauck-Kühne (1850–1917), who is said

to have been an important founding figure first of the Protestant women's movement and afterward of the Catholic women's movement.[9] Provided that there was a social and cultural milieu in which the unmarried state was not negatively connoted, the decision to remain unmarried relieved women explicitly of the "subordination under the man in the family,"[10] although not of subordination under the priest.

2. The German or Protestant gender model drafted a female life as one that took place first and foremost within the family. Life in the public, however, was not absolutely ruled out, if the borders of the gender model were not transgressed. But professional and paid female work outside the family—common in the lower classes—was not appreciated by the middle classes or the bourgeoisie. The Catholic female virtues were also not oriented toward the public, but beyond; and, last but not least, living in a convent ranked much higher than acting within the family, and, what is more important, as members of a convent, women were able to practice a profession, such as a nurse or a teacher. In this way, the Catholic Church offered a space in which women could have a profession and practice it in public. These circumstances might explain the sarcasm, for example, with which the Catholic female teachers' movement commented on the secular (Protestant) discussions among German (male) teachers and pedagogues in the late nineteenth century about the ability of women to work in secondary schools. "We (the Catholics) have been able to demonstrate women's ability to teach since many centuries," stressed Pauline Herber (1852–1921), for example, who founded the Verein katholischer deutscher Lehrerinnen (Association of Catholic German Female Teachers) in 1885.[11] And it is interesting to note that this association commenced its activities five years before the famous Allgemeiner Deutscher Lehrerinnenverein (General Association of German Female Teachers) of the women's movement was founded.

The bourgeois gender concept—designated secular but in fact Protestant—described above existed throughout the nineteenth century, together with the rejection of the Catholic gender model. It had, last but not least, specific consequences for the political rights of women and the school education of girls. It was only in 1919 that female Germans got the right to vote. Only male pupils had access to higher education for nearly the whole nineteenth century. It was not before 1900 that universities were opened to women. In general, female education was defined as a lower or middle education, which was never to reach the male education level. And when we compare the development of female denominational school education in early modern times with that of the nineteenth century, we can see that in the course of the Enlightenment, the primacy of Catholic female higher education vanished.[12] A comparison of this development with the developments in other European countries, for example in Italy, shows that the gender model of the Enlightenment influenced all European countries and did not depend on denominational predominance. But what is a specific characteristic of Germany in the era of the newly founded Empire is a combination of the so-called secular (Protestant) gender model with its rejection of the Catholic gender model and Catholic distance from the nation, which in the Catholic view was a Protestant nation. This combination created specific denominationally influenced educational systems and specific denominationally determined conditions for female agency, which will be described in the following.

By bringing together the leading role of the (Protestant) gender model with the politics of the *Kulturkampf* in the founding period of the German Empire between 1871 and 1878, we find that an image of Catholics as unpatriotic and outmoded became widespread not least because of the appreciation of monastic and unmarried life by Catholics. Of course, German patriotism was problematic in Catholic culture, because the Catholic community defined itself as a European or a world community. The nation seemed to rank second in this interpretation of cultural or religious loyalties. Especially during the period of the *Kulturkampf*, loyalty to the nation was a big problem for Catholic women—and for Catholic men as well, because of the violent conflict between the state and the officials of the Catholic Church.[13] In this period, it was a common assumption in Germany that Catholics could not be loyal to the nation because they had to obey the ultramontane pope. Similarly, it was common to assume that Catholics were less educated than Protestants because Catholicism supposedly preferred stupid obedience. And it was common to declare monastic and therefore unmarried life an antiquated idea.

The Syllabus for German History of the *Volksschule* in the German Empire

What do we know about the importance of the educational system with regard to the creation of good male and female patriots? Most German pupils only attended the so-called *Volksschule*, a school delivering a low educational level, in which male and female pupils were instructed together. Only in bigger towns were there separate classes for girls and boys. Therefore, we can say that most German pupils—male and female—got the same lessons from the same schoolbooks. German historians characterize the nineteenth century as the century of education.[14] Compulsory schooling was established early in this century. More or less all children, male and female, went to school (together) at the latest since the 1880s. From the middle of the century on, we can see attempts by the state to standardize and control the syllabuses. But it is important to know that the various German territories were autonomous with regard to the organization of their school systems. This independence remained even after the German Empire was founded in 1871. There was, however, a general development: religious education (Catholic and/or Protestant) lost its importance in the course of the nineteenth century. In Italy, this was perhaps different.

How were the syllabus of the German *Volksschule* and its patriotic aims constructed? When we analyze the development of the syllabus of (primarily Protestant) Prussia, we find that patriotism had been growing in importance as one of the main aims of education since the 1850s.[15] Soon after the founding of the German Empire, Prussia issued a new decree in 1872 concerning the school system and the syllabus, the Allgemeine Bestimmungen (General Regulations). Now, history was especially assigned the goal of patriotic education.[16] The decree reads, "In history the pupils of the *Volksschule* are to be instructed by means of historical biographies from the ancient history of Germany and Prussia."[17] Modern history was to be presented by the teachers especially via biographies of the Prussian monarchs. Here and in later decrees, the history of the Prussian dynasty and the history of wars were intended to be the main topics of history lessons. Additionally, from 1890 onward, the pupils had to learn that the Prussian kings—now the German emperors—had always sought to care for the property and health of their subjects and that there was no need for a socialist party. Specifically, "The pupils are to learn how the devoted and hard-working Prussian princes developed Prussia and how the wisdom and work of the Prussian princes and kings led to the German Empire, and how it has developed by the activities of Emperor Wilhelm I and by the unanimity of the German princes and peoples. The merits of the Prussian rulers concerning the prosperity of the people are to be emphasized as well."[18]

Which topics were to be taught? The following table compares the courses of instruction for history lessons in (Protestant) Prussia and (Catholic) Bavaria at the turn of the century.

Let us first analyze the Prussian instructions. This table shows that history was taught through the (male) biographies of Prussian rulers. Prussian and Protestant history were dominant. The history of other German countries, especially of the first German Empire in the Middle Ages and in early modern times, was neglected. Obviously, Prussian history was defined as German history long before the founding of the German Empire. Questions of the expansion of the territory, the Reformation, wars, and, topical then, loyalty toward the Prussian kings in personal union with the

Table 8.1. *Contents of the courses of instruction for history lessons in the German Volksschule in Prussia and Bavaria.*

Prussia (1892) [19]	Bavaria (1907) [20]
Antiquity and Middle Ages	**Antiquity and Middle Ages**
Biography of Emperor Wilhelm II and his family	
Ancient Germans	Ancient Germans
	Roman culture in Bavaria
"Hermannsschlacht"(Battle of the Teutoburg Forest)	"Hermannsschlacht"
Bonifatius	The introduction of Christianity to Germany, especially in Bavaria (Erhardus, Severin), and Bonifatius, the apostle of the Germans, the cultural work of the monasteries
Emperor Charlemagne	Emperor Charlemagne
Emperor Heinrich I (876–912), *seen as first "German" emperor*	Otto the Great (912–73), *who expanded the Empire to the south and Italy, was seen as "savior of Christianity"*
Friedrich Barbarossa (1122–90), *myth of national unity*	Friedrich Barbarossa (1122–90), *myth of national unity*
Albrecht I von Brandenburg (1100–1170), *founder of Brandenburg*	Otto von Wittelsbach (1117–83), *the first of the Bavarian dynasty of Wittelsbach*
The Crusades	
The Teutonic Order in Prussia	
The Hansa	The golden age of the cities, one city in the Middle Ages: Nuremberg
Friedrich I of Brandenburg (1371–1440), *first electoral prince of the Prussian dynasty of Hohenzollern*	The decline of the power of emperors and its restoration
Inventions and discoveries	Inventions and discoveries
Martin Luther and the Reformation	The separation of the Christian churches
Joachim I von Brandenburg (1484–1535), *enemy of the Reformation*, and Joachim II von Brandenburg (1505–71), *who supported the Reformation*	Rudolf I von Habsburg, *first German emperor from the Austrian house of Habsburg*, Ludwig IV: the Bavarian (1282–1347), *German emperor from the Bavarian house of Wittelsbach*
The Thirty Years War	The Thirty Years War

(continued)

Table 8.1. *continued*

Prussia (1892)	Bavaria (1907)
Modern times (1893)	**Modern times (1907)**
Guiding Ideas:	Guiding Ideas:
The focus is on the Prussian dynasty since early modern times and their work for the German Empire. "The pupils are to learn how the devoted and hard-working Prussian princes developed Prussia, and how the wisdom and work of the Prussian princes and kings led to the German Empire, and how it has developed by the activities of Emperor Wilhelm I and by the unanimity of the German princes and peoples. The merits of the Prussian rulers concerning the prosperity of the people are to be emphasized as well."[21]	"History lessons in the *Volksschule* are to teach the main events in the development of the German people. They should help to understand the present political, ecclesiastical, and social institutions, promote the taste for the good and the fine, and educate to active patriotism."[22]
These ideas could be exemplified as follows:	These ideas could be exemplified as follows:
	The decline of the German Empire
	Bavarian princes
Emperor Wilhelm II, youth and education, his work for peace, and social work for the workers; his family life	The German emperor, Bavaria as part of the Empire, Prince Regent Luitpold (Bavaria)
Empress Augusta Viktoria, religious sense, children . . .	
	The foreign rule in Germany, the French Revolution, the Confederation of the Rhine, the end of the German Empire, the Kingdom of Bavaria, the liberation of Germany
Emperor Wilhelm I, his hard youth, prince of Prussia, 1848, Prince regent, coronation	Bavaria's development as constitutional state, 1848 and agrarian/social reforms, Bavarian kings
Emperor Wilhelm I, wars, his clemency, his humble lifestyle, the attempts on his life, care for the working class	The reconstruction of the German Empire, the German war of brothers (1866), the German-French war of 1870/71; the new German Empire
Additional biographies: Friedrich Karl, Bismarck, Roon, Moltke, Empress Augusta	
	Second epoch of inventions and discoveries

German emperors were emphasized. How did this course of instruction influence the rules in other German countries?

In general, historical research into the school systems of the other countries of Germany explores their similarities with the Prussian system. The findings show that patriotism had the same importance everywhere. But in emphasizing the patriotic aspect, these analyses neglect regional and religious variations.[23] If we analyze, for example, the syllabus of Bavaria, a German country deeply influenced by Catholicism (see table 8.1), we can see that the guidelines of 1907 are in fact influenced by the Prussian guidelines, but we also see that they did not merely replace Prussian with Bavarian rulers. In the Bavarian syllabus, the German Empire of the Middle Ages and early modern times is not a German-Prussian empire but a Roman-German empire. Whereas the Prussian syllabus emphasizes the Reformation, the Bavarian syllabus emphasizes Christianity. And while patriotism in Prussia means loyalty to the ruling (Protestant) dynasty, this is not the case to the same degree in Bavaria. Furthermore, Bavarian patriotism could not be interpreted as German patriotism, as was the case in Prussia. In Catholic Bavaria, especially at the time of the French Revolution, the destruction of the old German Empire and the founding of a new kingdom of Bavaria under Napoleon's influence played an important role. This interpretation of history had severe consequences for patriotism. That is why the famous patriotic (Prussian) fights for freedom against Napoleon, which were understood as the founding acts of the nation, could not be interpreted in the same way in Bavaria, a country that was very long associated with France. While the Prussian guidelines neglected the fight between Prussia and the German south in 1866—five years before the founding of the new German Empire—the Bavarian guidelines had to include these events as well as the Bavarian defeat by Prussia. Even in 1907, patriotism in Bavaria had to manage a balancing act between Bavarian (Catholic) patriotism and German (Prussian and Protestant) loyalties.

What are the gender aspects? In both the Protestant and the Catholic syllabus, the history of male rulers and the Empire dominated. Wars as a field of male agency were also important (though more important in Prussia than in Bavaria). Some lessons about cultural questions gave the opportunity to talk about civil agrarian and urban life, but, in general, there was no place for female agency—be it Protestant or Catholic—in history lessons. The contemporaneous syllabus of female higher school education included the biographies of the rulers' wives. These biographies allowed the teaching of female virtues. But in the lower school syllabus, they were neglected. Of course, some teachers might have included female biographies into their lessons. But this cannot be proved. If we search for themes of history that made it possible for girls and young women to identify with female role models in general or female patriotic role models in particular, we have to analyze reading materials from outside the school lessons. Because it was common to teach history and virtues through historical biographies, I will additionally look at some examples of published historical biographies that were dedicated to the private reading of German (= Protestant) and Catholic female youths.

Female Biographies as Reading Material for the Female Youth

I will start with the German/Prussian example of Amanda Sonnenfeld, whose pen name was Amanda Sonnenfels. She was born in 1868 in Upper Silesia (Prussia). The daughter of a manor owner and well educated by private teachers, she was active as a speaker for the Gesellschaft für die Verbreitung von Volksbildung (Society for the Furthering of Public Education) and engaged in the women's movement.[24] Her denomination is not known.[25] Her 1910 book *Deutsche Frauengestalten* (German Women) became very famous: there were four editions until 1948; the last one was published in 2013. The book presented ten biographies of outstanding women as lessons for girls.

The author wrote in the preface that readers should be impressed not by the fame of these women but by their female virtues. What kind of women did Sonnenfeld portray as German female models? There is one unmarried woman and nine who are married; seven Protestants and three Catholics, among them two Protestant mothers of their country who defended their country against Napoleon; a famous poet's mother and a famous poet's wife; six female artists; and one female entrepreneur. With the exception of the two mothers of their country, no woman showed particular commitment to national politics or patriotism, but some of them admired the Prussian ruler Frederick the Great. They are all characterized as kind, gentle, industrious, and loyal to their families. None of them violated the postulated female gender role. They were either devoted mothers, whether of their families or of their countries, or they were "allowed" to work in the artistic area. The only woman working in business was from the sixteenth century. These biographies are presented as German biographies, but they seem to be much closer to the Protestant female gender role than to the Catholic or south German gender roles.

I will contrast these biographies with a specific Catholic version of admirable female biographies, which are presented in a book by the Catholic priest Konstantin Holl (1869–1919). In the early twentieth century, the priest from Hechingen was a very famous author of books for young readers.[26] In 1912, he published *Die Jugend großer Frauen* (The Youth of Great Women). The book contained forty female biographies and was

Table 8.2. *German historical biographies for girls.*

Amanda Sonnenfels, *Deutsche Frauengestalten*, Stuttgart 1910	
Queen Luise of Prussia (1776–1810) (Protestant)	Married "mother of her country," symbolic figure of the so-called war of liberation against Napoleon
Grand-Duchess Luise of Sachsen-Weimar (1757–1830) (Protestant)	Married "mother of her country" who is said to have protected her country and dynasty against Napoleon
Mrs. Councillor Goethe[27] (1731–1808) (Protestant)	Mother of the poet Wolfgang von Goethe
Bettina von Arnim (1785–1859) (Catholic)	Married writer
Charlotte von Schiller (1766–1826) (Protestant)	Wife of Friedrich Schiller
Karoline von Wolzogen (1763–1847) (Protestant)	Married writer and sister of Charlotte von Schiller
Anette von Droste-Hülshoff (Catholic)	Unmarried poetess
Anna Luise Karsch (1722–91) (Protestant)	Married poetess
Angelika Kauffmann (1741–1807) (Catholic)	Married European painter
Barbara Uttmann (1515–74)[28] (Protestant)	Married businesswoman who is said to have brought bobbin lace-making to the Erzgebirge

very famous. It had eleven editions until 1929. About twenty-five thousand copies were sold.[29]

A look at the biographies shows that they were not exclusively German. Less than 40 percent dealt with German women. Furthermore, the bourgeois gender model was not dominant. Sixty percent of the women were noble or princesses from sovereign houses. About three out of four were nuns, secular nuns, or congregational foundresses, as for example Angela Merici (1474–1540) or Maria Ward (1585–1645), who were engaged in congregational female youth education. Additionally, the author mentions decidedly Catholic female writers, as for example the convert Luise Hensel (1798–1876). The author informs his female readers that the biographies were extraordinary and that contemporary women would not at all be able to act in exactly the same way as the women he presented. But the female reader would nevertheless find enough great and beautiful things worthy of admiration and imitation.

What are, in the author's view, the characteristics of a great woman? The most important criterion is the welfare of the Catholic Church. This

Table 8.3. Die Jugend großer Frauen *(The Youth of Great Women)*, Konstantin Holl, 1912.

Name	Born	Nationality	Social Status	Profession
Elisabeth von Thüringen	1207	Germany	Princess	Sovereign, secular nun
Katharina of Siena	1347	Italy	Middle classes	Nun
Angela Merici	1474	Italy	Peasant	Nun
Theresia (Teresa of Ávila)	1515	Spain	Noble	Nun
Maria the Catholic (Mary Tudor)	1516	England	Princess	Sovereign
Margareta of Austria	1567	Germany	Princess	Nun
Luise of Carvajal	1568	Spain	Noble	Secular nun
Johanna Franziska of Chantal	1572	France	Noble	Congregational foundress, nun
Maria Ward	1585	England	Noble	Failed with congregational founding
Louise of Marillac	1591	France	Noble	Congregational foundress
Christine of Sweden	1626	Sweden	Princess	Sovereign
Kreszentia Höß	1682	Germany	Middle classes	Nun
Emanuela Therese of Bavaria	1696	Germany	Princess	Nun
Maria Franziska of the Five Wounds (Anna Maria Gallo)	1715	Italy	Middle classes	Secular nun
Louise of France	1737	France	Princess	Nun
Amalie von Gallitzin	1748	Germany	Noble	Court lady
Maria Magdalena Postel	1756	France	Middle classes	Congregational foundress
Anna Maria Taigi	1769	Italy	Middle classes	Secular nun
Anna Katharina Emmerich	1774	Germany	Peasant	Nun
Magdalena Sophie Barat	1779	France	Peasant	Nun
Emilie of Rodat	1787	France	Noble	Congregational foundress, nun
Kaiserin Karolina Augusta	1792	Austria	Princess	Sovereign

Name	Born	Nationality	Social Status	Profession
Maria Salesia Chappuis	1793	Switzerland	Middle classes	Nun
Anette von Droste-Hülshoff	1797	Germany	Noble	Poetess
Luise Hensel	1798	Germany	Middle classes	Poetess
Paulina Maria Jaricot	1799	France	Middle classes	Independent gentlewoman
Maria of Olivary	1802	France	Noble	Nun
Maria Theresia Dubouché	1809	France	Middle classes	Congregational foundress, nun
Maria Christina of Savoy	1812	Italy	Princess	Sovereign
Georgiana Fullerton	1812	England	Noble	Poetess
Maria Agnes Klara Steiner	1813	Austria	Peasant	Nun
Angela von Cordier	1813	Germany	Noble	Nun
Klara Fey	1815	Germany	Middle classes	Congregational foundress, nun
Pauline von Mallinckrodt	1817	Germany	Noble	Congregational foundress
Franziska Schervier	1819	Germany	Middle classes	Congregational foundress
Maria Karolina Frieß	1824	France	Middle classes	Nun
Maria Gonzaga von Loe	1826	Belgium	Noble	Nun
Emilie Ringseis	1831	Germany	Noble	Poetess
Ferdinande von Brackel	1835	Germany	Noble	Poetess
Maria Droste zu Vischering	1863	Germany	Noble	Nun

dedication to the Catholic Church is more important than concern for the family or the nation. More often than not, dedication to Catholicism requires resistance against the parents. Fighting for the Catholic Church, social work, a high level of education, and pedagogical commitment are especially important. These virtues make women strong. In summary, the female virtues presented by Holl had nothing to do with patriotism, the German Empire, or Prussia. In the framework of the Church, he offered a broader range of female agency than that presented in the German/Protestant female biographies. In particular, it was possible in his examples for women to carry out qualified work if they were not married. These women were *not* considered old maids.

Consequences for the Agency of Protestant and Catholic Feminists in the National State

As we know, the German feminist movement defined itself as a patriotic and secular movement. This might not be surprising, because there is a long German tradition of associating religious attitudes with antimodern or antifeminist behavior.[30] But if we analyze the networks of the so-called secular women's movement and the religious women's movements, we can see that it was definitely possible and common to be a leading and patriotic figure of the secular women's movement and to be simultaneously engaged as a Protestant (or sometimes as a Jew). This was significantly less possible for Catholics. On the one hand, we observe a Catholic distance toward the German Empire as well as a preference by Catholics for autonomous female organizations under the umbrella of the Church as demanded by the latter. On the other hand, the secular women's movement declared that there were insurmountable differences between their movement and Catholicism because of the Catholic doctrine of the primacy or supremacy of husbands over their wives. By emphasizing the gender hierarchy in the Catholic concept of family and family law, the secular (Protestant) women's movement neglected the agency of unmarried women in Catholicism. But in many areas, the Catholic women's movement effectively worked at the same borderlines as the secular women's movement. In the fields of female education, social work, and female professionalism, they were engaged in similar ways. Especially in the fight to open the universities to female students, the Catholic women's movement was even more effective than the secular women's movement.[31] Against the background of the severe problems of the Catholics during the *Kulturkampf*, the Catholic women's movement was able to organize support from the Catholic (male) movement for female enrollment at the universities. Close alliances of Catholic priests and monks representing one influential political wing of Catholicism and the Catholic women's movement working for the extension of professional opportunities for women were not unusual in the effort to strengthen Catholic opposition against Prussia and counter the anti-Catholic politics of the German Empire. Thus we can say that the Catholic distance toward the nation provided arguments for widening Catholic female agency.

Therefore, we can conclude that national and patriotic education in the German Empire during the nineteenth century was much more linked with Protestant ideas than with Catholic ideas. And it seems that the

Catholic female gender role allowed more female agency than the Protestant model. But the limits of Catholic female agency might be reached if Catholic women tried to free themselves from the dictates of the Catholic Church. For Catholic feminists who got rid of the influence of the Catholic Church, there was obviously only one model left in the German Empire: the secular and patriotic gender role, which in fact was a Protestant model. The question arises: where was the political place for secular feminists with a Catholic background in the German Empire?

Sylvia Schraut is professor of nineteenth- and twentieth-century German and European history at the Bundeswehr University Munich. Among others, her research areas are gender history and the history of political violence and terrorism. Her most recent publications are *Terrorismus und politische Gewalt* (Göttingen: Vandenhoeck & Ruprecht, 2018) and *Erinnern, vergessen, umdeuten? Europäische Frauenbewegungen im 19. und 20. Jahrhundert*, edited together with Angelika Schaser and Petra Steymans-Kurz (Frankfurt am Main/New York: Campus, 2019).

Notes

1. Compare, for example, the two master narratives of German nineteenth-century history: Thomas Nipperdey, *Deutsche Geschichte*, 2 vols. (Munich: C. H. Beck, 1990), and Hans-Ulrich Wehler, *Deutsche Gesellschaftsgeschichte*, vols. 2–3 (Munich: C. H. Beck, 2008).
2. In general, older studies about the development of the German educational system interpret the development of the school system from a Protestant perspective. See Karl-Ernst Jeismann and Peter Lundgreen, eds., *Handbuch der deutschen Bildungsgeschichte*, vol. 3, and Christa Berg, ed., *Handbuch*, vol. 4 (Munich: C. H. Beck, 1987; 1991); Reinhart Koselleck, ed., *Bildungsbürgertum im 19. Jahrhundert*, vol. 2: *Bildungsgüter und Bildungswissen* (Stuttgart: Klett-Cotta, 1990). New perspectives are provided by Anne Conrad, "Konfession und Geschlecht: Bildung von der Reformation bis zur Aufklärung," and Ute Gause, "Konfessionelle Bildung im 19. Jahrhundert," in *Gender, Religion, Bildung*, ed. Annebelle Pithan, Silvia Arzt, Monika Jakobs, and Thorsten Knauth (Gütersloh: Gütersloher Verlaghaus, 2009), 151–62; 163–68.
3. There are two examples among many others. In Gisela Wilkending, ed., *Mädchenliteratur der Kaiserzeit: Zwischen weiblicher Identifizierung und Grenzüberschreitung* (Stuttgart: J. B. Metzler, 2003), religious aspects were completely neglected. See Jennifer Drake Askey, *Good Girls, Good Germans: Girls' Education and Emotional Nationalism in Wilhelminian Germany* (Rochester, NY: Camden House, 2013).
4. Jean-Jacques Rousseau, *Émile oder über die Erziehung* (1762; Paderborn: Ferdinand Schöningh, 2001); Barbara Schneider-Taylor, *Jean-Jacques Rousseaus Konzeption der "Sophie": Ein hermeneutisches Projekt* (Hamburg: Verlag Dr. Kovac, 2006).

5. See Johann Heinrich Pestalozzi, *Wie Gertrud ihre Kinder lehrt: Ein Versuch den Müttern Anleitung zu geben, ihre Kinder selbst zu unterrichten, in Briefen* (Bern: Heinrich Gessner, 1801), http://reader.digitale-sammlungen.de/resolve/display/bsb11301318.html.
6. The new European gender model was developed during the French Revolution. It was formulated, for example, in 1793, when female political clubs were forbidden. Jean Pierre André Amar et. al., 9th Brumaire II (October 30, 1793), in Susanne Petersen, *Marktweiber und Amazonen: Frauen in der Französischen Revolution*, 3rd ed. (Cologne: Pahl-Rugenstein, 1991), 222. See also, Archives Parlementaires de 1787 à 1860, Rapport du 9 brumaire an II sur l'interdiction des clubs des femmes, http://gallica.bnf.fr/ark:/12148/bpt6k42696s.
7. Wolfgang Gippert, "Nation und Geschlecht," in *Geschlechtertypisierungen im Kontext von Familie und Schule*, ed. Sabine Andresen and Barbara Rendtorff (Opladen: Barbara Budrich, 2006), 91–103; Bettina Brandt, *Germania und ihre Söhne: Repräsentationen von Nation, Geschlecht und Politik in der Moderne* (Göttingen: Vandenhoeck & Ruprecht, 2010).
8. Hilde Lion, *Zur Soziologie der Frauenbewegung: Die sozialistische und die katholische Frauenbewegung* (Berlin: F. A. Herbig Verlagsbuchhandlung, 1926), 159.
9. Helene Simon, *Elisabeth Gnauck-Kühne*, vol. 1: *Ein Pilgerfahrt* (M. Gladbach: Volksvereins Verlag, 1928), 162–76.
10. Marie Bernays, *Die deutsche Frauenbewegung* (Leipzig, Teubner, 1920), 30.
11. Pauline Herber, "Ziele und Aufgaben des Vereins katholischer deutscher Lehrerinnen in der Gegenwart," *Mädchenbildung auf christlicher Grundlage* 2 (1905–6): 566f.
12. A thorough case study on denominational female education in early modern times and during the nineteenth century is Maria Anna Zumholz, *"Das Weib soll nicht gelehrt seyn": Konfessionell geprägte Frauenbilder, Frauenbildung und weibliche Lebensentwürfe* (Munich: Aschendorff, 2016).
13. Manuel Borutta, *Antikatholizismus: Deutschland und Italien im Zeitalter der europäischen Kulturkämpfe* (Göttingen: Vandenhoeck & Ruprecht, 2010); Andreas Holzem, "Krieg und Nation: Protestantische und katholische Befindlichkeiten um 1914," in *Handbuch der Religionsgeschichte im deutschsprachigen Raum*, vol. 6/1: *20. Jahrhundert: Epochen und Themen*, ed. Volkhard Krech and Lucian Hölscher (Paderborn: Ferdinand Schöningh 2015), 28–43.
14. Compare, for the nineteenth century, the introduction to *Handbuch der deutschen Bildungsgeschichte*, vol. 3, ed. Karl-Erst Jeismann and Peter Lundgreen (Munich: C. H. Beck, 1987). For an overview, especially of the educational system of the German Empire, see Heinz-Elmar Tenorth, "Schule im Kaiserreich," in *Schule und Unterricht im Kaiserreich*, ed. Reinhard Dithmar (Ludwigsfelde: Ludwigsfelder Verlagshaus, 2006), 11–31.
15. "Regulativ über die Einrichtung des evangelischen Seminar-, Präparanden- und Elementarschulunterrichts vom 1., 2. und 3. Oktober 1854," in Ferdinand Stiehl, *Die drei preußischen Regulative vom 1., 2. und 3. Oktober 1854*, 7th ed. (Berlin: Wilhelm Hertz, 1864). See also *Aktenstücke zur Geschichte und zum Verständnis der drei Preußischen Regulative vom 1., 2. und 3. October 1854*, ed. Ferdinand Stiehl (Berlin: Hertz, 1855).
16. "Allgemeine Bestimmungen des Königl. Preuß. Ministers . . . Betreffend das Volksschul-. Präparanden- und Seminar-Wesen," in *Centralblatt für die gesamte Unterrichts-Verwaltung in Preußen* (1872), 585–646.

17. Ibid., 596.
18. "Allerhöchster Erlaß vom 13. Oktober 1890," in *Centralblatt* (1890), 703ff., cited by Dörte Gernert, ed., *Schulvorschriften für den Geschichtsunterricht* (Cologne: Polygram, 1994), 88.
19. *Lehrpläne für den Geschichtsunterricht in den Volks- und Mittelschulen (Verordnungen betreffend das Schulwesen des Regierungsbezirks Breslau nebst einer mit Rücksicht auf die Provinz Schlesien getroffenen Auswahl gesetzlicher Bestimmungen über das Volksschulwesen*, ed. Eduard Sperber (Breslau: Hirt, 1898), 496ff. The basis was the Prussian "Verfügung vom 25. Juni 1892."
20. "Lehrordnung für die Volksschulen des K. Bayer: Regierungsbezirks Niederbayern, Amtliche Ausgabe Landshut 1907," in Gernert, *Schulvorschriften für den Geschichtsunterricht*, 164–66.
21. "Kabinett-Rescript Abt.II. B.II. 16745. Arnsberg, den 28. Dezember 1893," cited in Gernert, *Schulvorschriften für den Geschichtsunterricht*, 103.
22. Ibid., 164.
23. See Gerhard Schneider, "Geschichtsdidaktik und Geschichtsunterricht am Ende des Kaiserreiches," and Falk Pingel, "Geschichtslehrbücher zwischen Kaiserreich und Gegenwart," in *Geschichtsunterricht und Geschichtsdidaktik vom Kaiserreich bis zur Gegenwart: Festschrift des Verbandes der Geschichtslehrer Deutschlands zum 75jährigen Bestehen* (Stuttgart: Klett, 1988), 54–67; 242–60.
24. Franz Brümmer, *Lexikon der deutschen Dichter und Prosaisten vom Beginn des 19. Jahrhunderts bis zur Gegenwart*, 6th ed. (Leipzig: Philipp Reclam, 1913), 6:461–62.
25. She was perhaps Jewish or had Jewish ancestors. The name "Amanda Sonnenfels" is at least listed in a paper of the Reichschriftkammer 1937 as that of a Jewish writer. Published in Volker Dahm, *Das jüdische Buch im Dritten Reich*, 2nd ed. (Munich: C. H. Beck, 1993), 508.
26. For more information, see DBA II 609, 94–97.
27. Katharina Elisabeth Goethe.
28. Actually Barbara von Uthmann.
29. Konstantin Holl, *Die Jugend großer Frauen: Sonntagslesungen für Jungenfrauen* (Freiburg im Breisgau: Herdersche Verlagshandlung 1912); 2nd–3rd eds., 1913; 4th–5th eds., 1917; 6th–7th eds., 1920; 8th–10th eds., 1921; 11th ed., 1929 (23,000–25,000).
30. Anne Taylor Allen, "Religion und Geschlecht," in *Geschichte und Geschlechter*, ed. Karem Hagemann and Jean H. Quataert (Frankfurt am Main: Campus Verlag, 2008), 205–26.
31. Sylvia Schraut, "Bildung, Konfession, Geschlecht: Der Zugang von Frauen zu Universitäten und Wissenschaft," in *Vom Wandel eines Ideals: Bildung, Universität und Gesellschaft in Deutschland*, ed. Nikolaus Buschmann and Ute Planert (Bonn: Dietz, 2010), 29–45.

Bibliography

Allen, Ann Taylor. "Religion und Geschlecht." In *Geschichte und Geschlechter*, edited by Karen Hagemann and Jean H. Quataert, 205–26. Frankfurt am Main: Campus Verlag, 2008.

"Allgemeine Bestimmungen des Königl. Preuß. Ministers . . . Betreffend das Volksschul-. Präparanden- und Seminar-Wesen." In *Centralblatt für die gesamte Unterrichts-Verwaltung in Preußen* (1872), 585–646.

Archives Parlementaires de 1787 à 1860, Rapport du 9 brumaire an II sur l'interdiction des clubs des femmes. http://gallica.bnf.fr/ark:/12148/bpt6k42696s.

Askey, Jennifer Drake. *Good Girls, Good Germans: Girls' Education and Emotional Nationalism in Wilhelminian Germany*. Rochester, NY: Camden House, 2013.

Berg, Christa, ed. *Handbuch der deutschen Bildungsgeschichte*. Vol. 4: *1870–1918: Von der Reichgründung biz zum Ende des Ersten Weltkriegs*. Munich: C. H. Beck, 1991.

Bernays, Marie. *Die deutsche Frauenbewegung*. Leipzig: Teubner, 1920.

Borutta, Manuel. *Antikatholizismus: Deutschland und Italien im Zeitalter der europäischen Kulturkämpfe*. Göttingen: Vandenhoeck & Ruprecht, 2010.

Brandt, Bettina. *Germania und ihre Söhne: Repräsentationen von Nation, Geschlecht und Politik in der Moderne*. Göttingen: Vandenhoeck & Ruprecht, 2010.

Brümmer, Franz. *Lexikon der deutschen Dichter und Prosaisten vom Beginn des 19. Jahrhunderts bis zur Gegenwart*. 6th ed. Vol. 6. Leipzig: Philipp Reclam, 1913.

Conrad, Anne. "Konfession und Geschlecht: Bildung von der Reformation bis zur Aufklärung." In *Gender, Religion, Bildung*, edited by Annebelle Pithan, Silvia Arzt, Monika Jakobs, and Thorsten Knauth, 151–62. Gütersloh: Gütersloher Verlaghaus, 2009.

Dahm, Volker. *Das jüdische Buch im Dritten Reich*. 2nd ed. Munich: C. H. Beck, 1993.

DBA II 609.

Gause, Ute. "Konfessionelle Bildung im 19. Jahrhundert." In *Gender, Religion, Bildung*, edited by Annebelle Pithan, Silvia Arzt, Monika Jakobs, and Thorsten Knauth, 163–68. Gütersloh: Gütersloher Verlaghaus, 2009.

Gernert, Dörte, ed. *Schulvorschriften für den Geschichtsunterricht*. Hamburg: Polygram, 1994.

Gippert, Wolfgang. "Nation und Geschlecht." In *Geschlechtertypisierungen im Kontext von Familie und Schule*, edited by Sabine Andresen and Barbara Rendtorff, 91–103. Opladen: Barbara Budrich, 2006.

Herber, Pauline. "Ziele und Aufgaben des Vereins katholischer deutscher Lehrerinnen in der Gegenwart." *Mädchenbildung auf christlicher Grundlage* 2 (1905–6): 566f.

Holl, Konstantin. *Die Jugend großer Frauen: Sonntagslesungen für Jungenfrauen*. Freiburg im Breisgau: Herdersche Verlagshandlung, 1912.

Holzem, Andreas. "Krieg und Nation: Protestantische und katholische Befindlichkeiten um 1914." In *Handbuch der Religionsgeschichte im deutschsprachigen Raum*. Vol. 6/1: *20. Jahrhundert: Epochen und Themen*, edited by Volkhard Krech and Lucian Hölscher, 28–43. Paderborn: Ferdinand Schöningh, 2015.

Jeismann, Karl-Erst, and Peter Lundgreen, eds. *Handbuch der deutschen Bildungsgeschichte*. Vol. 3: *1800–1870: Von der Neuordnung Deutschlands bis zur Gründung des Deutschen Reiches*. Munich: C. H. Beck, 1987.

Koselleck, Reinhart, ed. *Bildungsbürgertum im 19. Jahrhundert*. Vol. 2: *Bildungsgüter und Bildungswissen*. Stuttgart: Klett-Cotta, 1990.

Lion, Hilde. *Zur Soziologie der Frauenbewegung: Die sozialistische und die katholische Frauenbewegung*. Berlin: F.A. Herbig Verlagsbuchhandlung, 1926.
Nipperdey, Thomas. *Deutsche Geschichte*. 2 vols. Munich: C. H. Beck, 1990.
Pestalozzi, Johann Heinrich. *Wie Gertrud ihre Kinder lehrt: Ein Versuch den Müttern Anleitung zu geben, ihre Kinder selbst zu unterrichten, in Briefen*. Bern: Geßner, 1801. http://reader.digitale-sammlungen.de/resolve/display/bsb11301318.html.
Petersen, Susanne. *Marktweiber und Amazonen: Frauen in der Französischen Revolution*. 3rd ed. Cologne: Pahl-Rugenstein, 1991.
Pingel, Falk. "Geschichtslehrbücher zwischen Kaiserreich und Gegenwart." In *Geschichtsunterricht und Geschichtsdidaktik vom Kaiserreich bis zur Gegenwart: Festschrift des Verbandes der Geschichtslehrer Deutschlands zum 75jährigen Bestehen*, edited by Paul Leidinger, 242–60. Stuttgart: Klett, 1988.
Rousseau, Jean Jacques. *Émile oder über die Erziehung*. 1762. Paderborn: Ferdinand Schöningh, 2001.
Schneider, Gerhard. "Geschichtsdidaktik und Geschichtsunterricht am Ende des Kaiserreiches." In *Geschichtsunterricht und Geschichtsdidaktik vom Kaiserreich bis zur Gegenwart: Festschrift des Verbandes der Geschichtslehrer Deutschlands zum 75jährigen Bestehen*, edited by Paul Leidinger, 54–67. Stuttgart: Klett, 1988.
Schneider-Taylor, Barbara. *Jean-Jacques Rousseaus Konzeption der "Sophie": Ein hermeneutisches Projekt*. Hamburg: Verlag Dr. Kovac, 2006.
Schraut, Sylvia. "Bildung, Konfession, Geschlecht: Der Zugang von Frauen zu Universitäten und Wissenschaft." In *Vom Wandel eines Ideals: Bildung, Universität und Gesellschaft in Deutschland*, edited by Nikolaus Buschmann and Ute Planert, 29–45. Bonn: Dietz, 2010.
Simon, Helene. *Elisabeth Gnauck-Kühne*. Vol. 1: *Ein Pilgerfahrt*. M. Gladbach: Volksvereins Verlag, 1928.
Sperber, Eduard ed. *Lehrpläne für den Geschichtsunterricht in den Volks- und Mittelschulen: Verordnungen betreffend das Schulwesen des Regierungsbezirks Breslau nebst einer mit Rücksicht auf die Provinz Schlesien getroffenen Auswahl gesetzlicher Bestimmungen über das Volksschulwesen*. Breslau: Hirt, 1898.
Stiehl, Ferdinand, ed. *Aktenstücke zur Geschichte und zum Verständnis der drei Preußischen Regulative vom 1., 2. und 3. Oktober 1854*. Berlin: Hertz, 1855.
———. *Die drei preußischen Regulative vom 1., 2. und 3. Oktober 1854*. 7th ed. Berlin: Hertz, 1864.
Tenorth, Heinz-Elmar. "Schule im Kaiserreich." In *Schule und Unterricht im Kaiserreich*, edited by Reinhard Dithmar and Hans D. Schulz, 11–31. Ludwigsfelde: Ludwigsfelder Verlagshaus, 2006.
Wehler, Hans-Ulrich. *Deutsche Gesellschaftsgeschichte*. Vols. 2–3. Munich: C. H. Beck, 2008.
Wilkending, Gisela, ed. *Mädchenliteratur der Kaiserzeit: Zwischen weiblicher Identifizierung und Grenzüberschreitung*. Stuttgart: J. B. Metzler, 2003.
Zumholz, Maria Anna. *"Das Weib soll nicht gelehrt seyn": Konfessionell geprägte Frauenbilder, Frauenbildung und weibliche Lebensentwürfe*. Münster: Aschendorff, 2016.

CHAPTER 9

Women for the Homeland
Comparing Catholic and Protestant Female Education in Italy (1848–1908)

Liviana Gazzetta

Notwithstanding the plethora of studies on female involvement in the idea of national ancestry as the basis of the Italian Risorgimento, the analysis of the proposals—chiefly issued by religious groups stemming from the two main Christian communities in Italy—regarding the patriotic function of women is still pretty fragmentary.[1] This is a problematic deficiency. In no other country, in fact, did the process of *nation-building* encounter such strong opposition from the dominant Church, with the consequent positioning of religious minorities in support of the national state; in no other country, therefore, did the female involvement in this process have such deep religious valences. In the absence of a consolidated picture emerging from studies, I shall proceed to make use of actual evidence in the course of this contribution, following the suggestions offered by a nucleus of sources of educational writing: I shall consider both overtly instructional material (speeches and teaching materials directed at girls or young women) and particularly significant periodicals aimed at women or at families with an educational objective in view. Through these we shall seek, specifically, to discern the ideal-typical features of female education in the Catholic and Protestant areas. The main Protestant groups in nineteenth-century Italy regarded Waldensians, Lutherans, Anglicans, Methodists, Baptists, as well as members of the Free Church movement.[2] After defining the frame of reference within which the comparison shall be made, I shall proceed to identify the main points that I believe prove definitively that female involvement in the Risorgimento process in the Protestant world promoted proximity to and often involvement in the feminist movement, unlike what tended to happen in the Catholic world.

It is undeniable—although for reasons that cannot be reconstructed here—that the relationship between the Catholic religion and the nation was unique and not easily comparable with other Catholic national contexts. On the other hand, in the nineteenth century, a controversial relationship between religion and nation undoubtedly arose within the Italian Catholicism of the period. To define the situation in what is perforce a very summary manner, one could say that the guiding idea of a Catholic nation,[3] which implied that Catholicism was a constituent characteristic of the Italian nation, was to assume crucial importance in the Risorgimento phase and later. The great predecessor of all successive variations of this canon was the Neo-Guelphism movement in the early 1800s, based on the tenet that established the genetic relationship between the Catholic religion and Italian civilization as the focal point of European Christian civilization at large and as a counterpoint to the rational/enlightenment idea of civilization.

But beyond this common base, the Catholic nation was defined according to uneven assumptions right from the beginning; within the idea of the civilizing mission of Italy as a Catholic nation, two prevailing trends seem to have been current. The first was based on the conviction that the Reformation had implemented a fundamental interruption of medieval Christianity; this interruption had given rise not only to an individualistic and materialistic modern society but to the very phenomenon of international disorder in relationships between states. The second, implying that European civilization itself was derived from Christianity, was inclined to recognize the Christian imprint in some of the legislation and values of modern societies and states. These two ways of understanding the Catholic nation parted company considerably after the 1848 revolution; on the one hand, the canon of the Catholic nation centered on papal authority and the need for the absolute confessional attributes of social and political legislation, giving rise to the intransigent movement and causing profound divisions with the Risorgimento state; on the other hand, an area of public opinion recognized itself as belonging to the liberal Catholic movement and (after unification) of conciliatory Catholicism, which was one of the strong points of the liberal governing class that led the unification process. It is therefore within this framework that we can attempt to investigate the horizons of an educational approach as regards women, as concerns the construction of a national state, in order to compare it to the situation in the Protestant world. We make this attempt in the awareness that our comparison is forced into a paradox—in fact, it was also with the support of liberal Catholicism that religious emancipation was granted to Italian Protestants (and Jews), while precisely this emancipation gave rise to the theory of a liberal, Protestant, and masonic conspiracy to harm the Church and the "real" nation supported by the majority of Italian Catholics.[4]

Elements to Be Analyzed: The Liberal Catholics

The conciliatory strategy of the liberal Catholics, as opposed to intransigent catholic culture and staunch adherents of the pope, aimed at preventing state lay radicalism and exerted a great deal of energy in favor of popular culture in the ethical-educational field; material destined to be read or heard by women was a fundamental part of this project. They managed to achieve what amounted to a substantial integration into the prevailing pedagogical-educational canon of liberal Italy during the second part of the nineteenth century, partly by blending in the values of self-helpism, the educational principle of helping people to help themselves. Ardent supporters of the much-desired regeneration of the homeland, starting with the family but first of all attributing value to the national religious tradition, liberal Catholics demanded improved education and—within limits—instruction for females as a reaction to the superficial or, worse still, frivolous upbringing that earlier generations had considered a suitable education for women.

However, like the intransigent Catholics, the liberal Catholics considered religious formation to be the foremost element in female education, even from a nationalist standpoint. The *Manuale per le giovinette italiane* (Manual for the Young Girls of Italy) by Luisa Paladini (which enjoyed great success) was the educational model as regards the central role played by religious formation and as regards the canon of the "strong woman," an authentic *topos* of Catholicism between the nineteenth and twentieth centuries. According to Giulia Molino Colombini, the three-centuries-long slumber of Italy had been caused by women's lack of religious faith, which had made them incapable of carrying out their domestic priesthood, as "only the Catholic religion is capable of knitting together political and moral opinions in order to achieve unity of identical persuasion in all."[5]

Women, according to these ideas, were effectively supposed to direct all their energies into the fundamental task of averting the basic disagreements between state and Church that plagued Italian society from 1848 and even more so from 1861 onward, without, however, allowing the state to separate itself from its faith. An effort had to be made to amalgamate freedom of conscience and rejection of agnosticism; the unitary liberal state had to find forms of conciliation with the Catholic "physiognomy" of the nation. If, therefore, all educational material in the nineteenth century invariably propounds that the fundamental aim of female activity is to guarantee "domestic peace" and to "maintain concord in the family,"⁶ the liberal Catholics held that it meant that wives and mothers were the best mediators in the conflict between faith and politics that rent the country and so often led to interfamilial conflict. It was a truly widespread concern among the liberal forces, who feared that the "domestic hearth" would be undermined by subterranean conflicts over religion between husband and wife.

In the 1880s, Ambrogio Garavaglia, in his famous text *Della educazione religiosa e civile delle fanciulle in conformità alle attuali condizioni d'Italia* (Of the Religious and Civic Education of Young Girls in Conformity with the Present Conditions in Italy)—criticized by the Jesuit *Civiltà Cattolica*—offered a fruitful summary of this thesis. The importance of female religious formation as a civic function is restated, as civic education is "an inefficient or even dangerous or deadly factor, if not illuminated and vivified by religion."⁷ As, in fact, there is a close relationship between the history of the various religions and the history of the nations they have modeled, so there is a close interdependence between the type of religion and the type of female: only the Christian woman, who knows how to live enclosed by the sanctuary of her domestic walls, according to Garavaglia, becomes the honor of society at large, guaranteeing "virginal reserve, holy modesty, maternal love, and conjugal love."⁸ Therefore, a woman can exercise a beneficial effect on society when she bases her virtue entirely on the tenets of faith (and here he introduces a series of examples of female patriotism) and can thereby prove the mutual interdependence of faith and politics: "Thus, Religion and the Homeland, the Nation and the Church, the Gospels and the Constitution are the fundamental principles of this education, which must, therefore, be in full accord with the present situation of Italy."⁹

The concept that "the future of children is in the hands of the mother" is ubiquitous, but the female mission had to be based on ethical-religious formation and had to take place strictly within the family walls. Don Vincenzo Papa, in his speech "La giovinetta e l'amor di patria" (Young Girls and Patriotism) once again underlines these points:

> Thus, you should once more exhibit your love for your homeland; your heart should be, as I should say, the altar on which these conflicts rest, to hold each other in the embrace of peace. . . . Say, with the sweet and powerful music of your lyrical accents, say that religion and homeland are two sisters, both always and only daughters of God; say that they cannot be enemies on earth, as a single thought and a single love unites them in friendship in heaven.¹⁰

Herein lay the true civic role of women, according to this view. This was a role that did not exclude knowledge of the order of the state, from an educational perspective, but it did not include any political participation therein: "To know the laws of their country, I believe, would be useful to women, so that they may be able to educate their children to respect and observe such provisions. I think that it would be necessary for the population in general,"[11] said Luisa Paladini in her *Manuale*. Her position totally accorded with the editorial position of *La Donna e la Famiglia* (The Woman and the Family), an important Catholic periodical published in Genoa that proclaimed the following in its first issue: "We would like to exclude politics completely, but we do not banish the principles and rules for a healthy patriotism. We would like, as our archbishop suggested, to be the bearers of a remedy against the roots of evil: within the family."[12] Due to its longevity (1862–1917) and the stature and authority of its contributors, the Genoese monthly can, in fact, be considered emblematic of these positions and of their evolution.

If "preserving and increasing private virtues is the part that divine and human laws assign to women,"[13] only religion is the true, sole defender of female dignity that no emancipation can replace, as Caterina Franceschi Ferrucci stressed in *Alle madri e alle giovinette d'Italia* (To the Mothers and Young Women of Italy): "We were freed by the Gospel!"[14] It was a female task of post-Unification mediation that gradually, thanks to the evolution of society and culture, incorporated the idea of public female activity in charity work, teaching, and philanthropy. This type of civic activity recurs as the only form of female self-helpism recognized by such illustrious Catholic authors as Augusto Alfani, for instance, in *Battaglie e vittorie* (Battles and Victories),[15] that only recognizes the value of female heroism in the fields of popular education and public or private charity. It would only be with the phenomena of Christian democracy and Catholic feminism between the nineteenth and twentieth centuries that minority sectors of Catholicism would accept that the civic and political formation of women could be necessary to religious faith itself in order to transform society. In these groups, the spirit of interfaith collaboration would combine with the critique of traditional female education and of the split between Church and nation-state, open issues since the Risorgimento, culminating in their acceptance, in 1907, of the Programma minimo femminista (Minimum Feminist Program) with democratic, radical, and socialist members.[16]

Protestantism in Nineteenth-Century Italy

Within Italian nineteenth-century Protestantism, the spiritual imprint of Evangelical revival became profoundly intertwined with the ideals of a nation-state. Carried on the wave of a romantic rediscovery of the Gospel, the Protestant churches aimed at a new form of Christianity that was to be born (or reborn) together with a united and free Italy. Furthermore, the letters patent of 17 February 1848, whereby Carlo Alberto granted civic rights to the Waldensians, created an inseparable link between the Risorgimento forces and the historical Protestant Church in Italy (the Waldensians) as well as the other existing Protestant entities, who were mainly present in the Piedmontese and Tuscan areas; at the end of the nineteenth century, Italian Protestants would number sixty-five thousand in an overall population of thirty-two million.[17]

Although the Protestant communities were structurally in favor of the Risorgimento, they were, nonetheless, affected by denominational differences; as regards culture and teaching methods, they were widely influenced by Francophone and Anglo-Saxon models, authors, and themes. One has to recall, however, that with regard to education, the various Protestant communities produced a "unitary" effort: a periodical named *La Scuola della domenica*, later called *L'Amico dei Fanciulli* (The Young Persons' Friend), that was first published in 1863 in Florence after an interdenominational assembly. The first interdenominational association experiences brought forth educational material. These were the Associazioni Cristiane dei Giovani, the Italian branch of the Young Men's Christian Association, established in 1887, followed by an analogous female organization; in 1894, the Unione cristiana delle giovani (Young Women's Christian Association) was founded in Turin, and in 1895, the Italian section of the Association internationale des amies de la jeune fille, which had been founded in 1877[18] after the first international abolitionist congress, was initiated.

Influenced by transnational liberal models, the Italian Protestant population—mostly bourgeois but also including peasant components especially in southern Italy and in the Piedmont area—saw the basic connection necessary to the construction of a nation not as ethnic or religious but as voluntary and contractual. Accustomed as they were to identifying each other as brothers on the basis of their faith, they certainly envisaged the nation as a family (and adopted a large-scale organizational project to suit this vision), but a family founded, paradoxically enough, on pacts: the pact between Protestants and the Crown, starting with emancipation; the pact between the diverse religious communities existing in the country; the pact between forces based on different ideological orientations; the pact, finally, between husband and wife within the family, which was the foundation of the national society.[19] For this reason, too, the Protestant world identified one of the greatest dangers to the new state as being the socially divisive factors produced by Roman Catholicism, with the traditional clerical influence it wielded over married women and its denial of the value of a civil union.

With this perspective, many Protestant members participated in anti-Catholic and anticlerical polemics with liberal, secular, and radical intellectual exponents.[20] The theme of diverse positions on religion between men and women, which we have seen as one of the most central debating points for the less intransigent Catholics, was openly debated in the Protestant press from completely the opposite point of view: the first thing to be pointed out was the responsibility of the clergy in "adamantly" opposing civil marriage, which had been introduced by Unification legislation. Women, especially young women, were invited to change their religious views, accepting the principle of freedom in the spiritual dimension as well: "Protestantism forms the family, and the family forms nations. Catholicism divides husband and wife. Protestantism unites them. Become Protestant, in order to become truly Christian. . . . You will have saved your homeland, tearing it from the grip of its greediest and deadliest enemies: the Jesuits and Rome."[21]

Such an appeal to "modernize" religion by the interdenominational educational press was echoed by structural attention to mixed education and by quoting active female models who tended to promote greater equality with the male status, often supported by examples relating to Protestant countries in northern Europe. Organically addressed to both genders, *L'Amico dei fanciulli* proposed educational models based on the celebration of the Risorgimento process and on respect for the Savoy family, but also on the invitation to prepare oneself to be a committed citizen: "Strive therefore to become useful, good citizens and thus primarily good Christians. Although the Christian knows he has a 'better homeland' in Heaven, nonetheless he loves his earthly homeland and strives to serve it with all his strength."[22]

It was an invitation to be a consciously committed and useful citizen, also classified according to gender, as a number of significant episodes show. One of the most significant concerned Lidia Poët, a Waldensian who became a symbol of the emancipation movement because she tried to enter the ranks of the Lawyers' Roster of Turin in 1883. In her thesis, at her qualifying exam for the doctor at law degree that was presented on 17 June 1881, Poët defined the state as a "great whole of families": by uniting the respective qualities of men and women, one could attain greater levels of harmony within the state as well as within the family. The complementary qualities of the characters and of the roles did not—as represented by Catholic teaching—imply the rigid separation of public and private spheres. If one believed that women could help to shape patriotism and civic virtues, observed Poët, one could not think that women should be excluded *a priori* from citizenship: "How will she recognize which public virtues are those she herself must support and fortify along with others?"[23] And as life in a state does not only imply rights, women too should serve their country.

She was, in other words, outlining a proposed female civic service, similar to that carried out by men: a female draft, whereby young women would be asked to devote a number of hours every day to public charity or assistance activities. It was an idea inspired by a concept of the complementary qualities of characters and roles between the sexes that was understandable also in view of the female anthropological model publicized by the Protestant press, a model in which features of relatively greater "emancipation" were present, compared to the general national context, but at the same time devoid of any aggressive claim staking. That the idea of a female militia complementary to the male one was a concept circulating among Italian Protestants can be proved by the fact that almost thirty years later, Poët's view was explicitly shared by another Waldensian national celebrity, Amilda Pons. In 1908, in her book *Studio della morale nel suo svolgimento religioso e scientifico* (Study on the Religious and Scientific Development of Morality), Pons too suggested the institution of female civic service in public assistance or teaching activities.[24] Without questioning the role women play in the family, the idea of a female militia to serve society and the state seems peculiar to the Protestant context, where gender relationships were conceived in what might be defined as complementary egalitarian terms. The extension of female capacities from home to society was the privileged ground on which a convergence with feminism was being developed within Protestant associations, unlike what was happening in most of the Catholic world.

Plutarchan Collections and Female Models

One should specify that it is not easy to identify precise mindset differences within the enormously abundant instructional material addressed to women that was produced throughout the second half of the nineteenth century. During the first decades after the unification of Italy, there was widespread approval and a sort of convergence of opinion between the lay, moderate circles and the liberal Catholics, and at times between the lay moderates and the Protestant circles, as regards the exemplary figures of Erminia Fuà Fusinato,[25] Caterina Percoto,[26] and Caterina Franceschi Ferrucci.[27] Regarding Erminia Fuà Fusinato, who often features among contemporary Catholic protagonists, it is interesting to note that she was born Jewish and had converted to Catholicism in 1856 in order to marry the patriotic poet Arnaldo Fusinato. These literary ladies were held to embody patriotic and family concepts and to show what the correct education and instruction for women should be—the kind of education and instruction that would perfect both intellectual and moral faculties without, however, upsetting the balance of the family or rejecting religious convictions in the name of national patriotism. The exemplary influence of Fuà Fusinato's biography seems to have gained a foothold even in Protestant circles, at the very least because the well-known poetess could be portrayed as a "martyr" to her love for instruction and education, as other female Protestant reformers had been.[28] On the other hand, whereas totally lay behavioral manuals were somewhat exceptional, especially if addressed to women, Protestant educational production in Italy inevitably ended up reflecting models and teaching perspectives that were not strictly Italian. It was thus that the all-pervasive Catholic model of the "strong woman"[29] also inspired well-established female authors by the introduction, at times, of suitable youthful examples.[30] These took the form of female Plutarchan collections: biographies of illustrious women to be presented as examples to young women, which were widely circulated throughout the nation during the second half of the nineteenth century, with the objective of building up a common historical memory and disseminating an elementary teaching method for the new Italian female citizens.[31]

As regards the delicate ground of female education, these Plutarchan compilations helped to build up a climate of syncretized integration between Catholic traditional models and lay virtuous models of domesticity—the kind of integration that, on one side, bypassed any political disagreements with the Church, and on the other was often the subject of criticism by intransigent Catholics. Francesco Berlan, the author of a publication on male exemplary figures that preceded his successful manual *Le fanciulle celebri* (Famous Young Women), presented a civilizing handbook, or *oecumene*, for the education of women that was certainly attentive to religious values inasmuch as it included exemplary saints, as well as female scientists, heroines of chastity, and heroines of the Italian unification wars.[32]

Clemente Rossi wrote the famous *Il tesoro delle giovinette* (Treasury for Young Girls), which was no less ecumenical and went through several editions; right from the start, it was positively reviewed by *Civiltà Cattolica* because of the educational importance attributed to religion. The early twentieth-century edition presented a series of famous women, starting from Roman history and continuing down to the actress Carlotta Marchionni, uniting religious with artistic or even political exemplary figures, like Eleonora Fonseca. However, if one examines the text carefully, the biographical content is only a marginal part of it, and, in the more treatise-like sections, the prevailing female models are always based on figures of the religious tradition. In the 1909 edition, there is also a chapter devoted to the illustration of the social rights and duties of Italian women; in this context, analysis of the burning question of marriage—hotly debated by the liberal state and the Church—is "solved" by the author when he admonishes women as to its inherent dangers. Although Rossi stressed that the Civil Code did not disapprove of religious marriage, he nonetheless bade young women beware of possible cases of men who had gone through a religious marriage ceremony and then undertook a second civil marriage: "You have been warned: nothing would excuse you."³³

The famous *Plutarch*, or biographical compendium, by Eugenio Comba adheres fairly closely to the Italian Protestant mindset, although it is by no means strictly confessional; his *Donne illustri italiane proposte ad esempio alle giovinette* (Illustrious Italian Women Presented as an Example to Young Women) was dedicated to Queen Margherita of Savoy. He hastens to preface that his compilation is based on the need to prove the importance of a "healthy" educational culture for women, particularly in view of their role in the education of the population. The majority of the models he proposes are thus women of culture, although he takes care to balance out his selection with exemplary female figures who led retiring lives, often devoted to self-sacrifice, from the medieval Pisan Kinzica de' Sismondi to a group of "illustrious living women"—which includes the unmissable Caterina Percoto—without, however, excluding a personality like Erminia Manelli, who gained fame for having joined the army in 1866 in her brother's stead. The presence of a biographical cameo of Olimpia Morata is also worthy of note; she supported the sixteenth-century Protestant Reformation and is described as a strongly gifted woman of great culture who overcame with tenacity the many adversities she encountered. The presence of this portrait underlines the peculiarity of Comba's *Plutarch*, resulting in the Italian Protestant schools considering him suitable to be adopted among their textbook authors.³⁴

Among the foreign writers who were referred to in Italian Protestant circles as authors of instructional material, special attention should be paid to the French pastor Adolphe Monod, a successful preacher and the author of two discourses on women, as well as to the Swiss pastor Frank Thomas. Both clearly upheld, unlike Catholic instructors, that Christ was the ideal for the lives of both sexes. In this way, they indicated a general human mission that pertained in equal measure to both sexes, and they always advocated coeducation. The latter was a peculiar aspect of Protestant educational models that gained ground, although it did so without detracting from the conviction as to the natural and spiritual diversity of women and men; it was the very complementary quality of the two sexes that was supposed, according to this thinking, to assist in the regular introduction of mixed-sex schools based on the American model. Scholastic coexistence and coeducation was held to be the best way of preparing young boys and girls for mutual respect, for knowledge of the strengths and weaknesses of each sex, and generally for living with each other.³⁵ Without radically overturning the asymmetrical positions and roles of the two sexes, matrimony was no longer held to be the only female destination; the choice of an unmarried life could gain value in study, in charitable activities for society, and in working as a deaconess;³⁶ and it was considered that careers hitherto denied to women should be opened to them, without, however, introducing them into active political life. In view of these ethical and legislative horizons, and with a willingness to renegotiate as regarded certain individual points, the Young Women's Christian Union joined the federation of the National Council of Women in 1908, as we shall see later.

Educational Renewal and Feminism

The interchanges between Protestantism and women's movements in the nineteenth and twentieth centuries can be confirmed by one of the most widespread stereotypes in the intransigent Catholic world of the time, which viewed the women of the religious minorities as the hidden but real source of feminism as well as of the masonic intrigues against the "national religion." In Italy, according to this theory, freemasonry was "in furious pursuit of women and young people to fill their lodges,"[37] finding ready consent among Jewesses and Protestants, chiefly in order to entrap teachers and educators, thus guaranteeing their control over the younger generations.

In the educational field, the first synergistic elements between the Protestant world and feminism had emerged in the 1870s with the Froebel movement,[38] which attempted to satisfy the country's need to modernize, starting by improving education and redesigning the civic role of the family. A movement had gathered around the introduction of the Froebel method as well as around a series of initiatives in which the leftist forces forged by the Risorgimento events were associated with the majority of the positivistic educational and justice system members, the more enlightened circles of the religious minorities in Italy, and the women's movement.

Centered on play activities and thematic conversations instead of lessons, the Froebel kindergartens were not intended to replace absent mothers but to operate as proper educational institutions that explicitly favored coeducation of the sexes; religious education—which was one of the aspects included in the scheme—was not supposed to be directed toward confessional ends. As the Froebel ideas spread, and after the experimental opening of Venice's first kindergarten in 1869, a lively debate on the educational role of nursery schools arose all over Italy, and Catholic public opinion veered against the Froebel perspective inasmuch as it was suspected of being a channel for the spread of Protestantism.

On the other hand, alongside a group of representatives of the Jewish middle class,[39] there was a circle of Protestant women who actively promoted the spread of nursery schools and a general renewal of the education system. They were, moreover, not Waldensian Protestants but of

English, American, and German provenance, and close to the Evangelical persuasion. Some of them were married to Italian patriots and intellectuals implicated in the Risorgimento. Stéfanie Etzerodt Omboni, Maria Boorman Wheeler Ceccarini, Emily Colton Bliss Gould, and Giorgina Craufurd Saffi[40] all took an active part, together with representatives of feminism or in their own capacity as members of the women's movement, in the creation of new educational structures and in the spread of nursery schools.

Almost immediately after promoting these activities, the Evangelical circles and the feminist activists joined forces in a campaign for the abolition of state prostitution that was developing all over Europe. One of the leaders of nineteenth-century feminist Protestantism, Josephine Butler, had founded the Ladies' National Association for the Repeal of the Contagious Diseases Acts and had then extended the initiative beyond its English confines by constituting the British, Continental and General Federation, a structure that was able to act as a catalyst, even on a general level, for elaborations and proposals in favor of female emancipation. In the same way as the kindergarten movement, the abolitionist campaign found support among the personalities and organizations of radical feminism, political opposition, and religious minorities. It was within these circles that the Italian branch of the Association internationale des amies de la jeune fille was founded toward the end of the century (the already-mentioned Associazione delle amiche della giovane was founded in 1877).

Protestant representatives were later present in the context of the Union for the (Greater) Good (together with representatives of a beginning Catholic feminism[41]) and finally, and most especially, in the Consiglio Nazionale delle Donne Italiane (National Council of Italian women). Officially founded in 1903 as a federation of associations that were chiefly social/assistance oriented and of moderate political color, the Consiglio Nazionale delle Donne included many aristocratic and bourgeois members close to the Liberal Party and linked to the Catholic faith without being aligned with liberal or intransigent Catholics.[42] This association was partly the result of the International Council of Women, an organization born in the United States in 1888 that, thanks to its inclination not to be aligned with any religion or political party and thanks to its moderate positions, had become well embedded within Anglo-Saxon Protestant feminist circles.

When the national congress of Italian women was called in Rome by the Consiglio Nazionale delle Donne in April 1908,[43] the presence of representatives linked to the Waldensian and Protestant worlds was significant both numerically and regarding quality; in addition to the by-then-well-known Lidia Poët and Amilda Pons, an important role was played by

Berta Turin, delegate for the Amiche della giovane, Lisa Noerbel, Alice Schiavoni Bosio, Luisa Giulio, and Carolina Amari. The occasion was marked by the presence of representatives from the two feminist Protestant structures then in existence: the Unione cristiana delle giovani and the Associazione internazionale delle amiche della giovane. Unlike what happened in Catholic circles, these Protestant organizations did not attempt to distinguish themselves as a separate front and, above all, did not oppose the order of the day presented by Linda Malnati against the teaching of any one religion in the schools. The 1908 congress was considered the official entrance of Protestant female organizations into the feminist movement; as Alice Schiavoni Bosio, who was responsible for the Roman section of the Unione cristiana delle giovani, stated on the pages of the national organ of the association,

> The time has come for the Christian Unions in Italy to be numbered among the Italian female activist entities; . . . the time has come, finally, for the unions to study and select what is beautiful, good, and just in the present female movement in Italy and, by joining it, in order to achieve the great ideal, come down into the battlefield, bringing with them their dispassionate and serene minds, that breadth of vision, that spirit of charity and sacrifice that they have drawn, that they must have drawn from the true source.[44]

It was on this very occasion, however, that the intransigent component took control of the whole female Catholic movement, radically opposing any collaboration with feminism and pushing the Catholic feminists (who were prepared to discuss the demands of the non-Catholic movements) off the stage.[45] We may conclude that national and patriotic female education in Italy during the nineteenth century was strictly linked with Catholic values and ideas, but only a part of the Catholic world was available to collaborate on the liberal state. In general, similarly to the Jewish situation,[46] the Protestant female gender role allowed for more agency in the public sphere than the liberal Catholic model—even though there was ample convergence on female educational values. While Protestant female organizations played an important role in the Italian feminist movement, the Catholic feminists were forced into silence.

Liviana Gazzetta is a PhD in European social history from the Middle Ages to the contemporary age at Venice University. Her research activity has developed around the themes of women's history and women's movements in the contemporary age. Among her publications are *Cattoliche durante il fascismo: Ordine sociale e organizzazioni femminili nelle Venezie* (Rome: Viella, 2011) and *Orizzonti nuovi: Storia del primo femminismo in Italia 1865–1925* (Rome: Viella, 2018).

Notes

1. For a discussion of the relationship between gender and the process of *nation-building* in Italy, see Rosanna De Longis, "Maternità illustri: Dalle madri illuministe ai cataloghi ottocenteschi," in *Storia della maternità*, ed. Marina D'Amelia (Rome: Laterza, 1997), 184–207; Ilaria Porciani, *Famiglia e nazione nel lungo Ottocento italiana: Modelli, strategie e reti di relazioni* (Rome: Viella, 2006); Marina Bonsanti, "Amore familiare, amore romantico e amor di patria," in *Storia d'Italia. Annali 22. Il Risorgimento*, ed. Alberto Mario Banti and Paul Ginsborg (Turin: Einaudi, 2007), 131–43; Silvana Patriarca, "Italiani/Italiane," in *Atlante culturale del Risorgimento: Lessico del linguaggio politico dal Settecento all'Unità*, ed. Alberto Mario Banti and Marco Meriggi (Rome: Laterza, 2011), 199–213.
2. See Giorgio Spini, *Risorgimento e protestanti*, 3rd ed. (Turin: Claudiana, 2008), and Giorgio Spini, *Italia liberale e protestanti* (Turin: Claudiana, 2002).
3. See Guido Formigoni, *L'Italia dei cattolici: Fede e nazione dal Risorgimento alla Repubblica* (Bologna: Il Mulino, 1998); Francesco Traniello, *Religione cattolica e Stato nazionale: Dal Risorgimento al secondo dopoguerra* (Bologna: Il Mulino, 2007).
4. For these aspects of the Italian Catholic movement, see Renato Moro, "Le chiese, gli ebrei e la società moderna: L'Italia," in *Integrazione e identità: L'esperienza ebraica in Germania e Italia dall'Illuminismo al fascismo*, ed. Mario Toscano (Milan: Franco Angeli, 1998), 167–82.
5. Giulia Molino Colombini, *Sulla educazione della donna: Pensieri* (Turin: Fory e Dalmazzo, 1851), 12.
6. Luisa A. Paladini, *Manuale per le giovinette italiane* (Florence: Le Monnier, 1857), 91.
7. Ambrogio Garavaglia, *Della educazione religiosa e civile delle fanciulle in conformità alle attuali condizioni d'Italia* (Milan: Dumolard, 1884), 35.
8. Ibid., 17.
9. Ibid., 227.
10. Vincenzo Papa, *La giovinetta e l'amor di patria* (Turin: Speirani, 1886), 12.
11. Paladini, *Manuale*, 92.
12. Fortunata Bottaro, "Letter" [1862?], in Marina Milan, *Donna, famiglia, società: Aspetti della stampa femminile cattolica in Italia tra Otto e Novecento* (Genoa: Ecig, 1983), 63.
13. Luisa A. Paladini, "Pensieri," *Letture femminili*, 1865, in Milan, *Donna, famiglia, società*, 17.
14. Caterina Franceschi Ferrucci, "Alle madri e alle giovinette d'Italia," *La donna e la famiglia*, January 1874.
15. Augusto Alfani, *Battaglie e vittorie: Nuovi esempi di "Volere è potere"* (Florence: Barbera, 1890).
16. See Francesco M. Cecchini, *Il femminismo cristiano: La questione femminile nella prima democrazia cristiana 1898–1912* (Rome: Editori Riuniti, 1979).
17. See Giorgio Spini, *Studi sull'evangelismo italiano tra Otto e Novecento* (Turin: Claudiana, 1994); Gian Paolo Romagnani, "Italian Protestants," in *The Emancipation of Catholics, Jews and Protestants*, ed. R. Liedtke and S. Wendehorst (New York: Manchester University Press, 1999), 148–68.

18. See Margherita Gay Meynier, *Breve storia della YWCA italiana dalle origini ad oggi*, s.l., s.n.
19. See Eugenio Biagini, "La nazione sinodale: Patria e libertà nella retorica protestante italiana, 1848–1866," in *Il protestantesimo italiano nel Risorgimento: Influenze, miti, identità*, ed. Simone Maghenzani (Turin: Claudiana, 2012), 89–111.
20. See Guido Verucci, *L'Italia laica prima e dopo l'Unità 1848–1876: Anticlericalismo, libero pensiero e ateismo nella società italiana* (Rome: Laterza, 1996).
21. "La moglie e il prete," *La famiglia cristiana*, 14 June 1878.
22. "Vittorio Emanuele II in Campidoglio," *L'Amico dei fanciulli*, July 7, 1871.
23. Lidia Poët, *Studio sulla condizione della donna rispetto al diritto costituzionale* (Pinerolo: Chiantore, 1881), 15.
24. Amilda Pons, *Studio della morale nel suo svolgimento religioso e scientifico* (Turin: Paravia, 1908), 125.
25. See Maria Cristina Leuzzi, *Erminia Fuà Fusinato: Una vita in altro modo* (Rome: Anicia, 2008); Nadia M. Filippini, "Amor di patria e pratiche di disciplinamento: Erminia Fuà Fusinato," in *Di generazione in generazione: Le italiane dall'Unità ad oggi*, ed. Maria Teresa Mori, Alessandra Pescarolo, Anna Scattigno, and Simonetta Soldani (Rome: Viella, 2014), 73–86.
26. See Adriana Chemello, "Caterina Percoto e l'educazione della donna," in *Donne al lavoro: Ieri oggi domani*, ed. Saveria Chemotti (Padua: Il Poligrafo, 2009), 305–33.
27. See Clotilde Barbarulli, "Caterina Franceschi Ferrucci accademica della Crusca: Il sapere di una donna nell'800," in *La Crusca nella tradizione letteraria e linguistica italiana* (Florence: Accademia della Crusca, 1985), 335–56.
28. Pietro P. Pons, "Erminia Fuà Fusinato ed Emilia Gould," *La Rivista cristiana*, 1877.
29. See Giorgio P. Camaiani, "L'immagine femminile nella letteratura e nella trattatistica dell'800: La 'donna forte' e la 'donna debole,'" in *Santi, culti, simboli dell'età della secolarizzazione 1815–1915*, ed. Emma Fattorini (Turin: Rosenberg & Sellier, 1997), 431–47; Liviana Gazzetta, "Ideologia e organizzazione della donna cattolica," in *Elena Da Persico*, ed. Liviana Gazzetta (Verona: Cierre, 2005), 47–90.
30. See, for example, Maria Bobba, *Donnina forte . . . racconto per le giovinette* (Turin: Paravia, 1894); Sofia Bisi Albini, *Donnina forte* (Florence: Bemporad, 1903).
31. See Ilaria Porciani, "Il Plutarco femminile," in *L'educazione delle donne: Scuole e modelli di vita femminile nell'Italia dell'Ottocento*, ed. Simonetta Soldani (Milan: Franco Angeli, 1991), 297–317; Anna Ascenzi, *Il Plutarco delle donne* (Macerata: EUM, 2009).
32. Francesco Berlan, *Le fanciulle celebri e l'infanzia delle donne illustri d'Italia antiche e moderne* (Milan: Agnelli, 1878).
33. Clemente Rossi, *Il tesoro delle giovinette* (Milan: Agnelli, 1909), 215.
34. Andrea Mannucci, "Il contributo protestante," in *Modelli e progetti educativi nell'Italia liberale*, ed. Giulia Di Bello (Florence: Centro editoriale toscano, 1998), 318.
35. Frank Thomas, "Nos filles," in *La famille* (Geneva: Jheber, 1903), 170–71.
36. Adolphe Monod, *La femme: Deux discours* (Paris: Ducloux, 1848), 84–106.
37. Giuseppe G. Franco, *Massone e Massona descritti dai documenti autentici dei settarii: Racconto storico* (Prato: Giachetti, 1889), 235.
38. See Enzo Catarsi, *L'asilo e la scuola dell'infanzia: Storia della scuola "materna" e dei suoi programmi dall'Ottocento ai nostri giorni* (Florence: La Nuova Italia, 1994); Tiziana Pironi, *Percorsi di pedagogia al femminile* (Rome: Carocci, 2014), 19–39.

39. See Clotilde Barbarulli, "Dalla tradizione all'innovazione: La 'ricerca straordinaria' di Elena Raffalovich Comparetti," in Soldani, *L'educazione delle donne*, 425–43.
40. About these themes, see Liviana Gazzetta, "'Nel campo della lotta': Organizzazioni femminili evangeliche e movimento delle donne in Italia tra Otto e Novecento," *Cristianesimo nella storia* 37, no. 1 (2016): 121–45.
41. See Roberta Fossati, "Modernismo e questione femminile," in *Il modernismo tra cristianità e secolarizzazione*, ed. Alfonso Botti and Rocco Cerrato (Urbino: Quattroventi, 2000), 673–90.
42. See Claudia Gori, *Crisalidi: Emancipazioniste liberali in età giolittiana* (Milan: Franco Angeli, 2003); Fiorenza Taricone, *Teoria e prassi dell'associazionismo italiano nel XIX e nel XX secolo* (Cassino: Università degli studi, 2008).
43. See Claudia Frattini, *Il primo congresso delle donne italiane, Roma 1908* (Rome: Biblink, 2008).
44. A. S. B., "L'ora è venuta," *L'Alba: Organo dell'unione cristiana delle giovani*, 1 January 1908.
45. See Paola Gaiotti De Biase, *Le origini del movimento cattolico femminile* (Brescia: Morcelliana, 1963); Cecilia Dau Novelli, *Società, Chiesa e associazionismo femminile: L'Unione fra le donne cattoliche d'Italia 1902–1919* (Rome: AVE, 1988).
46. For these themes, see *Donne nella storia degli ebrei d'Italia: Atti del IX Convegno internazionale "Italia Judaica,"* ed. Michele Luzzati and Cristina Galasso (Florence: Giuntina, 2007); Monica Miniati, *Le emancipate: Le donne ebree in Italia nel XIX e XX secolo* (Rome: Viella, 2008).

Bibliography

Alfani, Augusto. *Battaglie e vittorie: Nuovi esempi di "Volere è potere."* Florence: Barbera, 1890.

Ascenzi, Anna. *Il Plutarco delle donne*. Macerata: EUM, 2009.

A. S. B. "L'ora è venuta." *L'Alba: Organo dell'unione cristiana delle giovani*, 1 January 1908.

Barbarulli, Clotilde. "Caterina Franceschi Ferrucci accademica della Crusca: Il sapere di una donna nell'800." In *La Crusca nella tradizione letteraria e linguistica italiana*, 335–56. Florence: Accademia della Crusca, 1985.

———. "Dalla tradizione all'innovazione: La 'ricerca straordinaria' di Elena Raffalovich Comparetti." In *L'educazione delle donne*, edited by Simonetta Soldani, 425–43. Milan: Franco Angeli, 1989.

Berlan, Francesco. *Le fanciulle celebri e l'infanzia delle donne illustri d'Italia antiche e moderne*. Milan: Agnelli, 1878.

Biagini, Eugenio. "La nazione sinodale: patria e libertà nella retorica protestante italiana, 1848–1866." In *Il protestantesimo italiano nel Risorgimento: Influenze, miti, identità*, edited by Simone Maghenzani, 89–111. Turin: Claudiana, 2012.

Bisi Albini, Sofia. *Donnina forte*. Florence: Bemporad, 1903.

Bobba, Maria. *Donnina forte . . . racconto per le giovinette*. Turin: Paravia, 1894.

Bonsanti, Marina. "Amore familiare, amore romantico e amor di patria." In *Storia d'Italia: Annali 22. Il Risorgimento*, edited by Alberto Mario Banti and Paul Ginsborg, 131–43. Turin: Einaudi, 2007.

Borutta, Manuel. "La 'natura' del nemico: Rappresentazioni del cattolicesimo nell'anticlericalismo dell'Italia liberale." *Rassegna storica del Risorgimento* 58 (2001): 117–36.

Bounous, Clara. *La toga negata: Da Lidia Poet all'attuale realtà torinese*. Pinerolo: Alzani, 1997.

Camaiani, Giorgio P. "L'immagine femminile nella letteratura e nella trattatistica dell'800: La 'donna forte' e la 'donna debole.'" In *Santi, culti, simboli dell'età della secolarizzazione 1815–1915*, edited by Emma Fattorini, 431–47. Turin: Rosenberg & Sellier, 1997.

Catarsi, Enzo. *L'asilo e la scuola dell'infanzia: Storia della scuola 'materna' e dei suoi programmi dall'Ottocento ai nostri giorni*. Florence: La Nuova Italia, 1994.

Cecchini, Francesco M. *Il femminismo cristiano: La questione femminile nella prima democrazia cristiana 1898–1912*. Rome: Editori Riuniti, 1979.

Chemello, Adriana. *"Libri di lettura" per le donne: L'etica del lavoro nella letteratura di fine Ottocento*. Alexandria: Edizioni dell'Orso, 1995.

———. "Caterina Percoto e l'educazione della donna." In *Donne al lavoro: Ieri oggi domani*, edited by Saveria Chemotti, 305–33. Padua: Il Poligrafo, 2009.

Colombini, Giulia Molino. *Sulla educazione della donna: Pensieri*. Turin: Fory e Dalmazzo, 1851.

Dau Novelli, Cecilia. *Società, Chiesa e associazionismo femminile: L'Unione fra le donne cattoliche d'Italia 1902–1919*. Rome: AVE, 1988.

De Longis, Rosanna. "Maternità illustri: Dalle madri illuministe ai cataloghi ottocenteschi." In *Storia della maternità*, edited by Marina D'Amelia, 184–207. Rome: Laterza, 1997).

Ferrari, Silvio, and Andrea Zanotto. "Famiglia e diritto di famiglia nel conflitto tra Stato e Chiesa." In *Il "Kulturkampf" in Italia e nei paesi di lingua tedesca*, edited by Rudolf Lill and Francesco Traniello, 421–49. Bologna: Il Mulino, 1992.

Filippini, Nadia M. "Amor di patria e pratiche di disciplinamento: Erminia Fuà Fusinato." In *Di generazione in generazione: Le italiane dall'Unità ad oggi*, edited by Maria Teresa Mori, Alessandra Pescarolo, Anna Scattigno, and Simonetta Soldani, 73–86. Rome: Viella, 2014.

Formigoni, Guido. *L'Italia dei cattolici: Fede e nazione dal Risorgimento alla Repubblica*. Bologna: Il Mulino, 1998.

Fossati, Roberta. *Elites femminili e nuovi modelli religiosi nell'Italia fra Otto e Novecento*. Urbino: Quattroventi, 1997.

———. "Modernismo e questione femminile." In *Il modernismo tra cristianità e secolarizzazione*, edited by Alfonso Botti and Rocco Cerrato, 673–90. Urbino: Quattroventi, 2000.

Franchini, Silvia. "Moda e catechismo civile nei giornali delle signore italiane." In *Fare gli italiani: Scuola e cultura nell'Italia contemporanea*, edited by Simonetta Soldani and Gabriele Turi, 341–83. Bologna: Il Mulino, 1983.

Franco, Giuseppe G. *Massone e Massona descritti dai documenti autentici dei settarii: Racconto storico*. Prato: Giachetti, 1889.

Frattini, Claudia. *Il primo congresso delle donne italiane, Roma 1908*. Rome: Biblink, 2008.

Gaiotti De Biase, Paola. *Le origini del movimento cattolico femminile*. Brescia: Morcelliana, 1963.

Garavaglia, Ambrogio. *Della educazione religiosa e civile delle fanciulle in conformità alle attuali condizioni d'Italia*. Milan: Dumolard, 1884.

Gazzetta, Liviana. "Ideologia e organizzazione della donna cattolica." In *Elena Da Persico*, edited by Liviana Gazzetta, 47–90. Verona: Cierre, 2005.

———. "'Nel campo della lotta.' Organizzazioni femminili evangeliche e movimento delle donne in Italia tra Otto e Novecento." *Cristianesimo nella storia* 37, no. 1 (2016): 121–45.

Gibson, Mary. *Stato e prostituzione in Italia 1860–1915*. Milan: Il Saggiatore, 1995.

Gori, Claudia. *Crisalidi: Emancipazioniste liberali in età giolittiana*. Milan: Franco Angeli, 2003.

———. "Oltre domani: Futuro, progresso e divino nell'emancipazionismo italiano tra Otto e Novecento." *Storia delle donne* 1, no. 1 (2005): 239–55.

Leuzzi, Maria Cristina. *Erminia Fuà Fusinato: Una vita in altro modo*. Rome: Anicia, 2008.

Macrelli, Rina. *L'indegna schiavitù: Anna Maria Mozzoni e la lotta contro la prostituzione di stato*. Rome: Editori Riuniti, 1981.

Luzzati, Michele, and Cristina Galasso, eds. *Donne nella storia degli ebrei d'Italia: Atti del IX Convegno internazionale "Italia Judaica."* Florence: Giuntina, 2007.

Mannucci, Andrea. "Il contributo protestante." In *Modelli e progetti educativi nell'Italia liberale*, edited by Giulia Di Bello, 257–359. Florence: Centro editoriale toscano, 1998.

Menozzi, Daniele. *La Chiesa cattolica e la secolarizzazione*. Turin: Einaudi, 1993.

Milan, Marina. *Donna, famiglia, società: Aspetti della stampa femminile cattolica in Italia tra Otto e Novecento*. Genoa: Ecig, 1983.

Miniati, Monica. *Le emancipate: Le donne ebree in Italia nel XIX e XX secolo*. Rome: Viella, 2008.

Monod, Adolphe. *La femme: Deux discours*. Paris: Ducloux, 1848.

Moro, Renato. "Le chiese, gli ebrei e la società moderna: L'Italia." In *Integrazione e identità: L'esperienza ebraica in Germania e Italia dall'Illuminismo al fascismo*, edited by Mario Toscano, 167–82. Milan: Franco Angeli, 1998.

Paladini, Luisa A. *Manuale per le giovinette italiane*. Florence: Le Monnier, 1857.

Papa, Vincenzo. *La giovinetta e l'amor di patria*. Turin: Speirani, 1886.

Patriarca, Silvana. "Italiani/Italiane." In *Atlante culturale del Risorgimento: Lessico del linguaggio politico dal Settecento all'Unità*, edited by Alberto Mario Banti and Marco Meriggi, 199–213. Rome: Laterza, 2011.

Pazzaglia, Luciano. *Chiesa e prospettive educative in Italia tra Restaurazione e Unificazione*. Brescia: La Scuola, 1994.

Pera, Isabella. *"Camminare col proprio tempo": Il femminismo cristiano di primo Novecento*. Rome: Viella, 2016.

Peyrot, Bruna. "Verso le madri antiche: Alla ricerca delle donne nella storia Valdese." In *Vite discrete: Corpi e immagini di donne valdesi*, edited by Graziella Bonansea and Bruna Peyrot, 11–102. Turin: Rosenberg & Sellier, 1993.

Pironi, Tiziana. *Percorsi di pedagogia al femminile*. Rome: Carocci, 2014.

Poët, Lidia. *Studio sulla condizione della donna rispetto al diritto costituzionale*. Pinerolo: Chiantore, 1881.

Pons, Amilda. *Studio della morale nel suo svolgimento religioso e scientifico*. Turin: Paravia, 1908.

Pons, Pietro G. "Erminia Fuà Fusinato ed Emilia Gould." *La Rivista cristiana*, 1877.

Porciani, Ilaria. "Il Plutarco femminile." In *L'educazione delle donne: Scuole e modelli di vita femminile nell'Italia dell'Ottocento*, edited by Simonetta Soldani, 297–317. Milan: Franco Angeli, 1991.

———. *Famiglia e nazione nel lungo Ottocento italiana: Modelli, strategie e reti di relazioni*. Rome: Viella, 2006.
Romagnani, Gian Paolo. "Italian Protestants." In *The Emancipation of Catholics, Jews and Protestants*, edited by R. Liedtke and S. Wendehorst, 148–68. New York: Manchester University Press, 1999.
Rossi, Clemente. *Il tesoro delle giovinette*. Milan: Agnelli, 1909.
Savelli, Laura. "Assistenza alle lavoratrici migranti e battaglie civili: Le 'Amiche della giovinetta' (1877–1914)." *Passato e presente* 95, no. 1 (2015): 49–74.
Scaraffia, Lucetta. "Emancipazione e rigenerazione spirituale: Per una nuova lettura del femminismo." In *Donne ottimiste: Femminismo e associazioni borghesi nell'Otto e Novecento*, edited by Lucetta Scaraffia and Anna Maria Isastia, 19–126. Bologna: Il Mulino, 2002.
Simonetti, Simonetta. *Luisa Amalia Paladini: Vita e opera di una donna del Risorgimento*. Lucca: Pacini Fazi, 2012.
Spini, Giorgio. *Studi sull'evangelismo italiano tra Otto e Novecento*. Turin: Claudiana, 1994.
———. *Italia liberale e protestanti*. Turin: Claudiana, 2002.
———. *Risorgimento e protestanti*. 3rd ed. Turin: Claudiana, 2008.
Taricone, Fiorenza. *Teoria e prassi dell'associazionismo italiano nel XIX e nel XX secolo*. Cassino: Università degli studi, 2008.
Thomas, Frank. "Nos filles." In *La famille*, 170–71. Geneva: Jheber, 1903.
Traniello, Francesco. *Religione cattolica e Stato nazionale: Dal Risorgimento al secondo dopoguerra*. Bologna: Il Mulino, 2007.
Valerio, Adriana. "Pazienza, vigilanza, ritiratezza: La questione femminile nei documenti ufficiali della Chiesa (1848–1914)." *Nuova DWF* 16 (1989): 60–79.
Verucci, Guido. *L'Italia laica prima e dopo l'Unità 1848–1876: Anticlericalismo, libero pensiero e ateismo nella società italiana*. Rome: Laterza, 1996.

Section 4
POLITICS OF WOMEN'S EMANCIPATION

CHAPTER 10

Denomination Matters
Strategies of Self-Designation of the German Women's Movement

Anne-Laure Briatte

What was actually the matter with the German word *Emanzipation* that none of the members of the German middle-class women's movement wanted to use it? Let's listen to Franziska Tiburtius (1843–1927),[1] who denied being emancipated her whole life, though she went abroad to study medicine at a time when women were not allowed to study in Germany, became one of the first female doctors in Germany, and successfully ran her own policlinic for women in Berlin:

> Around the middle of the last century, "women's emancipation" began to be spoken of in Germany—a hideous term! Most people on hearing it can only think of loud, flashy, overexcited behavior, or of a mode of living not totally in accord with the prevailing morals. One who looks a little more deeply had better speak of the "women's movement." I would add that in my earliest youth, even skating, gymnastics, and horseback riding were considered emancipated.[2]

According to Franziska Tiburtius, *Emanzipation* was thus an "ugly" word, and it was associated with conspicuous, hysterical behavior and a morally dubious way of life. With critical undertones, she notes that even ice skating, gymnastics, and horseback riding were regarded as "emancipated" activities for women. For "deeper" matters, the word *Frauenbewegung* (women's movement), which is actually not the same thing, seemed to her more suitable.

In this quotation, Franziska Tiburtius refers to the negative connotations of the word "emancipation" in Germany.[3] Not only this word but also others related to the emancipation of women bore an unfavorable semantic resemblance to other contemporary phrases, which referred to perceived social problems, or at least challenges, in nineteenth-century Germany:

- the word "emancipation" recalled the *Judenemanzipation*, the emancipation of the Jews;
- the phrase "the women's question" (*Frauenfrage*) was inspired by the contemporary workers' question and the Jewish question (*soziale Frage; Judenfrage*), and
- the women's movement (*Frauenbewegung*) referred explicitly to the labor movement and the trade union movement (*Arbeiter- und Gewerkschaftsbewegungen*), the two biggest social movements that marked the second half of the nineteenth century.

In each case, these words brought the women close to social, religious, and political minorities: the Jews, the workers, and the unionists, all of whom were seen as a danger by the supporters of law and order.

There was indeed a great deal at stake in how the German middle-class women's movement named itself and its goals, because this would determine the way it was perceived by public opinion, by social reformers and politicians, and by the other wings of the women's movement. If it was too explicit about its goals, it risked alienating public sympathy, and it didn't need bad press. On the other hand, if it was too cautious, it ran the risk of being overlooked and its goals not being discussed in the public sphere. And the point was, to get bad press was still better than to get no press at all.[4] Consequently, it seems to make sense to interrogate how the German women's movement denominated itself and its goals. Firstly, the German middle-class women's organizations were obviously concerned about disguising, or at least minimizing, their goals in order not to be considered dangerous to the social order. But—and this will be the second step of my demonstration—another strategy consisted in suggesting emancipation without spelling it out, through historical parallels, iconography, alternative ways of life, and female biographies. Furthermore, to characterize oneself and one's goals was the opportunity for the different wings of the German women's movement to distinguish themselves from the others and to sharpen their profile among the women's movements in Germany. I will show this last point with the example of the radical wing of the German middle-class women's movement.

Don't Be Conspicuous!

The Harmless Names of the First Women's Associations

In October 1865, the Allgemeiner Deutscher Frauenverein (ADF; General German Women's Association) was founded in Leipzig by women who were active in the 1848 revolution, especially Louise Otto-Peters (1819–95) and Auguste Schmidt (1833–1902). Even before national unity in 1871, these women had the vision of an association of women from all German states. The ADF strove to promote the free development of women's talents. Its statutes claimed "the liberation of female work from all the obstacles standing opposed to its development."[5] It presented itself as devoted purely to women's education, employment opportunities, and working conditions. The emphasis on education was closely linked to the perceived necessity of extending female employment at a time when industrialization was speeding up. As Otto-Peters said in 1866, "The only emancipation that we pursue for our women is the emancipation of their work."[6] This, and more generally the goals of the ADF, may seem quite modest to us in the twenty-first century, but in nineteenth-century Germany, they were daring enough to worry many conservative male members of the educated classes. In the following five decades or more of its existence, the ADF developed a large network of charity and self-help associations, thus laying the foundations for a German movement for the emancipation of women.[7]

Twenty years later, in 1888, the women's association Frauenwohl was founded in Berlin by Minna Cauer (1841–1922), a future leader of the "radical" wing of the German women's movement. *Frauenwohl* merely means "women's welfare," but the women involved in this association and the sister groups founded in the following years across the German states[8] had an extended definition of this term. They fought not only for the core causes of better education and employment opportunities for women but also for access to university and higher professions, for gender equality in civil law (especially in marriage and family law), for legal protection of expectant or nursing mothers, for legal equality for illegitimate children, for equal suffrage rights, and for the abolition of state-regulated prostitution. Who could—from such a name—have had an inkling that the small women's association in Berlin was to become the headquarters of the radical wing of the middle-class women's movement?[9]

If women set such great store by going unnoticed, this was largely due to the association laws in the German states, which banned women from membership and participation in any association or meeting of a political nature. Until the association law was reformed in 1908, it hung like a sword of Damocles over their associations and meetings, which could be dispersed at any time.[10] But even if women had been allowed to identify their goals by name, they would certainly have avoided the term *Emanzipation* anyway, which had been brought into disrepute in Germany.

Emanzipation *in Disrepute*

The so-called *Meyers Konversations-Lexikon*, meant for a broad public and first published between 1839 and 1855, was the most comprehensive lexicon in the German language in the nineteenth century. Its various editions are very useful today for appreciating the contemporary meanings and connotations of concepts that were used then and whose meanings might differ from today's.

In the edition of 1885–92, which appeared at a peak of growth in the German women's movement, the entry "Emanzipation" first explains the meaning of the word in the context of ancient Roman law. Then, the meanings appearing in "the latest times" are mentioned and briefly commented on. Very interestingly, the first modern meaning named is "the emancipation of the flesh" (*Emanzipation des Fleisches*); that is, the liberation of sensual and sexual desire, which is immediately put in opposition to morals and religion.[11] The next meaning mentioned is "women's emancipation" as the liberation of the female sex from the limits that social and natural factors put to that gender; so, as it is explained, one can speak of "emancipated women" when the latter conspicuously and deliberately go beyond those limits.[12] Further mentions of modern uses of the word *Emanzipation* are: the emancipation of the schools (from the rule of the Catholic Church) and the emancipation of the Jews—that is, their investment with equal civil rights—and of the Catholics in Great Britain and Ireland. Regarding the emancipation of the flesh and women's emancipation, moral disapproval is not to be overlooked, and the important place given to this point in the entry reveals the explosive character of the topic at that time.

In her book *European Feminisms*, Karen Offen underlines the longevity of the sexual connotation of the word "emancipation," which can be put down to the discussion of "free love" among the Saint-Simonians and the Fourierists in France and elsewhere in the 1830s, whereby mutual sexual or affective attraction should be the only reason for two persons to make a couple, without regard for the social or economic needs of their families. In particular, the 1829 plea of Prosper Enfantin (1796–1864), a leader among the Saint-Simonians, for the "rehabilitation of the flesh" in relation to the mind, had scandalized many of his followers and led to court actions for offense against public morality. For decades after those widely publicized trials in Paris, the term "emancipation" would remain associated with immoral practices of sexuality and, therefore, with provocation and even danger.[13]

In 1852, when the conservative journalist and sociologist Wilhelm Heinrich Riehl (1823–97) denounced the "emancipated women" who took part in the revolution of 1848, he insisted on the "natural vocation" of their gender.[14] In his work on the family, which appeared years later (1855) as the third volume of his *Naturgeschichte des Volks als Grundlage einer deutschen Sozialpolitik* (1851–69), he even suggested that the idea of women's emancipation was foreign to the German identity and thus could not be a goal for a German woman.[15]

In the context of nationalisms in the late nineteenth century, the French term "emancipation" was avoided not only by German feminists but also by the Danish women's rights lawyer Pauline Worm (1825–83), for example, who bound the word to a loosening of morals comparable to the French vindication of emancipation.[16] According to Karen Offen, the German feminists in particular felt very uncomfortable with "emancipation," which, after the episode of the Commune in Paris in 1870–71, was definitely associated with the so-called *pétroleuses*—real or supposed female fire-raisers on public buildings during the "bloody week" of the Commune in May 1871, a figure associated with women involved in politics and the women's movement—and what they perceived as French female extremism.[17]

Under these conditions, the German feminists were evidently forced to ban the word *Emanzipation* if they did not want to be suspected of advocating loose morals, the abolition of the institution of the family, and political extremism, destruction, and chaos. But this raised the question: how to appear in the public sphere and communicate one's goals without using the "E word"?

Strategies of Implying Emancipation without Using the Word

Forced to be cautious in the denomination of their goals, the middle-class German feminists found several ways to suggest the idea of emancipation without actually uttering the word. To this purpose, they used (1) historical parallels with other cases of emancipation and (2) a universal iconographic language to imply emancipation; last but not least, (3) they demonstrated what they were claiming through their way of life: emancipation from guardianship in wedlock, but also from financial and social dependency, and the liberation of their bodies.

Historical Parallels

The choice of terms in pleas for equal rights offered subtle possibilities for suggesting parallels to similar cases of emancipation in the history of mankind, like the emancipation of the Jews—which was topical in the nineteenth-century German states—and the abolition of slavery.

One of the first pleas for equal civil rights for women in the German countries was published by the Prussian lawyer and statesman Theodor von Hippel (1741–96) under the odd title *Über die bürgerliche Verbesserung der Weiber* (On the Civil Improvement of Females, Berlin, 1792). The title was directly inspired by another publication that had appeared a good ten years earlier: *Über die bürgerliche Verbesserung der Juden* (On the Civil Improvement of the Jews, 1781) by Christian Konrad Wilhelm von Dohm (1751–1820). This famous plea for equal civil rights for the Jews initiated a broad discussion in Christian and Jewish intellectual circles in the German countries on the best ways to improve the social status of the Jews.[18] The fact that Hippel first published his innovative demand for the legal emancipation of women anonymously shows how explosive the claim was. In opposition to the emancipation of women, Jewish emancipation was realized in Prussia in 1812 in the context of the modernization of the Prussian state.

Regarding the abolition of slavery, the reference was explicit and meant not to be overlooked. At the end of the nineteenth century, the movement for the abolition of state regulation of prostitution, born in England and led by Josephine Butler (1828–1906), expanded in 1875 to the British, Continental and General Federation for the Abolition of Government Regulation of Prostitution, later to be known as the International Abolitionist Federation.[19] The German middle-class women's movement—mostly members of its radical wing—took an active part in this "abolitionist movement," as it was called.[20] It is no accident that the name of this organization for the rights of girls and women recalled the antislavery movement. The comparison between slave traffic and traffic in women and girls even stood in the statutes of the International Abolitionist Federation.[21] While stressing the similarity between the two abolitionist movements, the women condemned their situation as slaves in modern times. Emancipation meant nothing else than the liberation from slavery; the members of the International Abolitionist Federation fought for the emancipation of the female sex from unequal rights in the context of sexual morals and practices.

The "Iconographic Turn" of the German Women's Movement

Enlightenment symbols for the emancipation of individuals. The "visual century," which manifested with new imagistic techniques (e.g. photographs and films) and the development of mass media to broadcast them, had its roots in the late nineteenth century, and the feminists took an active part in this medial innovation by using pictures for propaganda goals. Around 1900, the German feminists began to use pictures to underline their intentions, especially in their numerous press organs. In the *Zeitschrift für Frauenstimmrecht* (Women's Suffrage Magazine), founded in 1907 by the radical feminists, the front page was ornamented with a vignette showing a woman breaking chains over her head and with a rising sun in the background (figure 10.1). This picture became the emblem

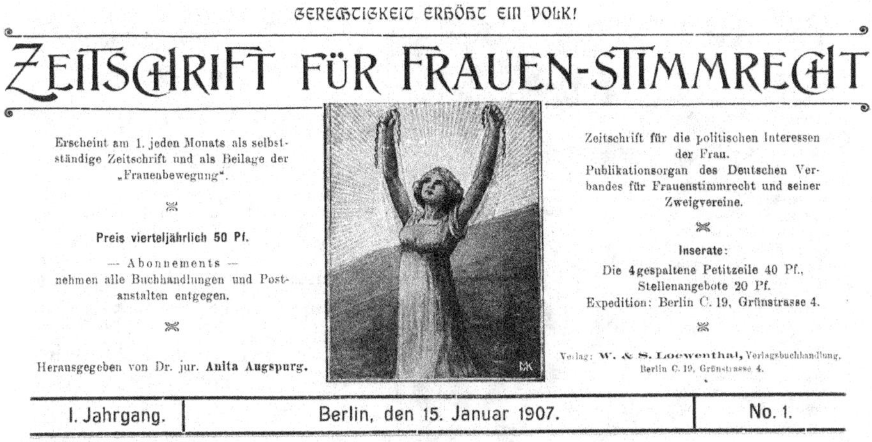

GERECHTIGKEIT ERHÖHT EIN VOLK!

ZEITSCHRIFT FÜR FRAUEN-STIMMRECHT

Erscheint am 1. jeden Monats als selbstständige Zeitschrift und als Beilage der „Frauenbewegung".

Preis vierteljährlich 50 Pf.

— Abonnements — nehmen alle Buchhandlungen und Postanstalten entgegen.

Herausgegeben von Dr. jur. **Anita Augspurg.**

Zeitschrift für die politischen Interessen der Frau. Publikationsorgan des Deutschen Verbandes für Frauenstimmrecht und seiner Zweigvereine.

Inserate: Die 4gespaltene Petitzeile 40 Pf., Stellenangebote 20 Pf. Expedition: Berlin C. 19, Grünstrasse 4.

Verlag: **W. & S. Loewenthal,** Verlagsbuchhandlung, Berlin C. 19, Grünstrasse 4.

I. Jahrgang.	Berlin, den 15. Januar 1907.	No. 1.

Figure 10.1. *Front page of* Zeitschrift für Frauenstimmrecht *(Women's Suffrage Magazine), 1. Jg., 1907, Nr. 1, Header. Collection AddF—Archiv der deutschen Frauenbewegung, Kassel.*

of the Deutscher Verband für Frauenstimmrecht (German Association for Women's Suffrage) and was printed on cards and stamps advertised for as "excellent means of propaganda" among the suffragists (figure 10.2). With its high symbolic character, it used the well-known iconography of the Enlightenment, just like in the painting *La Déclaration des Droits de l'Homme et du Citoyen* (1791) by Jean-Jacques Le Barbier (figure 10.3). In this painting, the shining sun symbolizes the light that is the power of reason on mankind, and the woman breaking chains symbolizes emancipation—from slavery, from ignorance, as well as from any form of guardianship.

Toward a professional use of pictures. Over the years, the German middle-class feminists developed sophisticated techniques in public relations,[22] which included the skillful use of images at strategic moments. Thus, each women's conference was documented by a photograph showing an assembly of women, suggesting that the women's movement was about to become a major movement of the century, like the labor or the trade union movements (for the international conference of the International Council of Women in Berlin in 1904[23] or the International Women's Peace Congress in The Hague, 1915; see figure 10.4).

In 1896, on the occasion of the International Women's Conference held in the German capital, the *Berliner Illustrirte Zeitung* (Berlin Illustrated News), the biggest mass magazine of the time, put a portrait of twelve "pioneers" of the German women's movement on its front page,

aus: Die Frauenbewegung, 11. jg., 1905, Nr. 21 (1. November 1905), S 167; Bestand Addf, Kassel

Figure 10.2. *Emblem of Deutscher Verband für Frauenstimmrecht (German Association for Women's Suffrage), advertisement for the suffrage stamp,* Die Frauenbewegung, *11. Jg., 1905, Nr. 21 (1. November 1905), p. 167; Collection AddF—Archiv der deutschen Frauenbewegung, Kassel.*

together with their names: Henriette Goldschmidt, Gräfin (countess) Viktorine Butler, Lina Morgenstern, Anna Schepeler-Lette, Helene Lange, Minna Cauer, Lily Braun-Gizycki, Emilie Kempin, Marie Stritt, Hanna Bieber-Böhm, Jeanette Schwerin, and Anita Augspurg.[24] In 1904, the third International Women's Conference was held in Berlin again under the auspices of the Union of German Women's Associations (Bund Deutscher Frauenvereine, BDF), founded ten years earlier. On the opening day, a portrait photograph of Marie Stritt, president of the BDF and of the conference, covered the whole front page of the *Berliner Illustrirte Zeitung*.[25] In the weekly journal *Die Woche*, a whole page was devoted to photographs of nine leaders of the German and international women's movements.[26] This gave the movement a face and increased its presence in the media.

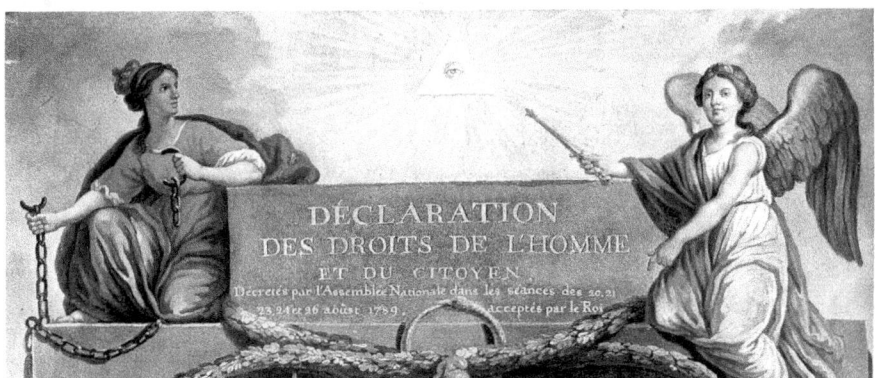

Figure 10.3. *Jean-Jacques Le Barbier, La Déclaration des Droits de l'Homme et du Citoyen, 1791, depicting the tables of the Declaration of Human and Citizens' Rights, adopted 26 August 1789. On the top, allegories of France (left), which breaks the chains, and of Justice (right), under the eye of the Supreme Being. Musée Carnavalet, Paris. Wikimedia Commons.*

Sophia Goudstikker (1865–1924) and Anita Augspurg (1857–1943), both involved in the middle-class women's movement and the latter a leader of its radical wing, had learned photography and ran a successful business in the Atelier Elvira in Munich, the first studio managed by women. Some of the individual and group portraits of the radical wing of the German women's movement came from this studio.[27] The well-known series of group portraits of five leaders of the middle-class women's movement—Anita Augspurg, Marie Stritt, Lily von Gizycki, Minna Cauer, and Sophia Goudstikker—dating from around 1894 (see figure 10.5), are posed "to capture moments of playful conspiracy."[28]

Figure 10.4. *International Women's Peace Conference in The Hague, April–May 1915. LSE Library via Wikimedia Commons.*

Figure 10.5. From left to right: *Anita Augspurg, Marie Stritt, Lily von Gizycki, Minna Cauer, and Sophia Goudstikker, around 1894. Photograph by Hofatelier Elvira, München; Bestand AddF, Kassel; International Instituut voor Sociale Geschiedenis, Collection Minna Cauer; ref.: BG A63/242.*

Marti L. Lybeck analyzes the photograph above as follows: "In one, all five women hold pencils to their chins in the pose of intrepid journalists. The pose enacts a masculine professional identity as it simultaneously foregrounds their identity as writing women. Their facial expressions range from mock seriousness to open amusement."[29] The women there are not just appearing to enjoy the transgression of gender roles and postures for the duration of the photo shoot—they actually emancipated themselves from gender roles in many regards in real life. They were successful businesswomen, women's rights activists, and journalists, and they documented this with such photographs.

Living Emancipation

To some extent, German middle-class feminists did more than claim the emancipation of women; they literally showed the way with their alternative lifestyles and biographies, which demonstrated in concrete terms what they were fighting for.

Emancipation from wedlock and husband's guardianship (*Ehevormundschaft*). Although it didn't represent the majority, an above-average proportion of feminists were unmarried. Some of them were married and had children (e.g. Hedwig Dohm, Marie Stritt, Auguste Kirchhoff), in accordance with the norms of bourgeois German society.[30] But many active feminists lived either as single women (e.g. Minna Cauer, Anna Pappritz, Alice Salomon, Franziska Tiburtius, Ottilie Hoffmann)—willingly or not—or with another woman (Helene Lange and Gertrud Bäumer, Anita Augspurg and Lida Gustava Heymann, Käthe Schirmacher and Clara Schleker). Helene Stöcker (1869–1943), who lived unmarried with a man for years, was an exception.[31] In so doing, she and her partner escaped a conventional way of life that did not correspond to their ideal of free individual development.[32] Franziska Tiburtius, for example, could not get married because she wanted to practice the medical profession and to run her own polyclinic in Berlin. By getting married, she would have lost the right to determine where to live, what to do with her money, and the full right to earn money at all; this was traditional civil law in the German states, confirmed in the united civil law, the *Bürgerliches Gesetzbuch* of 1900.[33] Anita Augspurg and her friend and comrade-in-arms Lida Gustava Heymann lived and worked together for more than forty years, and they lived as much as possible according to their convictions and ideals.[34] This would not have been possible had they been married, as they were perfectly aware.

Emancipation from economic and social dependency. The German women's movement called for better education and better professional opportunities for women in order to eradicate female financial dependency. In their self-help associations, like the Allgemeiner Deutscher Lehrerinnen-Verein (ADLV; General German Women Teacher's Association), founded in 1890 by Helene Lange (1848–1930), and the Kaufmännischer Hilfsverein für weibliche Angestellte (Business Benevolent Society for Female Employees), founded one year before by Minna Cauer and Julius Meyer, women worked to improve female professional qualifications, and through this activity they became professionals themselves. Only a very small number of German feminists, like Alice Salomon (1872–1948) or Dorothee von Velsen (1883–1970), could afford not to work for a living, because they came from well-off families. Hedwig Heyl (1850–1934) and Lida Gustava Heymann (1868–1943) both inherited substantial fortunes and became generous patrons of and—especially Heyl—efficient fundraisers for the German women's movement, but they were exceptional. Most of the German middle-class feminists had to earn their livings as journalists, authors, or teachers, and often lived in quite Spartan conditions.[35]

Not only did it turn out that women were able to manage money, and sometimes very successfully, but they also launched some initiatives aimed at liberating women from economic dependence. The Berlin Women's Bank (Berliner Frauenbank), founded in Berlin in 1910, was one of those feminist projects, where women worked to teach other women how to handle money and to make them more self-confident.[36] This bank run by women for women, established in the Motzstraße in Berlin, had about sixty employees who gave professional advice on legal questions related to money, mortgages, property management, credits, trust funds, and stocks and shares. Though the women's bank was run successfully, it went bankrupt during the war (in November 1915) for reasons that remain unclear.[37]

"The liberation of the body" was neither an explicit nor really an implicit goal of the German women's movement; at least it was not formulated in those terms, and it was not its priority.[38] Nevertheless, some feminists, mainly in the radical wing of the bourgeois women's movement, took the first step in this direction. Helene Stöcker, a prominent activist for "sexual reform," Sophia Goudstikker, and Anita Augspurg wore "Reformkleidung," i.e. "reform clothes," which were simple and functional, did not unduly compress the bust and the waist, and made it much easier to move. But both the leaders of the moderate wing of the German middle-class women's movement, Helene Lange and Gertrud Bäumer (1873–1954), also wore "reform clothes," the former because she found them more comfortable and practical, the latter because she appreciated their elegancy and simple beauty.[39] Beyond those practical and aesthetic considerations, the German middle-class women's movement criticized women's fashion because it had been proved unhealthy, and it supported reform clothes because they were healthier and allowed freedom of movement.[40] Moreover, Goudstikker and Augspurg practiced "unwomanly" activities, like riding and cycling, and allowed themselves to be seen smoking in public spaces.[41] The three women, Stöcker, Goudstikker, and Augspurg, also wore their hair short, an additional sign of liberation and bodily freedom.

Extended female mobility. To some extent, the feminists conquered spatial mobility, too. The delegates for international women's conferences often had to make long journeys across countries and continents. It did not matter if they traveled alone or with other women, they did not travel accompanied by men. The fact that Anita Ausgpurg and Lida Gustava Heymann learned to drive and got a license in 1927—Augspurg at the age of sixty-nine!—and traveled in their own car in Europe, North Africa, and the Middle East[42] is additional evidence of new female mobility and emancipation from their traditionally narrow sphere of activity.

Suggestion, illustration, and demonstration: with these elements of a communication policy, the German feminists advocated for women's emancipation without spelling it out. The strategy of showing how it looked when women lived and worked as emancipated individuals can be considered an aspect of the strategy "deeds, not words." Through the manner in which the German middle-class feminists formulated their goals, and in their choice of name for their organization, they marked themselves out from the other wings of the women's movements and sharpened their own profile.

Delimitations and Profiling
"Radical" vs. "Moderate"

After the foundation of the ADF in 1865, many women's associations were founded with a more or less charitable and emancipative character. Most of them were then gathered into the umbrella organization Bund deutscher Frauenvereine (BDF, League of German Women's Associations), founded in 1894, which claimed to represent the whole German women's movement—except the socialist women's movement, which was not invited to take part in the inaugural meeting. Very quickly, some more vindictive feminists, mostly from the Berlin association Frauenwohl, felt hindered by the directors of the BDF, whose policy seemed too cautious to them and its management of the women's associations too authoritarian.[43] As early as the inaugural meeting of the BDF, and then in every annual general assembly, they criticized the board members of the BDF as excessively cautious, frightened by reforms, and ultimately conservative.[44] In the meantime, they presented themselves indirectly as courageous, the initiators of reform, and responsible for bringing new ideas into discussion. Finally, they styled themselves as the "progressive minority" in the middle-class women's movement, with all the victim attitudes this allowed.

These women called themselves "radical," in opposition to the "moderates," and defined themselves and most of their goals (e.g. in the abolitionist movement, in the suffrage movement) in distinction from the moderate majority; the relationality of their self-denomination was an inherent part of their identity as "opposition" within the middle-class women's movement. A few years later, when they concentrated their work on the "politicization" of women and their political education, they presented themselves as the political women's movement, which they claimed to be the only legitimate women's movement, while they characterized the "moderate" BDF, which they had left in 1899, as backward and incapable of professional political practices.[45] Thus, they strove to stylize themselves as the avant-garde of the German women's movement at a time of fierce competition between its different wings.

Claiming women's suffrage had been for some years one of the numerous—real or exaggerated—demarcation lines between the "radical" and the "moderate" German women's movements. Helene Lange was the one who first brought forward for discussion the claim for an unrestricted and democratic women's suffrage.[46] After her, the "radical" feminists (first Lily von Gizycki, then Minna Cauer, Anita Augspurg, Lida Gustava Heymann, etc.) claimed it forcefully in the public space from the mid-1890s on. They held out with this public claim until 1908, which they were quite proud of. But the hardening of the British women's suffrage movement over the years forced them to draw limits and to be more precise regarding their own positions.

British Suffragettes vs. German Suffragists

The German "radical" feminists were obviously pleased to present themselves as the avant-garde of the German women's movement, which was not afraid to use unconventional methods in order to draw public attention to the causes they fought for.[47] Lida Gustava Heymann implemented her own mobilization methods from the Anglo-Saxon women's suffrage movement, like the campaign "No taxation without representation" in North America in the 1850s and especially in the 1870s.[48] Thus, she refused to pay her taxes if she were still refused the right to vote, which she had, according to the laws in the State of Hamburg, since she was settled there. But the German feminists did not adopt every mobilization method from abroad. According to the analysis of Susanne Kinnebrock, they adapted the subjects, the strategies, and even single arguments depending on whether they were likely to be accepted by German public opinion.[49]

The German "radical" feminists eventually found feminists who were more "fearless" than themselves: the British suffragettes. First, they admired the British suffragettes for their innovative methods and their largely publicized actions, such as the Women's Coronation Procession in 1911, where forty thousand women marched in a procession more than five miles long through the streets of London. But arguing for female rights was obviously not enough to initiate reform, and the suffragettes put the dictum "deeds, not words" into use; they began to use violence, went to prison, went on hunger strikes, and went to prison again if necessary.[50] Consequently, the British suffragettes received very bad press in Germany, and the German middle-class feminists hesitated over the appropriate reaction to it. Only Käthe Schirmacher (1865–1930), Anita Augspurg, and Lida Gustava Heymann continued to support them, while the BDF, which had always been skeptical toward them, distanced itself officially in

1913.⁵¹ Anita Augspurg eventually published some tendentious articles in which she lost contact with objectivity and seemed to flirt with violence as a means of action, and so she ceased to care about German opinion. As a result, she lost her good reputation as a critical but serious journalist and found herself marginalized, together with Lida Gustava Heymann, in the German women's and suffrage movements, as well as in public opinion.⁵²

Conclusion

The members of the German middle-class women's movement were mobilized for female emancipation from all sorts of subordinations and dependencies. Nevertheless, they were not tempted to use the word "emancipation," which was linked to merely negative associations: loose manners, broken families, political extremism, and even revolutions. On the contrary, they were most evidently concerned about their acceptance in German liberal, middle-class society and wanted no trouble in order to protect themselves from dissolution by authorities. But after the liberalization of the political context after 1890 and the reform of association law in 1908, it became possible to speak out more about their claims and goals. The German feminists used different strategies to express their goals. In doing so, they emancipated themselves from the rules of respectability and from laws that excluded women from public debates, and they convincingly paved the way for female emancipation.

Anne-Laure Briatte, the holder of a doctorate in Germanic studies and history, is lecturer in German history and civilization at the Sorbonne University in Paris. Her research focuses on German feminisms during the nineteenth and twentieth centuries. She is notably the author of *Citoyennes sous tutelle: Le mouvement féministe "radical" dans l'Allemagne wilhelmienne* (Berne: Peter Lang, 2013), and a coeditor of *L'Europe, une chance pour les femmes? Le genre de la construction européenne* (Paris: Editions de la Sorbonne, 2019), with Éliane Gubin and Françoise Thébaud. In her ongoing research, she is working on sexual violence in the French zone of military occupation in Germany after 1945.

Notes

1. See Christiane Lange, "Nur ein unzeitgemäßer Scherz? Akademikerinnen im Deutschland des späten 19. Jahrhunderts—Franziska Tiburtius u. a.," in *Geschriebenes Leben: Autobiographik von Frauen*, ed. Michaela Holdenried (Berlin: Erich Schmidt, 1995), 226–43; Johanna Bleker, "Vorspiel: Deutsche Ärztinnen mit

ausländischem Doktorgrad 1871–1901," in *Ärztinnen aus dem Kaiserreich: Lebensläufe einer Generation*, ed. Johanna Bleker and Sabine Schleiermacher (Weinheim: Deutscher Studienverlag, 2000), 11–34.
2. "Um die Mitte des vorigen Jahrhunderts fing man an in Deutschland von 'Frauenemanzipation' zu reden—gräßliches Wort! Die meisten konnten sich dabei nichts weiter denken als ein lautes, auffälliges, aufgeregtes Benehmen oder eine Lebenshaltung, die mit der herrschenden Sitte nicht ganz im Einklang stand. Wer etwas tiefer schaute, sprach lieber von "Frauenbewegung." Ich bemerke übrigens, daß in meiner ersten Jugend sogar Schlittschuhlaufen, Turnübungen und Reiten für emanzipiert galt." Franziska Tiburtius, *Erinnerungen einer Achtzigjährigen*, 3rd ed. (Berlin: C. A. Schwetschke & Sohn Verlagsbuchhandlung, 1929), 118.
3. See the illuminating reflections of Gisela Bock on the historical meanings and stakes of the concept of "emancipation" related to women's emancipation movements: Gisela Bock, "Begriffsgeschichten: 'Frauenemanzipation' im Kontext der Emanzipationsbewegungen des 19. Jahrhunderts," in *Geschlechtergeschichten der Neuzeit: Ideen, Politik, Praxis*, ed. Gisela Bock (Göttingen: Vandenhoeck & Ruprecht, 2014), 100–152.
4. "Die Bewegung hat bei den Massenmedien viel erreicht, wenn sie Aufmerksamkeit findet. Die schlechteste Nachricht ist keine Nachricht." Joachim Raschke, *Soziale Bewegungen: Ein historisch-systematischer Grundriss*, 2nd ed. (Frankfurt am Main: Campus Verlag, 1988), 344.
5. In German: "Der Allgemeine Deutsche Frauenverein hat die Aufgabe, für die erhöhte Bildung des weiblichen Geschlechts und die Befreiung der weiblichen Arbeit von allen ihrer Entfaltung entgegenstehenden Hindernissen mit vereinten Kräften zu wirken." Quoted in Angelika Schaser, *Frauenbewegung in Deutschland 1848–1933* (Darmstadt: WBG, 2006), 41.
6. Quoted in Carole Elisabeth Adams, *Women Clerks in Wilhelmine Germany: Issues of Class and Gender* (Cambridge: Cambridge University Press, 1988), 41.
7. Irene Stoehr, *Emanzipation zum Staat? Der Allgemeine Deutsche Frauenverein (1893–1933)* (Pfaffenweiler: Centaurus, 1990).
8. Petra Pommerenke, "Organisation und Bewegung: Die Frauenwohl-Vereine 1888–1914" (unpublished manuscript, Magisterarbeit at Johann Wolfgang Goethe University, Frankfurt am Main, 1996).
9. Female workers' associations usually named themselves with strikingly harmless names as well. Early female workers' associations were called, for example, Verein zur Fortbildung und geistigen Anregung der Arbeiterfrauen (1869–1871) (Association for the Training and Intellectual Stimulation of Working-Class Women) or Arbeiterfrauen- und Mädchenverein (Association for Working-Class Women and Girls) (1872–74) in Berlin. Even later, when female workers' associations had a more clearly class-conscious character, the names still sounded voluntarily harmless. The Frauen-Bildungsverein (Association for Women's Education), for example, founded in 1892 in Berlin, not only strove to increase women's education but also wanted to involve women in state and society issues and to free them from their outcast status. Especially the female labor associations had to be extremely cautious because of the so-called *Sozialistengesetz* (socialist law), adopted in 1878 and renewed many times until 1890. It aimed at hindering the development of the socialist movement and outlawed every socialist, social-democrat, and political labor organization and press organ.

10. See Ute Gerhard, ed., *Frauen in der Geschichte des Rechts von der Frühen Neuzeit bis zur Gegenwart* (Munich: C. H. Beck, 1997); Schaser, *Frauenbewegung in Deutschland*.
11. "So kamen in der neuern Zeit zur Sprache: E. des Fleisches oder die Befreiung der sinnlichen, auf Befriedigung durch materielle Genüsse gerichteten Begierden von den Schranken, welche ihnen auf der einen Seite Sitte und Religion, auf der andern soziale Verhältnisse entgegenstellen." Entry "Emanzipation" in *Meyers Konversationslexikon*, vol. 5, 4th ed. (Leipzig and Vienna: Verlag des Bibliographischen Instituts, 1885–92), 591, retrieved 19 April 2018 from http://www.retrobibliothek.de/retrobib/seite.html?id=104999.
12. "E. der Frauen oder die Befreiung des weiblichen Geschlechts von den Beschränkungen, mit welchen es natürliche und soziale Verhältnisse umgeben, daher man von emanzipierten Frauen dann zu sprechen pflegt, wenn sich dieselben in auffallender Weise geflissentlich über jene Schranken hinwegsetzen." Ibid.
13. Karen Offen, *Les féminismes en Europe 1700–1950*, trans. Geneviève Kniebiehler (Rennes: Presses Univ. de Rennes, 2012), 150 f.; 167.
14. R. (Wilhelm Heinrich Riehl), "Die Frauen: Eine sozial-politische Studie," *Deutsche Vierteljahrsschrift* 3, no. 3 (1852): 236–96.
15. Wilhelm Heinrich Riehl, *Die Naturgeschichte des Volkes als Grundlage einer deutschen Social-Politik*, vol. 3: *Die Familie* (Stuttgart and Augsburg: J. G. Cotta'scher Verlag, 1855), 18.
16. Offen, *Les féminismes*, 207.
17. Ibid., 207 ; 213.
18. Friedrich Battenberg, "Judenemanzipation im 18. und 19. Jahrhundert," in European History Online (EGO), Institute of European History (IEG), Mainz, 3 December 2010, retrieved 19 April 2018 from http://www.ieg-ego.eu/battenbergf-2010-de.
19. Melissa Hope Ditmore and Helen J. Self, "Abolition," in *Encyclopedia of Prostitution and Sex Work*, vol. 1, A–N, ed. Melissa Hope Ditmore (Westport, CT: Greenwood Press, 2006), 3–4; Frédéric Regard, ed., *Féminisme et prostitution dans l'Angleterre du XIXe siècle: la croisade de Josephine Butler* (Lyon: ENS éditions, 2013); Anne-Laure Briatte-Peters and Yannick Ripa, "La prostitution révélatrice de la condition feminine: Une lecture abolitionniste du réglementarisme au XIXe siècle (France, Allemagne, Angleterre)," in *La "condition féminine": Feminismus und Frauenbewegung im 19. und 20. Jahrhundert / La "condition féminine": Féminismes et mouvements de femmes au XIXe–XXe siècles*, ed. Françoise Berger and Anne Kwaschik (Stuttgart: Franz Steiner Verlag 2016), 55–66.
20. On the German involvement in the international abolitionist movement, see Bettina Kretzschmar, *"Gleiche Moral und gleiches Recht für Mann und Frau": Der deutsche Zweig der Internationalen abolitionistischen Bewegung (1899–1933)* (Sulzbach im Taunus: Helmer, 2014). Anna Pappritz was one of the female experts in the subject of prostitution and the abolition of state regulation; see Kerstin Wolff, *Anna Pappritz, 1861–1939: Die Rittergutstochter und die Prostitution* (Sulzbach im Taunus: Helmer, 2017).
21. Anna Pappritz, "Die Teilnahme der Frauen an der Sittlichkeitsbewegung," in *Handbuch der Frauenbewegung, II. Teil: Frauenbewegung und soziale Thätigkeit in Deutschland nach Einzelgebieten*, ed. Helene Lange and Gertrud Bäumer (Berlin: W. Moeser Verlagsbuchhandlung, 1901), 162.

22. Ulla Wischermann, *Frauenbewegungen und Öffentlichkeiten um 1900: Netzwerke—Gegenöffentlichkeiten—Protestinszenierungen* (Königstein im Taunus: Helmer, 2003).
23. See the photograph in Ute Gerhard, *Unerhört: Die Geschichte der deutschen Frauenbewegung* (Reinbek bei Hamburg: Rowohlt, 1990), 208f.
24. Front page of the *Berliner Illustrirte Zeitung*, 20 September 1896, retrieved 19 April 2018 from http://www.gettyimages.fr/detail/photo-d'actualité/titelseite-der-illustrirten-zeitung-vom-20-09-1896-photo-dactualité/542346415?#titelseite-der-illustrirten-zeitung-vom-20091896-berlin-zum-in-picture-id542346415.
25. See the cover in Elke Schüller, *Marie Stritt: Eine "Kampffrohe Streiterin" in der Frauenbewegung (1855—1928)*, with the first printing of the uncompleted memoir of Marie Stritt (Königstein im Taunus: Helmer, 2005), 142.
26. The legend under the portraits was "Abbildungen zum III. Internationalen Frauenkongreß in Berlin (1904)," in *Die Woche*, no. 23 (1904), 1003.
27. Susanne Kinnebrock, *Anita Augspurg (1857–1943): Feministin und Pazifistin zwischen Journalismus und Politik, eine kommunikationshistorische Biographie* (Herbolzheim: Centaurus-Verlag, 2005).
28. Marti M. Lybeck, *Desiring Emancipation: New Women and Homosexuality in Germany, 1890–1933* (Albany, NY: SUNY Press, 2014), 62.
29. Ibid., 62.
30. Sylvia Schraut portrays traditional women's life patterns in bourgeois milieus. Sylvia Schraut, *Bürgerinnen im Kaiserreich* (Stuttgart: Kohlhammer, 2013).
31. See my paper at the last conference of this DFG-Network, Munich, April 2015: "Endangering the Institution of Family? Emancipation and Family in the Radical Women's Movement in Wilhelmian Germany (1890–1918)," which was published in French: Anne-Laure Briatte-Peters, "Mariage, famille et sexualité vus par les féministes radicales dans l'Allemagne wilhelmienne (1890–1918)," *Revue d'Allemagne et des Pays de langue allemande* 48 (2016): 427–37.
32. Reinhold Lütgemeier-Davin and Kerstin Wolff, eds., *Lebenserinnerungen, Die unvollendete Autobiographie einer frauenbewegten Pazifistin, Helene Stöcker*, in Kooperation mit der Stiftung Archiv der deutschen Frauenbewegung, Kassel (Vienna: Böhlau, 2015).
33. Gerhard, *Frauen in der Geschichte des Rechts*, esp. 633–58.
34. Anne-Françoise Gilbert, "Frauenfreundschaft und frauenpolitischer Kampf im Kaiserreich: Das Beispiel von Lida Gustava Heymann und Anita Augspurg," *Ariadne—Forum für Frauen- und Geschlechtergeschichte* 40 (2001): 26–31.
35. Wischermann, *Frauenbewegungen*, 165–67.
36. Ibid., 170–71; Gilla Dölle, *Die (un)heimliche Macht des Geldes: Finanzierungsstrategien der bürgerlichen Frauenbewegung in Deutschland zwischen 1865 und 1933* (Frankfurt am Main: dipa-Verlag, 1997).
37. Wischermann, *Frauenbewegungen*, 172.
38. The liberation of the body was much more a topic for the so-called *Lebensreformbewegung*, the multifaceted movement for life reform. Among many other topics, the *Lebensreformbewegung* included a movement for the reform of dress codes and habits (*Reformkleiderbewegung*) and another one for nudism as a movement to reconnect to nature (*Freikörperkultur*). See Diethart Krebs and Jürgen Reulecke, ed., *Handbuch der deutschen Reform-Bewegungen 1880–1933* (Wuppertal: Hammer, 1998); Cornelia Klose-Lewerentz, "Befreite Körper? Die Lebensreformbe-

wegung und ihre Bedeutung für die Vorstellungen vom Körper zu Beginn des 20. Jahrhunderts," *Ariadne* 55 (2009): 54–59.
39. Gisela Jaacks and Angelika Schaser, "Vom kreativen Umgang mit Quellen und Lücken: Geschichtswissenschaft an Universitäten und Museen," in *Geisteswissenschaften in der Offensive: Hamburger Standortsbestimmungen*, ed. Jörg Dierken (Hamburg: EVA 2009), 311–12.
40. Karen Ellwaner and Elisabeth Meyer-Renschhausen, "Kleidungsreform," in Krebs and Reulecke, *Handbuch*, 87–102.
41. Kinnebrock, *Anita Augspurg*, 118.
42. Ibid., 470.
43. Lily von Gizycki, "Stimmungsbilder aus der General-Versammlung des Bundes deutscher Frauenvereine in München," *Die Frauenbewegung* 9 (1895): 69–70.
44. For example Minna Cauer, "Die Vereine und die Frauenbewegung," *Die Frauenbewegung* 12 (1895): 92.
45. Anne-Laure Briatte-Peters, *Citoyennes sous tutelle: Le mouvement féministe "radical" dans l'Allemagne wilhelmienne* (Bern: Peter Lang, 2013), 304–7.
46. Angelika Schaser, "Zur Einführung des Frauenwahlrechts vor 90 Jahren am 12. November 1918," *Feministische Studien* (2009): 102.
47. Concerning the public relations strategy and especially the technique of "scandalization," see Wischermann, *Frauenbewegungen*; for the self-representation of the radical wing of the German women's movement, see Anne-Laure Briatte-Peters, "Sie stand sich selbst im Weg: Die radikale Frauenbewegung im Verhältnis zu den anderen und zu sich selbst," in *Ariadne—Forum für Frauen- und Geschlechtergeschichte* 67–68 (2015): 80–88.
48. About this campaign, see Juliana Tutt, "'No Taxation without Representation' in the American Woman Suffrage Movement," *Stanford Law Review* 62 (2010): 1473–510.
49. Susanne, Kinnebrock, "'Wahrhaft international?' Soziale Bewegungen zwischen nationalen Öffentlichkeiten und internationalen Bewegungsverbund," in *Politische Netzwerkerinnen: Internationale Zusammenarbeit von Frauen 1830–1960*, ed. Eva Schöck-Quinteros et al. (Berlin: trafo, 2007), 27–55.
50. Silke Hanschke, "Der Kampf um das Frauenwahlrecht in Großbritannien: Emmeline Pankhurst, die Womens' Social and Political Union, und was daraus wurde," in *"Heraus mit dem Frauenwahlrecht": Die Kämpfe der Frauen in Deutschland und England um die politische Gleichberechtigung*, ed. Christl Wickert (Pfaffenweiler: Centaurus, 1990), 13–50.
51. Wischermann, *Frauenbewegungen*, 86.
52. Kinnebrock, *Anita Augspurg*, 333.

Bibliography

Adams, Carole Elisabeth. *Women Clerks in Wilhelmine Germany: Issues of Class and Gender*. Cambridge: Cambridge University Press, 1988.
Battenberg, Friedrich. "Judenemanzipation im 18. und 19. Jahrhundert." In European History Online (EGO), Institute of European History (IEG), Mainz, retrieved 19 April 2018 from http://www.ieg-ego.eu/battenbergf-2010-de.

Bleker, Johanna. "Vorspiel: Deutsche Ärztinnen mit ausländischem Doktorgrad 1871–1901." In *Ärztinnen aus dem Kaiserreich: Lebensläufe einer Generation*, edited by Johanna Bleker and Sabine Schleiermacher, 11–34. Weinheim: Deutscher Studienverlag, 2000.

Bock, Gisela. "Begriffsgeschichten: 'Frauenemanzipation' im Kontext der Emanzipationsbewegungen des 19. Jahrhunderts." In Gisela Bock, *Geschlechtergeschichten der Neuzeit: Ideen, Politik, Praxis*, 100–152. Göttingen: Vandenhoeck & Ruprecht, 2014.

Briatte-Peters, Anne-Laure. *Citoyennes sous tutelle: Le mouvement féministe "radical" dans l'Allemagne wilhelmienne*. Bern: Peter Lang, 2013.

———. "Sie stand sich selbst im Weg: Die radikale Frauenbewegung im Verhältnis zu den anderen und zu sich selbst." *Ariadne—Forum für Frauen- und Geschlechtergeschichte* 67-68 (2015): 80–88.

———. "Mariage, famille et sexualité vus par les féministes radicales dans l'Allemagne wilhelmienne (1890–1918)." *Revue d'Allemagne et des Pays de langue allemande* 48 (2016): 427–37.

Briatte-Peters, Anne-Laure, and Yannick Ripa. "La prostitution révélatrice de la condition feminine: Une lecture abolitionniste du réglementarisme au XIXe siècle (France, Allemagne, Angleterre)." In *La "condition féminine": Feminismus und Frauenbewegung im 19. und 20. Jahrhundert / La "condition féminine": Féminismes et mouvements de femmes au XIXe–XXe siècles*, edited by Françoise Berger and Anne Kwaschik, 55–66. Stuttgart: Franz Steiner Verlag, 2016 (SR des Deutschfranzösischen Historikerkomitees; 12).

Ditmore, Melissa Hope, and Helen J. Self. "Abolition." In *Encyclopedia of Prostitution and Sex Work*. Vol. 1: A–N, edited by Melissa Hope Ditmore. Westport, CT: Greenwood Press, 2006.

Dölle, Gilla. *Die (un)heimliche Macht des Geldes: Finanzierungsstrategien der bürgerlichen Frauenbewegung in Deutschland zwischen 1865 und 1933*. Frankfurt am Main: dipa-Verlag, 1997.

Gerhard, Ute, ed. *Frauen in der Geschichte des Rechts von der Frühen Neuzeit bis zur Gegenwart*. Munich: C. H. Beck, 1997.

———. *Unerhört: Die Geschichte der deutschen Frauenbewegung*. Reinbek bei Hamburg: Rowohlt, 1990.

Gilbert, Anne-Françoise. "Frauenfreundschaft und frauenpolitischer Kampf im Kaiserreich: Das Beispiel von Lida Gustava Heymann und Anita Augspurg." In *Ariadne* 40 (2001): 26–31.

Hanschke, Silke. "Der Kampf um das Frauenwahlrecht in Großbritannien: Emmeline Pankhurst, die Womens' Social and Political Union, und was daraus wurde." In *"Heraus mit dem Frauenwahlrecht": Die Kämpfe der Frauen in Deutschland und England um die politische Gleichberechtigung*, edited by Christl Wickert, 13–50. Pfaffenweiler: Centaurus, 1990.

Jaacks, Gisela, and Angelika Schaser. "Vom kreativen Umgang mit Quellen und Lücken: Geschichtswissenschaft an Universitäten und Museen." In *Geisteswissenschaften in der Offensive: Hamburger Standortsbestimmungen*, edited by Jörg Dierken, 299–321. Hamburg: EVA 2009.

Kinnebrock, Susanne. *Anita Augspurg (1857–1943): Feministin und Pazifistin zwischen Journalismus und Politik, eine kommunikationshistorische Biographie*. Herbolzheim: Centaurus-Verlag 2005.

———. "'Wahrhaft international?' Soziale Bewegungen zwischen nationalen Öffentlichkeiten und internationalen Bewegungsverbund." In *Politische Netzwerkerinnen: Internationale Zusammenarbeit von Frauen 1830–1960*, edited by Eva Schöck-Quinteros, Anja Schüler, Annika Wilmers, and Kerstin Wolff, 27–55. Berlin: trafo, 2007.

Klose-Lewerentz, Cornelia. "Befreite Körper? Die Lebensreformbewegung und ihre Bedeutung für die Vorstellungen vom Körper zu Beginn des 20. Jahrhunderts." *Ariadne—Forum für Frauen- und Geschlechtergeschichte* 55 (2009): 54–59.

Krebs, Diethart, and Jürgen Reulecke, eds. *Handbuch der deutschen Reform-Bewegungen 1880–1933*. Wuppertal: Hammer, 1998.

Kretzschmar, Bettina. *"Gleiche Moral und gleiches Recht für Mann und Frau": Der deutsche Zweig der Internationalen abolitionistischen Bewegung (1899–1933)*. Sulzbach im Taunus: Helmer, 2014.

Lange, Christiane. "'Nur ein unzeitgemäßer Scherz? Akademikerinnen im Deutschland des späten 19. Jahrhunderts—Franziska Tiburtius u. a." In *Geschriebenes Leben: Autobiographik von Frauen*, edited by Michaela Holdenried, 226–43. Berlin: Erich Schmidt, 1995.

Lütgemeier-Davin, Reinhold, and Kerstin Wolff, eds. *Lebenserinnerungen, Die unvollendete Autobiographie einer frauenbewegten Pazifistin, Helene Stöcker*. In Kooperation mit der Stiftung Archiv der deutschen Frauenbewegung, Kassel (L'Homme Archiv 5). Vienna: Böhlau, 2015.

Lybeck, Marti M. *Desiring Emancipation: New Women and Homosexuality in Germany, 1890–1933*. Albany, NY: SUNY Press, 2014.

Offen, Karen. *Les féminismes en Europe 1700–1950*. Translated by Geneviève Kniebiehler. Rennes: Presses Univ. de Rennes, 2012.

Pappritz, Anna. "Die Teilnahme der Frauen an der Sittlichkeitsbewegung." In *Handbuch der Frauenbewegung, II. Teil: Frauenbewegung und soziale Thätigkeit in Deutschland nach Einzelgebieten*, edited by Helene Lange and Gertrud Bäumer, 154–92. Berlin: W. Moeser Verlagsbuchhandlung, 1901.

Pommerenke, Petra. "Organisation und Bewegung: Die Frauenwohl-Vereine 1888–1914." Unpublished manuscript, Magisterarbeit at Johann Wolfgang Goethe University Frankfurt am Main, 1996.

Raschke, Joachim. *Soziale Bewegungen: Ein historisch-systematischer Grundriss*. 2nd ed. Frankfurt am Main: Campus Verlag, 1988.

Regard, Frédéric, ed. *Féminisme et prostitution dans l'Angleterre du XIXe siècle: la croisade de Josephine Butler*. Lyon: ENS éditions, 2013.

Riehl, Wilhelm Heinrich. "Die Frauen: Eine sozial-politische Studie." *Deutsche Vierteljahrsschrift* 3, no. 3 (1852): 236–96

———. *Die Naturgeschichte des Volkes als Grundlage einer deutschen Social-Politik*. Vol. 3: *Die Familie*. Stuttgart and Augsburg: J. G. Cotta'scher Verlag, 1855.

Schaser, Angelika. *Frauenbewegung in Deutschland 1848–1933*. Darmstadt: WBG, 2006.

———. "Zur Einführung des Frauenwahlrechts vor 90 Jahren am 12. November 1918." *Feministische Studien* (2009): 97–110.

Schüller, Elke. *Marie Stritt: Eine "Kampffrohe Streiterin" in Der Frauenbewegung (1855–1928)*. With the first printing of the uncompleted memoir of Marie Stritt. Königstein im Taunus: Helmer, 2005.

Schraut, Sylvia. *Bürgerinnen im Kaiserreich*. Stuttgart: Kohlhammer, 2013.

Stoehr, Irene. *Emanzipation zum Staat? Der Allgemeine Deutsche Frauenverein (1893–1933)*. Pfaffenweiler: Centaurus, 1990.
Tutt, Juliana. "'No Taxation without Representation' in the American Woman Suffrage Movement." *Stanford Law Review* 62 (2010): 1473–510.
Wischermann, Ulla. *Frauenbewegungen und Öffentlichkeiten um 1900: Netzwerke—Gegenöffentlichkeiten—Protestinszenierungen*. Königstein im Taunus: Helmer, 2003.
Wolff, Kerstin. *Anna Pappritz, 1861–1939. Die Rittergutstochter und die Prostitution*. Sulzbach im Taunus: Helmer, 2017.

CHAPTER 11

German and Italian Advocates for Women's Emancipation at the International Congress on Women's Achievements and Women's Endeavors in Berlin (1896)

Magdalena Gehring

Introduction

From the mid-nineteenth century onward, women in many European countries and further afield were developing organizations to fight for their legal and political rights and for better opportunities in education and occupation. By the end of the century, an organized international women's movement had started to grow. This chapter examines the women's movement in Germany and Italy and focuses on the Internationaler Kongreß für Frauenwerke und Frauenbestrebungen (International Congress on Women's Achievements and Women's Endeavors), the first international conference of this kind to be staged in Germany.

A comparison between the Italian and German women's movements in the context of the international women's movement addresses an apparent gap in the research. While there has been extensive investigation into the two national women's movements and their development, goals, and strategies, comparative studies are very rare.[1] Gabriele Boukrif gives a detailed view of the fight for the vote for women in both countries and compares two well-known advocates of women's suffrage, Hedwig Dohm and Anna Maria Mozzoni.[2] Karen Offen's overview, *European Feminisms, 1700–1950*, includes coverage of developments in Italy, but the temporal and geographical range of the study does not permit an in-depth examination of each individual national story.[3] The comparative volume on European women's movements edited by Sylvia Paletschek and Bianka Pietrow-Ennker unfortunately omits the Italian perspective.[4] Just two articles, by Donna Gabaccia and Elisabeth Dickmann, refer to the international context of the Italian women's movement.⁵ As a result, there is good reason to bring a comparative focus to the German and Italian women's movements at the end of the nineteenth century.

The social and political circumstances in Italy and Germany, their influence on the national women's movements, and the structure of the movements themselves are discussed in the first section, thus placing the positions, goals, and strategies of the advocates for women's rights within the broader context. The arrangements for the international congress in Berlin are then described: its setting, themes for debate, and speakers. The focus is on the discussion about the "woman question" and its solution, with particular attention to the speeches by Lina Morgenstern, Marie Stritt, Paolina Schiff, and Maria Montessori. These texts provide deeper insights not only into the self-perception of the women's movements and the specific conditions of women in the two countries but also into the divergences both between and within the different national movements. This leads to discussion of the direct confrontation between Germany's middle-class women and its socialist contingent during the congress in Berlin. In the conclusion, the results of this investigation are placed in the broader context.

The main source for the discussion is the record of the congress proceedings, which includes all the speeches and debates that took place, for the most part reproduced in full, edited by Rosalie Schoenflies.⁶ The speeches were given in German, English, Italian, and French, reflecting the education of the women participants and the international atmosphere. Reports on the congress in different publications within the German women's movement, such as the journal of the radical wing of the middle-class women's movement *Die Frauenbewegung* (The Women's Movement) and *Die Gleichheit* (Equality), edited by the socialist Clara Zetkin, were also consulted.⁷ In addition, reference is made to personal memoirs by advocates for women's rights.

The aim of this chapter is to provide a fuller understanding of how the different national settings influenced the women from the two nations in their goals, endeavors, and strategies. The hypothesis is that, firstly, the absence of a national umbrella organization and, secondly, regional diversity allowed there to be more radical feminist actors in the Italian women's movement than in its German counterpart. In light of the broader international movement, questions about the different loyalties of the women are raised. Did they mainly see themselves and their endeavors in a national context, as German or Italian, in a social context, as members of the middle class, or in a wider context, as women within the so-called "universal sisterhood"? Finally, consideration is given to whether and how the first international congress held within the German Empire influenced the national women's movement at the end of the nineteenth century.

The Social and Political Context of the Women's Movements in Germany and Italy

At first glance, it might seem that the histories of the two young nations were relatively similar. Germany and Italy both understood themselves as "cultural nations," which is to say that their history and culture constituted the basis for their establishment as a political nation. Both had strong civil national movements and were formed by unification wars driven from above, Italy in 1861, and the German Empire in 1871. Particularist systems were transformed into constitutional monarchies with fixed centers of power, respectively in Rome and in Berlin.[8]

However, there were some significant differences.[9] Germany was ruled by the Protestant Prussians and had to deal with a rigid class segregation, in which the aristocracy and military constituted the top level of society above a heterogeneous middle class, and then, the proletariat. In this Protestant-dominated culture, the Catholic and Jewish minorities had to endure discrimination and exclusion, although religion became less important toward the end of the nineteenth century.[10] In contrast, Italian culture continued to be influenced by the Catholic Church, and the Vatican strove to exert its spiritual authority over the people's moral conduct and social life. At the same time, Italian politics, especially during the first decades of the kingdom, was significantly coined by anticlerical tendencies. Quite apart from the presence of this second authority in Rome, Italy also had substantial internal differences in culture, language, education, social structure, and industrial development between the north and the south.[11] This kind of difference also existed in Germany but was less marked; this can be seen in the issue of national languages. In Italy, the *questione della lingua* (language question) remained a significant concern after the country's political unification, because the different regional dialects were the basis of regional cultures and identities.[12] These regional identities were thus of greater significance than in Germany. In Italy, as elsewhere, there were matters to be addressed that related to increasing class consciousness, but relationships between the middle class and the working class were not fundamentally antagonistic.

This hypothesis is borne out in the example of the middle-class women's movement in both countries. The beginning of an organized women's movement in Germany can be traced to the foundation of the Allgemeiner Deutscher Frauenverein (ADF; General German Women's Association) by Louise Otto-Peters in 1865 in Leipzig. It brought together women mostly from middle-class intellectual and liberal families. Right from the beginning, the association's aim was explicitly to bring all German women together, even though the national state did not yet exist.[13] The stated objectives of the ADF included women's access to higher education and their rights to have a profession and earn their own living. Suffrage was a longer-term goal, pursued by progressive women such as Hedwig Dohm and, from the 1890s on, by a radical wing that had formed around Minna Cauer; as a formal demand, it did not appear until 1902.[14] In 1894, the national umbrella organization Bund Deutscher Frauenvereine (BDF; Federation of German Women's Associations) was founded; with the exception of the socialist and Catholic women's groups, this brought together nearly all Germany's women's associations and started the organized work within the international women's movement.[15] As discussed later, there was a considerable gap between the middle-class and the socialist women; this widened during the congress in Berlin in 1896, where Clara Zetkin, the leader of the socialist women, proclaimed the doctrine of "reinliche Scheidung" (clean separation between the classes) in the presence of the international audience.[16]

In Italy, by contrast, organization of the women's movement started in 1880, when Anna Maria Mozzoni and Paolina Schiff founded the Lega Promotrice degli Interessi Femminili (League for the Promotion of Women's Interests) in Milan, the country's industrial center. The league was influenced by left-wing politics, and it brought together women from different social backgrounds; they fought for the complete equality of their sex including with respect to the vote, the improvement of women's lives in general, and the visibility of women in public life and leading positions. During the 1890s, the movement was growing, but it also split into many different groups whose interests varied according to their location.[17] The women active in Rome, for example, were generally from aristocratic backgrounds and were involved in educational issues. Some nonaristocratic women, like the famous educationalist Maria Montessori, led their own kind of emancipated life, which was not possible for women of a lower social status. At the start of the twentieth century, after the repression of the labor movement and left-wing political groups in the aftermath of the *fatti di maggio* (events of May 1898), the unification of the movement began with the foundation of the Consiglio Nazionale Donne Italiane (National Council of Italian Women) in 1903.[18] As in the German movement, there were evident political and social differences within the Italian women's movement, but the way of dealing with this diversity was not the same; left-wing groups, for example, were more readily accepted in Italy.

Although the Italian women's movement was not organized at a national level, Italian campaigners for women's rights were active in the nascent international women's movement and confidently presented their ideas and opinions. In 1878, for example, Anna Maria Mozzoni gave the opening speech at the Women's Rights Congress in Paris, an event hosted by Maria Deraismes at the time of the city's International Exposition.[19]

Fanny Zampini Salazaro sent her report on the conditions of women in Italy to the first meeting of the International Council of Women (ICW) in 1888 in Washington, DC, apologizing for not being able to attend in person.[20]

The German women were initially more reluctant to take part in the international women's movement; once they had decided to become involved, however, the German movement was one of the first national women's movements to join the ICW.

The International Congress on Women's Achievements and Women's Endeavors

The first international women's congress to be held in Germany, the Internationaler Kongreß für Frauenwerke und Frauenbestrebungen, took place in Berlin from 19 to 26 September 1896. It was organized by a small group of women active in Berlin and not by a women's association or the umbrella organization BDF. The idea of hosting an international women's conference had come from Lina Morgenstern, a longstanding member of the middle-class women's movement with a Jewish background. Her activities in supporting women were very broad: she was involved in initiatives with working-class women and was also the founder of the Berliner Hausfrauenverein (Association of the Housewives of Berlin).[21] In France and the United States, women had previously made effective use of trade fairs as the setting for international women's events.[22] The organizing committee represented the diversity within the German middle-class women's movement and included women with international experience. It was led by Morgenstern and the radicals Hedwig Dohm and Minna Cauer, who had founded the progressive association Verein Frauenwohl (Association for Women's Well-Being), and also brought in members of the more moderate wing of the movement, such as Jeanette Schwerin and Marie Stritt from the board of the BDF and Hanna Bieber-Böhm from the ADF. Bieber-Böhm had been a member of the first delegation to represent the German women's movement internationally, at the ICW in Chicago in 1893. The committee secretary, Eliza Ichenhäuser, was also an advocate for internationalism and helped to develop the German movement's international network; in 1899, she was to be elected as chair of the ICW's press committee.[23]

More than ten thousand invitations were sent out to women's associations in countries all over the world. Aside from the international aspect, the particular feature of the event was that all groups of every political persuasion within the women's movement were invited, from conservatives to radicals. The goal was "to create harmony between the women's movements of all countries and lead the whole of humanity to a better future." This was to be achieved "through justice for everybody, and the . . . liberation of women from illiberality, prejudice, ignorance, and disrespect."[24] The women's aspiration to work together irrespective of political, national, religious, and class distinctions was very progressive and tried to bring the idea of universal sisterhood to life.

The congress was a success, in numerical terms at least. The German women played host to about seventeen hundred delegates from Belgium, Denmark, England, Finland, France, the Netherlands, Austria, Russia and its provinces, Sweden, Switzerland, Hungary, the United States, and Italy in Berlin's magnificent town hall. In addition, more than two hundred observers, including journalists and members of the public, attended the open discussions.[25] Use of the venue represented a great honor for the women, and Minna Cauer described it as a "happy omen for the future."[26] The importance of this sign of acceptance and official support for women from the city of Berlin should not in fact be underestimated, because the women became visible in the public sphere.

The themes of the ninety-six speeches on the extensive program included the situation and development of the women's movement in different countries; childcare and education; women's access to higher education; training for women in the professions; healthcare and social care; women's position in regard to civil rights; women's employment and working conditions; women in arts, science, and literature; and the participation of women in the peace movement. Even the controversial topic of political participation and the right to vote were included in the program. This was a brave step by the German organizers, because the Prussian Law of Association, which remained in force until 1908, forbade women from taking part in any political activity, especially in societies and political parties, and from participation in political events in public.[27]

All these topics were aspects of the "woman question," a term that was used thirty-nine times in the speeches and discussions. In contrast, the term "women's emancipation" was used only eleven times. The texts provide no clear definition of either; it would seem that the speakers knew or assumed that the audience could understand the terms in the way intended, which was potentially problematic in this international and politically diverse environment.[28]

At the time, opinions about this congress were divided, just as they have been among scholars. Alice Salomon, who was active in the international women's movement, wrote in her memoirs that it was "an irrelevant issue, because the relationships between women from different countries were still haphazard."[29] Gertrud Bäumer's evaluation of the event in the *Handbuch der Frauenbewegung* (Manual of the Women's Movement) was also not entirely positive. She wrote that "overall the congress has been a great contribution as a means of attracting public attention, although the program had some deficiencies and its strong point was the overall impression rather than the thematic discussion. Ultimately, the congress started a broad discussion about the woman question."[30]

In contrast, Minna Cauer wrote in *Die Frauenbewegung*, which she edited, that "for the first time, German women are acting like women from other countries and invite people to a gathering, and for the first time they have the courage to engage in an exchange of ideas about their work and endeavors."[31] Notwithstanding the criticism voiced by German feminists, the event was given positive coverage in the German and international press by publications with positions ranging from the conservative to the revolutionary. For example, one of the most important German magazines of the time, the *Berliner Illustrirte Zeitung* (Berlin Illustrated News), printed photographs of twelve important representatives of the German women's movement attending the congress.[32] The diverse groups within the German women's movement seized this opportunity and, with a new self-confidence, took up their position in the public discussion of the time.

Karen Offen says that the event "greatly energized" German feminists; they were exposed to activists such as Eugénie Potonié-Pierre, who claimed at the congress that she and her French colleagues had invented the progressive term *feminisme*.[33] As it progressed, however, the tense relationship between the German middle-class and socialist women deteriorated rapidly. At the end of the congress, Cauer concluded that "I stay with my belief and express it here again, women are the only people who can still build a bridge from one side of the river to the other."[34] Ute Gerhard has therefore questioned whether the congress was a moment of glory or a missed opportunity for the women's movement in Germany.[35]

In the sections that follow, I focus on the representatives of the Italian and German women's movements and the dispute between Germany's middle-class and socialist women.

The Italian Representatives at the Congress

As mentioned earlier, the Italian women were actively involved in the nascent international women's movement. The diversity of the Italian women's movement was represented in Berlin by the inclusion of protagonists such as Maria Montessori, a qualified medical doctor, Paolina Schiff, a university lecturer, Rea Silvia Petrini, a headmistress, and Emma Castelbolognesi, an expert on German literature and a headmistress as well.

Paolina Schiff was born in 1841 to a German-Jewish family. At the time of the congress, she was a university lecturer in Italy and, as a pioneer of the Italian women's movement, was the first secretary of the Lega per la

Tutela degli Interessi Femminili (League for the Defense of Women's Interests) in Milan.[36] In this latter position, she was qualified to provide an overview of the women's movement in the industrialized region of northern Italy. Her speech was actually read by Rosalie Schoenflies, but she was present in the auditorium. She highlighted the early achievements of the movement and expressed her pride in its continued growth. She introduced the topics of interest in nine points, focusing on successful social projects to help working-class women; discussions about improvements to women's legal status; better female education, employment opportunities, and income; and women's participation in the peace movement.[37] Although she did not address the issue of women's political participation and suffrage, this too was an important topic in the discussions in Italy.

Schiff's report was followed by a description of the situation in Rome by the young Maria Montessori, the subsequently very well-known progressive educationalist who was born in 1870 to a middle-class intellectual family and who had just completed her doctoral dissertation in medicine. She described the situation in the "ancient city of Rome," where "the women's movement had just appeared." The newly formed Associazione femminile di Roma (Women's Association of Rome) brought together women who were mainly aristocratic and wealthy, in contrast to the socialist-oriented movement in Milan and the middle-class women's movement in Germany. She stressed the particular role of those women who supported "the emancipation of our sex with their action," giving the pioneering women who had attended the universities as an example. Montessori reminded her audience about the difficulties these women had had to face, including their near expulsion from society. Fifteen years later, the situation was vastly different: for a mother, their daughter's university degree was now a matter of pride.[38] This illustrated how women's courageous action and strong will could change society, and gave hope for further improvements. In Montessori's eyes, these women were exemplary role models because they had tried to solve an aspect of the woman question by practicing female emancipation. She believed that women's emancipation included their intellectual, financial, and social independence, and she thought that change would come through access to higher education and would be brought by confident women who were not afraid to challenge social norms. These women had shown the younger generation new opportunities and ways of achieving an independent life. Their brave behavior had resulted in a growing number of women teachers in girls' schools, and women physicians, lawyers, and scholars in the natural sciences. Although the legacy of the Roman past and the papacy weighed down upon them, Montessori was proud of the first steps that the women of Rome had taken to change their situation.³⁹ The emancipated woman that she portrayed in her speech corresponded to her own path of emancipation by means of education and professional qualification, which differed from the approach that Milan's Lega had adopted and was clearly connected to a wealthy and intellectual background. Her rhetorical skills and attractive appearance captured the attention not only of the women at the congress but also of the press, which she had strong feelings about: she wanted to be respected for her work and not because she was a young and good-looking woman.⁴⁰

In the session on "Women in Commerce, Industry, and Business," Montessori gave a much-noticed lecture on "Wages of Working Women," providing a detailed picture of the situation of working-class women in Italy supported by statistics. This highly educated woman was also concerned about the destiny of the majority of Italian women, who had to face hard work in the fields or the factory and lived in conditions of poverty. Montessori gave her speeches in Italian but handed out German translations beforehand.⁴¹

Rea Silvia Petrini and Emma Castelbolognesi had submitted a paper about education and the status of women teachers in Italian high schools. Castelbolognesi was born into a Jewish family in Modena. She spent most of her life in Germany. At the end of the nineteenth century, she lived in Berlin and was therefore present at the congress, but because of a timing issue she could not present their speech, and it therefore only appeared in the published proceedings in a shortened version.⁴² To date, unfortunately, no further information has emerged about Rea Silvia Petrini, illustrating the need for more biographical research into the early women's rights activists.

Rosalie Schoenflies also read the "Greetings of Peace" from the Comitato delle Signore per la Pace e l'Arbitrato Internazionale di Palermo (Palermo's committee of women for peace and international arbitration). Involvement in the peace movement was an important element of the women's movement in Italy because of the continuing colonial war in Ethiopia. The opposing parties signed a peace treaty in October 1896, confirming Ethiopia's independence.⁴³

The Italian women appeared as confident actors on the international floor. They were proud of the achievements of a new movement within the young nation, but they also called attention to Italy's social and gender-based injustices and proposed strategies to address these problems. Among themselves, these women had different approaches to dealing with the social, political, and religious differences in Italy at the time. Their main focuses were improvements in women's living conditions and education, and the achievement of suffrage and equality between the sexes.

The German Representatives at the Congress

Due to the large number of German participants, they cannot all be named in this chapter. The more prominent delegates representing German women included Marie Stritt, Johanna Goldschmidt, Käthe Schirmacher, Anita Augspurg, and Hanna Bieber-Böhm. The focus will be on the opening speech by Lina Morgenstern and the description of the German women's movement by Marie Stritt.

The chairwoman of the congress, Lina Morgenstern, born in 1831 and one of the pioneers and intriguing characters with the women's movement, recalled in her opening address the beginnings of women's attempts to change their own situation in 1848.[44] During the revolution in Germany of 1848–49, the term "emancipation" was "still a phantasm for the advocates of old opinions, prejudices, and customs." Now, however, it was no longer a "hallucination," as the success of the international congress showed: a small group of committed women in Berlin had been able to bring together many like-minded people from different countries. This allowed her to hope that "there will be a time when a peaceful gathering of the nations and the sexes will be possible."[45] Toward the end of the century, women's emancipation was in fact no longer just the fantasy of some eccentric women but increasingly approaching a reality.

The speech by Marie Stritt, a former opera singer, member of the ADF, founder of the Rechtsschutzverein (Rights Protection Association) in Dresden in 1894, and later the chairwoman of the BDF from 1899, focused on the development and current position of the German middle-class women's movement.[46] She opened with a rigorous critique of this, lamenting the slowness of development and lack of interest within wider German society, even though there was much discussion of the woman question in some circles. Furthermore, she declared "a general ignorance and distressing misunderstanding about the impact and goals of the movement," especially in intellectual circles.[47]

For Stritt, the woman question included issues such as the unfettered access of middle-class women to employment, high school education, and the universities, as well as society's double standards in relation to the conduct of men and women. In regard to this latter point, she was identifying an issue then at the heart of the woman question.[48] Her address also covered the debate over civil rights, female political participation, and votes for women.

Stritt saw the slow development of the women's movement as a major problem and spoke openly about it. She criticized the closed minds of ignorant people who discussed the woman question without any proper knowledge in the fear that women's demands were either excessive or were risky "experiments," pointing out that these critics seemed unaware that these "doubtful experiments" had already been successfully implemented in other countries.[49] In Stritt's view, the woman question encapsulated a number of social problems that affected the quality of women's lives. The task of the women's movement was to make society aware of these problems so that they could be resolved. Her critical assessment of her own national movement illustrates its character, which was not as confident as the Italian women's movement.

Like the Italian women's movement, the German movement included women from both Jewish and Christian backgrounds; their religious differences did not seem as important as the common injustice experienced in view of their sex. In her study on the Jewish middle class, Marion Kaplan suggests that involvement in the women's movement may have been a key moment for the integration of Jewish women in German society.[50] It is interesting that the middle-class women's movement was unable to accommodate Germany's socialist women in the same way, as can be seen in the next section.

The Dispute with the Socialist Women: A German Issue?

The invitation from the Berlin women had been extended to people of all political persuasions within the women's movement in Germany, from conservatives to radicals. Only one Protestant group of feminists and the country's socialist women declined the official invitation to the congress and refused to participate as speakers, even though the topic of working-class women was on the agenda.[51] Maria Montessori, Therese Schlesinger-Eckstein from Vienna, an active member of Austria's Sozialdemokratische Arbeiterpartei (Social Democratic Workers' Party), and Florence Routledge, who was to join the Women's Trades Union League in London in 1897, gave striking portrayals of the miserable conditions of working-class women in their respective countries.[52] In her detailed report on the congress, Minna Cauer was severely critical of the behavior of Lily Braun, one of her former allies who was now a member of the socialist women's movement; she seems to have been personally affronted by Braun's decision not to attend to give her speech.[53] It is necessary to explore why the socialist women did not make use of this opportunity to increase middle-class women's awareness of the poor living conditions of their working-class counterparts.

Braun's memoirs provide some interesting insights into the decision by the social democratic women to boycott the congress. She herself was born in 1865 into the family of an aristocratic officer but then started an independent life and was active in the radical wing of the women's movement. In 1896, she married the social democrat Heinrich Braun and joined the Social Democratic Party, marking a radical break with her origins.[54] At the point when the socialist women decided not to attend the "middle-class congress," because it would be against the "Klassenkampf" (class struggle), Braun had already announced that she would be addressing the congress on "The Female Labor Question." Under pressure from Wanda Orbin, the chair of Berlin's socialist women, she withdrew her contribution against her own inclinations. Years later, she still regretted not having addressed the congress.[55] The public explanation given was that the "middle-class committee" had not allotted enough time for presentation of the topic, a spurious reason, as the timing of other speeches showed.[56]

On the final day, the situation deteriorated further during the session on "Volkserziehung und Arbeiterinnenfrage" (popular education and women's labor question). Janette Schwerin was discussing the issue of "Which areas are suitable for the collaborative work of all women?" when Clara Zetkin intervened—"not as a participant in the congress but as a guest and an opponent"—and rejected any cooperation between the middle-class women and socialist women in Germany.[57] Although Zetkin found words to praise the success of the congress, she held onto the doctrine of the "reinliche Scheidung" (clean separation) between the two classes and indicated the shortcomings of the middle-class women's movement. Her rigid approach is interesting, because she herself had a middle-class background and friends in the middle-class movement.[58] The congress in Berlin made evident the large gap between the middle-class and socialist women within Germany, a feature that some international delegates found hard to understand. Baroness Alexandra Gripenberg, a Finnish social activist and women's rights advocate, expressed her incomprehension and described the fruitful cooperation between her country's middle-class and working-class women.[59]

Germany's socialist women, however, were not the only people who struggled to engage in cooperation. Although some middle-class women attempted to be open to cooperation with their socialist counterparts and worked to improve the living conditions of working-class women, their speeches highlighted the class differences in their lives. Maria Montessori, for example, talked about working-class women in Italy and regretted their lack of representation at the congress, but she still set the woman question apart from the issues that working-class women faced.[60] While it is clear that she sought solutions that would also help working-class women, her lifestyle and personal experiences of discrimination as a woman had nothing to do with the situation that working-class women had to face. Marie Stritt also emphasized the need for different solutions to the woman question in regard to middle-class and working-class women.[61] These examples illustrate the marked degree of routine social segregation. Social structures and hierarchies were not easy to overcome, and it is very probable that people feared losing social privileges. In this regard, the utopian vision of universal sisterhood failed.

Conclusion

Brief analysis of the representatives of the German and Italian women's movements at the international congress in Berlin has shown that both were religiously diverse. Each was fighting for the social, economic, and legal independence of women by means of better education, access to the professions, and changes to legislation. Although their goals and methods were similar, the women from the two countries expressed their situation and the development of their movement very differently, reflecting the disparities in each country's position and the structure of their movements. Paolina Schiff and Maria Montessori represented different parts of Italy and different aspects of its women's movement. Both were proud of the progress achieved, and each was convinced that further change would come. The relatively recent organization of the Italian women's movement at a national level had allowed more flexibility and different regional developments. In contrast, Marie Stritt was very critical of the movement in Germany and demanded a more serious effort from the German women. The tone of her speech foreshadowed her future role as chairwoman of the BDF, a position with responsibility and power.

The closing address by Minna Cauer illustrated the strong national identity of the German women, even though they had invited the international community to this progressive congress. She said that "every country has its own national woman question and every country has to find its own way of addressing, developing, and resolving this. Indeed, we can learn from our brave and inspiring sisters from other countries, but to imitate them would be mistaken."[62] In Cauer's view, the international exchange between women could not be more than an inspiration, because the national situations and needs were too different. Regular international exchange could support development of the national movements, and in so doing could improve women's rights worldwide. Although awareness of the shared battle for women's rights was an encouragement, universal sisterhood—surpassing national, social, religious, and ethnic boundaries—appeared at that point to be an unachievable utopia. This reality became apparent in the dispute between Germany's middle-class and socialist women, who did not want to work together for the liberation of women irrespective of differences in social class. The practice in Italy and other countries showed that cooperation between the classes was possible and could help to improve the quality of women's lives.

The German women had placed themselves confidently on the international stage, grasping the opportunity to meet women from a range of countries, with different experiences and political ideas, in order to raise the consciousness and develop the approach of the advocates of the women's movement. As Cauer concluded, however, there was still a long way to go: "The days that signaled tremendous advances for the women's movement in Germany are now behind us. It has taken the place it merits in the cultural movement of the world. This place must now be maintained."[63]

Magdalena Gehring completed her studies on modern/contemporary history and German literature at the TU Dresden in 2009. From 2013 to 2016 she held a position as research associate at the professorship of economic and social history in Dresden. In the academic year 2014–15, she was awarded a grant by the Leibniz-Institute of European History in Mainz. She has worked on several research projects, contributed at international conferences, and published several articles. In August 2018 she defended her dissertation and is currently working on its publication.

Notes

1. On the German women's movement, see Angelika Schaser, *Frauenbewegung in Deutschland, 1848–1933* (Darmstadt: WBG, 2006); Ute Gerhard, "The Women's Movement in Germany in an International Context," in *Women's Emancipation Movements in the Nineteenth Century: A European Perspective*, ed. Sylvia Paletschek and Bianka Pietrow-Ennker (Stanford, CA: Stanford University Press, 2004), 102–22; Ute Gerhard, *Frauenbewegung und Feminismus: Eine Geschichte seit 1789*, 2nd ed. (Munich: C. H. Beck, 2012); Ute Gerhard, *Unerhört: Die Geschichte der deutschen Frauenbewegung* (Hamburg: Rowohlt, 1990). On the Italian women's movement, see Franca Pieroni Bortolotti, *Alle origini del movimento femminile in Italia 1848–1892* (Turin: Einaudi, 1963); Annarita Buttafuoco, *Cronache femminili: Temi e momenti della stampa emancipazionista in Italia dall'Unità al fascismo* (Siena: Università degli studi di Siena, 1988); Perry Willson, *Women in Twentieth-Century Italy* (Basingstoke: Palgrave Macmillan, 2010); Elisabeth Dickmann, *Die italienische Frauenbewegung im 19. Jahrhundert* (Frankfurt am Main: Domus Editoria Europaea, 2002).
2. Gabriele Boukrif, *"Der Schritt über den Rubikon": Eine vergleichende Untersuchung zur deutschen und italienischen Frauenstimmrechtsbewegung (1861–1919)* (Münster: LIT, 2006); Gabriele Boukrif, "Anna Maria Mozzoni und Hedwig Dohm: Zwei Vorreiterinnen für das Frauenstimmrecht," in *Geschlechtergeschichte des Politischen: Entwürfe von Geschlecht und Gemeinschaft im 19. und 20. Jahrhundert*, ed. Gabriela Boukrif et al. (Münster: LIT, 2002), 19–49.
3. Karen Offen, *European Feminisms, 1700–1950: A Political History* (Stanford, CA: Stanford University Press, 2000).

4. Sylvia Paletschek and Bianka Pietrow-Ennker, *Women's Emancipation Movements in the Nineteenth Century: A European Perspective* (Stanford, CA: Stanford University Press, 2004).
5. Donna Gabaccia, "In the Shadow of the Periphery: Italian Women in the Nineteenth Century," in *Connecting Spheres: European Women in a Globalizing World, 1500 to the Present*, 2nd ed., ed. Marilyn J. Boxer and Jean H. Quataert (New York: Oxford University Press, 2000), 194–203; Elisabeth Dickmann, "Über die Grenzen: Die Italienerinnen in der frühen internationalen Frauenbewegung," in *Politische Netzwerkerinnen: Internationale Zusammenarbeit von Frauen 1830–1960*, ed. Eva Schöck-Quinteros et al. (Berlin: trafo, 2007), 207–28.
6. Rosalie Schoenflies, *Der internationale Kongress für Frauenwerke und Frauenbestrebungen in Berlin, 19. bis 26. September 1896: Eine Sammlung der auf dem Kongress gehaltenen Vorträge und Ansprachen* (Berlin: Hermann Walther, 1897).
7. The radical feminist journal *Die Frauenbewegung* was published in Berlin from 1895 to 1919. On the congress, see Minna Cauer, "Der Internationale Kongreß für Frauenwerke und Frauenbestrebungen in Berlin 19. bis 26. September," *Die Frauenbewegung* 18 (1896): 165–67; Minna Cauer, "Der Internationale Frauenkongreß in Berlin, September 1896," *Die Frauenbewegung* 19 (1896): 177–81. Articles in *Die Gleichheit* included the unattributed "Kleine Nachrichten: Der internationale Kongreß bürgerlicher Frauenrechlerinnen," *Die Gleichheit* 18 (1896): 143–44; "Der internationale Kongreß für Frauenwerke und Frauenbestrebungen," *Die Gleichheit* 21 (1896): 166–68.
8. Boukrif, *"Der Schritt über den Rubikon,"* 9. For an overview of the two national histories, see Volker Ullrich, *Die nervöse Grossmacht 1871–1918: Aufstieg und Untergang des deutschen Kaiserreichs* (Frankfurt am Main: Fischer, 2013); Denis Mack Smith, *Modern Italy: A Political History*, 2nd ed. (New Haven, CT: Yale University Press, 1997).
9. On this argument, see also the article by Amerigo Caruso in this volume.
10. Volker Ullrich, *Deutsches Kaiserreich* (Frankfurt am Main: Fischer, 2006), 7–10; Gerd Fesser, *Das Deutsche Kaiserreich, 1871–1914* (Cologne: PapyRossa, 2015), 47–50.
11. Willson, *Women in Twentieth-Century Italy*, 4–5.
12. Ibid.; Carsten Weber, *Das italiano-Projekt: Morphologie des Italienischen mit JSLIM* (Erlangen: CLUE, 2010), 13–14.
13. Ever since the revolution of 1848, the chairwoman of the ADF, Louise Otto-Peters, had believed in the unification of the German nation as well as the unity of German women. This aspiration is clearly expressed in the sentence, "Das ganze Deutschland soll es sein!" (Germany should be complete!); see Louise Otto-Peters, *Das erste Vierteljahrhundert des Allgemeinen deutschen Frauenvereins gegründet am 18. Oktober 1865 in Leipzig* (Leipzig: Moritz Schäfer, 1890), 4. See also Susanne Schötz, "Die Gründerinnen und Gründer des Allgemeinen Deutschen Frauenvereins: Neuere Forschungsergebnisse," in *Frauenaufbruch in die Moderne: Zum 140. Jahrestag der Gründung des ADF*, ed. Genka Lapön (Leipzig: Referat für Gleichstellung von Frau und Mann, 2000), 6–16.
14. Schaser, *Frauenbewegung in Deutschland*, 51.
15. Ibid., 42–44.
16. Gisela Bock, "Begriffsgeschichten: 'Frauenemanzipation' im Kontext der Emanzipationsbewegungen des 19. Jahrhunderts," in *Geschlechtergeschichten der Neu-*

zeit: Ideen, Politik, Praxis, ed. Gisela Bock (Göttingen: Vandenhoeck & Ruprecht, 2014), 149.
17. Willson, Women in Twentieth-Century Italy, 24–27.
18. Ibid., 27, 34.
19. Offen, European Feminisms, 151.
20. Ibid., 175; International Council of Women and National Woman Suffrage Association (U.S.), Report of the International Council of Women, Assembled by the National Woman Suffrage Association, Washington, D.C., U. S. of America, March 25 to April 1, 1888 (Washington, DC: Rufus H. Darby, 1888), 208–14.
21. Gerhard, Unerhört, 93–94.
22. Two specific examples are the congress in Paris in 1878, hosted alongside the International Exposition, and the second meeting of the ICW in Chicago in 1894, which was part of the World's Columbian Exposition.
23. Sophie Pataky, Lexikon deutscher Frauen der Feder: Vollständiger Neusatz beider Bände in einem Buch (Berlin: Hofenberg, 2014), 287–88; Gerhard, Unerhört, 245.
24. Schoenflies, Der internationale Kongress, 5. Translated by Magdalena Gehring.
25. Ibid., preface.
26. Cauer, "Der Internationale Frauenkongreß," 177.
27. Gerhard, Frauenbewegung und Feminismus, 42–43. In 1902, the BDF adopted a resolution to put the demand for women's suffrage on its formal program. Schaser, Frauenbewegung in Deutschland, 51.
28. Anne-Laure Briatte provides a detailed definition of the term "women's emancipation" in her chapter in this volume.
29. See Alice Salomon, Lebenserinnerungen: Jugendjahre, Sozialreform, Frauenbewegung, Exil, ed. Alice Salomon Hochschule (Berlin: Brandes & Apsel, 2008), 58.
30. See Gertrud Bäumer, "Die Geschichte der Frauenbewegung in Deutschland," in Handbuch der Frauenbewegung: Die Geschichte der Frauenbewegung in den Kulturländern, ed. Helene Lange and Gertrud Bäumer (Berlin: W. Moeser, 1901), 1:153.
31. Cauer, "Der Internationale Kongreß," 165.
32. Cauer, "Der Internationale Frauenkongreß," 179–80; front page of the Berliner Illustrirte Zeitung, 20 September 1896. See also the chapter by Anne-Laure Briatte in this volume.
33. Offen, European Feminisms, 205, 184.
34. Schoenflies, Der internationale Kongress, 350.
35. Gerhard, Frauenbewegung und Feminismus, 67.
36. Ruth Nattermann, "Vom Pazifismus zum Interventionismus: Die italienische Frauenrechtlerin Paolina Schiff (1841–1926)," in Frauen und Frieden? Zuschreibungen—Kämpfe—Verhinderungen, ed. Franziska Dunkel and Corinna Schneider (Berlin: Barbara Budrich, 2015), 73–85.
37. Schoenflies, Der internationale Kongress, 45.
38. Ibid., 47–48.
39. Ibid.
40. Ibid., 202–12. See Ingeborg Waldschmidt, Maria Montessori: Leben und Werk, 2nd ed. (Munich: C. H. Beck, 2006), 17.
41. Schoenflies, Der internationale Kongress, 47. Montessori also mentioned the property rights of women in Italy.

42. Ibid., 145–47. After the promulgation of the racial laws in November 1938, Castelbolognesi returned to Italy and taught German and French in the Jewish local school in Modena.
43. Bruce Vandervort, *Wars of Imperial Conquest in Africa, 1830–1914* (London: UCL Press, 1998), 156–66; John Foot, *Modern Italy* (New York: Palgrave Macmillan, 2003), 23.
44. Schoenflies, *Der internationale Kongress*, 5–7.
45. Ibid., 7.
46. Gerhard, *Unerhört*, 176–77; Elke Schüller, *Marie Stritt: Eine "kampffrohe Streiterin" in der Frauenbewegung (1855–1928)* (Königstein im Taunus: Ulrike Helmer, 2005).
47. Schoenflies, *Der internationale Kongress*, 8.
48. Ibid., 13.
49. Ibid., 15.
50. Marion Kaplan, *Jüdisches Bürgertum: Frau, Familie und Identität im Kaiserreich* (Hamburg: Dölling und Galitz, 1997), 271.
51. "Der internationale Kongreß für Frauenwerke und Frauenbestrebungen," 166.
52. Schoenflies, *Der internationale Kongress*, 191–212.
53. Cauer, "Der Internationale Frauenkongreß," 180.
54. Gerhard, *Unerhört*, 197–99; Elisabeth Fetscher, "Einleitung," in *Memoiren einer Sozialistin*, ed. Elisabeth Fetscher (Munich: Piper, 1985), 7–23.
55. Fetscher, *Memoiren einer Sozialistin*, 273–77.
56. Schoenflies, *Der internationale Kongress*, 202.
57. Ibid., 393–94.
58. "Der internationale Kongreß für Frauenwerke und Frauenbestrebungen," 166–68; Christina Klausmann, *Politik und Kultur der Frauenbewegung im Kaiserreich: Das Beispiel Frankfurt am Main* (Frankfurt am Main: Campus Verlag, 1997), 138; Gerhard, *Unerhört*, 197. In her report, Minna Cauer describes a discussion with Clara Zetkin in which the two women had tried to clarify the situation. Cauer, "Der Internationale Frauenkongreß," 180.
59. Schoenflies, *Der internationale Kongress*, 396–99. See also Tiina Kinnunen, "History as Argument—Alexandra Gripenberg, Ellen Key and the Notion of True Feminism," in *Gendering Historiography: Beyond National Canons*, ed. Angelika Epple and Angelika Schaser (New York: Campus Verlag, 2009), 181–207.
60. Ibid., 203, 396–99.
61. Ibid., 13.
62. Ibid., 351.
63. Cauer, "Der Internationale Frauenkongreß," 181.

Bibliography

Bäumer, Gertrud. "Die Geschichte der Frauenbewegung in Deutschland." In *Handbuch der Frauenbewegung: Die Geschichte der Frauenbewegung in den Kulturländern*, edited by Helene Lange and Gertrud Bäumer, 1:125–57. Berlin: W. Moeser, 1901.

Bock, Gisela. "Begriffsgeschichten: 'Frauenemanzipation' im Kontext der Emanzipationsbewegungen des 19. Jahrhunderts." In *Geschlechtergeschichten der Neuzeit:*

Ideen, Politik, Praxis, edited by Gisela Bock, 100–167. Göttingen: Vandenhoeck & Ruprecht, 2014.

Boukrif, Gabriele. "Anna Maria Mozzoni und Hedwig Dohm. Zwei Vorreiterinnen für das Frauenstimmrecht." In *Geschlechtergeschichte des Politischen: Entwürfe von Geschlecht und Gemeinschaft im 19. und 20. Jahrhundert*, edited by Gabriela Boukrif, Claudia Bruns, Kirsten Heinsohn, Claudia Lenz, Katrin Schmersahl, and Katja Weller, 19–49. Münster: LIT, 2002.

———. *"Der Schritt über den Rubikon": Eine vergleichende Untersuchung zur deutschen und italienischen Frauenstimmrechtsbewegung (1861-1919)*. Münster: LIT, 2006.

Buttafuoco, Annarita. *Cronache femminili: Temi e momenti della stampa emancipazionista in Italia dall'Unità al fascismo*. Siena: Università degli studi di Siena, 1988.

Cauer, Minna. "Der Internationale Kongreß für Frauenwerke und Frauenbestrebungen in Berlin 19. bis 26. September." *Die Frauenbewegung* 18 (1896): 165–67.

———. "Der Internationale Frauenkongreß in Berlin, September 1896." *Die Frauenbewegung* 19 (1896): 177–81.

Dickmann, Elisabeth. *Die italienische Frauenbewegung im 19. Jahrhundert*. Frankfurt am Main: Domus Editoria Europaea, 2002.

———. "Über die Grenzen: Die Italienerinnen in der frühen internationalen Frauenbewegung." In *Politische Netzwerkerinnen: Internationale Zusammenarbeit von Frauen 1830-1960*, edited by Eva Schöck-Quinteros, Anja Schüler, Annika Wilmers, and Kerstin Wolff, 207–28. Berlin: trafo, 2007.

Fesser, Gerd. *Das Deutsche Kaiserreich, 1871–1914*. Cologne: PapyRossa, 2015.

Fetscher, Elisabeth. "Einleitung." In *Memoiren einer Sozialistin*, edited by Elisabeth Fetscher, 7–23. Munich: Piper, 1985.

Foot, John. *Modern Italy*. New York: Palgrave Macmillan, 2003.

Gabaccia, Donna. "In the Shadow of the Periphery: Italian Women in the Nineteenth Century." In *Connecting Spheres: European Women in a Globalizing World, 1500 to the Present*, 2nd ed., edited by Marilyn J. Boxer and Jean H. Quataert, 194–203. New York: Oxford University Press, 2000.

Gerhard, Ute. *Unerhört. Die Geschichte der deutschen Frauenbewegung*. Hamburg: Rowohlt, 1990.

———. "The Women's Movement in Germany in an International Context." In *Women's Emancipation Movements in the Nineteenth Century: A European Perspective*, edited by Sylvia Paletschek and Bianka Pietrow-Ennker, 102–22. Stanford, CA: Stanford University Press, 2004.

———. *Frauenbewegung und Feminismus: Eine Geschichte seit 1789*. 2nd ed. Munich: C. H. Beck, 2012.

International Council of Women and National Woman Suffrage Association (U.S.). *Report of the International Council of Women, Assembled by the National Woman Suffrage Association, Washington, D.C., U. S. of America, March 25 to April 1, 1888*. Washington, DC: Rufus H. Darby, 1888.

Kaplan, Marion. *Jüdisches Bürgertum: Frau, Familie und Identität im Kaiserreich*. Hamburg: Dölling und Galitz, 1997.

Kinnunen, Tiina. "History as Argument—Alexandra Gripenberg, Ellen Key and the Notion of True Feminism." In *Gendering Historiography: Beyond National Canons*, edited by Angelika Epple and Angelika Schaser, 181–207. New York: Campus Verlag, 2009.

Klausmann, Christina. *Politik und Kultur der Frauenbewegung im Kaiserreich: Das Beispiel Frankfurt am Main*. Frankfurt am Main: Campus Verlag, 1997.

Mack Smith, Denis. *Modern Italy: A Political History*. 2nd ed. New Haven, CT: Yale University Press, 1997.
Nattermann, Ruth. "Vom Pazifismus zum Interventionismus: Die italienische Frauenrechtlerin Paolina Schiff (1841–1926)." In *Frauen und Frieden? Zuschreibungen—Kämpfe—Verhinderungen*, edited by Franziska Dunkel and Corinna Schneider, 73–85. Berlin: Barbara Budrich, 2015.
Offen, Karen. *European Feminisms, 1700–1950: A Political History*. Stanford, CA: Stanford University Press, 2000.
Otto-Peters, Louise. *Das erste Vierteljahrhundert des Allgemeinen deutschen Frauenvereins gegründet am 18. Oktober 1865 in Leipzig*. Leipzig: Moritz Schäfer, 1890.
Paletschek, Sylvia, and Bianka Pietrow-Ennker. *Women's Emancipation Movements in the Nineteenth Century: A European Perspective*. Stanford, CA: Stanford University Press, 2004.
Pataky, Sophie. *Lexikon deutscher Frauen der Feder: Vollständiger Neusatz beider Bände in einem Buch*. Berlin: Hofenberg, 2014.
Pieroni Bortolotti, Franca. *Alle origini del movimento femminile in Italia 1848–1892*. Turin: Einaudi, 1963.
Salomon, Alice. *Lebenserinnerungen. Jugendjahre, Sozialreform, Frauenbewegung, Exil*, edited by Alice Salomon Hochschule. Berlin: Brandes & Apsel, 2008.
Schaser, Angelika. *Frauenbewegung in Deutschland, 1848–1933*. Darmstadt: WBG, 2006.
Schoenflies, Rosalie. *Der internationale Kongress für Frauenwerke und Frauenbestrebungen in Berlin,19. bis 26. September 1896: Eine Sammlung der auf dem Kongress gehaltenen Vorträge und Ansprachen*. Berlin: Hermann Walther, 1897.
Schötz, Susanne. "Die Gründerinnen und Gründer des Allgemeinen Deutschen Frauenvereins: Neuere Forschungsergebnisse." In *Frauenaufbruch in die Moderne: Zum 140. Jahrestag der Gründung des ADF*, edited by Genka Lapön, 6–16. Leipzig: Referat für Gleichstellung von Frau und Mann, 2000.
Schüller, Elke. *Marie Stritt: Eine "kampffrohe Streiterin" in der Frauenbewegung (1855–1928)*. Königstein im Taunus: Ulrike Helmer, 2005.
Ullrich, Volker. *Deutsches Kaiserreich*. Frankfurt am Main: Fischer, 2006.
———. *Die nervöse Grossmacht 1871–1918: Aufstieg und Untergang des deutschen Kaiserreichs*. Frankfurt am Main: Fischer, 2013.
Vandervort, Bruce. *Wars of Imperial Conquest in Africa, 1830–1914*. London: UCL Press, 1998.
Waldschmidt, Ingeborg. *Maria Montessori: Leben und Werk*. 2nd ed. Munich: C. H. Beck, 2006.
Weber, Carsten. *Das italiano-Projekt: Morphologie des Italienischen mit JSLIM*. Erlangen: CLUE, 2010.
Willson, Perry. *Women in Twentieth-Century Italy*. Basingstoke: Palgrave Macmillan, 2010.

Section 5
PATRIOTISM AND GENDER

CHAPTER 12

Historian between Two Fatherlands
Robert Davidsohn and World War I

Martin Baumeister

Robert Davidsohn is not a prominent representative of nineteenth- and early twentieth-century German historiography. He is remembered mainly by experts in the fields of the history of historiography and medieval and Renaissance Italy due to his impressive research on Florence in the Middle Ages, published in two major multivolume works: *Forschungen zur Geschichte von Florenz*, a collection of archival sources published between 1896 and 1908, and his more than four-thousand-page study *Geschichte von Florenz*, published between 1896 and 1927.[1] In one of the few recent studies in which Davidsohn's name appears, Ulrich Wyrwa considers him a paradigmatic Jewish historian who refused any narrow nationalist stance, an example of a European intellectual, and one who is at home in various worlds. According to this view, Davidsohn's work as a scholar was embedded in European networks, and he thereby contributed to the transfer of historical dialogue in Europe as one of the Jewish historians who "can be considered pioneers of a European 'histoire croisée.'"[2]

This chapter sets out from this interpretation of Davidsohn as a forerunner of a transnational, particularly European, utopia in the era of nationalism, which was realized, at least partially, only after World War II. First, it traces briefly Davidsohn's rather unusual career as a historian, and then it focuses on his activities and experiences during World War I. Davidsohn, indeed, was apparently a successful *Grenzgänger*, crossing social, professional, geographical, and national boundaries and gaining high social respectability and international academic recognition before 1914, even though he was a former outsider due to his Jewish origins, his left-wing inclinations, and the lack of a formal academic position. The chapter will analyze World War I as a testing ground for such border crossing under the conditions of mobilization and war nationalism in order to understand to what extent bourgeois Jews could consider themselves integrated into European societies after the outbreak of military hostilities. In such a perspective, the war in particular is revealed as a challenge to Davidsohn's ideals of national belonging, to his self-concept as a scholar and a historian, and to his unspoken ideas of bourgeois male identity. The chapter is based on hitherto unknown, unpublished sources: Davidsohn's autobiographical writings, his war diaries and his memoir, his private correspondence, and also his practically unknown wartime publications.[3]

Crossing Borders

In 1886, when Robert Davidsohn began to study history at the University of Heidelberg at the age of thirty-three, a whole professional life already lay behind him.[4] At the age of twenty, after early work experiences as a commercial clerk, he began a career as a journalist at the *Berliner Börsen-Courier*, a left-liberal daily newspaper founded some years earlier by his brother George, eighteen years his senior. Robert quickly rose to the position of editor and later even that of the daily's owner, all while contributing significantly to transforming it into one of the newspapers with the widest circulations in the capital of the young German nation-state. During these highly intensive years, Davidsohn wrote about financial and economic matters as a journalist, as well as literature, theater, and other cultural topics, and moved within a wide network of personalities from the political, economic, social, and cultural elites of the Kaiserreich.

Davidsohn had grown up in a Jewish middle-class family in the port city of Danzig in the province of West Prussia, the youngest of eight brothers and sisters, menaced by social descent as a result of his father's severe illness, who had to rely on the economic support of his sons. It was through the support of his two oldest brothers, George and Paul, that Robert was able to earn the basic high school diploma of *Einjährig-Freiwilliger* at the Königliche Realschule in Berlin in 1867, although Davidsohn himself considered it only as a sign of *Halbbildung* (superficial education). He complained later that his education was stopped abruptly, that he had to go without the *Abitur*, the coveted graduation from the *Gymnasium*: "I was destined to become a merchant, although I didn't have any interest in the profession."[5] Thanks to his brother George, however, who gave him the opportunity to work as a journalist and introduced him into the social life of the vibrant capital city that was about to transform into a modern European metropolis, Robert Davidsohn escaped what seemed to be the family destiny. At the same time, he shared his family's main aspiration to combine economic success and independence with the search for cultural refinement and distinction after leaving behind the narrow world of their provincial hometown. George, who had begun his professional life in the commercial and banking sector, became a renowned theater and music critic, maintaining friendships with prominent musicians and composers, and, as the first president of the Berlin Richard Wagner-Verein, fervently promoted Wagner's music. Paul, the second of the Davidsohn brothers, had immigrated as a young man to the United Kingdom and then to Vienna, making a fortune as a businessman. At the same time, he was a passionate art connoisseur, building up a huge collection of antique etchings. The third brother, Arnold, after moving to the United States, became a successful lawyer in New York, while his daughter made a name for herself as a painter. Two of Robert's sisters became teachers. One of them, Clara Beate, who married a Berlin publisher, pioneered in the fields of child welfare and feminism.

The Davidsohn siblings' grandfather had still been deeply rooted in the traditional pre-emancipatory Jewish community, while their father had embraced German patriotism and identified with the ideals of a democratic liberalism that included the full emancipation of the Jewish minority. Robert had assumed his father's conviction of a secular national civil identity, which he saw best represented in *Freisinn* left-wing liberalism.[6] His distance from traditional Judaism, however, did not mean formally leaving the Jewish community. Neither in his memoirs nor in his wartime diary did Davidsohn comment on his relationship to Judaism and the Jewish community. There is a single personal document that demonstrates that in Florence, where he lived for almost forty years, he was registered as a member of the local Jewish community and regularly paid his fee.[7] In his autobiographical writings, Davidsohn remains silent as far as his attitudes regarding Judaism as well as antisemitism are concerned. The same goes for his relationship with the person closest to him, his wife Philippine Collot, whom he married in 1881 and with whom he shared the remaining fifty-six years of his life. Davidsohn clearly did not want to give an account of what he considered his sphere of intimacy in his personal writings. He did not hide his Jewish origins, and he engaged in the battle against antisemitism as a journalist, most prominently in the notorious Berlin "Antisemitismusstreit" of 1879–81, where the Davidsohn brothers' *Berliner Börsen-Courier*, according to an antisemitic pamphlet "together with the *Berliner Tageblatt*, the most Jewish newspaper in Germany," was one of the sharpest critics of Heinrich Treitschke and his followers[8]—a battle that earned Robert Davidsohn the cynical recognition by the antisemitic *Deutsches Tageblatt* as a person who "fears neither God nor men."[9]

Through his marriage with Philippine, an actress from a Catholic family of itinerant theater players, he distanced himself from his own social world in a certain way, choosing a wife from a milieu of problematic respectability, according to bourgeois standards, with whom he did not even share his Jewish origins. Only three years after his marriage, in 1884, he decided to begin a completely new life after a severe illness, which probably resulted from burnout. Indeed, he had spent more than ten years of frantic activity in the highly competitive Berlin newspaper industry and faced hard struggles as a critical journalist, including the continuous menace of censorship, searches of the newspaper offices, judicial charges, heavy fines, and even jail—Robert and George made the acquaintance of all of these. By retiring from the *Börsen-Courier*, which was transformed into a corporation, Davidsohn, still relatively young, made a fortune that guaranteed him and his wife economic independence and a bourgeois way of life. The Davidsohns did not retire, however, to the life of leisure of a couple of private means; instead, Davidsohn chose the way of hard work, becoming an independent scholar—a decision by which he meant to overcome a deep spiritual crisis. "I have spent much, most of my life in newspaper offices, and I know how abominably one believes oneself to stand a clear height above existence there, and how one looks down on all existence from this physically and intellectually misty atmosphere."[10]

As he was used to doing in his former career as a journalist, Davidsohn now concentrated all his energies on his new goal of becoming a scholar. After only one and half years of studying history at the University of Heidelberg, he earned his PhD with a doctoral thesis in medieval French history. The model for his new life was the late Ferdinand Gregorovius, known for his monumental history of Rome in the Middle Ages, with whom Davidsohn shared his national and liberal convictions, including his sympathies for the democratic ideals of the revolution of 1848–49 (in which Gregorovius had participated as a young man), the idea of historiography as a literary praxis, and the position of a *Privatgelehrter* (independent scholar), an academic outsider.[11] It was Gregorovius who recommended Davidsohn study the history of Florence. The city at the Arno, in his view, did not have the "world horizon of the Eternal City, but the horizon of the Renaissance."[12]

In contrast to Gregorovius, who always had to struggle hard to earn his livelihood as an independent scholar through his own publications, particularly his travel features, Davidsohn had laid a sound economic foundation for his new life and could even afford an affluent bourgeois lifestyle. For him and his wife, this meant practicing an intensive sociability with the local and foreign aristocratic and bourgeois elites, fascinated by the historic and artistic treasures of the Tuscan city and its growing fame as a cultural center of Italy, and attending sophisticated salons and international circles that gathered there.[13] In 1889, Davidsohn and his wife definitively took up residence in Florence, which on his first journey to Tuscany had appeared to him, according to a common romanticized stereotype, an "earthly paradise."[14] The new center of his life seemed the opposite of Berlin, an alternative to the emblematic site of a pernicious industrial modernity, characterized by, among other things, the superficiality of commerce, finance, and mass media—which in the antisemitic imagination were closely linked with Jews and Judaism.

It was not only the cultural and aesthetic values, however, that attracted the newborn historian. Following the example of Gregorovius's Rome, he chose Florence in the Middle Ages as his major lifelong historiographical project. Similar to how Gregorovius viewed the Eternal City, Davidsohn considered Florence, "in its development and significance for world culture—except perhaps for the unique case of Athens—the richest urban community,"[15] as a historical paradigm, the place of origin of a specifically civic culture where the ascending urban *Bürgertum* with its republican traditions had laid the foundations of Western modernity: "The history of Florence is mainly the history of its people and of the struggle against all kinds of domination which threatened to hamper its development; although confined to a narrow space, it merits general attention, because the whole splendor of our culture's dawn relies upon it."[16]

At the beginning of his studies in the Florentine archives and libraries, Davidsohn was seen as an intruder by local erudite circles and by the academic establishment. However, after many years of research and the publication in 1896 of the first volumes of the *Forschungen* and the *Geschichte* of medieval Florence, his reputation began to increase continually. This manifested itself as he began to be elected to Italian historical and cultural associations and the most prestigious academies of science in Italy and abroad.[17] Some twenty years after his move to Florence, Davidsohn reached the height of professional recognition among his academic peers as well as among political authorities in Italy and Germany, receiving a whole series of eminent honors and awards.[18] According to his friend Aby Warburg, whom he had met for the first time in an archive in Florence in 1894[19] and who shared with him his Jewish origins, his passion for Florence and Italy, and the position of a *Privatgelehrter*, Davidsohn was the only German scholar in the Tuscan city who enjoyed an undisputed reputation "earned by superb, selfless endeavor."[20] Among the German scholars living and working in Italy, Davidsohn was one of the very few who succeeded in integrating into his host country, building close relationships and friendships with Italians and members of the city's international community. This was the opinion still expressed by the Florentine newspaper *Nazione* in the obituary dedicated to Davidsohn in 1937, in the thick of the Fascist regime: "Roberto Davidsohn was one of the strangers who have most loved Italy . . . loved her, while making their lives ours, living always among us."[21] This judgment corresponds to Davidsohn's quest to harmonize his historiographical project of unraveling the origins of republican, civic modernity epitomized by medieval Florence with his life in the circles of a cosmopolitan, educated elite, fascinated by the "genius" of the city.[22] On the eve of the World War I, at the age of sixty, Davidsohn could be proud of his achievements of some twenty-five years of living and working in his "fatherland by adoption,"[23] marked by social integration and rather spectacular professional success. The outsider, a German Jew and former journalist, had become "our illustrious fellow citizen"[24] in his chosen city and an internationally renowned, highly appreciated historian.

His career as a historian appears to completely confirm Wyrwa's assessment of Davidsohn as a pioneer of a non-nationalist European history, one at home in several various worlds and acting as a mediator between Germany and Italy, driven by a deep optimism and a liberal credo of liberty and progress. He expressed this latter point in a poem written for a New Year's Eve party at the Florentine house of his friend Aby Warburg, reciting it on the eve of the new century while looking back on the passing one:

> Ave! Nineteenth Century, / which has seen the birth of all of us—
> Much criticized, much admired / you are approaching your end . . .
> Great things did you achieve, / great things have been entrusted to you . . .
> You have compelled steam and lightning / into humanity's servitude,
> And from the depths of the earth / now we can look freely at the sun![25]

"Perhaps we were a rehearsal for the Europeans of the day after tomorrow."[26] This nostalgic reminiscence of the utopian experience of a cosmopolitan community of artists, intellectuals, and politicians in Florence before World War I, published one year after the historian's death by one of his closest friends, the writer Isolde Kurz, seems congenial to Robert Davidsohn's idea of history as evoked by Wyrwa. The evolution of a European historiography by Jewish historians, based, inter alia, on this kind of transnational sociability described by Kurz, was destroyed in the Shoah, as Wyrwa argues consistently. It was, however, already World War I that not only put an end to this experiment but revealed its fragility, its inherent ambiguities, and its deep contradictions, as the case of Robert Davidsohn shows.

Taking Sides

In summer 1914, the Davidsohns' Italian dream ended twenty-five years after they had chosen Florence as their home. On 28 July, the day of the Austrian declaration of war against Serbia, Robert Davidsohn wrote to Isolde Kurz from his Swiss summer holiday resort of Pontresina and disclosed his doubts about staying in Italy. He supposed that Italy, due to its conflicts of interest and its aversion to Austria, would not remain alongside its partners in the Triple Alliance. "I only know that we would not be able to remain in an Italy that turns against the Germanic world. . . . My psychic and intellectual existence in the country of our love, the position I have created for myself, are based on the spiritual balance between the Italian and the Germanic world." Davidsohn was already seriously afraid that part of "his life's work" could be destroyed by "unstoppable forces."[27] A few days later, on 1 August, when news of the Italian declaration of neutrality arrived in Pontresina, the moment he feared had arrived. The balance that Davidsohn had mentioned in his letter to Isolde Kurz had been broken. Italian neutrality, for Davidsohn as for the majority of the German intellectual and political elites, meant betrayal; and some months later, in his war diary, the historian described his reaction in terms of the death of a beloved person: "On that evening, I cried for a long time into the summer night, and I am not ashamed of myself. I had lost a lot in this moment!"[28] Driven by this experience of loss, the Davidsohns decided to give up their voluntary extraterritoriality and return to Germany after a quarter of century "to be in the fatherland in the hour of need,"[29] or, as Davidsohn wrote to his friend Warburg using an almost mystical metaphor to describe the union between the individual and the collective, at that moment there could be no other place for him than Germany, "where one's own heartbeat shares the rhythm of the heartbeat of the millions."[30] While Davidsohn never commented on his own feelings and intimacy in his personal writings, the war opened up a new situation in which matters of politics, of national community, belonging, and identity became central topics to be dealt with—without "shame," as the otherwise sober historian emphasized—in a highly emotional way, analogous to interpersonal human behavior and directly related to issues of gender.

After returning to Germany, to a forced "exile" in their own fatherland, Davidsohn and his wife took up residence in Munich and tried to reconstruct their social network with members of the educated, political, and economic elites in the Bavarian capital, now in a completely German ambience. Robert Davidsohn suffered a serious interruption to his activities as a historian, but he was able to return to his former activity as a journalist. Aged sixty-one, like many other bourgeois men too old for active service in the army, he felt useless and marginalized, perhaps particularly anxious because of his Jewish origins in the face of common antisemitic prejudices against "unmanly" Jews. He had to struggle hard to find a way to participate in the German war effort, being convinced that just like the younger ones, older men should also be at the disposal of the fatherland for whatever purposes they might be usable for.[31] "One only does one's duty," he assured Aby Warburg, who for his part was driven by the same concerns, but remarked with a certain irony: "So everybody does what he can—and is not able to do."[32] There was, however, still another dimension to Davidsohn's war effort. Since the beginning of December 1914, after taking up residence in Munich, he dedicated a considerable amount of time to penning his "wartime memories," filling six notebooks with more than eleven hundred pages. He considered himself a privileged observer of the war "with insights into many affairs which were denied to other hundreds of thousands," invoking at the same time the duty of the historian "to write down his observations for posterity."[33] Davidsohn's *Erinnerungen der Kriegszeit*, a mixture of review and war diary, are a very particular document of his personal commitment to the "war of spirits,"[34] of his way of perceiving and interpreting the war, as well as of his changing moods, between high and low spirits, between hope and dejection.

In order to fulfill his self-imposed national duty, Davidsohn chose the form of *Gelehrtenpolitik* (scholarly politics), following a model common among German academic elites in the Kaiserreich by combining scientific expertise, public political commitment, and cooperation with political authorities.[35] He built on his specific proficiency as a historian intimately familiar with Italy, his experience as a journalist, and his wide network of acquaintances and friends. He engaged in his war service by intellectual means in the firm conviction that he was among those "who are called to represent the German people intellectually" and "have the right to speak in its name in decisive moments."[36]

Until the Italian declaration of war against Austria-Hungary on 23 May 1915, Davidsohn, on the one hand, concentrated his efforts on trying to influence public opinion in Italy to maintain the country's neutrality, doing so in opposition to the increasing mobilization of the *interventisti*, those advocating Italy to enter the war on the side of the Entente.[37] On the other hand, he tried to inform the German public on Italy, using historical arguments in order to explain the current political situation. Regarding his former "country of love"—like his friend Warburg[38]—he wanted to struggle against what he considered lies and falsifications by means of which the Italians' hatred was being stirred up against Germany, and at the same time he intended to improve the Germans' understanding of Italy in view of the fact that "in Germany, notwithstanding the widespread love for country and people, there has been only poor knowledge about modern Italy."[39]

From its beginnings, this rather disparate enterprise was doomed to failure. First of all, Davidsohn concentrated much more on his German public, publishing in the most important liberal newspapers, such as *Berliner Tageblatt*, *Frankfurter Zeitung*, and *Münchener Neueste Nachrichten*,[40] while Italy, supposedly his main target, stayed in the background. This was due, among other reasons, to his limited access to Italian newspapers, which in their majority soon distanced themselves from Germany, if they did not take an openly anti-German stance.[41] And finally, like his compatriots who tried to gain Italians for the German cause, Davidsohn had to enter into an argumentative vicious circle, "namely by discussing the Belgian problem."[42] This became evident in his most important attempt to present the German point of view to an Italian audience, introducing himself as "a German who feels with the heart of an Italian."[43] His main point was the defense of the German invasion of Belgium and the justification of the "sad events in Louvain" by referring to Germany's legitimate "infallible and irresistible instinct of conservation" and countering the accusation of atrocities by Germans against Belgian civilians with similar accusations against the victims themselves as the true guilty parties.[44] Davidsohn tried to explain international relations on a psychological level, arguing that a widespread Italian aversion for Germany in many cases had become open hatred. As far as the Germans were concerned, he declared that their real hatred did not go against France but rather against Russia, under the spell of Slavic anti-German hatred, and England, which, according to him, tried to safeguard its commercial hegemony through the sacrifice of an immense amount of blood. For Italian commentators, for their part, it was rather easy to turn Davidsohn's argument against Germany itself by condemning Germany's spirit of conquest that was solely guided by the right of its conquering force.[45]

In discussing practices and effects of propaganda with Aby Warburg, Davidsohn maintained the crucial importance of "plain interests" hidden behind a thin curtain of emotions.[46] His article on "Italia e Germania" reveals the dilemma contained in this point of view by highlighting the role of emotional factors in politics. Davidsohn himself did not escape from the trap of highly emotionalized war nationalism. In the abovementioned letter to his friend, while reasoning on the significance of national aspirations and interests, he congratulates Warburg on the second issue of his *Rivista illustrata*, an illustrated review edited by Warburg and aimed at influencing Italian public opinion in favor of Germany and neutrality, or, as Warburg put it ironically, "to sing a sweet lullaby to our Italian adulterer in order to prevent him at least from leaving us ill-intentionedly."[47] The *Rivista* reproduced a photograph taken in a German POW camp that had struck Davidsohn more than any other: "A zoological garden full of the wild beasts put into Germany. This document of Anglo-French culture indeed merits the widest possible dissemination."[48] Already in a letter to Isolde Kurz, shortly before the outbreak of hostilities, he had claimed the high superiority of the German world over the Slavic, which he saw as a menace to European civilization.[49] His binational career, his cosmopolitan sociability, his passion for Italy, his positive view of the liberal political culture of Italy (which in his eyes had achieved democracy), and his distance from the authoritarian anti-liberal traditions of Wilhelmine Germany did not prevent him from such openly racist declarations, though he also took a largely uncritical stance toward the official German interpretation of the war as a defensive struggle against an overwhelmingly hostile alliance that wanted to crush his country in a deadly embrace. From the very beginning of hostilities, he firmly believed in the just German cause as declared by the military and political establishment and considered the conflict a struggle for survival by the German nation surrounded by a huge enemy coalition headed by perfidious Great Britain.[50] In this way, he dissociated himself from his own left-liberal credo, criticizing the members of the *Freisinn* for whom a German victory could lead to the rule of reaction and orthodoxy. Against these "partisan anxieties," he claimed an unconditional will to save the fatherland from the threatening dangers "without wondering what political side effects could accompany this means of saving the nation."[51] He turned aggressively against the liberal press and referred critically to Theodor Wolff, the well-known chief editor of the liberal daily *Berliner Tageblatt*, who had lived in Paris as a young journalist: as Davidsohn remarked, Wolff maintained certain international attitudes "much more than I do, who have lived five times longer in a foreign country than he did. His love for Germany is not passionate enough, although there can't be any doubt that he wishes for his fatherland's victory or has even been longing for it with all his heart."[52] Pacifists for him were "well-intentioned but uncritical fanatics," their publications "extremely silly concoctions."[53] And he did not mince his words in his critique of Chancellor Bethmann Hollweg, a "dwarf" who presumed to do "titans' work,"[54] just the opposite of the heroic Hindenburg, to whom Davidsohn dedicated a poem praising the *Generalfeldmarschall* as the victor of Tannenberg and Germany's savior from the barbarian Russian menace.[55]

Davidsohn's war nationalism also became manifest in a whole range of nationalist stereotypes he used in his political deliberations, particularly with regard to Italy in the months and weeks before the country's decision to abandon neutrality. For him, the Italian national character was a strange mix of unrestrained passion and a cool and calculated manner, as he observed a few days before the Italian declaration of war.[56] At the same time, he referred to Italy's reputation of being "una nazione da carnevale."[57] Immediately before the Italian declaration of war, he complained about "the Jesuitic character" of the Italians, of many of his former friends and acquaintances, and the contradiction between what they said and what they really did: "Now many let fall their masks . . . much old hatred which had been hidden under smiling friendliness is coming to the fore."[58] He got so excited that in a letter to a close friend, he expressed the desire to give Peppino Garibaldi and his father Ricciotti a sound beating, both of them, grandson and son of Giuseppe Garibaldi, aggressive advocates of an Italian intervention, which Peppino realized by fighting alongside the

French even before Italy's entry into the war.[59] Here Davidsohn, at least in his imagination, crossed the threshold toward the physical violence he was excluded from as a "home-front warrior."

Notwithstanding these fits of nationalist anger, Davidsohn succeeded in giving some clear-sighted judgments, for example about the consequences of an Italian war intervention. In a letter to Aby Warburg in early May 1915, he compared the imminent Italian entry into the war with the wars of the Risorgimento: while these had been struggles to liberate an oppressed people, now the country was pushing toward war because of extreme nationalism in order to conquer new territories, "which even in the best case are not worth the immense stake, even if one doesn't take the betrayal into account. Even if Italy won the war, it would go toward economic ruin and terrible inner struggles as soon as inebriation and frenzy were followed by disillusionment."[60]

Davidsohn's clairvoyance and his harsh critique of "extreme nationalism," however, by no means included Germany. While in May 1915 he bitterly complained of "the vain megalomania, the nationalist desire for expansion of a people drunk on itself" as the reason for Italy to enter the war,[61] he himself, already at the beginning of hostilities, had imagined as a positive outcome of a German victory a European *Pax Germanica*, a "soft" German hegemony. The Reich would continue to control Belgium directly and impose its will on France and the rest of continental Europe, which would be organized as a highly autarkic European customs union, with the exclusion of "maritime" England and "semi-Asian" Russia, strengthening common economic and political interests on the continent and so banishing the threat of future wars and the self-destruction of Europe.[62] Alienated from his prewar liberalism, Davidsohn found "strange bedfellows," as he observed, quoting Shakespeare. In October 1917, he welcomed the foundation of the ultranationalist Fatherland Party despite the fact that he disagreed with it in the area of domestic policy.[63] Still, in the fourth year of the conflict, he saw each attempt to finish the war by means of negotiations, such as that proposed by the German parliament's peace resolution of July 1917 or Pope Benedict's peace plan of August 1917, as threatening to result in Germany's "self-emasculation." According to Davidsohn, Germany must continue to fight if it did not want to surrender unconditionally. All discussions about peace would damage the people's eagerness to continue to wage war.[64]

In his unconditional support of the German war effort, Davidsohn did not shrink from justifying the most radical forms of unrestricted warfare, be they submarine, aerial, or chemical. As he remarked in February 1916, "All knowledge and all human intelligence is currently focused on the most dreadful instruments of destruction. But there is no other way to avert damage than by increasing damage. Only by applying decisive means and striking decisive blows can the most terrible war the world has ever seen be brought to an end. . . . Struggling for her survival, Germany uses every means."[65] Before a Belgian colleague, he defended the German invasion of the neutral country and the violence and destruction caused by the German military,[66] while in one of his few critical assessments, he disagreed with the deportation of Belgian forced labor to Germany in the course of the so-called Hindenburg program: "Even in a war, utility must not be the only law; the victor's will must not be unrestrained and absolute. Such an attitude could be criticized as ideological, and at this time one cannot even voice it in public without great danger, but Germany in the future will be heavenly burdened by the responsibility for violent measures of this kind!"[67]

Davidsohn's scarce references to the situation of the Jews in the war, without any hint as to what he felt personally, came equally as a critique of the infringement of fundamental rights in the form of antisemitism. He criticized German war propaganda plans to win over the support of Italian Jews as completely inappropriate: Italian Jews, according to him, were even more patriotic than other groups; they held high offices, and there was no hatred against them because of their race or religion. They also deeply mistrusted Germany, where the antisemitic movement had its origins.[68] Concerning the notorious "Jewish census" in the Prussian army of 1916, we find only a brief aside in his diary from November, where he worries about dangers for the rule of law: as he remarks, the debates in parliament about preventive detention, censorship, and the treatment of Jews in the army had revealed a really alarming situation.[69]

The Great Illusion

Undoubtedly, these critical judgments were more than mere residues of Davidsohn's liberalism. His war experience did not prompt a definitive break with his convictions but rather reinforced some opinions and beliefs he had held already before 1914, certainly at the expense of his former left reformist ideals and his national loyalty shared between his German homeland and his Italian "fatherland by adoption." Davidsohn completely identified uncritically with the official interpretation of the war as a struggle for survival by a Germany menaced by a "world of enemies." When even his beloved Italy joined on the side of Germany's foes in 1915, he suffered, after the Italian declaration of neutrality, his second "war trauma": "Something very dear has died in our hearts. This void can never be filled again. . . . 'Torn are the bonds of love and life.'"[70] Davidsohn experienced the war situation as a highly emotionalized crisis of national belonging that appeared at the same time as a crisis of masculinity, with which he tried to come to terms in the categories and ideas of the nationalist right, stressing "unconditional will" and "strength" in the conflict that had become a *Durchhaltekrieg* (war of holding out) and judging political behavior by concepts such as "honor" and "shame."[71] In order to reaffirm his virility (being unable to enter active military service), he offered his expertise in the "war of spirits," which he understood as elitist "scholarly politics," as expressed by a friend of his serving in Hindenburg's staff: "We need men whose powerful words—as sharp as the German sword—are able to express an uncompromising will, based on a comprehensive education, and to ultimately win through."[72]

Undoubtedly, one can understand this commitment as part of a more general behavior on the part of members of the educated elite in Germany in the context of a "people's war," reacting against progressive status loss by means of a "spiritual crusade to restore the values of the *Bildungsbürgertum* to their rightfully dominant place."[73] For Davidsohn, however, the "state of emergency" was a fundamental challenge to his existential project, which could be described as what Sigmund Freud in 1915 had called "Kulturweltbürgertum," an ideal transnational, cosmopolitan community of the Western educated elite.[74] Freud described the outbreak of war as the destruction of this ideal and the great disillusionment of the "Kulturweltbürger," "his great fatherland destroyed, the common cultural possessions wasted, the fellow citizens divided and humiliated!"[75] Davidsohn reacted to this situation by exchanging his Florentine ideal world for an exclusive dedication to the German nation as a decidedly male project, with its absolute priority of external strength and power at the expense of his (former) ideas of democracy, civil rights, and progress. Aby Warburg shared his friend's preoccupations and personal war effort as an independent scholar and German patriot of Jewish origins with a passionate love for Italy. Contrary to Davidsohn, his patriotism was severely affected by his understanding of the war, in Freud's vein, as a radical break in civilization where *Bildung* had become a "crime or at least an unnatural state," while the "unleashed beast" wanted to drink more and more blood.[76] And he warned his friend against an exclusivist nationalist stance. "Don't we have to stress . . . that it is the idea of the good Western European which is our remedy, and not the German as he is[?]"[77] Warburg, who had defined himself in Italian in his diary some years before the war as an "Ebreo di sangue, Amburghese di cuore, d'anima Fiorentino" (by blood a Jew, at heart a native of Hamburg, in spirit a Florentine),[78] even in the "state of emergency" referred to the ideals of occidental rationality and civilization and pursued research into reason and superstition, logic and magic, enlightenment and counterenlightenment in culture and politics[79] as his project, likewise under conditions of war.

It is difficult to assess what sense Robert Davidsohn made of his war experience after the end of hostilities. In any case, his interpretation of the conflict and his war nationalism hardly justify his characterization as a Jewish historian acting as a pioneer of European history in the sense of an open "histoire croisée."[80] Rather, they show the fragility and contradictions of his transnational biography and professional project. After the war, Davidsohn tried to continue what he had done before summer 1914. For him, however, the outcome of the war not only meant painful military defeat but also almost catastrophic material loss due to inflation, which destroyed a major part of his fortune, and deep disillusionment. Thanks to the help of a wealthy American friend, James Loeb, he and his wife were able to return to Italy, where he finished his monumental work on medieval Florence and tried to regain his lost "earthly paradise." He saw the rise of Fascism and, at the same time, increasingly feared the menace of Nazism. His sympathies had now shifted definitively away from Germany to Italy. His ideas about strong, "masculine" national politics, however, had not vanished. In 1933, at the age of eighty, Davidsohn had to welcome the first refugees from Nazi Germany. His "fatherland by adoption" had now unexpectedly become his exile. Military invasion and the Italian victory in Abyssinia in 1935–36 were hailed by Davidsohn as the deeds of the "most influential statesman of recent times," who, according to him, had organized such a colonial war as there had never been before.[81] Davidsohn hoped that Fascist Italy under its Duce, as the strongest power in Europe, could be the remedy against Nazi Germany, "the only means to put an end to this whole brood in Germany!" as he told a German émigré.[82] Dying in 1937, he was spared the Italian racial laws and the beginning of World War II, which would bring the Italo-German alliance Davidsohn had dreamed of in 1914, but which, in this form, would have been for him the most terrible of all nightmares.

Martin Baumeister has been the director of the German Historical Institute in Rome since 2012. From 2003 until 2017, he held the chair in contemporary European history at the Ludwig-Maximilians-Universität of Munich. His current research interests are the history of contemporary Southern Europe and the Mediterranean, urban history, the history of religion, and the history of historiography. Among his recent publications is included an annotated edition of *Robert Davidsohn, Menschen, die ich kannte: Erinnerungen eines Achtzigjährigen* (Berlin: Duncker & Humblot, 2020), edited together with Wiebke Fastenrath Vinattieri in collaboration with Wolfram Knäbich.

Notes

1. Robert Davidsohn, *Forschungen zur Geschichte von Florenz*, 4 vols. (Berlin: Mittler, 1896–1908), and *Geschichte von Florenz*, 4 vols. in 7 parts (Berlin: Mittler, 1896–1927). Up to now, there is very little biographical information available on Davidsohn. For a first comprehensive biographical assessment, see Steffi Roettgen, "Dal 'Börsen-Courier' di Berlino al 'genio' di Firenze: Lo storico Robert Davidsohn e il suo inedito lascito fiorentino," in *Storia dell'arte e politica culturale intorno al 1900: La fondazione dell'Istituto Germanico di Storia dell'Arte di Firenze*, ed. Max Seidel (Venice: Marsilio, 1999), 313–38. See also *Robert Davidsohn (1853–1937): Uno spirito libero tra cronaca e storia. I. Atti della giornata di studio*, ed. Wiebke Fastenrath Vinattieri and Martina Ingendaay Rodio (Florence: Olschki, 2003).
2. Ulrich Wyrwa, "Die europäischen Seiten der jüdischen Geschichtsschreibung," in *Judentum und Historismus: Zur Entstehung der jüdischen Geschichtswissenschaft in Europa*, ed. Ulrich Wyrwa (Frankfurt am Main: Campus Verlag, 2003), 35f.
3. Robert Davidsohn, *Menschen, die ich kannte: Erinnerungen eines Achtzigjährigen*, typescript, 556 pp., completed 1937; *Erinnerungen der Kriegszeit* (1914–1919), manuscript, 6 notebooks (NB), 1160 pp. (Bayerische Staatsbibliothek Munich. Handschriftenabteilung, Sign.: Cgm 7915 1–6). Currently an annotated edition of both texts is being prepared: *Menschen, die ich kannte: Erinnerungen eines Achtzigjährigen*, ed. Martin Baumeister and Wiebke Fastenrath Vinattieri in collaboration with Wolfram Knäbich (Berlin: Duncker & Humblot, 2020) (Deutsche Geschichtsquellen des 19. und 20. Jahrhunderts, published by the Historische Kommission der Bayerischen Akademie der Wissenschaften; 76). *Erinnerungen der Kriegszeit* is published as an annotaded online edition by the German Historical Institute in Rome 2020, ed. Martin Baumeister and Wolfram Knäbich in collaboration with Wiebke Fastenrath Vinattieri. https://davidsohn-edition.dhi-roma.it/. I wish to express my gratitude to Wiebke Fastenrath Vianttieri and Wolfram Knäbich for supplying me with rich information from their bibliographical and archival research on Davidsohn.
4. For detailed information on Davidsohn's biography, see Martin Baumeister, Wiebke Fastenrath Vinattieri and Wolfram Knäbich, "Einleitung," in Davidsohn, *Menschen, die ich kannte*, 40.
5. Davidsohn, *Menschen, die ich kannte*, 40.
6. For the general context of Davidsohn's political attitudes, see Jacob Toury, *Die politischen Orientierungen der Juden in Deutschland: Von Jena bis Weimar* (Tübingen: Mohr, 1966).
7. See Robert Davidsohn to Comunità Ebraica di Firenze, 14 September 1934, letter printed in Wiebke Fastenrath Vinattieri, "Robert Davidsohn: La sua amicizia con la scrittrice Isolde Kurz e i suoi scritti del lascito della Biblioteca Comunale di Firenze," in *Robert Davidsohn (1853–1937)*, ed. Wiebke Fastenrath Vinattieri and Ingendaay Rodio, 116. It seems highly significant that we are informed about Davidsohn's affiliation in a letter of protest to the Comunità Ebraica, where he bitterly complains about receiving Zionist propaganda from the community.
8. See the articles in the annotated edition by Karsten Krieger, *Der "Berliner Antisemitismusstreit" 1879–1881: Eine Kontroverse um die Zugehörigkeit der deutschen Juden zur Nation. Eine kommentierte Quellenedition im Auftrag des Zentrums für Antisemitismusforschung*, 2 vols. (Munich: K.G. Saur, 2003), 1:21–23; 2:570–72,

618–20, 626–32, 647–55, 760–63. The antisemitic verdict against the *Berliner Börsen-Courier* from *Veri: Lexicon der Juden*. *Ph. Stauff's Semi-Kürschner*, 2nd ed. (1929; 1st ed. 1913), is quoted in Roettgen, "Dal Börsen-Courier," 333n17: "Nächst dem BT [*Berliner Tageblatt*] das jüdischste Blatt Deutschlands."

9. "... eine Person, die 'weder Gott noch Menschen fürchtet.'" *Deutsches Tageblatt*, 24 April 1882. All quotations translated into English by Martin Baumeister unless otherwise noted.

10. "Ich habe einen großen Theil, den größten meines Lebens in Redactionsstuben verbracht, und ich weiß, wie abscheulich man da auf einer lichten Höhe des Daseins zu stehen vermeint, und wie man aus dieser physisch und intellectuell dunstigen Atmosphäre auf alles Dasein herabsieht." Robert Davidsohn to Julius Rodenberg, Heidelberg, 23 June 1887, Robert Davidsohn: Nachlass Julius Rodenberg. GSA 81/II.4.13, Klassik Stiftung Weimar.

11. See Ferdinand Gregorovius, *Geschichte der Stadt Rom im Mittelalter: Vom V. bis zum XVI. Jahrhundert*, 8 vols. (Stuttgart: Cotta, 1859–1872). On Gregorovius, see Arnold Esch and Jens Petersen, eds., *Ferdinand Gregorovius und Italien: Eine kritische Würdigung* (Tübingen: Niemeyer, 1993); on the relationship between poetry and history in Gregorovius, see Norbert Miller, "Poetisch erschlossene Geschichte: Ferdinand Gregorovius' 'Wanderjahre in Italien' und seine Dichtung über den Garten von Ninfa," *Quellen und Forschungen aus italienischen Archiven und Bibliotheken* 96 (2016): 389–411.

12. Ferdinand Gregorovius to Robert Davidsohn, 11 March 1886, in Johannes Hönig, "Der Geschichtsschreiber der Stadt Rom an den Geschichtsschreiber von Florenz: Briefe von Ferdinand Gregorovius an Robert Davidsohn," *Deutsche Rundschau* 196 (1923): 152, quoted by Roettgen, "Dal 'Börsen-Courier,'" 322.

13. On Germans in Florence during the nineteenth and early twentieth centuries, see Rotraut Fischer and Christina Ujma, "Fluchtpunkt Florenz—Deutsch-Florentiner in der Zeit des Risorgimento zwischen Epigonalität und Utopie," Marburger Forum online 2014, http://tuprints.ulb.tu-darmstadt.de/4108/1/Fluchtpunkt_Florenz.pdf; Bernd Roeck, *Florenz 1900: Die Suche nach Arkadien* (Munich: C. H. Beck, 2001).

14. Robert Davidsohn, *Vom Nordcap bis Tunis: Reisebriefe von Norwegen, Italien und Nord-Afrika* (Berlin: Freund & Teckel, 1884), 59.

15. "... des in seiner Entwickelung und Bedeutung für die Weltcultur—vielleicht das einzige Athen ausgenommen—reichsten städtischen Gemeinwesens." Review of the first volume of Davidsohn's *Geschichte von Florenz* by Cornel von Fabriczy, *Repertorium für Kunstwissenschaft* 20, no. 3 (1897): 215.

16. "Die Geschichte von Florenz ist vorwiegend die seines Volksthums und des Kampfes gegen jede Art von Uebermacht, die dessen Entwickelung zu hemmen drohte; obwohl auf engen Raum beschränkt, verdient sie die allgemeine Theilnahme, weil vom Morgenrothe unserer Kultur auf ihr der volle Abglanz ruht." Davidsohn, *Geschichte von Florenz. I. Aeltere Geschichte*, IIIf.

17. In 1898, he was elected a member of the Deputazione di Storia Patria della Toscana; in 1902, he was among the first members of the exclusive Società Leonardo da Vinci (1902). He was nominated for membership in the Accademia della Crusca in Florence in 1903, the Accademia delle Scienze di Torino in 1908, and the Accademia dei Lincei in Rome in 1910. In 1909, he became a corresponding member of the Bayerische Akademie der Wissenschaften in Munich and a regular member in 1915 after he moved to Munich. As late as 1935, he

was elected, together with Benedetto Croce, a corresponding fellow of the British Academy.
18. In 1908, the Prussian Kultusministerium awarded him the title "Königlicher Professor." That same year, he received an official certificate from the City Council of Florence congratulating him for his publications. In 1912, he was awarded the silver Leibniz-Medaille of the Prussian Academy of Sciences.
19. Robert Davidsohn to Aby Warburg, 29 November 1894, Robert Davidsohn–Aby Warburg Correspondence 1894–1929, Warburg Institute Archive, University of London.
20. "... ein unbestrittenes, 'durch überlegene, selbstlose Arbeit erworbenes' Ansehen." Quoted by Roeck from a letter of Aby Warburg to Wilhelm Bode, dated 4 March 1903: *Florenz 1900*, 80.
21. "Roberto Davidsohn è stato uno degli stranieri che più abbiano amato l'Italia ... l'hanno amato facendo della nostra vita la vita loro, vivendo sempre fra noi." *La Nazione*, 21 September 1937, 4, quoted by Roettgen, "Dal 'Börsen-Courier,'" 317.
22. Davidsohn had dedicated the first volume of his *Geschichte von Florenz*, IV, to the "Genius von Florenz" (see also Roettgen, "Dal 'Börsen-Courier,'" 313).
23. "Adoptiv-Vaterlande": Robert Davidsohn to Wilhelm Walter Goetz, Munich, 14 January 1915, Nachlass Goetz, Korrespondenz, fol. 310, Bundesarchiv Koblenz.
24. "[N]ostro concittadino illustre": *La Nazione*, 24 February 1912, 3, quoted by Roettgen, "Dal Börsen-Courier," 314.
25. Have! Neunzehntes Jahrhundert, / Das uns Alle werden sah—
Viel gescholten, viel bewundert / Bist du deinem Ende nah ...
Grosses hast du selbst geschaffen, / Grosses ward dir anvertraut,
...
Du hast Dampf und Blitz gezwungen / In der Menschen Sklaverei,
Und aus Erden-Niederungen / Ward der Blick zur Sonne frei!
The poem (WAI 10.1, 31 December 1899) is quoted by Roeck, *Florenz 1900*, 11.
26. Isolde Kurz, *Die Pilgerfahrt nach dem Unerreichlichen: Lebensrückschau* (Tübingen: Wunderlich, 1938), 102, quoted by Roeck, *Florenz um 1900*, 267.
27. "Mein seelisches und intellektuelles Dasein im Lande unserer Liebe, die Stellung, die ich mir geschaffen, beruhen auf dem geistigen Gleichgewicht der italienischen und germanischen Welt.... ein Stück meiner Lebensarbeit ... wäre durch unhemmbare Gewalten vernichtet." Robert Davidsohn to Isolde Kurz, 28 July 1914, in Fastenrath Vinattieri, "Robert Davidsohn," 113.
28. "Ich habe an jenem Abend lange in die Sommernacht hinausgeweint und schäme mich Dessen nicht. Ich habe da viel verloren!" Davidsohn, *Erinnerungen*, NB 1, fol. 4 (5 December 1914).
29. Davidsohn, *Menschen, die ich kannte*, 329.
30. "... in Deutschland, wo der eigene Herzschlag den Rhyt[h]mus des Herzschlages der Millionen teilt." Robert Davidsohn to Aby Warburg, 24 September 1914, Robert Davidsohn–Aby Warburg Correspondence 1894–1929, WIA.
31. Davidsohn, *Erinnerungen*, NB 1, fol. 74 (late March 1915).
32. "Nur seine Pflicht tut man." Robert Davidsohn to Aby Warburg, 24 September 1914, Robert Davidsohn–Aby Warburg Correspondence 1894–1929, WIA; "So thut jeder was er kann und—nicht vermag," Aby Warburg to Robert Davidsohn, 15 November 1914, copybook of outgoing letters, V, 447, WIA. On Warburg's personal commitment in World War I, which in many ways resembles Davidsohn's, see Anne Spagnolo-Stiff, "L'appello di Aby Warburg a un'intesa

italo-tedesca: 'La guerra del 1914–15. Rivista illustrata,'" in *Storia dell'arte e politica culturale*, 249–69; Dorothea McEwan, "Due missioni politiche di Aby Warburg in Italia nel 1914–15," *Schifanoia* 42–43 (2012): 57–79.
33. Davidsohn, *Erinnerungen*, NB 1, fol. 2 (5 December 1914).
34. Regarding the "Krieg der Geister," see Kurt Flasch, *Die geistige Mobilmachung: Die deutschen Intellektuellen und der Erste Weltkrieg. Ein Versuch* (Berlin: Fest, 2000); for German-Jewish intellectuals see Ulrich Sieg, *Jüdische Intellektuelle im Ersten Weltkrieg: Kriegserfahrungen, weltanschauliche Debatten und kulturelle Neuentwürfe* (Berlin: Akademie Verlag, 2001).
35. Rüdiger vom Bruch, *Gelehrtenpolitik, Sozialwissenschaft und akademische Diskurse in Deutschland im 19. und 20. Jahrhundert* (Stuttgart: F. Steiner, 2006), 22.
36. ". . . diejenigen, die geistig das deutsche Volk zu vertreten berufen seien, diejenigen, denen das Recht zustehe, in entscheidenden Augenblicken in seinem Namen zu sprechen." Davidsohn, *Erinnerungen*, 17 April 1915.
37. On the struggle between *interventisti* and their opponents in Italy, see Brunello Vigezzi, *L'Italia di fronte alla prima guerra mondiale*, vol. 1: *L'Italia neutrale* (Milan: R. Ricciardi, 1966). On the struggle between "germanofili" and "neutralist" versus anti-German Italian nationalists during World War I, see Klaus Heitmann, *Das italienische Deutschlandbild in seiner Geschichte*, vol. 3: *Das kurze zwanzigste Jahrhundert (1914–1989). 1. Italien gegen Deutschland* (Heidelberg: Winter Verlag, 2012).
38. See Spagnolo-Stiff, "L'appello," and McEwan, "Due missioni," on Warburg's different projects of fighting lies, superstitions, and barbarism by collecting material for his "war archive," launching his *Rivista illustrata* in Italy, and preparing a manual, bibliography, and museum of lies.
39. ". . . daß in Deutschland bei aller sehr weit verbreiteten Liebe für Land und Volk ein geringes Verständnis für das eigentliche Wesen des modernen Italien bestanden hat." Robert Davidsohn, "Ein Wort für Italien," *Berliner Tageblatt*, 6 October 1914, morning edition, 1.
40. I identified fifteen articles concerning Italy written by Davidsohn, some of them published anonymously or written under pseudonyms, in these three newspapers between September 1914 and October 1916; however, I found only one major article published by him in an Italian newspaper: *Nazione* [Florence], September 1914.
41. On the poor, often counterproductive, results of German attempts to influence the Italian press in favor of the Reich, see Patrick Ostermann, *Duell der Diplomaten: Die Propaganda der Mittelmächte und ihrer Gegner in Italien während des Ersten Weltkrieges* (Weimar: VDG, 2000), 100–116, 122–39, 153–72; see Davidsohn's comment on *Nazione*: "Until recently the city's most important newspaper . . . [it is now] . . . struggling for survival because of its pro-German attitude and is maintained by the Germans," Robert Davidsohn to Harry Bresslau, 21 January 1915, in Anna Maria Voci, "'Anche la scienza ha perduto la sua serena imparzialità': una lettera di Robert Davidsohn a Harry Breslau (21 gennaio 1915)," *La Cultura* 38 (2000): 152; on German influence on *Nazione* see Ostermann, *Duell*, 101. Regarding Davidsohn's deep indignation about the venality of Italian journalists, see *Erinnerungen*, NB 1, fol. 33 (January 1915?).
42. "Nämlich durch Erörterung des belgischen Problems." Robert Davidsohn to Aby Warburg, 10 April 1915, Robert Davidsohn–Aby Warburg Correspondence 1894–1929, WIA.

43. "... un Tedesco che però sente con cuore d'Italiano." Robert Davidsohn, "Italia e Germania," *Nazione*, 16–17 September 1914, 1; see also Davidsohn, *Erinnerungen*, NB 1, fol. 16 (December 1914?).
44. On the German invasion of Belgium and the ensuing international propaganda battles, see John Horne and Alan Kramer, *German Atrocities, 1914: A History of Denial* (New Haven, CT: Yale University Press, 2001).
45. See Giulio Caprin, "Della Germania e dell'Italia. A Roberto Davidsohn," *Il Nuovo Giornale* [Florence], 21–22 September 1914, 2nd. ed., 1f.
46. "Die Stimmung sah ich ... stets nur als einen dünnen Vorhang an, hinter dem sich sehr nüchterne, wenn auch leidenschaftlich verfolgte Interessen bergen." Robert Davidsohn to Aby Warburg, 3 April 1915, Robert Davidsohn–Aby Warburg Correspondence 1894–1929, WIA.
47. "... singen wir jetzt unserem italienischen Ehebrecher ein sanftes Wiegenlied, um ihn wenigstens vor böswilligem Verlassen zu beschützen." Aby Warburg to Robert Davidsohn, 15 November 1914, copybook of outgoing letters, V, 447, WIA.
48. "[E]in zoologischer Garten voll der auf Deutschland losgelassenen wilden Bestien. Dieses Zeugnis englisch-französischer Kulturleistung verdient wirklich weiteste Verbreitung." Robert Davidsohn to Aby Warburg, 3 April 1915, Robert Davidsohn–Aby Warburg Correspondence 1894–1929, WIA. For the propagandistic use of pictures of colonial soldiers in Germany during World War I, see Benedikt Burkard, ed., *Gefangene Bilder: Wissenschaft und Propaganda im Ersten Weltkrieg* (exhibition catalogue, Historisches Museum Frankfurt, Petersberg: Imhof, 2014).
49. Robert Davidsohn to Isolde Kurz, 28 July 1914, in Fastenrath Vinattieri, "Robert Davidsohn," 113.
50. As a first step toward his commitment to propaganda, see Robert Davidsohn, "Offener Brief an den Lordkanzler Haldane," *Frankfurter Zeitung*, 16 August 1914, 1; Davidsohn, *Erinnerungen*, NB 1, fol. 9 (December 1914).
51. "... parteipolitischen Beklemmungen," Davidsohn, *Erinnerungen*, NB 1, fol. 36 (January 1915?); "... ohne zu fragen, welche Nebenwirkungen mit der Art der Errettung verknüpft sein möchten," fol. 37 (January 1915?).
52. "... in unvergleichlich höherem Maße, als etwa mir, der ich doch wohl fünf Mal so lange im Auslande gelebt habe. Seine Liebe für Deutschland zeigte sich nicht eben als eine stürmische, obwohl er zweifellos seinem Vaterlande von ganzem Herzen den Sieg wünschte, ja diesen herbeisehnte," Davidsohn, *Erinnerungen*, NB 1, fol. 36 (January 1915?). On Theodor Wolff, see Bernd Sösemann, *Theodor Wolff: Ein Leben mit der Zeitung* (Stuttgart: Steiner, 2012). Some examples of his radical critique of liberal newspapers include Davidsohn, *Erinnerungen*, NB 3, fol. 82 (25 April 1916: *Frankfurter Zeitung* "in ihrer ganz ehrlosen Gesinnung"); fol. 89 (6 May 1916: *Berliner Tageblatt* "[v]aterlandesverräterisch"; fol. 91 (10 May 1916: *Münchener Neueste Nachrichten* "lendenlahm").
53. "... wohlmeinende, doch kritiklose Fanatiker," Davidsohn, *Erinnerungen*, NB 2, fol. 32 (5 September 1915); "Machwerk von nicht zu überbietender Albernheit," NB 4, fol. 18 (7 July 1916).
54. Davidsohn, *Erinnerungen*, NB 5, fol. 49 (17 July 1916).
55. "An General von Hindenburg," *Frankfurter Zeitung*, 21 September 1914, quoted by Davidsohn himself in his, *Erinnerungen*, NB 1, fol. 20 (December 1914?).
56. Davidsohn, *Erinnerungen*, NB 1, fol. 85 (11 April 1915); see also his article "Vom Mittelalter zu unseren Tagen," written immediately after Italy's entry into

the war, where Davidsohn highlights a supposed disposition in Italian politics toward "Rausch und Taumel" (inebriation and frenzy), deeply rooted in the country's history: *Süddeutsche Monatshefte* 12, no. 5 (1915): 396. Only some weeks earlier, however, he had stated that "Man unterschätzt in Deutschland stets die Sachlichkeit und den Realismus der Italiener, die nur durch überzeugende Argumente des Verstandes oder durch Tatsachen zu beeinflussen sind, nicht durch nebelhafte Wortschälle" (Germans generally underestimate the practicality and the realism of the Italians, who can be influenced only by convincing reasonable arguments or facts, not by nebulous phraseology), Davidsohn, *Erinnerungen*, NB 1, fol. 71 (24 March 1915).
57. Davidsohn, *Erinnerungen*, NB 1, fol. 97 (4 May 1915).
58. "Es fällt jetzt manche Maske, die mit ganz italienischer Geduld durch Jahrzehnte getragen wurde, es bricht viel alter Haß hervor, der unter lächelnder Freundlichkeit verborgen war." Davidsohn, *Erinnerungen*, NB 2, fol. 10 (22 May 1915).
59. Davidsohn, *Erinnerungen*, NB 1, fol. 84 (11 May 1915). For the Garibaldi brothers volunteering in the French Foreign Legion, see Hubert Heyriès, *Les garibaldiens de 14: Splendeurs et misères des chemises rouges en France de la Grande Guerre à la Seconde Guerre mondiale* (Nice: Serre, 2005).
60. This is Davidsohn's summary of the letter in his *Erinnerungen*, NB 1, fol. 97 (3 May 1915): ". . . die im besten Falle den unerhörten Einsatz nicht wert sind, selbst wenn man von dem Treubruch absieht. Italien würde, selbst wenn es siegreich aus dem Kampf hervorginge, dem wirtschaftlichen Ruin und furchtbaren inneren Kämpfen entgegengehen, sobald dem Rausch und Taumel die Ernüchterung folgt!" This, however, is not in accordance with the original. Robert Davidsohn to Aby Warburg, 2 May 1915, Robert Davidsohn–Aby Warburg Correspondence 1894–1929, WIA.
61. ". . . die eitle Großmannssucht, das nationalistische Ausdehnungsbegehren eines von sich selbst trunkenen Volkes," Robert Davidsohn to Aby Warburg, 2 May 1915, Robert Davidsohn–Aby Warburg Correspondence 1894–1929, WIA.
62. Davidsohn, *Erinnerungen*, NB 1, fol. 28 (December 1914?).
63. ". . . seltsame Bettgenossen," Davidsohn, *Erinnerungen*, NB 5, fol. 60 (6 October 1917); for the Fatherland Party, see Heinz Hagenlücke, *Deutsche Vaterlandspartei: Die nationale Rechte am Ende des Kaiserreichs* (Dusseldorf: Droste, 1997).
64. "Selbstentmannung," Davidsohn, *Erinnerungen*, NB 5, fol. 59 (6 October 1917).
65. "Alles Wissen und aller Menschenwitz ist auf die furchtbarsten Instrumente der Vernichtung gerichtet. Und dennoch gibt es keinen anderen Weg, das Unheil zu enden, als indem das Unheil gesteigert wird. Nur durch Anwendung entscheidender Mittel und durch entscheidende Schläge kann der furchtbarste Krieg, den die Welt erlebt hat, seinem Ende entgegengeführt werden. . . . Um sein Dasein ringend, wendet Deutschland jedwedes Mittel an." Davidsohn, *Erinnerungen*, NB 3, fol. 38f (1 February 1916); see also *Erinnerungen*, NB 3, fol. 79 (23 April 1916) for his justification of aerial and submarine warfare, and NB 5, fol. 68f. (4 November 1917) for his justification of the use of poisonous gas.
66. Robert Davidsohn to Jacques Mesnil [i.e. Jean-Jacques Dwelshauvers], 24 April 1915, Davidsohn, *Erinnerungen*, NB 1, fol. 92 (24 April 1915).
67. "Auch im Kriege darf die Nützlichkeit nicht das einzige Gesetz, der Wille des Siegers darf nicht schrankenlos und allmächtig sein. Solche Gesinnungen mögen als ideologisch verschrieen werden und man kann sie in dieser Zeit nicht einmal öffentlich äußern, aber Deutschland wird in Zukunft schwer an der Last solcher

gewaltsamen Maßnahmen zu tragen haben!" Davidsohn, *Erinnerungen*, NB 4, fol. 79 (28 November 1916); for the deportation of Belgian forced labor, see Jens Thiel, *"Menschenbassin Belgien": Anwerbung, Deportation und Zwangsarbeit im Ersten Weltkrieg* (Essen: Klartext, 2007), 57–162.
68. Davidsohn, *Erinnerungen*, NB 1, fol. 52 (January 1915?).
69. Davidsohn, *Erinnerungen*, NB 4, fol. 70 (5 November 1916). For the "Judenzählung," see Jacob Rosenthal, *Die Ehre des jüdischen Soldaten: Die Judenzählung im Ersten Weltkrieg und ihre Folgen* (Frankfurt am Main: Campus Verlag, 2007).
70. "Etwas sehr Liebes ist uns gestorben. Die Lücke ist nicht wieder auszufüllen. . . . 'Zerrissen ist der Liebe, wie des Lebens Band!'" Davidsohn, *Erinnerungen*, NB 2, fol. 14 (24 May 1915). The last phrase is a quotation from Goethe's *Faust*, part 2.
71. "Die Deutsche und oesterreichische Diplomatie bedeck sich mit Unehre," Davidsohn, *Erinnerungen*, NB 3, fol. 22 (31 December 1915); "würdelos töricht," fol. 83 (25 April 1916: Österreich); "für alle Zeit mit Schande bedeck," fol. 93 (12 May 1916: Deutschland).
72. "Wir fordern Männer, deren beherrschende Rede,—dem deutschen Schwerte ebenbürtig scharf—einen auf umfassender Bildung gestützten unbeugsamen Willen zum Ausdruck zu bringen und endgiltig durchzusetzen vermag!" Walther Huth to Robert Davidsohn, 24 March 1915, Davidsohn, *Erinnerungen*, NB 1, fol. 74 (late March 1915).
73. Peter Jelavich, "German Culture in the Great War," in *European Culture in the Great War: The Arts, Entertainment, and Propaganda, 1914–1918*, ed. Aviel Roshwald and Richard Stites (Cambridge: Cambridge University Press, 1999), 43.
74. Sigmund Freud, "Zeitgemäßes über Krieg und Tod (1915)," in Sigmund Freud, *Studienausgabe IX: Fragen der Gesellschaft. Ursprünge der Religion* (Frankfurt am Main: S. Fischer, 2000), 35–40.
75. ". . . sein großes Vaterland zerfallen, die gemeinsamen Besitztümer verwüstet, die Mitbürger entzweit und erniedrigt!" Ibid., 40.
76. "Die entfesselte Bestie muss erst noch mehr Blut gesoffen haben; [Bildung] ist eben Frevel, mindestens ein [unnatürlicher] Zustand," Aby Warburg to Robert Davidsohn, 16 April 1915, copybook of outgoing letters, VI, 59, 58, WIA.
77. ". . . aber muß jetzt nicht mit allem Nachdruck gesagt werden . . . das [*sic*] es die Idee des guten Westeuropaers [*sic*] ist an der wir genesen wollen, nicht am Deutschen, wie er ist," Aby Warburg to Robert Davidsohn, 15 November 1914, copybook of outgoing letters, V 446, 447, WIA.
78. Diary entry from 1 June 1906, quoted in Dorothea McEwan and Alessandro Scafi, "Warburg and D'Annunzio in Defence of Truth: On Modern Literature and Alleged Jewishness," *Schifanoia* 52–53 (2017): 259–79. However, Davidsohn never referred to his Jewish origins in the sense of belonging to a particular community—be it religious, ethnic, or cultural.
79. Ibid.
80. See Wyrwa, "Die europäischen Seiten."
81. Mussolini as "einflußreichste[r] Staatsmann neuester Zeiten"; "eines Kolonialkrieges zu bewältigen, wie noch nie einer durchgeführt wurde." Davidsohn, *Menschen, die ich kannte*, addition [Beiblatt] to 542.
82. ". . . das einzige Mittel, um der ganzen Zucht in Deutschland ein Ende zu setzen!" Ernst Feder, unpublished diary, 28 August 1935, Leo Baeck Institute, New York, quoted in Klaus Voigt, *Zuflucht auf Widerruf* (Stuttgart: Klett Cotta, 1989), 1:193.

Bibliography

Burkard, Benedikt, ed. *Gefangene Bilder: Wissenschaft und Propaganda im Ersten Weltkrieg*. Exhibition catalogue. Historisches Museum Frankfurt. Petersberg: Imhof, 2014.

Caprin, Giulio. "Della Germania e dell'Italia: A Roberto Davidsohn." *Il Nuovo Giornale*, 21–22 September 1914.

Davidsohn, Robert. *Vom Nordcap bis Tunis: Reisebriefe von Norwegen, Italien und Nord-Afrika*. Berlin: Freund & Teckel, 1884.

———. Aby Warburg Correspondence, 1894–1929. Warburg Institute Archive, University of London.

———. *Forschungen zur Geschichte von Florenz*. 4 vols. Berlin: Mittler, 1896–1908.

———. *Geschichte von Florenz*. 4 vols. in 7 parts. Berlin: Mittler, 1896–1927.

———. "Offener Brief an den Lordkanzler Haldane." *Frankfurter Zeitung*, 16 August 1914.

———. "Italia e Germania." *Nazione*, 16–17 September 1914.

———. "Ein Wort für Italien." *Berliner Tageblatt*, 6 October 1914.

———. "Vom Mittelalter zu unseren Tagen." *Süddeutsche Monatshefte* 12, no. 5 (1915): 395–420.

———. *Erinnerungen der Kriegszeit* [1914–1919]. Online annotated edition. Edited by Martin Baumeister and Wolfram Knäbich in collaboration with Wiebke Fastenrath Vinattieri. Rome: German Historical Institute in Rome, 2020. https://davidsohn-edition.dhi-roma.it/.

———. *Menschen, die ich kannte: Erinnerungen eines Achtzigjährigen*, edited by Martin Baumeister and Wiebke Fastenrath Vinattieri in collaboration with Wolfram Knäbich. Berlin: Duncker & Humblot, 2020 (Deutsche Geschichtsquellen des 19. und 20. Jahrhunderts, published by the Historische Kommission bei der Bayerischen Akademie der Wissenschaften; 76).

———. Robert Davidsohn Letters. Julius Rodenberg Estate. Klassik Stiftung Weimar.

Esch, Arnold, and Jens Petersen, eds. *Ferdinand Gregorovius und Italien: Eine kritische Würdigung*. Tübingen: Niemeyer, 1993.

Fastenrath Vinattieri, Wiebke, and Martina Ingendaay Rodio, eds. *Robert Davidsohn (1853–1937): Uno spirito libero tra cronaca e storia. I. Atti della giornata di studio*. Florence: Olschki, 2003.

Fischer, Rotraut, and Christina Ujma. "Fluchtpunkt Florenz—Deutsch-Florentiner in der Zeit des Risorgimento zwischen Epigonalität und Utopie." In *Marburger Forum Online* 2014. http://tuprints.ulb.tu-darmstadt.de/4108/1/Fluchtpunkt Florenz.pdf.

Flasch, Kurt. *Die geistige Mobilmachung: Die deutschen Intellektuellen und der Erste Weltkrieg. Ein Versuch*. Berlin: Fest, 2000.

Freud, Sigmund. *Fragen der Gesellschaft: Ursprünge der Religion. Studienausgabe IX*. Frankfurt am Main: S. Fischer, 2000.

Goetz, Wilhelm Walter. *Correspondence*. Goetz Estate. Bundesarchiv Koblenz.

Gregorovius, Ferdinand. *Geschichte der Stadt Rom im Mittelalter: Vom V. bis zum XVI. Jahrhundert*. 8 vols. Stuttgart: Cotta, 1859–1872.

Hagenlücke, Heinz. *Deutsche Vaterlandspartei: Die nationale Rechte am Ende des Kaiserreichs*. Dusseldorf: Droste, 1997.

Heitmann, Klaus. *Das italienische Deutschlandbild in seiner Geschichte*. Vol. 3: *Das kurze zwanzigste Jahrhundert (1914–1989). 1. Italien gegen Deutschland*. Heidelberg: Winter Verlag, 2012.

Heyriès, Hubert. *Les garibaldiens de 14: Splendeurs et misères des chemises rouges en France de la Grande Guerre à la Seconde Guerre mondiale*. Nice: Serre, 2005.

Hönig, Johannes. "Der Geschichtsschreiber der Stadt Rom an den Geschichtsschreiber von Florenz: Briefe von Ferdinand Gregorovius an Robert Davidsohn." *Deutsche Rundschau* 196 (1923): 143–60.

Horne, John, and Alan Kramer. *German Atrocities, 1914: A History of Denial*. New Haven, CT: Yale University Press, 2001.

Jelavich, Peter. "German Culture in the Great War." In *European Culture in the Great War: The Arts, Entertainment, and Propaganda, 1914–1918*, edited by Aviel Roshwald and Richard Stites, 32–57. Cambridge: Cambridge University Press, 1999.

Krieger, Karsten. *Der "Berliner Antisemitismusstreit" 1879–1881: Eine Kontroverse um die Zugehörigkeit der deutschen Juden zur Nation. Eine kommentierte Quellenedition im Auftrag des Zentrums für Antisemitismusforschung*. Munich: K. G. Saur, 2003.

Kurz, Isolde. *Die Pilgerfahrt nach dem Unerreichlichen: Lebensrückschau*. Tübingen: Wunderlich, 1938.

McEwan, Dorothea. "Due missioni politiche di Aby Warburg in Italia nel 1914–15." *Schifanoia* 42–43 (2012): 57–79.

McEwan, Dorothea, and Alessandro Scafi. "Warburg and D'Annunzio in Defence of Truth: On Modern Literature and Alleged Jewishness." *Schifanoia* 52–53 (2017): 259–79.

Miller, Norbert. "Poetisch erschlossene Geschichte: Ferdinand Gregorovius' 'Wanderjahre in Italien' und seine Dichtung über den Garten von Ninfa." *Quellen und Forschungen aus italienischen Archiven und Bibliotheken* 96 (2016): 389–411.

Ostermann, Patrick. *Duell der Diplomaten: Die Propaganda der Mittelmächte und ihrer Gegner in Italien während des Ersten Weltkrieges*. Weimar: VDG, 2000.

Roeck, Bernd. *Florenz 1900: Die Suche nach Arkadien*. Munich: C. H. Beck, 2001.

Roettgen, Steffi. "Dal 'Börsen-Courier' di Berlino al 'genio' di Firenze: Lo storico Robert Davidsohn e il suo inedito lascito fiorentino." In *Storia dell'arte e politica culturale intorno al 1900: La fondazione dell'Istituto Germanico di Storia dell'Arte di Firenze*, edited by Max Seidel, 313–38. Venice: Marsilio, 1999.

Rosenthal, Jacob. *Die Ehre des jüdischen Soldaten: Die Judenzählung im Ersten Weltkrieg und ihre Folgen*. Frankfurt am Main: Campus Verlag, 2007.

Sieg, Ulrich. *Jüdische Intellektuelle im Ersten Weltkrieg: Kriegserfahrungen, weltanschauliche Debatten und kulturelle Neuentwürfe*. Berlin: Akademie Verlag, 2001.

Sösemann, Bernd. *Theodor Wolff: Ein Leben mit der Zeitung*. Stuttgart: Steiner, 2012.

Spagnolo-Stiff, Anne. "L'appello di Aby Warburg a un'intesa italo-tedesca: 'La guerra del 1914–15; Rivista illustrata.'" In *Storia dell'arte e politica culturale intorno al 1900: La fondazione dell'Istituto Germanico di Storia dell'Arte di Firenze*, edited by Max Seidel, 249–69. Venice: Marsilio, 1999.

Thiel, Jens. *Anwerbung, Deportation und Zwangsarbeit im Ersten Weltkrieg*. Essen: Klartext, 2007.

Toury, Jacob. *Die politischen Orientierungen der Juden in Deutschland: Von Jena bis Weimar*. Tübingen: Mohr, 1966.

Vigezzi, Brunello. *L'Italia di fronte alla prima guerra mondiale*. Vol. 1: *L'Italia neutrale*. Milan: R. Ricciardi, 1966.

Voci, Anna Maria. "'Anche la scienza ha perduto la sua serena imparzialità': una lettera di Robert Davidsohn a Harry Breslau (21 gennaio 1915)." *La Cultura* 38 (2000): 141–57.
Voigt, Klaus. *Zuflucht auf Widerruf*. Vol. 1. Stuttgart: Klett Cotta, 1989.
vom Bruch, Rüdiger. *Gelehrtenpolitik, Sozialwissenschaft und akademische Diskurse in Deutschland im 19. und 20. Jahrhundert*. Stuttgart: F. Steiner, 2006.
von Fabriczy, Cornel. Review of *Geschichte von Florenz*, Vol. 1, by Robert Davidsohn. *Repertorium für Kunstwissenschaft* 20, no. 3 (1897): 215–27.
Wyrwa, Ulrich. "Die europäischen Seiten der jüdischen Geschichtsschreibung." In *Judentum und Historismus: Zur Entstehung der jüdischen Geschichtswissenschaft in Europa*, edited by Ulrich Wyrwa, 9–36. Frankfurt am Main: Campus Verlag, 2003.

CHAPTER 13

Between Motherhood and Patriotic Duty
Marital Correspondence as a Key Source for the Understanding of French-Jewish Women's Perspectives on World War I

Marie-Christin Lux

"You will tell me *everything*, won't you. Because I'm capable, I think, of hearing everything."[1] In her 11 September 1914 letter, Alice Hertz, a Jewish woman from Paris, urges her husband Robert not to keep anything from her. Ever since he was mobilized in August 1914, she had constantly asked him to share all of his experiences on the Western Front with her. She explains that as his wife, she feels ready to hear everything he goes through during his military service. At the same time, however, the insertion of the words "I think" reveals her uncertainty about whether she is able to handle every detail of what her husband might tell her.

This inner struggle between curiosity and fear that Alice Hertz reveals in her short statement is characteristic of the complex narratives that couples created within their marital wartime correspondences. While husbands and wives alike depended on information and emotional support from their spouses, husbands did not want to alarm their families at home, and wives did not want to weaken the morale of their husbands at the front. Both partners therefore needed to keep the balance between opening up about their hopes and fears and lifting the spirits of their partner.

In this field of tension, couples like Alice and Robert Hertz created a link between their separated lives and discussed their perspectives on the war.[2]

Wartime Letters as Historical Sources

Historians have long debated the methodological challenges that must be considered when working with wartime letters. In France in particular, these ego documents, whether written by soldiers from the front or by wives and family members behind the lines, have been criticized as problematic sources. This critique goes back to Jean Norton Cru, who only reluctantly integrated letters into his groundbreaking study *Témoins*.[3] Cru, who was a veteran of the war himself, did not qualify letters as reliable testimonies, as he was convinced that neither soldiers nor the recipients at home wrote openly about their experiences and that they censored themselves to protect their spouses and families. His caution and skepticism regarding the source value of private letters was also based on the assumption that not only self-censorship but also censorship imposed by the state prevented the authors from revealing any deeper insights into their war experiences.[4]

However, studies using records from the postal control service have proved that while there were soldiers who did not share anything but banalities in their letters, the majority of them also wrote about their anxieties and the horrors they experienced on the battlefield. Many of the soldiers serving in their countries' armies used the almost daily correspondences to confide to their wives at least certain aspects of what they saw.[5] In a similar way, women who wrote to their men at the front often defied the official recommendations to not write about unsettling topics.[6] Just like their husbands, who took the demands of their wives for honesty seriously, they answered questions about the family members' health, well-being, and safety, even if the news was upsetting.[7]

Marital Correspondences as Spaces of Negotiation

Despite the controversial discussions regarding the value of letters as historical sources, wartime correspondences have inspired a vast number of publications and letter editions. Especially regarding studies on the two World Wars, letters from the battlefields have appeared as prominent sources since the 1960s. But despite the methodological diversity that scholars have applied when working with wartime letters, most of the studies have focused on male realms of experience.[8]

Although there have been tendencies to integrate the dimension of gender into the mainstream research on wartime letters since the 1990s, the majority of monographs within this field of research still ignored the female perspective within the correspondences. Over the past years, however, a number of studies have helped to broaden scholars' perspectives by introducing female voices into their analysis. Monographs and articles especially focusing on the affectionate character of marital wartime correspondences respond to their dialogical structure and present intermeshed analyses of male and female perspectives.

In their studies on the culture of letter writing, Christa Hämmerle and Ingrid Bauer stress the unique insights into female realms of experience that can be gathered through marital correspondences.[9] For France, Martha Hanna and Clémentine Vidal-Naquet's studies have shown impressive results on the maintenance and creation of intimacy and love in wartime, illuminating how marital correspondences offer insights into an intimate sphere of war as well as into interactions of men and women.[10]

Based on these intermeshed analyses of male and female perspectives, correspondences appear as spaces of communication that allowed but also forced husbands and wives to articulate their thoughts and emotions. Couples used their letters to each other to confirm their love and relationship during their separation. At the same time, however, wartime correspondences created spaces of negotiation in which the spouses shared but also challenged each other's thoughts and reflections on the conflict, their own roles in it, and their relationship to each other.

Jewish Women's Perspectives: Untold Stories of World War I

In the field of Jewish history, however, correspondences have rarely been used to explore the dynamics of marital relationships or to raise questions about female Jewish perspectives. Despite the wide range of controversial discussions, conferences, and publications that have emerged within the field of World War I studies since the centenary of 2014, Jewish women's experiences during the conflict still remain one of the untold stories of the war. While studies on the involvement of Jewish soldiers in the armies and societies of the belligerent nations and empires offer detailed insights into male military and civil war engagement, very little has been said about the experiences of their female counterparts.[11] Especially regarding the French case, Jewish women only appear in the context of simplistic generalizations and are mostly presented as a homogenous group of passive bystanders whose roles are vaguely defined as mothers, wives, and charity workers.[12]

The previous neglect of French-Jewish women's perspectives regarding the war is the starting point of this chapter. On the basis of marital wartime correspondences, it aims at exploring the diversity of female Jewish war experiences and breaking the habit of talking about women instead of listening to them. These letters that spouses wrote to each other on an almost daily basis offer complex insights into the thoughts and reflections of their authors. They are therefore key sources for a more differentiated analysis of female Jewish war experiences. However, previous editions of correspondences dealing with Jewish perspectives mainly focus on letters written by male Jewish soldiers and intellectuals like, for instance, Marc

Bloch.[13] The voices of female authors or correspondents on the other hand are not edited and remain mostly unheard. These women are reduced to the role of passive recipients, and the complex dialogues between two individuals are cut down to one-sided monologues. But in order to understand the complexity of Jewish World War I experiences, it is necessary to consider and listen to both sides of the dialogue. Private wartime letters allow scholars to follow personal narratives and deconstruct one-dimensional portrayals of Jewish women.

Alice Hertz and Laure Isaac: The Cases of Two French-Jewish Women

In contrast to previous editions and studies, this chapter therefore focuses on the female half of the correspondences and discusses the particular inner struggles Jewish women had to deal with during the war period. On the exemplary basis of the letters of Alice Hertz and Laure Isaac, this chapter asks how women tried to define themselves and their role within the war effort between being a mother, a French citizen, and a Jewish woman.[14] Although the cases chosen for this chapter only allow us to listen to two voices, they give us a first glimpse into the complexity of female Jewish perspectives.

Our first protagonist is Alice Hertz. Born Alice Sarah Bauer in 1877, she was the daughter of a Jewish merchant. She grew up in Paris, where she lived with her parents and her brothers, Edmond and Paul, and also spent the majority of her adult life. Just like her siblings, Alice attended public schools and enjoyed a secular education based on the laical values of the Third French Republic.[15]

After initially basing her studies on biology and natural sciences, Alice developed a keen interest in pedagogy. During a stay in London, where she accompanied her husband in 1904, she further engaged with new methodologies within this field and became a strong supporter of Friedrich Fröbel's concepts on early childhood education. Determined to adapt Fröbel's kindergarten concepts to the French educational system when she returned to Paris in 1905, she developed the first private kindergarten groups in her Parisian neighborhood. Together with Thérèrese Sance, the director of the prestigious *Collège de Sévigné* since 1909, Alice then went on to further the kindergarten concept in France and to train teachers in educational theory—a work that she also continued during the war.[16]

Although the sources do not tell us more about Alice's religious education or her family's ties to the Jewish community, her marital wartime correspondence suggests that she did not practice her religion, as neither she nor her husband Robert Hertz refer to any Jewish holidays or religious practices. Nevertheless, Alice and Robert both refer to themselves as Jewish in their letters. Their references to their own Jewishness are, however, rather based on belonging to a minority that had to prove their gratefulness and loyalty to France than to a religious group.[17]

Just like his wife, Robert Walter Hertz was born to Jewish parents but received his education in the French secular school and university system. After graduating from the École Normale Supérieure in 1904, he became part of Émile Durkheim's research group. As an ambitious sociologist and ethnologist, he soon made a name for himself within the group.[18]

At the same time, however, he dedicated himself to his political beliefs. Since his youth, Robert Hertz was a staunch socialist and friends with several members of the British Fabian Society. By founding the Groupe d'études socialistes in 1908, a forum for scholars modeled on the Fabian Society, he created his own political organization that attracted numerous intellectuals, especially from among the so-called *durkheimiens*.[19]

This combination of political engagement and academic studies characterized Robert Hertz's work until his mobilization in August 1914. When he left his Parisian home in order to fight in the French infantry, he continued these discussions in the letters to his wife and even started an ethnological study on his comrades in the army.[20]

After Robert's mobilization, Alice Hertz and her son Antoine moved from Paris to the Bretagne. In order to escape the danger of a German attack, they left the capital and stayed with Robert's family in the small town of Morgat. At the beginning of the university year in October 1914, however, Alice and Antoine moved back to Paris, where she continued her work as a professor at the Collège de Sévigné. In April 1915, Robert Hertz was killed during a German attack near Verdun. His death marks the sudden end of their wartime correspondence.[21]

Just like her friend Alice, our second protagonist, Laure Isaac, had a bourgeois Jewish family background. Born as Laure Ettinghausen in 1878 in Paris, she was the daughter of a German-born banker.[22] She went on to become an artist and was one of the students of the famous French painter Eugène Carrière. Laure's specialty was portraits, but during the war she used her creative talent to support her family as a cartoonist for several French newspapers. In 1902, she married the historian Jules Isaac at the synagogue of Saint-Étienne.[23]

Apart from this commitment to the Jewish faith, the sources do not tell us much about Laure's religious background. However, the facts that her and Jules Isaac's three children, Juliette, David, and Jean-Claude, did not receive any religious education and that all married non-Jews indicate that Laure did not practice her religion.[24]

In their marital wartime correspondence, Laure and Jules do, however, reveal a different form of spirituality. As the couple rejected the Jewish and Christian religions as too dogmatic and faulty, they created their own belief system that was based on their love for each other, a "religion du couple."[25] Their attitude toward their own Jewishness must therefore be described as ambiguous. Similar to Alice and Robert Hertz, they did not practice their religion, nor were they active members of the Jewish community. At the same time, they identified themselves as Jews and were part of a Jewish family network.

Based on his family background, Jules's distanced attitude toward religion is not self-evident. Born in 1877 in Rennes as the youngest of three children, he grew up in a bourgeois Jewish family that valued the French Republic and its principles just as much as Jewish traditions. His father was an Alsatian major and a member of the Légion d'Honneur[26] who taught him respect for the French army, while his mother took care of his religious education.[27] Despite this upbringing, Jules broke with his religion when he lost his parents at the age of fourteen, but his loyalty and respect for the French Republic and its army remained intact.

After his parents' death in 1891, his brother-in-law and his older sister Laure became his guardians. They sent him to the boarding school Lycée Lakanal in Sceaux, where he stayed until he moved to Lycée Henri IV in Paris in 1896. There, he met his former classmate Charles Péguy, who inspired him to become a socialist and even convinced him to join the Dreyfusards in 1898.[28]

Simultaneously with his political activism, Jules Isaac started studying history at the Sorbonne in 1898 and became a history and geography teacher in 1902.[29] For his first teaching position, Laure and Jules left Paris and moved to Nice. They changed their home residence several times and lived in Sens, Saint-Étienne, and Lyon before returning to Paris in 1914.[30]

In August 1914, Jules Isaac was mobilized and served in the French infantry and artillery at the Western Front until being severely injured and hospitalized in June 1917.[31] After her husband's mobilization, Laure Isaac fled Paris and moved to Saint-Étienne. She and her two children Juliette and Daniel stayed with Laure's sister Rosa before going to Lyon and then back to Paris. In Lyon, Laure volunteered in a hospital and worked as a freelance cartoonist for different newspapers. In 1918, she gave birth to her third child, a son named Jean-Claude. For the majority of the conflict, Laure and Jules Isaac remained separated and relied only on their letters to each other.

Motherhood versus Active Engagement in the War

Alice Hertz and Laure Isaac both had to face challenges and responsibilities on numerous levels. They took care of their children and had to cope with the likely possibility of losing their partners. They worked and volunteered to actively support their countries' war efforts and to prove their patriotism. And finally, they tried to define their roles as Jewish women and as Jewish citizens within a society at war. In the letters to their husbands, Alice and Laure constantly reflected on their own roles within the conflict and within French society. They tried to define themselves, explained their thoughts and actions, and discussed their views and beliefs with their partners.

Especially during the first months of the war, both women constantly refer to their motherhood as their central responsibility. In almost every letter, they reassure their partners about the well-being of their children and emphasize their physical and mental strength. In this spirit, Alice Hertz wrote on 29 August 1914,

> I feel strong like a rock and I will try to protect our little one. Nothing bad will happen to us.[32]

The soothing yet confident tone of the statement is characteristic for her reaction to the new responsibilities she took on following her husband's mobilization. Alice does not leave any room for doubt that she will take care of her son's safety. She even seems to draw strength from her role as a mother and the new responsibilities that came with the absence of her partner.

Looking at her letters from the early phase of the war, her motherhood appears to be her central frame of reference. Her main concern is to raise and teach her five-year-old son, Antoine, whose physical and intellectual development she proudly describes in each letter. In several of her letters from this period however, her self-portrayal as a mother goes even further. On 31 August 1914, Alice even addresses her husband Robert with the words "my little son, my beloved, in this moment I feel more like your mother than your wife."[33]

Her motherhood is at the center of her self-definition and her concept of patriotism.[34] On 20 August 1914, Alice even expresses this link between motherhood and patriotism on a metaphorical level by comparing the war to the process of giving birth:

> I feel like giving birth, so full of hope, so full of good, of drive toward the future, that the current suffering doesn't count; it is almost good and salutary.[35]

But despite this attempt at defining herself as the mother and protector of the family, Alice struggles with her limited activity in the war effort. Especially during her stay in the Bretagne, she often fantasizes about taking "a more active part in the war—to work, help, prove one's love, one's trust in another way than by being just patient and excited."[36] After her husband's transfer to the front lines, she expresses her discontent at not being part of the active war effort even further. On 22 November 1914, she explains:

> One would like to be a bit more involved in the events, live a bit more in the atmosphere back there—there where these destroyed villages are that you talk to me about . . .—I am almost jealous of Claire Halphen who is a nurse in Dijon in her husband's hospital or of Mme Guyesse Pélissieri who also helps her husband. But don't worry. I will not do anything because first and foremost I have to take care of our little Tonie, I have to protect him—and that excludes the rest.[37]

The letter illustrates the inner struggle Alice had to deal with. On the one hand, she openly proclaims her wish to experience the war alongside her husband; on the other hand, she refers to her motherly duties, which according to her made it impossible to get involved with any active war efforts.

In a similar manner, Laure Isaac constantly compared her engagement to that of other women and declared her willingness to do more than be a mother. On 12 September 1914, she tells her husband about aid projects that have been set up by local women and brings up the possibility of volunteering at an ambulance:

> They are creating an ambulance next to our place . . . maybe I could make myself a bit useful. Mme Brahmet and others organize relief actions for the refugees in the train stations.[38]

But despite her efforts, Laure faced the same struggle as Alice. Her wish to prove her courage and patriotism clashed with her private responsibilities. Just like her friend Alice, she felt limited in her ability to be more active and measured herself against the involvement of other women. On 19 September 1915, she shares her disappointment:

> Louise prepares for a nursing exam, which will allow her to be closer to Henri. I understand that she tries everything for that. Sadly, it is necessary to have been a nurse in a hospital on a regular basis, and with my children I am not able to do that.[39]

But although both women quarreled with their role in the conflict and wished for more ways to prove themselves, they still wanted to be acknowledged as participants in the war. They wanted to make sure that especially their husbands who were fighting in the trenches knew that they were fighting and suffering as well. After Jules Isaac had told his wife in January 1916[40] that he believed the war only changed the lives of the men in the army, Laure harshly criticizes him and responds:

> What you are telling me about the combatants' esprit does not surprise me; I don't think that we are that different; we have also changed, we changed while seemingly leading the same lives as before; I think that the women who are behind the lines

have a lot more in common with the poilus of the trenches than with the civilians—from before.⁴¹

Laure does not share her husband's perspective on male and female war experiences. She strongly disagrees with Jules's idea that only the combatants experience the war as a transformative moment. By stretching the similarities between men and women, Laure Isaac openly opposes gender-related stereotypes. She even implies that the war equalizes women and men.⁴²

On 10 November 1914, Alice Hertz argues in a very similar way and insists that everyone is equally part of the war effort:

> I know that the destiny of our country not only depends on those who fight but also on the attitude of those who wait and hope. All of us can contribute to the force or weakness of our nation.⁴³

By stressing their commitment to their family as well as their devotion to the French Republic, both women tried to define themselves in the field of tension between being a loving mother and a patriotic French citizen. In this regard, their efforts and argumentations do not differ from those of most other French women of non-Jewish faith.

Jewish Women and the Narrative of Self-Sacrifice

But as Jewish women, they had to deal with yet another challenge. Most studies on Jewish experiences of war in France stress the narrative of a Jewish population that felt indebted to France and tried to achieve full integration into French society by willingly sacrificing themselves on the battlefields.⁴⁴ A critical reading of personal sources, especially of ego documents by Jewish women, however, shows that this one-dimensional narrative does not correspond with the complexity of Jewish perspectives on the war. In their correspondences, Alice and Laure rarely discuss their Jewishness.⁴⁵ While questions about motherhood and being a woman in general are aspects both women frequently focus on, they almost never initiate conversations about their roles as Jewish women.

In contrast to her husband Robert Hertz, who was an eager supporter of the concept of Jewish self-sacrifice, Alice only partially agreed with the idea. In her response to Robert's letter in which he solemnly declares his willingness to die as a Jew for France,⁴⁶ it becomes clear that she only supported his ideas as long as they did not affect her personally.

> Everything you told me, beloved, I felt and understood it. The other day I wrote to Andrée: what a joy, for us other Jews, to be able to shed our blood! It's true I added selfishly: I just rather wish it would be my blood instead of Robert's.⁴⁷

At first sight, it seems that Alice agreed with Robert and that she understood his urge to prove his unlimited devotion for France. Looking carefully at her response, however, it becomes clear that Alice was not at all willing to sacrifice her husband. When talking about Robert's life, Alice drew the line and clearly chose his well-being over any abstract demand for Jewish self-sacrifice. Neither Alice nor Laure corresponded to the narrative of French Jews willingly sacrificing their lives or those of the people they cared about in order to prove their unconditional love for France. Both women were proud that their husbands fought in the French Army and accepted the fear and suffering that came with it, but they also wanted to protect their families.

Yet they were still aware that being Jewish put them in a sensitive position. Although neither Laure nor Alice put a special emphasis on their Jewishness within the correspondences, they repeatedly pointed out how grateful they were to be part of the French Republic. Their deep connection to the values of the Republic and their fear for the system's stability become apparent in a letter Laure wrote on 26 November 1917. In this letter, she recalls a conversation she had with a group of friends about the current state of the war that left her deeply worried.

> On Tuesday, I was at Laure's where I spent the afternoon. Louise, Ellen, and Claire were there. Can you believe that in this milieu, that more than any other should know why we fight and what the Republic represents for us, they are pining for any kind of change, which according to them should bring any kind of solution, and I was the only one defending our Republic, which despite its faults is our reason to live, and finally I had to silence myself under the jeers of all the women present who are full of questions but blind and who don't understand. I am well aware that this is only a small bourgeois circle, but if they talk like that how can you not fear what the women who neither have the instruction nor the race think about that?[48]

Laure is deeply troubled by her friends' war fatigue and the fact that they openly questioned their loyalty to the Republic. As a Jewish woman, she passionately defended the French state to which she felt such a strong connection. Her reaction shows that despite her rejection of the concept of Jewish self-sacrifice, she still felt the need to prove her unconditional devotion to the Republic. Just like her friend Alice, she was torn between her love for her country and her love for her family.

Conclusion

In their ambiguity, the two cases of Alice Hertz and Laure Isaac offer a first glimpse into the complexity of Jewish women's perspectives on and during World War I. The exemplary study of their letters shows how marital correspondences can be used to gain a deeper understanding of the different struggles and challenges Jewish women had to deal with. In their letters, these women openly wrote about the war as they saw and experienced it. Although they rather tried to boost the morale of their husbands and therefore often hid their fears behind patriotic slogans, they also wanted their partners to understand what they were going through. Marital correspondences are therefore key sources for the analysis of female Jewish war experiences. In the same way as these private letters enable scholars to gain a deeper understanding of intimacy and love in wartime, they can also be used to open up new perspectives regarding Jewish experiences of World War I.

Through the equal study of the letters of both spouses, marital correspondences form a unique basis for an intermeshed analysis of female and male realms of experience. They allow scholars to broaden their perspectives beyond trenches and battlefields and to deconstruct the binary concept of front and home front. By using wartime correspondences as central sources, scholars can paint a more differentiated picture of Jewish war experiences than previous studies have done. By pointing out these benefits of marital correspondences as key sources for the understanding of French-Jewish women's perspectives on World War I, this chapter ultimately calls for new methodological approaches and analytical concepts that embrace the multiperspectivity of Jewish experiences instead of oversimplifying them.

Marie-Christin Lux is currently completing her PhD in history at the Center for Research on Antisemitism (Zentrum für Antisemitismusforschung, TU Berlin) in Berlin about the multiperspectivity of French-Jewish experiences during World War I. She has a BA in history and French literature from the University of Constance and a joint master's degree in history from the École des Hautes Études en Sciences Sociales in Paris and the University of Heidelberg. She is a member of the research group Der Erste Weltkrieg und die Konflikte der europäischen Nachkriegsordnung (1914–1923) at the Center for Research on Antisemitism, and was a visiting scholar at the Leibniz Institute of European History in Mainz.

Notes

1. Alice to Robert Hertz, 11 September 1914, Collège de France, Archives Laboratoire d'anthropologie sociale/Fonds Robert Hertz.
2. See Christa Hämmerle, "Entzweite Beziehungen? Zur Feldpost der beiden Weltkriege aus frauen- und geschlechtergeschichtlicher Perspektive," in *Schreiben im Krieg Schreiben vom Krieg: Feldpost im Zeitalter der Weltkriege*, ed. Veit Didczu-

neit, Jens Ebert, Thomas Jander (Essen: Klartext Verlag, 2011), 246–47; Martha Hanna, "War Letters: Communication between Front and Home Front," in *1914-1918-Online: International Encyclopedia of the First World War*, ed. Ute Daniel, Peter Gatrell, Oliver Janz, Heather Jones, Jennifer Keene, Alan Kramer, and Bill Nasson, issued by Freie Universität Berlin, 10 October 2014, doi: 10.15463/ie1418.10362.

3. Jean Norton Cru, *Témoins: Essai d'analyse et de critique des souvenirs de combattants édités en français de 1915 à 1928* (1929; Paris: Eurédit, 2015).
4. Some of this skepticism toward family correspondences still prevails in the works of Frédéric Rousseau. See, for instance, Frédéric Rousseau, *La guerre censurée: Une histoire des combattants européens de 14-18* (Paris: Le Seuil, 1999), 42–44.
5. See, for instance, John Horne, "Soldiers, Civilians and the Warfare of Attrition: Representations of Combat in France, 1914–1918," in *Authority, Identity and the Social History of the Great War*, ed. Frans Coetzee and Marilyn Shevin-Coetzee (Providence, RI: Berghahn Books, 1995), 223–49; Jean Nicot, *Les poilus ont la parole: Dans les tranchées; lettres du front 1917–1918* (Brussels: Éditions complexe, 1998).
6. In most countries, there were guidelines published in newspapers explaining how women should write to their husbands who were serving in the armies. Women were supposed to refrain from sharing any information that could upset their husbands. Instead, they were required to comfort them with their letters. One of these instructions on letter writing that was published in France was "Pour Celles qui écrivent aux Soldats," written by Marcel Prévost of the Académie Française. Marcel Prévost, "Pour Celles qui écrivent aux Soldats," *Le Petit Parisien*, 29 September 1917.
7. Hanna, "War Letters."
8. Due to limited space, it is not possible to present an extensive bibliography. The following examples can therefore only give an idea of the vast research on wartime letters: Hanna, "War Letters"; Sylvie Housiel, *Dire la guerre: Le discours épistolaire des combattants français de 14-18* (Limoges: Lambert-Lucas, 2014); Martyn Lyons, *The Writing Culture of Ordinary People in Europe, 1860–1920* (New York: Cambridge University Press, 2013); Veit Didczuneit, Jens Ebert, and Thomas Jander, eds., *Schreiben im Krieg—Schreiben vom Krieg: Feldpost im Zeitalter der Weltkriege* (Essen: Klartext Verlag, 2011); Bernd Ulrich and Benjamin Ziemann, *German Soldiers in the Great War: Letters and Eyewitness Accounts* (Barnsley: Pen & Sword Military, 2010); Benjamin Ziemann, *War Experiences in Rural Germany, 1914–1923* (New York: Berg, 2007); Rémy Cazals and Frédéric Rousseau, *14-18: Le cri d'une génération* (Toulouse: Privat, 2003); Gerald Lamprecht, *Feldpost und Kriegserlebnis: Briefe als historisch-biographische Quelle* (Innsbruck: Studien Verlag, 2002); Klaus Latzel, "Vom Kriegserlebnis zur Kriegserfahrung: Theoretische und methodische Überlegungen zur erfahrungsgeschichtlichen Untersuchung von Feldpostbriefen," *Militärgeschichtliche Mitteilungen* 56, no. 1 (1997): 1–30; Bernd Ulrich, *Die Augenzeugen: Deutsche Feldpostbriefe in Kriegs- und Nachkriegszeit 1914–1933* (Essen: Klartext, 1997); Peter Knoch, "Feldpost—eine unentdeckte historische Quellengattung," *Geschichtsdidaktik* 11 (1986): 154–71.
9. See, for example, Ingrid Bauer and Christa Hämmerle, eds., *Liebe schreiben: Paarkorrespondenzen im Kontext des 19. Und 20. Jahrhunderts* (Göttingen: Vandenhoeck & Ruprecht, 2017); Christa Hämmerle and Edith Sauer, eds., *Briefkulturen und ihr Geschlecht: Zur Geschichte der privaten Korrespondenz vom 16. Jahrhundert bis

heute, L'Homme Schriften 7 (Vienna: Böhlau, 2003); Christa Hämmerle, "'You Let a Weeping Woman Call You Home?': Private Correspondences during the First World War in Austria and Germany," in *Epistolary Selves: Letters and Letter-Writers, 1600–1945*, ed. Rebecca Earle (Brookfield, VT: Ashgate, 1999), 152–82.

10. Martha Hanna, "A Republic of Letters: The Epistolary Tradition in France during World War I," *American Historical Review* 108, no. 5 (2003): 1338–61; Martha Hanna, *Your Death Would Be Mine: Paul and Marie Pireaud in the Great War* (Cambridge, MA: Harvard University Press, 2008); Clémentine Vidal-Naquet, *Couples dans la Grande Guerre: Le tragique et l'ordinaire du lien conjugal* (Paris: Les Belles Lettres, 2014).

11. While female Jewish perspectives only play a minor role within the French historiography, studies focusing on other European cases like the Austro-Hungarian Empire, Germany, and Italy have already started to integrate Jewish women into their narratives. See, for instance, for the Austro-Hungarian Empire: Marta Markova, "Alice Rühle-Gerstel und der geistige Aufstand europäischer Kulturschaffender gegen Krieg und Militarismus," in *Jüdische Publizistik und Literatur im Zeichen des Ersten Weltkriegs*, ed. Petra Ernst and Eleonore Lappin-Eppel (Innsbruck: Studienverlag, 2016), 233–46; Dieter Hecht, *Zwischen Feminismus und Zionismus: Anitta Müller-Cohen (1890–1962); Die Biographie einer Wiener Jüdin*, L'Homme Schriften 15 (Vienna: Böhlau, 2008); Marsha L. Rozenblit, "For Fatherland and Jewish People: Jewish Women in Austria during World War I," in *Authority, Identity, and the Social History of the Great War*, ed. Frans Coetzee and Marilyn Shevin-Coetzee (Providence, RI: Berghahn Books, 1995), 199–222. For Germany, Dorothee Wierling followed the family of the feminist Lily Braun: "Imagining and Communicating Violence: The Correspondence of a Berlin Family, 1914–1918," in *Gender and the First World War*, ed. Christa Hämmerle, Oswald Überegger, and Birgitta Bader Zaar (New York: Palgrave Macmillan, 2014), 36–51, and *Eine Familie im Krieg: Leben, Sterben und Schreiben 1914–1918* (Göttingen: Wallstein Verlag, 2013). Regarding the Italian case, Ruth Nattermann published several studies dealing with the experiences of Italian-Jewish women. See, for instance, her contribution to this volume, as well as "The Female Side of War: Experience and Memory of the Great War in Italian-Jewish Women's Ego Documents," in *The Jewish Experience of the First World War*, ed. Edward Madigan and Gideon Reuveni (New York: Palgrave Macmillan, 2018), 233–54; "Zwischen Pazifismus, Irredentismus und nationaler Euphorie: Italienische Jüdinnen und der Erste Weltkrieg," in *Jüdische Publizistik und Literatur im Zeichen des Ersten Weltkriegs*, ed. Petra Ernst and Eleonore Lappin-Eppel (Innsbruck: Studienverlag, 2016), 247–63.

12. Very few studies have concentrated their analysis on Jewish experiences in France during World War I. Although the period between 1914 and 1918 is a well-researched field in French historiography, Jewish experiences and perspectives have only been at the center of a small number of articles and monographs. In his work of reference *Les Juifs de France et la Grande Guerre: Un patriotisme républicain 1914–1941*, as well as in his articles dealing with World War I and its aftermath, Philippe E. Landau focuses on male actors and their roles and experiences within Jewish institutions, the French army, and French society as a whole. Jewish women, on the other hand, only appear on the sidelines. In her article on Jewish historians and sociologists, Annette Becker refers to marital correspondences of Jewish intellectuals, but she does not cite the letters of their wives. Despite the

in-depth analysis of male realms of experience, previous studies therefore only treat Jewish women as minor characters. See Philippe Landau, "La communauté juive de France et la Grande Guerre," *Annales de démographie historique* 103, no. 1 (2002): 91–106; Philippe Landau, *Les Juifs de France et la Grande Guerre: Un patriotisme républicain 1914–1941* (Paris: CNRS Éditions, 1999); Annette Becker, "De quelques historiens, sociologues et ethnologues juifs en Grande Guerre: Entre Sciences sociales, République, Union sacrée et barrésisme," *Archives juives* 36, no. 2 (2003): 68–85.

13. Marc Bloch, *Écrits de guerre (1914–1918): Textes réunis et présentés par Étienne Bloch; Introduction par Stéphane Audoin-Rouzeau* (Paris: Armand Colin Masson, 1997).

14. The two correspondences chosen for this article are also referenced in my dissertation project, in which I study the multiperspectivity of wartime experiences within correspondences of French-Jewish and non-Jewish couples. The current title of the project, which is advised by Prof. Dr. Werner Bergmann and Prof. Dr. Ulrich Wyrwa at the Center for Research on Antisemitism (Technical University Berlin), is *Als Jude, als Frau, als Intellektueller—Die Vielstimmigkeit von Kriegserfahrungen in den Korrespondenzen französischer jüdischer und nicht-jüdischer Ehepaare (1914–1918)*. The more than three hundred letters of the wartime correspondence between Alice and Robert Hertz are maintained as part of the Fonds Robert Hertz at the Archives Laboratoire d'anthropologie sociale (Collège de France, Paris). The private letters of Laure and Jules Isaac have been transferred as part of the Fonds Jules Isaac from the Bibliothèque Méjanes in Aix-en-Provence to the Bibliothèque nationale de France. The correspondence, which comprises thirteen volumes with more than twenty-five hundred letters, has been digitalized and can be accessed via Gallica, https://gallica.bnf.fr.

15. See Extrait d'acte de naissance d'Alice Bauer, Collège de France. Archives Laboratoire d'anthropologie sociale/Fonds Robert Hertz; Robert Parkin, *The Dark Side of Humanity: The Work of Robert Hertz and its Legacy* (New York: Routledge, 2006), 187.

16. See Marcel Mauss, "Notice biographique: Alice Robert Hertz," in Robert Hertz, *Sociologie religieuse et folklore* (Paris: Librairie Félix Alcan, 1928), 12–13; Parkin, *Dark Side of Humanity*, 187.

17. See, for instance, Robert's letter to Alice from 3 November 1914 and her response from 14 November 1914; Robert to Alice Hertz, 3 November 1914, and Alice to Robert Hertz, 14 November 1914, Collège de France. Archives Laboratoire d'anthropologie sociale/Fonds Robert Hertz.

18. See Émile Durkheim, "Notice biographique sur Robert Hertz.—Le souvenir d'un des talents le plus confirmés de l'École française de sociologie, disparu tout jeune dans la Grande Guerre," in Émile Durkheim, *Textes: 1. Éléments d'une théorie sociale; Présentation de Victor Karady* (Paris: Éditions de Minuit, 1975), 439–40; Marcel Fournier, *Émile Durkheim (1858–1917)* (Paris: Fayard, 2007), 593–95.

19. See Parkin, *Dark Side of Humanity*, 5–7; Alexander Riley and Philippe Besnard, eds., *Un ethnologue dans les tranchées, août 1914—avril 1915: Lettres de Robert Hertz à sa femme Alice* (Paris: CNRS Éditions, 2002), 8, 16.

20. See Robert Hertz, "Contes et dictons recueillis sur le front, parmi les poilus de la Mayenne et d'ailleurs (1917)," in Hertz, *Sociologie religieuse et folklore*, 144–77.

21. See Parkin, *Dark Side of Humanity*, 9–10, 12–14, 187, 190; Riley and Besnard, *Un ethnologue dans les tranchées*, 10–11; Mauss, "Notice biographique," 12–13.

22. See Laure Ettinghausen 24 March 1878, Acte de naissance 2. Arrondissement 1878 (Cote V4E 2644), Archives de Paris, Registres d'actes d'état civil (1860–1902); Maurice Ettinghausen 24 October 1899, Acte de décès 17. Arrondissement 1899 (Cote V4E 10212), Archives de Paris, Registres d'actes d'état civil (1860–1902).
23. See Muriel Pichon, *Les Français juifs 1914–1950: Récit d'un désenchantement* (Toulouse: Presses Universitaires du Mirail, 2009), 257; Jules Isaac, *Un historien dans la Grande Guerre, Lettres et carnets 1914–1917, introduction par André Kaspi, présentation et notés par Marc Michel* (Paris: Armand Colin, 2004), 7; André Kaspi, *Jules Isaac: Historien, acteur du rapprochement judéo-chrétien* (Paris: Plon, 2002), 44, 247.
24. See Pichon, *Les Français juifs*, 257.
25. See, for instance, Laure to Jules Isaac, 24 January 1917, Bibliothèque nationale de France, Archives et manuscrits NAF 28655 Fonds Jules Isaac, Correspondance échangée entre Jules et Laure Isaac, 1914–1918; Jules to Laure Isaac 6 February 1917, ibid.
26. See Procès-Verbal de Réception d'un Officier de la Légion d'honneur, Archives Nationales, Leonore (Dossier LH/1335/74); Extrait des Registres des Actes des naissances de la ville de Metz Marx Isaac, Archives Nationales, Leonore (Dossier LH/1335/74); Acte de naissance Jules Marx Isaac, 20 November 1877, Archives de Rennes, Registre des naissances (1877) (Cote 2E85); Isaac, *Un historien dans la Grande Guerre*, 5–6; Kaspi, *Jules Isaac*, 14–15.
27. See Jules Isaac, *Expériences de ma vie: Péguy* (Paris: Calmann-Lévy, 1959), 20–24; Isaac, *Un historien dans la Grande Guerre*, 6.
28. See Kaspi, *Jules Isaac*, 15–16, 40–41; Isaac, *Expériences de ma vie*, 35–36, 69, 91, 123.
29. Isaac, *Un historien dans la Grande Guerre*, 7.
30. Kaspi, *Jules Isaac*, 44–50.
31. See Isaac, *Un historien dans la Grande Guerre*, 23, 28–29; Kaspi, *Jules Isaac*, 48–49; Pichon, *Les Français juifs*, 257.
32. Alice to Robert Hertz, 29 August 1914, Collège de France, Archives Laboratoire d'anthropologie sociale/Fonds Robert Hertz.
33. Alice to Robert Hertz, 31 August 1914, Collège de France, Archives Laboratoire d'anthropologie sociale/Fonds Robert Hertz.
34. By centering her role within the war effort as well as her expression of patriotism on the concept of motherhood, Alice Hertz satisfied the mainstream definition of female contribution to the war within French society. See Susan Grayzel, "Mothers, Marraines, and Prostitutes: Morale and Morality in First World War France," *International History Review* 19, no. 1 (1997): 66–82, 67. For a deeper discussion on the discursive meaning of motherhood in France and Great Britain, see Susan Grayzel, *Women's Identities at War: Gender, Motherhood, and Politics in Britain and France during the First World War* (Chapel Hill: University of North Carolina Press, 1999).
35. Alice to Robert Hertz, 20 August 1914, Collège de France, Archives Laboratoire d'anthropologie sociale/Fonds Robert Hertz.
36. Alice to Robert Hertz, 19 September 1914, Collège de France, Archives Laboratoire d'anthropologie sociale/Fonds Robert Hertz.
37. Alice to Robert Hertz, 22 November 1914, Collège de France, Archives Laboratoire d'anthropologie sociale/Fonds Robert Hertz.

38. Laure to Jules Isaac, 12 September 1914, Bibliothèque nationale de France, Archives et manuscrits NAF 28655 Fonds Jules Isaac, Correspondance échangée entre Jules et Laure Isaac, 1914–1918.
39. Laure to Jules Isaac, 19 September 1915, Bibliothèque nationale de France, Archives et manuscrits NAF 28655 Fonds Jules Isaac, Correspondance échangée entre Jules et Laure Isaac, 1914–1918.
40. Jules to Laure Isaac, 1 January 1916, Bibliothèque nationale de France, Archives et manuscrits NAF 28655 Fonds Jules Isaac, Correspondance échangée entre Jules et Laure Isaac, 1914–1918.
41. Laure to Jules Isaac, January 4, 1916, Bibliothèque nationale de France, Archives et manuscrits NAF 28655 Fonds Jules Isaac, Correspondance échangée entre Jules et Laure Isaac, 1914–1918.
42. Although this argumentation by Laure Isaac suggests a shift in masculine and feminine identities, studies on war and gender have shown that the war rather helped to maintain existing gender models than to dissolve them. See, for instance, Françoise Thébaud, "La Grande Guerre: le triomphe de la division sexuelle," in *Histoire des femmes en Occident*, ed. Georges Duby and Michelle Perrot (Paris: Plon, 1992), 31–74, as well as Margaret R. Higonnet's and Patrice L.-R. Higonnet's reflections on the process of negotiating and renegotiating gender boundaries, "The Double Helix," in *Behind the Lines: Gender and the Two World Wars*, ed. Margaret R. Higonnet, Jane Jenson, Sonya Michel, and Margaret C. Weitz (New Haven, CT: Yale University Press 1987), 31–47.
43. Alice to Robert Hertz, 10 November 1914, Collège de France, Archives Laboratoire d'anthropologie sociale/Fonds Robert Hertz.
44. Despite Jean-Jacques Becker's study of reference on France's entry into the war, in which he shows that the majority of the population did not enthusiastically welcome the war, most works on the experiences of France's Jewish population paint a less multilayered picture. Although Philippe Landau points out that the majority of French Jews experienced the war in the same way as the non-Jewish population of France, he still focuses on source material that perpetuates the image of an exceptional Jewish patriotism. See Jean-Jacques Becker, *Comment les français sont entrés dans la guerre* (Paris: Les Presses de Sciences Po, 1977); Landau, *Les Juifs de France et la Grande Guerre*. However, recent studies on German and European Jews suggest that this narrative also needs to be called into question for the French case. See Sarah Panter, *Jüdische Erfahrungen und Loyalitätskonflikte im Ersten Weltkrieg* (Göttingen: Vandenhoeck & Ruprecht, 2014), 40–41; Ulrich Sieg, *Jüdische Intellektuelle im Ersten Weltkrieg: Kriegserfahrungen, weltanschauliche Debatten und kulturelle Neuentwürfe* (Berlin: Akademie Verlag, 2008), 53–61.
45. The fact that these bourgeois, acculturated Jewish women did not put an emphasis on their Jewishness corresponds to Muriel Pichon's analysis of France's Jewish population. She stresses that especially acculturated Jews did not primarily consider their military service as a means of proving their devotion to France but as their civic duty (see Pichon, *Les Français juifs*, 37–38, 43–44). Furthermore, these acculturated Jewish women did not suffer from antisemitic attacks as did, for instance, Jewish soldiers who were serving in colonial companies and the Foreign Legion or Jewish migrants living in Paris. In their correspondences, antisemitism therefore does not appear as a direct threat that they have to discuss with their partners. Direct questions about belonging or feeling excluded from society be-

cause of their Jewishness are rather absent from their letters and therefore mark blank spaces within their part of the correspondences.

46. Robert to Alice Hertz, 3 November 1914, Collège de France, Archives Laboratoire d'anthropologie sociale/Fonds Robert Hertz.
47. Alice to Robert Hertz, 14 November 1914, Collège de France, Archives Laboratoire d'anthropologie sociale/Fonds Robert Hertz.
48. Laure to Jules Isaac, 26 April 1917, Bibliothèque nationale de France, Archives et manuscrits NAF 28655 Fonds Jules Isaac, Correspondance échangée entre Jules et Laure Isaac, 1914–1918.

Bibliography

Bauer, Ingrid, and Christa Hämmerle, eds. *Liebe schreiben: Paarkorrespondenzen im Kontext des 19. und 20. Jahrhunderts*. Göttingen: Vandenhoeck & Ruprecht, 2017.
Becker, Annette. "De quelques historiens, sociologues et ethnologues juifs en Grande Guerre: Entre Sciences sociales, République, Union sacrée et barrésisme." *Archives juives* 36, no. 2 (2003): 68–85.
Becker, Jean-Jacques. *Comment les français sont entrés dans la guerre*. Paris: Les Presses de Sciences Po, 1977.
Bloch, Marc. *Écrits de guerre (1914–1918): Textes réunis et présentés par Étienne Bloch; Introduction par Stéphane Audoin-Rouzeau*. Paris: Armand Colin Masson, 1997.
Cazals, Rémy, and Frédéric Rousseau. *14–18: Le cri d'une génération*. Toulouse: Privat, 2003.
Cru, Jean Norton. *Témoins: Essai d'analyse et de critique des souvenirs de combattants édités en français de 1915 à 1928*. Paris: Eurédit, 2015, 1st edition 1929.
Didczuneit, Veit, Jens Ebert, and Thomas Jander, eds. *Schreiben im Krieg—Schreiben vom Krieg: Feldpost im Zeitalter der Weltkriege*. Essen: Klartext Verlag, 2011.
Durkheim, Émile. "Notice biographique sur Robert Hertz.—Le souvenir d'un des talents le plus confirmés de l'École française de sociologie, disparu tout jeune dans la Grande Guerre." In *Textes: 1. Éléments d'une théorie sociale; Présentation de Victor Karady*, edited by Émile Durkheim, 439–45. Paris: Éditions de Minuit, 1975.
Fournier, Marcel. *Émile Durkheim (1858–1917)*. Paris: Fayard, 2007.
Grayzel, Susan. "Mothers, Marraines, and Prostitutes: Morale and Morality in First World War France." *International History Review* 19, no. 1 (1997): 66–82.
———. *Women's Identities at War: Gender, Motherhood, and Politics in Britain and France during the First World War*. Chapel Hill: University of North Carolina Press, 1999.
Hämmerle, Christa. "'You Let a Weeping Woman Call You Home?': Private Correspondences during the First World War in Austria and Germany." In *Epistolary Selves: Letters and Letter-Writers, 1600–1945*, edited by Rebecca Earle, 152–82. Brookfield, VT: Ashgate, 1999.
———. "Entzweite Beziehungen? Zur Feldpost der beiden Weltkriege aus frauen- und geschlechtergeschichtlicher Perspektive." In *Schreiben im Krieg Schreiben vom Krieg: Feldpost im Zeitalter der Weltkriege*, edited by Veit Didczuneit, Jens Ebert, and Thomas Jander, 241–52. Essen: Klartext Verlag, 2011.
Hämmerle, Christa, and Edith Sauer, eds. *Briefkulturen und ihr Geschlecht: Zur Geschichte der privaten Korrespondenz vom 16. Jahrhundert bis heute*. L'Homme Schriften 7. Vienna: Böhlau, 2003.

Hanna, Martha. "A Republic of Letters: The Epistolary Tradition in France during World War I." *American Historical Review* 108, no. 5 (2003): 1338–61.

———. *Your Death Would Be Mine: Paul and Marie Pireaud in the Great War*. Cambridge, MA: Harvard University Press, 2008.

———. "War Letters: Communication between Front and Home Front." In *1914-1918-Online: International Encyclopedia of the First World War*, edited by Ute Daniel, Peter Gatrell, Oliver Janz, Heather Jones, Jennifer Keene, Alan Kramer, and Bill Nasson. Issued by Freie Universität Berlin, 10 October 2014. doi: 10.15463/ie1418.10362.

Hecht, Dieter. *Zwischen Feminismus und Zionismus: Anitta Müller-Cohen (1890–1962); Die Biographie einer Wiener Jüdin*. L'Homme Schriften 15. Vienna: Böhlau, 2008.

Hertz, Robert. "Contes et dictons recueillis sur le front, parmi les poilus de la Mayenne et d'ailleurs (1917)." In *Sociologie religieuse et folklore*, edited by Robert Hertz, 144–77. Paris: Les Presses universitaires de France, 1928.

Higonnet, Margaret R., and Patrice L.-R. Higonnet. "The Double Helix." In *Behind the Lines: Gender and the Two World Wars*, edited by Margaret R. Higonnet, Jane Jenson, Sonya Michel, and Margaret C. Weitz, 31–47. New Haven, CT: Yale University Press, 1987.

Horne, John. "Soldiers, Civilians and the Warfare of Attrition: Representations of Combat in France, 1914–1918." In *Authority, Identity and the Social History of the Great War*, edited by Frans Coetzee and Marilyn Shevin-Coetzee, 223–49. Providence, RI: Berghahn Books, 1995.

Housiel, Sylvie. *Dire la guerre: Le discours épistolaire des combattants français de 14–18*. Limoges: Lambert-Lucas, 2014.

Lyons, Martyn: *The Writing Culture of Ordinary People in Europe, 1860–1920*. New York: Cambridge University Press, 2013.

Isaac, Jules. *Un historien dans la Grande Guerre, Lettres et carnets 1914–1917, introduction par André Kaspi, présentation et notés par Marc Michel*. Paris: Armand Colin, 2004.

Kaspi, André. *Jules Isaac: Historien, acteur du rapprochement judéo-chrétien*. Paris: Plon, 2002.

Knoch, Peter. "Feldpost—eine unentdeckte historische Quellengattung." *Geschichtsdidaktik* 11 (1986): 154–71.

Lamprecht, Gerald. *Feldpost und Kriegserlebnis: Briefe als historisch-biographische Quelle*. Innsbruck: StudienVerlag, 2002.

Landau, Philippe. *Les Juifs de France et la Grande Guerre: Un patriotisme républicain 1914–1941*. Paris: CNRS Éditions, 1999.

———. "La communauté juive de France et la Grande Guerre." *Annales de démographie historique* 103, no. 1 (2002): 91–106.

Latzel, Klaus. "Vom Kriegserlebnis zur Kriegserfahrung: Theoretische und methodische Überlegungen zur erfahrungsgeschichtlichen Untersuchung von Feldpostbriefen." *Militärgeschichtliche Mitteilungen* 56, no. 1 (1997): 1–30.

Markova, Marta. "Alice Rühle-Gerstel und der geistige Aufstand europäischer Kulturschaffender gegen Krieg und Militarismus." In *Jüdische Publizistik und Literatur im Zeichen des Ersten Weltkriegs*, edited by Petra Ernst and Eleonore Lappin-Eppel, 233–46. Innsbruck: Studienverlag, 2016.

Mauss, Marcel. "Notice biographique: Alice Robert Hertz." In Robert Hertz, *Sociologie religieuse et folklore*. Paris: Librairie Félix Alcan, 1928.

Nattermann, Ruth. "Zwischen Pazifismus, Irredentismus und nationaler Euphorie: Italienische Jüdinnen und der Erste Weltkrieg." In *Jüdische Publizistik und Literatur im Zeichen des Ersten Weltkriegs*, edited by Petra Ernst and Eleonore Lappin-Eppel, 247–63. Innsbruck: Studienverlag, 2016.

———. "The Female Side of War: Experience and Memory of the Great War in Italian-Jewish Women's Ego documents." In *The Jewish Experience of the First World War*, edited by Edward Madigan and Gideon Reuveni, 233–54. New York: Palgrave Macmillan, 2018.

Nicot, Jean. *Les poilus ont la parole: Dans les tranchées: lettres du front 1917–1918*. Brussels: Éditions complexe, 1998.

Panter, Sarah. *Jüdische Erfahrungen und Loyalitätskonflikte im Ersten Weltkrieg*. Göttingen: Vandenhoeck & Ruprecht, 2014.

Parkin, Robert. *The Dark Side of Humanity: The Work of Robert Hertz and Its Legacy*. New York: Routledge, 2006.

Pichon, Muriel. *Les Français juifs 1914–1950: Récit d'un désenchantement*. Toulouse: Presses universitaires du Mirail, 2009.

Prévost, Marcel. "Pour Celles qui écrivent aux Soldats." *Le Petit Parisien*, 29 September 1917.

Riley, Alexander, and Philippe Besnard, eds. *Un ethnologue dans les tranchées, août 1914—avril 1915: Lettres de Robert Hertz à sa femme Alice*. Paris: CNRS Éditions, 2002.

Rozenblit, Marsha L. "For Fatherland and Jewish People: Jewish Women in Austria during World War I." In *Authority, Identity, and the Social History of the Great War*, edited by Frans Coetzee and Marilyn Shevin-Coetzee, 199–222. Providence, RI: Berghahn Books, 1995.

Rousseau, Frédéric. *La guerre censurée: Une histoire des combattants européens de 14-18*. Paris: Le Seuil, 1999.

Sieg, Ulrich. *Jüdische Intellektuelle im Ersten Weltkrieg: Kriegserfahrungen, weltanschauliche Debatten und kulturelle Neuentwürfe*. Berlin: Akademie Verlag, 2008.

Thébaud, Françoise. "La Grande Guerre: Le triomphe de la division sexuelle." In *Histoire des femmes en Occident*, edited by Georges Duby and Michelle Perrot, 31–74. Paris: Plon, 1992.

Ulrich, Bernd. *Die Augenzeugen: Deutsche Feldpostbriefe in Kriegs- und Nachkriegszeit 1914–1933*. Essen: Klartext, 1997.

Ulrich, Bernd, and Benjamin Ziemann. *German Soldiers in the Great War: Letters and Eyewitness Accounts*. Barnsley: Pen & Sword Military, 2010.

Vidal-Naquet, Clémentine. *Couples dans la Grande Guerre: Le tragique et l'ordinaire du lien conjugal*. Paris: Les Belles Lettres, 2014.

Wierling, Dorothee. *Eine Familie im Krieg: Leben, Sterben und Schreiben 1914–1918*. Göttingen: Wallstein Verlag, 2013.

———. "Imagining and Communicating Violence: The Correspondence of a Berlin Family, 1914–1918." In *Gender and the First World War*, edited by Christa Hämmerle, Oswald Überegger, and Birgitta Bader Zaar, 36–51. New York: Palgrave Macmillan, 2014.

Ziemann, Benjamin. *War Experiences in Rural Germany 1914–1923*. New York: Berg, 2007.

Section 6
WAR AND VIOLENCE

CHAPTER 14

"An Expression of Horror and Sadness"?
(Non)Communication of War Violence against Civilians in Ego Documents (Austria-Hungary)

Christa Hämmerle

It is well known that World War I was a "people's war" (*Volkskrieg*). The years of 1914–18 brought the catastrophic realization of a totalizing concept of "modern" warfare, which had arisen since the late eighteenth century, during the Revolutionary and Anti-Napoleonic Wars, and had become hegemonic in Europe during the late nineteenth century.[1] It was based on the principle of mobilizing the entire society: men had to follow universal conscription in the event of war as "citizen-soldiers," and women, children, and the elderly had to support such mass armies as much as they could as the "home front." This also meant, in the words of the historian John Horne, that "if the aim of mobilization is to involve the population as a whole, a similar aim must be assumed for the enemy, whose entire society then becomes a potential war target." Such a view also triggered the phenomenon that "a language of outright hostility flourished in the belligerent states, transforming the enemy into a Manichean barbarian to save the nation from whom only total commitment to the war effort was adequate."[2]

As a result of these developments, the distinction between soldiers and civilians was erased, and the civilian population also became a target of warfare—despite being protected by The Hague Convention of 1907, which foresaw and tried to avoid the events of World War I.[3] From the very beginning of this war, civilians had to experience many forms of violence to an extent hitherto unknown, ranging from rape to famishment, displacement, internment, the shooting or hanging of thousands of men and women, air raids, etc.[4] These realities of World War I—consequences of its disastrous character as a "laboratory of violence"[5]—insistently prove what gender historians have long argued and examined during the last two decades, both theoretically and empirically: society in World War I cannot be divided into two separated spheres of the front as an exclusively male-defined realm on the one hand and a predominantly female-connoted home (front) on the other. On the contrary, these spheres were entangled in many ways, as the war was waged everywhere.[6] This of course had various manifestations, as civilians also experienced the war differently, depending on, among other factors, where and how far away they lived from the combat areas. In the most extreme cases close to these vast regions, they suffered related forms of violence.

In her chapter in this volume, Nadia Maria Filippini describes this situation in depth for the Italian districts of Venetia and Friuli, which became war zones even before Italy entered the war.[7] Later this included, as Filippini also analyzes, many war atrocities against the local civilian population in the context of invasion and occupation. Unlike the historiographies of Italy, Belgium, or the Western Front, such developments in regard to the Austro-Hungarian army have been studied more closely only during the last years. The same is true for what happened in Serbia, Montenegro, and other regions of the Balkans as well as in occupied Russian areas, where officers and soldiers of the k. & k. Army or its often brutal and arbitrarily acting system of military justice also committed many war crimes against enemy civilians.[8] Besides, whole regions of the vast Habsburg Monarchy itself—above all Galicia, Bukovina, and the area around Trieste, Gorizia, and the Isonzo River—remained devastated after military operations and changes in the occupying regimes during the war.[9] There and elsewhere in the rear of the moving fronts/mobile warfare, the "own" civilian population—if not on the run or evacuated[10]—was subjected to harsh military control and the dictate of the drumhead courts martial, which—in the words of the photo historian Arno Holzer—"can be rightly referred to as a systematic war against the civilian population."[11] This also resulted in persecution and excesses of violence, even to the extent of mass executions of members of the own side's local population, which in these regions often consisted of ethnic or religious minorities. Therefore, the k. & k. Army was responsible for frequent transgressions of war norms and even for atrocities against parts of its own people, which had become an "inner enemy" due to resentments and suspicion of espionage or collaboration with the hostile Russians, Serbs, and Italians.[12]

On the whole, lots of different people populated these areas: military of all sorts, people working for the military, relatives such as officer wives, as well as the large staff of different forms of battlefield hospitals and thousands of wounded or ill soldiers including POWs, as well as many civilians fleeing advancing or retreating troops, etc. Often, all of them were under threat due to artillery bombing or air raids that became increasingly frequent the longer the war lasted. We therefore have to conceptualize the regions behind the moving front lines, generally referred to as the rear area, as theaters of war where modern warfare with its integration of and menace to the civilian population in general, and women and children in particular, became most obvious, most dramatic during World War I—however, having said that, civilians in the so-called hinterland were also threatened by war violence.[13]

In what follows, I will focus on these areas of mobile warfare and investigate traces of various forms of war-related violence against civilians in ego documents, which have hitherto been largely ignored by Austrian historiography.[14] Some of these autobiographic texts have survived in family archives or institutionalized collections;[15] some, although not many, were published or self-published. Do these primary sources tell us anything about the excesses of violence against civilians during World War I, be it at the hands of their own or enemy troops? Was this topic, as Arno Holzer has argued based on only some isolated examples written by combatants,[16] indeed communicable to a broader extent, and if so, which words, in which ways, related to which events? Are established enemy stereotypes to be found in the ego documents? Do they show signs of patriotism and nationalism, the official discourse suggesting that the own troops waged a "clean" and defensive war, whereas it was the enemy that committed atrocities against civilians? And are there differences between various forms of ego documents—war correspondences on the one hand and war diaries or diary-like texts on the other? What can we learn from such a comparison related to genre definitions and the much-disputed question of truth content of ego documents?

It is obviously extremely difficult to answer these questions based on contemporary ego documents written by civilians who were massively affected by war-related violence themselves, as they had to flee or were interned, bombed, raped, etc. Such sources, or protocols with reports from the victims themselves, which Nadia Fillipini was able to investigate for the Italian case,[17] could not be taken into account here—though that does not mean that the public had no knowledge of them. On the contrary, the Austrian Reichsrat (Imperial Assembly) controversially discussed these topics after its establishment in May 1917 and in the course of the postwar Kommission zur Erhebung militärischer Pflichtverletzungen (Committee for the Inquiry into the Violation of Military Duty) from late 1918 to 1922.[18] As often in history, the victims had no voice, or if they did, their voices were hardly heard, hardly communicated.[19] Against this background, I began to search for traces of acts of violence against civilians in various ego documents I have read during the last years from different thematic angles. This source material consists, firstly, of a comprehensive sample of couple correspondences that I have also examined in the context of a research project funded by the Austrian Science Funds for a study on

"Violence and Love—Entangled," focusing on World Wars I and II.[20] Secondly, I will also examine some diaries or diary-like texts that, in contrast to letters, were not subject to institutionalized censorship, although war propaganda tried to instrumentalize this kind of private writing as well.[21] Such sources are still quite rare in the Austro-Hungarian context, at least in regard to examples written by noncombatants who were stationed behind the battlefronts. Therefore, my analysis will include some remarkable texts that originate from war diaries of nurses or assistance nurses. In most cases, these accounts have been self-published in the years after the war. They are organized in a diary-like fashion; therefore, we can define them as hybrids, fluctuating between the diary form and the memoir form.

The Language of War Correspondences

Let us turn first to war correspondences. As early research on this dialogically structured source material has established, this type of correspondence mostly followed the conventional rules of masking the physical, often killing- and war-related violence among soldiers and, even more so, against civilians. For the combatants, and much cited until today, Isa Schikorsky has described this tendency by defining five "maxims of conversation," namely "concealment," "belittlement," "poetization," the "use of phrases" ("Phraseologisierung"), and "image cultivation" ("Imagepflege"). According to Schikorsky, the horrors of war were more or less "indescribable."[22] Later, more micro-level studies have added that this "indescribability" was primarily due to the main functions of war correspondences: the need to bridge war-related separation, to continue private relations and a dialogue between families, couples, and relatives. This strengthened the tendency of maintaining the normality of everyday life despite the situation of war. Therefore, many war letters—and couple correspondences in particular—indeed prioritized such topics over the description of war-related violence, all the more so since many soldiers tended to adopt the hegemonic ideal of militarized masculinity, including heroism, patriotism, officially propagated views on the war, and enemy stereotypes. Women at home, on the other hand, were also confronted with gendered propaganda that urged them not to erode the combatants' morale, and thus to send them only positive letters.[23]

Despite certain ambivalences and some undermining countertendencies that will be discussed later, it is easy to imagine that this situation, together with censorship, primarily resulted in violence-concealing war correspondences—at least if we look at the most frequently surviving war letters and cards from bourgeois strata.[24] Women in the hinterland, as the main addressees of these writings, followed similar discursive patterns in their replies, all the more so as their only other sources on what happened during the advancement or retreat of troops or on the battlefields and in the occupied areas were usually censured newspapers of the home front, which they frequently read. Often, the reports of the male partners from the theaters of war did not include much more than these official communiqués, as the fiancée of the reserve officer Leopold Wolf, who served as an artillerist of a mortar unit from the very beginning of the war, once explicitly wrote. In his correspondence about his participation in conquering Belgium in summer 1914, and from the rear area of the Eastern and later the Southern Front, Leopold only very rarely addressed the topics of real danger, war destruction, or violence. Besides, and probably also due to censorship, he hardly mentioned precise locations where this could have or had happened; his short references on war violence indeed followed the abovementioned narrative strategies.[25] Or he simply told his fiancée, Christl Lang, to get the relevant information from the newspapers. In a letter from December 1916, when he was involved in the Isonzo battles, she answered him: "Dear Olly [for Leopold, C. H]. You referred me to the papers, but they don't say much. As long as the offensive lasted, one could read quite often about the southern wing of the Karst plateau, but now they always say 'situation/position unchanged, nothing new.' That's all. . . . I think that you have moved around quite a bit since you've been down there, haven't you? I assume that you are now close to Sistiana, . . . approximately."[26]

It is not surprising that civilians threatened by military operations were hardly ever mentioned in this correspondence. This applies to both fellow and enemy nationals. It is as if they had never been where Leopold Wolf was, apart from one or two hints such as: "Even the otherwise intimidated civilians have the courage to come out and go to church, festively dressed and in endless groups."[27] Two further examples demonstrate how the officers' wives at the home front responded in this respect. In general, they tended to use rather empty phrases, like Lilly Weber, whose husband had, most probably, never raised the subject during his war deployment in occupied Serbia, where the troops of the Habsburg Monarchy committed many war crimes against civilians who lived in these areas. This is also true for October and November 1915, when Serbia was finally conquered by the Austro-Hungarian and the German armies. Without considering what this could mean for the enemy civilians, Lilly Weber wrote to Friedrich Weber from Vienna that "the situation is favorable for us in Serbia, so you will surely come back soon."[28] And in November 1917, just after the Italian defeat of Caporetto that caused a disaster for the civilian population of the newly occupied Italian regions,[29] another woman from an Austrian provincial capital hoped, "What do you think, [Alfred], will the colossal victories in the South bring peace closer?"[30]

We do not know if this topic would have been expressed differently from the perspective of immediate danger. The inhabitants of Austrian cities in the hinterland suffered from hunger and the disastrous shortage of nearly everything from 1916 at the latest,[31] but they were not threatened by direct artillery bombing or air raids. To be sure, people were fully aware that this happened elsewhere and that they could potentially face a similar situation. Some of them, such as Anna and Alfred Ertl, mentioned concerns along these lines in their correspondence. Alfred, who was positioned in Italy, often witnessed air bombings, and he discussed these experiences in his letters. He reassured his wife, "If airplanes really came to G., the region where we live would be completely safe, no military building. Thus, don't be afraid!"[32]

Like Anna Ertl and her children, millions of civilians in the Habsburg Monarchy faced a different menace. From 1916 at the latest, they suffered from the already mentioned disastrous lack of food and commodities, which above all affected Vienna and other Austrian cities as well as industrial regions. Many soldiers knew about this situation from reports of their relatives or their furlough. If possible, therefore, they dispatched large quantities of parcels, be it from Romania, Ukraine, Northern Italy, or other occupied regions.[33] To help their beloved ones they sent home cheaply purchased or plundered foodstuff and goods, which caused dramatic shortages for the enemy population. Once again, these repercussions were not mentioned at all in the letters, apart from very rare exceptions. Alfred Ertl, for instance, sent home whatever he could in 1917 and 1918, despite his wealthy background. It added up to huge amounts of different items, all the more because Ertl moved around in the rear area of the Austro-Italian front lines. I quote one example, which again refers to the situation of the Austrian army in Italy after Caporetto: "Today, I have again prepared a parcel . . ., it contains not even half of what I bought. . . . We had another very pleasant surprise today, as the officers of the command received some gifts: 1 Italian winter blouse, 1 summer blouse, 1 pair of summer trousers . . ., 2 bed linen, 1 padded headrest and 15 sandbags. . . . All from Italian loot."[34]

But despite such contents, the war correspondence between Alfred and Anna Ertl also contains counternarratives. Isa Schikorsky and other researchers have long overlooked such antagonistic tendencies, which have become clearer only through recent micro-level studies. These ambivalences have been proved mainly for the Western Front and France, where ample scholarship exists on various genres of ego documents of World War I in general and war correspondences in particular. In many cases, the latter also include the mentioning of violence, as John Horne, Martha Hanna, and others have shown.[35] Their studies also investigate ambivalences, or rather an inherent tension between coded and decoded experiences of violence. According to these findings, ego documents of World War I should be seen as the continual attempt to cope with societal or discursive taboos, with the rule of patriotism and nationalism and related stereotypes of the enemy on the one hand and military or self-censorship as well as concepts of militarized masculinity and womanhood on the other. Without doubt, these aspects shaped the language of contemporaries to a very large extent, as we have seen. But—and this is important—all these discursive offers for making sense of the catastrophe of war could also fail or clash with the wish to write truly, at least to some extent, about what happened, and this occurred more frequently the longer the war lasted.[36] This is mostly true for battlefield violence and related dying or killing,[37] which so many soldiers had to suffer on a regular basis. In certain situations, they broke their silence and stopped masking such horrors, mostly before offensives or after days of continual threat and destruction.

In some cases, such a tendency toward openness also occurred in regard to observed war violence against civilians—although this happened only very rarely in the war letters I have read and examined. The example of Alfred and Anna Ertl is, therefore, exceptional, as they even communicated about war violence against civilians, which is only one topic among many others in their hundreds of letters, such as—above all—love, longing, sorrow, and illness, the upbringing of their children, their material situation, etc. In late July 1917, for instance, Alfred described the enemy aircrafts as "even quite beautiful" when they "withdraw calmly in a high altitude."[38] Only a few days later, he experienced heavy bombardment at close range around Cepovan. He then wrote a letter to his wife to assure her that he was no longer in danger, as his division would be transferred "from the battle zone to the well-deserved reserve" in the following days. Then he described frankly what had happened not only to soldiers, but also to some civilians:

> In this moment, the aircrafts already began their horrible work and a bomb was falling; the whole house shook in its foundations, we ran out of the door, to a door downstairs leading into an arched tavern, where we were relatively safe, and waited there, helplessly, for the bombing to end; these were indeed uncomfortable moments, without the possibility of doing anything; bombs hitting the ground, explosions, the poor women screaming,—war is something horrible. There have certainly been 30 bombs, 2 houses burnt down, a one year old child burnt. . . .[39]

And a few months later, when the Habsburg Army devastated the Italian regions behind Caporetto, Alfred Ertl "moved to places of the most terrible battles in the Karst area." His wife, Anna, answered him, driven by her wish to be always with him: "My dear! . . . I am with you amidst rubble and ruins, amidst the relicts of prospering life, I see how you arduously search for accommodation, and I see in your beloved eyes the expression of horror and sadness."[40]

This example is very instructive. It makes us expect other similar cases of such a communication between front and home front for the Austrian context—a communication that did not only mask war-related experiences of violence in various forms—although this tendency seems to have clearly dominated and supported the hegemonic interpretation that war was only fought between male soldiers, male armies. If further research takes both aspects into consideration—that is, the masking of war violence against civilians as well as more openly expressed or even empathic descriptions that might occur simultaneously—we will probably better understand why the latter did not have a long-lasting and decisive impact. As it seems, this has much to do with the genre of war correspondences. On the one hand, war letters were written in an atmosphere dominated by censorship, publicly propagated patriotism, nationalism, and enemy stereotypes. On the other hand, they aimed to create a comprehensible communication, normality, and intimacy. Apparently, this could only be achieved by masking the most troubling and shocking experiences of war.

Diaristic War Accounts

What can be said about diaries or diary-like accounts that in most cases had no actual addressee and were therefore not subject to censorship? Did they contain more glimpses of the real war drama, also in regard to the topic of this chapter, even though they were nevertheless often motivated by propaganda or meant as patriotic accounts of the war experience? What follows can offer only some preliminary observations by underlining the need for further research on this topic. In this respect, we should, as the following examples suggest, not only rely on officers' diaries, which are more likely to have survived and been passed on and which according to my experience do not reveal much about the war against civilians, but also concentrate on other accounts. Some of them have been published only recently. I will argue that these diaristic texts can in fact contrast main narratives of war correspondences to a certain degree—although they also mask war violence or adopt official or hegemonic discourses on this topic at the same time.

Let us first look at an example written by a combatant, the diary of Hans Haugeneder, which was published in 2010. This one-year volunteer was enlisted in the Seventieth Infantry Regiment and kept notes from June 1916 until July 1918. He first participated in the campaign against Russia in the course of the Brusilov Offensive, then came to the Romanian battlefront in early 1917 and later that year engaged in the Eleventh and

Twelfth Isonzo Battles. Haugeneder then witnessed the advance of the k. & k. troops to the Piave River, where he fell ill and was sent back to a field hospital. At the end of 1917, he was promoted to second lieutenant of the reserve before he was redeployed, which brought him to Szegedin, Zagreb, Carinthia, etc.[41] His war diary is written in an often pathetic, florid style, full of metaphors, and contains vivid descriptions of what he observed and experienced. Most of the time, the events are described without judgment or empathy, as the following passages from 11 and 12 August 1916, when the k. & k. Army was winning ground against the Russians, demonstrate: "Nesterovce, the former residence of the regimental staff, with its marvelous gardens, was hit by fire grenades that torched everything in a blink of an eye. Machine gun bullets relentlessly hit scads of soldiers, civilians, and cattle, bring thousandfold death accompanied by the terrible weeping and screaming of the victims."[42] And the next day, now in Kudenovce, Haugender wrote, "An unforgettable sight met my eye. Eerily beautiful fireworks of burning villages and bridges in the wider vicinity, in addition the enormous detonations from the ammunitions dumps and the quarries which were blown up at the last moment. The day awakes in blood-red firelight."[43]

It was only after the extensively described Twelfth Isonzo Battle, in the course of the advance through northern Italy toward the Piave River, that this soldier—who clearly interpreted the events of these dramatic days as rightful "revenge"[44] and "great retaliatory strike"[45] against the "traitor country"[46]—also mentioned some acts of violence against civilians more explicitly. Those accounts were juxtaposed with haunting depictions of the soldiers' "dehumanized face-to-face fighting and murdering,"[47] including vivid descriptions of the fatal consequences of gas attacks, exploding shells, mines, etc. Also, Haugeneder noted lootings and related activities, characterizing them as "a hearty refreshment with cheese, beer, meat, and wine from the enemy supplies,"[48] and, by using the following euphemism: "But the prosaic stomachs of the victors care little about the poetic landscape and swaying palm trees, their hearts and minds are completely at all those crawling and flying mammals, at Capitoline geese, irredentist chicken, posh aristocratic peacocks . . ."[49] And he continues: "A new life joyfully pulsates through the veins, laughing human faces again; drums drumming and pipes piping: these two cronies that have been burnt a long time ago have joined us again as good comrades. . . ."[50]

But there are still rare glimpses of criticism of what happened that sometimes burst forth through the otherwise dominant view of war as a natural condition of mankind:

> Night quarters in the castle of the Duke of Aosta in Soleschiano. The finest undergarments, clothes, tools, and objects of arts lie around everywhere in large quan-

tities and fall into the hands of our troops, who are unfortunately often up to mischief and senseless activities. . . .

Lestizzo [Lestizza, C. H.] and Flambro look terrible. Horrible scenes took place there. The restlessly fleeing remnants of the second Italian army, together with the civilian population of these two villages, put up a fight. But the unstoppable and fast advance of the pursuers swept over them, brought bloody death to their lines, and randomly smashed them to the ground, in and near streets, in ditches, in alleys and corners. Now, there are endless rows of fully packed baggage train wagons everywhere with uniforms, weapons, kitchenware and food, long-necked cannons of all calibers, and hundreds of dead horses in jumbled piles. A cruel judgment![51]

It is only recently that I came across another edited war diary written by a man, which is very rich in content regarding our topic. It is from a noncombatant, the field chaplain Karl Gögele from South Tyrol, who from August 1914 onward was responsible for the Hospital No. 4 of the German Order, which was stationed "behind the fronts of Galicia" as part of the Fourth Army.[52] Until September 1915, this hospital and its ten cleric nurses Gögele supervised were often moving around, similar to many other parts of the heterogeneous field sanitary apparatus, troops moving backward, military administrative units, and many civilians. In so doing, they all had to cope with the consequences of mobile warfare in this hard-fought Eastern theater of war, as entire cities and regions were occupied, first by the Russians, then the Allied Powers, and vice versa several times over. Despite their enormous losses and defensive operations after the so-called breakthrough near Gorlice and Tarnów in May 1915, the Allied Powers were able to occupy some Russian areas for longer periods, which to some degree outlasted the Russian Brusilov Offensive of mid-1916.[53] Therefore, Gögele and "his" field hospital came to Kovel in Russian Poland (Volhynia), where they stayed for more than two years until March 1918, when they were recalled to Pordenone in Italy. In Galicia and Kovel, they not only were responsible for hundreds of soldiers but also looked after ill or wounded hospitalized prisoners of war and civilians—many of them Jewish. Often, they were billeted in the homes of the local population, which created a closer contact. All this is also documented in the hundreds of photos Karl Gögele took throughout the war.

As expected, these extraordinary records contain much about the civilian population in the Galician and Russian war regions where Gögele was stationed. Many a time, he mentions, for example, their escape and evacuations, such as at the beginning of September 1914 near Rawa-Ruska, where he observed not only "military trains, full of soldiers who cheerfully went into battle" but also many "lines of refugees, stricken by misery and hardship, carrying all sorts of trash and junk, with grief-stricken mothers and screaming children and nosy girls."[54] Subsequently, Gögele extensively described his experiences with the Jewish population of this region, the so-called "Ostjuden," or, more precisely, his views on these people, which were mainly along the lines of contemporary antisemitism. And when he mentions the "enemy troops," they are sometimes described as soldiers raping innocent people and torching entire villages, as in the first half of October 1914 when he and the hospital of the German Order came through Rzeszow: "We were told that the Russians occupied [the town, C. H.] for 16 days. At their arrival they gave a banquet for the officers in the city hall and immediately started to make themselves at home. The Cossacks are said to have stolen and robbed many valuables and watches, whereas the rest of the troops at least paid a bit, albeit not the asking price. Several of those who laid ill in the hospital also witnessed that girls have been raped. Many citizens kept their daughters locked at home during the whole time of the occupation."[55] On the other hand, his depictions of the Russian POWs in "his" hospital do not contain common enemy stereotypes but follow the dominant neutral and factual style of his accounts.

The topic of the Russian enemy torching or destroying entire villages occurs again in a later passage of these remarkable war accounts, which also describes that many civilians became direct victims of warfare, having been killed by bombs or bullets when too close to the firing lines. For Beszczyna in the south of Austro-Galician Bochnia, this is reported in 1915: "But how the nice Beszczyna looked! Most of the houses were shot and burnt. . . . Unfortunately, not all the people had fled and several lost their lives. We were told that a mother with her child in her arms left her hiding place for a moment. That same moment the child was hit by a bullet and died. There was still debris in the fields from the fighting everywhere."[56]

Last but not least, Karl Gögele also reported the execution of civilians. In the first volume of his diaries, this is mentioned only very rarely,[57] but it becomes a frequent topic in the second part, which is mainly about his time in occupied Kovel, where such executions happened on a regular basis.[58] As a military chaplain, it was one of Gögele's responsibilities to accompany these people to their deaths—provided they were Catholics.[59] As his diary shows, he was convinced that they were enemy civilians who had worked as spies or against the occupation, or were thieves, etc. His convictions against supposed "inner enemies," however, remained vague, if referred to at all. Gögele described all this without critical reflection or expressions of empathy; for him, executing civilians seems to have been a natural consequence of war, and as such indisputable.

But this matter-of-course tone that clearly dominates other Austrian war diaries as well can occasionally also turn into more ambivalent narratives. Such a tendency becomes visible in a sample of diary-like texts which were written by former war nurses who did "frontline nursing" for longer periods,[60] and who therefore witnessed how civilians were affected by the war in many ways in the areas directly behind the front lines. Admittedly, these women, who in former Austria mostly served for the Red Cross or the Maltese Order and were subjected to military law, identified themselves with the aims and the enemy stereotypes of their respective warring nations to a certain degree—but not completely, as I have analyzed in detail elsewhere.[61] Let us therefore focus here on the fact that we can also find criticism in nurses' diary-based war accounts, or even harsh accusations, not least in relation to our topic. In the words of Agathe Fessler, who served at several places in Galicia for a long time from October 1914 onward, this tendency reads as such:

> Then the deportation of the civilian population from the outskirts of Cracow began. We had to give out bread and black coffee to these poor people who were sitting in the trains passing through. Deeply sad scenes unfolded here: . . . How many children got lost in the indescribable turmoil. . . . An old, fragile woman could not get a place in any of the trains. She was sitting on the ground with tears frozen on her cheeks, because it was bitterly cold. . . . It was a horrible time. . . .[62]

Another example is R. M. Konrad, who decided to move toward the battlefronts in late 1915, because she, in her own words, "wanted to directly participate in caring for the wounded in the field," to "search" for them immediately "after the battle," and to "apply the first emergency dressing." She remembered in detail, for instance, how the surgery in Ljubljana, where she worked in December of the same year, was "bombed" and became "a heap of rubble." This was a life-threatening situation for the nurses, and some people were even killed.[63] In her diary, which she had bought before leaving the hinterland in order to note "little war episodes"[64] and which most evidently served as the primary text source of her self-published war accounts, this Red Cross nurse also jotted down other similar events.

Agathe Fessler and R. M. Konrad, like some other war nurses, could only self-publish their diary-like texts after the end of the war. My last example comes from Eveline Hrouda, who in contrast succeeded in finding a publishing house for her war account—which was an absolute exception in postwar Austria. The publication of her book *Barmherzigkeit: Als freiwillige Malteserschwester im Ersten Weltkrieg* (Compassion: A Voluntary Maltese Nurse in the Great War) is probably due to the fact that at this time, in 1935, the Austro-Fascists had already abolished the first Austrian Republic and replaced it with the "Corporate State" (*Ständestaat*). Austro-Fascism supported an extensive remilitarization and heroization of the war experience and remembrance; in this revisionist context, even nurses were sometimes included in the construction of the alleged "front community."[65] Eveline Hrouda's diary-like war account in many ways adopts such narratives, underlines contemporary patriotism, and points out the alleged necessity to serve the warring fatherland as far as possible—but again, this is not the whole story. The counternarratives to this tendency culminate in her depictions of the events after the Italian defeat at Caporetto in the Twelfth Isonzo Battle, for example in the region of Udine, where Hrouda—by this time completely exhausted—was stationed in November 1917. She wrote, for example, about looting Austro-Hungarian soldiers: "So many valuables were destroyed, it beggars all description. The soldiers looted and acted like vandals. They vandalized pictures, mirrors, and everything else; if a door was locked, they just broke it open, and if a lock resisted—a blow of an axe or a butt opened the chest or the shelf, and if firewood was needed—there was enough furniture. . . . Udine is a beautiful town, where they wreaked havoc."[66] After these events, Eveline Hrouda remained stationed in occupied Italy, where "her" field hospital was also responsible for Italian civilians, which she remembered not without empathy, as it seems: "At the beginning of May [1918], they brought us an Italian woman, who was badly wounded because of shell shooting which had injured both legs. The poor woman had to undergo an emergency surgery, although she was pregnant. A few days after she had luckily survived the operation . . ., she gave birth to a weak child, but this premature infant, our candidate for baptism, lived only for a few days."[67]

Conclusion

How to summarize all these findings of (non)communication of violence against civilians in a quite heterogeneous sample of ego documents of World War I? Is it worthwhile to deepen research by further expanding the corpus of such texts? Or does this source material offer no relevant insights at all, as it largely follows given discursive patterns, which were saturated with elements of nationalist war perceptions or war propaganda?

Altogether, the ego documents of World War I presented above seem to confirm that—even for women who worked as noncombatants in war zones—war violence against civilians was a topic characterized by a silence that was culturally rooted and by euphemisms, mere hints, and short sentences, or was altogether tabooed instead of being comprehensively and openly elaborated. But some references to these events, which run counter to the tendency of masking the topic, do in fact exist, as we have seen. They are, however, all in all exceptional, given the current state of research and the existing available ego documents I have read during the last years.

It has also become obvious that we cannot use this source material as a reservoir of facts—needless to say, this applies to ego documents in general. The narratives of these texts often omitted the fact that World War I had also been waged against civilians, which holds true both for war correspondences and for diaries or diary-like war accounts. This becomes most evident in regard to all acts of sexual or sexualized violence against women, from the forced medical examinations of women suspected of prostitution to the dramatic extent of (mass) rapes—which indeed occurred a thousand times over on all sides of the conflict. If at all, such rapes were only mentioned as having been committed by the enemy and never by the home armies or soldiers. This in the end followed the subtext of contemporary war propaganda that ascribed brutish, ferocious, and primitive behavior to the enemy.[68]

Without doubt, these tendencies were also the result of long-standing enemy stereotypes and the powerful "male" myth that war was fought to protect the fatherland and its "womenandchildren"[69]—a term coined by Cynthia Enloe. Written as one word, it indicates the stereotypical use of such a justification of war. During World War I, this myth had lost its credibility. The reality, however, if realized at all, seemed to have been rather inexpressible, or at least noncommunicable, and only mentioned in private diaries or diary-like war accounts. Whereas in war correspondences empathy for women and children who were affected or even killed in the course of hostile actions is expressed very rarely, these diaristic texts do refer to such events more often—albeit mostly in the form of single phrases or a few sentences and predominantly without any moral judgment, that is, in a matter-of-course tone and justified by the situation of war. In the sources examined here, only a few remarks addressed executions of the civilian population or criticized soldiers of the home army who looted the occupied territories. These dispersed hints can easily be overlooked or sink into oblivion again, but they are valuable source material for historians.

In my interpretation, the ambivalences I have described point to what is expressible in various forms of ego documents and what is not, and how nondisclosure relies on authorship, time, and context of writing. They also prove the difficulties in finding a coherent language for the war experiences of 1914–18, as given discursive sense-making practices were often not adequate. For some of the writers I have introduced, war-related confusion, fear, or shock may have resulted in adopting the public war discourse to an even higher degree, whereas others—primarily, but not exclusively, noncombatants and women who had no public voice—tried to find a different language, at least to some extent, and included counternarratives in their depictions. However, these discursive struggles in war diaries and diary-like compilations had no lasting resonance as it seems, since they remained private also in the postwar era, when such texts were not published or could only be self-published, and therefore had no impact on the public memory at all. The new First Austrian Republic only saw a short period of pacifism, harsh war criticism, and accusations against those who were held responsible for the catastrophe, the war atrocities, and the army's violations of war norms. This became clear in the course of sessions of the abovementioned Committee for the Inquiry into the Violation of Military Duty, established in December 1918 and dissolved in February 1922. Only very few of the 484 cases investigated resulted in a conviction.[70] In parallel and after the political influence of the Social Democrats, who saw themselves as advocates for the victims of war, diminished rapidly, yet another shift in the language of noncommunication of war-related violence in public discourse occurred: it was silenced again.

This was all the more the case as former officers gradually monopolized the historiography of World War I, and, as a result, the hegemonic culture of war remembrance became increasingly revisionist by glorifying the defeated Habsburg Army and by reestablishing the figure of the soldier-hero. At the same time, society underwent a process of remilitarization and remasculinization, a topic that is well researched.[71] It also triggered the tendency that "own" civilian victims were forgotten or not mentioned at all, which—as we have seen—happened already in many ways during the war. In the Austrian context after 1918, the fact that these victims predominantly belonged to non-German ethnicities or were—often Jewish—refugees from "mixed" areas of the Habsburg Monarchy that no longer belonged to the new Austrian state underpinned this development. During the 1920s, it culminated in completely tabooing this dimension of modern warfare in the context of war remembrance, apart from the realm of fictional literature and very rare examples.

Christa Hämmerle is professor of modern history and women's and gender history at the University of Vienna. She is cofounder and coeditor of *L'Homme: Europäische Zeitschrift für Feministische Geschichtswissenschaft* and chair of the Sammlung Frauennachlässe (collection of women's personal papers). Among her fields of research are gender and war (especially World War I, the Austro-Hungarian military from 1868 to 1914), the history of auto/biographical writings, and the history of love. Among her latest publications are *Heimat/Front: Geschlechtergeschichte/n des Ersten Weltkriegs in Österreich-Ungarn* (Vienna: Böhlau 2014); "1914/18—Revisited," special issue, *L'Homme Z.F.G.* 29, no. 2 (2018), edited with Ingrid Sharp and Heidrun Zettelbauer.

Notes

1. Cf., for example, Karen Hagemann, *"Mannlicher Muth und Teutsche Ehre": Nation, Militär und Geschlecht zur Zeit der Antinapoleonischen Kriege Preußens* (Paderborn: Ferdinand Schöningh, 2000); Karen Hagemann, *Revisiting Prussia's Wars*

against Napoleon: History, Culture and Memory (Cambridge: Cambridge University Press, 2015); Stig Förster and Jörg Nagler, eds., *On the Road to Total War: The American Civil War and the German Wars of Unification, 1861–1871* (Cambridge: Cambridge University Press, 1997).
2. John Horne, "Civilian Populations and Wartime Violence: Towards an Historical Analysis," *International Social Science Journal* 174 (2002): 484.
3. Cf., for example, the early work of Jost Dülffer, *Regeln gegen den Krieg? Die Haager Friedenskonferenzen 1899 und 1907 in der internationalen Politik* (Berlin: Ullstein, 1981).
4. Cf., for example, the summary of Stéphane Audoin-Rouzeau and Annette Becker, *14–18: Understanding the Great War*, trans. from the French by Catherine Temerson (New York: Hill and Wang, 2000), 45–69, for all belligerent countries.
5. See Benjamin Ziemann, *Gewalt im Ersten Weltkrieg: Töten—Überleben—Verweigern* (Essen: Klartext Verlag, 2013), esp. 7–21.
6. Cf., for example, Susan Grayzel, *Women and the First World War* (New York: Pearson Education, 2002); Christa Hämmerle, *Heimat/Front: Geschlechtergeschichte/n des Ersten Weltkriegs in Österreich-Ungarn* (Vienna: Böhlau, 2013).
7. See Nadia Maria Filippini, "Hunger, Rape, Escape: The Many Aspects of Violence against Women and Children in the Territories of the Italian Front," in this volume.
8. The earliest important articles on these topics are from Hans Hautmann, for example: "Kriegsgesetze und Militärjustiz in der österreichischen Reichshälfte 1914–1918," in *Justiz und Zeitgeschichte: Symposiumsbeiträge 1976–1993*, ed. Erika Weinzierl, Oliver Rathkolb, Rudolf G. Ardelt, and Siegfried Mattl (Vienna: Jugend & Volk, 1995), 73–85; "Zum Sozialprofil der Militärrichter im Ersten Weltkrieg," in *Richter und Gesellschaftspolitik: Symposion Justiz und Zeitgeschichte, 12. und 13. Oktober 1995 in Wien*, ed. Erika Weinzierl, Oliver Rathkolb, Siegfried Mattl, and Rudolf G. Ardelt (Innsbruck: Studien-Verlag, 1997), 21–29; "Die österreichisch-ungarische Armee auf dem Balkan," in *Kriegsverbrechen in Europa und im Nahen Osten im 20. Jahrhundert*, ed. Franz W. Seidler and Alfred M. de Zayas (Hamburg: Mittler & Sohn, 2002), 36–41. See also Jonathan E. Gumz, *The Resurrection and Collapse of Empire in Habsburg Serbia, 1914–1918* (Cambridge: Cambridge University Press, 2009); Anton Holzer, *Das Lächeln der Henker: Der unbekannte Krieg gegen die Zivilbevölkerung 1914–1918* (Darmstadt: Primus, 2008); Hannes Leidinger, Verena Moritz, Karin Moser, and Wolfram Dornik, *Habsburgs schmutziger Krieg: Ermittlungen zur österreichisch-ungarischen Kriegsführung 1914–1918* (St. Pölten: Residenz Verlag, 2014); Oswald Überegger, "'Verbrannte Erde' und 'baumelnde Gehenkte': Zur europäischen Dimension militärischer Normübertretungen im Ersten Weltkrieg," in *Kriegsgreuel: Die Entgrenzung der Gewalt in kriegerischen Konflikten vom Mittelalter bis ins 20. Jahrhundert*, ed. Sönke Neitzel and Daniel Hohrath (Paderborn: Ferdinand Schöningh, 2008), 241–78; Jochen Böhler, Włodzimierz Borodziej, and Joachim von Puttkamer, eds., *Legacies of Violence: Eastern Europe's First World War* (Munich: De Gruyter Oldenbourg, 2014).
9. Cf., for example, Mark von Hagen, *War in a European Borderland: Occupations and Occupation Plans in Galicia and Ukraine, 1914–1918* (Seattle: University of Washington Press, 2007); Hermann J. W. Kuprian, and Oswald Überegger, eds., *Katastrophenjahre: Der Erste Weltkrieg und Tirol* (Innsbruck: Universitätsverlag Wagner, 2014).

10. According to estimates, for example, more than two hundred thousand mostly Jewish refugees came to Vienna alone in winter 1914–15; others came from areas behind the Italian front, etc.
11. Holzer, *Lächeln*, 19. All German quotes are translated by the author of this chapter. Many thanks to Christine Brocks, Sheffield, for her revisions.
12. This primarily, albeit not solely, affected the Jewish, Polish, and Ruthenian populations of Bukovina and Galicia.
13. We do not know how many civilian fatalities Austria-Hungary suffered. Estimates put the figure at four hundred thousand; the real extent, however, is probably much higher.
14. The German term *populare Autobiographik*, coined by Bernd Jürgen Warneken in 1985, refers to research on various forms of ego documents written by less-educated people who were not part of the elites; see Bernd Jürgen Warneken, *Populare Autobiographik: Empirische Studien zu einer Quellengattung der Alltagsgeschichtsforschung* (Tübingen: Tübinger Vereinigung für Volkskunde 1985).
15. The majority of these sources are collected in the Sammlung Frauennachlässe (Collection of Women's Personal Papers, hereafter cited as SFN) of the Department of History, University of Vienna; see http://www.univie.ac.at/Geschichte/sfn/.
16. Holzer, *Lächeln*, 20, 66–86.
17. In the main, these are protocols from an examination of 1919 on war atrocities of the k. & k. Army after the Twelfth Isonzo Battle.
18. See note 70.
19. See for occupied France, where such diaries were already discovered and researched, the work of Manon Pignot, published for example as "French Boys and Girls in the Great War: Gender and the History of Children's Experiences, 1914–1918," in *Gender and the First World War*, ed. Christa Hämmerle, Oswald Überegger, and Birgitta Bader-Zaar (New York: Palgrave, 2014), 163–75.
20. Christa Hämmerle, "Gewalt und Liebe—ineinander verschränkt: Paarkorrespondenzen aus zwei Weltkriegen: 1914/18 und 1939/45," in *Liebe schreiben: Paarkorrespondenzen im Kontext des 19. und 20. Jahrhunderts*, ed. Ingrid Bauer and Christa Hämmerle (Göttingen: Vandenhoeck & Ruprecht, 2017), 171–231. The title of the research project was "Writing (about) Love? Historical Analysis Regarding the Negotiation of Gender Relations and Positions in Couple Correspondence of the 19th and 20th Century."
21. See Christa Hämmerle, "Diaries," in *Reading Primary Sources: The Interpretation of Texts from 19th and 20th Century History*, ed. Miriam Dobson and Benjamin Ziemann (New York: Routledge, 2008), 141–59; Christa Hämmerle, "Between Instrumentalisation and Self Governing: (Female) Ego-Documents in the European Age of Total War," in *The Uses of First Person Writings: Africa, America, Asia, Europe/Les usages des écrits du for privé: Afrique, Amérique, Asie, Europe*, ed. François Joseph Ruggiu (Brussels: Peter Lang, 2013), 263–84.
22. Isa Schikorsky, "Kommunikation über das Unbeschreibbare: Beobachtungen zum Sprachstil von Kriegsbriefen," *Wirkendes Wort* 42, no. 2 (1992): 295–315.
23. See, for example, Ines Rebhan-Glück, "Eifersucht—(k)ein Gefühl in Feldpostbriefen aus dem Ersten Weltkrieg," in Bauer and Hämmerle, *Liebe schreiben*, 123f.; Hämmerle, *Gewalt und Liebe*, 182f.
24. In contrast to the well-represented side of officers or NCOs and their families, war correspondences written by common soldiers or their addressees have survived in much smaller numbers. There are exceptions, but often only in the form

of fragments or single pieces from a correspondence. See, for example, Benjamin Ziemann, "Geschlechterbeziehungen in deutschen Feldpostbriefen des Ersten Weltkriegs," in *Briefkulturen und ihr Geschlecht: Zur Geschichte der privaten Korrespondenz vom 16. Jahrhundert bis heute*, ed. Christa Hämmerle and Edith Saurer (Vienna: Böhlau Verlag, 2003), 261–82; and the edition of Doris Kachulle, Anna Pöhland, Robert Pöhland et al., eds., *Die Pöhlands im Krieg: Briefe einer sozialdemokratischen Arbeiterfamilie aus dem Ersten Weltkrieg* (Cologne: PapyRossa Verlag, 2006).

25. See in detail Hämmerle, *Gewalt und Liebe*; Christa Hämmerle, "'You Let a Weeping Woman Call You Home?' Private Correspondences during the First World War in Austria and Germany," in *Epistolary Selves: Letters and Letter-Writers, 1600–1945*, ed. Rebecca Earle (Aldershot: Ashgate, 1999), 152–82; Rebhan-Glück, "Eifersucht."
26. Christl Lang to Leopold Wolf, 13 December 1916, in SFN, NL 14.
27. Leopold Wolf to Christl Lang, 4 April 1915, written somewhere from the region behind the fortress Przemysl in Galicia, after the capitulation of the k. & k. troops there; in SFN, NL 14.
28. Lilly Weber to Friedrich Weber, 3 December 1915, in SFN, NL 21 II.
29. Cf. also the chapter of Nadia Filippini in this volume.
30. Anna Ertl (pseud.) to Alfred Ertl (pseud.), 4 November 1917, in SFN, NL 174.
31. Cf. for Vienna for example Alfred Pfoser and Andreas Weigl, eds., *Im Epizentrum des Zusammenbruchs: Wien im Ersten Weltkrieg*, 2nd ed. (Vienna: Metroverlag 2013), especially 132–98, 556–77. This is a frequent topic in many couple correspondences of the time.
32. Alfred Ertl to Anna Ertl, 4 September 1917, in SFN, NL 174.
33. Hämmerle, *Gewalt und Liebe*, 193–97.
34. Alfred Ertl to Anna Ertl, 16 March 1918, in SFN, NL 174.
35. Audoin-Rouzeau and Becker, *14–18*; John Horne, "Soldiers, Civilians and the Warfare of Attrition: Representations of Combat in France, 1914–1918," in *Authority, Identity and the Social History of the Great War*, ed. Frans Coetzee and Marilyn Shevin-Coetzee (Providence, RI: Berghahn Books, 1995), 223–49; Martha Hanna, "A Republic of Letters: The Epistolary Tradition in France during World War I," in *American Historical Review* 108, no. 5 (2003), 1338–61.
36. This assumption basically follows Klaus Latzel's and Michael Humburg's approaches on war correspondences based on the sociology of knowledge. Cf. Klaus Latzel, *Deutsche Soldaten—nationalsozialistischer Krieg? Kriegserlebnis—Kriegserfahrung 1939–1945* (Paderborn: Ferdinand Schönigh, 1998); Klaus Latzel, "Kriegsbriefe und Kriegserfahrung: Wie können Feldpostbriefe zur erfahrungsgeschichtlichen Quelle werden?," *Werkstatt Geschichte* 22 (1999): 7–23; Martin Humburg, *Das Gesicht des Krieges: Feldpostbriefe von Wehrmachtsoldaten aus der Sowjetunion 1941–1944* (Wiesbaden: Westdeutscher Verlag, 1998).
37. For former Austria, not enough letters written by common soldiers have survived to differentiate this between officers and the rank and file.
38. Alfred to Anna Ertl, 29 July 1917, in SFN, NL 174.
39. Alfred to Anna Ertl, 3 August 1917, in SFN, NL 174.
40. Anna to Alfred Ertl, 16 January 1918, in SFN, NL 174.
41. Hans Haugeneder, *Gestern noch auf stolzen Rossen: Tagebuch eines Kriegsteilnehmers 1916-1918*, foreword by Peter Schubert (Klagenfurt: Verlag Hermagoras, 2017), 7–9.

42. Ibid., 29f.
43. Ibid., 31.
44. Ibid., 87.
45. Ibid., 91.
46. Ibid., 110.
47. Ibid., 95.
48. Ibid., 99.
49. Ibid., 104.
50. Ibid., 105.
51. Ibid., 105f.
52. *Hinter den Fronten Galiziens: Feldkaplan Karl Gögele und sein Verwundentenspital; Aufzeichnungen 1914–1915*, ed. Monica Mader (Bozen: Edition Raetia, 2016). This volume contains the first part of Gögele's chronologically organized war accounts, all of which are based on the diaries he kept during wartime; see ibid, 330. It covers the period until the beginning of his time in Kovel. The second volume, containing Gögele's notes from 26 September 1915 to 12 November 1918 was published in January 2018 under the title *Raues Leben, großes Sterben: Feldkaplan Karl Gögele und sein Deutschordensspital. Kriegstagebücher 1915–1918*, ed. Monika Mader (Bozen: Edition Raetia, 2018). I had the chance to read the manuscript before writing this chapter, but I could not quote from the final, printed version. Therefore, what follows focuses on the first volume.
53. Cf. Erwin A. Schmidl, "Der Kriegsschauplatz Galizien," in Mader, *Hinter den Fronten*, 36–45.
54. Gögele in Mader, *Hinter den Fronten*, 102.
55. Ibid., 173. See also ibid., 219. Here, Gögele describes how Bochnia has been looted by the Russians during three weeks in early 2015.
56. Ibid., 236.
57. Ibid., 176.
58. Ibid.
59. In some cases, Gögele did the same for people of other confessions, if he was asked.
60. Cf., for example, Margaret R. Higonett, ed., *Nurses at the Front: Writing the Wounds of the Great War* (Boston: Northeastern University Press, 2001).
61. For an analysis of these texts, see Christa Hämmerle, "'Mentally Broken, Physically a Wreck . . .': Violence in War Accounts of Nurses in Austro-Hungarian Service," in Hämmerle, Überegger, and Bader-Zaar, *Gender and the First World War*, 89–107; Christa Hämmerle, "Counter-Narratives of the Great War? War Accounts of Nurses in Austro-Hungarian Service," in *Inside World War One? The First World War and Its Witnesses*, ed. Richard Bessel and Dorothee Wierling (Oxford: Oxford University Press, 2018), 143–66.
62. Agathe Fessler, *Aus der Mappe einer Armeeschwester* (Bregenz; self-published brochure, Stadtarchiv Bregenz, Nachlaß Agathe Fessler, 1919), 9, referring to winter 1914.
63. R. M. Konrad, *Schwestern als Menschen: Aus den Aufzeichnungen einer Armeeschwester* (Innsbruck: self-published, printed Friedr. Sperl, 1922), 15.
64. Ibid., 4.
65. See the analysis in Hämmerle, *Counter-Narratives*.
66. Eveline Hrouda, *Barmherzigkeit: Als freiwillige Malteserschwester im Weltkrieg* (Graz: Leykam, 1935), entry of 17 November 1917.

67. Hrouda, *Barmherzigkeit*, 42.
68. See, among others, John Horne and Alan Kramer, *German Atrocities 1914: A History of Denial*. New Haven, CT: Yale University, 2001.
69. Cynthia Enloe, "The Gendered Gulf," in *Collateral Damage: The "New World Order" at Home and Abroad*, ed. Cynthia Peters (Boston: South End Press, 1992), 93–110.
70. Holzer, *Lächeln*, 133–39.
71. Cf. above all Oswald Überegger, "Vom militärischen Paradigma zur 'Kulturgeschichte des Krieges'? Entwicklungslinien der österreichischen Weltkriegsgeschichtsschreibung zwischen politisch-militärischer Instrumentalisierung und universitärer Verwissenschaftlichung," in *Zwischen Nation und Region: Weltkriegsforschung im interregionalen Vergleich; Ergebnisse und Perspektiven*, ed. Oswald Überegger (Innsbruck: Universitätsverlag Wagner, 2004), 63–122.

Bibliography

Audoin-Rouzeau, Stéphane, and Annette Becker. *14–18: Understanding the Great War*. Translated from the French by Catherine Temerson. New York: Hill and Wang, 2000.

Böhler, Jochen, Włodzimierz Borodziej, and Joachim von Puttkamer, eds. *Legacies of Violence: Eastern Europe's First World War*. Munich: De Gruyter Oldenbourg, 2014.

Dülffer, Jost. *Regeln gegen den Krieg? Die Haager Friedenskonferenzen 1899 und 1907 in der internationalen Politik*. Berlin: Ullstein, 1981.

Enloe, Cynthia. "The Gendered Gulf." In *Collateral Damage: The "New World Order" at Home and Abroad*, edited by Cynthia Peters, 93–110. Boston: South End Press, 1992.

Fessler, Agathe. *Aus der Mappe einer Armeeschwester*. Bregenz: self-published brochure, Stadtarchiv Bregenz, Nachlaß Agathe Fessler, 1919.

Förster, Stig, and Jörg Nagler, eds. *On the Road to Total War: The American Civil War and the German Wars of Unification, 1861–1871*. Cambridge: Cambridge University Press, 1997.

Grayzel, Susan. *Women and the First World War*. New York: Pearson Education, 2002.

Gumz, Jonathan E. *The Resurrection and Collapse of Empire in Habsburg Serbia, 1914–1918*. Cambridge: Cambridge University Press, 2009.

Hämmerle, Christa. "'You Let a Weeping Woman Call You Home?' Private Correspondences during the First World War in Austria and Germany." In *Epistolary Selves: Letters and Letter-Writers, 1600–1945*, edited by Rebecca Earle, 152–82. Aldershot: Ashgate, 1999.

———. "Diaries." In *Reading Primary Sources: The Interpretation of Texts from 19th and 20th Century History*, edited by Miriam Dobson and Benjamin Ziemann, 141–59. London: Routledge, 2008.

———. "Between Instrumentalisation and Self Governing: (Female) Ego-Documents in the European Age of Total War." In *The Uses of First Person Writings: Africa, America, Asia, Europe/Les usages des écrits du for privé: Afrique, Amérique, Asie, Europe*, edited by François Joseph Ruggiu, 263–84. Brussels: Peter Lang, 2013.

———. *Heimat/Front: Geschlechtergeschichte/n des Ersten Weltkriegs in Österreich-Ungarn*. Vienna: Böhlau, 2013.

———. "'Mentally Broken, Physically a Wreck . . .': Violence in War Accounts of Nurses in Austro-Hungarian Service." In *Gender and the First World War*, edited by Christa Hämmerle, Oswald Überegger, and Birgitta Bader-Zaar, 89–107. New York: Palgrave, 2014.

———. "Gewalt und Liebe—ineinander verschränkt: Paarkorrespondenzen aus zwei Weltkriegen: 1914/18 und 1939/45." In *Liebe schreiben. Paarkorrespondenzen im Kontext des 19. und 20. Jahrhunderts*, edited by Ingrid Bauer and Christa Hämmerle, 171–231. Göttingen: Vandenhoeck & Ruprecht, 2017.

———. "Counter-Narratives of the Great War? War Accounts of Nurses in Austro-Hungarian Service." In *Inside World War One? The First World War and Its Witnesses*, edited by Richard Bessel and Dorothee Wierling, 143–66. Oxford: Oxford University Press, 2018.

Hagemann, Karen. *"Männlicher Muth und Teutsche Ehre": Nation, Militär und Geschlecht zur Zeit der Antinapoleonischen Kriege Preußens*. Paderborn: Ferdinand Schöningh, 2000.

———. *Revisiting Prussia's Wars against Napoleon: History, Culture and Memory*. Cambridge: Cambridge University Press, 2015.

Hagen, Mark. *War in a European Borderland: Occupations and Occupation Plans in Galicia and Ukraine, 1914–1918*. Seattle: University of Washington Press, 2007.

Hanna, Martha. "A Republic of Letters: The Epistolary Tradition in France during World War I." In *American Historical Review* 108, no. 5 (2003): 1338–61.

Haugeneder, Hans. *Gestern noch auf stolzen Rossen: Tagebuch eines Kriegsteilnehmers 1916–1918*. Foreword by Peter Schubert. Klagenfurt: Verlag Hermagoras. 2017.

Hautmann, Hans. "Kriegsgesetze und Militärjustiz in der österreichischen Reichshälfte 1914–1918." In *Justiz und Zeitgeschichte: Symposiumsbeiträge 1976–1993*, edited by Erika Weinzierl, Oliver Rathkolb, Rudolf G. Ardelt, and Siegfried Mattl, 73–85. Vienna: Jugend & Volk, 1995.

———. "Zum Sozialprofil der Militärrichter im Ersten Weltkrieg." In *Richter und Gesellschaftspolitik: Symposion Justiz und Zeitgeschichte, 12. und 13. Oktober 1995 in Wien*, edited by Erika Weinzierl, Oliver Rathkolb, Siegfried Mattl, and Rudolf G. Ardelt, 21–29. Innsbruck: Studien-Verlag, 1997.

———. "Die österreichisch-ungarische Armee auf dem Balkan." In *Kriegsverbrechen in Europa und im Nahen Osten im 20. Jahrhundert*, edited by Franz W. Seidler and Alfred M. de Zayas, 36–41. Hamburg: Mittler & Sohn, 2002.

Higonett, Margaret R., ed. *Nurses at the Front: Writing the Wounds of the Great War*. Boston: Northeastern University Press, 2001.

Holzer, Anton. *Das Lächeln der Henker: Der unbekannte Krieg gegen die Zivilbevölkerung 1914–1918*. Darmstadt: Primus, 2008.

Horne, John. "Soldiers, Civilians and the Warfare of Attrition: Representations of Combat in France, 1914–1918." In *Authority, Identity and the Social History of the Great War*, edited by Frans Coetzee and Marilyn Shevin-Coetzee, 223–49. Providence, RI: Berghahn Books, 1995.

———. "Civilian Populations and Wartime Violence: Towards an Historical Analysis." *International Social Science Journal* 174 (2002): 483–90.

Horne, John, and Alan Kramer. *German Atrocities 1914: A History of Denial*. New Haven, CT: Yale University Press, 2001.

Hrouda, Eveline. *Barmherzigkeit: Als freiwillige Malteserschwester im Weltkrieg*. Graz: Leykam, 1935.
Humburg, Martin. *Das Gesicht des Krieges: Feldpostbriefe von Wehrmachtsoldaten aus der Sowjetunion 1941–1944*. Wiesbaden: Westdeutscher Verlag, 1998.
Kachulle, Doris, Anna Pöhland, Robert Pöhland et al., eds. *Die Pöhlands im Krieg: Briefe einer sozialdemokratischen Arbeiterfamilie aus dem Ersten Weltkrieg*. Cologne: PapyRossa Verlag, 2006.
Konrad, R. M. *Schwestern als Menschen: Aus den Aufzeichnungen einer Armeeschwester*. Innsbruck: self-edited, printed Friedr. Sperl, 1922.
Kuprian, Hermann J. W., and Oswald Überegger, eds. *Katastrophenjahre: Der Erste Weltkrieg und Tirol*. Innsbruck: Universitätsverlag Wagner, 2014.
Latzel, Klaus. *Deutsche Soldaten—nationalsozialistischer Krieg? Kriegserlebnis—Kriegserfahrung 1939–1945*. Paderborn: Ferdinand Schönigh, 1998.
———. "Kriegsbriefe und Kriegserfahrung: Wie können Feldpostbriefe zur erfahrungsgeschichtlichen Quelle werden?" *Werkstatt Geschichte* 22 (1999): 7–23.
Leidinger, Hannes, Verena Moritz, Karin Moser, and Wolfram Dornik. *Habsburgs schmutziger Krieg: Ermittlungen zur österreichisch-ungarischen Kriegsführung 1914–1918*. St. Pölten: Residenz Verlag, 2014.
Mader, Monika, ed. *Hinter den Fronten Galiziens: Feldkaplan Karl Gögele und sein Verwundentenspital. Aufzeichnungen 1914–1915*. Bolzano: Edition Raetia, 2016.
———, ed. *Raues Leben, großes Sterben: Feldkaplan Karl Gögele und sein Deutschordensspital. Kriegstagebücher 1915–1918*. Bolzano: Edition Raetia, 2018.
Pfoser, Alfred, and Andreas Weigl, eds. *Im Epizentrum des Zusammenbruchs: Wien im Ersten Weltkrieg*. 2nd ed. Vienna: Metroverlag 2013.
Pignot, Manon. "French Boys and Girls in the Great War: Gender and the History of Children's Experiences, 1914–1918." In *Gender and the First World War*, edited by Christa Hämmerle, Oswald Überegger, and Birgitta Bader, 163–75. New York: Palgrave, 2014.
Rebhan-Glück, Ines. "Eifersucht—(k)ein Gefühl in Feldpostbriefen aus dem Ersten Weltkrieg." In *Liebe schreiben: Paarkorrespondenzen im Kontext des 19. und 20. Jahrhunderts*, edited by Ingrid Bauer and Christa Hämmerle, 113–38. Göttingen: Vandenhoeck & Ruprecht, 2017.
Schikorsky, Isa. "Kommunikation über das Unbeschreibbare: Beobachtungen zum Sprachstil von Kriegsbriefen." *Wirkendes Wort* 42, no. 2 (1992): 295–315.
Schmidl, Erwin A. "Der Kriegsschauplatz Galizien." In *Hinter den Fronten Galiziens: Feldkaplan Karl Gögele und sein Verwundentenspital. Aufzeichnungen 1914–1915*, edited by Monika Mader, 36–45. Bolzano: Edition Raetia, 2016.
Warneken, Bernd Jürgen. *Populare Autobiographik: Empirische Studien zu einer Quellengattung der Alltagsgeschichtsforschung*. Tübingen: Tübinger Vereinigung für Volkskunde 1985.
Überegger, Oswald. "Vom militärischen Paradigma zur 'Kulturgeschichte des Krieges'? Entwicklungslinien der österreichischen Weltkriegsgeschichtsschreibung zwischen politisch-militärischer Instrumentalisierung und universitärer Verwissenschaftlichung." In *Zwischen Nation und Region: Weltkriegsforschung im interregionalen Vergleich; Ergebnisse und Perspektiven*, edited by Oswald Überegger, 63–122. Innsbruck: Universitätsverlag Wagner, 2004.
———. "'Verbrannte Erde' und 'baumelnde Gehenkte': Zur europäischen Dimension militärischer Normübertretungen im Ersten Weltkrieg." In *Kriegsgreuel: Die Entgrenzung der Gewalt in kriegerischen Konflikten vom Mittelalter bis ins 20.*

Jahrhundert, edited by Sönke Neitzel and Daniel Hohrath, 241–78. Paderborn: Ferdinand Schöningh, 2008.

Ziemann, Benjamin. "Geschlechterbeziehungen in deutschen Feldpostbriefen des Ersten Weltkriegs." In *Briefkulturen und ihr Geschlecht: Zur Geschichte der privaten Korrespondenz vom 16. Jahrhundert bis heute*, edited by Christa Hämmerle and Edith Saurer, 261–82. Vienna: Böhlau Verlag, 2003.

———. *Gewalt im Ersten Weltkrieg: Töten—Überleben—Verweigern*. Essen: Klartext Verlag, 2013.

CHAPTER 15

Hunger, Rape, Escape

The Many Aspects of Violence against Women and Children in the Territories of the Italian Front

Nadia Maria Filippini

Across Europe, commemoration of the centenary of World War I has generated new research and historical reassessment, not least as regards the history of women and gender, an area that had been somewhat neglected in the historiography. Significantly, four important national conferences were organized on this theme in Italy in 2014 and 2015; in addition, there were various other initiatives of a more regional nature, and increased interest has also been reflected in other events and publications.[1]

The complex nature of the various investigative approaches has become evident. These have related not just to the political and social arena but also to the spheres of representation, the collective imaginary, behavioral and psychological developments, and individual agency. In contrast to the traditional and more markedly homogenizing interpretation, the full variety of women's experiences has emerged; in 1992, the French historian Françoise Thébaud was already arguing that recognition of these differences within the world of women was essential for any proper historical assessment.[2]

In this regard, geographical location, particularly in a time of war, proved to be of crucial importance. The populations of border areas, living in the territories cut through by the front or immediately behind it, were exposed to experiences that were profoundly different from the inhabitants of the rest of the country. They were drawn into the conflict in various ways and had a foretaste of the implications of total war: militarization of the land, interaction with the troops, bombing, forced evacuation, and violence in its many aspects.[3] The traditional distinction between the "home front" and the "military front," customarily used for gendered readings of the war, thus proves entirely inappropriate for these situations.⁴

My contribution examines these aspects, focusing on the situation in the area of the Veneto and Friuli, which right from Italy's entry into the war was hit by a full-blown "social earthquake" that seriously disturbed every aspect of daily existence and had a profound impact on the lives of women and children.

It needs to be said, first of all, that the repercussions of the European conflict were already being felt before Italy actually entered the war, during the months of its controversial neutrality, in cities and towns such as Venice and Chioggia, whose economies were based on port activities, fishing, tourism, and exports. In Venice, closure of the port and tight restrictions on fishing, imposed by a port authority regulation issued on 7 August 1914, led to a serious economic crisis: by October, there were already as many as 6,650 people unemployed in the city, and by the beginning of 1915, the figure had risen to 10,000. The consequences of the deterioration in the population's living conditions, which the municipal coffers were unable to cope with, included serious social tension, with strikes, demonstrations, and attacks on bakeries, as discussed in the research by Bruna Bianchi.⁵ The arrival of refugees from the territories over the border contributed to a worsening of the situation: about 180,000 people originally from the Veneto, of whom about 150,000 were unemployed, returned home in 1914. This made it necessary, in August 1914, to set up a special Committee for Recalled Soldiers, the Unemployed, and Emigrants, which subsequently became a Committee for Civilian Preparation.

The situation was of course to further worsen when Italy entered the war, especially regarding daily life, which experienced radical upheaval as a result.

Many towns and cities saw changes to their layout and arrangements due to the requirements of the war, which had a clear impact on the residents: particular mention should be made of Udine, the city that hosted the Italian High Command during the war, and Padua after Caporetto.⁶ The militarization of the territories of Friuli and the Veneto, which were regarded as war zones and placed under military authority, subjected their entire populations to oppressive restrictions on their individual liberty: bans on strikes and demonstrations, no free movement after curfew, the suspension of rights, checks and arrests based on mere suspicion, requisition of foodstuff and buildings, and the imposition of semi-compulsory labor.

The phenomenon of deportation and the mass internment of civilians, which is still largely to be investigated, should also be highlighted. According to Giovanna Procacci, thousands of women from Friuli, Belluno, and the Trento area, in places adjacent to the border such as Cortina and

Valsugana, especially during the first year of the war, were interned under charges of being "Austrian sympathizers" or of "suspected complicity with the enemy," simply because their first language was German.[7] Other women were interned as a precautionary measure because they held prominent positions, such as schoolteachers or hotelkeepers, and were thought to be capable of espionage or propaganda activity.

An enormous quantity of troops flooded into this area, not only along the front line but also behind the lines; the consequences of this great intermingling of soldiers and civilians included those of a social nature. Among those that should be highlighted was the phenomenon of prostitution; this was not confined to the "war brothels" allowed for by Prime Minister Antonio Salandra but was more widely distributed across the territory in semi-clandestine fashion, encouraged by the increasing poverty of the population. This topic is still to be thoroughly studied, as the research carried out by Emilio Franzina at the end of the 1990s has not been followed by any further investigations.[8]

Alongside the soldiers, another army flooded into these lands: that of the "civilian laborers" who were employed in the war sites, overseen by the military authorities, on the establishment of the logistical infrastructure needed by the army. According to estimates by Matteo Ermacora, about six hundred thousand people were involved across the whole war period.[9] This number included women from the Carnia, Belluno, and Trento areas who were taken on to carry supplies to the troops; it is not known to what extent this was voluntary or semi-compulsory, but every day they walked up into the mountains with panniers full of armaments and supplies for the soldiers. According to a rough estimate, there were about four thousand of these young women, who had to endure extremely difficult working conditions and rigid discipline, often having to go into high-risk areas. This was demonstrated by the tragic case of Maria Plozner Mentil from Timau, Udine, a young mother of four children who was killed by a sniper in February 1916 and became the symbol of the *portatrici* (women porters), but was recognized as a war casualty and awarded a gold medal only eighty-one years later.[10]

To this picture should be added the experience of aerial bombing raids, which for the first time in history also hit civilians living and working in areas relatively far away from the military front line. The whole area of Friuli and the Veneto, from Udine to Verona, was subjected to regular aerial bombardment from the very first day of the war, with Venice bombed on 24 May 1915, and experienced the destruction of residential dwellings, factories, churches, and hospitals. The cities that were worst hit included Udine and Padua, but also Treviso, Vicenza, and Venice, where as many as forty-two air raids were recorded. One single raid on Padua, on 3 November 1915, gave rise to ninety-three deaths and ninety-six people wounded.

The coverage that the newspapers gave to these attacks underlined their powerful impact on a population that was totally unprepared and largely unprotected. Giovanni Scarabello, the Venetian author who described exactly where the bombs fell on his city, gave his book the title *Martirio di Venezia* (The Martyrdom of Venice), which emphasizes the assault on an unarmed and unprotected civilian population.[11]

To the dire poverty and anxiety over the fate of family members was added the sense of vulnerability and destruction. It is thus not surprising that some women experienced such a degree of mental distress that they were admitted to the psychiatric hospital, as can be seen in the clinical records of the San Clemente hospital in Venice. However, the hardest hit were the children: the rate of infant mortality under five years of age almost doubled between 1914 and 1916, rising from 24.8 to 41 percent of all deaths recorded.[12]

A real social tsunami, however, was caused by the military defeats that left vast areas of the mountains and plains of Friuli and the Veneto exposed to the enemy advance. The Austrian *Strafexpedition* (punitive counterattack) of May 1916, in the first place, and then, and above all, the rout of Caporetto in October 1917 provoked a hurried flight that involved the forced evacuation of not only the land that the enemy occupied but also a much larger area deemed to be at risk; this included cities in the plain such as Treviso and Venice, two-thirds of whose population was evacuated in November 1917, as well as areas on the left bank of the Piave River.[13] The striking extent of this exodus, which the government was not ready to deal with, has been reconstructed by Daniele Ceschin, who has estimated that the overall number of refugees during the war, when the various waves are added together, was about six hundred thousand.[14] This constituted a real "human flood," as it was described by Ardengo Soffici in his book *La ritirata del Friuli*, an account of the disaster of Caporetto first published in 1919.[15]

This phenomenon was quickly erased from public memory, with the emphasis given to the celebrations of victory, and only recently has it been brought back into the spotlight in its full dramatic nature. Primary sources such as diaries, letters, and appeals for civilian participation, patiently brought together from the archives, have with their harsh detail gone beyond the social context to bring back the personal lives of people who were forced to abandon their homes in haste and to face long, exhausting, and dangerous journeys without any provisions, assistance, or hope of shelter.

In many cases, hunger and destitution were compounded by the tragic dispersal of family units; for example, many children became lost during the flight, and there were also many who did not survive because of the difficult conditions of the journey. This is described in entries in the diary of Antonietta Giacomelli:

> They arrive soaked through by the rain and covered in mud, bringing with them only a few possessions that they had gathered together in a hurry and often at random; separated families, parents who have lost children along the way, children who have lost parents. Children aged three, two, or one are brought to us by women who don't know who they are. . . . There is an endless stream of old people, women, children, and babies, many of them ill.[16]

For many, the end of this odyssey was only the beginning of a new Calvary: dispatched to regions that were sometimes far away, including Sicily, assigned to houses that were often in decay and without electricity and water, and supported by derisory financial aid, they found themselves obliged to accept work in conditions of oppressive exploitation. In addition, in many cases they also had to face the mistrust, if not open hostility, of the local population, which spoke a different language and saw them as dangerous competitors in a poor and insecure labor market; the refugees, despite being Italian, were assigned all the negative attributes that mark out those who are "different," and were cast as beggars, thieves, uncouth, and so on.[17]

The refugees, including women, addressed many complaints and appeals to the authorities, reporting the degrading conditions and the disappointment of those who had expected to be welcomed by the solidarity of their fellow Italians. This can be seen in the account of a woman refugee from Vicenza, given lodgings in a village in the province of Benevento:

> We are looked at like animals and badly regarded by the local people. They tell us that we are Austrians; but never mind. God provides even for us poor unfortunates.[18]

Another testimony confirms the labeling of refugees as "Austrians" and "Germans":

> They call us "tedeschi" (Germans) only because we have a language that's different from the others, and because they can't understand what we're saying . . . in Tuscany we're believed to be cannibals . . . and everywhere they see us as outsiders, killjoys, and the cause of the war.[19]

One woman wrote that "the refugees were treated worse than by the Austrians," implying that she would have stayed in her own area if she had known how she was going to be treated.[20] In actual fact, those who stayed behind were subjected to much more serious acts of violence, as occurred in occupied territory across Europe: assault, rape, looting, and systematic requisition of property.

The Royal Commission of Inquiry into the Violation of People's Rights, set up by the Italian government on 15 December 1918 soon after the war had ended, collected numerous statements across different towns and villages from mayors, doctors, parish priests (who often performed the functions of the civilian authority), and ordinary men and women. These were published in seven volumes; the inquiry's proceedings are now conserved in a series of large folders in the Archivio Centrale dello Stato (Italy's central state archives).[21]

Don Valentino Liva, the canon of Cividale who carried out many of the mayor's duties during the months of enemy occupation, gave this account:

> The first troops to enter Cividale were German, but then four days later the Austrians installed themselves on the left bank of the Natisone, so that for some time the Austrians were on the left and the Germans on the right bank of the Natisone, until 22 December when the Germans left. . . . There were very many incidents of theft with violence committed against people, so many that it's impossible to give all the details. . . . During the first week of the enemy occupation, I don't know whether under orders, both the German and Austrian soldiers ransacked the city and its outer districts. . . . In August 1918, with the officer Eltza in command of the area, goods were systematically seized from all the houses, and when people complained, his reply was that this had been done to replenish supplies in Gradisca and Gorizia; however, the goods were never distributed and neither were they paid for or returned.[22]

"The early days were truly hellish: girls, women, and children were fleeing from their houses and running through the fields and woods screaming with terror," according to Don Carlo De Nardi, the parish priest of Pieve di Soligo.[23] In his own collection of statistics compiled "family by family," he then detailed the extent of the seizure of livestock, valuable items, and money just in the agricultural areas within his district:

> Cattle: 1437 animals; horses: 50; pigs: 1838; sheep: 98; poultry: 13,311; corn: 5,394 *quintali*; wheat: 1541 q.; hay: 18,651 q.; wine: 5,336 hundred liters; cash: 52,254 lire; objects of value: 1,039; bicycles: 192; furniture: 1039 items; linen: 24,496 items.
>
> I believe I can state, without checks or more detailed information that I will provide later, that prior to the invasion there were about 4,000 head of cattle in the district, of which the enemy took away 3,400; the remainder were saved only because they were hidden. As far as I know, about 2,200 pigs were taken.[24]

Not even the churches were spared: in Conegliano, in the province of Treviso, the priest was forced to leave his church accommodation, and the church was stripped of all its furnishings and paintings:

> From those interminable months I have just one memory of terror. The darkest period was the first invasion. It was 9 November when the first swarms of German soldiery arrived. I know that I saw my church house invaded, and that I saw the orgy continuing for many days around me. I was thrown out. An officer told me to go and sleep in the cowshed. With difficulty, I managed to find lodgings with a greengrocer. In the village, there were only the shouts of soldiers drunk on wine,

looting, destruction, and fires. In the area around, there were assaults, robberies, and acts of violence . . . In the pillage, nothing was spared. I saw the most sacred items disappear from my church: two paintings . . . candlesticks, stoles, sacred objects. Their total value was 50,000 lire.[25]

The homes of refugees were especially plundered and destroyed, with the removal not only of objects and linen but also of locks, doorframes, and beams, for use as firewood.

In Pordenone, a flourishing industrial area in Friuli, the factories were stripped of equipment, as described by Umberto Castellani and Federico Cammeo, both prominent local citizens:

We could see a continual passage of lorries heading for the station loaded with every kind of machinery. The Amman cotton mill, the Veneziano cotton mill, the factories of Torre and Rosai, the former Lustig paper mill, the fertilizer factory, the brickworks of Villanova, Pordenone's printing institute: all were in turn completely ransacked, and are now almost completely lacking in machinery. It was the same fate for the Licinio engineering workshop.[26]

Every component part of the occupying army was implicated in the witness statements: Germans, Austrians, and Hungarians. The mayors and parish priests proved to be fairly attentive in distinguishing between these various affiliations and in specifying their particular behavior; this is illustrated by the statements from the canon of Cividale and from the Conegliano priest, who detailed how the departure of the Germans (who had arrived in the village on 9 November) was followed by the arrival of the Austrians, without the general situation changing very much; rather, the arrival of troops of a different nationality meant that the raids and requisitions were renewed with a greater intensity:

After the Austrians had replaced the Germans in January, things did not change. With some degree of increased formality, the stripping of properties essentially became harsher and more oppressive. Gradually, everything was seized. Provisions, linen, furniture, door handles, window closings. The purchase of wheat was prevented, and use of the mills forbidden.[27]

The progressively stricter rationing of foodstuffs, in addition to the raids, resulted in a real "starvation of the population" and "hunger regime," as it was described by the inquiry's president Giorgio Mortara.[28] According to Marco Mondini, the orders issued by Field Marshall Boroevic, the commander of the Austro-Hungarian forces, authorized every soldier "to freely take possession of goods up to a total of 25 kilograms of food and 80 of various commodities, or instead works of art and furniture, while the bread ration for Italians was reduced to 150 grams per day, and finally to only 50."[29]

The suffering endured by the population is portrayed in numerous reports. The director of the hospital in Belluno, for example, wrote that "in the months from April to July, the population's dietary situation was indescribably difficult. Hunger had forced people to eat even alfalfa and other plants normally only consumed by the livestock," with the inevitable consequences of gastrointestinal diseases, hydremia, and pellagra.[30]

The parish priest of Pieve di Soligo stated that "there were countless victims of starvation in Pieve di Soligo, Farra, Rolle, Miane, Combai, Revine, Farra, Vittorio Veneto, and Fregona. The people of Piave and Cadore, in particular, seemed more like walking skeletons than human beings."[31]

Protests by the authorities and the priests were to no avail. The priest just quoted made reference to the responses from the military command, which seemed almost designed to emphasize the stereotype of a cruel and "barbarous" enemy, scornful of every norm and humanity, which occurred throughout the wartime propaganda, especially in the final years of the conflict. This image encouraged the *Leghe antitedesche* (anti-German leagues) and the *Fascio femminile interventista antitedesco* (women's anti-German action group), which were spreading quickly in Italian territory after Caporetto, to such an extent that they won over associations for women's emancipation such as the Unione Femminile:

> To us priests, begging for pity for the starving populations, came the response: "It's war. It's not important whether the civilian population lives. It's better that a hundred civilians die rather than a horse." The commanding officer in Farra di Soligno, when a woman asked him for a bit of bread for her starving children, responded: "For you Italians, we just need to leave your eyes for crying."[32]

In the areas directly affected by the conflict, malnutrition and disease caused a sudden increase in the civilian mortality rate, which rose to about double that of the prewar period: it went from an average of seventeen per one thousand in the period 1912–14 to between thirty and forty per one thousand in 1918, markedly higher than in other Italian regions (twenty-eight per one thousand).[33] The highest mortality rates were recorded in the municipalities close to the Piave line. The Commission of Inquiry estimated that about ten thousand people had died of starvation.[34]

In the areas occupied by enemy troops, women were raped. This also occurred in war zones across Europe, from the Northwest to the Eastern Front, although comparative research has shown that the characteristics of this phenomenon varied.[35] The bodies of the enemy's womenfolk were regarded as war booty; their appropriation was an act that signified conquest, including from a symbolic point of view. This was the implication of the episodes that took place particularly often during the early days of the retreat from Caporetto, and were evidently permitted by the military command.[36]

In most cases, women were raped at night by groups of solders who forced their way into houses, especially the more isolated ones, and put their menfolk (fathers and husbands) out of action. In other cases, women were attacked and raped out in the street, while going to work or looking for food. Should any of them react or attempt to defend themselves, they were beaten and at risk of being killed or injured, as these accounts illustrate:

> On 17 November, 1917, at about 10.30 pm, three German soldiers arrived at our house in Carpesica [Vittorio, Treviso], broke through the main entrance, came up to the first floor and entered my room. I was in bed and was woken up by the presence of these three soldiers. I shouted out to my father, who was sleeping in an adjoining room, and meanwhile one of them punched me in the face. My father came in and asked the three soldiers why they were there. One of them took out a dagger and stabbed my father in the heart; he fell backwards to the floor. Then my mother arrived as well and carried off my father, who was bleeding and at risk of death. The soldiers stayed in the room and once again approached my bed, uncovered me, and ripped off my nightgown. I tried to get away, but I was caught by the three of them and thrown back down naked on the bed. I fainted, and all three raped me in turn. I could distinctly feel that they despoiled my body, and the traces of my violated virginity were left on the bed. Then the three of them quickly left.[37]

> On the night of 4 November '17, five Austrian soldiers came into the room where I was sleeping and using threats and violence abused my body. Two children who cried out, frightened by this savagery, were beaten on the bed. These soldiers, who had thrown my husband out of the room and kept an eye on him while they carried out their crime, did not hesitate in doing this in the presence of my little girls, who were forced to keep quiet by threats and blows with a rifle butt. This terrible event left its mark on my nerves for a long time.[38]

The presence of small children often led the women to avoid offering resistance for fear of them suffering reprisals or revenge, as can be seen in Regina's statement:

> On 4 November '17, at 11.00 pm, I was at the house of C. Antonio, in Ronchis, when six Austrian soldiers came in. They first seized my sister Luigia, thirty-two years old, taking her into the yard where all six of them in turn spent their lust on her, not without first hitting her many times. Afterwards, my sister was unwell for a long time as a result of the beating, the shock to her nerves, and most of all from the syphilis that she was given by one of her abusers. An hour later, they came back into the room where they had surprised my sister Luigia and took out B. Antonio, forcibly shutting him into a nearby room, with two guards on the door with bayonets at the ready. They then took hold of me and two of them had their way with me in the presence of all the rest of the family who had remained in the same room. Before they violated me I had my six-month-old baby girl held tight in my arms, and they threatened to kill her if I didn't put her down in order to surrender to their wishes.[39]

Some women, who were younger and without children, saved themselves by escaping through the window and hiding in the woods, with neighbors, or in the parish church; this is apparent both from their direct testimony, and in statements by priests and other witnesses. Others were saved by many neighbors rushing to their assistance.

It has been convincingly argued by Ceschin that there does not seem to have been a deliberate plan behind the episodes of sexual violence, nor an intention to use sexual assault as a weapon of war within an "ethnic cleansing" approach.[40] These events seem to have been the outcome of spontaneous ventures by the soldiers and of a basic mindset that equated the enemy's women to "objects" for the taking, at the disposal of the conquerors, like war booty. Their actions were clearly permitted by the tolerant attitude taken by the military command, which let things happen without interfering or subsequently punishing those responsible: when the parish priest of Pieve di Soligo went to the local military commander to report these episodes, he was told that "even the soldiers have to enjoy themselves."[41]

There are no precise statistics for this phenomenon, not least because many women declined to make public an event that would have dishonored both themselves and their family, as both priests and others observed: "It is natural that through an innate and profound sense of modesty our women stay silent about certain disgraces."[42]

The inquiry carried out by the Royal Commission confirmed 735 cases of rape, with 165 detailed reports; however, it was not so much the figures that it brought into the spotlight but rather the dramatic situations of those who were the victims: women of all ages, including girls and elderly women, attacked in their homes and raped, often in full view of children and elderly parents. Whoever reacted or tried to defend themselves was hit and risked death; fifty-three women were killed for precisely this reason. Many statements emphasize the physical and psychological trauma that resulted: "After this event I fell sick and was close to dying, to the extent that I was given the last rites."[43] In some cases these assaults resulted in the contraction of venereal diseases, as in the account reproduced earlier.

In many cases the silence of the victim was not enough, as the rapes were followed by the birth of babies, poignantly known as *figli di guerra* (war children); some of the statements tell of this sequence of events:

> On the evening of 9 November 1917, when the Germans had just entered Conegliano, a soldier wearing a red cross on his arm, who had taken lodgings on the floor below mine, came into my room at midnight and wanted to lie with me against my will. I tried to fight against this in every way, and to free myself from his grip, but he got on top of me and abused my body for two hours. After this he went back to the floor below and the following morning he left with his other comrades.

> My impression is that the person who raped me was the head of the group. I had been a virgin and unfortunately the consequence of this violent encounter was that I became pregnant, while being forty-two years old, and nine months later, on 10 August, I gave birth to a baby girl whom I am raising with great difficulty because of my weak physical state.[44]

The arrival of these children forced moral dilemmas on the mothers and their husbands, families, and communities, causing further tragedy and hardship.

In 1918, in view of these situations, the priest Don Celso Costantini founded the Ospizio dei figli della Guerra (home for war children), subsequently renamed the Istituto San Filippo Neri, in Portogruaro. Between 1918 and 1922, this orphanage took in 355 children, most of whose mothers were married women (244) or widows (25), and only a minority unmarried (61).[45] Some were the children of refugees, and some of girls who had been seduced by soldiers stationed in their village.

The archives reveal that it was often the husband, returning from the front, who could not accept the situation; on other occasions it was the woman herself, and there were also cases in which the whole family forced the mother to abandon her child, or threw her out if she refused to do this. In every case, it meant that the women were subjected to additional and more subtle forms of violence, as can be seen in the following accounts:

> Virginia G., who had remained in the village of Enemonzo during the enemy invasion while her proper husband found himself on the other side of the Piave River, came to conceive a child who was born in the January that followed the liberation. This event gave rise to disastrous conflict between the married couple, and the wife was disowned. Now forced to work in order to procure food for herself, and for her child, she finds this impossible, having to attend to the care of the child.[46]

> Until now, the presence of the aforementioned bastard child has been tolerated within the family, but now the [mother's] three brothers, discharged from military service, no longer want anything to do with the "tedesco" (German) [their name for the child], and want him to be completely removed from the paternal house.[47]

> During the first year one still saw the arrival of some women, their faces hidden by a handkerchief, who were truly unable to relinquish their child in their heart, and the moment that their husband went away for two days to Udine or Treviso, they would travel miles and miles on foot and, exhausted, would plead: Let me kiss him. How is he? Is he well? Has he grown?[48]

These accounts tell us that in these areas, the period after the war also had its particular and very problematic features; it was necessary to accommodate the slow and laborious return of both the soldiers and the civilian refugees, which was drawn out over many months. As these people returned, they had to deal with houses and villages that had been plundered and destroyed, and with deep residual wounds that were mental as well as physical; the reconstruction required was not only material but also social, emotional, and psychological.

These events profoundly affected women's lives: not only did they experience the indirect effects of the war but also its brutality, its torment, and death. The price they paid was very high.

However, it should also be emphasized that an interpretation solely in terms of victimhood would be misleading, and would not give a proper explanation of the complexity and multifaceted nature of this experience: these events were not just about suffering, trauma, and violence. They also tell us about strength, courage, and the extraordinary capacity of women to react, resist, and start again in order to protect their children and families as well as themselves. They give us stories of anonymous heroines, as well as of victims. This courage shown by women, who had to commit themselves on a daily basis to the struggle to survive, was to be the starting point for something more important than the material reconstruction of the postwar period: its spiritual and affective reconstruction.

Nadia Maria Filippini, lecturer in women's history at the University of Ca' Foscari in Venice, is a founder member of the Società Italiana delle Storiche and coordinator of its Venice chapter. She has devoted her research to women's history, with particular reference to the themes of the body and the relationship "women-nation." She has written on the topic of women in World War I: "Nei territori del fronte. L'area veneta," in *La Grande guerra delle italiane: Mobilitazioni, diritti, trasformazioni* (Rome: Viella, 2016), 229–48. She edited the volume *Donne dentro la guerra: Il primo conflitto mondiale in area veneta*, which contains her essay "Le donne nei Comitati di assistenza e difesa civile in Veneto" (Viella, 2017).

Notes

This chapter has been translated from the Italian by Stuart Oglethorpe.
1. The conferences have included the following: "Vivere la guerra: Pensare la pace (1914–1921). Le esperienze delle donne, il pensiero femminista e le relazioni internazionali" (Living War: Thinking Peace (1914–1921). Women's Experiences, Feminist Thought and International Relations), Venice, 26–28 November 2014, organized by the University of Ca' Foscari (Dipartimento di Studi Linguistici e Culturali Comparati); "Donne e scuola nella Grande Guerra: Profili biografici e percorsi didattici" (Women and School in the Great War: Biographical Profiles and Didactic Programs), Padua, 3 November 2014, organized by the Società Italiana delle Storiche (Veneto branch); "Donne e Prima Guerra mondiale in area Veneta," (Women and War in the Veneto Region), Venice, 26 February 2015, organized by the Società Italiana delle Storiche (Veneto branch) (proceedings

published as Nadia Maria Filippini, ed., *Donne dentro la guerra: Il primo conflitto mondiale in area veneta* [Rome: Viella, 2017]); "La grande guerra delle italiane: Mobilitazioni, diritti, trasformazioni," Rome, 24–25 September 2015, organized by the Società italiana delle Storiche (proceedings published as Stefania Bartoloni, ed., *La grande guerra delle italiane: Mobilitazioni, diritti, trasformazioni* [Rome: Viella, 2016]); "Le donne nel primo conflitto mondiale: Dalle linee avanzate al fronte interno; La Grande Guerra delle italiane," Rome, 25–26 November 2015, organized by the Ufficio Storico dello Stato maggiore della Difesa (proceedings published as Ufficio Storico, Stato maggiore della Difesa, ed., *Le donne nel primo conflitto mondiale: Dalle linee avanzate al fronte interno; la Grande Guerra delle italiane; Atti del congresso di studi storici internazionali* [Rome: Stato maggiore della Difesa, 2016]). See also the following, published to mark the centenary of World War I: Roberto Bianchi and Monica Pacini, eds., "Donne 'comuni' nell'Europa della Grande Guerra," *Genesis: Rivista della Società Italiana delle storiche* 15, no. 1 (special issue) (2016); Stefania Bartoloni, *Donne di fronte alla guerra: Pace, diritti e democrazia* (Rome: Laterza, 2017).
2. "This experience was neither uniform nor unambiguous, in that depending on a woman's nation, age cohort, and social background it brought varying degrees of independence, suffering, and overwork." See Françoise Thébaud, "La Grande Guerra: Età della donna o trionfo della differenza sessuale?," in *Storia delle donne*, ed. Georges Duby and Michelle Perrot, vol. 5: *Il Novecento*, ed. Françoise Thébaud (Rome: Laterza, 1992), 81. See also Françoise Thébaud, "Femmes et genre dans la guerre," in *Encyclopédie de la Grande Guerre*, ed. Stéphane Audoin-Rouzeau and Jean-Jacques Becker (Montrouge: Bayard, 2004), 613–25.
3. On women in the Veneto region, see Nadia Maria Filippini, "Nei territori del fronte: L'area veneta," in Bartoloni, *La Grande guerra delle italiane*, 229–48; Nadia Maria Filippini, "Il Veneto in guerra: Le donne delle province nord-orientali al fronte e nelle retrovie," in Ufficio Storico, Stato maggiore della Difesa, *Le donne nel primo conflitto mondiale*, 137–52.
4. This issue has been discussed by Perry Willson, *Women in Twentieth-Century Italy* (Basingstoke: Palgrave Macmillan, 2010), 43–44.
5. Bruna Bianchi, "Venezia nella Grande Guerra," in *Storia di Venezia: L'Ottocento e il Novecento*, 3 vols., ed. Mario Isnenghi and Stuart Woolf (Rome: Istituto della Enciclopedia Italiana, 2002), 1:349–407.
6. Matteo Ermacora, "Udine, capitale della guerra," in *Fronti interni: Esperienze di guerra lontano dalla guerra, 1914–1918*, ed. Andrea Scartabellati, Matteo Ermacora, and Felicita Ratti (Naples: Edizioni Scientifiche Italiane, 2014), 109–28.
7. Giovanna Procacci, "L'internamento di civili in Italia durante la prima guerra mondiale: Normativa e conflitti di competenza," *DEP: Deportate, esuli, profughe; Rivista telematica di studi sulla memoria femminile* 5–6 (2006): 33–66. Available online at: www.unive.it/pag/fileadmin/user_upload/dipartimenti/DSLCC/documenti/DEP/numeri/n5-6/3_Procacci.pdf.
8. Emilio Franzina, *Casini di guerra: Il tempo libero dalla trincea e i postriboli militari nel primo conflitto mondiale* (Udine: Gaspari, 1999); Emilio Franzina, "Le fabbriche dell'amore castrense: Case e casini del soldato," in *La memoria della Grande Guerra nelle Dolomiti*, ed. Isabella Bossi Fedrigotti, Luciana Palla, Giovanna Procacci, and Antonio Gibelli (Udine: Gaspari, 2001), 151–73.
9. Ermacora says that "the military detachments were complemented by on average between 130,000 and 150,000 'operai borghesi' (civilian workers). During the

war, just the provision of services and execution of defense works required a vast number of workers, both civilian and military, ranging between 300,000 and 500,000 men, to which should be added the troops who carried out the work on the front line." See Matteo Ermacora, *Cantieri di guerra: Il lavoro dei civili nelle retrovie del fronte italiano (1915–1918)* (Bologna: Il Mulino, 2005), 68.

10. See Francesca Sancin, "Le portatrici carniche: Maria Plotzner Mentil," in *Donne nella Grande Guerra*, ed. Marta Boneschi et al. (Bologna: Il Mulino, 2014), 51–66. See also Franca Cosmai, "Le portatrici carniche e cadorine: Una peculiare forma di mobilitazione femminile nella zona di guerra," in Filippini, *Donne dentro la guerra*, 187–202. On women porters in Trentino, see Nicola Fontana, "L'impiego della manodopera femminile nei lavori di fortificazione sul fronte trentino," in *Donne in Guerra, 1915–1918: La Grande Guerra attraverso l'analisi e le testimonianze di una terra di confine*, ed. Paola Antolini et al. (Trento: Centro Studi Judicaria, 2006), 49–68; Matteo Ermacora, "Frauen im Krieg: Das Fallbeispiel Friaul (1915–1917)," in "Krieg und Geschlecht/Guerra e genere," ed. Siglinde Clementi and Oswald Überegger, special issue, *Geschichte und Region/Storia e Regione* 23, no. 2 (2014): 98–117; Matteo Ermacora, "Women Behind the Lines: The Friuli Region as a Case Study of Total Mobilization, 1915–1917," in *Gender and the First World War*, ed. Christa Hämmerle, Oswald Überegger, and Birgitta Bader Zaar (New York: Palgrave Macmillan, 2014), 16–35.

11. Giovanni Scarabello, *Il martirio di Venezia durante la Grande Guerra e l'opera di difesa della marina italiana*, 2 vols. (Venice: Tipografia del Gazzettino Illustrato, 1933).

12. See Bruna Bianchi, "Vivere a Venezia durante la guerra: Le donne, la povertà, il trauma, la protesta (1914–1919)," in Filippini, *Donne dentro la guerra*, 119–38.

13. On the causes, dimensions, and social consequences of this defeat, see Nicola Labanca, *Caporetto: Storia e memoria di una disfatta* (Bologna: Il Mulino, 2017).

14. Daniele Ceschin, *Gli esuli di Caporetto: I profughi in Italia durante la Grande Guerra* (Rome: Laterza, 2006); Daniele Ceschin, "Profughe: Donne in fuga dalla zona di guerra," in Ufficio Storico, *Le donne nel primo conflitto mondiale*, 153–70; Daniele Ceschin, "Dopo Caporetto: Donne in fuga e vittime di violenza," in Filippini, *Donne dentro la guerra*, 203–18.

15. Ardengo Soffici, *La ritirata del Friuli: Note di un ufficiale della seconda armata* (Florence: Vallecchi, 1919).

16. Antonietta Giacomelli, *Vigilie (1914–1918)*, ed. Saveria Chemotti (1919; Padua: Il Poligrafo, 2014), 251 (31 October 2017), 256 (3 November 1917).

17. See Ceschin, *Gli esuli di Caporetto*; Daniele Ceschin, "L'esilio in Italia: I profughi di guerra," in *Gli italiani in Guerra: Conflitti, identità, memorie dal Risorgimento ai nostri giorni*, 5 vols., ed. Mario Isnenghi, vol. 3: *La Grande Guerra: Dall'intervento alla "vittoria mutilata,"* ed. Mario Isnenghi and Daniele Ceschin (Turin: UTET, 2008), part 1, 260–73. See also Luciana Palla, "Scritture di donne: La memoria delle profughe trentine nella prima guerra mondiale," *DEP: Deportate, esuli, profughe; Rivista telematica di studi sulla memoria femminile* 1 (2004): 45–52.

18. Ceschin, *Gli esuli di Caporetto*, 193.

19. Ibid.

20. Ibid., 196.

21. On the work of the Commission of Inquiry, see Labanca, *Caporetto*, 88–99.

22. Archivio Centrale dello Stato (ACS), *Reale Commissione d'Inchiesta*, b. 1, testimonianza di Don Liva Valentino, canonico di Cividale e funzionate da sindaco nei mesi dell'occupazione nemica, 21 December 1918.

23. ACS, *Reale Commissione d'Inchiesta*, b. 3, testimonianza di Don Carlo De Nardi, sacerdote di Pieve di Soligo, 9 January 1919.
24. ACS, *Reale Commissione d'Inchiesta*, b. 1, testimonianza di Don Liva Valentino, canonico di Cividale, 21 December 1918.
25. ACS, *Reale Commissione d'Inchiesta*, b. 1, testimonianza di Don Vincenzo Botteon, parroco di San Marino in Conegliano, 20 December 1918.
26. ACS, *Reale Commissione d'Inchiesta*, b. 1, testimonianza del Cav. Umberto Castellani e Federico Cammeo, Pordenone, 24 November 1918.
27. ACS, *Reale Commissione d'Inchiesta*, b. 1, testimonianza di Don Vincenzo Botteon, parroco di San Marino in Conegliano, 20 December 1918.
28. Filippini, "Nei territori del fronte," 233.
29. Marco Mondini, *La guerra italiana: Partire, raccontare, tornare, 1914–18* (Bologna: Il Mulino, 2014), 283.
30. Quoted in Filippini, "Il Veneto in guerra," 144.
31. ACS, *Reale Commissione d'Inchiesta*, b. 3, testimonianza di Don Carlo De Nardi, sacerdote di Pieve di Soligo, 9 January 1919.
32. ACS, *Reale Commissione d'Inchiesta*, b. 3, testimonianza di Don Carlo De Nardi, sacerdote di Pieve di Soligo, 9 January 1919.
33. Giorgio Mortara, *La salute pubblica in Italia durante e dopo la guerra* (Bari: Laterza, 1925), 110, and chap. 9 ("Cause di morti per regione"). The author's analysis compares data from across the country. See also Giovanna Procacci, "Il fronte interno e la società italiana in Guerra," in *La guerra italo-austriaca (1915–18)*, ed. Nicola Labanca and Oswald Überegger (Bologna: Il Mulino, 2014), 215–37.
34. Mortara, *La salute pubblica*, 103.
35. See John Horne, "Atrocité et exactions contre les civils," in *Encyclopedie de la Grande Guerre: Histoire et culture; 1914–18*, ed. Stéphane Audoin-Rouzeau and Jean-Jacques Becker, 2nd ed. (Montrouge: Bayard, 2013), 367–79; Bruna Bianchi, *Crimini di guerra e contro l'umanità: Le violenze ai civili sul fronte orientale (1914–1919)* (Milan: Unicopli, 2012); Bruna Bianchi, ed., *La violenza contro la popolazione civile nella Grande Guerra: Deportati, profughi, internati* (Milan: Unicopli, 2006).
36. On violence on the Italian front, see Antonio Gibelli, "Guerra e violenze sessuali: Il caso veneto e friulano," in *La memoria della Grande Guerra nelle Dolomiti*, ed. Isabella Bossi Fedrigotti, Luciana Palla, Giovanna Procacci, and Antonio Gibelli (Udine: Gaspari, 2001), 195–206; Daniele Ceschin, "L'estremo oltraggio: La violenza alle donne in Friuli e in Veneto durante l'occupazione austro-germanica (1917–1918)," in Bianchi, *La violenza contro la popolazione civile*, 165–84; Laura Calò, "Le donne friulane e la violenza di guerra durante l'occupazione austro-tedesca 1917–1918: Alcuni esempi per la Carnia," in *Carnia invasa, 1917–1918: Storia, documenti e fotografie dell'occupazione austro-tedesca della Carnia e Friuli*, ed. Enrico Folisi (Tolmezzo: Arti Grafiche Friulane, 2003), 111–32.
37. ACS, *Reale Commissione d'Inchiesta*, b. 1, testimonianza di A. D. T., Vittorio Veneto, 15 December 1918.
38. ACS, *Reale Commissione d'Inchiesta*, b. 1, testimonianza di F. R., Ronchis di Torreano, 24 January 1919.
39. ACS, *Reale Commissione d'Inchiesta*, b. 1, testimonianza di C. G., Ronchis di Torreano (Udine).
40. Ceschin, "Dopo Caporetto."

41. ACS, *Reale Commissione d'Inchiesta*, b. 3, testimonianza di Don Carlo De Nardi, sacerdote di Pieve di Soligo, 9 January 1919.
42. ACS, *Reale Commissione d'Inchiesta*, b. 1, testimonianza del sig. Mandruzzato di Belluno.
43. ACS, *Reale Commissione d'Inchiesta*, b. 1, testimonianza di A. D. T., Vittorio Veneto.
44. ACS, *Reale Commissione d'Inchiesta*, b. 1, testimonianza di M. E., Conegliano, 29 December 1918
45. On the orphanage in Portogruaro, see Andrea Falcomer, "Gli 'orfani dei vivi': Madri e figli della guerra e della violenza nell'attività dell'Istituto San Filippo Neri (1918–1947)," *DEP: Deportate, esuli, profughe* 10 (2009): 76–93. See also Calò, "Le donne friulane e la violenza di guerra," which also drew on the archive of the orphanage. On "war children" elsewhere in Europe, see Ruth Harris, "The 'Child of the Barbarian': Rape, Race and Nationalism in France during the First World War," *Past & Present* 141 (1993), 170–206; Stéphane Audoin-Rouzeau, *L'enfant de l'ennemi, 1914–1918: Viol, avortement, infanticide pendant la Grande Guerre* (Paris: Aubier, 1995).
46. Falcomer, "Gli 'orfani dei vivi,'" 85.
47. Ibid., 84.
48. Ibid., 89.

Bibliography

Audoin-Rouzeau, Stéphane. *L'enfant de l'ennemi, 1914–1918: Viol, avortement, infanticide pendant la Grande Guerre*. Paris: Aubier, 1995.

Bartoloni, Stefania, ed. *La grande guerra delle italiane: Mobilitazioni, diritti, trasformazioni*. Rome: Viella, 2016.

———. *Donne di fronte alla guerra: Pace, diritti e democrazia*. Rome: Laterza, 2017.

Bianchi, Bruna. "Venezia nella Grande Guerra." In *Storia di Venezia: L'Ottocento e il Novecento*, 3 vols., edited by Mario Isnenghi and Stuart Woolf, 1:349–407. Rome: Istituto della Enciclopedia Italiana, 2002.

———, ed. *La violenza contro la popolazione civile nella Grande Guerra: Deportati, profughi, internati*. Milan: Unicopli, 2006.

———. *Crimini di guerra e contro l'umanità: Le violenze ai civili sul fronte orientale (1914–1919)*. Milan: Unicopli, 2012.

———. "Vivere a Venezia durante la guerra: Le donne, la povertà, il trauma, la protesta (1914–1919)." In *Donne dentro la guerra: Il primo conflitto mondiale in area veneta*, edited by Nadia Maria Filippini, 119–38. Rome: Viella, 2017.

Bianchi, Roberto, and Monica Pacini, eds. "Donne 'comuni' nell'Europa della Grande Guerra." *Genesis: Rivista della Società Italiana delle storiche* 15, no. 1 (special issue) (2016).

Calò, Laura. "Le donne friulane e la violenza di guerra durante l'occupazione austro-tedesca 1917–1918: Alcuni esempi per la Carnia." In *Carnia invasa, 1917–1918: Storia, documenti e fotografie dell'occupazione austro-tedesca della Carnia e Friuli*, edited by Enrico Folisi, 111–32. Tolmezzo: Arti Grafiche Friulane, 2003.

Ceschin, Daniele. "L'estremo oltraggio: La violenza alle donne in Friuli e in Veneto durante l'occupazione austro-germanica (1917–1918)." In *La violenza contro la popolazione civile nella Grande Guerra: Deportati, profughi, internati*, edited by Bruna Bianchi, 165–84. Milan: Unicopli, 2006.

———. *Gli esuli di Caporetto: I profughi in Italia durante la Grande Guerra*. Rome: Laterza, 2006.

———. "L'esilio in Italia: I profughi di guerra." In *Gli italiani in Guerra: Conflitti, identità, memorie dal Risorgimento ai nostri giorni*, 5 vols., edited by Mario Isnenghi. Vol. 3: *La Grande Guerra: Dall'intervento alla "vittoria mutilata*,*"* edited by Mario Isnenghi and Daniele Ceschin, part 1, 260–73. Turin: UTET, 2008.

———. "Profughe: Donne in fuga dalla zona di guerra." In *Le donne nel primo conflitto mondiale: Dalle linee avanzate al fronte interno; la Grande Guerra delle italiane; Atti del congresso di studi storici internazionali*, edited by Ufficio Storico, Stato maggiore della Difesa, 153–70. Rome: Stato maggiore della Difesa, 2016.

———. "Dopo Caporetto: Donne in fuga e vittime di violenza." In *Donne dentro la guerra: Il primo conflitto mondiale in area veneta*, edited by Nadia Maria Filippini, 203–18. Rome: Viella, 2017.

Cosmai, Franca. "Le portatrici carniche e cadorine: Una peculiare forma di mobilitazione femminile nella zona di guerra." In *Donne dentro la guerra: Il primo conflitto mondiale in area veneta*, edited by Nadia Maria Filippini, 187–202. Rome: Viella, 2017.

Ermacora, Matteo. *Cantieri di guerra: Il lavoro dei civili nelle retrovie del fronte italiano (1915–1918)*. Bologna: Il Mulino, 2005.

———. "Frauen im Krieg: Das Fallbeispiel Friaul (1915–1917)." In "Krieg und Geschlecht/Guerra e genere," edited by Siglinde Clementi and Oswald Überegger, Special issue, *Geschichte und Region/Storia e Regione* 23, no. 2 (2014): 98–117.

———. "Udine, capitale della guerra." In *Fronti interni: Esperienze di guerra lontano dalla guerra, 1914–1918*, edited by Andrea Scartabellati, Matteo Ermacora, and Felicita Ratti, 109–28. Naples: Edizioni Scientifiche Italiane, 2014.

———. "Women behind the Lines: The Friuli Region as a Case Study of Total Mobilization, 1915–1917." In *Gender and the First World War*, edited by Christa Hämmerle, Oswald Überegger, and Birgitta Bader Zaar, 16–35. New York: Palgrave Macmillan, 2014.

Falcomer, Andrea. "Gli 'orfani dei vivi': Madri e figli della guerra e della violenza nell'attività dell'Istituto San Filippo Neri (1918–1947)." *DEP: Deportate, esuli, profughe; Rivista telematica di studi sulla memoria femminile* 10 (2009): 76–93.

Filippini, Nadia Maria, ed. *Donne dentro la guerra. Il primo conflitto mondiale in area veneta*. Rome: Viella, 2017.

———. "Il Veneto in guerra. Le donne delle province nord-orientali al fronte e nelle retrovie." In *Le donne nel primo conflitto mondiale: Dalle linee avanzate al fronte interno; la Grande Guerra delle italiane; Atti del congresso di studi storici internazionali*, edited by Ufficio Storico, Stato maggiore della Difesa, 137–52. Rome: Stato maggiore della Difesa, 2016.

———. "Nei territori del fronte. L'area veneta." In *La grande guerra delle italiane: Mobilitazioni, diritti, trasformazioni*, edited by Stefania Bartoloni, 229–48. Rome: Viella, 2016.

Fontana, Nicola. "L'impiego della manodopera femminile nei lavori di fortificazione sul fronte trentino." In *Donne in Guerra, 1915–1918: La Grande Guerra attra-*

verso l'analisi e le testimonianze di una terra di confine, by Paola Antolini, Gunda Barth-Scalmani, Matteo Ermacora, Nicola Fontana, Diego Leoni, Paolo Malni, and Anna Pisetti, 49–68. Trento: Centro Studi Judicaria, 2006.

Franzina, Emilio. "Le fabbriche dell'amore castrense: Case e casini del soldato." In *La memoria della Grande Guerra nelle Dolomiti*, edited by Isabella Bossi Fedrigotti, Luciana Palla, Giovanna Procacci, and Antonio Gibelli, 151–73. Udine: Gaspari, 2001.

———. *Casini di guerra: Il tempo libero dalla trincea e i postriboli militari nel primo conflitto mondiale*. Udine: Gaspari, 1999.

Giacomelli, Antonietta. *Vigilie (1914–1918)*. Edited by Saveria Chemotti. 1919. Reprint, Padua: Il Poligrafo, 2014.

Gibelli, Antonio. "Guerra e violenze sessuali: Il caso veneto e friulano." In *La memoria della Grande Guerra nelle Dolomiti*, by Isabella Bossi Fedrigotti, Luciana Palla, Giovanna Procacci, and Antonio Gibelli, 195–206. Udine: Gaspari, 2001.

Harris, Ruth. "The 'Child of the Barbarian': Rape, Race and Nationalism in France during the First World War." *Past & Present* 141 (1993), 170–206.

Horne, John. "Atrocité et exactions contre les civils." In *Encyclopedie de la Grande Guerre. Histoire et culture. 1914–18*, 2nd ed., edited by Stéphane Audoin-Rouzeau and Jean-Jacques Becker, 367–79. Montrouge: Bayard, 2013.

Labanca, Nicola. *Caporetto: Storia e memoria di una disfatta*. Bologna: Il Mulino, 2017.

Mondini, Marco. *La guerra italiana: Partire, raccontare, tornare, 1914–18*. Bologna: Il Mulino, 2014.

Mortara, Giorgio. *La salute pubblica in Italia durante e dopo la guerra*. Bari: Laterza, 1925.

Palla, Luciana. "Scritture di donne: La memoria delle profughe trentine nella prima guerra mondiale." *DEP: Deportate, esuli, profughe; Rivista telematica di studi sulla memoria femminile* 1 (2004): 45–52.

Procacci, Giovanna. "L'internamento di civili in Italia durante la prima guerra mondiale: Normativa e conflitti di competenza." *DEP: Deportate, esuli, profughe; Rivista telematica di studi sulla memoria femminile* 5–6 (2006): 33–66. Available online at: www.unive.it/pag/fileadmin/user_upload/dipartimenti/DSLCC/documenti/DEP/numeri/n5-6/3_Procacci.pdf.

———. "Il fronte interno e la società italiana in Guerra." In *La guerra italo-austriaca (1915–18)*, edited by Nicola Labanca and Oswald Überegger, 215–37. Bologna: Il Mulino, 2014.

Sancin, Francesca. "Le portatrici carniche: Maria Plotzner Mentil." In *Donne nella Grande Guerra*, edited by Marta Boneschi et al., 51–66. Bologna: Il Mulino, 2014.

Scarabello, Giovanni. *Il martirio di Venezia durante la Grande Guerra e l'opera di difesa della marina italiana*. 2 vols. Venice: Tipografia del Gazzettino Illustrato, 1933.

Soffici, Ardengo. *La ritirata del Friuli: Note di un ufficiale della seconda armata*. Florence: Vallecchi, 1919.

Thébaud, Françoise. "La Grande Guerra: Età della donna o trionfo della differenza sessuale?" In *Storia delle donne*, edited by Georges Duby and Michelle Perrot. Vol. 5: *Il Novecento*, edited by Françoise Thébaud, 25–90. Rome: Laterza, 1992.

———. "Femmes et genre dans la guerre." In *Encyclopédie de la Grande Guerre*, edited by Stéphane Audoin-Rouzeau and Jean-Jacques Becker, 613–25. Montrouge: Bayard, 2004.

Ufficio Storico, Stato maggiore della Difesa, ed. *Le donne nel primo conflitto mondiale: Dalle linee avanzate al fronte interno; la Grande Guerra delle italiane; Atti del congresso di studi storici internazionali*. Rome: Stato maggiore della Difesa, 2016.

Willson, Perry. *Women in Twentieth-Century Italy*. Basingstoke: Palgrave Macmillan, 2010.

Section 7

WAR EXPERIENCE AND MEMORY

CHAPTER 16

The Construction of the Enemy in Two Jewish Writers
Carolina Coen Luzzatto and Enrica Barzilai Gentilli

Tullia Catalan

Introduction

In the Austrian Littoral area, including the cities of Gorizia and Trieste, the years preceding and during World War I were characterized by a bitter struggle of a national nature between Italians, Slovenians, and Croats, accompanied in irredentist areas by a strong anti-Austrian sentiment. The cultural and artistic circles as well as the national political associations and representations were by preponderance middle class, largely composed of members of the free professions, and motivated by the desire for their own national claims to prevail over those of the other side, if not even to declare, as in the case of the philo-Italian national liberals, their own cultural supremacy in Trieste.[1] In this climate of tension and competition over political and cultural hegemony, the role of intellectuals became crucial by virtue of their influence on public opinion, which at the time was more literate than in the Kingdom of Italy.[2]

During the second half of the nineteenth century and up until the eve of World War I, the political struggle saw all possible means of propaganda pressed into service, as has been noted, with copious use of journals, romances, and poetic and dramaturgical productions to convey the most important themes of Italian patriotism and thus make them palatable to the rest of the population.[3] These were the privileged channels in the Upper Adriatic for spreading the stereotypical image of the political enemy, both internal and external, identified in the so-called "Slavs" already at the end of the 1870s.[4] During the war, there was a propaganda campaign against the Austrians in irredentist circles in exile in the Kingdom of Italy, alongside their campaign against the "Slavic" enemy, while among the Italian nationalists the enemy was primarily identified as German.[5]

Some irredentist intellectuals in this border area between Italy and Austria also contributed to delineation of the enemy's characteristic features and then used them in the propagandistic work of delegitimating the enemy through construction of a public narrative that often propounded the same negative stereotypes. These irredentist intellectuals included, for example, Carolina Coen Luzzatto of Gorizia and Enrica Barzilai Gentilli of Trieste, who I am about to examine. Together with other female writers like Ida Finzi (pen name Haydée), Elody Oblath, and Rina del Prado,[6] they enthusiastically participated in the political struggle to claim Trieste and Gorizia for Italy and used their literary abilities journalistically and narratively to provoke a broader mobilization and in order to include women and the younger generations in support of the cause.[7] The public they addressed was primarily women and children, through novels and pedagogical writings used to educate the new generation to the nation.[8] Some of these writers were Austrian citizens; others were *regnicole*, meaning they had Italian citizenship although they lived in Trieste or Gorizia. These latter were compelled to abandon Austrian territory along with their families and reenter the Kingdom of Italy when war broke out.

The present research begins with some questions regarding the role of female intellectuals in Adriatic irredentism, with particular attention to the manner of their participation in the political conflict before and during World War I.[9] I have investigated their contribution, through narrative and journalism, to constructing an image of the enemy that would survive the war and evolve with much more violent overtones during the Fascist period. I have asked how these women positioned themselves with respect to the climate of violence that permeated the political debate in this border area while contributing through their literary productions to consolidating a political culture of exclusion of the other that would become radicalized in the wartime years. The period of war represented a moment of change in this field too, since the initial hostility toward the enemy rapidly transformed into authentic hatred that was destined to endure in the following decades.

I have focused my attention on Carolina Coen Luzzatto and Enrica Barzilai Gentilli, whose careers as intellectuals in a border context, educated as they were in the multiethnic and multireligious Habsburg region, emerge clearly from their intellectual and political as well as their familial biographies. The cultural Jewish roots they shared, although manifesting in very different ways in their lives, took a toll especially on Carolina when the Christian Social Party—which advocated political antisemitism even in Trieste and Gorizia, places that were so different from Vienna at the time—came to power in Austria.[10]

Carolina Coen Luzzatto and Enrica Barzilai Gentilli: Two Female Jewish Writers in a Border Region

In this chapter, I examine the activities of two Jewish intellectuals originally from Trieste[11] and analyze their intellectual careers in the light of the presence—albeit one in the minority—of a current of political antisemitism in the Austrian Littoral area[12] in an attempt to infer the motivations for their assuming such a radical stance as they did against the Slovenians and Austrians. The chapter centers on some salient moments in the biographies of Carolina Coen Luzzatto (1837–1919)[13] and Enrica Barzilai Gentilli (1859–1936),[14] residents respectively of Gorizia and Trieste, two cities on the border between Austria and Italy. Their journalistic and literary productions are analyzed to determine their contribution, through their writings and publications, to the construction of the political enemy, focusing on the war period, especially in the case of Enrica. Therefore, I have paid attention to the manner in which the two writers were able to mobilize people on the topics dear to their hearts. Both were ardent supporters of irredentism and were also involved (Carolina more so than Enrica) in the female emancipation movement, but they belonged to two different generations, with different experiences of political militancy, although they reached the same conclusions during the war.

Sara, called Carolina, daughter of Isach Sabbadini and Stellina Estella Norsa, was born in Trieste in 1837 to a middle-class family of stockbrokers of Sephardic origin; she was more than twenty years older than Enrica Barzilai Gentilli. She received a Jewish education from her family from an early age in a Trieste that was still cosmopolitan and a fully developed commercial center. The port city provided her the opportunity to come into contact with the Italian literary tradition through the Piedmontese professor Marco Tedeschi, who was chief rabbi of the local Jewish community at the time, while she simultaneously received a solid patriotic Italian education.[15] In the following decades, which she spent in neighboring Gorizia where she moved after her marriage to Salomon Girolamo Coen Luzzatto in 1856, Carolina did not distance herself from the Jewish religion but continued to be observant.[16] This constant respect for the Jewish tradition showed itself in the education she provided her children, and also from small hints that can be derived from the correspondence of her nephew, Carlo Michelstaedter, who mentions more than once his recollection of some Jewish festivity at Aunt Carolina's.[17]

Three children were born of the marriage of Carolina and Girolamo: Graziadio, Cornelia, and Ada, but her private life was not devoid of suffering, despite the friendly ties maintained with her husband's entire family, among them the Michelstaedters.[18] Relations with her children were tormented and worsened by the suicide of her younger daughter, Ada, while she never achieved a full and harmonious union with her husband despite good grounds for one, particularly on the intellectual level; and thus for some years Carolina also lived through the pain of an impossible love. One could say that Carolina fulfilled herself mostly outside of the family sphere, in her cultural and political activity as a writer and, above all, as an indefatigable journalist; indeed, she was the first woman to direct an Italian-language political journal, *Il Corriere di Gorizia*, which she did with steadfastness and passion.[19]

For her part, Enrica (Enrichetta) Barzilai Gentilli had better fortune in family affections, although we know unfortunately little about her private life. Born in Trieste in 1859, she too was a member of a Sephardic group; she was the daughter of Elena Saraval and Giuseppe Barzilai, an orientalist philologist, literato, and much-esteemed biblical commentator. A lawyer by profession, he was also chancellor of the Jewish community of Trieste and fervently Italian, to the point that in 1866, he chose to become a citizen of the kingdom and thus forfeited his right to practice as a lawyer in Austrian territory. Enrica was raised, like Carolina, in a family with Italian sentiments that had maintained its ties with the Mosaic religion. In 1884, Enrica was married in Trieste, in a Jewish ceremony, to her coreligionist, the journalist Alberto Gentilli, an Austrian subject. The two young people were known within one of the Triestine literary salons, that of Elisa Tagliapietra Cambon, which was frequented by philo-Italian intellectuals and irredentists. Gentilli was a fervent irredentist and, from 1890 up until the outbreak of war, the editor and editor in chief of *Il Piccolo*, Teodoro Mayer's daily newspaper that was very widely circulated in the city and was sympathetic to the liberal-nationalist position.[20]

After his hasty flight to Italy on 21 May 1915 to join his wife, who had already left at Christmas 1914, and to avoid capture by the Austrian police who had been informed of his "radical Italian" sentiments,[21] Gentilli worked as an editor on important nationalist papers like *La Tribuna* and, after the war, the *Messaggero*.

Family life was very fulfilling for Enrica, who was deeply bonded to her husband through affection and shared political ideals. They had two daughters, Rina and Nella. Her special bond of affection with and mutual admiration for her brother, Salvatore Barzilai, was also important; he was a deputy, a mason, and, during World War I, minister without portfolio in the Salandra government, nominated a senator of the kingdom in 1920.[22] Enrica was always very close to him, more so than to her other four siblings.

Coming as they did from the same city and the same Jewish community, which was one of the most dynamic in the Habsburg Empire at the time, and with both of them actively involved in many irredentist initiatives in Trieste and Gorizia, the two women had thus already approached the theme of the enemy prior to the outbreak of war.

Participation in and organization of public readings in salons and Italian-minded cultural circles frequented by the liberal bourgeoisie; conferences; involvement in artistic and literary productions, sometimes also in the presence of intellectuals from the Kingdom of Italy: this was the terrain in which to take the measure of the intended cultural mediation between Italy and the Italians of Austria, as Carolina Coen Luzzatto, for example, did for years. Endowed with great charisma and organizational skills, she stood out among irredentist women of the Gorizian and Triestine bourgeoisie for her ability to play her part in favor of Italy on two levels: that of the female emancipationist and that of the masculine political world, especially through her directorship of, first, the *Corriere di Gorizia* and later the *Corriere Friulano*, but also due to her frequent contributions to various papers in the kingdom, especially those of neighboring Friuli, where she could claim a solid relationship with several noted intellectuals, including the journalist Pacifico Valussi and the writer Giuseppe Marcotti.[23]

Less of a protagonist of the public irredentist scene in Trieste in the years before the war, Enrica Barzilai Gentilli was initially active primarily in literature for children and women; then, during the war and her exile in Rome, she entered a group of nationalist women and became very active in propaganda against the German enemy, to the point of being registered during the years of fascism as a Roman heroine during the conflict.[24]

At the end of the nineteenth century and the beginning of the twentieth, the political activity of both women was marked by some crucial phases that determined their turn in a radical direction, inserting them into a nationalist and xenophobic stream of interventionist nationalism characterized by violent language.[25] These new sentiments typified Carolina's contributions to the press in the years before the war, while for Enrica, expressions of hatred toward the enemy came later, coinciding with her abandonment of Trieste when war broke out and her arrival in Rome. Her insertion into the nationalist feminist environment came quickly; she was received with open arms both in the circle of the Lyceum and in the Comitato Nazionale Femminile Interventista Antitedesco (National Feminine Anti-German Interventionist Committee). Enrica's path was probably facilitated by her close relationship with Salvatore Barzilai, which opened the doors of the capital's political circles to her.

Although they both campaigned in the irredentist ranks and both belonged to the Jewish minority of the Littoral, it is not clear that the two women were in close contact, although they seem to have been distantly related.[26] We do know for certain that Carolina Coen Luzzatto appreciated the writings of Enrica Barzilai Gentilli; she expressed a positive opinion on "Confidenze Muliebri," one of Enrica's first literary essays, in the "Biblioteca del Corriere" column of the *Corriere di Gorizia*.[27]

In any case, in this crucial period for irredentism and for nationalism, with key topics closely related to the context of sentiment and female intimacy (albeit with constant attention to female emancipation), both of them dedicated themselves to the political struggle, inspired by deep-seated patriotic feelings for Italy. Both lived the battle of propaganda against the supposed "enemies of the homeland" unstintingly, to the point of spending all their energies on the political and nationalist effort. For Carolina, the principal enemy was the Slav, while for Enrica, it was the Slavs and the Germans who became the main objective of her writings in *L'Unità d'Italia* during her militancy in the Comitato Nazionale Femminile Interventista Antitedesco. Thus, with the instruments at their disposal, both contributed to the construction and dissemination in contemporary irredentist and nationalist circles of anti-Slav and anti-German stereotypes that were destined to endure over time.

From Children's Writers to Political Struggle against the Enemy: The Themes Addressed

Carolina and Enrica followed the same path into the world of letters: both of them wrote children's books, producing novels, narratives, and comedies with the pedagogical goal of educating the Italian, not the Austrian, nation.[28]

In her production for children, which she began in 1868, Carolina dealt with themes linked to the role of bourgeois women in modern society, paying special attention to the education of children. In her view, the love of the fatherland should be imparted to them from a young age, they should demonstrate attention and a charitable spirit toward those less well-off and endowed, and they should grow up honest. The role of the family was markedly central in this early work; education, for Carolina Coen Luzzatto, was the principal means through which to become a good Italian citizen, in that all her references to the classics of literature always point to works in Italian and never to those in German.

Furthermore, as Ziani and Curci emphasize, an educational method emerges in these writings characterized by a fundamental harshness that does not pardon any error, but even exalts in the inflexibility of customs and in loyalty to the fatherland and religion.[29] Another theme that was dear to her was that of female emancipation, reinforced by her ties with the writer Malvina Frank and the Italian women's press. She contributed to Gualberta Beccari's journal *La Donna* and during this period also translated a series of novels from German into Italian, bearing witness to the linguistic cosmopolitanism that characterized many of these women of the border region.

In his preface to a collection of Carolina's writings posthumously published in 1924, Ugo Pellis remarks, with the nationalist rhetoric of the day, on her patriotic commitment to childhood education, "to mold Italian boys and Italian girls of nobly human and sincerely Italian character, especially in irredentist country; here is the program that the writer of comedies, an excellent mother and excellent citizen, has proposed and accomplished with nobility and pride."[30] However, Carolina's intellectual capabilities were better expressed in her activities as a journalist and cultural mediator, contexts in which her irredentist political vision succeeded in captivating a large public in the philo-Italian circles of Trieste and Gorizia, where she was highly esteemed for her polemical capabilities and organizational tenacity.

Enrica Barzilai Gentilli's literary production began in 1896, when she was already the mother of two little girls. She often focused on the maternal role, on innovative topics like divorce, on which she expressed positions very critical of its consequences for the family, and on questions related to the class struggle. We learn from contemporary critics that Enrica's most successful literary productions were for the theater; she wrote comedies centered on current events and episodes drawn from popular life. The frequent setting of her works in Venice is considered a sort of homage and reminiscence of the beloved Italian identity.[31] Differently from Carolina, Enrica engaged with political journalism during the war, not before.

The education of little children, as well as of older boys and girls, was seen by both of them as one of the pillars of nation-building, and it was not by chance that literature on childhood at the time constituted a privileged domain for irredentist writers. During this period, this was the theater of action for other Triestine Jewish literati. Haydée (Ida Finzi) and Rina Del Prado, for example, wrote short stories and novels for the smallest children whose central message was the defense of the Italian nationalist identity against the Austrians and the threat of Germanization.[32] On the eve of World War I, many of these writers took a significant anti-German and anti-Slovenian turn on this subject, and beside the stereotype of the little "kraut-eating" German we find the coarse and perfidious Slovene urchin, devoid of culture and sensitivity when compared to the delicate and sensitive Italian child.

Enrica and Carolina, from two different generations, arrived at their radical anti-Slav and anti-German positions via different time frames and biographical courses. Carolina got there first, having passed through a greater number of phases, and her anti-Slavism had its roots in the consequences of political antisemitism at the end of the century, whose repercussions were felt in Gorizia. The antisemitic campaign carried out during the period of the Dreyfus Affair by the Slovenian Catholics in Gorizia against Carolina Luzzatto, and her strong influence on the local liberal press, played an important part in changing her attitude toward the Slovenian people. Meanwhile, Enrica assumed radical anti-German positions during the war and anti-Slav positions after the war, having come into closer contact with Italian nationalist currents during her exile in the Kingdom of Italy during the conflict. It is important to emphasize that antisemitism played no role in her case, but Italian propaganda against the enemy had a lot to do with it.[33] Both of their literary productions involved stereotypes and language proper to racial discrimination. We will first examine Carolina C. Luzzatto's intellectual and political trajectory in Gorizia at the end of the nineteenth and beginning of the twentieth centuries.

In turn-of-the-century Gorizia, Carolina was well ensconced in liberal-nationalist circles, of which she quickly became a noted animator. Her salon rapidly became famous in Gorizia, and her network of contacts surpassed its borders—on one side, Austria, and on the other, Italy—with the frequent presence of writers from the kingdom. For the topic under discussion here, her connection with the writer Giuseppe Marcotti was particularly important; he was the author of a violently anti-Slav novel, *L'Oltraggiata*, published in Italy in 1905 and immediately seized by the Austrian censors for its incitement to hatred.[34] All of the themes of anti-Slavism can be found in its pages. It tells of the rape of a young Italian woman from Gorizia by a corrupt Slovene priest. The woman, not coincidentally, is named Giulia, and the image intended to be evoked in the Italian readers of the novel is that of the irredentist lands of Venezia Giulia, violated by the presence of the Slavic enemy.

Carolina was involved in circulating the book clandestinely in Trieste, convinced that it was one of the most effective representations of the Slav threat to the so-called Italianness of the zone. In my view, the most important point is the reversion in this novel to the metaphor of the violated woman to deepen the image of the offended nation in the reader.[35]

Beginning in the 1870s, the journalist brought to life about a dozen associations in Gorizia with literary, artistic, and sporting focuses, all of them characterized by the Italianness of their constituencies. She had particular investment in two associations very close to irredentist ideals: the Pro Patria and the Lega Nazionale, both of them secretly financed by the Grand Orient of Italy. It was in these associations that anti-Slavism began to come up in conversations among members beginning in the second half of the nineteenth century. Carolina was able to maintain constant contact with Triestine and Udinese intellectuals throughout this period characterized by political conflict initially with Austria and then also with the Slovene community.

These contacts confirmed her in a profound anticlericalism against the Slovene clergy. The education of the Slovenian younger generation, which was frequently provided by clergy, was of great concern to Carolina C. Luzzatto, who was aware of how the educational context could become the ground for inculcating a nationalist identity. She frequently returns to this theme and to the necessity to be more dynamic and proactive as irredentists, including in her correspondence with Marcotti. Reading between the lines, one can sometimes discern her fundamental dissatisfaction at having been born a woman in a society in which women were excluded from political involvement. It is not by chance that she sadly remarked to Ugo Pellis, during the sole interview released on her life, "Pecà che non son giovine e che no son un omo."[36]

Despite this difficulty, she headed three journals, of which the most important and longest lived was *Il Corriere di Gorizia*, which lasted from 1883 to 1899. It was in this periodical that Carolina published many of her political articles under the pseudonym Arcolani, apparently out of a desire to conceal the fact that she was a woman. Carolina's progressive transformation into one of the greatest supporters of anti-Slavism in the Adriatic irredentist context got underway in the pages of this periodical. During the last years of the century, her attitude toward the Slovenes underwent a progressive transformation that we can sum up in three phases. The first phase featured an inclusive spirit, close to the ideals of Mazzini, that had her, in the first years of the 1870s, looking upon the Slovene population's self-affirmation process with admiration, although her conviction is also clear from articles published in Triestine and Gorizian periodicals that the Italian language and culture belonged to a superior civilization.[37] During the 1880s, the first fears emerge in Carolina's writings published in the *Corriere di Gorizia* in the face of an increasingly aggressive Slovene presence in the cultural and economic arena. In fact, the journalist was clearly aware that the Slovenes were already a group no longer to be identified exclusively with the peasant class except by forcing the paradigm. A growing Slovene bourgeoisie was active in Gorizia at the time and was becoming significant even on the political stage. Therefore, Carolina began to mobilize the supporters of the Italian cause with articles and conferences organized ad hoc to continue the struggle to defend the Italianness that was threatened, in her view, by Slovene enterprise. She saw it as crucial for the irredentist cause to hinder the spread of Slovene schools in the territory, and it also became vital to completely oppose the Slovene clerical component, which she viewed as a prime obstacle to progress and modernity.

In an 1883 article, for example, Carolina emphasizes Austria's differential treatment of nationalist claims by Italians and Slovenes, whereby the latter were always preferentially satisfied in their requests compared to the Italians:

> The axiom of two weights and two measures has thus been peacefully developed among us, as if it were the law or the right of the Slovenes. They have broken through open doors and passed onward, taking advantage not only of their nationality but also clearly seeking to trample on ours. ... Let us not begrudge them, but, now awakened from our drowsiness, let us ask for ourselves what should be denied them.[38]

The third and final phase of her political activism was characterized by a turn to join the ranks of the nationalist and xenophobic irredentists, appropriating their topics and discriminatory language.[39] This radical change, which can be verified from Carolina's writings, may be attributed to the harsh antisemitic attacks of which the Jewish writer was the subject in the Gorizian Slovene Catholic press in the Christian Social context, during a period in which the Christian Social Party was establishing itself in Austria and the Dreyfus Affair was underway.[40] For her part, Carolina never considered renouncing her Judaism, unlike other irredentists, and countered the charges with similarly violent language, unleashing outbursts of outright anti-Slavism.

Thus, we come to a period in which the opposition of the two nationalisms manifested in reciprocal demonization, the one of the other, with the "other" portrayed as an enemy to be annihilated. These positions did not change in the first years of the twentieth century, and Carolina stood firm in her violently anti-Slavic positions until the outbreak of World War I, as we can see in all her correspondence with Marcotti, as well as in her articles in the *Corriere Friulano*, the periodical to which she assiduously contributed until the outbreak of war.[41]

In November 1915, at seventy-nine years old, she was arrested, together with other Gorizian irredentists, and imprisoned by the Austrian authorities as a political danger. Carolina C. Luzzatto was incarcerated at Göllersdorf together with her faithful friend and collaborator Costantina Furlani,[42] who was willing to follow her to prison at all costs. Even in the wretched conditions of imprisonment,[43] and notwithstanding her old age, her capacity to maintain contacts was not diminished. Unfortunately, nothing remains of her private letters, because the house in Gorizia was destroyed by bombardments during the war. However, we learn the record of this period of imprisonment from the recollections of many former political prisoners in Austria, where her combative character and her ability to bring people together through her political passion come to the fore. Thus, when news of the Italian conquest of Gorizia arrived in 1916, one of her companions in Göllersdorf, Nicolò Cobol of Trieste, recalls:

> Carolina Luzzatto, the esteemed Gorizian writer, whom Austria deported to Göllersdorf despite her age of 80 years, her blindness, and the ailments that keep her in bed or in the armchair for much of the day, is also delighted by the taking

of Gorizia, for whose Italianness she had fought and suffered. Today, the nearly underground cell where she is confined that receives just a little light from a small window furnished with a huge grate, is the destination of a continuous pilgrimage of prisoners who come to meet and congratulate her. . . . One who goes to visit the cell in which the Teutonic barbarism has confined this prisoner is amazed by the solemn austerity that the noble figure of this writer confers on the poor, sad surroundings. The mayor of Gorizia visits Mrs. Luzzatto daily, and they spend hours and hours reminiscing together about the affairs, persons, and events of their Gorizia. The circle of visitors is not numerous because the environment is so constrained . . ., but it comprises the best elements among the prisoners. The conversations sometimes take on the most elevated tones, but it is the patriotic note that predominates. Luzzatto, courageous and combative fighter for the irredentist ideas, despite her age and her ailments still maintains her pristine energy.[44]

In the recollections of her contemporaries, Carolina C. Luzzatto is always described as a woman of great character and political passion. After being transferred to Oberhollabrunn in 1916 because of her precarious state of health, she was able to reenter Gorizia in October 1918, from where she then moved to Trieste in November, to be hosted by a relative who was very dear to her, her nephew Salvatore Sabbadini, an important figure in the Triestine Jewish community and noted irredentist in his own right.[45] In January 1919, having received the news of her son Graziadio's death in Athens, she decided to return to Gorizia, where she died in the same month. Her patriotism accompanied her to the grave; she requested to be buried wrapped in the tricolor, like a soldier.[46]

Ugo Pellis, remembering her also with regard to her anti-Slav passion, wrote:

> In politics, she had a practical directive, suitable to the needs and the times, with simple and restrained contours. For her, there was one enemy, one principal danger: the greed of the Slav, favored by the government and eager to take over the city. And indeed, the national struggle in Gorizia, and in the region as a whole, was a struggle, daggers drawn, with the "Slavs."[47]

Different and less well known, due to the absence of sources and monograph studies, was the experience of Enrica Barzilai Gentilli, for which we can identify two phases. The first took place in Trieste with her participation in the irredentist conspiracy in the first years of the twentieth century, together with her husband Alberto Gentilli, at a time when, as already mentioned, he was editor in chief of the *Piccolo*, Trieste's biggest daily. Both of them attended the literary salon of Elisa Tagliapietra Cambon, one of the city's centers of Italianness, where they came into contact with all the liberal-nationalist-minded intellectuals, with numerous representatives of the local Jewish community among them. In this period, we can discern some hints of anti-Slavic prejudice (which was already widespread in the city in liberal-nationalist environments) in some of her short stories, with Slovene children described as coarse, uncivil, and quarrelsome; these stereotypes were reiterated virulently in the immediate postwar period in the pedagogical context for the education of the new generation.[48] However, during this period in Trieste, she did not express such violently anti-Slavic positions as those already adopted by Carolina C. Luzzatto in her journal articles. Her turn in a more discriminatory and outright violent direction is rather to be seen in the second phase, coinciding with her exile to Rome with her family to avoid imprisonment and deportation by the Austrians, as actually happened to Carolina. She had no difficulty rapidly integrating herself into the political environment of the capital and very quickly became one of the protagonists of a group of nationalist women with whom she contributed to the press and to propaganda campaigns in support of the war. The experience of the war also brought her to change her mind, as shown by Monica Miniati, on the equality of men and women.[49]

In Rome, she joined the "Lyceum" circle,[50] the Lega Patriottica Femminile,[51] and later the Comitato Nazionale Femminile Interventista Antitedesco, and contributed to two periodicals: *L'Unità d'Italia: Organo del Comitato nazionale femminile per l'intervento italiano*, directed by Beatrice Sacchi and founded in July 1915 under the strong influence of French anti-German propaganda,[52] and *La Madre Italiana: Rivista mensile per orfani della Guerra*, which began publication in May 1916. It was the war that caused the hatred of Germans and Slavs to take root in Enrica, a common course for many other irredentist women in the Adriatic area, such as Luisa Carniel Slataper, the wife of Scipio Slataper, and also Ida Finzi (Haydée).[53] The women who gathered in Rome in the Comitato antitedesco, which had about 250 members, mostly came from the emancipationist bourgeoisie and aristocracy and were motivated by the idea of the superiority of the Latin race and animated by a radicalized hatred of the Germans, including Germans who had lived in Italy for years.[54] Very early on in the twentieth century, the irredentist women of Trieste and Gorizia had settled into an attitude of rejection toward the German element and one of distance toward the Slovenes, at a time in which the self-assertion of the Slovene bourgeoisie had been flagged as a danger to the Italian cultural hegemony in the two cities. This experience, matured ahead of time and already partially structured in its repertoire of topics and language to be used against the enemy, was now put in the service of war propaganda. It can thus be declared that the irredentist world, both male and female, had already learned to sharpen their weapons against their adversaries. The Jewishness of both our writers does nothing to detract from their assuming these positions; for both of them, the two arenas of fatherland and religious faith were clearly distinct, and the second belonged to the dimension of the family, not the public sphere.

Referring to the Comitato Nazionale Femminile Interventista Antitedesco and the positions it took in the press during the war, Laura Guidi clearly highlights the racist drift, illuminating how the war also gave rise to a discourse on race aimed at achieving greater national cohesiveness:

> The war was a double benefit, in their eyes: on the one hand, it reinforced and expanded the frontier with the Austro-German minority, and on the other it mobilized the "bloodline" against the common enemy of the race . . . it allowed one to look to a new national cohesiveness, hierarchically structured on the military model. This was an absolute conception that did not allow for shading or internal differentiations, and it rejected every critical manifestation without tolerance.[55]

Enrica Barzilai Gentilli joined this nationalist current with great enthusiasm, as can be seen in her articles published in *L'Unità d'Italia* and her important participation in the second congress of the Comitato in May 1918, where her discourse on safeguarding the purity of the Italian stock from possible German contamination assumed violent and racist tones.[56] The chief objects of her attacks were the German women present in Italy during the war because of marital ties or work obligations, and even the families in the kingdom who continued to buy German toys for their children.

The voice of Anna Maria Mozzoni had already been heard calling into question mixed marriages between Italians and Germans in a 1915 article in very violent tones, permeated with racism. The article is worth quoting from here, as it epitomizes all the propaganda in the journals on this theme, showing that this was a political angle shared by several contributors to this element of the press. For Mozzoni, between the Germans and the Italians there was an

> incompatibility of race; no harmonious combination has ever been possible between them, for historical reasons and, perhaps fatally, for reasons of nature. . . . It is difficult to imagine two mentalities, two consciences, two traditions, two races more incompatible and mutually repellent. . . . Violence alone is reasonable, necessary, and moral, to break up relationships that nature repudiates.[57]

The stereotypical baggage adopted to outline the figure of the enemy was already well known among irredentists, who had been making liberal use of it since the end of the nineteenth century; the Germans, like the Slavs, were duly defined as barbarian and cruel. Even their God was different from the God of the Latins, French, and Italians, as Enrica herself makes very clear in an article on the theme of Christmas in 1915.[58] Reading her considerations, one can intuit the writer's path toward progressive intolerance for all that was not Italian or Latin. For example, she demonizes German-manufactured toys; in her view, the very features of the dolls reveal the coarseness of the Germans: "The Teutonic dolls, with their too-blue eyes, their too-chubby cheeks, their hair too much like straw, should be substituted with Italian dolls, which are prettier and more natural."[59] She further charges all those who continue to have contact with the German world despite the war, for whatever reason, with lack of patriotism. Thus, Enrica throws herself at consumers of German-brand chicory, the coffee substitute still sold by merchants too little attentive to the fate of their fatherland; also under attack are the bakers who continued to call their panini burrati "Vienna." Finally, theatrical and musical shows and programs that included German composers come under scrutiny, even those internationally recognized for their artistic value.[60]

The topic on which Barzilai Gentilli was most insistent, both in journal articles and during the second congress of the Comitato in May 1918, was that of mixed marriage. According to the Triestine writer, German women were naturally tyrannical toward Latin spouses: "The German woman . . . changes completely when she becomes the spouse of an Italian or a Frenchman; now, in the marital home, she becomes the dominatrix, the tyrant, the one who holds the scepter of power in her hand. . . ."[61] In her view, such unions represented a genuine danger to the purity of the Italian bloodline, and it was necessary to take all steps to prevent them, including by penalizing German women who had already become Italian citizens, legally, after marrying an Italian.[62]

The end of the war and Italian victory did nothing to change the proportion of violent tones in the narrative language of Enrica Barzilai Gentilli. In her later pedagogical output, the writer harped on the contrast between Italians and Slavs, exalting the superiority of the Italian race and civilization over the Slavic. There is no doubt that the war and the climate of violence it generated continued to impact the construction of the Slavic enemy in the eastern border area during the Fascist period.

Conclusion

Despite their different life experiences and their belonging to two different generations, it seems to me that Carolina Coen Luzzatto and Enrica Barzilai Gentilli display common elements in their militancy for Adriatic irredentism. These two border-region writers, both of them Jewish, although they lived their faith in the private sphere, were affected to different degrees by the political antisemitism present in Gorizia and Trieste at the end of the century. In that period, this antisemitism targeted the liberal-national irredentists, and Carolina, as a well-known public personage in Gorizia and Trieste, immediately became one of the targets of the Catholic press, especially the Slovene. At that time, the young Enrica Barzilai Gentilli was taking her first steps in producing literature for children and women, and, while she frequented Triestine irredentist environments along with her husband, she did not constitute an obvious target for the antisemites like Carolina. Both, however, breathed the climate of tension fed by the nationalist conflict between Slovenes and Italians in the two cities, and this influenced and radicalized their Italian patriotism. In both of them, the idea became progressively entrenched that the internal enemy should be combated with all possible means, and the experience of war constituted the crucial turning point that marked, especially for Enrica, the embracing of strongly racist positions against the German enemy. This was also facilitated by her coming into contact with an Italian nationalist milieu permeated with anti-German propaganda that was aggravated and violent in tone.

Thus, for both of them, the passage from anti-Slav prejudice, which is clearer in Carolina's case and also structured in her narratives and language, to a stereotyped image of the enemy that contained racist contours was a process that began at the turn from the nineteenth century to the twentieth and came to fruition during the war.

Tullia Catalan is associate professor of contemporary history at the University of Trieste (Department of Humanities). Her research interests include the history of the Jewish community of Trieste from 1789 to World War II; Italian Jews in the 1848 Revolution; antisemitism and Catholicism at the turn of the twentieth century and in the 1930s; the narratives and representations of anti-Slavism in the Upper Adriatic area; and the European Jewish philanthropic associations in the nineteenth and twentieth centuries. She is a member of the editorial boards of the journals *Quest: Issues in Contemporary Jewish History* and *Memoria e Ricerca*, and scientific supervisor of the Jewish Museum Carlo and Vera Wagner in Trieste.

Notes

This chapter has been translated from the Italian by Ela Harrison.
1. See Marina Cattaruzza, *L'Italia e il confine orientale: 1866–2006* (Bologna: Il Mulino, 2007), 63–70. On Slovenes in Trieste, see Marta Verginella, *Il confine degli altri: La questione giuliana e la memoria slovena* (Rome: Donzelli, 2008).
2. On irredentist intellectuals, see Angelo Ara and Claudio Magris, *Trieste: Un'identità di frontiera* (Turin: Einaudi, 1982); Roberto Pertici, ed., *Intellettuali di frontier: Triestini a Firenze (1900-1950)*, 2 vols. (Florence: Olschki, 1985); Renate Lunzer, *Irredenti redenti: Intellettuali giuliani del '900* (Gorizia: Lint Editoriale, 2009); Katia Pizzi, *A City in Search of an Author: The Literary Identity of Trieste* (London: Sheffield Academic Press, 2001). Always important on irredentism: Angelo Vivante, *Irredentismo Adriatico* (1912; Trieste: Edizioni Italo Svevo, 1984).

3. On the use of literature for patriotic purposes, see Alberto M. Banti, *La nazione del Risorgimento: Parentela, santità e onore alle origini dell'Italia unita* (Turin: Einaudi, 2000); Alberto M. Banti, *Sublime madre nostra: La nazione italiana dal Risorgimento al fascismo* (Rome: Laterza, 2011).
4. See Luca Giuseppe Manenti, "Geografia e politica nel razzismo antislavo: Il caso dell'irredentismo italiano (secoli XIX–XX)," in *Fratelli al massacre: Linguaggi e narrazioni della Prima guerra mondiale*, ed. Tullia Catalan (Rome: Viella, 2015), 17–38.
5. I have analyzed elsewhere this mechanism of creating an internal and external enemy in the Austrian Littoral: Tullia Catalan, "Linguaggi e stereotipi dell'antislavismo irredentista dalla fine dell'Ottocento alla Grande Guerra," in Catalan, *Fratelli*, 39–68. On this theme of the construction of the enemy in wartime, see Nicola Labanca and Camillo Zadra, eds., *Costruire un nemico: Studi di storia della propaganda di guerra* (Milan: Edizioni Unicopli, 2011); Angelo Ventrone, *Il nemico interno: Immagini, parole e simboli della lotta politica nell'Italia del Novecento* (Rome: Donzelli, 2005); Angelo Ventrone, *La seduzione totalitaria: Guerra, modernità, violenza politica (1914–1918)* (Rome: Donzelli, 2003).
6. On female irredentist writers, see Cristina Benussi, "Scrittrici a Trieste: Per una storia," in *Le triestine donne volitive: Presenza e cultura delle donne a Trieste tra Ottocento e Novecento*, ed. Anna Di Gianantonio and Marina Rossi (Trieste: Istituto Regionale per la Storia del movimento di liberazione in Friuli Venezia Giulia, 2006), esp. 66–69; Gabriella Ziani, "Letterate e artiste tra Otto e Novecento," in Di Gianantonio and Rossi, *Le triestine*, 107–25. See also Pizzi, *City in Search*.
7. For a general contextualization of the involvement of Italian women in World War I: Stefania Bartoloni, ed., *La Grande Guerra delle italiane: Mobilitazioni, diritti, trasformazioni* (Rome: Viella, 2016); Stefania Bartoloni, *Donne di fronte alla guerra: Pace, diritti e democrazia* (Rome: Laterza, 2017).
8. Pizzi, *City in Search*; Di Gianantonio and Rossi, *Le triestine*; Roberto Curci and Gabriella Ziani, *Bianco rosa e verde: Scrittrici a Trieste fra '800 e '900* (Trieste: Lint, 1993).
9. There is still no analytical study dedicated to the participation of women in the irredentist movement, despite the strong presence of women among the "irredenti" exiles and the numerous criminal proceedings against them during the wartime years when they were suspected of treason by Austria. Lunzer's book on irredentist intellectuals, *Irredenti*, pays no attention to women's contributions. The sole and fundamental text at our disposal, composed of biographical sketches, is Curci and Ziani, *Bianco*.
10. For a general background on the Triestine Jewish community that also takes account of the political antisemitism of the period, see Tullia Catalan, *La Comunità ebraica di Trieste 1781–1914: Politica, società e cultura* (Trieste: Lint, 2000). For the Jewish community of Gorizia, see Adonella Cedarmas, *La Comunità israelitica di Gorizia 1900–1945* (Udine: Istituto friulano per la storia del movimento di liberazione, 2000); Marco Grusovin, ed., *Cultura ebraica nel Goriziano* (Udine: Forum, 2007).
11. On Triestine Jewish women, see Tullia Catalan, "Donne ebree a Trieste fra Ottocento e prima guerra mondiale," in *Donne nella storia degli ebrei d'Italia: Atti del IX Convegno internazionale "Italia Judaica," Lucca, 6–9 giugno 2005*, ed. Michele Luzzati and Cristina Galasso (Florence: La Giuntina, 2007), 347–71. Fundamental on Jewish women in Italy: Monica Miniati, *Le emancipate: Le donne*

ebree in Italia nel XIX e XX secolo (Rome: Viella, 2008); for the participation of intellectual Jewish women in World War I, see Ruth Nattermann, "Zwischen Pazifismus, Irredentismus und nationaler Euphorie: Italienische Jüdinnen und der Erste Weltkrieg," in *Jüdische Publizistik und Literatur im Zeichen des Ersten Weltkriegs,* edited by Petra Ernst and Eleonore Lappin-Eppel (Innsbruck: Studienverlag 2016), 247–63; Monica Miniati, "Donne in guerra: Il contributo femminile ebraico nella Prima Guerra Mondiale," in *Gli ebrei italiani nella grande guerra (1915–1918): Atti del Convegno del Museo Ebraico, Bologna, 11 novembre 2015,* ed. Caterina Quareni and Vincenzo Maugeri (Florence: Giuntina, 2017), 127–47.

12. See Catalan, *La Comunità,* 251–302.
13. On Carolina Coen Luzzatto, see the biographical profile by Maddalena Del Bianco, "Luzzatto Coen Carolina, giornalista e patriota," in *Nuovo Liruti: Dizionario biografico dei friulani,* vol. 3: *L'Età contemporanea,* ed. Cesare Scalon, Claudio Griggio, and Giuseppe Bergamini (Udine: Forum, 2011) 1986–91. See also the fundamental volume by Maria Bozzini La Stella, *Carolina Coen Luzzatto* (Monfalcone: Edizioni della Laguna, 1995). See also Diego Redivo, "Tra ebraismo e irredentismo a proposito di una recente biografia di Carolina Luzzatto," *Quaderni Giuliani di Storia* 1 (1998), 155–63; Curci and Ziani, *Bianco,* 187–90.
14. On Enrica Barzilai Gentilli, see Curci and Ziani, *Bianco,* 87–96, where her literary and theatrical production is also examined. On Alberto Gentilli, see Enrica Barzilai Gentilli, *Nell'ottantesimo anniversario di Alberto Gentilli nato il 19 dicembre 1952, morto il 14 maggio 1932, dedica alla venerata memoria sua la vedova* (Trieste: s.n., 1932).
15. See Bozzini La Stella, *Carolina,* 17–22.
16. See ibid. 22–27.
17. See Carlo Michelstaedter, *Epistolario,* ed. Sergio Campailla (Milan: Adelphi, 1983), 292–95.
18. See Bozzini La Stella, *Carolina,* 28–29.
19. On the Gorizian press of the period, see Jolanda Pisani (Cassandra), "La stampa a Gorizia dal 1800 ai giorni nostri," *Studi Goriziani* 1 (1956): 39–49.
20. On the Triestine press, see Silvana Monti Orel, *I giornali triestini dal 1863 al 1902* (Trieste: Lint, 1976); Silvio Benco, ed., *Il "Piccolo" di Trieste: Mezzo secolo di giornalismo* (Rome: Treves, Treccani, Tumminelli, 1931). When Italy entered the war in May 1915, Alberto Gentilli fled Trieste immediately and took refuge in Italy, where his wife and children had moved some months earlier. There is a dossier on him in the Archivio di Stato di Trieste (henceforth ASTs) *I.R. Direzione di Polizia: Presidiali Riservati,* b. 412, fasc. Alberto Gentilli.
21. It appears from the documentation collected in the ASTs, *I.R. Direzione di Polizia: Presidiali Riservati,* b. 412, fasc. Alberto Gentilli, that when he fled, Gentilli did not possess excess wealth but only some savings. It also emerges from Austrian records that his wife was an Italian subject before their marriage. Trieste, 4 November 1915, letter from the I.R. Police Directorate of Trieste to the lieutenancy.
22. On Salvatore Barzilai: Emilio Falco, *Salvatore Barzilai: Un repubblicano moderno tra massoneria e irredentismo* (Rome: Bonacci, 1996).
23. Carolina's journalistic activity began with an apprenticeship at Giuseppe Caprin's "Il Progresso" in Trieste, part of the Garibaldine-Mazzinianine liberal-nationalist current. We can trace her activity in Gorizia from the end of the 1860s in the pages of *Isonzo,* of which she took charge for its final period until it ceased publication in March 1880. Through initiatives of Carolina C. Luzzatto, this periodical

was followed by *L'Imparziale* and *Il Raccoglitore*, both of them philo-Italian and both short lived, beginning and ceasing publication during the year 1880. It was the establishment of *Il Corriere di Gorizia* in Gorizia in 1883 that brought the real qualitative leap forward in Carolina's political journalism. She directed the periodical with great attentiveness and authority until it closed in 1899. Thereafter, she contributed assiduously to the *Corriere Friulano* until it closed in 1914. See Bozzini La Stella, *Carolina*, 103–33.

24. Costanzo Premuti, *Eroismo al fronte, bizantinismo all'interno* (Rome: Tipografia Italiana, 1924), 370.
25. I have analyzed Carolina C. Luzzatto's transition in Catalan, *Linguaggi e stereotipi*, 59–63.
26. A distant relationship between the two women is noted in Bozzini La Stella, *Carolina*, 116, but without specific details.
27. See ibid., 116.
28. For an overview of Carolina C. Luzzatto's literary production for children, see Bozzini La Stella, *Carolina*, 53–64. The education of children was a theme very dear to the Jewish-Italian community. Some Jewish women, like Adele Levi Della Vida, for example, as well as Elena Raffalovich Comparetti, were genuine pioneers of the Froebel Kindergartens in Italy. See Jole Ceccon, "Adele Levi della Vida e la sua opera in alcuni inediti," *Rassegna di pedagogia* 2 (1955): 120–32; Clotilde Barbarulli, "Dalla tradizione all'innovazione: 'La ricerca straordinaria' di Elena Raffalovich Comparetti," in *L'educazione delle donne: Scuole e modelli di vita femminile nell'Italia dell'Ottocento*, ed. Simonetta Soldani (Milan: Angeli, 1989), 425–43. See also James C. Albisetti, "Froebel Crosses the Alps: Introducing the Kindergarten in Italy," *History of Education Quarterly* 2 (2009): 159–69.
29. See Curci and Ziani, *Bianco*, 189–90.
30. See Ugo Pellis, *Prefazione a Carolina C. Luzzatto, Teatro educativo: Prose e poesie varie; Edite e inedite* (Trieste: casa ed. C.U.Trani, 1923), 10.
31. See Curci and Ziani, *Bianco*, 90–91. At the time, the issue of divorce was one of the most discussed themes in the Jewish world. See, for example, Vittorio Polacco, *La questione del divorzio e gli israeliti in Italia* (Padua-Verona: Fratelli Drucker, 1894). For the relation between Jewish Italians and the state, see Carlotta Ferrara degli Uberti, "Libertà di coscienza e modelli di cittadinanza nell'Italia liberale: Ebrei e Comunità ebraiche nel rapporto con le istituzioni statali," *Società e Storia* 118 (2007): 699–724.
32. On Ida Finzi and Rina Del Prado, see Ilona Fried, "L'immagine della donna nella narrativa femminile ebraica: Haydée, Rina Del Prado, Elody Oblath," in *Shalom Trieste: Gli itinerari dell'ebraismo*, ed. Adriano Dugulin (Trieste: Comune di Trieste, 1998), 189–98; Katia Pizzi, "Verso una pedagogia dell'unificazione: Allieve di quarta di Haydée e l'italianità ebraica a Trieste," in *Donne delle minoranze: Le ebree e le protestanti d'Italia*, ed. Claire E. Honess and Verina R. Jones (Turin: Claudiana, 1999), 271–80. Biographical sketches of all the authors mentioned are also contained in Ziani and Curci, *Bianco*.
33. See Labanca and Zadra, *Costruire un nemico*.
34. I have covered the whole matter in detail in Catalan, *Linguaggi e stereotipi*.
35. Here, I refer to Alberto Mario Banti, *L'onore della nazione: Identità sessuali e violenza nel nazionalismo europeo dal 18° secolo alla grande guerra* (Turin: Einaudi, 2005).

36. Pellis, *Prefazione a Carolina*, 6. The expression is in Triestine dialect, meaning, "It's a shame that I'm not young and that I am not a man."
37. Fundamental in this connection are her writings in *L'Isonzo* during the 1870s. For a deeper exploration, see Barbara Vallati, "Carolina Coen Luzzatto (1837–1919): Il percorso di una giornalista tra irredentismo e ebraismo" (thesis presented to the University of Trieste, academic year 2006–7).
38. Carolina C. Luzzatto, "Perché combattiamo?" *Il Corriere di Gorizia*, 24 March 1883.
39. I have analyzed this phase in detail in Catalan, *Linguaggi e stereotipi*, 62.
40. The harshest attacks were against *Il Rinnovamento* (Slovene Catholic journal in Gorizia) and *L'Eco del Litorale* (Catholic journal of the Austrian Littoral) during the 1890s. See Vallati, "Carolina Coen Luzzatto," 93–101.
41. See Bozzini La Stella, *Carolina*, 129–30.
42. Costantina Furlani was also an irredentist and was a German teacher in Gorizia at the Istituto femminile. See Antonella Gallarotti, ed., *Donne per Gorizia* (Gorizia: Edizioni della Laguna, 1993), 60.
43. See Franco Cecotti, ed., *"Un esilio che non ha pari" 1914–1918: Profughi, internati ed emigrati di Trieste, dell'Isontino e dell'Istria* (Gorizia: LEG, 2001), which contains a good description of the conditions of the Italian internees during the war.
44. See Nicolò Cobol, *Memorie del mio esilio* (Milan: Caddeo Editore, 1924), 138–39.
45. On Sabbadini: Michela Andreatta and Claudia Morgan, eds., *La biblioteca e l'archivio del Fondo Salvatore Sabbadini dei Civici musei di storia ed arte di Trieste* (Trieste: Civici musei di storia ed arte, 2003).
46. See Bozzini La Stella, *Carolina*, 168–69.
47. See Pellis, *Prefazione a Carolina*, 8
48. See Enrica Barzilai Gentilli, *Piccole storie della Venezia Redenta: Racconti per ragazzi* (Florence: Bemporad, 1920).
49. See Miniati, *Donne in guerra*, 143–44.
50. On the Lyceum, an international club founded in 1908, see Mirka Sandiford, ed., *Lyceum club internazionale di Firenze: 1908–2008; Cento anni di vita culturale del primo circolo femminile italiano* (Florence: Polistampa, 2008); Simona Maionchi, "Un Club femminile del Novecento: Il Lyceum dalla fondazione agli anni Settanta," *Carte di donne: Per un censimento della scrittura delle donne dal XVI al XX Secolo*, ed. Alessandra Contini and Anna Scattigno (Rome: Edizioni di Storia e Letteratura, 2005).
51. See Katja Gerhartz, "Le madri della Patria. Bürgerliche Frauenbewegung, Nationalismus und Krieg in Italien (1900–1922)" (doctoral thesis, Heinrich Heine University, Düsseldorf, 2003), 256.
52. See Emma Schiavon, "Il movimento suffragista, 1895–1918," in Bartoloni, *La Grande Guerra*, 147. On women's associations during the war, see Stefania Bartoloni, "L'associazionismo femminile nella Prima guerra mondiale e la mobilitazione per l'assistenza civile e la propaganda," in *Donna Lombarda 1860–1945*, ed. Ada Gigli Marchetti and Nanda Torcellan (Milan: Franco Angeli, 1992), 65–91.
53. See Gerhartz, "Le madri della Patria," 158–59, for a treatment of the anti-German politics in the journals. See Nattermann, *Zwischen Pazifismus*.
54. See Laura Guidi, "Un nazionalismo declinato al femminile (1914–1918)," in *Vivere la guerra: Percorsi biografici e ruoli di genere tra Risorgimento e primo conflitto mondiale*, ed. Laura Guidi (Naples: Clio-Press, 2007), 97.

55. See Guidi, "Un nazionalismo," 96.
56. See Comitato nazionale femminile interventista-antitedesco, *Atti del secondo congresso nazionale di azione antitedesca: Roma 5, 6, 7 maggio 1918* (Rome: Tip. L. Adrini, 1918).
57. Anna Maria Mozzoni, "Le razze," *L'Unità d'Italia*, no. 3, 1915.
58. Enrica Barzilai Gentilli (E. B. G.), "Natale del 1915," in *L'Unità d'Italia*, no. 6, 1915.
59. E. B. G., "Un nostro dovere," in *L'Unità d'Italia*, no. 1, 1916.
60. See ibid.; E. B. G., "Il Giuocattolo," in *L'Unità d'Italia*, no. 2, 1918.
61. See E. B. G., "Donne tedesche," in *L'Unità d'Italia*, no. 10, 1917.
62. See Comitato nazionale femminile interventista-antitedesco, *Atti del secondo congresso*.

Bibliography

Albisetti, James C. "Froebel Crosses the Alps: Introducing the Kindergarten in Italy." *History of Education Quarterly* 2 (2009): 159–69.
Andreatta, Michela, and Claudia Morgan, eds. *La biblioteca e l'archivio del Fondo Salvatore Sabbadini dei Civici musei di storia ed arte di Trieste*. Trieste: Civici musei di storia ed arte, 2003.
Ara, Angelo, and Claudio Magris. *Trieste: Un'identità di frontiera*. Turin: Einaudi, 1982.
Banti, Alberto M. *La nazione del Risorgimento: Parentela, santità e onore alle origini dell'Italia unita*. Turin: Einaudi, 2000.
———. *L'onore della nazione: Identità sessuali e violenza nel nazionalismo europeo dal 18° secolo alla grande guerra*. Turin: Einaudi, 2005.
———. *Sublime madre nostra: La nazione italiana dal Risorgimento al fascismo*. Rome: Laterza, 2011.
Barbarulli, Clotilde. "Dalla tradizione all'innovazione: 'La ricerca straordinaria' di Elena Raffalovich Comparetti." In *L'educazione delle donne: Scuole e modelli di vita femminile nell'Italia dell'Ottocento*, edited by Simonetta Soldani, 425–43. Milan: Angeli, 1989.
Bartoloni, Stefania. "L'associazionismo femminile nella Prima guerra mondiale e la mobilitazione per l'assistenza civile e la propaganda." In *Donna Lombarda 1860–1945*, edited by Ada Gigli Marchetti and Nanda Torcellan, 65–91. Milan: Franco Angeli, 1992.
———, ed. *La Grande Guerra delle italiane: Mobilitazioni, diritti, trasformazioni*. Rome: Viella, 2016.
———. *Donne di fronte alla guerra: Pace, diritti e democrazia*. Rome: Laterza, 2017.
Barzilai Gentilli, Enrica. *Piccole storie della Venezia Redenta: Racconti per ragazzi*. Florence: Bemporad, 1920.
———. *Nell'ottantesimo anniversario di Alberto Gentilli nato il 19 dicembre 1952, morto il 14 maggio 1932, dedica alla venerata memoria sua la vedova*. Trieste: s.n., 1932.
Benco, Silvio, ed. *Il "Piccolo" di Trieste: Mezzo secolo di giornalismo*. Rome: Treves, Treccani, Tumminelli, 1931.
Benussi, Cristina. "Scrittrici a Trieste: Per una storia." In *Le triestine donne volitive: Presenza e cultura delle donne a Trieste tra Ottocento e Novecento*, edited by Anna Di

Gianantonio and Marina Rossi, 57–87. Trieste: Istituto Regionale per la Storia del movimento di liberazione in Friuli Venezia Giulia, 2006.
Bozzini La Stella, Maria. *Carolina Coen Luzzatto*. Monfalcone: Edizioni della Laguna, 1995.
Catalan, Tullia. *La Comunità ebraica di Trieste 1781–1914: Politica, società e cultura*. Trieste: Lint, 2000.
———. "Donne ebree a Trieste fra Ottocento e prima guerra mondiale." In *Donne nella storia degli ebrei d'Italia: Atti del IX Convegno internazionale "Italia Judaica," Lucca, 6–9 giugno 2005*, edited by Michele Luzzati and Cristina Galasso, 347–71. Florence: La Giuntina, 2007.
———. "Linguaggi e stereotipi dell'antislavismo irredentista dalla fine dell'Ottocento alla Grande Guerra." In *Fratelli al massacro: Linguaggi e narrazioni della Prima guerra mondiale*, edited by Tullia Catalan, 39–68. Rome: Viella, 2015.
Cattaruzza, Marina. *L'Italia e il confine orientale: 1866–2006*. Bologna: Il Mulino, 2007.
Ceccon, Jole. "Adele Levi della Vida e la sua opera in alcuni inediti." *Rassegna di pedagogia* 2 (1955): 120–32.
Cecotti, Franco, ed. *"Un esilio che non ha pari" 1914–1918: Profughi, internati ed emigrati di Trieste, dell'Isontino e dell'Istria*. Gorizia: LEG, 2001.
Cedarmas, Adonella. *La Comunità israelitica di Gorizia 1900–1945*. Udine: Istituto friulano per la storia del movimento di liberazione, 2000.
Cobol, Nicolò. *Memorie del mio esilio*. Milan: Caddeo Editore, 1924.
Comitato nazionale femminile interventista-antitedesco. *Atti del secondo congresso nazionale di azione antitedesca: Roma 5, 6, 7 maggio 1918*. Rome: Tip. L. Adrini, 1918.
Curci, Roberto, and Gabriella Ziani. *Bianco rosa e verde: Scrittrici a Trieste fra '800 e '900*. Trieste: Lint, 1993.
Del Bianco, Maddalena. "Luzzatto Coen Carolina, giornalista e patriota." In *Nuovo Liruti: Dizionario biografico dei friulani*. Vol. 3: *L'Età contemporanea*, edited by Cesare Scalon, Claudio Griggio, and Giuseppe Bergamini, 1986–91. Udine: Forum, 2011.
Falco, Emilio. *Salvatore Barzilai: Un repubblicano moderno tra massoneria e irredentismo*. Rome: Bonacci, 1996.
Ferrara degli Uberti, Carlotta. "Libertà di coscienza e modelli di cittadinanza nell'Italia liberale: Ebrei e Comunità ebraiche nel rapporto con le istituzioni statali." *Società e Storia* 118 (2007): 699–724.
Fried, Ilona. "L'immagine della donna nella narrativa femminile ebraica: Haydée, Rina Del Prado, Elody Oblath." In *Shalom Triestee: Gli itinerari dell'ebraismo*, edited by Adriano Dugulin, 189–98. Trieste: Comune di Trieste, 1998.
Gallarotti, Antonella, ed. *Donne per Gorizia*. Gorizia: Edizioni della Laguna, 1993.
Gerhartz, Katja. "Le madri della Patria: Bürgerliche Frauenbewegung, Nationalismus und Krieg in Italien (1900–1922)." Doctoral thesis, Heinrich Heine University, Düsseldorf, 2003.
Grusovin, Marco, ed. *Cultura ebraica nel Goriziano*. Udine: Forum, 2007.
Guidi, Laura. "Un nazionalismo declinato al femminile (1914–1918)." In *Vivere la guerra: Percorsi biografici e ruoli di genere tra Risorgimento e primo conflitto mondiale*, edited by Laura Guidi, 93–118. Naples: Clio Press, 2007.
Labanca, Nicola, and Camillo Zadra, eds. *Costruire un nemico: Studi di storia della propaganda di guerra*. Milan: Edizioni Unicopli, 2011.
Lunzer, Renate. *Irredenti redenti: Intellettuali giuliani del '900*. Gorizia: Lint Editoriale, 2009.

Maionchi, Simona. "Un Club femminile del Novecento: Il Lyceum dalla fondazione agli anni Settanta." *Carte di donne: Per un censimento della scrittura delle donne dal XVI al XX Secolo*, edited by Alessandra Contini and Anna Scattigno, 297–316. Rome: Edizioni di Storia e Letteratura, 2005.

Manenti, Luca Giuseppe. "Geografia e politica nel razzismo antislavo: Il caso dell'irredentismo italiano (secoli XIX–XX)." In *Fratelli al massacre: Linguaggi e narrazioni della Prima guerra mondiale*, edited by Tullia Catalan, 17–38. Rome: Viella, 2015.

Michelstaedter, Carlo. *Epistolario*. Edited by Sergio Campailla. Milan: Adelphi, 1983.

Miniati, Monica. "Donne in guerra: Il contributo femminile ebraico nella Prima Guerra Mondiale." In *Gli ebrei italiani nella grande guerra (1915–1918): Atti del Convegno del Museo Ebraico, Bologna, 11 novembre 2015*, edited by Caterina Quareni and Vincenzo Maugeri, 127–47. Florence: Giuntina, 2017.

———. *Le emancipate: Le donne ebree in Italia nel XIX e XX secolo*. Rome: Viella, 2008.

Monti Orel, Silvana. *I giornali triestini dal 1863 al 1902*. Trieste: Lint, 1976.

Nattermann, Ruth. "Zwischen Pazifismus, Irredentismus und nationaler Euphorie: Italienische Jüdinnen und der Erste Weltkrieg." In *Jüdische Publizistik und Literatur im Zeichen des Ersten Weltkriegs*, edited by Petra Ernst and Eleonore Lappin-Eppel, 247–63. Innsbruck: Studienverlag 2016.

Pellis, Ugo. *Prefazione a Carolina C. Luzzatto, Teatro educativo: Prose e poesie varie; Edite e inedite*. Trieste: casa ed. C.U.Trani, 1923.

Pertici, Roberto, ed. *Intellettuali di frontiera. Triestini a Firenze (1900–1950)*. 2 vols. Florence: Olschki, 1985.

Pisani (Cassandra), Jolanda. "La stampa a Gorizia dal 1800 ai giorni nostril." *Studi Goriziani* 1 (1956): 39–49.

Pizzi, Katia. "Verso una pedagogia dell'unificazione: Allieve di quarta di Haydée e l'italianità ebraica a Trieste." In *Donne delle minoranze: Le ebree e le protestanti d'Italia*, edited by Claire E. Honess and Verina R. Jones, 271–80. Turin: Claudiana, 1999.

———. *A City in Search of an Author: The Literary Identity of Trieste*. London: Sheffield Academic Press, 2001.

Polacco, Vittorio. *La questione del divorzio e gli israeliti in Italia*. Padua-Verona: Fratelli Drucker, 1894.

Premuti, Costanzo. *Eroismo al fronte, bizantinismo all'interno*. Rome: Tipografia Italiana, 1924.

Redivo, Diego. "Tra ebraismo e irredentismo a proposito di una recente biografia di Carolina Luzzatto." *Quaderni Giuliani di Storia* 1 (1998): 155–63.

Sandiford, Mirka, ed. *Lyceum club internazionale di Firenze: 1908–2008; Cento anni di vita culturale del primo circolo femminile italiano*. Florence: Polistampa, 2008.

Schiavon, Emma. "Il movimento suffragista, 1895–1918." In *La Grande Guerra delle italiane: Mobilitazioni, diritti, trasformazioni*, edited by Stefania Bartoloni. Rome: Viella, 2016.

Vallati, Barbara. "Carolina Coen Luzzatto (1837–1919): Il percorso di una giornalista tra irredentismo e ebraismo." Thesis presented to the University of Trieste, academic year 2006–7.

Ventrone, Angelo. *La seduzione totalitaria: Guerra, modernità, violenza politica (1914–1918)*. Rome: Donzelli, 2003.

———. *Il nemico interno: Immagini, parole e simboli della lotta politica nell'Italia del Novecento*. Rome: Donzelli, 2005.

Verginella, Marta. *Il confine degli altri: La questione giuliana e la memoria slovena*. Rome: Donzelli, 2008.

Vivante, Angelo. *Irredentismo Adriatico*. 1912. Reprint, Trieste: Edizioni Italo Svevo, 1984.

Ziani, Gabriella. "Letterate e artiste tra Otto e Novecento." In *Le triestine donne volitive: Presenza e cultura delle donne a Trieste tra Ottocento e Novecento*, edited by Anna Di Gianantonio and Marina Rossi, 107–25. Trieste: Istituto Regionale per la Storia del movimento di liberazione in Friuli Venezia Giulia, 2006.

CHAPTER 17

Heroic Fathers, Patriotic Mothers, Fallen Sons

National Belonging and Political Positioning in Italian-Jewish Families' Versions of World War I

Ruth Nattermann

In March 1942, the Italian-Jewish writer and art critic Margherita Sarfatti (1880–1961) filed an application with the infamous General Division of Demography and Race of the Interior Ministry, known as Demorazza, asking to be officially regarded as not belonging to the "Jewish race." At that time, the Fascist regime's attack on Jewish rights, which had steadily intensified since the promulgation of the Racial Laws in 1938, was reaching its climax.[1] Sarfatti, Mussolini's former mistress, was already living in South American exile. For most people, the ongoing atrocities of the current war had overshadowed the memory of the so-called Great War. Still, in Sarfatti's long plea about her Italian patriotism, her attachment to Catholicism, and her deep loyalty toward fascism, she explicitly referred to the death of her eldest son Roberto in World War I. She wrote, "Throughout her whole life [Margherita Sarfatti], and likewise her late husband Cesare Sarfatti, had showed the most absolute indifference toward the principles of Jewish solidarity, while she had constantly allied herself to the cause of 'italianità.' Needless to recall [her] patriotic mission and the sacrifice of the heroic Roberto Sarfatti [in World War I]."[2]

Margherita's eldest son had enrolled as a voluntary soldier and was killed at the age of just seventeen in January 1918. Subsequently, the sophisticated writer, together with Mussolini himself, stylized young Roberto as the first martyr of fascism. Herein lies the origin of Margherita Sarfatti's influence on the symbolism and forms of representation of fascism, which was to increase over the following years.[3] World War I had represented a turning point in her personal as well as her political identity.

An entirely different personal and ideological development can be found in Sarfatti's Italian-Jewish contemporary Amelia Rosselli (1870–

1954), mother of the resistance fighters Carlo and Nello, whose eldest son Aldo fell in 1916.[4] In sharp contrast to the theatrical, public celebration of Roberto Sarfatti's death, Amelia Rosselli and her sons continued to cherish Aldo's memory mostly in private, while their political commitment against fascism intensified significantly. In September 1928, Nello Rosselli, who had just been released after over a year's political detention, visited his brother's grave in the small village of Timau, near Udine. His delicately guarded letter to his mother reads, "Others have their inherited soil; we will have this dear grave, these mountains that Aldo has defended, this small village where it seems that the dead of the cemetery may live again."[5] For Nello, his brother's soul had become a natural part of the place that did not require artificial and pompous monuments, as his memory would be kept alive by the family.[6]

As was the case for Margherita Sarfatti, World War I marked a turning point in the lives of Amelia Rosselli and her sons, but one that led in the opposite direction. Amelia, who like Margherita Sarfatti had sympathized with nationalism and irredentism, abandoned these ideas after Aldo's death. Her younger sons Carlo (1899–1937) and Nello Rosselli (1900–1937), who were called up to the army in 1917 and 1918 respectively, began to reflect more consciously on the patriotic passion their mother had transmitted to them.[7] In the immediate postwar period, Nello joined republican circles, whereas Carlo became interested in socialism. It was the beginning of their fervent commitment against fascism, which in 1937 was violently and irretrievably ended when they were killed in Bagnoles-de-l'Orne by fascist henchmen. After the assassination of her sons, Amelia Rosselli went into exile, but even from Switzerland and the United States, she contributed considerably to the spread of the transnational networks of antifascists, often Jewish intellectuals, that her family had helped to establish since the early years of Mussolini's dictatorship. Rosselli remained loyal to her Jewish origins and cultural heritage, which she closely associated with her ideals of justice and freedom.[8]

This chapter aims to explain the reasons for different ideological developments in Italian-Jewish individuals and families, which were closely connected to World War I Based on unpublished wartime correspondence and autobiographical as well as contemporary literary and historical works, the focus is on three middle-class Italian-Jewish families: Amelia and Aldo Rosselli, their close friends Gina Lombroso and her husband Guglielmo Ferrero, and Margherita and Roberto Sarfatti. The assumption is that the experience of World War I was decisive in influencing or changing long-term political positions and attitudes as regarded national belonging and Jewish loyalties. The ideological choices the protagonists of this study made are representative for the political options of contemporary Italian Jewry in general; in the postwar period and the early years of Mussolini's regime, fascist and antifascist positions developed within Italian-Jewish families in quite the same way as in the non-Jewish Italian population.[9] In 1938, however, the situation for Italian-Jewish protagonists changed irrevocably. Hence, the versions of World War I they created in retrospect were the result of two entangled processes: their war experience and the more recent experience of exclusion under fascism. In this context, the article inquires into the impact of present political circumstances as well as personal needs for meaning on the intricate dynamics of war narratives and memories.

War Narratives in Italian-Jewish Families as an Expression of National Belonging

The many ways in which Jewish individuals and families in Italy experienced and remembered World War I have been widely ignored in historical research. For decades, relevant historiography focused on the political and military contribution of Italian-Jewish men to the war effort[10] without much considering more intimate primary sources such as war correspondence between husbands and wives and mothers and sons, war diaries, or memoirs by Jewish protagonists.[11] This is partly due to the generally difficult accessibility of these kinds of documents; the main reason, however, is surely more profound. Similarly to the German and the Austrian context, Italian Jews' recollections of World War I were overlain or even destroyed by the devastating experience of the World War II and the Shoah.[12] Memories of the *Grande Guerra* vanished materially as well as mentally in view of persecution, emigration, expulsion, and deportation in the crucial period between 1938 and 1945. Hence, the significant impact that World War I had on ideological developments and transformations as well as concepts of Jewish identities faded into the background. Tullia Catalan is among the very few historians to have included political attitudes and discourses of female protagonists in relevant new Italian studies as well.[13] A recent publication by Petra Ernst-Kühr and Eleonore Lappin-Eppel focusing on Jewish literature during World War I from a transnational perspective emphasizes the importance of discovering and highlighting the rich facets of self-images as well as political and cultural viewpoints that emerged in the course of the global conflict.[14] As the opposite examples of Margherita Sarfatti and Amelia Rosselli suggest, questions regarding diversity and ambiguity in historical processes and developments of historical protagonists need to be applied to studies on the history of World War I in the Italian-Jewish context, too. Precisely for this purpose, it is worth analyzing the origins and transformations of war narratives as they can be identified in surviving ego documents and writings.

In the eyes of most Italian Jews, World War I represented the first outstanding opportunity to prove their national solidarity toward the *patria e gran madre Italia*, as well as their gratitude toward the royal house of Savoy, which had emancipated Italian Jewry.[15]

In 1915, barely one year after the beginning of World War I, Gina Lombroso's book on her prominent father Cesare's life and work appeared in its first edition.[16] At that time, the question of Italian intervention in the war was becoming more and more acute. In May 1915, Italy officially withdrew from the Triple Alliance with Germany and Austria-Hungary after the Entente had made considerable concessions to the country in the treaty of London. Old anti-Austrian sentiments began to reemerge in Italian society to a significant degree, also in middle-class Italian-Jewish families such as the Lombrosos, who had often been closely involved in the Italian wars of independence. The dangerous fascination which interventionism and irredentism exerted on many Jewish protagonists was based above all on the memory of their ancestors' commitment to Italian unification, with its inherent project of Jewish emancipation.[17]

Female protagonists, journalists and writers especially who were committed to the contemporary women's movement, tied in with their fathers' war effort during the Risorgimento. The memory of ancestors and their commitment to the creation of an Italian nation were part of secular Jewish identity, which defined the self-image and accomplishments of most Italian-Jewish activists within contemporary feminist organizations. Although they had distanced themselves from Jewish religion and customs, middle-class protagonists such as Amelia Rosselli and Gina Lombroso maintained a profoundly Jewish consciousness, based to a considerable extent on ethical values, ideas of a common origin, and the preservation and communication of family memories. Significantly, in Cesare Lombroso's biography, which Gina Lombroso dedicated to her son Leo Ferrero, she included a long chapter about the "Lombroso soldato," describing how her father had enrolled as a volunteer in the Piedmontese army in 1859 "in order to beat Austria."[18] Allusions to fathers' heroic commitment to the Risorgimento and their fervent war effort for liberation from the Austrian subjugation also appear in ego documents that relate to World War I from a temporal distance. Relevant texts written during the Fascist period reveal a particularly urgent tendency to highlight the family's participation in the national project, thus implicitly defending an Italian national identity that was discredited and eventually brutally denied by the Fascist dictatorship. The Venice-born Amelia Rosselli, who looked back at Aldo's soldierly sacrifice for Italy in her memoirs, wrote with patriotic emphasis about "[Leone] Pincherle, my father's uncle, a close friend of Daniele Manin, who had participated in the triumvirate of the provisional government [of the Repubblica di San Marco]."[19] Similarly, Rosselli's friend, the author

Laura Orvieto (1876–1953),[20] dedicated significant space to the period of World War I in her autobiography, also writing about Aldo and his young friends who fell in the war. She, too, alluded to her father Achille Cantoni's patriotic passion, to which he testified as a *volontario garibaldino* in the Italian wars of independence.[21] Father figures were central in the creation of war narratives in Italian-Jewish families, which accentuated the idea of World War I as the completion of the Risorgimento, at the same time celebrating the families' direct involvement in Italian nation-building. The stylization of the fathers as heroic soldiers fighting for Italian freedom and unity against Austrian rule became a recurrent theme in journalistic and literary texts written by Italian-Jewish women during and after World War I. They were part of the overall contemporary attitude of the Italian middle class with reference to the celebration of the families' contribution to the nation and their participation in the Risorgimento.[22] At the same time, texts by Italian-Jewish protagonists assumed a particular quality because of the characteristic interrelationship between national reunification and Jewish emancipation. Writing about their ancestors' political achievements became a vivid expression and self-reassurance as to national belonging in a time of political and personal crisis.

Experiencing and Communicating the Horror of War: Guglielmo Ferrero's Letters to Gina Lombroso

As for Gina Lombroso, it was not only in her writings that she was committed to the national cause. As early as the beginning of 1915 she traveled to France, symbol of the resistance against the central powers, and visited Red Cross units, schools, and shelters.[23] Gina's aversion to Austria and Germany, as well as her unconditional support for the Entente, resulted to a considerable extent from her family background and upbringing. Her father Cesare Lombroso (1835–1909), descendant of a Sephardic Jewish family, was born in Verona, which remained Austrian until 1866. He himself had fought for Italian independence and liberation from Habsburg rule. Gina's sophisticated mother Nina De Benedetti, on the other hand, came from an affluent family of Jewish merchants from Piedmont who had been significantly influenced by the nearby French culture.[24] France continued to be an important political and cultural reference point within the Lombroso family. Gina herself had grown up in Turin, where Cesare Lombroso had held the chair in medical jurisprudence since 1876. She and her sister Paola enjoyed a thorough and liberal education, highly stimulated by their father's intellectual influence and his scholarly friendships. The encounter with the Russian-Jewish feminist and doctor Anna Kuliscioff (1857–1925), who had moved to Turin at the end of the 1880s in order to specialize in gynecology, was crucial for Gina and Paola's growing interest in the contemporary women's emancipation movement, left-wing politics, and social work.[25] In 1897, Gina Lombroso graduated in literature and philosophy at the University of Turin; four years later, she also took her exams in medicine there. She married the eminent historian and writer Guglielmo Ferrero (1871–1942), her father's pupil, in the same year. This highly educated woman became Ferrero's closest intellectual collaborator and ideological companion.[26]

The letters Gina Lombroso received from her husband during World War I on his long journeys to France and Northern Italy, where he visited the front, were decisive for her personal perception of the war. Ferrero's unpublished war correspondence with his wife represents an important ego document for the history of experience of World War I, although it has been widely ignored in relevant research. The direct experience of the horrors of war caused a change in Ferrero's personal outlook and political attitude, which was to influence Gina Lombroso's awareness of the conflict as well. As soon as hostilities commenced, Guglielmo Ferrero began to support Italy's entering the war as an ally of France and Great Britain.[27] He belonged to the group of so-called democratic interventionists, whose political faith in revolutionary France, together with anti-Austrian sentiments and a strong aversion toward Germanism, led at first to an idealization of the war as a means of creating a new democratic European order.[28] At the time, Ferrero was writing for the important newspaper of democratic alignment *Il Secolo*, based in Milan, providing a critical assessment of the developing conflict. As a correspondent for the newspaper, Ferrero traveled to France many times and sometimes for several months, between autumn 1914 and spring 1919, talking to politicians and military staff as well as visiting the front lines. In contrast to his traditional image as a patriarchal husband, faithful to Cesare Lombroso's thesis of the intellectual inferiority of women, the numerous unpublished letters he wrote to Gina during his travels reveal that he held her political knowledge and judgement in high esteem, and that a close and trusting relationship existed between husband and wife. Moreover, Ferrero did not shrink from describing the physical horrors of war he witnessed, such as injuries, corpses, and stenches, to his wife, an experienced doctor. In this way, Gina, who stayed with their children, Leo and Nina, in Florence, where the family had moved from Turin in 1916, shared her husband's thoughts and feelings, at the same time gaining immediate insight into the harsh realities of the war.

In September 1916, just a few weeks after the Sixth Battle of the Isonzo in which the Italians had conquered Gorizia, Ferrero went on a long excursion to the Basso Isonzo, also visiting the trenches in the Carso area. He was horrified by the obvious presence of death and destruction, writing to Gina that "the most terrible thing was the stench that came from all the trenches, and after 12 hours I still smell it. The six thousand corpses that the hill hides have not been able to be buried . . . they are under piles of stones . . . [there is] a smell that one feels in the entire mountain, especially on hot and sticky days like yesterday. It seems to me that the poor soldiers have a great desire that the war end soon."[29]

In view of the horrors he witnessed, Ferrero's estrangement from his ideal of a just war under a democratic banner is clearly perceptible in his letters. What is more, the real, immediate contact with young Austrian and German soldiers made him increasingly question his anti-Germanic sentiments, realizing that they had been based on political tendencies and stereotypes but not on universal human principles. During his excursion to the Basso Isonzo, he encountered a group of prisoners and addressed a seventeen-year-old German soldier, a grammar school student "with a kind and sweet face," who reminded him of his almost coeval nephew, as he wrote to his wife.[30] Significantly, in the same days his repulsion for the fighting reached its climax. "What a horror," Ferrero wrote to Gina after witnessing an Italian soldier being torn to pieces by an exploding grenade during a battle he had watched from a nearby hill.[31] Only four days later, he stated with unmistakable weariness: "I really have a great desire to return home. . . . The tempest of the war . . . is reaching its climax."[32]

By this time, if not before, and in the face of the extreme cruelties he had seen, Ferrero must have felt that he had been wrong in his interventionist attitude and the belief that the war was eventually going to lead to an overall democracy. He explicitly admitted this mistake many years later in his autobiography,[33] written during the 1930s when he and his wife Gina were living in Swiss exile, excluded from the national community because of their antifascist commitment. But already in his 1923 book on the horrendous consequences of the Treaty of Versailles, *La tragedia della pace*, which appeared one year after Mussolini had come to power in Italy, he referred to the democratic ideal he had associated with World War I as an illusion.[34]

Gina Lombroso, who had closely participated in her husband's war experience, shared his attitude, convinced of the wrongness of the conflict. In the course of the war, she had distanced herself altogether from her former distinctly interventionist attitude, which had been based to a considerable extent on the memory of her father's participation in the Risorgimento, fighting for national independence and unity as well as for Jewish emancipation. In view of the increasing power of fascism, the image of World War I as a completion of the Risorgimento, resulting in a democratic European order, had lost its significance for her. During the 1920s, Gina Lombroso actively participated in the construction and support of antifascist intellectual networks in Florence, which also involved Amelia Rosselli and her sons Carlo and Nello.[35]

Two Mothers' Crossroads during Wartime: Margherita Sarfatti's and Amelia Rosselli's Political Choices

Whereas the experience of war had led the married couple Guglielmo Ferrero and Gina Lombroso from an interventionist to an antimilitarist attitude, Margherita Sarfatti's ideological development took an entirely different course. In her case, too, it was her personal war experience that exercised a decisive influence on her political positioning. Margherita Sarfatti, née Grassini, came from a sophisticated, affluent Jewish family. She was born in the Venetian Ghetto Vecchio in 1880. The talented girl enjoyed an excellent education and, at an early age, began to write articles on social issues for the socialist press and as an art critic. At the age of nineteen, she married the Jewish lawyer Cesare Sarfatti (1866–1924), a committed socialist, who was aiming at a political career. They moved to Milan, the center of contemporary Italian socialism.[36] The subsequent commitment of Margherita Sarfatti to women's associations such as the Unione Femminile Nazionale, to the socialist press, and to futurist and avant-garde circles is well known. She met Mussolini for the first time in 1912, when he was among the leading figures of the Socialist Party and about to become editor in chief of its journal *Avanti*. Over the following years, Sarfatti shared all his important political and private decisions. Though she had originally supported pacifism, she turned to the interventionist wing of the Socialist Party in 1915, tempted by Italian nationalist aspirations toward the so-called *terre irredente*.[37] Her encounter with Mussolini and the subsequent personal as well as ideological convergence between the two politically ambitious and prominent figures were decisive for Sarfatti's supportive attitude toward Italian intervention, strengthened further by her idea that the German "barbarians" threatened the superior Latin culture and civilization.[38]

In 1917, influenced by his mother's nationalist attitude, Margherita's eldest son Roberto, a rather restless and adventurous seventeen-year-old boy, decided to enroll as a volunteer. He was killed in the first battle of the Three Mountains in January 1918. Margherita Sarfatti, numb with grief and feeling complicit in his death, decided to commemorate him as a hero. Mussolini himself supported the creation of the myth of the young fallen soldier, and particularly the definition of Sarfatti herself as the hero's mother sacrificing her son for the *patria* as a national symbol.[39] Only a few days after Roberto's death, he published an article in *Il Popolo d'Italia* in which he epitomized the young soldier as the incarnation of the courageous *Ardito*.[40] Roberto's death originated the fascist cult of the fallen soldier, at the center of which stood the heroic, masculine experience of war. Margherita herself contributed significantly to the creation of Roberto's myth. In 1919, she edited a volume of Roberto's letters,[41] and in 1921, she published a book of poems dedicated to her dead son.[42] His memory became an editorial project. As opposed to the widespread individual mourning practice in Italy, which was expressed in private publications of commemorative volumes that were distributed among family members and friends and remained in a private space, Sarfatti made her grief decidedly public. Within the male-dominated cult of the fallen, which had developed in Italy as in most European countries,[43] Sarfatti made her voice heard, influencing significantly the discourse on an appropriate national commemoration. The semantics of voluntary soldierly sacrifice in the name of the *patria* became increasingly connected with the cult of heroic motherhood.[44]

Especially in her poems, Sarfatti celebrated the image of the courageous mother's sacrifice of her son for the creation of a new Italy, a new national community born out of the family's loss for the fatherland and the bonds of blood.[45] On the third anniversary of Roberto's death, Mussolini himself organized a public ceremony in Milan, at which fascists, legionaries, and futurists were present. Roberto became an icon on which the cult of the heroic youth, motherly sacrifice, and the new fascist nation, born out of the blood of young heroic fighters, could be constructed.[46] In April 1922, the "young avant-garde" of the Partito d'azione fascista in Milan wrote to Margherita Sarfatti, defining Roberto as the heroic example who had given their squadron, named after him, strength and honor.[47] His memory was explicitly included in the political culture of Fascist Italy, supported to a considerable extent by the publications and ceremonies staged by Mussolini and Sarfatti herself. On 19 April 1925, in the framework of another public ceremony, Roberto was posthumously awarded the gold medal for bravery, thus becoming the youngest soldier to receive the highest military decoration of World War I in Italy.[48] Ten years later, a funeral monument built on behalf of Margherita Sarfatti by the architect Giuseppe Terragni was solemnly inaugurated on Col d'Echele, in the immediate proximity of the place where Roberto had been killed. In sharp contrast to Aldo Rosselli, Roberto Sarfatti's death in World War I became a recurrent topic and visible part of the collective memory of the Great War during the fascist period.

Considering the commemoration of fallen soldiers as a political act, it becomes clear why the memory of ideologically opposed historical protagonists, such as Aldo Rosselli, was increasingly confined within the private sphere and eventually excluded from the official memory discourse during the fascist period. The cultural and political backgrounds of Sarfatti and Rosselli up to the beginning of the war, however, were not dissimilar. Like Sarfatti, Amelia Rosselli, née Pincherle, was born in Venice. She descended from a liberal, patriotic Jewish family and, similarly to Sarfatti, had been brought up in a profoundly anti-Austrian climate. It was this background that continued to influence her political attitude as well as the upbringing of her three sons in Florence, where the family resided from 1903 onward. Rosselli took an active part in the Italian women's emancipation movement and became head of the literary section of the Florentine Lyceum, an important cultural association for women.[49] Like Margherita Sarfatti, Gina Lombroso, and many other middle-class Jewish activists, Amelia Rosselli had reacted with enthusiasm to Italy's decision in May 1915 to enter the war on the side of the Entente. After the beginning of the war, Rosselli's antipathy for Germany and Austria, together with her profound sense of belonging to the Italian nation, strengthened her desire for Italy to join the war on the side of the democracies, France and Great Britain. The death of her son Aldo, however, changed her attitude decisively. In March 1916, the twenty-year-old fell in the region of Carnia on the Italian-Austrian front. The news of his death reached Rosselli as late as the beginning of April. In her memoirs, she dedicates a long passage to the reluctant and unbearably painful realization of her son's death.[50]

Unlike Sarfatti, Rosselli broke definitively with nationalism after Aldo's death, as her letters to Orvieto reveal.[51] In distinct contrast to Sarfatti's stylization of Roberto as the first martyr of fascism and symbol of a new national identity, Amelia linked her son's death with her family's memory of their fathers' soldierly effort for the creation of an Italian nation and the reward of emancipation. Apparently, she perceived Aldo's death on the battlefield and her own motherly sacrifice as proof of her family's irrefutable loyalty toward the Italian fatherland. While Sarfatti coped with her grief by politically exploiting her son's death, making it part of the public memory discourse, Amelia Rosselli and her sons Carlo and Nello remembered Aldo within the intimate sphere of the family. The opposite ways in which the two mothers mourned for their dead sons emphasize their profound ideological as well as individual differences.

Conclusion

As the examples of the Lombroso Ferrero, Rosselli, and Sarfatti families show, the experience of World War I proved decisive in influencing or changing political positions and attitudes between national identity and long-term Jewish loyalties. In all three cases, these developments had their origins within families, or rather within the interaction between family members. The immediate involvement in the war and the awareness of its horrors caused a profound change in Ferrero's interventionist attitude and national prejudices. He began to reject the idea that World War I would eventually lead to a new democratic European order. Ferrero's personal war experience, which he communicated extensively in his letters to Gina Lombroso, had a significant impact on her own changing perception of the conflict as well. Within the course of the war, the couple turned down the delusive concept of World War I as the completion of the Risorgimento, which Jewish middle-class families traditionally associated with Jewish emancipation and national belonging. Guglielmo and Gina's growing support of antimilitarist positions and rejection of power politics already foreshadowed their significant antifascist commitment during Mussolini's dictatorship.

Amelia Rosselli's and Margherita Sarfatti's ideological developments, on the other hand, resulted to a considerable extent from their individual war experience as soldiers' mothers. The deaths of their sons led to different ideological choices, which found their expression not least in their ways of mourning. Following Mussolini's example, Margherita Sarfatti assumed fascist positions. Amelia Rosselli instead distanced herself altogether from nationalism and irredentism. Over the following years, she actively supported her sons' increasing political commitment against fascism. Whereas Roberto Sarfatti's death was politicized, becoming part of the male-dominated cult of the fallen, Amelia Rosselli's grief and emotional anguish were given no public space. At the same time, Aldo's memory continued to be shared by the inner circle of his Jewish family and their friends. Laura Orvieto, in particular, participated in Amelia's memories, writing extensively about Aldo in her letters as well as in her autobiography. As a citizen-soldier he had proved his loyalty toward the nation his ancestors had helped to create. Fascism and the racial laws deprived Italian Jewry of this experience, which had represented the climax of their patriotism and consciousness of national belonging. Many years later, in 1947, when Amelia had returned to Florence from her American exile, she wrote to Laura Orvieto:

> And how many times . . . I think I must turn around to wait for Aldo, so I can walk beside him. . . . But then I realize that I am wrong, that he had already left beforehand, with his sacrifice, with the treasure of his immature twenty years in his hand, which he gave away all at once, so as to create a little piece of this Italy which they have taken away from us.[52]

Ruth Nattermann is assistant professor (Privatdozentin) at the Department of European History at the University of Munich. She held postdoctoral positions at the LMU Munich and the German Historical Institute in Rome, and has been principal investigator of the international DFG-network "Gender—Nation—Emancipation." Among her latest contributions is *Jüdinnen in der frühen italienischen Frauenbewegung 1861–1945. Biographien, Diskurse und transnationale Vernetzungen* (Rome: Bibliothek des Deutschen Historischen Instituts in Rom, 2020); "The Female Side of War: The Experience and Memory of the Great War in Italian-

Jewish Women's Ego-Documents," in *The Jewish Experience of the First World War*, ed. Edward Madigan and Gideon Reuveni (Basingstoke/New York: Palgrave Macmillan, 2018), 233–54.

Notes

1. On the development of antisemitic politics in Fascist Italy, see especially Enzo Collotti, *Il Fascismo e gli Ebrei: Le leggi razziali in Italia* (Rome: Laterza, 2004); Michele Sarfatti, *The Jews in Mussolini's Italy: From Equality to Persecution* (Madison: University of Wisconsin Press, 2006).
2. Archivio Centrale dello Stato (ACS), Fondo Ministero dell'Interno, Direzione Generale Demografia e Razza (DEMORAZZA), Fasc. 6037, Busta 79: Grassini in Sarfatti, Margherita di Amedeo, DCITT 1941–1942. Among the numerous works on Sarfatti, see Stefania Bartoloni, "Margherita Sarfatti: Una intellettuale tra Nazione e Fascismo," in *Di generazione in generazione: Le Italiane dall'Unità ad Oggi*, ed. Maria Teresa Mori et al. (Rome: Viella, 2014), 207–20; Simona Urso, *Margherita Sarfatti: Dal mito del Dux al mito americano* (Venice: Marsilio, 2003); Karin Wieland, *Die Geliebte des Duce: Das Leben der Margherita Sarfatti und die Erfindung des Faschismus* (Munich: Carl Hanser Verlag, 2004).
3. On this argument, see Bartoloni, "Margherita Sarfatti," 212; Mario Isnenghi, "Scenari dell'io nei racconti sociali della Grande Guerra," in *La Grande Guerra delle italiane: Mobilitazioni, diritti, trasformazioni*, ed. Stefania Bartoloni (Rome: Viella, 2016), 281–82; Urso, *Margherita Sarfatti*, 131–34.
4. On Amelia Rosselli, born Pincherle, see Dolara Vieri, "Amelia Rosselli Pincherle," *Quaderni del Circolo Rosselli* 3 (2006); Giovanna Amato, "Una donna nella storia: Vita e letteratura di Amelia Pincherle Rosselli," *Quaderni del Circolo Rosselli* 1 (2012); Amelia Rosselli, *Memorie*, ed. Marina Calloni (Bologna: Il Mulino, 2001).
5. Nello to Amelia Rosselli, Udine, 12 September 1928, in Zeffiro Ciuffoletti, ed., *I Rosselli: Epistolario familiare 1914–1937* (Milan: Mondadori, 1997), 390.
6. Monumental cemeteries were built in Italy especially from the beginning of the 1920s onward in order to celebrate soldiers' military and patriotic sacrifice in World War I. The Fascist regime exploited these commemorative places for propagandistic ends. See Patrizia Dogliani, "Redipuglia," in *I luoghi della memoria: Simboli e miti dell'Italia unita*, ed. Mario Isnenghi (Rome: Laterza, 2010), 425.
7. See Ciuffoletti, *I Rosselli*, 4, 69–71; Zeffiro Ciuffoletti and Nicola Tranfaglia, "Introduzione," in *Lessico familiare: Vita, cultura e politica della famiglia Rosselli all'insegna della libertà*, ed. Zeffiro Ciuffoletti and Gian Luca Corradi (Florence: Edimond, 2002), xiv–xv.
8. For Rosselli's antifascist networks in exile, see Marina Calloni and Lorella Cedroni, "Presentazione: Due famiglie in esilio," in *Politica e affetti familiari: Lettere di Amelia, Carlo e Nello Rosselli a Guglielmo, Leo e Nina Ferrero e Gina Lombroso Ferrero (1917–1943)*, ed. Marina Calloni and Lorella Cedroni (Milan: Feltrinelli, 1997), 21–27.
9. See Sarfatti, *Jews in Mussolini's Italy*, 54, 63–78.
10. See Felice Tedeschi, *Gli israeliti italiani nella guerra 1915–1918* (Turin: F. Servi, 1921); Mario Toscano, "Gli ebrei italiani e la prima guerra mondiale (1915–

1918): Tra crisi religiosa e fremiti patriottici," in *Ebraismo e antisemitismo in Italia: Dal 1848 alla guerra dei sei giorni*, ed. Mario Toscano (Milan: Franco Angeli, 2003), 110–22; Mario Toscano, "Ebrei ed ebraismo nell'Italia della grande guerra: Note su una inchiesta del Comitato delle comunità israelitiche italiane del maggio 1917," in Toscano, *Ebraismo e antisemitismo in Italia*, 123–54; Mario Toscano, "Religione, patriottismo, sionismo: Il rabbinato militare nell'Italia della Grande Guerra (1915–1918)," *Zakhor* 8 (2005): 77–133.

11. An important example for the war experience within a German-Jewish family is provided by Dorothee Wierling, "Imagining and Communicating Violence: The Correspondence of a Berlin Family, 1914–1918," in *Gender and the First World War*, ed. Christa Hämmerle, Oswald Überegger, and Birgitta Bader Zaar (New York: Palgrave Macmillan, 2014), 36–51. On the significance of war correspondence between husbands and wives, see Christa Hämmerle, "Gewalt und Liebe—ineinander verschränkt: Paarkorrespondenzen aus zwei Weltkriegen; 1914/18 und 1939/45," in *Liebe schreiben: Paarkorrespondenzen im Kontext des 19. und 20. Jahrhunderts*, ed. Ingrid Bauer and Christa Hämmerle (Göttingen: Vandenhoeck & Ruprecht, 2017), 171–230.

12. On historical and familial remembrance regarding World War I in general, see Jay Winter, *Remembering War: The Great War between Memory and History in the Twentieth Century* (New Haven, CT: Yale University Press, 2006), esp. 8–13. On the forgetting and the neglect of Jewish experience and memories of World War I in the Austrian context, see Petra Ernst, "Der Erste Weltkrieg in deutschsprachig-jüdischer Literatur und Publizistik in Österreich," in *Krieg: Erinnerung; Geschichtswissenschaft*, ed. Siegfried Mattl et al. (Vienna: Böhlau Verlag, 2009), 62–68. On German and Austrian historiography on Jews and World War I, see Petra Ernst, Jeffrey Grossman, and Ulrich Wyrwa, "Introduction," in "The Great War: Reflections, Experiences and Memories of German and Habsburg Jews (1914–1918)," ed. Petra Ernst, Jeffrey Grossman, and Ulrich Wyrwa, special issue, *Quest: Issues in Contemporary Jewish History; Journal of Fondazione CDEC* 9 (October 2016), http://www.quest-cdecjournal.it/index.php?issue=9.

13. See Tullia Catalan, "Linguaggi e stereotipi dell'antislavismo irredentista dalla fine dell'Ottocento alla Grande Guerra," in *Fratelli al massacro: Linguaggi e narrazioni della Prima Guerra Mondiale*, ed. Tullia Catalan (Rome: Viella, 2015), 39–69.

14. Petra Ernst and Eleonore Lappin-Eppel, eds., *Jüdische Publizistik und Literatur im Zeichen des Ersten Weltkriegs* (Innsbruck: Studienverlag, 2016). See in particular their "Vorwort," 7–10.

15. See Toscano, "Gli ebrei italiani," 285, 289–90, 292. The idea of the citizen-soldiers' national solidarity, "rewarded" with civil rights and political participation, had become central for the Jewish minorities in many European countries. Particularly on the Austrian context, see Gerald Lamprecht, "Kriegserinnerungs- und Identitätsdiskurse am Beispiel des 'Bundes jüdischer Frontsoldaten' und der Zeitschrift *Jüdische Front* 1932–1938," in Ernst and Lappin-Eppel, *Jüdische Publizistik und Literatur*, 168. On the German, Austrian-Hungarian, and French contexts, see Derek Penslar, *Jews and the Military: A History* (Princeton, NJ: Princeton University Press, 2013), 170–71.

16. Gina Lombroso Ferrero, *Cesare Lombroso: Storia della Vita e delle Opere* (Bologna: Zanichelli Editore, 1915). On the life and work of the prominent anthropologist Cesare Lombroso (1835–1909), see Mary S. Gibson, *Born to Crime: Cesare*

Lombroso and the Origins of Biological Criminology (Santa Barbara, CA: Praeger Press, 2002). On his daughters, the doctor and writer Gina (1872–1944) and the educationalist and writer Paola (1871–1954), see Delfina Dolza, *Essere figlie di Lombroso: Due donne intellettuali tra '800 e '900* (Milan: Franco Angeli, 1991).

17. On the frequent affinity between Italian Jews and irredentism, see Ulrich Wyrwa, *Gesellschaftliche Konfliktfelder und die Entstehung des Antisemitismus: Das Deutsche Kaiserreich und das Liberale Italien im Vergleich* (Berlin: Metropol Verlag, 2015), 83; Catalan, "Linguaggi," 54–55.
18. Gina Lombroso Ferrero, "Lombroso soldato (1859–64)," in Lombroso Ferrero, *Cesare Lombroso*, 89.
19. Rosselli, *Memorie*, 53. On the *Repubblica di San Marco*, see Paul Ginsborg, *Daniele Manin e la rivoluzione veneziana del 1848–49* (Turin: Einaudi, 1978).
20. On Orvieto, see "Laura Orvieto: La voglia di raccontare le 'Storie del Mondo,'" *Antologia Vieusseux* 18 (2012): 53–54; Ruth Nattermann, "The Italian-Jewish Writer Laura Orvieto (1876–1955) between Intellectual Independence and Social Exclusion," in "Portrait of Italian Jewish Life (1800s–1930s)," ed. Tullia Catalan and Cristiana Facchini, special issue, *Quest: Issues in Contemporary Jewish History; Journal of Fondazione CDEC* 8 (November 2015), http://www.quest-cdecjournal.it/focus.php?id=368.
21. Laura Orvieto, *Storia di Angiolo e Laura*, ed. Caterina Del Vivo (Florence: Leo S. Olschki, 2001), 52.
22. On the respective attitude of Italian middle-class families, see Oliver Janz, *Das symbolische Kapital der Trauer: Nation, Religion und Familie im italienischen Gefallenenkult des Ersten Weltkriegs* (Tübingen: Mohr Siebeck, 2009), 355–65.
23. See the report in "La Donna," 20 March 1915 and 15 April 1915; on the commitment of Italian-Jewish women to the national cause, see Bartoloni, "Margherita Sarfatti," 211; Monica Miniati, *Le emancipate: Le donne ebree in Italia nel XIX e XX secolo* (Rome: Viella, 2008), 211–24.
24. See Dolza, *Essere figlie*, 26.
25. On the prominent contemporary feminist Anna Kuliscioff, partner of Filippo Turati and cofounder of the Italian Socialist Party, see especially Marina Addis Saba, *Anna Kuliscioff: Vita privata e passione politica* (Milan: Mondadori, 1993).
26. See Dolza, *Essere figlie*, 140–50. On the historian and writer Guglielmo Ferrero, see especially Lorella Cedroni, *Guglielmo Ferrero: Una biografia intellettuale* (Rome: Aracne Editore, 2006); *Guglielmo Ferrero tra società e politica: Atti del convegno, Genova 4–5 ottobre, 1982*, ed. Rita Baldi (Genoa: ECIG, 1986).
27. There is no direct evidence in the sources that Ferrero reflected on the fact that the coalition with France and Great Britain also included Tsarist Russia, which had been following the most exclusionary policy toward its Jewish population. As late as July 1917, five months after the February Revolution, Ferrero admitted in a letter to Gina Lombroso that he felt very troubled about the news from Russia: "Seeing what the socialists are doing there, one is really horrified by this party and this order of ideas. And we ourselves even contributed to its accreditation!"; Guglielmo Ferrero to Gina Lombroso, 20 July 1917, Gabinetto G. P. Vieusseux, Firenze, Archivio Contemporaneo "Alessandro Bonsanti" (hereafter ACGV), Fondo Lombroso, GLF.II.2.441.
28. The most prominent representative of contemporary left-wing intellectuals who supported a democratic interventionism was the historian Gaetano Salvemini (1873–1957), a close friend of the Lombroso Ferreros; see Andrea Frangioni,

Salvemini e la Grande Guerra: Interventismo democratico, wilsonismo, politica delle nazionalità (Soveria Mannelli: Rubbettino, 2011).

29. Guglielmo Ferrero to Gina Lombroso, Udine, 11 September 1916, ACGV, Fondo Lombroso, GL.F.II.2.399.
30. Guglielmo Ferrero to Gina Lombroso, Udine, 18 September 1916, ACGV, Fondo Lombroso, GL.F.II.2.403.
31. Ibid.
32. Guglielmo Ferrero to Gina Lombroso, Milan, 22 September 1916, ACGV, Fondo Lombroso, GL.F.II.2.406.
33. Guglielmo Ferrero, *Pouvoir : Les génies invisibles de la cité* (New York: Brentano's, 1942).
34. Guglielmo Ferrero, *La tragedia della pace* (Milan: Edizioni Athena, 1923), 7f.
35. See Dolza, *Essere figlie*, 157–61.
36. On Sarfatti's Jewish family background, her youth in Venice, and early commitment to writing, see especially Urso, *Margherita Sarfatti*, 19–29.
37. See ibid., 29–35; Wieland, *Die Geliebte*, 145–47.
38. Sarfatti had been horrified when, in October 1915, the Germans executed the British nurse Edith Cavell, who had helped Allied soldiers escape from German-occupied Belgium. Her prejudices against the German "barbarians" were significantly influenced by this event. See Wieland, *Die Geliebte*, 145–46.
39. See ibid., 151–54, Urso, *Margherita Sarfatti*, 131–33. On the archaic figure of the stoic mother sacrificing her sons for the fatherland, see also Perry Willson, *Women in Twentieth-Century Italy* (New York: Palgrave Macmillan, 2010), 60–62.
40. *Il Popolo d'Italia*, 2 February 1918; Margherita Sarfatti, *Dux* (Milan: Mondadori, 1926), 194.
41. Margherita Sarfatti, *Roberto Sarfatti: Sue lettere e testimonianze di lui* (Milan: Istituto Editoriale Italiano, 1919). On the commemorative volume for Roberto, see Janz, *Das symbolische Kapital der Trauer*, 276–79.
42. Margherita Sarfatti, *I vivi e l'ombra: Liriche* (Milan: Facchi, 1921).
43. See Claudia Siebrecht, "The Female Mourner: Gender and the Moral Economy of Grief during the First World War," in Hämmerle, Überegger, and Bader Zaar, *Gender and the First World War*, especially 146, 148, 154f. On the widespread phenomenon of commemorative volumes in Italy, see Janz, *Das symbolische Kapital der Trauer*.
44. After World War I, the emphatic celebration of a collective sacrifice was supposed to create a new form of patriotism, associated with the "regeneration" and "rebirth" of the nation. Subsequently, the Fascist regime transformed the Festa della Vittoria into a celebration of heroism and martyrdom for the divinity of the *Patria*, analogous to the way Margherita Sarfatti represented her son's sacrifice. The connection created between nation and war moved into the center of the symbolic-liturgical construction of fascism. On this argument, see Guri Schwarz, *Tu mi devi seppellir: Riti funebri e culto nazionale alle origini della Repubblica* (Turin: Utet, 2010), 37f.; Nicola Labanca, "La prima guerra mondiale in Italia, dalla memoria alla storia, e ritorno," in *La Guerra Italo-Austriaca (1915–18)*, ed. Nicola Labanca and Oswald Überegger (Bologna: Il Mulino, 2014), 309–11; Roberta Suzzi Valli, "Il culto dei martiri fascisti," in *La morte per la patria: La celebrazione dei caduti dal Risorgimento alla Repubblica*, ed. Oliver Janz and Lutz Klinkhammer (Rome: Donzelli, 2008), 105–8.

45. "Il mio latte mutato in tuo sangue, figlio bianco e vermiglio, la mia carne che fu carne tua, scomparver sotterra, e con essi la mia gioventù"; Margherita Sarfatti, "San Silvestro 1918," in *I vivi e l'ombra*, 164f. The ancient topos of the mother's sacrifice of her son became a recurrent theme in literary and artistic works during World War I also outside Italy and within politically opposed contexts. A well-known example is the sculpture of the *Mourning Parents*, which the German artist Käthe Kollwitz created for her son Peter, who fell in October 1914 in the First Battle of Flanders; another example is her wartime diary, which includes numerous references to her motherly sacrifice. After Peter's death, his room in his parents' house assumed ritual significance. On the anniversary of his death, family members and friends commemorated him there by reading his letters and literary texts and lighting candles, thus participating in the sacral dimension of the event. Käthe Kollwitz seemed to be the "priest of this sanctuary," similarly to Margherita Sarfatti's symbolic role with regard to Roberto. Unlike the latter, the commemoration of Peter, however, continued to take place mainly within the private sphere. On Käthe Kollwitz's motherly sacrifice and the cult of her dead son, see Regina Schulte, "Käthe Kollwitz' Opfer," in *Die verkehrte Welt des Krieges: Studien zu Geschlecht, Religion und Tod*, ed. Regina Schulte (New York: Campus Verlag, 1998), 119–23. On the emotional connotations of sacrifice in the war, see Ute Frevert, "Ehre, Scham und die Wollust des Opferns = Honour, Shame and the Lust of Sacrificing," in *Der gefühlte Krieg: Emotionen im Ersten Weltkrieg/Feeling War: Emotions in the First World War*, ed. Jane Redlin and Dagmar Neuland-Kitzerow (Husum: Verlag der Kunst, 2014), 13–26.
46. Philip V. Cannistraro and Brian R. Sullivan, *Margherita Sarfatti: L'altra donna del duce* (Milan: Mondadori, 1993), 262; Urso, *Margherita Sarfatti*, 133.
47. See the letter by the Avanguardia giovanile del Partito d'azione fascista, sezione di Milano, to Margherita Sarfatti, 20 April 1922, in Urso, *Margherita Sarfatti*, 133.
48. See ibid., 131.
49. On Rosselli's family and upbringing, see Calloni, "Introduzione," in Rosselli, *Memorie*, 12–15; on her commitment to the Florentine Lyceum, see Patricia Bulletti, "Amelia nel Lyceum (1908–1937)," and Mirka Sandiford, "Il Lyceum di Firenze ai tempi di Amelia," *Quaderni del Circolo Rosselli* 3 (2006): 29–38; 39–48.
50. Rosselli, *Memorie*, 151–55. On Aldo Rosselli's death, see also Leo Valiani, "Introduzione," in Ciuffoletti, *I Rosselli*, x; Ruth Nattermann, "The Female Side of War: The Experience and Memory of the Great War in Italian-Jewish Women's Ego-Documents," in *The Jewish Experience of the First World War*, ed. Edward Madigan and Gideon Reuveni (New York: Palgrave Macmillan, 2018), 245–46.
51. See especially Amelia Rosselli to Laura Orvieto, s.d. (1919?), ACGV, Fondo Laura Orvieto, F.Or. 1.2059.
52. Amelia Rosselli to Laura Orvieto, Florence, 11 June 1947, ACGV, Fondo Laura Orvieto, F.Or. 1.2059.

Bibliography

Addis Saba, Marina. *Anna Kuliscioff: Vita privata e passione politica*. Milan: Mondadori, 1993.
Amato, Giovanna. "Una donna nella storia: Vita e letteratura di Amelia Pincherle Rosselli." *Quaderni del Circolo Rosselli* 1 (2012).

Baldi, Rita, ed. *Guglielmo Ferrero tra società e politica: Atti del convegno, Genova 4–5 ottobre, 1982*. Genoa: ECIG, 1986.

Bartoloni, Stefania. "Margherita Sarfatti: Una intellettuale tra Nazione e Fascismo." In *Di generazione in generazione: Le Italiane dall'Unità ad Oggi*, edited by Maria Teresa Mori, Alessandra Pescarolo, Anna Scattigno, and Simonetta Soldani, 207–20. Rome: Viella, 2014.

Bulletti, Patricia. "Amelia nel Lyceum (1908–1937)." *Quaderni del Circolo Rosselli* 3 (2006): 29–38.

Calloni, Marina, and Lorella Cedroni. "Presentazione: Due famiglie in esilio." In *Politica e affetti familiari: Lettere di Amelia, Carlo e Nello Rosselli a Guglielmo, Leo e Nina Ferrero e Gina Lombroso Ferrero (1917–1943)*, edited by Marina Calloni and Lorella Cedroni, 21–27. Milan: Feltrinelli, 1997.

Cannistraro, Philip V., and Brian R. Sullivan. *Margherita Sarfatti: L'altra donna del duce*. Milan: Mondadori, 1993.

Catalan, Tullia. "Linguaggi e stereotipi dell'antislavismo irredentista dalla fine dell'Ottocento alla Grande Guerra." In *Fratelli al massacre: Linguaggi e narrazioni della Prima Guerra Mondiale*, edited by Tullia Catalan, 39–69. Rome: Viella, 2015.

Cedroni, Lorella. *Guglielmo Ferrero: Una biografia intellettuale*. Rome: Aracne Editore, 2006.

Ciuffoletti, Zeffiro, ed. *I Rosselli: Epistolario familiare 1914–1937*. Milan: Mondadori, 1997.

Ciuffoletti, Zeffiro, and Nicola Tranfaglia. "Introduzione." In *Lessico familiare: Vita, cultura e politica della famiglia Rosselli all'insegna della libertà*, edited by Zeffiro Ciuffoletti and Gian Luca Corradi, xiv–xv. Florence: Edimond, 2002.

Collotti, Enzo. *Il Fascismo e gli Ebrei: Le leggi razziali in Italia*. Rome: Laterza, 2004.

Dogliani, Patrizia. "Redipuglia." In *I luoghi della memoria: Simboli e miti dell'Italia unita*, edited by Mario Isnenghi, 421–35. Rome: Laterza, 2010.

Dolza, Delfina. *Essere figlie di Lombroso: Due donne intellettuali tra '800 e '900*. Milan: Franco Angeli, 1991.

Ernst, Petra. "Der Erste Weltkrieg in deutschsprachig-jüdischer Literatur und Publizistik in Österreich." In *Krieg: Erinnerung; Geschichtswissenschaft*, edited by Siegfried Mattl, Gerhard Botz, Stefan Karner, and Helmut Konrad, 47–72. Vienna: Böhlau Verlag, 2009.

Ernst, Petra, and Eleonore Lappin-Eppel, eds. *Jüdische Publizistik und Literatur im Zeichen des Ersten Weltkriegs*. Innsbruck: Studienverlag, 2016.

Ernst, Petra, Jeffrey Grossman, and Ulrich Wyrwa. "Introduction." In "The Great War: Reflections, Experiences and Memories of German and Habsburg Jews (1914–1918)," edited by Petra Ernst, Jeffrey Grossman, and Ulrich Wyrwa, Special issue, *Quest: Issues in Contemporary Jewish History; Journal of Fondazione CDEC* 9 (October 2016). http://www.quest-cdecjournal.it/index.php?issue=9.

Ferrero, Guglielmo. *La tragedia della pace*. Milan: Edizioni Athena, 1923.

———. *Pouvoir: Les génies invisibles de la cite*. New York: Brentano's, 1942.

Frangioni, Andrea. *Salvemini e la Grande Guerra: Interventismo democratico, wilsonismo, politica delle nazionalità*. Soveria Mannelli: Rubbettino, 2011.

Frevert, Ute. "Ehre, Scham und die Wollust des Opferns = Honour, Shame and the Lust of Sacrificing." In *Der gefühlte Krieg: Emotionen im Ersten Weltkrieg/Feeling War: Emotions in the First World War*, edited by Jane Redlin and Dagmar Neuland-Kitzerow, 13–26. Husum: Verlag der Kunst, 2014.

Gibson, Mary S. *Born to Crime: Cesare Lombroso and the Origins of Biological Criminology*. Santa Barbara, CA: Praeger Press, 2002.
Ginsborg, Paul. *Daniele Manin e la rivoluzione veneziana del 1848–49*. Turin: Einaudi, 1978.
Hämmerle, Christa. "Gewalt und Liebe—ineinander verschränkt: Paarkorrespondenzen aus zwei Weltkriegen: 1914/18 und 1939/45." in *Liebe schreiben: Paarkorrespondenzen im Kontext des 19. und 20. Jahrhunderts*, edited by Ingrid Bauer and Christa Hämmerle, 171–230. Göttingen: Vandenhoeck & Ruprecht, 2017.
Isnenghi, Mario. "Scenari dell'io nei racconti sociali della Grande Guerra." In *La Grande Guerra delle italiane: Mobilitazioni, diritti, trasformazioni*, edited by Stefania Bartoloni, 273–94. Rome: Viella, 2016.
Janz, Oliver. *Das symbolische Kapital der Trauer: Nation, Religion und Familie im italienischen Gefallenenkult des Ersten Weltkriegs*. Tübingen: Mohr Siebeck, 2009.
Labanca, Nicola. "La prima guerra mondiale in Italia, dalla memoria alla storia, e ritorno." In *La Guerra Italo-Austriaca (1915–18)*, edited by Nicola Labanca and Oswald Überegger, 303–23. Bologna: Il Mulino, 2014.
Lamprecht, Gerald. "Kriegserinnerungs- und Identitätsdiskurse am Beispiel des 'Bundes jüdischer Frontsoldaten' und der Zeitschrift *Jüdische Front* 1932–1938." In *Jüdische Publizistik und Literatur, im Zeichen des Ersten Weltkriegs*, edited by Petra Ernst and Eleonore Lappin-Eppel, 167–86. Innsbruck: Studienverlag, 2016.
Laura Orvieto. "La voglia di raccontare le 'Storie del Mondo.'" *Antologia Vieusseux* 18 (2012): 53–54.
Lombroso Ferrero, Gina. *Cesare Lombroso: Storia della Vita e delle Opere*. Bologna: Zanichelli Editore, 1915.
Miniati, Monica. *Le emancipate: Le donne ebree in Italia nel XIX e XX secolo*. Rome: Viella, 2008.
Nattermann, Ruth. "The Female Side of War: The Experience and Memory of the Great War in Italian-Jewish Women's Ego-Documents." In *The Jewish Experience of the First World War*, edited by Edward Madigan and Gideon Reuveni, 233–54. New York: Palgrave Macmillan, 2018.
———. "The Italian-Jewish Writer Laura Orvieto (1876–1955) between Intellectual Independence and Social Exclusion." In "Portrait of Italian Jewish Life (1800s–1930s)," edited by Tullia Catalan and Cristiana Facchini. Special issue, *Quest: Issues in Contemporary Jewish History, Journal of Fondazione CDEC* 8 (November 2015). http://www.quest-cdecjournal.it/focus.php?id=368.
Orvieto, Laura. *Storia di Angiolo e Laura*. Edited by Caterina Del Vivo. Florence: Leo S. Olschki, 2001.
Penslar, Derek. *Jews and the Military: A History*. Princeton, NJ: Princeton University Press, 2013.
Rosselli, Amelia. *Memorie*. Edited by Marina Calloni. Bologna: Il Mulino, 2001.
Sandiford, Mirka. "Il Lyceum di Firenze ai tempi di Amelia." *Quaderni del Circolo Rosselli* 3 (2006): 39–48.
Sarfatti, Margherita. *Roberto Sarfatti: Sue lettere e testimonianze di lui*. Milan: Istituto Editoriale Italiano, 1919.
———. *I vivi e l'ombra: Liriche*. Milan: Facchi, 1921.
———. *Dux*. Milan: Mondadori, 1926.
———. *The Jews in Mussolini's Italy: From Equality to Persecution*. Madison: University of Wisconsin Press, 2006.

Schulte, Regina. "Käthe Kollwitz' Opfer." In *Die verkehrte Welt des Krieges: Studien zu Geschlecht, Religion und Tod*, edited by Regina Schulte, 117–51. New York: Campus Verlag, 1998.
Schwarz, Guri. *Tu mi devi seppellir: Riti funebri e culto nazionale alle origini della Repubblica*. Turin: Utet, 2010.
Siebrecht, Claudia. "The Female Mourner: Gender and the Moral Economy of Grief during the First World War." In *Gender and the First World War*, edited by Christa Hämmerle, Oswald Überegger, and Birgitta Bader Zaar, 144–62. New York: Palgrave Macmillan, 2014.
Suzzi Valli, Roberta. "Il culto dei martiri fascisti." In *La morte per la patria: La celebrazione dei caduti dal Risorgimento alla Repubblica*, edited by Oliver Janz and Lutz Klinkhammer, 102–19. Rome: Donzelli, 2008.
Tedeschi, Felice. *Gli israeliti italiani nella guerra 1915–1918*. Turin: F. Servi, 1921.
Toscano, Mario. "Ebrei ed ebraismo nell'Italia della grande guerra: Note su una inchiesta del Comitato delle comunità israelitiche italiane del maggio 1917." In *Ebraismo e antisemitismo in Italia: Dal 1848 alla guerra dei sei giorni*, edited by Mario Toscano, 123–54. Milan: Franco Angeli, 2003.
———. "Gli ebrei italiani e la prima guerra mondiale (1915–1918): Tra crisi religiosa e fremiti patriottici." In *Ebraismo e antisemitismo in Italia: Dal 1848 alla guerra dei sei giorni*, edited by Mario Toscano, 110–22. Milan: Franco Angeli, 2003.
———. "Religione, patriottismo, sionismo: Il rabbinato militare nell'Italia della Grande Guerra (1915–1918)." *Zakhor* 8 (2005): 77–133.
Urso, Simona. *Margherita Sarfatti: Dal mito del Dux al mito americano*. Venice: Marsilio, 2003.
Valiani, Leo. "Introduzione." In *I Rosselli: Epistolario familiare 1914–1937*, edited by Zeffiro Ciuffoletti, vii–xxvii. Milan: Mondadori, 1997.
Vieri, Dolara. "Amelia Rosselli Pincherle." *Quaderni del Circolo Rosselli* 3 (2006).
Wieland, Karin. *Die Geliebte des Duce: Das Leben der Margherita Sarfatti und die Erfindung des Faschismus*. Munich: Carl Hanser Verlag, 2004.
Wierling, Dorothee. "Imagining and Communicating Violence: The Correspondence of a Berlin Family, 1914–1918." In *Gender and the First World War*, edited by Christa Hämmerle, Oswald Überegger, and Birgitta Bader Zaar, 36–51. New York: Palgrave Macmillan, 2014.
Willson, Perry. *Women in Twentieth-Century Italy*. New York: Palgrave Macmillan, 2010.
Winter, Jay. *Remembering War: The Great War between Memory and History in the Twentieth Century*. New Haven, CT: Yale University Press, 2006.
Wyrwa, Ulrich. *Gesellschaftliche Konfliktfelder und die Entstehung des Antisemitismus: Das Deutsche Kaiserreich und das Liberale Italien im Vergleich*. Berlin: Metropol Verlag, 2015.

CHAPTER 18

The Commemoration of Jewish Soldiers in Austria

Gerald Lamprecht

In February 1915, Adolf Altmann, then rabbi of the Jewish community of Merano in South Tyrol as well as the military chaplain in the region, published an appeal in the Viennese Jewish journal *Dr. Bloch's oesterreichische Wochenschrift* with the title "Jewish Communities, Found War-Chronicles."[1] Referring to Shabbat Zachor and the biblical command to remember, he wrote, "God wishes that Israel would keep in mind the historical context of His national doings." Based on religious precepts, he claimed to be memorializing the Jewish war service and sacrifice and argued that it would be important in the future to document the Jewish suffering, merits, achievements, and rejections that occurred during the course of the war. He stated that he intended to write a Jewish history of warfare on a regional basis, with the aim of integrating Jewish history into general history, to embed Jewish memory into the Austrian collective memory. For Rabbi Altmann, this did not mean that Jews should disappear into non-Jewish society or its culture of memory. On the contrary, for him and many other Jews engaged in memory discourse, Jews were to be represented within the Austrian cultural memory as Jews: equal citizens, whose patriotism and loyalty should be honored by their fellow gentile citizens.

Jewish Soldiers and Austrian History

However, when we analyze memories, commemorative services, and memorial practices with regard to the military service of Jewish soldiers as members of the Austrian-Hungarian army over the past hundred years, it soon becomes evident that Rabbi Altmann did not achieve his aim. We can see that during both the war and the interwar period, neither the Jewish military service nor Jewish soldiers were naturally integrated into the Austrian collective memory. In particular, National Socialism and the

Holocaust created a rift that continues to exist today. This is because the almost-complete expulsion and killing of Austrian Jews that took place between 1938 and 1945 also led to the extinction of Judaism, Jewish history, and, thus, the expulsion of the memory of fallen Jewish soldiers from the Austrian cultural and collective memory. The National Socialists not only expelled and exterminated the Jews from the community of remembrance (*milieu de mémoire*) but also destroyed many of the material signs of memory (*lieu de mémoire*), such as war memorials or memorial plaques located in synagogues and Jewish cemeteries.

In post–World War II Germany, the first signs and activities of memory that refer to World War I and the Jewish soldiers who served in it appeared shortly after the end of the World War II, and mostly after the 1960s, as Tim Grady shows in his book.[2] In Austria, however, historical and social discussions about war memories and Jewish soldiers in particular, as well as Jewish history and culture in general, started much later. The earliest commemorative activities were conducted in the early 1980s, when the Austrian Jewish Museum in Eisenstadt was moved to the so-called Wertheimer House. This move was initiated by the well-known scholar from the University of Vienna and founder of the Austrian Jewish Museum, Kurt Schubert. Schubert wanted the museum to rebuild and reinstall the memorial plaque for the fallen Jewish soldiers of Eisenstadt, which had first been established in 1934 by the Federation of Jewish War Veterans of Austria and which was, in all probability, destroyed by National Socialists after the Austrian annexation to Nazi Germany in March 1938.[3]

From the 1982 inauguration of the memorial plaque in Eisenstadt on, and particularly since 1995, the Austrian army has integrated Jewish soldiers and those war memorials that still exist into their memorial activities for the fallen soldiers of both wars, which take place every year on All Saints' Day.[4] Every year on 1 November, soldiers of the Austrian army place a wreath in front of Jewish war memorials located in the Jewish cemeteries in Graz and Vienna. Although this is an important act of official recognition of the Jewish participation in World War I and of Jewish loyalty to the state, it is also important to note that public attention to these acts is still rather marginal in comparison to the public commemorative activities that are carried out in almost every Austrian town and village by local groups of the Austrian Veterans' Association.

Analyzing the academic historical discussions of this issue in Austria, it becomes evident that any historical engagement with Jewish participation in World War I, like the social and political commemoration activities, was late in starting. The first studies on this topic were conducted by authors, such as Wolfgang von Weisl,[5] István Déak, Marsha Rozenblit, and David Rechter, who were not affiliated with Austrian academic organizations and who consequently also published their books outside of Austria.[6] In general, books and articles that dealt with Jewish history and/or the history of persecution of Jews by the National Socialists were first published in the late 1960s, and almost exclusively by formerly persecuted persons.[7]

From the early 1980s onward, the number of publications increased, particularly those that dealt with various aspects of Jewish history and culture in the nineteenth and twentieth centuries, and especially with the fin de siècle and persecution during the NS regime. While many contemporary studies on these topics are available, a research gap still exists with regard to the question of Jewish war memory and military service in Austria during World War I. Besides those books mentioned above, few other studies were published during the late 1980s and early 1990s.[8] In fact, only the attention drawn to the centennial commemoration of the outbreak of war in 2014 directed more attention to Jewish soldiers. This relatively new focus is exemplified by a special exhibition at the Jewish Museum in Vienna, which included the exhibition catalogue,[9] as well as a revised re-edition of Erwin A. Schmidl's 1989 book with a new title—*Habsburgs jüdische Soldaten*[10]—and some other articles.[11]

This finding of new attention on Jewish soldiers must be modified when we analyze mainstream and official exhibitions as well as some recent books published after 2014.[12] For example, neither the largest exhibition in Austria in 2014, *Jubel & Elend: Leben mit dem Großen Krieg 1914–1918*,[13] nor the extensive essay collection *Im Epizentrum des Zusammenbruchs: Wien im Ersten Weltkrieg*[14] paid much attention to the faith of Jewish soldiers. In the exhibition, as in the book, Jews are only mentioned with regard to refugee care or in the context of refugee issues or problems. This means that they are either presented as victims of the war or as part of the social and political problems that arose during the course of the war. In all of these studies and exhibitions, Jews are presented as more or less passive objects of history, but never as active individuals or groups—participating actors or subjects with their own agency. In such a way, Jewish soldiers and Jews in general are located outside or on the fringes of the Austrian collective war memory. This marginalization, however, is not only the result of the annihilation and destruction by the National Socialists but also of the insufficiency or total lack of discussions and analyses carried out by Austria's postwar society with regard to its Nazi heritage.[15] The latter manifests itself, in particular, in the Austrian culture of war memory after 1945, which was, to a large extent, established by the Österreichischer Kameradschaftsbund (the Austrian Veterans' Association) and which has always been supported by large parts of Austria's society as well as by members of political parties. The Austrian Veterans' Association, which is well integrated into the Austrian political system and society, defined itself in the Austrian postwar era as a "community of fate of the war generation"[16] and consisted exclusively of former members of the German Wehrmacht. They commemorate first and foremost the soldiers who fell in World War II. Thus, World War I is eclipsed, and, consequently, no space remains for the particular commemoration of Jewish soldiers or the destruction of Jewish life by the National Socialists in Austrian society after World War II.

Jewish Soldiers and Memory Discourse from 1914 to 1938

While Jewish soldiers were marginalized after 1945 for the reasons mentioned above, it is possible to argue that a continuity of memory discourses exists during and after World War I. From 1914 to 1938, discourses about military service and acts of remembrance of the fallen soldiers were central both to political discussions and to the political culture. Referring to Reinhart Koselleck,[17] acts of war memory with the political "death cult" in the center are, in general, crucial for the political unit—normally the nation, state, or *Volk*—to legitimize or stabilize itself. Within this discourse of memory, questions of participation and inclusion within or exclusion from the political unit are negotiated. Individual soldiers' deaths on the battlefield were at the center of all these discourses and were, therefore, on the one hand, the ultimate evidence of each citizen's loyalty to the state, nation, *Volk*, and, on the other hand, capable of lending meaning to the individual soldiers' senseless deaths.[18]

From the late eighteenth century onward, military service became a central point of discussion during the formation of modern liberal and civil societies. The "citizen-soldier" displayed his willingness to die on the battlefield and, thus, his loyalty to the state; in return, the state guaranteed him the right to political participation, civil rights, and equality as a member of the community.[19] Thus, the issue of Jews in military service was closely tied to Jewish emancipation in Europe. Prussian councilor Christian Wilhelm Dohm's 1781 text, titled *Ueber die buergerliche Verbesserung der Juden* (On the Civil Improvement of the Jews) served as a guide in Germany and Austria in particular, as well as in other countries.[20] In his book, Dohm dedicates a whole chapter to the military service of Jews and specifies all of the arguments used by the opponents of Jewish emancipation for the first time. These opponents alleged that Jews were not fit for military service in general, due to the religious requirement that they observe the Sabbath as a day of rest, the Kashruth, their social segregation from gentiles, physical weakness, and their general observance of the religious principle that only a defensive war is a just war. Furthermore, they accused Jews of disloyalty and concluded that "citizens who do not defend the society to which they belong cannot be citizens like others; they cannot demand equal rights and have to accept oppressive differences."[21] Dohm countered these arguments, stating that it is

> correct to claim unrestricted military service from the Jews. Of course, currently they are not able to do this because they have lived for a very long time under oppression, which has suffocated their religious speculative philosophy, militant minds, and individual bravery. For one and a half millennia, they had no fatherland; how could they fight and die for it? But, I am convinced that they will do this with the same ability and fidelity as all others do it, just as we give them a fatherland.[22]

Dohm's text contains all of the essential elements of the discourses that deal with Jewish military service during the nineteenth and twentieth centuries, as well as those about the Jewish war memory. These discourses always consider the question of whether Jews can be equal citizens of the states in which they live and of which they truly were citizens. Thus, many Jews in Austria welcomed the war enthusiastically and hoped that they would be able to express their patriotism through their unrestricted military service as well as the supportive engagement of Jewish communities and associations. In doing so, they expected that the legal emancipation of Jews, which began in Austria in 1867, would come to fruition both over the course of and due to the war, resulting in their social acceptance by gentile Austrians.[23]

In contrast to these Jewish expectations, which were rooted deep in the history of emancipation, strong non-Jewish discourses concerning Jewish military service, Jewish refugees, and Jewish loyalty in general arose during the course of the war, which resulted in a considerable increase of and radicalization in antisemitism.[24] Although antisemitic agitations had already taken place when the Jewish refugees from Galicia and Bukovina arrived in German-speaking parts of the monarchy in 1914 and 1915, antisemitism became an even more important issue in public discourse from at least the midpoint of the war on. This was because the Austrian censorship board had tried to suppress antisemitism and attempted to preserve the party truce in the first years of the war. This stance underwent fundamental changes after the death of Emperor Franz Joseph I in November 1916 and at the reconvention of the Austrian parliament in May 1917. From that point on, and especially during the pivotal years of 1918 and 1919, antisemitism increased. Jews became the scapegoats for all social and political crises.[25] To antisemites, Jews were shirkers of duty, cowards, had no fatherland or patriotic feelings, and were accused of being war profiteers and instigating revolutionary uprisings and upheavals.[26] Antisemites could be found among members of political parties, on the editorial staff of newspapers and journals, and in various associations. For example, the Combatants Association of German-Austria was founded in 1920 and was, from that time on, one of the leading antisemitic organizations in Austria during the interwar period.[27]

All this led to a fundamental identity crisis for Jews, who were concerned about questions both of their Jewish self-identity and of their position in the state and society.[28] Another factor making the situation more complicated was that, after the downfall of the Habsburg Empire, the newly founded republic of German-Austria, and later Austria, established itself as a hegemonic German national state and had to redefine its relationships with its ethnic and religious minorities. Furthermore, the emerging republic was also attempting to distance itself from the monarchy, which affected the political practice of war remembrances in general, as well as the specific question of the Jewish position within them.

Agents, Spaces, and Media of Memory

Within the Jewish population, individual agents of memory became active from 1914 onward. They linked their war memories with specific concerns and expectations, and they interpreted the war and their war experiences within this specific Jewish framework. Apart from the families, for whom—according to Jay Winter[29]—war memory signified a way to grieve and come to terms with trauma in the first place, individual actors of memory were rabbis, Jewish military chaplains, Jewish religious communities, editors of journals and newspapers, individual intellectuals, and members of associations such as the Federation of Jewish War Veterans of Austria, which was founded in Vienna in 1932.[30]

In this context, it is striking to note that welfare associations for the victims of war, such as the Association of Jewish War Veterans, Widows, and Orphans,[31] did not perform specific acts of commemoration, such as erecting war memorials. The aforementioned association, which has its roots in an appeal made by Nathan Birnbaum that appeared in various German-Jewish journals from December 1917 on,[32] drew particular attention to survivors and wounded, mutilated soldiers, as well as to dependents of fallen soldiers. The organization initiated work programs and set up social support for its members. Although Nathan Birnbaum argued in 1917 that such an organization not only had to work for the "interest, the fame and honor of the combatants and war-disabled"[33] but also for the Jewish collective and its reputation in the years immediately after the war, there was no place for activities that concerned the symbolic recognition and representation of the Jewish soldiers and victims of war in the public sphere. This may be due to the fact that the economic and social crises required all the efforts of the Jewish communities and organizations, pushing all symbolic issues into the background. Another reason could be that in Austria, which had lost the war, the injured, disabled, or shell-shocked soldiers, especially Jewish ones, did not lend themselves to a national heroic narrative or the narrative of the "fallen hero," which would not exist in Austria until the establishment of the Austrian fascist regime in 1933–34. Furthermore, for such a narrative, only the ultimate sacrifice (that of the hero's death) counts, an observation that Derek Penslar also made of Germany, in contrast to what was seen in the victor states, France and England.[34]

From 1914 to 1938, many discourses that dealt with various topics concerning Jews and the war appeared in German-Jewish journals and publications or took place in synagogues, cemeteries, and during the process of creating war memorials and memorial plaques. Thereby, the German-Jewish journals published in Vienna played important roles. First and foremost was *Dr. Bloch's oesterreichische Wochenschrift*, which more or less represented the voice of the hegemonic, bourgeois Jewish groups in Vienna and Austria during wartime.[35] Other important journals were the *Wahrheit*, the *Jüdische Zeitung*, the *Jüdische Volksstimme*, and the *Jüdische Korrespondenz*.[36] All of these journals represented different Jewish groups and took up different positions; nonetheless, it could be stated that, disregarding their ideological differences, all German-Jewish journals stressed the service of loyal Jews for the fatherland. They all connected Jewish military service and other examples of Jewish sacrifice with their demand that the state and members of gentile society honor Jews and Jewish soldiers and guarantee them civil rights. All of these journals published more or less patriotic texts, in particular, *Dr. Bloch's oesterreichische Wochenschrift*, which also published the names of both fallen and decorated soldiers, biographies of Jewish heroes, and war letters in almost every issue. Rabbi Joseph Samuel Bloch, the editor of *Bloch's oesterreichischer Wochenschrift*, argued that he had to do this because, in 1915, the Austrian war ministry did not heed the Jewish demand that they publish statistics on the numbers of fallen and decorated Jewish soldiers in order to document Jewish patriotism.[37]

In addition to the journals mentioned above, specific commemorative publications were also printed, including the *Jüdisches Kriegsgedenkblatt*,[38] which was edited in six volumes between 1914 and 1917 by the Austrian journalist Moritz Frühling. Each volume collected biographies and documents from Jewish soldiers and war heroes. From May 1915 onward, the committee of the Jewish war archive, founded by certain Austrian Zionists, published the *Jüdisches Archiv* in nine volumes between 1915 and 1917; the journal was then reissued in 1920.[39] While the *Kriegsgedenkblatt* represented a paper memorial for Jewish soldiers, officers, and Emperor Franz Joseph I, the Zionist initiators of the *Jüdisches Archiv* were attempting to fight against antisemitism and the antisemitic accusations of alleged Jewish disloyalty and cowardice.[40] In addition to these publications, it is also important to name the journal of the Federation of Jewish War Veterans of Austria, *Jüdische Front*, published between 1932 and 1938, as well as some collections of sermons.

All these journals and publications had an almost exclusively Jewish readership, and the texts published in them attempted to convey the meaning of the war and the sacrifices made in the war to the Jewish community. These endowments of meaning were made using references to the political situation, in general, as well as to a specific Jewish context. For example, in December 1914, Rabbi Wilhelm Reich,[41] from Baden near Vienna, who was responsible for writing a series of patriotic articles in 1914 and 1915, published a text in *Dr. Bloch's oesterreichischer Wochenschrift* titled "Jewish War Heroes." In this text, he stated that

> the history of war in our times provides us with evidence that Jewish heroism in war didn't slip away. Hundreds and hundreds of our religious companions who are in the war were decorated on the field of honor; they are in no way inferior to any denomination or nation in the fight for the fatherland, and when the book of war is closed with the help of God, we will point with pride and satisfaction to the golden book, in which also a considerable number of names of Jewish heroes will shine for the glorification of Jewry. The names of the Jewish heroes are the dignified followers of the Maccabees.[42]

Rabbi Reich, as well as other authors writing in German-Jewish journals, put the war, military service, and deaths that occurred on the battlefield into a Jewish religious and/or historical context. In doing so, they lent meaning to the massive number of soldiers' deaths and also legitimized the war in general. For them, as well as for many other Jews all over Europe, the war against the Tsarist regime was seen as a holy war,[43] and the tsar himself was named "Amalek," the enemy of the Jewish people.[44] Therefore, the objectives of the Habsburg Monarchy in the war were also the objectives of the Austrian Jews. Jewish heroism, seen in the light of the tradition of the Maccabees, was equivalent to heroism with respect to the fatherland, the monarchy, and the faith and honor of Judaism. Jewish military service and the accompanying discourses, like Jewish heroism, counteracted antisemitism and accusations of Jewish cowardice, and also aimed to strengthen Judaism and Jewish identity. These discourses worked in the direction of Jewish and gentile collectives.

War Memorials and Military Cemeteries

Jewish memory discourses not only appeared in German-Jewish journals, publications, and sermons but also in the discussions that took place when Jewish communities and other members of Austrian towns and villages began planning the erection of military cemeteries or war memorials. In these activities, the state and the communities had to address the questions of how to bury the fallen soldiers in a dignified way as well as how to convey that the soldiers' deaths were of central importance.

During the course of the nineteenth century, and especially during World War I, the death of the individual soldier on the battlefield was considered to be the ultimate sacrifice for the nation or the fatherland, as a result of which the practices of remembrance for fallen soldiers changed fundamentally. Through a process of democratization and equalization, it was determined that all fallen soldiers should be remembered without emphasis on their ethnic, social, or military status, but rather as heroic sons of the fatherland and equal members of the nation. In connection with the collectively constructed, idealized trench experience, the equally idealized experience of comradeship, and the often-invoked picture of the party truce, all soldiers were to be seen as equal in death.[45]

This national endowment and the unprecedented number of soldiers who fell during World War I resulted in the design of military cemeteries and war memorials. "The immediate symbol of wartime camaraderie was the military cemetery: linking the living comradeship of the trenches with that of the fallen comrades."[46] Thus, not only generals, officers, and aristocrats were memorable; it was argued that every fallen soldier should get his own tombstone, which should be the same as that of his comrade. Furthermore, it was argued that the cemeteries should have uniform and predominantly geometric designs, which, with reference to George L. Mosse, often included Christian symbols; in many military cemeteries, a cross appeared in the center.[47]

While, in many cases, Jews and Jewish communities accepted the Christian symbolism in the cemeteries and in the rhetoric of public grief and commemoration,[48] we can also see that the erection of the interdenominational military cemeteries triggered fundamental discussions about Jewish particularity among the Jewish communities in Austria. These discussions concerned fundamental questions of the age of emancipation and focused on the difficult relationship between Jewish particularism and the national demand for equality, as well as the demand for complete assimilation. An example of all of this could be seen when the city of Vienna decided to erect an interdenominational war cemetery for all of the soldiers who had died in Vienna on the grounds of Vienna's central cemetery in 1914. To realize this plan, Richard Weiskirchner, the Christian Social mayor of the city of Vienna, wrote a letter to the Jewish community, inviting them to bury their fallen soldiers in this cemetery as well. In their first response, the board of the Jewish community seemed to welcome this idea rather enthusiastically and indicated their decision, as a result of this invitation, not to erect a separate burial ground for the Jewish soldiers in the Jewish section of the central cemetery.[49] They imposed only three conditions on the city of Vienna: that the Jewish soldiers should receive Jewish funerals and, if religious symbols were to appear on the tombstones, then Jewish tombstones should bear Jewish symbols. This stipulation meant that Jewish soldiers were to be identified with the Star of David and the common abbreviation of the benediction from the first book of Samuel, 25:29: "May his soul be bound up in the bond of life."[50] Furthermore, the city of Vienna was also asked to respect the wishes of parents if they wanted to bury their relatives in a Jewish cemetery.[51]

After a short while, however, the board of the Jewish community reconsidered their decision on the basis of various misgivings and instead planned to bury the Jewish soldiers in a specific heroes' section within the Jewish cemetery. In addition to concerns about the observance of religious rules and fulfilling the desires of the families to have a Jewish place to express their grief, another underlying reason for the change was clearly stated in a letter to the editor, published in *Dr. Bloch's oesterreichischer Wochenschrift* in January 1915:

> We appreciate the fact that the city of Vienna does not want to differentiate between the heroes who have sacrificed their lives for the fatherland. Nevertheless, I would like to suggest that the fallen Jewish soldiers should be buried, if possible, in a separate area, in the Jewish cemetery, because it should be possible, in the quieter times ahead, to also honor the Jewish cemetery through the erection of a war memorial. We should do this because the lack of a memorial shouldn't be criticized by the next or the next or even one generation, when the son asks his father: Didn't the Jews fight in the year 1914, because there isn't a war memorial in the Jewish cemetery?[52]

The Jewish communities in Vienna and other Austrian cities had already begun to fear existing and future antisemitism by the end of 1914 and the beginning of 1915. To prevent and check the growth of antisemitism, they needed to maintain the Jewish cemeteries and future war memorials as arguments against antisemitic attacks. They needed them as visible representations of the fallen Jewish soldiers, their sacrifice for the fatherland, and Jewish loyalty. Consequently, in almost every Austrian town that had a Jewish community, separate heroes' sections with war graves were built within the Jewish cemeteries.

In addition to their justified fear of antisemitism, Jewish communities also had reservations about Christian appropriation of fallen Jewish soldiers and their commemoration, which were not unfounded. In the Habsburg Monarchy, from the very beginning of the war, the commemorations and expressions of public grief for the mass deaths were composed of Christian, dynastic, and patriotic elements. The Habsburg soldiers died "for God, Emperor, and fatherland."[53] The official commemorations of fallen soldiers of the Habsburg Monarchy and, later, in the First Republic were influenced or informed by Christian practices for the commemoration of the dead. During the war, and increasingly after its end, war memorials were built around Christian churches and in Christian cemeteries in almost every Austrian town and village, and many of these displayed either nationalistic or Christian symbols. The sacrifice of the soldiers was equated to the sacrifice of Jesus Christ, as Heidemarie Uhl, Stefan Riesenfellner,[54] and Oswald Überegger[55] have all shown in their studies. Accordingly, the public commemoration ceremonies took place every year on All Saints' Day, when thousands of people in Vienna, for example, would make a pilgrimage to the central cemetery to commemorate the fallen soldiers at the abovementioned central war memorial, in which a temporary wooden cross had been erected at the center, and which was also located behind the so-called Lueger's Church.[56]

Although this hegemonic Christian commemorative practice did not carry the obligation of a governmental decree, the Jewish communities faced considerable public and political pressure to attend. For example, the military authority in Styria asked the Jewish community to hold an All Saints' Day commemorative service in the Jewish cemetery on 2 November 1916 to celebrate the Jewish soldiers buried there.[57] In his first response, Rabbi David Herzog, who had published his patriotic war sermons the year before,[58] did not have any objections, but he decided after a short time, by mutual consent with the board members of the Jewish community and the board members of the Chevra Kadisha, not to undertake this ceremony under any circumstances, due to general religious reservations.[59]

However, this does not mean that the Jewish communities excluded themselves from all public commemorative activities. On the contrary, they usually joined and supported all such activities and ceremonies, but they also sought to preserve their Jewish religious and ethnic particularism. For example, when the Committee for the Preservation of the War Graves in Austria pursued a joint objective to collect money for war graves during the commemorative services on All Saints' Day by organizing Public War Graves Day[60] in 1917, the German-Jewish journals also published advertisements for the Public War Graves Day.[61] Furthermore, both as individuals and members of Jewish communities and Jewish associations like the Federation of Jewish War Veterans of Austria, Jews participated in many of the public commemorative activities and ceremonies during and after the war, except for antisemitic agitations that excluded them. By attending these public commemorative activities, they demonstrated their belief that Jews were naturally an equal part of the Austrian society and state, and that they appreciated the Christian hegemony to some extent. Nevertheless, they also demanded that mainstream Christian society respect Jewish particularism, on the one hand, and Jewish loyalty, patriotism, and war sacrifices on the other.

Despite the fact that there were many interactions and overlaps between the Jewish and gentile political and public practices of commemoration, the primary places for Jewish war memory and memory discourses, both during and after the war, were the German-Jewish journals and, in particular, *memoire* publications, synagogues, and Jewish cemeteries. After the end of the war, war memorials or memorial plaques were erected in synagogues and Jewish cemeteries, normally in the middle of the war grave sections, in almost every Jewish community in Austria. At the center of all these memorials and plaques stood a list of the fallen soldiers, as in the gentile memorials, without reference to their military or social status. The inscribed names were usually framed by religious or patriotic symbols and followed by religious references to the book of Samuel—the more martial—or to the book of the prophet Isaiah, if the initiators of the memorial wished to lend a sense of peacekeeping to their commemoration.[62] All of these plaques and memorials had the typical inscriptions that appear on Jewish tombstones.

The best-known Jewish war memorial in Austria was inaugurated in the Jewish section of the central cemetery in Vienna in October 1929.[63] It included all of the abovementioned symbols and elements, and commemoration ceremonies took place in front of the war memorial every year until the annexation of Austria by Nazi Germany in March 1938.

Conclusion

Jewish war memory and commemoration practices in Austria had many elements that overlapped with and were similar to those of gentiles. By analyzing Jewish memory discourses, we can see that Jewish and gentile agents of memory used the same terms and strategies to lend meaning to the huge number of deaths that occurred in the course of World War I. They invoked the idealistic community and comradeship of the trenches and interpreted the deaths of the soldiers in both religious and political ways. Jews always participated or tried to participate in public and political memory activities in Austria, and, in doing so, they stated their intent and willingness to integrate into society, to join the national collective, and to fulfill the expectations of emancipation. This, however, did not mean that they were willing to abandon their Jewishness or give in to the pressures of equalization, which meant, for many gentile Austrians, total assimilation. On the contrary, they insisted on expressing their Jewish self-consciousness as loyal citizens and Austrian Jews.[64]

Thus, there are obvious differences in the historical references to specifically Jewish expectations about the war and Jewish military service. These expectations contributed to the particular history of Jewish emancipation and are linked to questions of Jewish self-identity, religious traditions, and political considerations, which recurred with specific regard to the position of Jews in state and society. In this, antisemitism played an important role. Over the course of the war, as well as during the interwar period, Jewish military service and war memory was always linked to a defense against antisemitism and to the pursuit of social acceptance and the state's formal guarantee and protection of civil rights. In contrast to gentile discourses, the commemoration of the Jewish memory of World War I has had a transnational perspective. Coming from various countries that were wartime enemies during World War I, Jewish veterans founded the World Federation of Jewish War Veterans in Paris in 1935 to fight against antisemitism and to protect Jewish honor and interests.[65]

Thus, various Jewish agents of commemoration initiated the erection of specifically Jewish war memorials and memorial plaques in Jewish cemeteries and synagogues. For them, commemoration of the fallen soldiers had to fulfill various tasks. Their military service represented arguments in debates about Jewish identity, politics, antisemitism, and Jews' position within society. Finally, both Austrian Jews and Christians had to deal with aspects of war memory in order to come to terms with the traumas associated with war, in order to be able to mourn the loss of fallen family members both within their families and in public. For Jews, as for gentiles, *private grief* and *public mourning*[66] were essential.

Gerald Lamprecht, PhD, is professor of Jewish history and contemporary history and head of the Center for Jewish Studies at the University of Graz. His research interests include Jewish history in the nineteenth and twentieth centuries in Central Europe, history of the Jewish soldiers in World War I, National Socialism and the persecution of the Jews, and memory studies. Among others, he is coeditor of the volume *Jewish Soldiers in the Collective Memory of Central Europe: The Remembrance of World War I from a Jewish Perspective* (Böhlau: Vienna-Cologne-Weimar, 2019), with Eleonore Lappin-Eppel and Ulrich Wyrwa.

Notes

1. Adolf Altmann, "Jüdische Gemeinden, leget Kriegschroniken an!" *Dr. Bloch's oesterreichische Wochenschrift*, 26 February 1915, 154–55.
2. Tim Grady, *The German-Jewish Soldiers of the First World War in History and Memory* (Liverpool: Liverpool University Press, 2011).

3. See *Neue Eisenstädter Zeitung*, 1 July 1934, 5; *Burgenländische Freiheit*, June 1982, 43.
4. See Manfred Oswald, "Traditionspflege von Widerstand und Verfolgung im österreichischen Bundesheer," *DÖW Jahrbuch* (1997): 182.
5. Wolfgang von Weisl, *Die Juden in der Armee Österreich-Ungarns* (Tel Aviv: Alamenu, 1971).
6. István Déak, *Beyond Nationalism: A Social and Political History of the Habsburg Officer Corps* (Oxford: Oxford University Press, 1990); David Rechter, *The Jews of Vienna and the First World War* (London: The Littman Library of Jewish Civilization, 2001); Marsha Rozenblit, *Reconstructing a National Identity: The Jews of Habsburg Austria during World War I* (Oxford: Oxford University Press, 2001).
7. See Gerald Lamprecht, "Jewish Studies at the University of Graz and in Austria," *Jewish Culture and History* 17, no. 3 (2016): 183–88.
8. To name only the most important authors, for example: Erwin A. Schmidl, *Juden in der k. (u.) k. Armee 1788–1918* (Eisenstadt: Österreichsiches Jüdisches Museum, 1989); Martin Senekowitsch, *Ein ungewöhnliches Kriegerdenkmal: Das jüdische Heldendenkmal am Wiener Zentralfriedhof* (Wien: Österreichisches Bundesheer, 1994); Martin Senekowitsch, *Verbunden mit diesem Lande: Das jüdische Kriegerdenkmal in Graz* (Graz: Militärkommando Steiermark, 1995); Beatrix Hoffmann-Holter, *"Abreisendmachen" Jüdische Kriegsflüchtlinge in Wien 1914 bis 1923* (Vienna: Böhlau Verlag, 1995); and currently, Sarah Panter, *Jüdische Erfahrungen und Loyalitätskonflikte im Ersten Weltkrieg* (Göttingen: Vandenhoeck & Ruprecht, 2014).
9. Marcus G. Patka, *Weltuntergang: Leben und Sterben im Ersten Weltkrieg* (Vienna: Styria premium, 2014).
10. Erwin A. Schmidl, *Habsburgs jüdische Soldaten 1788–1918* (Vienna: Böhlau Verlag, 2014).
11. For example, Gerald Lamprecht, Eleonore Lappin-Eppel, and Heidrun Zettelbauer, eds., "Der Erste Weltkrieg aus jüdischer Perspektive: Erwartungen—Erfahrungen—Erinnerungen," *Zeitgeschichte* 41, no. 4 (2014).
12. There are also some exceptions, such as Marsha Rozenblit, "Der Habsburg-Patriotismus der Juden," in *Die Habsburgermonarchie und der Erste Weltkrieg: Teil 2 Vom Vielvölkerstaat Österreich-Ungarn zum neuen Europa der Nationalstaaten*, ed. Helmut Rumpler (Vienna: Verlag der Österreichischen Akademie der Wissenschaften, 2016), 887–917.
13. Schallaburg Kulturbetriebsges. m.b.H., ed., *Jubel & Elend: Leben mit dem Großen Krieg 1914–1918* (Schallaburg: Schallaburg, 2014).
14. Alfred Pfoser and Andreas Weigl, eds., *Im Epizentrum des Zusammenbruchs: Wien im Ersten Weltkrieg* (Vienna: Metropolverlag, 2013).
15. See, for the Austrian historical consciousness, Heidemarie Uhl, *Zwischen Versöhnung und Verstörung: eine Kontroverse um Österreichs historische Identität fünfzig Jahre nach dem "Anschluß"* (Vienna: Böhlau Verlag, 1992).
16. Hans Klingbacher, "Der Österreichische Kameradschaftsbund: Organisation und Strukturen unter besonderer Berücksichtigung der historischen Entwicklung" (PhD diss., University of Vienna, 1987), 5.
17. Reinhart Koselleck, "Introduction," in *Der politische Totenkult: Kriegerdenkmale der Moderne*, ed. Reinhart Koselleck and Michael Jeismann (Munich: Bild und Text, 1994), 9.

18. See Ute Frevert, *Die Kasernierte Nation: Militärdienst und Zivilgesellschaft in Deutschland* (Munich: C. H. Beck, 2001), 9–17.
19. Cf., for example, Ute Frevert, "Bürgersoldaten—Die allgemeine Wehrpflicht im 19. und 20. Jahrhundert," in *Die Wehrpflicht und ihre Hintergründe: Sozialwissenschaftliche Beitrage zur aktuellen Debatte*, ed. Ines-Jacqueline Werkner (Erlangen: Verlag für Sozialwissenschaften, 2004), 48–49; Nikolaus Buschmann, "Vom 'Untertanensoldaten' zum 'Bürgersoldaten'? Zur Transformation militärischer Loyalitätsvorstellungen um 1800," *Jahrbuch des Simon-Dubnow-Instituts* 12 (2013): 105.
20. Christian Wilhelm Dohm, *Ueber die buergerliche Verbesserung der Juden* (Berlin: Friedrich Nicolai, 1871).
21. Ibid., 223.
22. "Man hat Recht, auch von den Juden ganz unbeschränkte Kriegsdienste zu fordern. Itzt können sie dieselben freylich nicht leisten, weil die Unterdrückung, in der sie so lange gelebt *Ueber die buergerliche Verbesserung der Juden*, den kriegerischen Geist und persönlichen Muth bey ihnen erstickt und ihre religiösen Spekulationen auf so ungeselige Paradoxen geleitet hat. Sie hatten seit anderthalb Jahrtausenden kein Vaterland, wie konnten sie also für dasselbe fechten und sterben? Aber ich bin überzeugt, daß sie dieses mit gleicher Fähigkeit und Treue, wie alle anderen, thun werden, sobald man ihnen ein Vaterland gegeben hat." Ibid., 236–37.
23. See Rozenblit, *Reconstructing a National Identity*, 39.
24. Peter Pulzer, *Die Entstehung des politischen Antisemitismus in Deutschland und Österreich 1867–1914* (Göttingen: Vandenhoeck & Ruprecht, 2004), 299–308; Bruce Pauley, *Eine Geschichte des österreichischen Antisemitismus: Von der Ausgrenzung zur Auslöschung* (Vienna: Kremayr & Scheriau, 1993), 100–131.
25. See, for example, Marsha L. Rozenblit, "Sustaining Austrian 'National' Identity in Crisis: The Dilemma of the Jews in Habsburg Austria, 1914–1919," in *Constructing Nationalities in East Central Europe*, ed. Pieter M. Judson and Marsha L. Rozenblit (New York: Berghahn Books, 2005), 185.
26. See Ezra Mendelsohn, "Zwischen großen Erwartungen und bösem Erwachen: Das Ende der multinationalen Reiche in Ostmittel- und Südosteuropa aus jüdischer Perspektive," in *Zwischen großen Erwartungen und bösem Erwachen: Juden, Politik und Antisemitismus in Ost- und Südosteuropa 1918–1945*, ed. Dittmar Dahlmann and Anke Hilbrenner (Paderborn: Ferdinand Schöningh Verlag, 2007), 13–30; Gerald Lamprecht, "Juden in Zentraleuropa und die Transformationen des Antisemitismus im und nach dem Ersten Weltkrieg," *Jahrbuch für Antisemitismusforschung* 24 (2015): 63–88.
27. See Frontkämpfervereinigung Deutsch-Österreichs: Wiener Stadt- und Landesarchiv (WStLA), A32-5442/1922.
28. According to Marsha Rozenblit, after the war, the narrative of the tripartite identity of Austrian Jews, for which the imperial dynasty had played a central role, came to an end. Rozenblit, "Sustaining Austrian 'National' Identity," 178–92.
29. Jay Winter, *Sites of Memory, Sites of Mourning: The Great War in European Cultural History* (Cambridge: Cambridge University Press, 1995); Jay Winter, *Remembering War: The Great War between Memory and History in the Twentieth Century* (New Haven, CT: Yale University Press, 2006).
30. Gerald Lamprecht, "Erinnerung an den Krieg: Der Bund jüdischer Frontsoldaten Österreichs 1932 bis 1938," in *Weltuntergang: Jüdisches Leben und Sterben im Ersten Weltkrieg*, ed. Marcus G. Patka (Vienna: Styria premium, 2014), 200–10.

31. See, for the Association of Jewish War Veterans, Widows, and Orphans, WStLA, A32-1807/1929.
32. See Nathan Birnbaum, "Verband jüdischer Kriegsteilnehmer und Kriegsbeschädigter," *Dr. Bloch's oesterreichische Wochenschrift*, 28 December 1917, 814–16.
33. "Verband jüdischer Kriegsteilnehmer und Kriegsbeschädigter," *Jüdische Zeitung: Nationaljüdisches Organ*, 21 December 1917, 1.
34. Derek Penslar, *Jews and the Military: A History* (Princeton, NJ: Princeton University Press, 2013), 169.
35. See Jacob Toury, *Die Jüdische Presse im Österreichischen Kaiserreich 1802–1918* (Tübingen: Mohr Siebeck, 1982), 82; Eleonore Lappin, "Zensur und Abwehr des Antisemitismus: Dr. Bloch's österreichische Wochenschrift im Ersten Weltkrieg," in *Judenfeindschaft und Antisemitismus in der deutschen Presse über fünf Jahrhunderte Band I*, ed. Michael Nagel and Moshe Zimmermann (Bremen: edition lumière, 2013), 299–316.
36. See Eleonore Lappin-Eppel, "Gedanken zu Judentum, Krieg und Frieden in der Wiener jüdischen Presse während des Ersten Weltkrieges am Beispiel von 'Die Wahrheit,' 'Jüdische Zeitung,' und 'Jüdische Korrespondenz,'" *Zeitgeschichte* 41, no.4 (2014): 200–221.
37. Joseph Samuel Bloch, "Die Österreichischen Juden im Weltkriege," in *Erinnerungen aus meinem Leben von Dr. Joseph Samuel Bloch*, ed. Morris Bloch (Vienna: Appel & Co Verlag, 1933), 3:228–29.
38. See Dieter Hecht, "Spuren der Vergessenen: Das 'Jüdische Kriegsgedenkblatt'— Ein Erinnerungsforum," *Zeitgeschichte* 41, no. 4 (2014): 222–41.
39. See Eleonore Lappin, "Zwischen den Fronten: Das Wiener Jüdische Archiv: Mitteilungen des Komitees Jüdisches Kriegsarchiv 1915–1917," in *Deutsch-jüdische Presse und jüdische Geschichte I: Dokumente, Darstellungen, Wechselbeziehungen*, ed. Eleonore Lappin and Michael Nagel (Bremen: edition lumière, 2008), 229–46.
40. "Mit einem Worte, wenn wir in unserem Kampfe gegen das Uebelwollen und für unser volles Recht gerüstet sein wollen, dann müssen wir das ‚Jüdische Kriegsarchiv' schaffen." "Die Mitarbeit am Jüdischen Archiv," *Jüdisches Archiv*, May 1915, 2–4.
41. See Thomas E. Schärf, *Jüdisches Leben in Baden: Von den Anfängen bis zur Gegenwart* (Vienna: Mandelbaum Verlag, 2005), 120–22. Reich was also responsible for erecting a Jewish war memorial in Baden in 1921. See "Kriegerdenkmaleinweihung in Baden bei Wien," *Die Wahrheit*, 7 July 1921, 11.
42. "Die Kriegsgeschichte unserer Zeit legt nun aber Zeugnis ab, daß das jüdische Kriegsheldentum nicht geschwunden ist; Hunderte und aber Hunderte unserer Glaubensgenossen, die im Kriege stehen, sind ausgezeichnet auf dem Felde der Ehre; sie stehen keiner Konfession und keiner Nationalität im Kampfe für das Vaterland nach, und wenn das Kriegsbuch dieser Zeit mit Gottes Hilfe geschlossen sein wird, werden wir mit Stolz und Genugtuung hinweisen können auf das goldene Buch, in welchem auch in stattlicher Zahl die Namen jüdischer Kriegshelden zur Verherrlichung der Judenheit fortleuchten werden! Die Namen jüdischer Kriegshelden als würdige Nachfolger der Makkabäer!" Wilhelm Reich, "Jüdische Kriegshelden," *Dr. Bloch's oesterreichische Wochenschrift*, 11 December 1914, 855.
43. "Die Söhne des jüdischen Volkes haben das lebendige Bewußtsein, daß für sie der Krieg gegen Rußland ein heiliger Krieg ist, und sie erinnern sich an all die Leiden und Drangsale namenloser Grausamkeit, welche ihre Brüder in Rußland

zu erdulden hatten." "Der Kaiser Franz Josef I.," *Dr. Bloch's oesterreichische Wochenschrift*, 14 August 1914, 1.
44. See Adolf Altmann, "Jüdische Gemeinden, leget Kriegschroniken an!" *Dr. Bloch's oesterreichische Wochenschrift*, 6 February 1915, 154.
45. See George L. Mosse, *Fallen Soldiers: Reshaping the Memory of the World Wars* (New York: Oxford University Press, 1990), 80–94.
46. George L. Mosse, "The Jews and the German War Experience, 1914–1918," In *Masses and Man: Nationalist and Fascist Perceptions of Reality*, George L. Mosse (New York: Howard Fertig, 1980), 268.
47. Mosse, *Fallen Soldiers*, 70–80.
48. See Mosse, "Jews and the German War Experience," 267.
49. See protocol of the board meeting, 22 September 1914. Central Archive for the History of Jewish People (CAHJP), Archiv der IKG Wien, A/W 1477.
50. Jewish community of Vienna to mayor, 13 September 1914. CAHJP, Archiv der IKG Wien. A/W 1477.
51. Protocol of the board meeting, 15 September 1914. CAHJP, Archiv der IKG Wien, A/W 1477.
52. Hermann Stern, "Ein jüdisches Kriegerdenkmal," *Dr. Bloch's oesterreichische Wochenschrift*, 8 January 1915, 24–25.
53. "Für Gott Kaiser und Vaterland." See Heidemarie Uhl, "Kriegsallerseelen 1914–1918," In *Im Epizentrum des Zusammenbruchs*, ed. Alfred Pfoser et al. (Vienna: Metropolverlag, 2013), 114.
54. See Stefan Riesenfellner and Heidemarie Uhl, eds., *Todeszeichen: Zeitgeschichtliche Denkmalkultur* (Vienna: Böhlau Verlag, 1994).
55. See Oswald Überegger, *Erinnerungskriege: Der Erste Weltkrieg, Österreich und die Tiroler Kriegserinnerung in der Zwischenkriegszeit* (Innsbruck: Universitätsverlag Wagner, 2011).
56. See, for example, "Allerseelenfeier für die verstorbenen Krieger," *Neue Freie Presse*, 2 November 1916, 3–4.
57. See protocol of the board meeting of the Chevra Kadisha, 23 October 1916. RGWA, 709-1-7.
58. See David Herzog, *Kriegspredigten* (Frankfurt am Main: Verlag von J. Kauffmann, 1915).
59. See protocol of the board meeting of the Chevra Kadisha, 6 November 1916. RGWA, 709-1-7.
60. See "Allgemeiner Kriegsgräbertag Österreich 1917," *Badener Zeitung*, 31 October 1917, 1.
61. See *Dr. Bloch's oesterreichische Wochenschrift*, 26 October 1917, 684; *Jüdische Zeitung*, 19 October 1917, 5.
62. See protocol of the meeting of the committee for the erection of the war memorial on the central cemetery, 4 April 1926, and the program of the call for bids, August 1926. CAHJP, Archiv der IKG Wien, A/W 1176 a-d.
63. See Gerald Lamprecht, "Erinnern an den Ersten Weltkrieg aus jüdische Perspektive 1914–1918," *Zeitgeschichte* 41, no. 4 (2014): 254–56.
64. See Marsha L. Rozenblit, "Jewish Ethnicity in a New Nation State: The Crisis of Identity in the Austrian Republic," in *In Search of Jewish Community: Jewish Identities in Germany and Austria, 1918–1933*, ed. Michael Brenner and Derek J. Penslar (Bloomington: Indiana University Press 1998), 135.
65. Sigmund Edler von Friedmann, the leader of the Federation of Jewish War Veter-

ans of Austria, was also the leader of the World Federation of Jewish War Veterans from 1935 to 1940. "Avissar Eitan (Friedman, Sigmund)," in *International Biographical Dictionary of Central European Emigrés 1933–1945*, vol. 1, ed. Herbert A. Strauss and Werner Röder (Munich: K G Saur, 1908), 27.
66. See Jay Winter, *Sites of Memory, Sites of Mourning: The Great War in European Cultural History* (Cambridge: Cambridge University Press, 1995).

Bibliography

Altmann, Adolf. "Jüdische Gemeinden, leget Kriegschroniken an!" *Dr. Bloch's oesterreichische Wochenschrift*, 26 February 1915, 154–55.
Birnbaum, Nathan. "Verband jüdischer Kriegsteilnehmer und Kriegsbeschädigter." *Dr. Bloch's oesterreichische Wochenschrift*, 28 December 1917, 814–16.
Bloch, Joseph Samuel. "Die österreichischen Juden im Weltkriege." In *Erinnerungen aus meinem Leben von Dr. Joseph Samuel Bloch*, edited by Morris Bloch, 3:228–41. Vienna: Appel & Co Verlag, 1933.
Buschmann, Nikolaus. "Vom 'Untertanensoldaten' zum 'Bürgersoldaten'? Zur Transformation militärischer Loyalitätsvorstellungen um 1800." *Jahrbuch des Simon-Dubnow-Instituts* 12 (2013): 105–26.
Déak, István. *Beyond Nationalism: A Social and Political History of the Habsburg Officer Corps*. Oxford: Oxford University Press, 1990.
Dohm, Christian Wilhelm. *Ueber die buergerliche Verbesserung der Juden*. Berlin: Friedrich Nicolai, 1871.
Frevert, Ute. *Die Kasernierte Nation: Militärdienst und Zivilgesellschaft in Deutschland*. Munich: C. H. Beck, 2001.
———. "Bürgersoldaten—Die allgemeine Wehrpflicht im 19. und 20. Jahrhundert." In *Die Wehrpflicht und ihre Hintergründe: Sozialwissenschaftliche Beitrage zur aktuellen Debatte*, edited by Ines-Jacqueline Werkner, 45–64. Erlangen: Verlag für Sozialwissenschaften, 2004.
Grady, Tim. *The German-Jewish Soldiers of the First World War in History and Memory*. Liverpool: Liverpool University Press, 2011.
Hecht, Dieter. "Spuren der Vergessenen: Das 'Jüdische Kriegsgedenkblatt'—Ein Erinnerungsforum." *Zeitgeschichte* 41, no. 4 (2014): 222–41.
Herzog, David. *Kriegspredigten*. Frankfurt am Main: Verlag von J. Kauffmann, 1915.
Hoffmann-Holter, Beatrix. *"Abreisendmachen": Jüdische Kriegsflüchtlinge in Wien 1914 bis 1923*. Vienna: Böhlauverlag, 1995.
Klingbacher, Hans. "Der Österreichische Kameradschaftsbund: Organisation und Strukturen unter besonderer Berücksichtigung der historischen Entwicklung." PhD diss., University of Vienna, 1987.
Koselleck, Reinhart. "Introduction." In *Der politische Totenkult: Kriegerdenkmale der Moderne*, edited by Reinhart Koselleck and Michael Jeismann, 9–20. Munich: Bild und Text, 1994.
Lamprecht, Gerald, Eleonore Lappin-Eppel, and Heidrun Zettelbauer, eds. "Der Erste Weltkrieg aus jüdischer Perspektive: Erwartungen—Erfahrungen—Erinnerungen." *Zeitgeschichte* 41, no. 4 (2014): 242–66.
Lamprecht, Gerald. "Erinnern an den Ersten Weltkrieg aus jüdischer Perspektive 1914–1918." *Zeitgeschichte* 41, no. 4 (2014): 254–56.

———. "Erinnerung an den Krieg: Der Bund jüdischer Frontsoldaten Österreichs 1932 bis 1938." In *Weltuntergang: Jüdisches Leben und Sterben im Ersten Weltkrieg*, edited by Marcus G. Patka, 200–10. Vienna: Styria premium, 2014.

———. "Juden in Zentraleuropa und die Transformationen des Antisemitismus im und nach dem Ersten Weltkrieg." *Jahrbuch für Antisemitismusforschung* 24 (2015): 63–88.

———. "Jewish Studies at the University of Graz and in Austria." *Jewish Culture and History* 17, no. 3 (2016): 183–88.

Lappin, Eleonore. "Zwischen den Fronten: Das Wiener Jüdische Archiv; Mitteilungen des Komitees Jüdisches Kriegsarchiv 1915–1917." In *Deutsch-jüdische Presse und jüdische Geschichte I: Dokumente, Darstellungen, Wechselbeziehungen*, edited by Eleonore Lappin and Michael Nagel, 229–46. Bremen: Edition Lumière, 2008.

———. "Zensur und Abwehr des Antisemitismus: Dr. Bloch's österreichische Wochenschrift im Ersten Weltkrieg." In *Judenfeindschaft und Antisemitismus in der deutschen Presse über fünf Jahrhunderte*, edited by Michael Nagel and Moshe Zimmermann, 1:299–316. Bremen: Edition Lumière, 2013.

———. "Gedanken zu Judentum, Krieg und Frieden in der Wiener jüdischen Presse während des Ersten Weltkrieges am Beispiel von 'Die Wahrheit,' 'Jüdische Zeitung,' und 'Jüdische Korrespondenz.'" *Zeitgeschichte* 41, no. 4 (2014): 200–21.

Mendelsohn, Ezra. "Zwischen großen Erwartungen und bösem Erwachen: Das Ende der multinationalen Reiche in Ostmittel- und Südosteuropa aus jüdischer Perspektive." In *Zwischen großen Erwartungen und bösem Erwachen: Juden, Politik und Antisemitismus in Ost- und Südosteuropa 1918–1945*, edited by Dittmar Dahlmann and Anke Hilbrenner, 13–30. Paderborn: Ferdinand Schöningh, 2007.

Mosse, George L. "The Jews and the German War Experience, 1914–1918." In *Masses and Man: Nationalist and Fascist Perceptions of Reality*, edited by George L. Mosse, 263–83. New York: Howard Fertig, 1980.

———. *Fallen Soldiers: Reshaping the Memory of the World Wars*. New York: Oxford University Press, 1990.

Oswald, Manfred. "Traditionspflege von Widerstand und Verfolgung im österreichischen Bundesheer." *DÖW Jahrbuch* (1997): 180–85.

Panter, Sarah. *Jüdische Erfahrungen und Loyalitätskonflikte im Ersten Weltkrieg*. Göttingen: Vandenhoeck & Ruprecht, 2014.

Patka, Marcus G. *Weltuntergang: Leben und Sterben im Ersten Weltkrieg*. Vienna: Styria Premium, 2014.

Pauley, Bruce. *Eine Geschichte des österreichischen Antisemitismus: Von der Ausgrenzung zur Auslöschung*. Vienna: Kremayr & Scheriau, 1993.

Penslar, Derek. *Jews and the Military: A History*. Princeton, NJ: Princeton University Press, 2013.

Pfoser, Alfred, and Andreas Weigl, eds. *Im Epizentrum des Zusammenbruchs: Wien im Ersten Weltkrieg*. Vienna: Metropolverlag, 2013.

Pulzer, Peter. *Die Entstehung des politischen Antisemitismus in Deutschland und Österreich 1867–1914*. Göttingen: Vandenhoeck & Ruprecht, 2004.

Rechter, David. *The Jews of Vienna and the First World War*. London: The Littman Library of Jewish Civilization, 2001.

Reich, Wilhelm. "Jüdische Kriegshelden." *Dr. Bloch's oesterreichische Wochenschrift*, 11 December 1914.

Riesenfellner, Stefan, and Heidemarie Uhl, eds. *Todeszeichen: Zeitgeschichtliche Denkmalkultur*. Vienna: Böhlauverlag, 1994.

Rozenblit, Marsha L. "Jewish Ethnicity in a New Nation State: The Crisis of Identity in the Austrian Republic." In *In Search of Jewish Community: Jewish Identities in Germany and Austria, 1918–1933*, edited by Michael Brenner and Derek J. Penslar, 134–53. Bloomington: Indiana University Press 1998.

———. *Reconstructing a National Identity: The Jews of Habsburg Austria During World War I*. Oxford: Oxford University Press, 2001.

———. "Sustaining Austrian 'National' Identity in Crisis: The Dilemma of the Jews in Habsburg Austria, 1914–1919." In *Constructing Nationalities in East Central Europe*, edited by Pieter M. Judson and Marsha L. Rozenblit, 178–91. New York: Berghahn Books, 2005.

———. "Der Habsburg-Patriotismus der Juden." In *Die Habsburgermonarchie und der Erste Weltkrieg*. Vols. 1–2: *Vom Vielvölkerstaat Österreich-Ungarn zum neuen Europa der Nationalstaaten*, edited by Helmut Rumpler, 887–917. Vienna: Verlag der österreichischen Akademie der Wissenschaften, 2016.

Schallaburg Kulturbetriebsges. m.b.H., ed. *Jubel & Elend: Leben mit dem Großen Krieg 1914–1918*. Schallaburg: Schallaburg Kulturbetriebsges, 2014.

Schärf, Thomas E. *Jüdisches Leben in Baden: Von den Anfängen bis zur Gegenwart*. Vienna: Mandelbaum, 2005.

Schmidl, Erwin A. *Juden in der k. (u.) k. Armee 1788–1918*. Eisenstadt: Österreichsiches Jüdisches Museum, 1989.

———. *Habsburgs jüdische Soldaten 1788–1918*. Vienna: Böhlau, 2014.

Senekowitsch, Martin. *Ein ungewöhnliches Kriegerdenkmal: Das jüdische Heldendenkmal am Wiener Zentralfriedhof*. Vienna: Österreichisches Bundesheer, 1994.

———. *Verbunden mit diesem Lande: Das jüdische Kriegerdenkmal in Graz*. Graz: Militärkommando Steiermark, 1995.

Stern, Hermann. "Ein jüdisches Kriegerdenkmal." *Dr. Bloch's oesterreichische Wochenschrift*, 8 January 1915, 24–25.

Strauss, Herbert A., and Werner Röder, eds. "Avissar Eitan (Sigmund Friedman)." *International Biographical Dictionary of Central European Emigrés 1933–1945*. Vol. 1. Munich: K. G. Saur, 1908.

Toury, Jacob. *Die Jüdische Presse im Österreichischen Kaiserreich 1802–1918*. Tübingen: Mohr Siebeck, 1982.

Überegger, Oswald. *Erinnerungskriege: Der Erste Weltkrieg, Österreich und die Tiroler Kriegserinnerung in der Zwischenkriegszeit*. Innsbruck: Universitätsverlag Wagner, 2011.

Uhl, Heidemarie. *Zwischen Versöhnung und Verstörung: Eine Kontroverse um Österreichs historische Identität fünfzig Jahre nach dem "Anschluß."* Vienna: Böhlau, 1992.

———. "Kriegsallerseelen 1914–1918." In *Im Epizentrum des Zusammenbruchs: Wien im Ersten Weltkrieg*, edited by Alfred Pfoser and Andreas Weigl, 114–21. Vienna: Metropolverlag, 2013.

von Weisl, Wolfgang. *Die Juden in der Armee Österreich-Ungarns*. Tel Aviv: Alamenu, 1971.

Winter, Jay. *Sites of Memory, Sites of Mourning: The Great War in European Cultural History*. Cambridge: Cambridge University Press, 1995.

———. *Remembering War: The Great War between Memory and History in the Twentieth Century*. New Haven, CT: Yale University Press, 2006.

Index

abolitionism, 203, 209, 224, 231
acculturation, 153, 165, 167
activism, political, 45, 107, 109, 114, 292, 362
Adams Lehmann, Hope Bridges, 125
Adélaïde, Stanislas Marie, 164
Adriatic Littoral, 353, 355, 357
affiliation, religious, 85, 86, 97, 119, 128, 129
agency, 8, 179, 180, 183, 187, 191–193, 210, 332, 397
Ahrens, Heinrich, 58
Alberto, Carlo, 203
Albo, Joseph, 141
Alexandria, 87, 88
Alfani, Augusto, 202
Algeria, 97
Algiers, 87
Allgemeine Bestimmungen, 184
Allgemeiner Deutscher Frauenverein, 11, 220, 243
Allgemeiner Deutscher Lehrerinnenverein, 182
Allied Powers, 318
Altmann, Adolf, 395
Altschul, Eduard, 152–153
Amadori, Rosy, 122
Amari, Carolina, 210
Amico dei Fanciulli, L', 203–204
Ancien Régime, 167
Anderson, Benedict, 59
Anglicans, 198
Anthony, Susan B., 125
anti-Catholic, 6, 193, 203
anti-cosmopolitanism, 14

antifeminism, 38, 64, 128, 130, 192
antisemitism, 7, 14, 17, 18, 127–128, 265, 274, 297, 319, 354, 355, 359, 360, 366, 367, 399, 401, 402, 404, 407
anti-Slavism, 359–362
archaeology, 73
Archivio Centrale dello Stato, 337
Armitage, David, 40
Arndt, Ernst Moritz, 1
Arnheim, Michael Aron, 150–151
Artom, Elia Samuele, 171–172
Artom, Isacco, 59
Ascoli, Isacco, 170
Ashkenaz, 142, 149, 151
Ashkenazi, Jacob ben Isaac, 151
assimilation, 60, 127, 139, 403, 406
  cultural, 6
Assing, Ludmilla, 112–113
  Ottilie, 112
Association internationale des amies de la jeune fille, 203
association laws. *See* Prussian Law of Association
Association of Jewish war veterans, widows and orphans, 400
Associazione femminile di Roma, 248
Associazione internazionale delle amiche delle giovani, 209–210
Augspurg, Anita, 226–228, 229, 230, 232–233, 250
Auschwitz, 89
Austria, 7, 13, 16, 18, 43, 88, 122, 180, 190, 246, 251, 268, 311, 313–314, 316, 319–320, 323,

334–338, 340, 353–354, 355–357, 359, 360–362, 364, 378, 379, 380, 382, 385, 395–398, 399–402, 403–407
Austria-Hungary, 15, 17, 48, 270, 309, 311, 314, 320, 335, 338, 379, 395
Austrian Littoral, 353, 355
Austrian Republic, 17–18, 320, 322–323
Austrian Veterans' Association, 396, 397
Avanti, 383

Baader-Meinhof Group, 35
Bacheracht, Therese von, 111–112
Bader Zaar, Birgitta, 13
Balkans, 310
Banti, Alberto, 38, 39
Baptists, 198
Barbier, Jean-Jacques Le, 225, 227
bar/bat mitzvah, 139, 146
Barrès, Maurice, 65
Barzilai, Salvatore, 356, 357
Barzilai Gentilli, Enrica, 353, 354–356, 357, 359, 363, 364, 366
Bauer, Ingrid, 289
Bäumer, Gertrud, 229, 230, 246
Bavaria, 43, 184, 185–187, 188, 269
Bebel, August, 128
Beccari, Gualberta Alaide, 358
Beecher-Stowe, Harriet, 124
Behrenbeck, Sabine, 2
Belgium, 71, 122, 191, 246, 271, 273, 310, 313
belonging, 16, 18, 41, 60, 74, 85, 141, 171, 172, 199, 269, 291, 376
  cultural, 7
  national, 7, 13, 14, 44, 264, 275, 377, 378, 380, 385, 386
Benedict XV, Pope, 273
Benso de Cavour, Camillo, 1, 59
Berlan, Francesco, 71, 206
Berlin, 2, 12, 44, 67, 111–113, 120–122, 141, 143, 146, 151, 219, 221, 225, 226, 229, 230, 231, 241–244, 245–246, 247, 249, 250–253, 264, 265, 266, 267
Berliner Börsen-Courier, 264, 265, 266
Berliner Frauenbank, 230

Berliner Hausfrauenverein, 245
Berliner Illustrirte Zeitung, 225, 226, 247
Berliner Tageblatt, 265, 270, 272
Bianchi, Bruna, 333
Bible, the, 127, 141, 145, 150–152, 170
Bieber-Böhm, Hanna, 125, 226, 245, 250
Bingham, George Caleb, 61
biography, 15, 40, 69, 70, 129, 143, 150, 180, 184, 185–186, 187–189, 191, 205, 206, 220, 228, 276, 379, 380, 382, 386, 401
Birnbaum, Nathan, 400
Bismarck, Otto von, 1, 12, 40, 66–67, 186
Bloch, Joseph Samuel, 401
Bloch, Marc, 289–290
Bluntschli, Johann Kaspar, 58
Boilly, Louis-Léopold, 63
Boroevic, Field Marshall, 338
Borrani, Odoardo, 63
Boukrif, Gabriele, 241
Bourget, Paul, 65
bourgeoisie, 6, 9, 10, 14–15, 17, 60, 61, 66, 68, 87, 88, 91, 106, 110, 113, 127, 139, 140, 146–148, 150, 151–153, 163, 167, 171, 180, 182, 189, 190, 191, 203, 208, 209, 229, 230, 242, 243, 250, 251, 263–264, 265, 266, 267, 269, 275, 291, 292, 296, 312, 353, 357, 358, 361, 364, 380, 401
boys, 68, 139, 144, 146, 150, 152, 174, 175, 183, 207, 359
Braun, Lily. *See* Gizycki, Lily von
Braun-Gizycki, Lily. *See* Gizycki, Lily von
Breuilly, John, 37
British Fabian Society, 291
Broers, Michael, 43
Brunamonti, Alinda, 122
Brunet, Francesca, 43
Büdinger, Moses, 148
Bukovina, 310, 399
Bund Deutscher Frauenvereine, 226, 231, 244
Bürgertum. *See* bourgeoisie
Burschenschaftler, 43

Butler, Gräfin Viktorine, 226
Butler, Josephine, 209, 224

Cairoli, Adelaide, 71
Cambon, Elisa Tagliapietra, 356, 363
Cammeo, Federico, 338
Campe, Emilie, 112
Campo, Marietta, 70
Canisius, Peter, 144
Caporetto, Defeat of, 313, 314, 321, 333, 335, 339
Carbonari, 43
Cardoso, Daniel, 89
Carducci, Giosuè, 69
Carpi, Leone, 88
Carrière, Eugène, 291
Castelbolognesi, Emma, 247, 249
Castellani, Umberto, 338
Castelnuovo, Giacomo, 88, 95
Catalan, Tullia, 17, 353, 378
catechism, 139, 170, 171
    Jewish, 9, 139, 140, 143–145, 146, 148, 149, 150–153, 163, 167, 169, 170–171
    Catholic, 8, 9, 60, 64, 97, 107, 108, 127, 165, 168, 169–171, 172, 174, 179, 180, 181–183, 184, 187–188, 189, 192, 193, 198, 199, 200, 202, 204, 205, 207–210, 222, 243, 244, 265, 319, 360, 362, 366
    Church, 70, 107, 163, 179, 180, 189, 191, 193, 222, 243
    role model, 9, 181–183, 188, 193, 206
Catholicism, 9, 108, 127, 180, 183, 187, 191, 199, 200, 202, 203, 204, 205, 367, 376
    conciliatory, 199, 200
    intransigent, 199, 200, 204, 206, 208, 209, 210
    liberal, 8, 199, 200, 201, 205, 209, 210
Cauer, Minna, 221, 226–229, 232, 244–247, 251, 253–254
Cavicchioli, Silvia, 72
Ceccarini, Maria Boorman Wheeler, 209
censorship, 71, 109, 266, 274, 288, 312, 313, 315, 316, 360, 399

Ceschin, Daniele, 335, 341
Chabod, Federico, 37
charity, 202, 205, 210, 221, 289
Charles Albert, King, 164
children, 8, 10, 17, 60, 62, 64, 65–66, 67–68, 69, 70, 86, 95, 106, 107, 120, 123, 124–125, 126, 130, 139, 143, 145, 148–149, 169, 173, 186, 201, 221, 229, 291, 293, 294, 314–315, 333–334, 354, 355, 357–358, 364, 365, 368, 381
    and education, 10, 108–110, 147, 148, 150, 151, 168–173, 181, 184, 202, 291, 354, 358, 359
    and war, 15, 16, 309, 311, 318, 320, 322, 332–333, 335–336, 337, 339, 340, 341–343
Christian-Social party, 354, 362
civilians, 15–16, 271, 295, 309–310, 311–319, 321, 333, 334, 339
Civiltà Cattolica, 201, 206
citizenship, 7, 11, 13, 62, 95, 164, 204, 354
class, 7, 8, 11–12, 13–15, 37, 42, 48, 49, 65–66, 68, 71, 87–91, 97, 105, 106, 108, 109–110, 111–112, 114, 127, 130, 163, 167, 172, 182, 186, 190, 191, 199, 208, 219–221, 223–225, 227–233, 242–253, 264, 353, 355, 361, 377, 379, 380, 385, 386
    struggle, 71, 97, 243, 252, 359
Clemens, Gabriele, 2
Cobol, Nicolò, 362
Code Civil, 65
Coen Luzzatto, Ada, 355
    Carolina, 353–364, 366, 367
    Cornelia, 365
    Graziadio, 365
    Salomon Girolamo, 365
Collot, Philippine, 265
colonialism, 95
Comba, Eugenio, 207
Combatants Association of German-Austria, 399
Comitato Nazionale Femminile Interventista Antitedesco, 357, 358, 364, 365

Comitato delle Signore per la Pace e l'Arbitrato Internazionale di Palermo, 249
commemoration, 17, 18, 40, 332, 384, 395–398, 400, 403, 404–405, 406, 407
Commune, the, 64, 65, 71, 223
consciousness, 12, 243, 254, 379, 386, 406
  national, 7, 386
Consiglio Nazionale delle Donne Italiane, 209, 244
Constantinople, 87
conversion, 127, 130, 165, 181
"Corporate State," 320
correspondence, 4, 94–96, 264, 287, 290, 296, 312, 355, 361, 362
  marital, 15, 287–290, 295, 297, 311, 312, 314. 381
  wartime, 15, 287–291, 295, 311–314, 316, 322, 377, 378, 381
Corriere Friulano, 357, 362
Corriere di Gorizia, 356–358, 361
Corriere Israelitico, 166
cosmopolitanism, 14–15, 275, 359
Costantini, Don Celso, 342
Craufurd Saffi, Giorgina, 209
Croce, Benedetto, 37, 44
Cru, Jean Norton, 288
culture, 4, 9, 10, 16, 37, 42–44, 66, 72, 85, 95, 105, 106, 111, 125, 127–129, 139, 152, 153, 164–66, 168, 171, 173, 179, 180–183, 185, 187, 200, 202, 203, 207, 243, 254, 264, 266, 267, 271, 275, 276, 289, 321, 323, 353, 354, 357, 359, 361, 364, 377, 378, 380, 383, 384, 395–398
  bourgeois, 10, 150
Cultural Studies, 40
Curci, Roberto, 358

D'Amelia, Marina, 108
Davidsohn, Robert, 14, 15, 263–276
Deák, István, 396
De Benedetti, Nina, 380
deculturation, 165
De Felice, Renzo, 2
Deraismes, Maria, 244

democracy, 35, 59, 60, 61, 65, 66, 69, 70, 113, 120, 202, 266, 271, 275, 381, 382, 385, 403
De Nardi, Don Carlo, 337
de' Sismondi, Kinzica, 207
Deutscher Flottenverein, 66
Deutscher Kolonialverein, 66
Deutscher Verband für Frauenstimmrecht, 225, 226
Deutsches Tageblatt, 265
De Viel-Castel, Horace, 110
de Zerbi, Rocco, 70
diaries, 275, 312, 316, 335
  wartime, 16, 264, 265, 269–270, 274, 311–312, 316–320, 322, 378
diaspora, 86, 87, 93, 94, 96
Dickmann, Elisabeth, 241
diplomacy, 38, 41
Dipper, Christof, 2
discrimination, 119, 243, 252
  racial, 360
diversity, 12, 69, 141, 165, 203, 207, 242, 244–247, 288, 289, 378
  cultural, 3
  religious, 3, 253
Di Vittorio, Giuseppe, 95
Dogliani, Patrizia, 2
Dohm, Christian Konrad Wilhelm, 224, 398–399
Dohm, Hedwig, 229, 241, 244, 245
domesticity, 59, 147, 206
Donna e la Famiglia, La, 202
Donna, La, 358
Donna Italiana, La, 109
Drago, Maria, 70
Dr. Bloch's Oesterreichische Wochenschrift, 395, 401–402, 404
Dreyfus Affair, 360, 362
Dubin, Lois, 4
Durkheim, Émile, 291
duty, 3, 71, 74, 110, 113, 130, 147, 149, 152, 166, 269, 270, 311, 323, 399
  national, 8, 110, 130, 270, 287

Economic Community, European, 2
education, 8–11, 46, 59, 60, 63, 68, 69, 71, 90, 95, 108–109, 119–120, 127–128, 143, 145, 147, 148,

149, 152, 153, 163–169, 171–
175, 183, 184, 186, 188, 191,
198–204, 206–209, 221, 229,
242–244, 246, 248, 249, 252,
291, 354, 355, 358, 359, 361,
364, 380, 381, 383
    academic, 119, 129
    denominational, 119, 174, 182
    female, 8, 11, 37, 46, 64, 71, 90,
108, 119, 129, 151–153, 174,
175, 182, 189, 192, 198–202,
205–207, 210, 221, 231, 241,
248, 250, 253, 264, 268, 269,
275, 290
    higher, 119, 127, 128, 129, 183, 187, 243, 246, 248
    informal, 127, 175
    national, 63, 192, 210
    non-formal, 175
    patriotic, 108–109, 181, 184, 186, 192, 210, 355
    religious, 10, 127, 139, 140, 142,
143, 146, 152, 163, 168, 170,
173, 174, 184, 206, 208, 290,
291, 292, 355
    women's (*see* education: female)
    -al system, 145, 167, 170, 172, 179, 180, 183, 208, 290
Educatore Israelita, L', 9, 166, 168, 169, 174
ego documents, 14, 16, 288, 295, 309, 311, 314–315, 321–322, 378, 379, 381
eheliche Vormundschaft, 10, 229
Elias, Norbert, 60
emancipation, 6–8, 10–12, 44, 119,
121, 128, 163–165, 167, 168,
172, 173, 175, 199, 202, 203,
205, 219–223, 225, 228, 244,
250, 385
    Age of, 6, 13, 403
    Jewish, 6, 7, 9, 10, 14, 127, 139, 145,
163–165, 167, 171–173, 175,
199, 220, 222, 224, 265, 379,
380, 382, 386, 398, 399, 406,
407
    of minorities, 5, 36, 49, 163, 199
    movement, 3, 10, 11, 13, 44, 204, 221, 355, 381, 385

    national, 5, 36
    women's, 3, 7, 10, 11, 12, 13, 14,
17, 38, 119, 121, 127, 128, 175,
209, 219, 221–225, 228, 229,
230, 231, 233, 241, 244, 246,
248–249, 250, 339, 355, 357,
358, 364, 381, 385
empire, 48, 70, 179, 185, 187, 289
    British, 48
empowerment, 8, 151, 152
Enfantin, Prosper, 222
Engländer, Hermann, 152
Enlightenment, The, 11, 147, 180, 181, 183, 199, 224–225
Enloe, Cynthia, 322
Entente Cordiale, 270, 379, 380
Ermacora, Matteo, 334
Ernst-Kühr, Petra, 13, 378
Ertl, Alfred, 314, 315
    Anna, 314, 315
Esposito, Anna, 4
Ethiopia, 249
ethnicity, 16, 37, 42, 46, 48, 74, 90, 96, 323
    situational, 85, 96
Etzerodt Omboni, Stéfanie, 209
Europe, 1, 2, 8, 10–12, 35–40, 42, 43,
46, 59, 72, 96, 97, 105–108,
120, 121, 127, 130, 139, 145,
150, 164, 167, 183, 204, 209,
230, 263, 273, 276, 309, 332,
336, 339, 398, 402
Evangelical Church, 107
exile, 17, 41, 48, 59, 68, 69, 88, 166,
172, 269, 276, 353, 357, 360,
364, 376, 377, 382, 386
extraterritoriality, 87, 269

family, 3, 4, 5–6, 7–10, 13, 14, 16,
17, 38, 39, 42, 44, 48, 58–74,
85–89, 91, 94–97, 105, 107,
109, 110, 112, 119, 122, 127–
130, 139, 140, 142, 147–150,
165, 168–170, 173, 181, 182,
185, 186, 188, 191, 192, 198,
200–205, 208, 221–223, 229,
233, 243, 247–249, 251, 264,
265, 287, 288, 290–293, 295,
296, 311, 312, 335, 336, 337,

340–343, 354–356, 358, 359,
364, 365, 376–381, 383–386,
400, 404, 407
Fanfani, Pietro, 71
Fanfulla, 92
fatherland, 14, 17, 43, 58–60, 63,
69–71, 73, 74, 263, 268, 269,
272–276, 320, 322, 358, 364,
366, 384, 385, 399, 401–404
Fascio femminile interventista antitedesco,
339
Fascism, 2, 17, 44, 89, 276, 320, 357,
376–378, 382, 385, 386
Fattiboni, Zellide, 70
fatti di maggio, 244
Febvre, Lucien, 60
Federation of Jewish War Veterans of
Austria, 396, 400, 401–402, 405,
407
feminism, 64, 205, 208, 209, 210, 222,
241, 247, 265
  Catholic, 193, 202, 209, 210
  first-wave, 11, 13
  Protestant, 192, 193, 198, 208, 209,
  210, 251
feminist, 8, 10, 13, 15, 38, 125, 180,
193, 209, 210, 224, 229, 230,
232, 357, 379, 380
  discourse, 10
  German, 11, 12, 192, 223–225, 228–
  233, 247
  Italian, 11, 12, 202, 210
  Jewish, 14, 380
  middle class, 11, 12, 225, 228, 229,
  231, 232
  movement, 8, 198, 210
  principles, 14
  radical, 12, 209, 224, 230–232, 242
Ferrero, Guglielmo, 377, 380–382, 383,
385
  Leo, 379, 381
  Nina, 381
Fessler, Agathe, 320
Filippini, Nadia Maria, 15, 16, 310
Finzi, Ida, 354, 359, 364
First World War. *See* World War I
Fischer, Fritz, 2
Florence, 14, 92, 175, 203, 263, 265–
268, 276, 381, 382, 385, 386

Foa, Anna, 173
Fonseca, Eleonora, 206
formation, 35, 38, 48, 71, 94, 200–202,
398
Foscolo, Ugo, 43, 68
Fourierists, 222
France, 1, 4, 5, 6, 11, 13, 43, 48, 61–
65, 71, 87, 88, 90, 92, 95, 96,
122, 187, 190, 191, 222, 227,
245, 246, 271, 273, 287, 289,
290, 291, 295, 296, 314, 380,
381, 385, 401
Franceschi Ferrucci, Caterina, 108, 202,
205
Francia, Enrico, 72
Frank, Malvina, 358
Frankfurter Zeitung, 270
Franzina, Emilio, 334
Franz Joseph I, Emperor, 399, 402
Frauenbewegung. *See* women's
movement
Frauenbewegung, Die (journal), 226,
242, 247
Frauenwohl, 221, 231, 245
Frederick the Great, 188
freemasonry, 90, 93, 208
Freisinn, 265, 272
French Third Republic, 48, 59, 64
Freud, Sigmund, 14, 275
Friedenthal, Markus Beer, 149
Friedländer, David, 151, 152
Friedländer, Saul, 3
Friuli, 16, 310, 333–335, 338, 357
Fröbel, Friedrich, 290
Froebel movement, 208
Fromm, Erich, 141
front, 15, 64, 65, 210, 287, 288, 292,
294, 297, 310, 313, 314, 316,
318–320, 332, 334, 339, 342,
381, 385
  home (*see* home front)
Frontoni, Giulia, 7, 8, 39, 105
Fruci, Gian Luca, 69
Frühling, Moritz, 401
Fuà Fusinato, Erminia, 205
Furlani, Costantina, 362
Fürth, Henriette, 125
Fusinato, Arnaldo, 205
Fusinato, Guido, 70

Gabaccia, Donna, 241
Galicia, 310, 318, 319, 320, 399
Gambetta, Léon, 65
Garavaglia, Ambrogio, 201
Garibaldi, Anita, 71
  Giuseppe, 58, 272
  Peppino, 272
  Ricciotti, 272
Gartenlaube, 66, 67
Gat, Azar, 47
Gazzetta Livornese, La, 92
Gelehrtenpolitik. *See* politics: scholarly
gender, 3, 5, 7, 8, 9, 12, 13, 16, 36–39, 46, 48, 49, 60, 67, 105, 106, 130, 139, 140, 149, 152, 153, 179, 181, 187, 204, 221, 249, 269, 288, 309, 312
  differences, 149
  hierarchy, 181, 192
  ideal, 9, 66, 105, 106, 153, 173, 207
  model, 8, 9, 48, 180, 181
    bourgeois, 180, 182, 189
    Catholic, 180, 182, 183, 193
    Christian European, 181
    diametrical, 181
    of the Enlightenment, 183
    European, 181
    female, 9, 181
    German, 3, 9, 180–182
    Protestant, 180–183, 193, 210
    secular, 181, 183
  normativity, 140
  order, 129, 139, 145, 147
  relationships, 145, 205
  roles, 8, 10, 37–39, 105, 107, 145, 147, 153, 188, 193, 210, 228
  stereotypes, 295
  and World War I, 332, 333
Gentilli, Alberto, 356, 363
  Enrica Barzilai (*see* Barzilai Gentilli, Enrica)
  Nella, 356
  Rina, 356
Gerhard, Adele, 8, 120–126, 128, 129
Gerhard, Ute, 247
Germany, 1–5, 7–11, 13, 14, 35–38, 40, 42–44, 47, 48, 61, 65–68, 73, 105, 107, 108, 111, 112, 114, 129, 139, 140, 142, 143, 179–181, 183–185, 187, 190, 191, 219–221, 223, 224, 229, 232, 241–245, 247–254, 265, 267–276, 366, 379, 380, 385, 396, 398, 401, 406
German Confederation, 7, 43, 179
German Empire, 6, 7, 9, 18, 62, 63, 128, 179–180, 183, 184, 185, 186, 187, 190–193, 242, 243, 270
German Order, 318, 319
  Wilhelmine, 271
Gerondi, Yonah, 151
Geschlechtsvormundschaft, 10
Gesellschaft für die Verbreitung von Volksbildung, 188
ghetto, 139, 164, 165, 168, 172, 173, 383
Giacomelli, Antonietta, 335
Gierke, Otto von, 68
Ginsborg, Paul, 3
Giolitti, Giovanni, 70
girls, 63, 68, 69, 90, 139, 144, 146, 150–153, 172, 173, 175, 187–189, 198, 200, 206, 224, 318, 319, 337, 340–342, 359
  and education, 63, 90, 174, 175, 182, 183, 201, 207, 248, 359
Giulio, Luisa, 210
Gizycki, Lily von, 226–228, 232, 251
Gleichheit, Die, 242
Gnauck-Kühne, Elisabeth, 181
Gögele, Karl, 318, 319
Goldschmidt, Henriette, 226
Goldschmidt, Johanna, 250
Gorizia, 310, 337, 353–364, 366, 381
Goudstikker, Sophia, 227, 228, 230
Gould, Emily Colton Bliss, 209
Gouges, Olympe de, 125
Grady, Tim, 396
grana, 85, 86, 88, 90–92, 94, 96, 97
Grand Orient of Italy, 360
Graz, 396
Great Britain, 222, 272, 381, 385
Great War. *See* World War I
Green, Abigail, 39
Gregorovius, Ferdinand, 266, 267
Gripenberg, Baroness Alexandra van, 252

Grossmann, Avraham, 149
Groupe d'études socialistes, 291
Guerrieri Gonzaga, Anselmo, 35
Guidi, Laura, 365

Habsburg Empire, 4, 13, 146, 171, 356, 400
Hagemann, Karen, 38, 39
Hague Convention, the, 309
halakhah, 142, 144, 145
Hale, Sarah Josepha, 62
Hamburg, 109, 110, 112, 146, 149, 232, 275
Hämmerle, Christa, 13, 15, 289, 309
Hanna, Martha, 314
Hardy, Frederick Daniel, 62
Hasdà, Salomone, 87
Hasidism, 139, 151
haskalah, 4, 146, 151, 152
Haugeneder, Hans, 316, 317
Hebrew, 97, 142, 143, 152, 153, 170
Heine, Heinrich, 112
Hensel, Luise, 189, 191
Herber, Pauline, 182
Herbert, Ulrich, 40, 47
Herkner, Heinrich, 121
Hertz, Alice, 15, 287, 290–296
    Robert, 15, 287, 290–293, 295
Herzog, Rabbi David, 405
Heyl, Hedwig, 229
Heymann, Lida Gustava, 229, 230, 232, 233
Hindenburg, Paul von, 272, 274, 275
Hippel, Theodor von, 223, 224
Hirsch, Samuel, 148, 150
Hirschi, Caspar, 47
histoire croisée, 45, 263, 276
historian, 2, 3, 13–15, 35–41, 43–49, 68, 70, 72, 106, 110, 146, 149, 179, 183, 263, 264, 267–270, 276, 287, 291, 309, 310, 322, 332, 378, 381
historiography, 1–3, 5, 12, 36, 39–43, 46–48, 164, 263, 266, 268, 311, 323, 332, 378
history, 4, 7, 36, 37, 39–41, 45, 46, 58, 59, 61, 67, 70, 73, 85, 86, 96, 97, 119, 121, 145, 165, 166, 167, 168, 184, 186, 187, 188, 206, 223, 243, 263, 264, 266–268, 292, 311, 332, 334, 378, 381, 395, 397, 399, 402
    of communication, 41
    comparative, 2–5, 35–38, 41, 45, 47, 48
    conceptual, 41
    cultural, 38, 40, 41, 46
    discipline of, 40, 41
    East Asian, 3
    entanglement, 36, 37, 41, 45, 48
    European, 1, 2, 39, 40, 45, 46, 47, 48, 268, 276
    family, 59, 73
    gender, 13, 16, 38, 332
    German, 2, 3, 4, 35, 37, 40, 42, 43, 47, 49, 183, 184
    global, 37, 41, 45, 46, 47, 48
    of historiography, 263
    of the Holocaust, 3
    imperial, 48
    integrated, 2, 3, 4
    intellectual, 41, 44
    Italian, 2, 3, 35, 37, 44, 47, 49, 166
    Jewish, 3, 4, 10, 13, 48, 141, 145, 166, 170, 289, 395, 396, 397, 407
    local, 46
    Mediterranean, 48
    national, 2–5, 35–38, 40, 41, 44–47, 49, 58, 59, 201, 243
    parallel, 2, 5, 35, 36, 37, 46, 49
    political, 41, 47, 48
    of religion, 141, 201
    transfer, 36, 37, 41, 45
    transatlantic, 48
    transnational, 5, 36, 37, 38, 44, 45, 48
Hoffmann, Ottilie, 229
Holl, Konstantin, 188, 190, 191
Hollweg, Chancellor Bethmann, 272
Holocaust, the, 3, 396
Hölscher, Lucian, 46
Holzer, Arno, 310, 311
Homberg, Naphtali Herz, 4, 146–147
home front, 15, 273, 297, 309, 310, 313, 316, 332
honor, 5, 39, 42, 59, 66, 144, 148, 152, 201, 246, 275, 384, 400, 402, 407

Horne, John, 309, 314
Hrouda, Eveline, 320, 321
human rights, 13

Ichenhäuser, Eliza, 245
ideal, 9, 10, 14, 42, 66, 105–111, 114, 142, 147, 150, 153, 173, 202, 207, 210, 229, 264–266, 274, 275, 312, 356, 360, 361, 377, 382
identity, 5, 9, 14, 38, 42, 43, 48, 49, 61, 85, 89, 91, 92, 94, 96, 228, 231, 243, 269, 400
  bourgeois male, 14, 15, 264
  collective, 5, 17, 36, 42, 48
  cultural, 17
  family, 96
  gender, 7, 38
  German, 67, 222
  historical, 37
  Italian, 7, 10, 85, 96, 166, 359, 379
  Jewish, 7, 10, 14, 67, 85, 96, 127, 128, 146, 165, 166, 169, 378, 379, 402, 407
  macro-, 92
  micro-, 92
  national, 5, 9, 17, 36, 38, 42, 44, 47, 64, 67, 86, 89, 253, 265, 359, 361, 379, 385
  political, 49, 105, 376
  religious, 7, 17, 67, 86
  social, 49
illiteracy, 167
India, 72, 97
Induno, Girolamo, 63
integration, 6, 7, 10, 11, 14, 16, 40, 47, 164, 165, 169, 171, 172, 173, 200, 206, 251, 268, 295, 311
intellectuals, 3, 4, 15, 107, 145, 209, 268, 289, 291, 353–357, 360, 363, 377, 400
International Abolitionist Federation, 224
International Council of Women, 209, 225, 245
nternationaler Kongreß für Frauenwerke und Frauenbestrebungen, 241, 245
interventionism, 13, 379

interwar period, 18, 395, 399, 407
Intransigent movement, 199, 200, 208, 210
irredentism, 354, 355, 358, 366, 377, 379, 386
Isaac, Laure, 15, 290–292, 294–296
  Jules, 15, 291, 292, 294
Isonzo, 310, 381, 382
  battles of, 16, 313, 317, 321, 381
Israel, 94
Isserles, Moses, 142
Istria, 4, 73
Italian Civil Code, The, 10, 206
Italy, 1, 2, 4–7, 9–14, 16–18, 35–38, 40, 42, 43, 44, 47, 48, 60, 63, 68, 69, 70, 86–90, 92–96, 108, 122, 143, 163–166, 168, 171, 173, 175, 180, 183, 184, 185, 190, 191, 198–203, 205, 206, 208, 210, 241–249, 252, 253, 263, 266–276, 310, 314, 317, 318, 321, 332, 333, 337, 354–358, 360, 364, 365, 378, 379, 381, 382, 384, 385, 386
  Kingdom of, 6, 62, 353, 354, 357, 360

Jagel de Gallichi, Abraham. *See* Yagel, Abraham ben Ḥenanyah
Janz, Oliver, 2
Japan, 72
Jerusalem, 87, 94
"Jewish census," 274
Jews, 3, 7, 10, 12, 14, 16, 17, 18, 44, 59, 60, 85, 86, 87, 88, 89, 93, 95, 97, 112, 119, 128, 129, 139, 140, 142, 144, 145, 152, 163, 164, 165, 172, 208, 220, 222, 223, 224, 263, 265, 267, 269, 274, 291, 292, 295–297, 323, 354, 356, 357, 359, 363, 380, 386, 395–407
  Ashkenazic, 142, 149
  central European, 3
  Eastern European, 4, 13, 139
  German, 3, 6, 7, 17, 67, 121, 143, 146, 150, 153, 224, 243, 247, 251, 265, 267, 268, 269, 275, 323, 401, 402, 405, 406

Italian, 6, 7, 44, 60, 85–87, 89, 90, 93, 95–97, 163–174, 199, 249, 274, 376, 377, 378, 379, 380, 386
  liberal, 127, 384
  orthodox, 127, 139, 143, 148–149, 152
  secular, 17, 127, 143, 146, 192, 379
  Sephardic, 380
  wandering, 142, 143, 171, 172
  war experiences, 13, 15, 289, 290, 297, 318, 376, 378, 395–407
  women, 8–11, 13–15, 17, 90, 119, 120, 127, 128, 140, 148–153, 172–175, 192, 205, 208, 245, 247, 249, 251, 287, 289–291, 293, 295, 296, 297, 355, 364, 366, 376, 380, 383, 384
Judaism, 4, 7, 9, 10, 112, 139–142, 145, 146, 149, 165, 166, 170–172, 174, 265, 267, 362, 396, 402
  Rabbinic, 144
Jüdisches Archiv, 401
Jüdische Front, 402
Jüdische Korrespondenz, 401
Jüdischer Frauenbund, 128
Jüdisches Kriegsgedenkblatt, 401
Jüdische Volksstimme, 401
Jüdische Zeitung, 401

k. & k. Army, 310, 317
Kaiserreich. *See* Germany: German Empire
Kaplan, Marion, 251
Karo, Yosef, 142
Kaufmännischer Hilfsverein für weibliche Angestellte, 229
Kemmerer, Edwin Walter, 122
Kempin, Emilie, 226
Kinnebrock, Susanne, 232
Kirchhoff, Auguste, 229
Kley, Eduard, 149
Kohler, George Y., 146
König, Gustav, 67
Konrad, R. M., 320
Koselleck, Reinhart, 398
Kühne, Gustav, 112
Kulisčioff, Anna, 380
Kulturkampf, 67, 179, 183, 192

"Kulturweltbürgertum," 14, 275
Kurz, Isolde, 268, 269, 271

Labriola, Teresa, 122
Lamprecht, Gerald, 13, 17, 18, 395
Lang, Christl, 313
Lange, Helene, 122, 123, 226, 229, 230, 232
language, 16, 40, 42, 62, 64, 66, 70, 88, 143, 145, 146, 153, 170, 171, 222, 223, 243, 309, 312, 315, 322, 323, 334, 336, 357, 360–362, 364, 366, 367
Lappin-Eppel, Eleonore, 13, 378
Lattes, Guglielmo, 170
Lega Nazionale, 360
Lega Patriottica Femminile, 364
Lega per la Tutela degli Interessi Femminili, 247–248
Lega Promotrice degli Interessi Femminili, 11, 244
legge Sacchi, 10
Leib, Glikl bas Judah, 150
Leipzig, 220, 243
Leonhard, Jörn, 45
Le Play, Frédéric, 64, 65
letters, 15, 16, 43, 66, 68, 69, 72, 94, 112, 181, 269, 271, 272, 273, 287–297, 312–316, 335, 362, 377, 380–383, 385, 386, 401, 403, 404
Levi, Adele, 174
Levi, Giuseppe, 166, 168
Levi D'Ancona, Luisa, 97
Levin, Rahel, 112
Lewald, August, 112
  Fanny, 112
liberal, 2, 7, 8, 12, 14, 42, 44, 70, 91, 108, 112, 113, 127, 167, 173, 179, 181, 199–201, 203, 205, 206, 209, 210, 233, 243, 264, 266, 268, 270–272, 353, 356, 357, 360, 363, 364, 366, 380, 384, 398
  -ism, 42, 44, 127, 265, 273, 274
"Liberation Wars," 42, 43, 66
Libya, 86, 89, 94, 95, 97
liberty, 59, 69, 268, 333
linguistic turn, the, 40

Liva, Valentino, 337
Livorno, 44, 85–88, 90–92, 96, 164
    State Archives, 7, 96
Loeb, James, 276
Lombroso, Cesare, 379–381
    Gina, 17, 377, 379–383, 385, 386
    Paola, 380
London and Westminster Review, 111
Louise of Prussia, 66
loyalty, 14, 16, 18, 42, 44, 47, 48, 49,
    61, 147, 149, 184, 187, 188,
    242, 291, 292, 296, 358, 376,
    377, 385, 395, 396, 398, 399,
    401, 404, 406
    cultural, 5, 36, 48, 183, 377
    national, 13, 16, 48, 61, 171, 183,
        274, 291, 385, 386
    political, 5, 36, 48
    social, 5, 36, 48
Luther, Martin, 67, 68, 185
Lutheran Church, 70, 198
Luzzatto, Samuel David, 4
Luzzatto Voghera, Gadi, 171
Lybeck, Marti L., 228
Lyceum, 357, 364, 385

Maccabees, 70, 402
Madigan, Edward, 13
Madre Italiana. Rivista mensile per orfani della Guerra, La, 364
Magee, John L., 61–62
Maghreb, 90, 97
Maimon, Salomon, 143
Maimonides, Moses, 141, 151, 170
Malnati, Linda, 210
Maltese Order, 320
Mameli, Goffredo, 69
Manelli, Erminia, 207
Mantua, 171
Marchionni, Carlotta, 206
Marcotti, Giuseppe, 357, 360, 361, 362
Margherita, Queen of Savoy, 207
Mario, Alberto, 69
marriage, 59, 62, 64, 66, 67, 68, 70, 85,
    124, 128, 144, 147, 173, 181,
    204, 206, 207, 221, 266, 355
    mixed, 58, 60, 265, 365, 366
Marseilles, 87
masculinity, 38, 39, 148, 275, 312, 315

maternity. *See* motherhood
Mayer, Teodoro, 356
Mazzini, Giuseppe, 1, 2, 3, 43, 70, 71, 361
Melfa, Daniela, 88
memoir, 69, 70, 242, 246, 251, 264,
    265, 312, 378, 379, 385, 406
memorial, 395, 396, 400–407
memory, 13, 43, 63, 72, 74, 94, 96,
    206, 337, 377, 379, 384, 386
    actor of, 400
    agent, 400, 406
    collective, 42, 72, 110, 206, 384, 395, 396
    discourse, 17, 384, 385, 395, 398, 402, 406
    family, 17, 377, 379, 382, 384–386
    public, 16, 17, 322, 335, 385, 406
    war, 13, 16, 18, 270, 376, 378, 384,
        395–400, 406, 407
Mendelssohn, Moses, 140, 141
Mentil, Maria Plozner, 334
Merici, Angela, 189, 190
Meriggi, Marco, 2, 43
Messaggero, Il, 356
metaphor, 58, 61, 62, 64, 68, 69, 107,
    110, 129, 269, 293, 317, 360
Methodists, 198
methodology, 35, 41
Mey, Henriette von der, 122
Meyer, Julius, 229
"Meyers Konversationslexikon," 221
Meysenburg, Malwida von, 108
Mezzogiorno, Il, 92
Michelet, Jules, 59
Michelstaedter, Carlo, 355
middle class. *See* bourgeoisie
Midrash, 145, 151
migration, 4, 7, 41, 48, 73, 86, 87, 88, 94
Milan, 244, 248, 249, 381, 383, 384
military service, 14, 18, 42, 275, 287,
    342, 395, 397–399, 401, 402, 407
Miniati, Monica, 165, 172, 173, 364
minorities, 3, 5, 6, 8, 16, 36, 41, 44, 48,
    49, 94, 119, 121, 127, 130, 163,
    164, 168, 198, 202, 208, 209,

220, 231, 243, 265, 291, 310, 342, 355, 357, 365, 400
Mishnah, 127, 152
modernity, 39, 42, 44, 46, 47, 94, 95, 174, 267, 361
Molino Colombini, Giulia, 200
monarchism, 42
monarchy, 7, 16–18, 38, 41, 43, 48, 59, 64, 69, 70, 96, 179, 184, 243, 310, 313, 314, 323, 399, 400, 402, 404, 405
Mondini, Marco, 338
Monod, Adolphe, 207
Montenegro, 310
Montessori, Maria, 242, 244, 247–249, 251–253
Monti, Rina, 122
morality, 66, 71, 139, 140, 143–146, 153, 168, 169, 173, 200, 205, 219, 222, 223, 243, 322, 342, 365
  national, 5, 64
Morata, Olimpia, 207
Moreno, 7, 44, 85, 86, 88–92, 95, 96, 97
  Aaron Daniele, 88, 89
  Giacomo, 89, 95
  Leone, 89, 94, 95
  Moisè, 85. 88, 89
  Raffaello, 89, 91, 92, 93, 95
  Sara, 88
  Ugo, 89, 95
Morgenstern, Lina, 226, 242, 245, 250
Moritz, Karl Philipp, 1
Mortara, Giorgio, 338
Mortara, Marco Mordekai, 60, 171
Mosse, George L., 38, 403
motherhood, 8, 60, 61, 63, 68, 69, 108, 120–126, 128–130, 287, 292, 293, 295, 384
  biological, 124–126
  spiritual, 125, 126
  and war, 292, 293
"mother of the nation," 8, 105–110, 114
movement, 1, 3, 8, 10, 38, 41, 44, 65, 70, 108, 112, 113, 146, 151, 152, 163, 180, 182, 192, 198, 199, 204, 208, 209, 210, 220, 224, 225, 231, 244, 246, 248, 249, 252, 254, 274, 355

national, 1, 8, 39, 72, 105–110, 112–114, 179, 242, 243, 251, 253
women's, 3, 8, 10–13, 45, 68, 119, 121, 122, 126–129, 179–182, 188, 192, 198, 208, 209, 210, 219–227, 229–233, 241–254, 355, 379, 381, 385
Mozzoni, Anna Maria, 11, 241, 244, 365
Mulazzi, Virginia, 122
Müller, Jürgen, 43
Münchener Neueste Nachrichten, 270
Munich, 227, 269, 270
museums, 72, 73, 74, 396, 397
Muslims, 97
Mussolini, Benito, 376–378, 382–384, 386

Napoleon, 42, 43, 61, 63, 66, 164, 187, 188, 189
  -ic Code, 10, 43, 62
  -ic Empire, 43
  -ic era, 42, 44, 63, 109, 309
  -ic occupation, 6
nation, 1–3, 5–8, 12, 13, 16, 35, 37–42, 46, 48, 58–66, 68–74, 85, 91, 94, 105–112, 114, 130, 163, 164, 179, 180, 181, 183, 187, 191, 192, 199–201, 203, 204, 206, 243, 249, 250, 272, 275, 289, 295, 309, 320, 354, 358, 360, 379, 380, 384–386, 398, 402, 403
  building, 1, 3–8, 35–39, 41–49, 58, 198, 359, 380
  state, 1, 5, 10, 14, 35–42, 44–48, 58, 59, 145, 179, 180, 198, 202, 243, 264, 400
national discourse, 5, 16, 105–107, 109, 110, 113
national duty, 8, 130, 270
nationalism, 1, 3–6, 13–18, 35–49, 59, 66, 72, 89, 95, 96, 105, 106, 112, 179, 200, 223, 263, 268, 271–273, 275, 276, 311, 315, 316, 321, 354, 356–365, 367, 377, 383, 385, 386, 405
  ideological, 35
  irredentist, 17, 358, 362, 377, 386

methodological, 5, 35, 36, 39–43, 45–49
origins of, 42, 46, 47
political, 42
and sexuality, 38
situational, 85, 96
national movement, 1, 8, 39, 72, 105–108, 110, 112–114, 179, 242, 243, 251, 253
German, 105, 107–110, 113
national principle, 13
National Socialism, 2, 35, 39, 73, 96, 276, 395–397, 406
Nattermann, Ruth, 1, 17, 39, 376
Nazione, La, 59, 267
Nazism. *See* National Socialism
Neo-Guelphism, 199
Niethammer, Lutz, 49
nineteenth century, 1, 2, 4–13, 35–41, 44, 46, 47, 48, 58, 60, 61, 63, 69, 85–91, 96, 97, 105–107, 110–112, 114, 119, 129, 139–141, 143, 145, 148, 149, 151, 163, 165, 166, 168–170, 172, 174, 175, 179–184, 192, 198, 199, 200, 202, 203, 205, 206, 208–210, 219–224, 241–243, 249, 263, 268, 309, 353, 357, 360, 365, 367, 397, 399, 403
Noerbel, Lisa, 210
North German Confederation, 7
Novalis, 66
Nützenadel, Alexander, 2

Oblath, Elody, 354
occupation, 8, 122–126, 128, 129, 130, 142, 165, 241
"productive," 123
"reproductive," 123
Offen, Karen, 64, 222, 223, 241, 247
Oppenheim, Moritz, 67
Orbin, Wanda, 252
Orvieto, Laura, 60, 380, 385, 386
Osterkamp, Jana, 48, 49
Ottoman Empire, 86
Otto-Peters, Louise, 11, 220, 221, 243

Padua, 4, 122, 333, 334
painting, 5, 63, 225, 337, 338

celebratory, 63
Paladini, Luisa, 200, 202
Paletschek, Sylvia, 10, 241
Panter, Sarah, 39
Papa, Don Vincenzo, 201
Pappenheim, Naphtali ben Samuel, 143
Pappritz, Anna, 229
Paris, 64, 222, 223, 227, 244, 272, 287, 290–292, 407
paternalism, 42
patriotism, 5, 14, 18, 38, 40, 42, 43, 48, 58, 60, 61, 63, 65, 66, 69, 70–73, 88, 92, 93, 95, 109, 110, 181, 183, 184, 186, 187, 191–193, 198, 201, 202, 204, 205, 209, 210, 265, 274, 275, 293–295, 353, 355, 358, 359, 363, 364, 366, 367, 376, 377, 379, 380, 384, 386, 395, 399, 401
national, 16, 43, 44, 110, 188, 192, 205, 265, 311, 315, 376
regional, 43
and war, 14–16, 65, 67, 275, 297, 312, 316, 320, 376, 399, 401, 402, 404–406
patriotic discourse, 5, 38, 42, 58
peace movement, 246, 248, 249
Pécout, Gilles, 41
pedagogy, 164, 290
Péguy, Charles, 292
Pellis, Ugo, 359, 361, 363
Pennacchio, Daniela, 87
pensions, 62
Penslar, Derek, 401
Percoto, Caterina, 205, 207
periodization, 5, 46
Petrini, Rea Silvia, 247, 249
Petrizzo, Alessio, 72
pétroleuse, 64, 223
Petuchowski, Jakob, 145
philanthropy, 90, 97, 202
Piave, 317, 335, 339, 342
Piccolo, Il, 356, 363
Piedmontese Code, The, 10
Pierson, Ruth Roach, 6
Pietrow-Ennker, Bianka, 10, 241
Pisanelli, Giuseppe, 70
Planck, Gottlieb, 68
Planert, Ute, 38, 42, 47

Plessner, Salomon, 152
Plutarchs, feminine, 71, 205–207
Poët, Lidia, 204, 209
Poincaré, Raymond, 65
Poland, 122, 318
"political lady," 8, 105, 106, 110, 111, 114
politics, 2, 11–13, 36, 38–41, 43, 44, 63, 69, 70, 72, 85, 88, 90, 92, 96, 105–107, 110, 111, 113, 114, 120, 139, 164, 179, 180, 181, 183, 188, 192, 201, 202, 206, 208, 209, 220, 223, 231, 233, 241, 243–246, 250, 269, 270–272, 275, 276, 291, 323, 332, 353–355, 357, 359, 360–363, 366, 376–378, 381, 383–386, 397, 398, 400, 406, 407
  scholarly, 270
Pons, Amilda, 205, 209
Popolo d'Italia, Il, 383
Porciani, Ilaria, 2–6, 38, 58, 92
postcolonial studies, 45, 106, 119
Potonié-Pierre, Eugénie, 247
Prado, Rina del, 354, 359
Prague, 4, 146, 152
Prévost, Eugène Marcel, 64
private sphere, 3, 38, 204, 366, 384
Procacci, Giovanna, 333
progress, 2, 42, 44, 46, 94, 95, 107, 147, 253, 268, 275, 361
progressive, 64, 231, 244, 245–248, 253
proletariat, 243
Pro Patria, 360
Protestant, 6, 8, 9, 37, 60, 67, 68, 107, 122, 127, 129, 163, 179–184, 187–189, 191–193, 198, 199, 202–210, 243, 251
  Church, 202, 203
  role model, 187–188
Prussia, 2, 7, 9, 38, 44, 65–67, 109, 112, 150, 179, 180, 184, 185–189, 191, 192, 223, 224, 243, 264, 274, 398
Prussian Law of Association, 246
public sphere, 8, 9, 12, 58, 90, 149, 153, 210, 220, 223, 246, 364, 400

race, 37, 73, 146, 274, 296, 364–366, 376
racial laws, Italian, 18, 89, 276, 376, 386
racism, 17, 36, 64, 271, 365, 367
Raj, Satiajit, 72
rape, 15, 309, 311, 319, 322, 332, 336, 339, 340–342, 360
Raphael, Lutz, 46
Rapoport, Salomo Judah, 4
Rechter, David, 396
Rechtsschutzverein, 250
reconciliation, 168
Red Brigades, 35
Red Cross, 90, 320, 380
reform, 4, 6, 10, 42–44, 68, 139, 146, 148, 149, 167, 186, 206, 221, 230–233, 274
  social, 121, 186, 220
Reformation, 67, 184, 185, 187, 199, 207
refugee, 16, 91, 276, 294, 318, 323, 333, 335, 336, 338, 342, 397, 399
Regime of Capitulations, 86
Reich, Rabbi Wilhelm, 402
Reichsverband gegen die Sozialdemokratie, 66
Reichsrat, Austrian, 311
religion, 3, 6–8, 13, 37, 42, 46, 48, 65, 67, 70, 71, 105, 127, 139–142, 164, 169, 171, 179, 180, 199, 201, 202, 204, 209, 210, 222, 243, 274, 292, 358
  Catholic, 169, 171, 199–201, 206, 208
  Jewish, 9, 10, 140, 143, 145, 148, 150–152, 170–172, 290–292, 355, 356, 379
  Protestant, 67
remembrance, 13, 18, 37
  community of, 396
  war, 13, 16, 320, 323, 398, 400, 403
republic, 4, 17, 61–65, 68, 70, 73, 320, 322, 400, 405
  French, 6, 15, 48, 59, 64, 65, 71, 290, 292, 295, 296
republican, 6, 15, 18, 59, 61, 63, 64, 65, 111, 267, 377
resistance, 2, 16, 17, 174, 191, 340, 377, 380

Restoration, age of, 60
Reuveni, Gideon, 13
Revival, Evangelical, 107, 202
revolution, 61, 63, 65, 142, 233
  of 1848/497, 11, 42, 110, 112, 113, 179, 199, 220, 222, 250, 266
  Age of, 42, 43
  American, 59, 61, 62
  French, 11, 59, 61–65, 106, 107, 145, 164, 181, 186, 187, 381
Rey, Luigi, 95
Riall, Lucy, 39
Riehl, Wilhelm Heinrich, 222
Riesenfellner, Stefan, 405
Risorgimento, the, 6, 8, 18, 40–42, 60, 69, 70, 72, 73, 88, 163, 164, 165, 167, 198, 199, 202–204, 208, 209, 273, 379, 380, 382, 386
Ristori, Adelaide, 122
Rivista Israelitica, La, 166
Romanticism, German, 1
Rome, 2, 4, 70, 91–93, 109, 204, 209, 243, 244, 248, 249, 266, 267, 357, 364
  Treaty of, 2
Rörig, Karoline, 39
Rosselli, Amelia, 17, 376–379, 382–386
  Aldo, 377, 379, 384–386
  Carlo, 377, 382, 385
  Nello, 377, 382, 385
Rossi, Clemente, 206
Rostand, Jean, 59
Rousseau, Jean Jacques, 63, 64, 173, 180, 181
Routledge, Florence, 251
Rozenblit, Marsha L.13, 396
Russia, 122, 246, 271–273, 310, 316–319, 380

Sabbadini, Salvatore, 363
Saint-Simonians, 222
Salandra, Antonio, 334, 356
Salomon, Alice, 229, 246
salon, 58, 106, 111, 112, 266, 356, 357, 360, 363
Sance, Thérèse, 290
Sardinia-Piedmont, Kingdom of, 6, 164
Sarfatti, Cesare, 376, 383
  Margherita, 17, 376,-378, 383–386
  Roberto, 376, 377, 383–386
Savoy, 191, 204, 207, 379
Scarabello, Giovanni, 335
Scardozzi, Mirella, 97
Schepeler-Lette, Anna, 226
Schiavoni Bosio, Alice, 210
Schieder, Theodor, 39
Schieder, Wolfgang, 2
Schiera, Pierangelo, 2
Schiff, Paolina, 11, 242, 244, 247, 248, 253
Schikorsky, Isa, 312, 314
Schirmacher, Käthe, 122, 229, 232, 250
Schleker, Clara, 229
Schlesinger-Eckstein, Therese, 251
Schlessinger, Wolf, 148
Schmidl, Erwin A., 397
Schmidt, Auguste, 11, 125, 220
Schmoller, Gustav, 120, 121
Schoenflies, Rosalie, 242, 248, 249
Schoppe, Amalia, 112
school, 10, 11, 69, 71, 91, 93, 95, 109, 119, 125, 142, 165, 167, 168, 172–174, 182–184, 187, 188, 207–210, 222, 249, 264, 291, 292, 361, 380
  boys', 151, 174, 175
  education, 119, 167, 182, 187, 250
  girls', 174, 175, 182, 187, 248, 250
  Jewish, 4, 10, 145, 151, 167, 169, 170, 172, 174
  public, 167, 171, 174, 290
  state, 168, 169
  syllabus, 95, 184, 187, 207
  Talmud Torah, 175
Schubert, Kurt, 396
Schulze Wessel, Martin, 48, 49
Schwerin, Jeanette, 226, 245, 252
Scodnik, Irma Melany, 122
Scuola della domenica, La, 203
Secolo, Il, 381
Second World War. *See* World War II
secularism, 139, 143, 146, 180
secularization, 139, 145, 153
self-helpism, 200, 202
Serbati, Antonio Rosmini, 168
Serbia, 268, 310, 313
Sering, Max, 121

Settembrini, Luigi, 70
Settimana Israelitica, La, 166
sexuality, 38, 39, 222
Sheffer, Gabriel, 93–94
Shoah, 268, 378
Shulḥan Arukh, 142–144
Simon, Helene, 8, 120–126, 128, 129
Simon, Jules, 64
Slataper, Luisa Carniel, 364
　Scipio, 364
Slavs, 271, 353, 354, 358–367
Slonik, Benjamin Aron ben, 151
Slovenes, 359–362, 364, 366, 367
social work, 181, 186, 191, 192, 381
social democrats, 121, 128, 251
Social Democratic Party, 127–129, 251, 252, 323
socialist, 64, 71, 125, 184, 202, 231, 242, 244, 247, 248, 251–253, 291, 292, 383
Soffici, Ardengo, 335
Soldani, Simonetta, 69
Sombart, Werner, 121
Sonderweg, 2, 4
Sonnenfeld, Amanda, 188
Sonsino, Grazia, 88
Spangenberg, Gustav, 67
SPD. *See* Social Democratic Party
Stanton, Cady, 125
stereotype, 37, 164, 171, 174, 208, 266, 272, 295, 311, 312, 315, 316, 319, 320, 322, 339, 354, 358–360, 364, 367, 382
Strafexpedition, 335
Stöcker, Helene, 229, 230
Stritt, Marie, 125, 226–229, 242, 245, 250–253
suffrage, 11, 221, 224–226, 231–233, 241, 244, 248, 249
Sulema, Ester, 91
　Pompeo, 91
synagogue, 92, 97, 139, 142, 165, 174, 291, 396, 401, 406, 407

Tagore, Rabindranath, 72
Taine, Hippolyte, 64
Talmud, 142–146, 149, 151, 152–153, 171

Taylor Allen, Ann, 108
Tedeschi, Marco, 355
teleological thinking, 5, 35, 36, 46, 47, 49
Terragni, Giuseppe, 384
testimonies, 15, 16, 288
　of Jewish soldiers, 13
Thébaud, Francoise, 332
Thomas, Frank, 207
Tiburtius, Franziska, 220, 229
time, 6, 36, 46, 48, 49, 72, 96, 127
　historical, 46
Tocqueville, Alexis de, 61
tolerance, 97, 165, 171, 365
　Edict of, 146
Torah, 9, 141, 143–144, 148, 171
Tortarolo, Edoardo, 2
trade, 87–90, 96, 245
　-s union, 48, 220, 225, 251
transnationalism, 4–7, 12–15, 36–42, 44, 45, 47–49, 203, 263, 268, 275, 276, 377, 378, 407
trauma, 16, 17, 35, 274, 341, 343, 400, 407
Treitschke, Heinrich von, 35, 37, 67, 265
Treviso, 334, 335, 337, 340, 342
Tribuna, La, 356
Trieste, 4, 73, 166, 310, 353–357, 359, 360, 362–364, 366
treue Zions-Wächter, Der, 149
Tsar, 402
Tsur, Yaron, 90
Tunis, 7, 44, 85–88, 90–93, 95, 96
Tunisia, 85–91, 95, 96, 97
Turin, 44, 95, 174, 203, 204, 380, 381
Turin, Berta, 210
twansa, 86, 88, 90, 96, 97

Überegger, Oswald, 13, 405
Udine, 321, 333, 334, 342, 360, 377
Uhl, Heidemarie, 405
unification, 43, 62, 243, 244
　Italian, 40, 63, 70, 71, 86, 92, 163, 167, 199, 202, 204, 205, 379
　national, 6, 44, 60, 380
　wars, 206, 243
Unione cristiana delle giovani, 203, 210

Unione, L', 91–95, 97
Unione Femminile Nazionale, 339, 383
Union for the (Greater) Good, 209
Unità d'Italia. Organo del Comitato nazionale femminile per l'intervento italiano, 364
United States, 5, 8, 10, 59, 61–63, 111, 120–122, 129, 163, 209, 245, 246, 265, 377
university, 59, 72, 120–122, 128, 129, 221, 247, 248, 264, 266, 291, 381, 396
Upper Adriatic, 353

Valussi, Pacifico, 357
Varnhagen, Rosa, 112
Varnhagen von Ense, August, 112
Vatican, the, 167, 243
Velsen, Dorothee von, 229
Veneto, 16, 333–335, 339
Venice, 143, 170, 208, 333, 334–335, 359, 379, 384
Verein katholischer deutscher Lehrerinnen, 182
Vessel, Eusèbe, 90
Vessillo Israelitico, Il, 9, 166, 173, 174
Vidal-Naquet, Clémentine, 289
Vienna, 139, 152, 251, 265, 313, 314, 354, 366, 396, 397, 400–406
 Congress of, 43, 44
violence, 13, 15–17, 38, 49, 167, 232, 233, 273, 274, 309–317, 321–323, 332, 336–338, 340–343, 354, 357, 362, 364–367
Volhynia, 318
Volkov, Shulamit, 127
Volksschule, 183–184, 185, 186
volunteers, 15, 37, 67, 173, 292–294, 316, 379, 383

Wagner, Adolph, 121
Wahrheit, Die, 401
Waldensians, 198, 203–205, 208, 209
Walters, Keith, 90
war, 3, 4, 6, 13–18, 38, 40, 42, 43, 61–67, 89, 109, 113, 184–187, 189, 206, 230, 243, 249, 264, 268, 269, 270, 272–276, 287–297, 309–313, 315–323, 332–336, 339, 341–343, 353–357, 359, 360, 362, 364–367, 376, 378–380, 382, 384–386, 395–402, 404–407
 Anti-Napoleonic, 61, 66, 309
 atrocities, 16, 310, 323
 correspondence, 264, 287–291, 297, 311, 312, 314, 316, 321–322, 377, 378
 experience, 13, 16, 274, 276, 288–290, 295, 297, 310, 316, 322, 364, 367, 378, 381–383, 386, 400
 letters, 15, 287, 288, 290, 293, 297, 312, 315, 316, 380, 381
 nationalism, 17, 263, 271, 272, 276, 321, 360, 365
 patriotism, 14, 15, 63, 109, 312, 366, 405
 remembrance, 13, 17, 18, 323, 378, 396–407
 Revolutionary, 309
Warburg, Aby, 267–271, 273, 275
Ward, Maria, 189, 190
warfare, 17, 273, 309, 311, 319, 323, 395
 mobile, 310, 311, 318
Webb, Beatrice, 122
Weber, Adelheid, 129
Weber, Friedrich, 313
 Lilly, 313
Weber, Marianne, 129
Weber, Max, 128
Wehler, Hans-Ulrich, 2
Wehrmacht, 398
Weisl, Wolfgang von, 396
Weiskirchner, Richard, 403
welfare, 8, 62, 97, 129, 130, 148, 189, 221, 265, 400
Wentscher, Else, 129
Werner, Anton von, 68
Werner, Michael, 45
Western Front, the, 15, 287, 292, 310, 314
Wetzlar, Isaac, 144
Winter, Jay, 400
Wissenschaft des Judentums, 4

Woche, Die, 226
Wolf, Leopold, 313
Wolff, Theodor, 272
womanhood, 9, 105, 106, 108, 110, 121, 129, 315
"woman question," 242, 246–248, 250–253
women, 3, 7–13, 15–17, 38–41, 59–66, 69–72, 86, 90, 94, 96, 105–114, 119–130, 139, 140, 144, 145, 147–153, 172, 174, 181, 182, 187–192, 198–202, 204–208, 219, 220, 222–224, 231, 232, 241–247, 249–254, 287–290, 294–296, 309, 311, 312, 315, 320–322, 332–334, 354, 357, 358, 361, 364, 367, 381, 383, 385
   Catholic, 107–108, 172, 174, 181, 183, 192, 193, 203, 206
   German, 8, 14, 110, 113, 114, 120, 153, 188, 189, 219, 221, 222, 228–232, 243, 245–248, 250–254, 365, 366
   Italian, 7, 13, 14, 60, 70, 109, 110, 172, 202, 206, 209, 243–245, 247, 249, 251–253, 333–337, 339–343, 357–359, 364, 380
   Jewish, 7–9, 11, 13–15, 17, 60, 120, 127, 128, 140, 150, 153, 172–175, 180, 192, 208, 245, 249, 251, 287, 289, 290, 293, 295–297, 380
   Protestant, 8, 9, 181, 192, 206, 208
women's movement, 12, 13, 68, 119, 121, 122, 126–129, 208, 209, 220, 223, 241, 246, 250, 251, 379
   Catholic, 182, 192
   emancipation, 3, 10–13, 127, 381, 385
   German, 12, 13, 119, 127, 179–182, 188, 219–222, 224–227, 229–232, 241–245, 247, 248, 250–254
   International, 45, 226, 230, 241, 244–246, 253
   Italian, 11–13, 241–245, 247–249, 251, 253, 385
   Protestant, 182, 192
   religious, 180, 192
   secular, 180, 192
   transnationalist orientation of, 13
Woodville, Richard Caton, 61
work, 12, 15, 66, 86, 87–88, 91, 93, 95, 106, 113, 119–121, 123, 125, 126, 128, 129, 140, 174, 181, 182, 184–186, 188, 191, 192, 202, 220, 221, 229, 230, 231, 244, 246, 247, 249, 252, 253, 263, 264, 266–269, 287–293, 310, 319–321, 334, 336, 338, 340, 342, 354, 356, 358, 359, 365, 377, 379, 381, 400
   intellectual, 8, 39, 119–130
   relief, 13, 129
working class, 186, 243, 245, 248, 249, 251, 252
World War I, 1, 4, 6, 11–17, 35, 36, 39, 59, 66, 67, 73, 89, 263, 268, 287–290, 296, 297, 309–312, 314, 315, 321–323, 332, 353, 354, 356, 359, 362, 376–382, 384, 385, 386, 396–398, 403, 406, 407
World War II, 2, 35, 37, 39, 59, 73, 96, 263, 276, 288, 312, 378, 396, 398
World Federation of Jewish War Veterans, 407
Worm, Pauline, 223
writers, 1, 4, 8, 17, 65, 66, 106–108, 110–114, 122–124, 126, 152, 165, 174, 189, 207, 268, 322, 353–360, 362–366, 376, 379, 381
writing, 4, 11, 40, 47, 49, 70, 106, 108–114, 120, 124, 125, 129, 144, 150, 198, 228, 264, 265, 269, 289, 312, 322, 354, 355, 357–359, 361, 362, 378, 380, 381, 386, 402
WWI. *See* World War I
WWII. *See* World War II
Wyrwa, Ulrich, 13, 263, 268

xenophobia, 357, 362

Yagel, Abraham ben Ḥenanyah, 143–145, 170
Young Germany movement, 112
Yuval-Davis, Nira, 106

Zampini Salazaro, Fanny, 245
Zeitschrift für Frauenstimmrecht, 224, 225

Zetkin, Clara, 122, 125, 242, 244, 252
Ziani, Gabriella, 358
Zimmermann, Bénédicte, 45
Zola, Émile, 64
Zuntz, Nathan, 121–122
Zunz, Leopold, 4